D1291870

Brandeis

A FREE MAN'S LIFE

Life is not a having and a getting;
but a being and a becoming.
Matthew Arnold.

Also by Alpheus Thomas Mason

ORGANIZED LABOR AND THE LAW, 1925

BRANDEIS: LAWYER AND JUDGE IN THE MODERN STATE, 1933

THE BRANDEIS WAY, 1938

BUREAUCRACY CONVICTS ITSELF, 1941

BRANDEIS

A Free Man's Life

BY ALPHEUS THOMAS MASON

New York

THE VIKING PRESS

1946

PRINTED IN U.S.A.

BY THE VAIL-BALLOU PRESS, INC.

To the Memory

of

Bernard Flexner

Acknowledgments

WORK on this book began early in 1940 when Justice Brandeis authorized its preparation and gave me full access to his public papers and documents. He also made available memoranda, diaries, notebooks, and personal correspondence. Brandeis had a natural archival bent and enjoyed filing significant materials. He began to gratify this trait as early as 1875, and by 1900 the habit was firmly fixed and fully indulged. The results are unique in the length of the period covered and in the formidable mass of papers accumulated.

Justice Brandeis's relatives, friends, colleagues and co-workers have lent me letters and documents, prepared memoranda, and discussed his career. To Mrs. Brandeis I am under a very special obligation. She made available letters and other material and was unfailingly responsive to any and all calls for help. The Justice's younger daughter, Elizabeth Brandeis Raushenbush, supplied the letter written by Samuel D. Warren on the occasion of her parents' engagement and permitted the use of the letter she herself wrote her father when he retired from the Court. Informal talks with her in July 1940 gave me many insights into her father's character and work.

There had been occasional interviews with the Justice since 1933; after 1940 these became more frequent. During his last years he seemed mellower, more relaxed. July 22–31, 1940, I saw him each day at Chatham. Laying aside his habitual reserve, he reminisced on various episodes. At morning and afternoon sessions he would often talk for an hour or more. Mrs. Brandeis was on guard to conserve his diminishing resources, but as the days passed the Justice himself decided when the session must end. Sometimes he would escape for an unscheduled talk in the little room at the back of the cottage, where I was examining papers. During these memorable days there was hardly a phase of his long career not touched upon, with illuminating comment on his heritage, his motivating creed, his likes and dislikes. He talked freely but never at random, intent, as always, to illustrate an idea or point a moral.

vii

Substantial assistance came from Louis B. Wehle, the Justice's nephew; Josephine and Pauline Goldmark, his wife's sisters; Edward F. McClennen and Jacob Kaplan, his former law partners; Miss E. Louise Malloch, his former secretary; Mrs. Alfred Brandeis, his sister-in-law; the Misses Fanny and Adele Brandeis, his nieces; Paul Freund and Willard Hurst, former law clerks; Mrs. Florence Boeckel and Mrs. Josephine January, close friends of the family; A. A. Berle, Sr., a co-worker in Boston public campaigns; Charles C. Burlingham of the New York Bar, a friend since law-school years; the late Richard W. Hale of the Boston Bar; and the late Joseph B. Eastman of the Interstate Commerce Commission.

Besides using the roomful of Brandeis papers at the University of Louisville, and numerous other sources friendly and unfriendly to the Justice and his work, I have worked through official records, reports, and pamphlets, scores of files of magazines and newspapers bearing upon his career. The effort has been to cover the entire field and to present the subject in a spirit of impartiality. In this endeavor many others have co-operated: George W. Alger, Beulah Amidon, F. F. Baldwin, Roger W. Baldwin, Jacob Billikopf, Raymond P. Brandt, Clarence S. Brigham, H. I. Brock, Robert W. Bruère, Clyde S. Casady, Lelia E. Colburn, Charles Townsend Copeland, John H. Cramer, Mrs. Jacob De Haas, Judd Dewey, Felicia Deyrup, Irving Dilliard, Justice William O. Douglas, Abram G. Duker, Lincoln Filene, Edward C. Finney, Abraham Flexner, Justice Felix Frankfurter, Elisha M. Friedman, Benjamin Goldstein, August Gutheim, Arthur D. Hill, Frederick M. Kerby, Paul Kellogg, Pennell C. Kirkbride, the late Louis E. Kirstein, Fola La Follette, Morris S. Lazaron, Max Lerner, Judge Louis E. Levinthal, Judge Julian W. Mack, Max Meyer, Richard Neuberger, George Wharton Pepper, Gifford Pinchot, James Morgan Read, Edward A. Richards, James L. Richards, Charles G. Ross, George Rublee, Mrs. Morris Saval, Harry A. Slattery, Mrs. Joseph B. Speed, Kenneth M. Spence, the late Harlan F. Stone, Robert S. Szold, Thomas E. Waggaman, Herbert White, and Robert W. Woolley.

The resources of various libraries have been freely and fully at my disposal. Grateful recognition is due to Miss Pearl Weiler, Librarian, and J. N. Lott, Jr., Dean, University of Louisville Law School, for supplying material from the Brandeis collection; to Mr. Malcolm O. Young, Reference Librarian, Princeton University, for innumerable services; and to Miss Katharine Brand, Special Custodian, Woodrow Wilson papers, Library of Congress, for making accessible the relevant documents in that collection.

Financial help, without which this book could not have been written, came from various institutions—The Rockefeller Foundation, Princeton University, and the Palestine Economic Corporation.

Princeton University students, graduate and undergraduate, have given me stout assistance in library exploration, in checking sources, and other tasks involved in a large research project. For this I am especially indebted to John Brigante, Frank Gray, and J. W. Peltason. Several undergraduates, writing senior theses under my supervision on various phases of Brandeis's public career, have done work of distinction and at the same time given this biography considerable help. Among these are Henry Lee Staples, Jr., John Pryor Furman, and Samuel Warren Seeman.

After the book was in manuscript and still in the plastic stage, I had the editorial assistance of Prof. Walter Lincoln Whittlesey of Princeton and Mr. William Miller of New York. Professor Whittlesey gave more than skillful editorial help. For his unfailing sympathy, suggestion, and inspiration, this book owes an unpayable debt. In preparing the manuscript for the printer the author is heavily obligated to Miss Jerry Heringman of The Viking Press for revisions, corrections, and uncanny detection of discrepancies.

Throughout the years since 1934, the author's wife, Christine Este Mason, has tolerantly borne the brunt of his struggle to understand and portray Brandeis, and has given assistance which no words of acknowledgment can adequately express.

A. T. M.

Princeton
March 11, 1946

Contents

List of Illustrations

xiii

Brandeis

A FREE MAN'S LIFE

Profile

WRITING his mother from Harvard Law School in March 1878, William E. Cushing sketched a fellow-student: "My friend Brandeis is a character in his way—one of the most brilliant legal minds they have ever had here. . . . Hails from Louisville, is not a college graduate, but has spent some years in Europe, has a rather foreign look and is currently believed to have some Jew blood in him, though you would not suppose it from his appearance—tall, well-made, dark, beardless, and with the brightest eyes I ever saw. Is supposed to know everything and to have it always in mind. The professors listen to his opinion with the greatest deference. And it is generally correct. There are traditions of his omniscience floating through the school. One I heard yesterday. A man last year lost his notebook of Agency lectures. He hunted long and found nothing. His friends said: 'Go and ask Brandeis—he knows everything—perhaps he will know where your book is.' He went and asked. Said Brandeis, 'Yes, go into the auditors' room, and look on the west side of the room, on the sill of the second window, and you will find your book.' And it was so." * 1

Famous at twenty-one years, and to the end of his days, Louis Dembitz Brandeis is among the most controversial public figures of our time. He was a great lawyer, uncommonly effective both as advocate and counselor. He was a great judge. But relentless curiosity and ardor for seeing things whole broke down the conventional barriers of his profession, drove him beyond the law into life itself, forcing him to see that no man, no group, can lay exclusive claim to truth. In working up his cases, whether private or public, he seized every opportunity to probe more deeply than the immediate litigation seemed to require. Often that was how he won his cases— by putting the human before the legal element. Thus he often roused personal enmity and baffled both friend and foe. His opponents started by hating his tactics and ended by hating the man himself. Like Lincoln, he

* All bibliographic references will be found at the end of this volume.

3

was bitterly despised, greatly loved, and also profoundly misunderstood. "Lonely is the man who understands," or, as Emerson says, "To be great is to be misunderstood."

All agree that Brandeis's achievements are remarkable, but as to the nature of his talents, as to the mainspring of his life and work, opinions are varying and contradictory. Some corporation heads and their "lawyer adjuncts" still see in him Machiavellian duplicity, see in his pose as champion of the people a device to gain notoriety and large fees.[2] Others in business and finance find him a dangerous radical, bent on destroying established institutions. Still others praise his crusading humanitarianism, his sacrifice of personal ambition to help the poor. Observers of more practical idealism see him as a dreamer. To other men he is an ingenious pioneer, dealing systematically and objectively with our complicated pecuniary culture, using the techniques of science to discover the sources of power in our society, and the methods of controlling that power for the public good. Some of his acts give credence to each of these verdicts.

Brandeis rarely failed to shift his position when the ground he was standing on went soft. Critics, as usual, leveled against him the charge of inconsistency. How, some still ask, could he score financial success as a big corporation lawyer only to become so fierce an opponent of bigness, monopoly, and the money trust? How, they inquire, could he serve corporations— his clients—and then battle them in the name of that vague entity—the people? How, with his heralded liberalism, could he maintain so lucrative a law practice and die a multimillionaire? And since he did, in fact, make a fortune during the period 1879–1907, the reasons for his *volte-face* were suspect. Why would he support a man at one time and later oppose him, defend a corporation and later prosecute it, simultaneously advise and oppose big business?[3] Plausibly enough, his enemies saw him as a bandwagon demagogue.

Each of these queries has a kernel of truth, making it easy for his enemies to accuse Brandeis of subordinating his principles to his purse. He was most conspicuous in the public eye when monopoly seemed to many the practicable solution for business depressions. Brandeis disagreed. He sought to block the trend toward bigness and monopoly as inimical to efficiency, individualism, true laissez faire, and democracy, as heading the nation precisely in the direction capitalists professed their desire to avoid—state socialism. Then he was fiercely denounced as playing both ends against the middle in an effort to line his own pocket. When he endorsed the social and economic value of trade unionism, and at the turn of the century pronounced the correction of irregular employment our most urgent task, spokesmen for labor claimed him as their own while corporation magnates labeled him an obstreperous agitator, inciting class hatred, inspiring false hopes. When, on the other hand, he argued in favor of the manufacturer's right to fix the price of trade-marked articles, or advocated the incorporation of unions, industrialists figuratively patted him on the back, while trade unionists turned hostile.

The evening of his judicial career came in the decade when Roosevelt's New Deal was to win for all men the more abundant life, the four freedoms, everywhere in the world. While strongly sympathizing with such noble purposes, Brandeis expressed doubt whether grandiose plans and a few fallible planners could achieve these commendable goals. He continued to voice unfaltering faith in little men and little institutions, while erstwhile friends accused him of clinging to obsolete views, of wishing to turn the clock back.

It seems not to have occurred to Brandeis's critics that inconsistency such as his may have resulted from his methods, his power to grow, from capacity to live and learn, from ability to win wider knowledge from broader experience. Critics did not see that his shifts of position were vitally related to that independent strength of mind manifest throughout his career—that persistent refusal to hunt with the pack. Experience taught him the fallacy of seeing any socio-political issue or proposed remedy as an absolute, in terms of black and white.

When theoretical molds are applied to particular situations, they seldom fit. Therefore the stand he took, after inquiry, was often unexpected. Since he had discredited Taft's conservation policy in 1910, it was assumed he would do it again later the same year when Taft's Department of the Interior again came under fire. Yet he refused, since examination of the facts failed to support the charges. Since he had opposed advanced railroad rates in 1911, it was expected he would do the same in 1914; yet it was the big shippers, not the railroads, he then opposed. Since he had associated himself with progressive Republicans, it was thought that he would join the Progressive Party; yet he came out for Wilson and the Democrats. In each case, facts, not abstract theory, determined his position. Only a man literally free from all political and financial obligation could act as Brandeis did.

America to him was the freest country on earth, yet even here men were only partially and relatively free. The worker whose best effort barely wins a livelihood is not free. Those who go through life in aimless search for pleasure, who live solely to impress others or to win their approval, are not free. The corporation executive whose thought is merely of profit and more profit is thereby enslaved. The lawyer whose life is spent showing corporations how they can evade the law is himself enchained. The politician bent on office and power is not his own man but his electorate's or his party's.

Brandeis began his career determined to create in his own circumstances the prerequisites for independence and freedom of action. He shied off from an attractive partnership with his brother-in-law and from establishing himself near his family. Success must be won independently. He deliberately achieved financial security for himself and his family; he sought out worth-while social contacts, built up professional and social prestige lest personal isolation hamper his quest for the good life.

To be really free, a man must be clear of physical appetite and passion, uncramped by social convention, immune to accepted dogmas and creeds. Brandeis saw freedom menaced by one's possessions as much as by financial dependence, endangered by security as well as insecurity, by power as well as weakness. No man is free, he said, if ambition masters him; all power-seekers are themselves enslaved. In time he discovered that by engaging in specific public causes he enjoyed a keen sense of duty done, of liberation— an enlargement of his own liberty.

It cannot be said that Brandeis was moved by an inner compulsion toward some perfectionist utopia; nor can he be considered solely as a champion of the underdog. His public activities were invariably undertaken on the initiative of others or grew out of his day-to-day law practice. He was neither blind to, nor neglectful of, corporate property rights. His career has been conspicuously identified with crucial social conflicts chiefly because so many able lawyers in his day actually were adjuncts of great corporations; they had lost sight of their opportunity, renounced a great obligation, "to protect *also* the interests of the people." [4] These interests Brandeis made his own.

Legal practice had become increasingly involved with business and finance, with relations between competing railroad systems, between great trusts and their consumers, between employers and employees—all rivaling in magnitude the affairs of state. Therefore the lawyer, Brandeis felt, must also be the statesman. Earlier in our history the legal profession had been approved as "a brake on democracy," "a ring in the nose of Leviathan." But Brandeis could not go along with this idea. Modern statesmanship, he held, required that lawyers redress the balance between corporate power and political democracy in favor of the latter. By leading the battle against human exploitation, lawyers could inform and temper popular protest, moderate political action. Only thus could a capitalist-democracy be preserved and kept on its path of progress "within the broad lines of existing institutions."

Viewing Brandeis in some such way as this, one may perhaps discover more consistency in his life and work, an integrated achievement true to its own purpose, as well as a closer kinship between the things he sought to win for his fellow-men and the growth he so arduously achieved for himself.

PART I

Heritage

CHAPTER ONE

In Quest of Freedom. The Forty-Eighters

IF LOUIS BRANDEIS knew how to use freedom, it was because his parents, Adolph Brandeis and Frederika Dembitz Brandeis, knew how to acquire it. Though neither family actively participated in the European revolutions of 1848, they suffered from the severity with which the revolutions were crushed. Along with thousands of other "Forty-eighters," Adolph and Frederika came to America, where they found some of the freedom Europe denied them; and here they passed along to their children much of the spirit that had made them rebels in Europe.

ADOLPH BRANDEIS (1822–1906)

Adolph Brandeis, son of Simon and father of Louis, was born in Prague, May 13, 1822, of an old Bohemian-Jewish family which traced back to the fifteenth century.

Adolph wanted to be a chemist, but he was never able to make the necessary preparation. He worked for a while as manager of his father's cotton-print mill in Prague. But there was no future in it, as the Brandeis handblock printing became less and less able to compete with machine methods. Adolph entered the local Technical School to study agriculture, estate management, and marketing. He was graduated with distinction in March 1843, but times were hard, and especially so for Jews, and he couldn't get a job. This was doubly disappointing because he had fallen in love.

Opposite the Brandeis factory stood the house of Amalia Wehle with whom Frederika Dembitz lived. Adolph called there often, and Frederika thought him "uncommonly charming, graceful, possessed of all the poetry of youth and unusually good manners." He thought equally well of her, and soon they were in love, "more deeply than they realized." [1] Talk of marriage followed, but first Adolph had to find suitable employment. Since Prague offered little, Adolph, in the spring of 1846, journeyed to Hamburg, only to be disappointed again. On June 16, 1846, he wrote his brother Samuel, a physician in Prague: "After my long journey I seem to have gone backward rather than forward, and to stand again at the very beginning of a career. . . . The pay of the best clerks is worse than in Prague, and as for any hope of independence, no one can talk about that. If everything fails, I cast my eyes on the near ocean and what lies beyond." [2]

America, however, had still to wait for the first of the Brandeises. Adolph found employment in a Hamburg grocery, and while this job was not sufficiently good to justify marriage, it kept him occupied and brought him experience of value later. His work took him to England, where he acquired knowledge of foreign trade, gained facility in the language, and became acquainted with Anglo-Saxon customs and institutions. The latter only increased his dissatisfaction with politics in Bohemia, and when revolution broke out there in 1848, he hurried home. Before he could join the rebels, however, he was stricken by typhoid fever. This turned out well, for when the Austrian Imperial government suppressed the revolt, Adolph's name was not among those proscribed. To him, as to so many others, 1848 was always the "wonderful year" when "the spirit of the Lord informed the peoples of Europe and His mighty voice overthrew the tyrants." [3] The next year was also wonderful, for then he married Frederika—in America.

FREDERIKA DEMBITZ (1829-1900)

Frederika was born in Prague, November 15, 1829, the daughter of Dr. Sigmund Dembitz and Fanny Wehle Dembitz. Both were the children of parents who had been ruined financially by the Napoleonic wars and who never recouped their wealth. Nor did their children—Sigmund and Fanny being in their usual straits when Frederika was born.

Sigmund, who wanted to practice medicine in Prague, then a part of Austria, took his medical degree at the University of Königsberg in Prussia—this despite the well-known Austrian law restricting the practice of medicine to graduates of Austrian schools. Sigmund and Fanny then moved from one little Polish town to another, never achieving anything notable in the way of a physician's practice. From time to time their prospects seemed to brighten, only too soon to be darkened by political unrest and not infrequently by the whim, eccentricity, or caprice of Sigmund. According to Frederika, her father was "unusually gifted, but irritable, passionate, and eccentric. Even at 62, he was handsome, tall, and stately. He was full of eloquence and enthusiasm, looked like a prince, and was more brilliant than most men. Unfortunately he was very impractical and inconsiderate, and although he was one of the first physicians of his day and especially famous as a surgeon, he could never maintain himself and never earned more than a meager livelihood." [4]

Dr. Dembitz and his family lived for a while in the Polish town of Zirke, near Posen, where he was physician to the Duke of Brunikowsky. To Frederika, Zirke was "the paradise of my childhood." Here the Dembitzes felt at home in "a circle consisting of German officials and small Polish nobility." [5] But the "circle" was broken by the revolution of 1831, which engendered so much hatred of Germans that Dr. Dembitz (though openly sympathetic with the Poles) felt impelled to move again—this time to Prussian Brandenburg. Thereafter life for the Dembitzes grew even more dismal, brightened only by occasional visits to the Wehle family at Prague. "As a little child," Frederika recalled in 1880, "I heard my parents speak of Prague again and again and heard it referred to with love and longing, as pious pilgrims must have felt for Jerusalem or Mecca." [6]

Frederika's only formal education was a term of six months at public school in the town of Müncheberg and about a year at a girls' high school in Frankfurt. French, writing, and arithmetic she learned from her father: "He was an excellent teacher and knew how to make the lessons very interesting—exciting our curiosity and introducing into every subject something beautiful and instructive." Frederika also had private tutors. A Lutheran clergyman named Waitzmann taught her, along with his daughter, ancient history and literature. From a Jewish tutor, Herr Edeles, who "in behavior and dress was reminiscent of the scholars of the ancient regime," she learned a little history and literature. An "old lady," Madame Sannet, "who was something of a despot," taught her French grammar and conversation, while various teachers contributed to her musical education. [7]

When Frederika was eleven her younger brother, Theodore, died of concussion when a nurse let him fall from a horse on the merry-go-round. The next year she lost her mother whom she idolized. "Let me be silent about those days and weeks," she wrote long afterward. "Did ever a twelve-year-old child feel more forsaken?" Her father tried vainly to keep his little family together. "If my mother's brothers had not supported us," Frederika recalled, "I do not know what would have become of us." [8] Thereafter she lived in Prague with her Aunt Amalia Wehle, whom Frederika described as "noble, helpful, and good."

Continuing her education, she studied drawing, went to dancing school, and took part in the performance of plays of her own composition: "When I think of the entertainments we arranged for ourselves, I must confess that they really were brilliant, and anyone who watched us might have expected us to do more than we accomplished later." [9] She steeped herself in Schiller and Goethe and read Karl Beck's poems, Bettina von Arnim's letters, and the rest of the romantic school; she joined a literary club and tried her hand at verse and the novel. Looking back later on this idyllic period, she wrote: "As in Italy when one wanders through the fields and mountain paths, every blooming bush, every broken piece of marble covered with climbing vines, every ruin which shows against the deep blue sky, the ragged, black-haired boy who leans lazily against the palm tree—all seem to compose into a charming sketch for the artist. In some such way, I adorned everything in my life with bright sparkling colors. The people whom I met, I compared with people in books. I idealized them 'to my heart's content, and so I really led a double life and my happy disposition and good health often helped me over many a domestic difficulty." [10]

Frederika was a voracious reader, and this literary interest she shared later with her children, especially with Louis. Writing him at Harvard she once reminisced: "I am pleased that Molière suits you so well. You know, he is my old friend. It also has something to do with the fact that my father first introduced me to him, I would say, made me feel at home in the circle so entirely new to the German child. Still today I remember certain passages in *Le Menteur, L'Avare, Tartuffe, Les Précieuses Ridicules,* and so on, which he explained to me, calling my attention to their good points, about which he himself burst into Homeric laughter again and again. I never read or hear Molière without remembering Father's study and my seat at the table, where I became acquainted for the first time with this amiable spirit. Do you know, that I was not yet ten years old?" [11]

FROM REACTIONARY EUROPE TO ADVANCING AMERICA

Frederika was nineteen when the revolutions broke out in 1848. The Dembitzes, Wehles, and Brandeises were not seriously implicated, yet they were concerned over the long and desolate reaction ahead if the revolutions failed. That they were Jews made their outlook even drearier, for they could be sure of increased racial prejudice once the reactionary tide set in.

Economically their prospects in the old world were no better than they were politically. The textile trade in which Frederika's uncle, Gottlieb Wehle, and the Brandeis family were engaged had been depressed for some time, and there was little hope of improvement. It was difficult, without experience, to shift to other lines that looked more promising than textiles. Only one escape seemed to be open to them—America, about whose resources they had heard so much and in whose freedom they hardly dared believe. Typically, these city people thought first of American land; like Jefferson, they associated freedom with agriculture. It was one thing to yearn for freedom in America and another to pull up all roots and move there, and especially to move there from European cities onto the land. But this they decided to do in 1848.

Of all the Wehles, Dembitzes, and Brandeises, only Adolph Brandeis, now engaged to Frederika, had any knowledge of farming, and this was largely academic. In the fall of 1848 the older members of the three families sent Adolph as envoy and scout to study American conditions and select a location.

Adolph arrived in New York, traveled for a while in the East, and then went on to the agricultural Middle West, visiting farms and villages along the way. Young Brandeis's pleasure and facility in travel were greatly enhanced by the companionship of a young friend of the Wehles then on a business trip to the United States to secure information about American investments for the House of Rothschild. Thanks to his companion's contacts and letters of introduction, Adolph saw places and met people not accessible to most foreigners. More important, Adolph, like de Tocqueville, caught the spirit of America and the motivation behind American democracy. He observed a people engrossed in achieving a livelihood, yet inspired by something greater than their own affairs. Even among the rank-and-file Americans he sensed the striving to build a free and great country. He wrote Frederika: "When you look at people and see how they work and struggle to make a fortune, you might think you were living among merely greedy speculators. But this is not true. It is not the actual possession of things but the achievement of getting them that they care for. I have often thought that even the hard work of these people is a kind of patriotism. They wear themselves out to make their country bloom, as though each one of them were commissioned to show the despots of the old world what a free people can do. . . ."[12]

Adolph also saw cruder sides of American life. After visiting Beaver, Pennsylvania, near Pittsburgh, he wrote less like de Tocqueville and more like Charles Dickens, Mrs. Trollope, or Harriet Martineau:

The most interesting and remarkable things here are the contrasts you keep meeting. Practical convenience has been carried to a stage that Europe may not reach in a century, but there are habits in social life and manners which recall the childhood of civilization and even savagery. The American is most unbearable at table, and I can't refrain from telling you about a table d'hôte which I saw at Pittsburgh. . . .

Imagine a very long room set for 200 persons. The corridors are full of people impatiently waiting for the dinner bell to ring. Finally the welcome sound is heard. Like raging lions they all rush in to get the best places. In a second they are all seated and are greedily pouring down the hot soup which stands before them. All the rest of the food has already been placed on the table in shining metal dishes (such as you have probably seen in North Germany).

About thirty very tall Negroes dressed in white linen are standing about the table. At the sound of a small bell they raise their right hands as to a solemn oath; at a second signal they put their hands on the covers; at a third, they swing the covers high over their heads and all march around the table and carry off the covers. Then everyone falls to and before you can recover from the extraordinary spectacle, the steaming roasts, the dainty pies, and the delicious fruit are gobbled up and in a few minutes you find yourself deserted and only the unsavory remnants remain—"only the ruins betray the presence of man." You wander into the next room and see the same people taking an afternoon nap with their chairs tipped back and their feet on the table.[13]

Yet crude as Americans were, they were also tolerant, free, and independent. This was a great thing to Adolph, so recently come from a Europe where police regulations stopped one at every step and espionage was one of the most important functions of government. Intoxicated by America, he promptly applied for first citizenship papers, and two months after his arrival he was already at the point where "politics over here interests me much more than European politics." [14]

"I already love our new country so much," he wrote Frederika in January 1849, "that I rejoice when I can sing its praises. . . . I have gotten hold of a book which contains the messages of all the Presidents. This week I have been reading of the progress made in Washington's day, and I felt as proud and happy about it as though it had all been my own doing, as though the statistics showed my own yearly balance sheet. Afterwards I laughed at myself, but there is something in it. It is the triumph of the rights of man which emerges and in which we rejoice. I feel my patriotism growing every day, because every day I learn to know the splendid institutions of this country better." [15]

FARMING: PROS AND CONS

But Adolph, after all, had come on a specific mission—to see if the proposed farm colony were practical, and if so, to find a suitable location. Wishing to learn directly about life on American land, he hired himself out as a farm worker in Butler County, Ohio. The experience was painful, and he began immediately to share his disillusionment with Frederika. Describing his room in the farmhouse, he wrote: "Climb up a little stairs to a large room with five windows and three beds (where I sleep with two laborers), where three broken chairs and two old clocks are the whole furniture, and you will find me sitting at a little table, writing these lines with tears in my eyes and the deepest love in my heart." [16]

Farmers, he thought at first, could be "the happiest of men." He observed,

above all, how the American farmer took "endless satisfaction in his extraordinary, indeed unrivalled independence," how he would "insist obstinately on doing without everything that makes him dependent on
others." He was also impressed by the fact that work on an American farm
did not seem so exhausting or endless. There might still be time in the
evening for reading, he believed at the start, time for continuing one's
education, and for the enjoyment of one's friends and neighbors. But
Adolph's good impressions did not last long. Farming, even in America,
could and did involve back-breaking toil, so much so that a "man could
sink to a mere beast of burden." Worse still, farming could, and not infrequently did, mean stultifying monotony, "tedium" that "can become the
most deadly poison in family life." [17]

Soon Adolph decided in his own mind that his city-bred kinsmen, especially the older members, would not be equal to the rigors of farm life.
And he undertook the delicate task of conveying this thought to his relatives in Europe:

I appreciate that you are very unwilling to give up this idea, for I was too, and
we are not the only ones; but you can be very sure that all considerations against
farming which I have expressed were not lightly uttered, that they rest on
exact proof in my own experience and that of others. . . .

The Dr. B's about whom I wrote you on Nov. 15th have given up their farms
and sawmills because they could not make a living out of them and they found
life in the forest unbearable. If ever city people seemed fit for American farm
life, it was these people, both the men and the women, and still they are giving
up their undertaking after dearly bought experience.[18]

To soften the blow, Adolph philosophized: "The good things are not
always as good, the bad seldom as bad, as expected." He was convinced
that there were "few dissatisfied people" among the newcomers. And this
was true, not so much because of the material gains won, but because of a
deeply felt spiritual transformation. "To your own surprise," Adolph told
Frederika, "you will see how all your hatred of your fellow-men, all your
disgust at civilization, all your revulsion from the intellectual life, will
drop away from you at once. You will appreciate the fact that these feelings are solely products of the rotten European conditions." [19]

Adolph by this time had discovered that farming by no means exhausted
America's possibilities. The country's unbounded resources enabled men
facing failure in one occupation to transfer to another and with reasonable
prospects of success. This he undertook to do himself, turning from the
land, of which he knew so little, to the more familiar market place. In
January 1849 he got a job in a Cincinnati grocery. The experience gained

in Hamburg and England began almost immediately to tell, and by the following May, when he was at last to meet his family in New York, his employer offered him a partnership.

But Adolph, before this, had decided that he could do much better for himself. "I have various plans," he wrote Frederika, January 13, 1849, "for our joint undertaking which promise well for us both." His major plan was the manufacture of starch, sugar, and soap—all "very lucrative" he pointed out. He asked Frederika and his brother Samuel to make a point of learning, before their departure, all they could about the Bohemian process of making starch from corn.

All Adolph's new and grand plans were received coldly in Europe. His family and friends were deeply disappointed, even offended. Despite Adolph's "experience, abundant inquiry and thought," they were most unwilling to give up their dream of exchanging "civilization for the wilderness." This romantic dream was still intact when the steamer *Washington* sailed from Hamburg, April 8, 1849, carrying the Wehles, Brandeises, and Dembitzes, twenty-six persons in all. Twenty-seven great chests contained their belongings, ranging from two grand pianos and a cheval glass to feather beds, copper pots and pans.

TRIAL AND FAILURE IN MADISON, INDIANA

Adolph met the group in New York full of enthusiasm for his adopted country, and with no "anxiety at all on our account or on anybody else's." He talked long and optimistically of business opportunities, the dawning prosperity of the Middle West, the thriving river traffic along the Ohio. In two weeks the group set out to see for itself. From New York the Wehles, Dembitzes, and Brandeises went by slow-moving barge up the Hudson through the Erie Canal to Buffalo, by Lake Erie steamer to Sandusky, and by rail to Cincinnati. Here Adolph had leased a four-storey house for a month, to enable his relatives to consider their future at leisure. They soon abandoned the farm project, and while the women, accustomed to many servants, wrestled unhappily with housekeeping, the men pondered America's business opportunities and the best locality in which to pursue them.

On his journeys through the Middle West, Adolph had been impressed by Madison, Indiana, on a bend of the Ohio River between Louisville and Cincinnati.[20] Its position made it a terminal for the first railroad built in the state, a transfer point between the railroad serving central Indiana and a busy region of the Ohio River. He anticipated, as did others, that Madison would soon become "the first city of Indiana, first in commerce, population, wealth, literature, laws, religion, politics, and social enjoyment." [21]

Madison also seemed blessed with a healthful climate, at that time a most important consideration. In near-by Cincinnati hundreds were dying daily of cholera, whereas Madison had so far escaped the scourge.[22] The Brandeis and Wehle families decided to settle there and build their factory for the manufacture of starch from corn. As a sort of lifeline for the new venture, they planned to start a grocery and general produce store under the name of G. & M. Wehle, Brandeis & Company.

Dr. Dembitz, Frederika's father, visualized better prospects for himself and his son Lewis, a lawyer, in the more populous city of Cincinnati. They did not go there, however, until Frederika married Adolph Brandeis on September 5, 1849. Actually it was a double wedding, Frederika's cousin Lotti marrying Adolph's brother Samuel at the same time. The young couples started housekeeping together in a small house in Madison near the Wehles.

The starch factory proved unsuccessful, and was sold out at a loss at the end of two years. The grocery and produce store, however, under Adolph's efficient management, fared better. He assumed much of the responsibility, especially in the purchase of stock, and traveled by buggy or on horseback through the Ohio Valley, buying crops, personally supervising the packing and shipping, talking to farmers, and studying the life and politics of the region. Evenings on these trips he joined discussions at local grocery stores or village taverns. "They cast lots or play dominoes," Adolph wrote his wife, "to decide who is to pay the reckoning for the beer; and as I always take part in the game and pay, and then leave my beer, I have made many good friends."[23] As a German he enjoyed a marked advantage in a section where Germans greatly outnumbered all other settlers. Not infrequently he would travel sixty to eighty miles through land inhabited exclusively by Germans, without hearing "a single word of English." Little wonder that Lincoln, at about that same time, trying law cases in similar country, "carried a German grammar and studied the language in a night class."[24]

A shrewd judge of men, Adolph Brandeis was himself being sized up by a contemporary observer, John Lysle King, a leading lawyer in Madison, a columnist, violinist, and later a member of the Indiana House of Representatives.[25] No doubt with others, as with himself, King passed for a wit. He became acquainted with Adolph before the rest of the clan reached America, and he recorded in his diary: "Brandeis, my Bohemian acquaintance, was in this afternoon and talked to me about himself. . . . We had some married people at our house to tea and I took Brandeis there with me. He is well bred, and has good manners. . . . He seems familiar with the great names, if not the literature of Germany. . . . He is betrothed to a maiden, who is a sister to the boy [Lewis Dembitz] he wishes to have read law in our office. . . . He represents her as accomplished, but not beautiful. . . . He says the doctor's [Samuel Brandeis] is the handsomest of the three girls, but that his betrothed is the cleverest and best educated." * [26]

King was favorably inclined to having his new friends settle in Madison, anticipating cultural and pecuniary advantages for himself: "I was round with Brandeis today looking for a house—saw none to be had for love or money. He went to Cincinnati this evening and will probably take a house there. I regret this; I should like the clan to settle here. If his intended brother-in-law [Lewis Dembitz] studied law with us I could absorb German from him." [27]

Soon after the clan's arrival, King recorded: "My German acquaintance Brandeis has been in again. . . . Two of the gentlemen of the family were with him and are gentlemen, intelligent, shrewd looking ones. I shall be glad when they come. They will be of some advantage to me both in the way of company and probably of business." [28]

Of Lewis Dembitz, Frederika's brother, who had attended the *Gymnasium* of Frankfurt-on-Oder at Glogau University, and had taken a law course of one semester in Prague, King wrote in his diary: "He is only 16 and is very boyish in appearance of manner and his juvenility escaped him in divers ways. But the child is already 'father to the man.' He is a prodigy of information and must have genius. He was born for distinction. . . . A foreigner making his acquaintance with things around him through the medium of a foreign tongue and of an age when the mind is least inquisitive about such things, he yet seems to be possessed himself of the spirit of our institutions and to have with quick comprehension grasped in a *coup d'oeil,* the main features of our whole legal and political system and to have learned them with the spirit of a philosopher and not the mere senseless curiosity of boyhood. It was wonderful to hear a boy of his age and his extreme youthful appearance expatiate on matters of state and of law with the familiarity of an old acquaintance of them. His knowledge is that of a man, his appearance that of a child. I am told that Judge Walker of Cincinnati, to whom he is a student, says that he is the brightest boy of his class and the brightest boy of his age that he knows. He sat in the office with me two hours. I wondered constantly at his resources." [29]

King was especially curious as to the women of the family: "The Brandeis and Wehle crowd are domiciled next door to Moore's house. I hoped to get a glimpse of some of the ladies, but the twilight shades deepened around too much into dimness to give me a good sight." [30] When

---

* Frederika wrote of herself in her *Reminiscences:* "I did not consider myself beautiful except for my hair and my eyes."

Adolph neglected to use the first opportunity to introduce him, he complained: ". . . the ladies returning passed into the house. I was not asked in to see them."

When King finally did meet them he was unimpressed: "I was round at Wehle's till 10 o'clock. The ladies came in and I was introduced. I didn't have much to say to them—as they understood English too imperfectly and are too diffident to use our tongue as well as they know how to keep up an animated conversation. . . . They dress in a very ordinary way, but otherwise must be very accomplished ladies." [31]

Madison must have been grateful for the presence of Adolph's brother, Dr. Samuel Brandeis, when, despite its reputed healthful climate, the town was stricken by cholera in the summer of 1849. "The cholera news is worse than it has been yet," King noted June 17, 1849. "Dr. Brandeis came in and said he had just been treating an Irish woman." Again, on July 14, King wrote: "Dr. Brandeis told me of a German girl who dreamed she and her sister were going to die. They were in perfect health. In four days she and her sister did die of cholera." Dr. Dembitz was also a godsend to near-by Cincinnati and later to Louisville. He had himself contracted the dread disease in an early epidemic, and the immunity thus gained increased his usefulness later on at the centers of greatest trouble.

Despite the neighborliness of a small town, life in Madison was lonely and devoid of cultural interest for people with the background of the Brandeises and the Wehles. Taking refuge in themselves, they devoted many a quiet evening to reading and music.

King's diary tells of such entertainment at the Wehles: "We soon grew sociable and familiar—had music on the piano. Mr. Adolph Brandeis's fingers first swept the keys. Maurice [King's cousin] then vocalized and did us 'Sweet Were My Dreams.' . . . Then there was a polka, waltz, and gallop instrumentation from Mrs. Moritz Wehle, who added in that way her quota of entertainment and made fascinating sound to wake from the vibrated strings in tones which went to our inner spirits and stirred them from their inner depths in compensation for the amount of sound which her inability in English deprived us from the organ of speech. She went well and familiarly through all the intricate passages and labyrinths of German music and executed Mozart and Beethoven with interpretations of Strauss, to our admiration and with spirit enough to start some of the company into the motions of a normal waltz and instrumental polka."

Beneath the genteel veneer of King's diary one senses the strangeness of the new environment to these cultured immigrants, their embarrassment in struggling with a foreign language. "It amuses and entertains me," King remarked, "to hear the [Wehle] ladies talk. They are a little shy to the use of our speech too—their coyness and diffidence on this score keeps the imagination active enough to render them decidedly entertaining. Helen spoke in French to them. They were so agreeably surprised to hear a language they understood that their gratification spontaneously revealed itself in joyous exclamations and they followed us to the gate with a new-born fervor expressing the happiness they would have in seeing her again." [32]

On their first New Year's Eve in America, the Wehles and Brandeises invited their American friends to celebrate with them "in something of the manner of the Fatherland." To the provincial King their festivities appeared "crude," almost outlandish. As a "Son of Temperance," King could hardly participate, but looked on, filled with a sense of tolerant superiority:

"Toward twelve . . . Mr. Wehle surmounted the table with a tureen of hot whiskey punch—the savory steams of which penetrated all my olfactories and led me to instant temptation, it was so very delicious. I knew from the ethereal particles which underwent distillation through the pores of my nasal affix that I realized the meeting of the members in all the essential points of Agrippa's fable in relation to my indulging. Before I could finally enforce the authority of my pledge, they assembled around the table, all standing, forming a social cordon—masculine and feminine—and joining arms held up their brimmers, raised a song with a full chorus, pledged healths and repeated many a time and oft. The boisterous refrains though unknown to me, intimated how turbulent the spirit of gaiety was within. I could scarcely be permitted to decline the glass which was filled for me. It touched but did not bedew my lips. . . . Still I held out. I stood by and listened to the merry clink of their oft replenished glasses and resisted the still more insidious and dangerous congruent of jovial spirits without compromising myself. Song followed song . . . and at one o'clock, after seeing the New Year welcomed duly with their *vivat,* but the mirth still going on, I left and turned homeward steps." [33]

The Brandeises and Wehles did not tarry long in Madison. As the much heralded prosperity did not materialize, people began to move away. The little town daily grew quieter and more monotonous; certain members of the family feared that "soon not a soul, except of course ourselves, will be left here." [34] Heeding the sign of the times, the Brandeis family moved in 1851 (shortly after the birth of Adolph and Frederika's first child, Fannie) to Louisville. A few years later the Wehles moved to New York.

CHAPTER TWO

Youth and Schooling in an Expanding World

LOUISVILLE in the fifties hummed with activity. Strategically located on the Ohio River in the heart of a rich agricultural section, it was a crossroad between North and South, between the industrial East and the pioneering West. Packet steamships plied the turgid Ohio on regular schedule between Louisville and New Orleans. To Louisville came southern planters to buy pork, hay, flour, and machinery for their cotton mills and sugar refineries; from Louisville northward flowed a steady stream of southern commodities—sugar, molasses, coffee, cotton. Wealth accumulated; and by the time the Brandeises arrived, rich merchants and manufacturers had already built many great mansions of limestone and brick with classic cornice and carved balustrade.

Into this thriving and proud community Louis David Brandeis was born, November 13, 1856, the youngest of Adolph's and Frederika's four children. Except Fannie, all were born in Louisville, in a little house on Center Street, between Chestnut and Walnut: Amy on April 9, 1852, Alfred on March 23, 1854. Louis came in on the rising tide of the family's fortunes, for his father was on the way to becoming a prosperous grain and produce merchant. Adolph had made the first wheat shipments from Kentucky to the eastern states in 1855, when the Genesee Valley wheat crop in New York failed. Thereafter, among the millers of the East, the reputation of Kentucky white wheat was established. To profit from this reputation and to develop other markets as well, Adolph formed a partnership in 1855 with Charles W. Crawford, and the new firm of Brandeis & Crawford gradually expanded. In a few years they were operating a flour mill, a tobacco factory, an eleven-hundred-acre farm, and a river freighter, the *Fanny Brandeis*.

Meanwhile other members of the family group had come to Louisville and begun successful professional careers. Adolph's brother Samuel built up a large medical practice, and in 1853 Lewis Dembitz began a notable legal career.

CIVIL WAR AND PROSPERITY

The tumultuous days of the Civil War, not family successes, were among Louis Brandeis's earliest recollections. "I remember helping my mother

carry out food and coffee to the men from the North," he recalled. "The
streets seemed full of them always. But there were times when the rebels
came so near that we could hear the firing. At one such time my father
moved us across the river. Those were my first memories." [1]

Shadows of the Civil War still hung over the Kentucky of Louis's youth.
Kentucky had been one of four slave states that remained loyal to the
Union and sent more men to the northern than to the southern armies;
but for twenty years after the war, Kentucky voted with the Solid South.
As ardent abolitionists, Louis's father and uncle held views contrary to those
prevailing in their adopted state. Yet the family fortunes were actually
improved by conditions growing out of the conflict. Previous to 1861 Brandeis & Crawford had carried on a large grain trade with the South; when
war broke out their business was transferred to the regions north of the
Ohio River. They were large contractors with the federal government
throughout the war. During these years the firm expanded enormously
and helped promote the growth of Louisville as an important grain center. Adolph and Frederika had early in 1860 bought a house on First Street,
which they modernized and completely remodeled. In a few years more,
reflecting their increased prosperity, they bought a lot on exclusive Broad-
way, built a large limestone-front house and staffed it with Negro servants,
including their first Negro coachman. [2]

In this atmosphere of comfort and success Louis enjoyed a normal boyhood. He played with dolls, burned himself with gunpowder, frightened
maids with straw dummies, teased little girls, and, as the youngest of the
gang with which he played, fought the "Little Lord Fauntleroys" of
Louisville.

Louis was devoted to his older brother Alfred, and the comradeship of
their youth developed into an affection which grew through the years. In
the eyes of their mother Alfred and Louis were to each other "as *Wall* and
Veit, twin brothers in the hobbledehoy years." "My heart rejoices," she
wrote to Louis, December 5, 1881, "when I see you happy together. It seems
to me that there never were two brothers who complemented one another
so perfectly and were so completely one as you two." [3]

Adolph Brandeis prospered enough to be able to give his family the
benefits of travel even during the war. In 1862 he sent them East to New
York to visit the Wehles, whom Frederika had not seen since the Madison
days. A favorite among the Wehles was Frederika's beautiful cousin Re-
gina, who had married Dr. Joseph Goldmark, Louis Brandeis's future
father-in-law. In the summer of 1864 the Brandeis family went East again,
this time to Newport. The following summer Alfred and Louis went with

their parents to Niagara Falls, to Canada, and again to Newport. In his eighty-fifth year Louis still remembered vividly the thrill of seeing the falls, the ocean, and "real Indians." [4]

At Newport the Brandeises boarded in the same house with several other Louisville families, including their aunt, Lotti Brandeis, who had made the trip with them. Adolph was particularly happy in the comradeship of a Prague boyhood friend, Dr. William Taussig, now of St. Louis. In writing her two little girls in Louisville, Frederika described Taussig as a worthy man, and told how "our good Papa sits with him recalling old stories of his youth and laughing till the tears run down." [5] These Newport days were full of swimming, boating, and fishing. The boys rode donkeys, read at the library, and readily became acquainted with the children of other vacationers. [6]

There were shorter trips also. St. Louis, a metropolis within easy reach of Louisville and the home of Dr. Taussig, was particularly attractive to the Brandeis family. In 1870, when Frederika was visiting there with Alfred, the fourteen-year-old Louis wrote her:

Louisville
September 7, 1870

My dear darling Ma:

As I can't write to you tomorrow morning, I use my time tonight to write a few lines and congratulate my dear Ma on her wedding day, the first one I have not been with you. I hope you are having a splendid time. I know Alfred is. We are all a little sick (home sick but not sick of home) today but otherwise are very well.

Today the regular lessons began and there was yawning done in our room which would have done justice to Pa. I study only French, Latin, Chemistry, German, Algebra, Composition, Trigonometry: Mathematics and Languages being the principal studies.

We went out riding with Aunt Rosa on the river road yesterday. Aunt Lotti and Mrs. Knefler were here this afternoon. Nora has started to our school. She is in the Kindergarten. Stella goes to the free school. Pa is at the Opera House meeting tonight. Fanny is going to the Prussian meeting tomorrow afternoon. Mr. Hirschbull is going to raffle off the picture HEIDELBERG he used to have hanging in his store, for the wounded. Has Pa written you of his proposed punishment for Napoleon? It is this: He should be put in prison with no book but Kinglake's Crimea. Amy is troubling me awful as she wants to write, so goodbye. Hoping you will soon be back to your

Loving son
Louis

PRE-EMINENCE IN ALL HIS STUDIES

In his schoolwork Louis stood out as an extraordinarily precocious child. Like his sisters and brother, he was given every educational advantage that Louisville could afford, and he made good use of all his opportunities. For a while he attended Miss Wood's private school, where he made his first excellent record. He used *Goodrich's New First School Reader,* one of whose advantages was the number of "lessons in rhyme" which it contained. Louis's copy of this reader, used by him at the age of seven, is preserved among his papers. Its illustrations bear evidence of the future Supreme Court Justice's early efforts with water colors.

At the German and English Academy of Louisville, Louis's grades, almost without exception, were 6, denoting perfection. On one occasion the principal made a point of stating that "Louis deserves special commendation for conduct and industry." [7] At the Louisville Male High School his grades for the sophomore year were mostly 6, none being as low as 5, on a scale in which 5 signified "excellent" and 6 "without fault." [8] In his sixteenth year Louis was awarded a gold medal "for pre-eminence in all his studies" by the University of the Public Schools in Louisville. [9]

Louis studied music as a matter of course, for a while devoting himself conscientiously to the violin. But he lacked real musical talent. His sister Fannie, on the other hand, was very gifted musically and tried to help him. Louis recorded in his diary of 1871: "Fannie promised to practice with me every Monday and Thursday and sometimes on Saturday. Wonder if she will do it regularly." His musical efforts, though discouraging, were not entirely fruitless. Writing Mrs. James B. Speed, March 11, 1933, Justice Brandeis recalled that "in the summer of grim 1875, Harry [Mrs. Speed's brother, Harry Bishop], Henry Watterson and I (as second fiddle) played the overture to *Zampa* in Mr. [Louis H.] Hast's Orchestra."

A GOODLY HERITAGE

In Louisville in the middle of the nineteenth century the Brandeises found a good deal of cultural stimulation. Among their friends were a group of Americans and some of the more intellectual forty-eighters who met regularly in the newly formed Louisville library. According to Dr. Abraham Flexner, then a youth of fifteen and part-time assistant in the library, this group was accustomed to gather at five-thirty in the afternoon "to read and discuss the daily papers, *The Nation,* and *The Saturday Review.* . . . I listened in and I have heard no better or more stimulating talk from that day to this." [10]

The families of the Brandeis brothers and Lewis Dembitz were a closely knit, idealistic, intellectually self-reliant group. Although prominent in the community life of Louisville, they found the most stimulating companionship among themselves, very much as in the old Wehle house at Prague. Lewis Dembitz was easily the dominating figure in the group. And it was largely admiration for this brilliant uncle that inspired Louis Brandeis to study law. In Lewis Dembitz's honor Louis changed his middle name of David to Dembitz.

Lewis Dembitz was a lawyer of uncompromising integrity. His extreme moral fastidiousness kept not a few clients from his door. He was an able and productive scholar, author of several authoritative legal works, notably *Kentucky Jurisprudence* and *Land Titles in the United States*. An enormously learned and versatile man, he was interested in almost anything that concerned human life. "To those of my generation," Justice Brandeis said of him many years later, he was "a living university. With him, life was unending intellectual ferment. . . . In the diversity of his intellectual interests, in his longing to discover truths, in his pleasure in argumentation and the process of thinking, he reminded one of the Athenians." [11]

Dembitz had a reading, if not speaking, knowledge of a dozen languages, including Hebrew and Arabic, and was sought out for his views on intricate philological questions. He contributed regularly to encyclopedias, and throughout his mature years corresponded widely with English and European scholars. Profoundly versed in the culture of Judaism, he had mastered its history, ritual, and theology. No problem of higher mathematics baffled him. Though astronomy was for him only a hobby, he forecast to the minute the total eclipse of the sun in 1869. Yet with all his scholarship he was not pedantic. He carried his learning lightly, delighting his friends with choice incidents of absent-mindedness that are still related in Louisville.

"The greatest combination of good fortune any man can have," Brandeis said later, "is a parentage unusual for both brains and character." In Louis the significant characteristics of both parents were blended in happy and well-balanced combination. From his father he inherited sound judgment, subtle wit, and a remarkable capacity for the persuasive management of men. From his mother stemmed a romantic strain, an insatiable desire to better conditions, unfaltering faith in his fellow-men. She possessed "preeminently," Justice Brandeis remarked, "a sense of duty to the community, not so much by preaching, but by practice." [12]

Neither parent professed formal religion. They held no membership in either church or synagogue. Frederika, in her *Reminiscences,* discussed why she brought up her children without formal religion:

"I do not believe that sins can be expiated by going to divine service and observing this or that formula; I believe that only goodness and truth and conduct that is humane and self-sacrificing towards those who need us can bring God nearer to us, and that our errors can only be atoned for by acting in a more kindly spirit. Love, virtue and truth are the foundation upon which the education of the child must be based. They endure forever. . . . And this is my justification for bringing up my children without any definite religious belief: I wanted to give them something that neither could be argued away nor would have to be given up as untenable, namely, a pure spirit and the highest ideals as to morals and love. God has blessed my endeavors." [13]

In Louis, Frederika saw all her "dreams of high ideals and purity united." For her, as for him, religion had nothing to do with dogma or ceremony; it was synonymous with generous and humane impulses, the basic moral virtues. By the time he was eighteen Louis himself felt keenly the desire to be of public service. In his youthful notebook he had copied Bacon's words: "In the theatre of human life, it is only for God and angels to be spectators." For his high sense of social obligation, for his zealous interest in the general welfare, credit—on his own testimony—is due most of all to his parents.

ECONOMIC COLLAPSE AND EUROPEAN TRAVEL

The financial good fortune which had attended Louis from birth ended in 1872 when Brandeis & Crawford suffered heavy losses through the failures of southern clients in the postwar depression. Unwilling to risk further loss in the economic crash he saw impending, Adolph decided to dissolve the firm of Brandeis & Crawford and await the return of better times. Yet even this redounded to Louis's benefit, for Adolph, prodded by Lewis Dembitz, decided to take his family on a visit to Europe. They left Louisville in May 1872, planning to spend fifteen months abroad. Their return, however, was postponed from time to time because of the illness of Louis's oldest sister, Fannie. Actually it was three years before they returned to America.

Louis, not yet sixteen, keenly enjoyed every minute of the trip. He began a diary on the day the S.S. *Adriatic* sailed, August 10, 1872, and went into great detail concerning ship and passengers:

At 9 o'clock A.M. Aug. 10th 1872 I arrived aboard the steamer at the W.S.L. docks, Jersey City, New Jersey. On board were all those intending to make the journey and their friends who came to see them off and the latter were by far the greater number. At 9:45 the bells for causing the visitors to leave were rung and at 10:12 we left the docks.

Our ship was a large ocean steamer, 4,000 tons, four hundred feet in length and said to be the fastest between England and America, having made one trip in 7 days and 8 hours. Our captain, a stout six-footer, is a jolly looking man and makes himself as agreeable as possible.

Soon after starting we caught up to the S.S. *Washington,* French Line, and a short time afterwards to the S.S. *Egypt,* National, and *City of New York,* Ismay Line, all of which we soon left behind. Later in the day, about 4 P.M., we saw the four, S.S. *Washington, City of New York, Egypt* and *Abyssinian,* Cunard Line, abreast.

The weather this day was clear, the water smooth and green in color. Everybody seemed well except a few who seemed to have made up their minds to be sick all the time and made themselves unwell by remaining in the berths. Everybody seemed delighted and surprised at not yet being sick and wondering how soon they would be.

The *Adriatic* reached Liverpool on August 18. After a brief stay the Brandeis family went to London for three days, thence via Dover to Ostend, Cologne, Frankfurt, and Stuttgart. Their longest sojourn was in Ischl, a Tyrolean summer resort, where they remained until mid-October.

Louis's original intention was to continue his schooling at the *Gymnasium* in Vienna, but despite a gold medal for distinguished work in Louisville, his preparation was not good enough for him to pass the entrance examinations. This too proved fortunate, as it let him spend 1872–73 in travel and self-education. He remained most of the winter in Vienna, taking private lessons and attending lectures at the University and enjoying those vital elements of German culture—music and the theater. On March 20, 1873, he started by way of Trieste on a visit to Italy, arriving in Venice on the 23rd. After a leisurely stay in the Adriatic capital, where his mother rejoiced in art treasures and architecture, the family visited Bologna, Naples, Genoa, Pisa, and Milan. Upon arriving in Milan late in May, Amy was stricken with typhoid fever, and they were unable to continue their journey until early in July, when they left for Switzerland via Como and the incomparable Italian lake country.[14]

There followed for Louis a memorable summer in Switzerland, rich in the companionship of his father and his brother. Both boys liked to go mountain climbing with their father, though Louis tired more easily than Alfred, loath as he was to admit it. One of their climbs in the Bernina Alps was to discover the source of the River Inn. While resting under a clump of trees, Alfred suggested they seek also the source of the River Adda. At this exhausted young Louis exclaimed, "I don't see why I should have to find the source of every damned river in Europe!" [15]

This year of stimulating travel Louis Brandeis remembered all his life. Letters to his brother covering nearly half a century are full of references to it, to innumerable incidents and the dates on which these occurred. In later life his wife's delicate constitution and the pressure of his own work prevented extensive travel. As compensation he read widely of foreign lands, their history and culture, and acquired an unusual knowledge of civilizations and peoples he had never seen.

In the fall of 1873 Alfred returned to Louisville to work, and Louis decided to try to enter the Annen-Realschule in Dresden by obtaining a waiver of examinations. Owing to his sister's illness, the family was unable to accompany him, and he was thrown upon his own resources. He had his first taste of independence in making the journey to Dresden alone. When a friend on whom he had depended for an introduction to the rector of the Annen-Realschule could not accompany him as promptly as he wished, he determined to brave the rector himself. Like a moth about a candle, he circled the school until he had mustered enough courage to enter. Finally he went right to the principal's office. The rector stated flatly that he could not admit a new pupil without examination. Louis was also informed that in addition to the examinations he would have to submit birth and vaccination certificates. To this the youth replied: "The fact that I'm here is proof of my birth and you may look at my arm for evidence that I was vaccinated." [16]

So successfully did Louis argue his case that the rector permitted him to matriculate without the required test. This was a tribute to the good judgment of the rector as well as early evidence of the future Supreme Court Justice's power of persuasion.

Louis rewarded the confidence of the rector. His notebooks, in his clear, beautiful hand, show the serious thought he put on his studies. In the three terms he attended the Annen-Realschule his grades hardly varied. The first term he had four grades of 2, denoting *gut,* and eight of 1, denoting *sehr gut.* The last terms he had three grades of 2 and nine of 1. While Louis took twelve courses at a time, he did not change from term to term, but continued the same program. No doubt this was essential for thorough grounding in his subjects, and perhaps he thus received an education of more value to his future career. His program included French, Latin, and German (the three subjects in which he was comparatively weak), literature, mineralogy, geography, physics, chemistry, and much mathematics.

A year and a half after entering the school, Louis won a prize which, according to custom, he could select for himself. Louis chose a book on Greek art, *Charakterbilder aus der Kunstgeschichte,* by A. W. Becker. On the fly leaf, yellow and musty with years, is a faint inscription in spidery German script:

A prize awarded out of the Heymann Endowment to the honor student, Louis Dembitz Brandeis, for industry and good behavior by the faculty of the Annen-Realschule, Dresden, March 19, 1875.

M. Job, Rector.

Schooling in Germany meant far more to him than the usual routine of subjects conventionally memorized and faithfully rehearsed. Many years later he told his secretary, Paul A. Freund, how he discovered the deductive process. "I heard him say," Mr. Freund relates, "that although he did well in his studies theretofore, it was not until he went to Dresden that he really learned to think. He said that in preparing an essay on a subject about which he had known nothing, it dawned on him that ideas could be evolved by reflecting on your material. This was a new discovery for him."

HOMESICK FOR AMERICA: IMMIGRANTS NO MORE

The years abroad deepened Louis's Americanism. Although appreciative of the great advantages derived from his European education, he rebelled against the Prussian ideals then coming to dominate Germany—the formalism, the rigid, almost military discipline which made the German *Gymnasium* such a model of efficiency. The Kentucky boy was irked by the authoritarian aspects of faculty-student relationships, the hat tipping and formal respect due the professors. In his own words: "I was a terrible little individualist in those days, and the German paternalism got on my nerves." [17] One night he returned to the school late and, discovering that he had forgotten his key, whistled loudly enough to awaken his roommate. For this offense he was taken to task by a stern *Schultzmann*. Years later, recalling this experience of his youth, he remarked: "This made me homesick. In Kentucky you could whistle! I wanted to go back to America and I wanted to study law. My uncle, the abolitionist, was a lawyer; and to me nothing else seemed really worth while." [18]

When in the spring of 1875 his parents decided to return home, Louis naturally was eager to go. Yet his keen interest in everything around him had not been dulled by intensive sightseeing and study, and as the return trip began, he had the fresh outlook of a person just arrived in Europe, not that of one on the verge of leaving it. He was delighted with Hamburg and with Le Havre, from which his family sailed May 5, 1875, his mother and Fannie traveling second class, his father, Amy, and himself third class. He wrote in his diary:

May 3rd. Quite bewildered by the noise and bustle of Hamburg, delighted with the lively business, beautiful houses, parks, etc.

May 8th. In Havre we took a carriage and rode around in town. Beautiful parks—splendid flowers in bloom. Grand docks—fine buildings, wide streets. Pa & I went to town again after supper—took coffee under the arcades near the theatre.

As on the trip over, Louis sized up his fellow-passengers with a shrewd and critical eye. On the whole he did not approve of them, recording in his diary:

The passengers of the 2nd cabin are on the whole rather unpleasant, very few interesting, very few fine, exceedingly many Jews. The nicest are Mr. Thomson, American engineer, who had been in a Russian armory three years & 1½ years in Germany; Mr. Steinmacher, goldsmith from New York, the Russian actress, who was going to Philadelphia for two years (came on board at Havre), Mr. Grabmann, formerly officer in the Austrian army, the most lively man on board; great talker, fine figure, reminds much of Chas. Morningstar, but is less fine, and more fussy—very courageous and impudent. His wife a ninny. Grabmann has quite much wit & is really funny. Mr. and Mrs. Schultz—geese. Kohler, Edelheim—quite nice.

The ship was a steamer which also carried sails, as was then the practice. It must have been a diminutive ship by present standards, for sails were hoisted to steady it, either against the rolling waves or the jolting of its engines.

As the journey progressed the notations in Louis's diary became briefer. In fact, many of them were apparently written later, possibly after he had returned to Louisville. But they remained discriminating and showed a deep, almost poetic appreciation of the sights of the voyage.

The ship reached New York Harbor on the evening of May 18, and the following day the Brandeis family disembarked. After a visit with friends in Brookline, Massachusetts, when Louis made plans for matriculating at Harvard Law School, they went on home, arriving in Louisville on June 1, 1875.

For the whole Brandeis family these three years in Europe, despite the beauties and intellectual delights, had but strengthened their devotion to America.

CHAPTER THREE

Cambridge and St. Louis in the 1870's

LOUIS, not yet nineteen, entered Harvard Law School, September 27, 1875. He was without college training and prepared directly for his new studies only by reading Kent's *Commentaries on American Law* that summer. His financial resources comprised a few hundred dollars borrowed from Alfred.

Louis loved life at Harvard, where he remained until 1878. Those were indeed "the wonderful years." Long letters to his family and friends in Louisville spoke in glowing terms of the advantages of studying at this "splendid institution." The fullest letters went to Otto Wehle, a young Louisville attorney, who later married Louis's sister Amy. "You have undoubtedly heard from others of my work here," Louis wrote Otto, March 12, 1876; "how well I am pleased with everything that pertains to the law; yet my own inclinations prompt me to repeat the same to you, though at the risk of great reiteration. My thoughts are almost entirely occupied with the law, and you know—*Wovon das Hertz voll ist, u.s.w.*" Of "inestimable value" were a "complete library of over fifteen thousand volumes" and the opportunity to "associate with young men who have the same interest and ambition, who are determined to make as great progress as possible in their studies and devote all their time to the same."

A question then much debated among lawyers and students was the relative advantage of study in law school as against "reading law" in a lawyer's office. In 1876 Louis had not made up his mind. "After one has grasped the principles which underlie the structure of the Common Law," he wrote Otto, "I doubt not that one can learn very much in an office. That first year at law is, however, surely ill-spent in an office."

He was still concerned over the question in 1889. "Undoubtedly," he then observed, "each offers advantages which the other does not possess. All lawyers concede that a short apprenticeship in the office of a practitioner is valuable; but a thorough knowledge of legal principles is essential to higher professional success, and this knowledge, which under all circumstances is difficult of acquisition, can rarely be attained except as the result of uninterrupted, systematic study, under competent guidance. For such training, the lawyer's office seldom affords an opportunity." [1]

JOINING THE LANGDELL REVOLUTION

Prior to 1870 law was taught at Harvard, as elsewhere, chiefly by lectures which explained and illustrated prescribed textbook reading. The student had no firsthand contact with court opinions as such. A few years before Brandeis matriculated, however, teaching methods had been radically changed by a New York lawyer, Christopher Columbus Langdell, who in 1870 became Dane Professor of Law at Harvard.

Langdell's appointment marked an epoch in legal education. He began at once to revise and stiffen requirements for admission, to reorganize and expand the course of study, and, more particularly, to apply the inductive method of modern science to the study of the law. Believing that textbooks, even though based on actual cases, did not effectively discipline the lawyer's mind, Langdell selected and compiled cases in various branches of the law. These actual cases he had the students analyze in class, by taking apart the arguments of counsel and the courts' opinions. In the language of one of Louis's professors, by Langdell's method "the case is 'eviscerated.'" [2] Langdell himself proclaimed the advantages of his new pedagogy in the preface to his *Selected Cases on Contracts,* October 1871—the first book of its kind ever published:

Law, considered as a science, consists of certain principles or doctrines. . . . Each of these doctrines has arrived at its present state by slow degrees: in other words, it is a growth, extending in many cases through centuries. This growth is to be traced in the main through a series of cases; and much the shortest and best, if not the only way of mastering the doctrine effectually is by studying the cases in which it is embodied. . . . To have such a mastery of these as to be able to apply them with constant facility and certainty to the ever-tangled skein of human affairs, is what constitutes a true lawyer; and hence to acquire that mastery should be the business of every earnest student of the law. [3]

Brandeis was among the first subjected to the new legal training, and he was glad of it. Even in its experimental years he had little or no misgiving as to the wisdom of the bold course Langdell had charted. "Some of our professors," he wrote Otto Wehle, March 12, 1876, "are trying to inculcate in us a great distrust of textbooks, and to prove to us the truth of the maxim *Melius est petere fontes quam sectari rivulos.** When one sees how loosely most textbooks are written and how many startling propositions are unsupported by the authorities cited to sustain them—the temptation to become a convert of Coke's is very great. Several textbooks, however, some late English ones, receive almost unqualified praise—among which is

* Better it is to seek the fountains than to follow the rivulets.

Leake's admirable work on contracts. Of course no one would dare detract from Stephen's fame, but to Parsons and even Story the epithet of 'loose' is not infrequently bestowed."

At first lawyers and professors looked askance at Langdell's innovation. Indeed, the Law School of Boston University was founded in protest against his methods. Nevertheless, the new system quickly showed results at Harvard and soon spread throughout the country. Brandeis himself was enthusiastic. "When the end of the chapter of cases is reached," he wrote, "the student stands possessed of the principles in their full development. Having attended as it were at their birth, having traced their history from stage to stage, the student has grown with them and in them; the principles have become a part of his flesh and blood; they have *pro hac vice* created a habit of mind. Like swimming or skating, once acquired, they cannot be forgotten; for they are a part of himself." [4]

Louis stressed the "intellectual self-reliance and spirit of investigation" which the inductive method engenders. He explained that a case, though selected as illustrating one stage in the development of a legal doctrine, may involve a dozen other points not directly connected with that doctrine, and these the student may follow up for himself. "The points thus incidentally learned are," he declared, "impressed upon the mind as they never could be by mere reading or by lectures; . . . for they occur as an integral part of the drama of life." [5]

The impact of the case method on Louis's intellectual development was the more significant in that it reinforced a natural bent toward inductive processes, which he had discovered for himself while at the Annen-Realschule in Dresden.

Louis also weighed the pros and cons of another controversy over teaching methods—the lecture system. "I remember," he wrote Otto, March 12, 1876, "a few Sundays before I left Louisville you, Al, and I were up in your room, comfortably reclining on the bed, and talking about lectures. You thought they were of no earthly use—and I almost agree with you now. A lecture alone is little better than the reading of textbooks, but such lectures as we have here in connection with our other work are quite different things. *Idem non est idem.*"

Harvard's law clubs also won Louis's praise. "Grand institutions," he called them, "a great incentive to labor, and the work for them is a pleasant change." These clubs were similar to present-day moot courts except that they were conducted entirely by the students. Cases were presented and argued by a few selected members, the rest of the club sitting as judges. Louis was a member of the Pow-Wow Club, and he prepared for its "courts" as thoroughly as he did for his professors' classes. He described one of his own cases for Otto in a letter on November 12, 1876: "I have spent a great deal of my time for several weeks on the subject of 'Declarations forming a part of the Res Gestae,' as I was of counsel on two cases involving that branch of the law of Evidence. One of the cases that we tried in our Club-Court was *Insurance Company* v. *Mosely & Wall 489,* which was decided, as is usual in Supreme Court (U.S.) cases, by a divided Court. I was counsel for the Company and am fully convinced of it, that the decision is utterly wrong, and I expect our Court, like that learned Judge in the English Exchequer, to decide 'that the case of the Plff (Mosely) so far as it relies on authority, fails in precedent, and so far as it rests on principle, fails in reason.' I am afraid those Supreme Court Judges will be refused admittance into Paradise for the bad law they have been promulgating in this life. Many of them surely deserve the most dreadful punishment."

But Harvard's greatest claim to distinction, as Louis saw it, was not law club, library, or "contacts." It was the "instruction of consummate lawyers, who devote their whole time to *you.*" Within six months Louis had marked certain of his professors for distinction. "The rising lights among our Professors," he observed, "are James B. Ames and John C. Gray, Sr.— the latter the editor of the last edition of Story on *Partnership,* and formerly editor of the *American Law Review;* the former, a graduate of Harvard College and Law School who has never practiced law, a man of the most eminent abilities as instructor, possessing an infallibly logical mind and a thorough knowledge of the Common Law. As R. C. B. would say— 'He'll make his mark.' "

Brandeis's second year at Harvard was much the same as his first, "only a little pleasanter." His courses were, as he listed them: "Equity Pleading (3 lectures a week), Evidence (2), Corporations and Partnership (2), Trusts and Mtges (2), Bills and Notes (1)." He thought the selection represented a "very judicious choice." By early November he was completely settled, "running along smoothly in the old grooves with so much to do" that he had "not time to become lazy." "The Law School," he wrote Otto, November 12, 1876, "is, unfortunately, very popular. We have an increase of nearly thirty students over last year's number and the library is consequently overcrowded." At times this inconvenienced individual students, but for Louis inconvenience was more than compensated by "the glory of the thing."

To accommodate the increased enrollment, which reflected the success of Langdell's method, notable additions were made to the faculty. Among these was Charles Saunders Bradley whom Louis described as "ex-Chief Justice of Rhode Island, the Bradley who figures so largely in Howard's, Black's, and the early numbers of Wallace's Reports." He is "undoubtedly," Louis wrote Otto, "a great acquisition for the Law School, and is very highly spoken of by every lawyer in this part of the country."

Louis was much impressed by the divergent points of view, sometimes very marked, among members of the faculty, for all of whom he had profound respect. In the November 12 letter he also wrote Otto: "It is very interesting to hear the different professors successively express their views on the same things or persons. Frequently they are diametrically opposed to one another. Last year, it seemed to be Ames's great aim and object to convince us that nine-tenths of the Judges who have sat on the English Bench and about ninety-nine-hundredths of the American Judges 'did not know what they were talking about'—that the great majority of Judges were illogical, inconsistent, and unreasonable, that there had been in fact only one man who understood his trade and profession, i.e., Baron Parke—that even the great Mansfield was a fraud, who stood convicted of the inexpiable crime of having introduced Equity doctrines into the sacred and immaculate Common Law, of having been the first to prepare for the eventual victory of the Roman Law in England. Under Bradley all this is different. He never lets an opportunity escape him for lauding the English and especially American Judges. Story and Marshall, Nelson and Grier, Mansfield and Eldon are repeatedly the subject of his praise. Ames would set up his own reasoning against that of a legion of Judges and scores of text-writers. Bradley in his deference to 'His Honor' even goes so far as to avoid offering any criticism on what has become settled by decisions, however unsupported by reason."

His letter solemnly continued: "On the other hand, Bradley is the greatest advocate of the Roman Law and of the Equity system in our jurisprudence, rejoices over the gradual growth of Equity doctrines in our law and the ultimate rule of real justice and right. Whatever is 'against conscience' is to him the subject of abhorrence. He desires that there should be no distinction between what is 'legally right' and what is 'morally right.' Ames is like the inflexible professor of the deductive method, who being timidly informed that his principles, if carried out, would split the world to pieces, answered carelessly: 'Let it split; there are enough more planets.' Ames also would have the world split, and leave the mending process to the legislature—rather than be guilty of an illogical conclusion. Bradley again, considering the aim and end of all law, to keep the world whole, shys at any conclusion which leads to palpable hardship."

And he concluded: "Ames wants to leave as much as possible to the *duodecim liberos et legales homines*. Bradley (who being a great Corporation lawyer has probably lost many verdicts) evidently thinks that juries in Civil Cases are an obsolete institution—or at least ought to be. Between these extremes, Ames and Bradley, there are of course the views of the three other Professors, each differing widely from the others."

READING MAKETH A FULL MAN

Though Louis loved the study of law enough to give practically all his time to it, he did find spare moments for other things. "Independent of my legal studies," he told Otto (November 12, 1876), "I have done comparatively little reading since I am here, and do not think I shall be able to spare more time from my law in the future than I have in the past. Nevertheless, I have managed to spend a little time every evening with English and German authors, and have at least the consolation that in course of time, 'Many a little will make a pickle.' I have been indulging in Emerson also—and can conscientiously say that my admiration for him is on the increase. I have read a few sentences of his, which are alone enough to make the man immortal."

Louis's interest in literature, though always utilitarian, was not new. Before going to Europe in 1872, he had acquired Dr. John Todd's *Index Rerum,* a blank index book for collecting and storing literary lessons. "Let a young man when he begins life," Dr. Todd advised, "be in the habit of making an index of all that he reads which is truly valuable (and he ought to read nothing else), and at the age of thirty-five or forty he has something of his own and which no price can purchase. Many would think hundreds of dollars well spent, could they purchase what they have thrown away; and what each one might most easily save for himself, and to aid in saving which, this book is prepared." Louis seemed determined to follow Dr. Todd's advice, for the first notation in the *Index Rerum* ran: "Remember that even if you are able to read a good book and understand it, even this is not all; you must think of it after you have ceased reading, and not allow your mind to be immediately taken up by your own little petty affairs the moment you set the book aside. To profit by what you read not only concentration of mind is necessary *whilst* reading but *after thought.*"

Except for this, and a single passage in German, however, the *Index Rerum* remained empty until Louis returned to America. Then legal material began to crowd its pages, but included also were Biblical quotations and a variety of quips and jokes. Each notation was carefully indexed by subject, and the source frequently added. The topics most thoroughly covered were "Law" and "Boston"—its political history, its growth in population, its schools, public institutions, streets, water supply.

For matters that did not fall easily into the classifications of an index, Brandeis started another notebook which he filled with references, quotations, and his own comments on books read. These included Shakespeare,

Swift, Horace Walpole, De Quincey, Lowell, Emerson, Matthew Arnold, Milton, Tennyson, Swinburne, Longfellow, Stevenson.

Emerson was now Louis's favorite author, and quotations from his work ranged from short excerpts to full pages. Louis copied, "They can conquer who believe they can." Also, "The Golden Age is not behind but before you." From Emerson, Brandeis learned the self-reliance he practiced all his life:

It is easy in the world to live after the world's opinion; it is easy in solitude to live after our own; but the great man is he who in the midst of a crowd keeps with perfect sweetness the independence of solitude.

Also:

Speak what you think now in hard words, and tomorrow speak what you think tomorrow in hard words again, though it contradict everything you said today.

In Emerson, Brandeis found a moral which he later tried to teach Big Business:

Every man takes care that his neighbor shall not cheat him. But a day comes when he begins to care that he does not cheat his neighbor. Then all goes well. He has changed his market cart into a chariot of the sun.

Other sayings also impressed themselves upon Louis's receptive mind. From Victor Cherbuliez's *Samuel Brohl and Partner* he recorded:

Napoleon I used to say that in giving battle he used to arrange to have 70 chances out of 100 in his favor; the rest he left to fate.
Our most sacred duty is to be resolutely unjust to our friends and enemies.
We ought to lay in a stock of absurd enthusiasms in our youth or else we shall reach the end of our journey with an empty heart, for we lose a great many on our way.
Arithmetic is the first of sciences and the parent of safety.

From Lowell he quoted at length:

The masses of any people, however intelligent, are very little moved by abstract principles of humanity and justice, until those principles are interpreted for them by the stinging commentary of some infringement upon their own rights. . . .[6]
The capacity of indignation makes an essential part of the outfit of every honest man, but I am inclined to doubt whether he is a wise one who allows himself to act upon its first hints.[7]

One of the strongest charges to be brought against Louis in later years was that of "inconsistency"—a topic fully considered in his notebooks.

From Emerson he culled: "A foolish consistency is the hobgoblin of little minds." From Lowell he took again: "The imputation of inconsistency is one to which every sound politician and every honest thinker must sooner or later subject himself. The foolish and the dead alone never change their opinion." [8]

Into the notebook also went a brief résumé of E. P. Whipple's essay, "Young Men in History," scathing passages from Swinburne's *Dante Gabriel Rossetti,* and a condensation of the Norwegian *Frithiof's Saga.* Despite Oliver Wendell Holmes's appraisal of Tennyson as "a stallfed poet," Louis made a synopsis of *The Princess,* on January 18, 1877, and took many quotations that seemed fine poetry, noting among others:

> Drink deep until the habits of the slave
> The sins of emptiness, gossip and spite,
> and slander die
>
> . . .
>
> For often fineness compensated size—
> Besides the brain was like the hand and grew
> with using
>
> . . .
>
> How'er you babble, great deeds cannot die
> They with the sun and moon renew their light
> Forever blessing those that look on them
>
> . . .
>
> That we might see our own work out, and watch
> The sandy footprints harden into stone
> For was and is and will be, are but is.

On February 10, 1877, he copied these lines from Matthew Arnold's "Sohrab and Rustum":

> For we are all like swimmers in the sea,
> Poised on the top of a huge wave of Fate,
> Which hangs uncertain to which side to fall.
> And whether it will heave us up to land,
> Or whether it will roll us out to sea,
> Back out to sea to the deep waves of death,
> We know not, and no search will make us know;
> Only the event will teach us in its hour.
> Truth sits upon the lips of dying men.

Louis's reading and quoting also stimulated him to write. Thus he entered into the notebooks a devastating criticism of De Quincey's *Philosophy of Roman History* which Louis thought did not differentiate the causes of Rome's decay from the effects. Later, however, he repented, noting that his criticism had been too severe.

He never did repent his opinion of De Quincey's "Plato's Republic," read in the summer of 1876. "Have just read this essay," he noted and "judging from which (I have no other source of information) Plato's ideal republic, which he himself thought too perfect ever to be realized, must be the most theoretically nonsensical plan that human ingenuity ever invented." He went further:

He [Plato] imagines a class of men in his society who possess all the physical power, who enjoy the respect and admiration of the state, but who nevertheless have no desire to accumulate property, who have no tendency towards despotism —and this, though all the nobler feelings which usually fill men's breasts have been killed at their birth or eradicated—although they have had no education in what is elevating and ennobling—on the contrary, whose greatest virtue is violence and brutality, whose pleasures, debauchery, the emoluments of whose profession are unlimited concubinage and mandatory infanticide. Such is the noble race of soldiers who are to be the guardians of Plato's Republic, who are to ensure its stability and greatness. Such are the men who are to be the terror of the enemy, the gods of their countrymen. Surely we must either accuse the creator of such anomalous men of endless incongruities and inconsistencies, or we cannot sufficiently admire the mind which can so successfully liberate itself from everything human as to imagine a new creature unaffected by what affects us, moved to good deeds by what leaves us cold—who is governed by our passions, our appetites and desires, not actuated by such motives as we are, but who is blessed with our virtues and cursed with our vices, which however the education devised by Plato is to eradicate. Indeed we are forced to exclaim: "Such is the ingenuity of man."

Other essays exhibit Louis's literary skill. His sketch of some Roman underground chapels, for instance, written apparently for his own pleasure and recounting an experience of his European tour, shows imagination, sensitivity, and discriminating use of language. Of the chapel Alla Morte on Ponte Sisto, he wrote: "The walls and ceilings . . . are ornamented with the most peculiar bas-relief, and covered with fantastic arabesques and mosaic work. One finds attached to the walls here and there nice flowers, rosettes . . . squares, crosses, and all kinds of ornaments as only an oriental imagination could invent. Everything is made of human bones carved and joined together with the utmost care and excellence."

The contrast between this chapel of the dead and its living worshipers horrified Louis:

One is tempted to distrust one's own eyes. Imagine a subterranean chapel in candlelight, built as it were of human skulls and skeletons, the walls decorated

with human bones, occupied by living beings—mostly girls and women, and
ladies dressed in silks—sitting in rows on chairs, healthy, laughing, tittering
faces leaning against dreary moldering bones in an atmosphere pervaded by
rottenness buried in a cloud of musty incense. I took a seat next to a young girl
who was seated just below a grinning skeleton and who was conversing with
her neighbor on very worldly topics; meditatively, frightened almost, I looked
at this skeleton and his youthful plunder over whom he was stretching both
hands—for the girl was sitting in such a position that it looked as if she had
dropped into the skeleton's arms. This was Holbein's Dance of Death in real
life. . . .

It is remarkable how what is naturally terrible disappears when clad in artistic forms in obedience to the laws of Esthetics. But it is repulsive, dreadful, to
think that art should use as the material for its beautiful figures and statues and
graceful arabesques . . . that which the earth would like to bury in beneficent
night. This seems to me to be the summit of the fanatical contempt of life, the
odd freak of the triumph over the terrors of death. . . .

Deeply impressed by the chaotic intermixture of these bones, Louis had
inquired of a Capuchin: " 'Padre, when all these skeletons and bones have
to seek their appurtenances, what a terrible confusion will there be!' 'Yes,'
replied the monk, 'on Doomsday when the dead come to life again, there
will be a terrible rattle here.' " In Louis's mind all this did not reflect credit
on Christianity. Not even the Egyptian religion, said to be the religion of
death, was so patently morbid.

HOBNOBBING WITH INTELLECTUALS

"Reading," Louis noted in his index, "equivalent to drinking, maketh a
full man." But good company makes him better still. The knowledge of
literature Louis gained while at Law School and in the few years immediately following, added to his personal charm and intelligence, soon earned
for him an enviable place among students and faculty at Harvard and
among intellectuals in Boston. Through his friendship with the Cochrans
of Brookline, he came to know James T. Field, the publisher, and other
leading literary people. During his first year in Law School he had the
good fortune to meet Denman Ross, the legal historian, who took him to
hear the last Harvard lectures of Henry Adams and Charles Eliot Norton.
Louis carefully noted the names and addresses of all these eminent people.

Besides Professor Ephraim Emerton of the college, whom Louis had
met in Europe, he was on very friendly terms with Professor Charles Saunders Bradley. At Bradley's house he met Professor Nathaniel Southgate
Shaler, a Kentuckian and well-known naturalist. Shaler was a brilliant
conversationalist, whose talk shone with "racy wit, homely shrewdness,

persuasive wisdom and poetic feeling. . . . His presence," wrote Charles Townsend Copeland, was "magnetic and heartening, his speech was wine, his laugh a cordial." [9] Naturally the Shaler house became a rendezvous for intellectuals. Here Louis became acquainted with educators of distinction. His notebook contains the wisdom of Professors Palmer, Childs, Bowen, and others. As pearls were dropped Louis picked them up, often to criticize them later in the privacy of his notes. He was ever mindful of Swift's remark: "That was excellently observed, say I, when I read a passage in an author where his opinion agrees with mine. When we differ— then I pronounce him to be mistaken." Professor Shaler's "persuasive wisdom" struck Louis most forcibly. He particularly noted these basic observations:

Cosmopolitanism, centralization, is objectionable, is to be avoided. It diminishes the probabilities of greatness. It contravenes Nature which stamps on all its creatures a local impression. . . . Every person, as every animal or plant, should upon examination disclose his habitation. . . .

The aim of civilization is the bettering of the condition of man and advancement of human happiness. This can only be attained by "rounding him off"— and only that degree of concentration of labor, specialism, is conducive to that end and purpose—to civilization itself—as maximizes this rounding off. Man is a complete organism intended to grapple with all questions and conditions of life; he is a world in himself and excessive specialism, individual or local, works against nature.

In the spring of 1878 Louis received this note from Professor James Bradley Thayer:

Mr. R. W. Emerson is to be at my home on Tuesday evening and will read a lecture to a few of our friends on "Education." If it would interest you to see him and hear him I wish you would come in at 8 o'c. He is, you know, old now, and perhaps one who had not seen him before would not quite understand the great charm that he and all he says have for his friends. But if you would like to see him it would give us great pleasure to have you come. There is no need of preparing for the occasion. I have never heard the lecture; but you and I ought to be interested in "Education."

Louis accepted the invitation, but the experience was noted curtly: "On March 11, 1878, I heard R. W. Emerson read an 'Essay on Education' at the house of Professor J. B. Thayer at Cambridge, Mass."

Louis wrote often to Louisville, telling in detail of his academic and social conquests, and received enthusiastic replies. "The account of your schedule is charming," his father wrote, October 7, 1877, "and if you were not my son and dearer to me than I myself, I would envy you. Enjoy this beautiful time to its fullest and with full knowledge; for it will not stay as beautiful as now . . . no matter how favorable good fortune may be."

His mother also encouraged him. "How pleasant your life in Cambridge is!" she wrote him on October 21, 1877. "How refreshing and wholesome this gay, intellectual atmosphere! I hope that you continue to write me about *yourself;* but everything, the disagreeable too, if it should come."

Through it all Louis kept a steady head. Never one to swallow the ideas of others, he repulsed domination by overweening Brahmins. In his notebook he recorded with contempt Cicero's remark that "he would rather be on the side of Plato, tho' he were thereby in the wrong, than be opposed to him and be in the right." Louis also noted: "It seems to be the prerogative of lofty minds not only to enlighten us with their wisdom, but also to enslave us with their authority."

Quick as he was to detect—and reject—domination, Louis was also quick to absorb information on practically any subject. With a laugh, no doubt, he passed on one such gem of knowledge to his brother-in-law, Otto Wehle, who had just become a father:

Providence
July 13th, '78

Dear Otto:

Hope you are bringing up little Fanny on the most approved theories of baby-training. I find discoveries in this important science have been very great within the past few years, all old methods having been superseded. Cradles are entirely condemned. Fathers, brothers, uncles, are not to be made miserable by the "Rock Me to Sleep." Baskets are the thing now. Babies don't cry now unless they are sick, and then not as an expression of pain, but merely to call attention to their condition, not yet having acquired articulate speech. The eternal cry for "Mamma" is put an end to.

I just tell you this for fear that these advances in science have not reached the shores of the Ohio and hope you will investigate this matter fully.

I don't want my niece to be behind the times.

Your bro.
Louis D. B.

When Amy and Otto's second child, a boy, was born, their choice of a name was almost a foregone conclusion. In reply to Otto's letter telling of Louis Brandeis Wehle's birth, Louis wrote:

Sept. 16th, '80

Dearest Amy and Otto:

Otto's letter reached me a few minutes ago and I need not tell you how happy it made me.

My *name* is in your hands.

Lovingly,
Louis

SETBACKS AND A TRIUMPHANT FINISH

Louis's years at Harvard Law School were not without difficulties. One problem was finances; another, ill-health and poor eyesight. Between the years 1875–78 his father just about managed to pay his debts. He could not offer Louis financial assistance, and made this clear on October 7, 1877, when he wrote: "The cotton business has been abandoned and the result is just as wretched as I expected. The act of winding up consists only in the attempt to collect bad debts, which up to now has been my only business. For nothing has yet been found. Being unemployed is naturally terribly distressing for me, but I swindle the day as best I can. My people maintain that I look very well, and so at least they cannot tell how it looks inside. . . . In spite of my lack of occupation I have not read anything worth-while since my return. To be sure, before supper every evening I go to the library, and since Otto takes *The Nation* and Alfred *The Saturday Review* there is enough reading matter at home."

On February 20, 1878, Adolph wrote again: "You ask me to write to you when I am 'in the humour.' To tell the truth, I always am. Really my disposition is on the whole not bad at all. I am about reconciled with my position and I live like a real proletarian from day to day. 'Misery likes company,' and I have it now and to spare; and the circle of miserable businessmen grows every day and becomes more respectable. You know how Dr. Goldmark in his day used to grieve every day about having lost so and so much money, because he had not bought any 'whiskey.' Thus I am daily pleased about my profit, because I did not buy any cotton and any pork. . . . Once in a while I succeed in earning a little something which is 'clear profit,' because I have no business 'expenses.' "

This reversal of fortune taught Louis thrift and resourcefulness. Alfred's loans tided him over for a while and at the end of the first year he applied for a scholarship. It was granted, but Professor Charles Saunders Bradley advised against accepting it. "Why not take up tutoring?" Bradley suggested. "You can begin with my boy." This Louis did, and by the beginning of his second year tutoring had become quite profitable. "It is marvelous," his father wrote him, October 7, 1877, "that your tutorship is turning out so well. Do not exert yourself too much."

Louis's father and mother always feared their son would overtax his physical strength. Louis also was aware of this danger. To keep fit he went regularly to the Hemmenway Gymnasium, which had just been opened to students, under the able direction of Dr. Dudley A. Sargent. According to Dr. Sargent, of all the students he examined, Brandeis was muscularly the weakest. Sargent was actually alarmed over his frail physique and prescribed a course of exercise. Louis thereafter never abandoned the habit of limited but regular exercise.

He also suffered from eye strain, an ailment fairly common among the Harvard law students of his day. Yet he read constantly under the blinding flicker of the old-time gas jet. The summer after his first year, however, while reading law with Otto Wehle in Louisville, Louis's eyes gave out. A prominent Cincinnati oculist warned him against further reading. "The physicians have prescribed," he wrote Otto, August 31, 1876, "total abstinence from law for me, for the present."

Nevertheless he returned to Boston that fall, and consulted Hasket Derby, who diagnosed the trouble as muscular and ordered a course of exercises. These helped a little, but Derby finally advised him to abandon his chosen career. This Louis couldn't do. He felt then as he did a few years later—"One mistress only claims me. The 'law' has her grip on me and I suppose I cannot escape her clutches." Into his notebook he copied at this time:

> For every evil under the sun,
> There is a remedy, or there is none.
> If there is one, try and find it,
> If there is none, never mind it.

Sir Thomas More's couplet, also copied, has the same spirit:

> If evils come not then our fears are vain;
> And if they do, fear but augments the pain.

The prospect of giving up the law was hardly more disappointing to Louis than to his father, who advised him to see Dr. Knapp, a well-known New York oculist. Knapp found nothing organically wrong with his eyes and sagely observed: "It won't hurt you to read less and think more." Louis thought this over and decided he could continue his law course by having fellow-students read to him. This helped him in another way, for it forced him to utilize to the full his already acute memory. Unable because of his eyes to rely on last minute cramming for examinations, he stored up legal principles in his head. This made him seem so learned, as indeed he was, that his tutoring business prospered.[10]

Among the students who read to Louis was his friend Samuel Dennis

Warren, Jr., son of a wealthy paper manufacturer. The service deepened their friendship and ultimately resulted in Warren and Brandeis becoming law partners.

But that was in the future. Louis completed his law course in the two years then required for the degree, and made a record for scholarship still unequaled. As of December 1941, Brandeis, according to Dean James M. Landis, was still the most brilliant student ever to have attended the Harvard Law School. " 'A' grades in those days," Landis explained, "began in the neighborhood of 90, as contrasted with the 75 of the present period, but Brandeis's two-year average stands at 97 and includes three marks of 100 and two of 99." [11]

University rules, however, stated that a student under twenty-one could not graduate. Louis had earned the right to be class valedictorian, but at twenty he was not even eligible to graduate, much less orate. At a hurried last minute conference Commencement morning the trustees agreed to suspend the rule and permit Louis to graduate.

Many years later his classmate Philip Alexander Bruce wrote of Brandeis: "We were members of the same law class at Harvard University about 1877. That class contained at least two hundred young men who had graduated very high in the different New England colleges, and who had been led by their unusual ability and culture to adopt law as their profession in life. I think it would be admitted by every surviving member of that class, however distinguished, that Mr. Brandeis, although one of the youngest men present, had the keenest and most subtle mind of all."

Continuing, Bruce observed: "Mr. Brandeis had hardly taken his seat in our class room before his remarkable talents were discovered and his claim to immediate distinction allowed. Nearly forty years have passed since I was present at those scenes in the Harvard class room, and yet I can recall as clearly as if it were yesterday the pleasant voice of the youthful student, his exact and choice language, his keen intellectual face, his lithe figure, his dark yet handsome aspect, and finally the unaffected suavity of his manner, that had in it something of the Old World. Intellect, refinement, an alert and receptive spirit, were written all over his attractive personality." [12]

Brandeis himself never forgot the keen pleasure of student days at Harvard. "Those years," he told Ernest Poole in 1911, "were among the happiest of my life. I worked! For me the world's center was Cambridge." [13]

Brandeis spent his summer vacations in Louisville reading law with Otto Wehle, and returned there after his graduation in 1877, when that city was the scene of violent railroad strikes. Louis and his brother Alfred came from a party one evening to find that the big front window of their own house on Walnut and First Streets had been smashed by a mob. Years later Justice Brandeis recalled having attended a public meeting that summer, called to consider ways and means of protecting life and property. The meeting ran on into the night and the brothers slept on a jury-room table. Some nights that week Louis patrolled the streets with a gun; and others he spent in a railroad shed. As he looked back in the summer of 1940 on this posse service, he recalled that the gun was probably more dangerous to himself than anyone else. At any rate, when order was finally restored, he turned in his munitions unused and himself unharmed, much to the relief of his family.[14]

The following year, 1877–78, Louis returned to Cambridge for a year of graduate work, living as before in 29 Thayer Hall, and supporting himself in various ways. When Professor Ephraim Emerton married in the spring of 1877, President Eliot appointed Louis a proctor in Harvard College in Emerton's place.[15] This eased his finances. As an incidental job he sat in on examinations at the rate of a dollar an hour. This helped too. So did the resumption of his tutoring. Indeed, things went so well that by the end of 1878 Louis had repaid his brother's loan and had, in addition, saved between twelve and fifteen hundred dollars.[16] He invested six hundred of this in an Atchison Railroad bond, which he continued to hold even after his fortune ran into millions.[17]

AN UNTOWARD BEGINNING IN ST. LOUIS

Louis's superb record at Harvard won him exceptional opportunities at the outset of his career. Among these was an offer of a partnership with Charles Nagel, later Secretary of Commerce and Labor in the Taft administration. Nagel had married Louis's favorite sister, Fannie, in 1877 and was already established in St. Louis. There was much to bring the two young men together. Nagel's parents were of solid German stock. They had settled in Texas where Charles's father practiced medicine and where Charles was born. A strong abolitionist, Dr. Nagel moved to St. Louis at the outbreak of the Civil War. There Charles was educated. He was uncommonly zealous in matters of public interest, a strong fighter for good government and civic improvement. All this appealed to Louis. But above and beyond this, Louis and Charles were brought together by their devotion to Fannie.[18]

Before Louis's student days drew to a close, Nagel prodded him for a decision. On November 10, 1877, he wrote: "Well, Louis, time is flying. What do you think about next year? I confidently expect you to come here; although I have no new reasons to urge; and stand just where I stood last year. Our city is overcrowded with lawyers, so far as numbers go; and there are enough lawyers of some ability to make it a matter of trial to get the business. My business is not large; but I think I have very respectable clients, with respectable cases; and this not only makes practice acceptable, but must in the end make it paying. . . .

"If you come here next year I expect, of course, that you would come into our office. Having two rooms, a good library and a good location, I think you could do better with us than elsewhere. The third year there [Harvard] will make it less desirable for you to go into an old office. . . . But naturally it would take something decided to keep us separated."

Louis refused to be hurried, and when he failed to respond, Nagel apparently felt he had put on too much pressure. He wrote again, disclaiming any intention of creating an "awkward situation":

D'Arcy & Nagel
Attorneys at Law
515 Pine Street

St. Louis, Nov. 27, 1877.

Dear Louis:

Your silence makes Fan feel somewhat uneasy. She fears that your eyes are bad. I hope that they are not and think that my letter may have caused you some trouble. Do not let it. If anything is awkwardly expressed, believe me now that everything was meant for the best.

I thought I might touch upon the subject mentioned without in any way creating an awkward situation. Do not forget that no one more than I concedes your chances! Gladstone the student was not yet premier and might never have been; so I tell Fan that you may never be Chief Justice; although I do think that your chances for excellence are fine. This, more than anything else, would satisfy me, that you should be bound to no one. I do not want to convince or persuade you as to place, time, or anything! What I said was said in the most unselfish spirit. Come and go, and always feel that I can assist by letting go as well as any one. I consider myself merely a decent young lawyer of ordinary ability, who will make an honest living if God will, who might do a little better than he does financially if he were not doing a higher duty in another direction. Fan herself cannot enjoy *your* victories more than I. I have said to you what I would do— it is for you to make your plans, to make your choice. You must remember that I cannot be hurt by your coming here, but that you well may be—therefore, I may say, "Come, if you can, and take what you will—we have little to choose from." And you may say just as well, "I can do better elsewhere." That ends it.

Try to understand me. You will. Fan does. I speak freely to her as you know, and she would brook no injustice to you from anyone, be it intended or not.

Much love to you, Louis. Fan is right well, and so is

Yours, etc.
Charlie

Louis had still not made up his mind, June 18, 1878, when Nagel wrote him, saying: "You seem in all things to be a privileged individual. It is our great longing to have you live with Fan and me—that is all; and you must give me credit for having begged you so little, when I wished you so much."

Toward the end of his last year at Harvard, Brandeis seems to have decided to go to St. Louis, but not with Nagel. Somehow he had clearly indicated that he did not wish to go into the proposed partnership, and asked his brother-in-law to look for something else for him. By early July Nagel discovered what seemed a likely opening with an uncle of the Harvard economist F. W. Taussig. Nagel wrote Louis, July 10, 1878: ". . . James Taussig is not talkative; he keeps a regular office boy who attends to all messages and I think to all copying. He has a class of practice which gives opportunity for the choicest law work. He has large cases, so that a man would have an opportunity to work at one case for some time and go to its foundation. He is slow and would, I think, give one ample time. No one is more anxious than I to have you in no way identified with the Taussigs. But I think you can take this position and preserve every kind of independence. The present incumbent does. And if upon trial you do not like the place, you need merely leave it. Please let me know what your opinion is so that I may be in a position to talk decisively with J. T. It will without doubt be difficult to find another place with compensation. Varrhes, it seems, cannot even find desk room. What Taussig pays I do not know. He said you must not expect to grow rich in a year. . . ."

In the hard times of the seventies Taussig's offer seemed the best, and Louis accepted it. His family regretted, of course, that he did not choose Louisville instead of St. Louis. With Alfred's aid, his father was once more slowly re-establishing himself in business, and in the course of a few years the new firm of A. Brandeis & Son became important as a receiver and shipper of grain. Louis could have had its law business. In Louisville too was brother-in-law Otto Wehle who already had a good practice. Nevertheless Louis thought St. Louis the more promising of the two cities and wrote his mother so. Then, overcome by doubt, he wrote again, on August 2, 1878:

Dearest Mamma:
  Since writing this letter I have doubted somewhat whether I was right in the course I pursued in this matter. If after reading the letter you think I was *wrong*, I most humbly beg your pardon.

Lovingly,
Louis

His mother replied on August 7: "I never felt prouder and happier about my boy." And on August 11 his father wrote: "I had given up hope a long time ago that you would settle here, and therefore the news that you had decided for St. Louis was not a very big disappointment. The reasons for this which you mention in your last letter are entirely convincing to me, especially your wanting to try your skill tilting with the world, before you decide to settle down to a purely scientific career. With your energy and with your persevering diligence you cannot, with the help of God, miss altogether in any career, and it is only a question of which gives you the best opportunity to express your talents. And this must always be tried out. I think that in this case you may follow your own inclination with assurance, and I am grateful that you spared us the struggle of the choice. For in the long run we could only have advised you against your inclination. Moreover, even if your reasons were not as strong as they are, you would be right just the same in following your inclination. For you are so young, that you can afford to risk something, and I do not doubt that, whatever you undertake, can turn out only to be a beneficial step in your development. Therefore I leave you to yourself with the most blissful confidence and send you my blessing. A temporary separation from any one of you is probably unavoidable and I only hope that we parents will be allowed to have you occasionally near us. . . ."

Brandeis's first year of practice started inauspiciously with an illness which kept him in Massachusetts until the end of September 1878. Taussig kindly held the position open, urging him "to take all the time necessary for a radical cure." [19] In November 1878 Louis was finally admitted, on motion, to the Missouri bar. His office was at 505 Chestnut Street. In 1936, on the twentieth anniversary of Justice Brandeis's appointment to the United States Supreme Court, the St. Louis Bar Association placed there a commemorative bronze tablet bearing this inscription:

On this site Louis Dembitz Brandeis, Justice of the Supreme Court of the United States, began the practice of law in 1878. From this spot spread the influence of a great lawyer, a social philosopher, and a wise and just judge. Presented by his friends, under the auspices of the Bar Association of St. Louis, 1936.[20]

Brandeis's St. Louis practice seemed ill-fated from the start. He tried for a while to console himself with the thought that the variety of his cases extended his knowledge and experience. By February 1879 his simulated optimism was fast ebbing away. He described his practice to Otto Wehle, February 10, 1879:

A great part of my work for Mr. Taussig consists in looking up the law on particular questions as they arise in the trial of cases below. Not infrequently, the search is confined to Missouri law and in these instances the work rarely extends to the writing of a brief. I think I am picking up a good deal of law in this way. The investigation is frequently hurried and very limited in its range, but always suffices to open my eyes to new points which I can settle for myself hereafter.

My own practice independently of what I get from . . . Taussig, is not very extensive. I got $5 (actually $4.75) the other day for legal advice to a woman who stumbled into my office asking for a "Notar"—*"Kennen Sie die Rechte?"*

Saturday, James T. turned over a $50 claim from a Baltimore party to me for collection, which I hope to get. Today an employee of the O. & M. R.R. stumbled in upon me with an old claim for services rendered in '75—which I probably shall not be able to collect. This is about all that has come to me. . . .

The quantity of young and old lawyers here without practice is appalling.

Apparently Louis's scruples, or at least Taussig's, did not preclude their taking cases in which right and justice lay on the opposite side. To Otto, he observed on April 1: "My case has ultimately been decided—but alas— against us—as right and justice demands. We have, of course, filed a motion for a re-hearing and may appeal. The Defendant based his defense on two grounds, the one impregnable, the other, I think, very weak. It is possible (for we have not yet learnt the grounds of the decision) that the Judge took the latter ground, as we endeavored very much to confuse him on the former, and if he did, we may have some chance above."

A SIGNIFICANT FIRST BRIEF

Young Brandeis's St. Louis practice, though mediocre on the whole, gave him some chance to develop those methods which distinguished him later. The quest for the underlying principles "became part of his flesh and blood." To find those principles he often had to go far beyond the usual authorities. An early case, involving the "liability of trust-estates on contracts made for their benefits," * gave him a chance to write about this to Otto Wehle in his letter of April 1. Here too the problem of ethics appeared: "I have for the past week devoted much of my time to the investigation and particularly meditation over the: 'Liability of Trust-Estates on Contracts Made for their Benefit' (i.e., By Trustee, Ex'tr, Adm'r, Guardian, Committee).

"The question has often attracted my attention but until recently I have never been able to find the point referred to, as the point, to my knowledge, has never been treated in textbooks and not even mentioned except in

* *Liability of Trust-Estates on Contracts Made for their Benefits,* in the Circuit Court, City of St. Louis, June Term, 1879, *Martin Michael v. Joseph H. Locke, Lunatic,* and *Richard D. Lancaster, Guardian of Joseph H. Locke.* L. D. Brandeis, James Taussig.

Lewin * & Perry † in a vague way and in half of one sentence. I wrote a little essay of about 14 pages on the subject with some idea of having it published in one of our Law Journals. The investigation was provoked by one of Mr. Taussig's cases and as I find that the result, as set forth by me, is not exactly favorable to his case, or at least might be giving weapons into the hands of the other side, I shall, of course, keep it under lock and key, or, rather, do as I have done, leave it in his safe.

"In your great lunacy practice you may have thought and found much on the subject. I wish you would give me what information you have on this very nice question. The matter is of such practical importance; I am astonished that there is so little law on it."

Later Taussig had Louis's brief "printed almost without change" and submitted it to the Missouri Court of Appeals with the object of presenting "a view of all sides of the question." [21] Brandeis finally wrote a scholarly article covering the entire subject. His paper was read in manuscript by Oliver Wendell Holmes, Jr.,[22] and published in the *American Law Review* of July 1881. With a scholar's impartiality, Brandeis added a footnote:

The writer wishes to state that he was of counsel for plaintiff in a cause still pending, requiring the advocacy of the equity herein suggested and that this investigation was made and his views were formed while acting in such capacity. Still it is believed that the subject is fairly treated, and that the collection of authorities on the mooted questions is complete.

The privilege of being able to deal with subjects "fairly" is not often given to the practicing lawyer. An impartial lawyer, devoted to the objective pursuit of truth, is indeed, from the point of view of clients, distinctly undesirable, and from the point of view of the Bar, shockingly irregular. The legal scholar, on the other hand, under no obligation to win cases, can afford to look at them dispassionately. This Louis longed to do. It was this longing that led him to play with the idea of returning to Harvard as a professor. That was what he meant by the "purely scientific career" referred to in his letter to his father telling of his St. Louis decision. Brandeis later did teach a few courses at Harvard, though he never gave his full time to it. He was able to get into teaching because he soon moved back to Boston.

BOSTON LURES HIM BACK

St. Louis never really satisfied Brandeis personally, professionally, or socially. He suffered periodically from malaria there. And while he suffered, he pined for the congenial puritan atmosphere of Boston. He liter-

* Thomas Lewin, *A Practical Treatise on the Law of Trusts and Trustees* (London, 1875).
† William Perry, *Treatise on the Law of Trusts and Trustees* (Boston, 1872).

ally became homesick for intellectual and cultural stimulation. He was bored with St. Louis social life—"dancing three nights out of six and one of these Sunday." "After that dose of dancing," he wrote his sister Amy, February 1, 1879, "I was heartily tired of ballroom conversation; in fact, was disposed to become melancholy and to moralize on the total depravity of man and woman." Then he added, "I suppose the Cambridge letters may have greatly conduced to my impatience with ballroom superficiality and vapidity. There are 'lots' of nice people in that Massachusetts town."

Thoughts of possible burial in the backwaters of a mid-western metropolis and of opportunities irretrievably lost ran through his mind as he copied into his notebook these lines from Shakespeare's *Julius Caesar:*

> There is a tide in the affairs of men,
> Which, taken at the flood, leads on to fortune;
> Omitted, all the voyage of their life
> Is bound in shallows and in miseries.

Had Brandeis remained in St. Louis, he would in time have built up a thriving practice. But at the moment conditions were by no means auspicious for advancement. To Otto Wehle on April 1, 1879, he wrote: "Am very glad to hear that your practice shows signs of revival and growth. Litigation and legal business is very much depressed here. Everybody complains and most with reason. Even in our office, business is poor. A host of *old* cases, dating from better times, alone serves to keep us occupied."

Brandeis's reprieve from St. Louis came in May 1879. His Boston classmate and friend, Samuel D. Warren, Jr., who had graduated second to him, and had taken a position with Shattuck, Holmes & Munroe, wrote suggesting a partnership of their own and the editorship of a law journal. This was tempting indeed, but Brandeis was cautious for several reasons. At the outset clients would have to come largely from Warren's social and business contacts. The editorship might require more time than he could afford as a practicing lawyer. Finally, could his eyes stand the combined strain of practice and editorial work? Still he reacted favorably and asked Warren for further information:

St. Louis
May 30th, 1879

My dear Warren,

Your letters of 22nd and 28th inst. duly received. In answer to the latter I telegraphed you this evening: "Shall write fully tonight. It seems a good thing." The proposition to assume the editorship of one of the law-periodicals undoubtedly deserves the greatest consideration.

If, as you suggest, it would give me a living salary—that would enable me to disregard what otherwise would be a great obstacle to my going into partnership with you. On the other hand the editorship must not defeat the main purpose for which it is invoked. It seems to me essential that the position should not monopolize our time and that we should have sufficient time to devote to the law business to enable us to work up a practice. For, although I am very desirous of devoting some of my time to the literary part of the law, I wish to become known as a practicing lawyer. As a means of existing while working up a practice and as a means of becoming favorably known to the legal fraternity and also because it affords an opportunity for law-writing I regard the suggested editorship as highly desirable; but it must be in aid of and incidental to our law partnership, and not in substitution of it. Furthermore, my eyes, though quite strong again, allowing me to work practically the whole day and as much as [is] ordinarily required in a lawyer's practice, must be still carefully used and would not, I fear, be able to stand much or regular night-work. Whether a legal editorship is compatible with these considerations I cannot here determine. I conceive that it might be and must beg you carefully to investigate whether it is.

If it is compatible with these considerations and you still hold the opinions expressed in your letters of May 5th and 22nd, I should be willing and feel justified in giving up my position here and removing to Boston. I have assumed throughout that the editorship could be had if desired. Of course I am aware that there is a mere *possibility* that it can be procured.

If I should decide to remove to Boston or if it were advisable for me to go to Boston for consultation, I could leave here on short notice.

If you are unable to get control of the editorship for us or find it unadvisable to accept the same for the reasons stated, I wish to postpone for a little while my final answer as to starting a firm together. I wish to wait particularly for your letter giving the results of our examination of the prospects of a young law firm and more particularly your own prospects of securing business through your social and financial position.

On the whole, the advantages of Boston seemed to outweigh any possible disadvantages, and by early July Brandeis had made up his mind to join his former classmate—as he put it, "to become known as a practicing lawyer." Nagel accepted the move unwillingly but in good spirit: "From the start," he wrote, July 5, 1879, "I have been divided with myself in reference to the question of change; my reason spoke for Boston; my heart was for St. Louis." Nagel disliked the tie-up with Warren. "I was strongly opposed to the Warren partnership, particularly after what I saw in your own letters; and still more was I opposed to a partnership commenced with the idea of an early disruption. Partnerships are not as unlike marriages as some people suppose. They are apt enough to turn out bad in the best cases, and should be entered into with every apparent reason for success on both sides." Nevertheless Nagel gamely conceded: "If Boston is a success nothing in St. Louis can compare with it.

"Yes," his letter concluded, "you seem one of those unfortunate individuals who are doomed for life to say which one of many good things they want. We rejoice with you, Louis; you cannot blame us for feeling the one regret, that you are to a great extent lost to the family, and to Fannie and me and the boy particularly."

CHAPTER FOUR

Boston: Hub of the Universe

CERTAIN that he had made the right decision, Brandeis set out for Boston early in the summer of 1879. Along in July, after less than a year in St. Louis, he formed the partnership with Warren, whose family's paper-mill business and other interests promised substantial practice at the outset.

The start was delayed a little, however, because Louis could not hang out his shingle until he was admitted to the Massachusetts Bar. Also some decision had to be reached as to the firm's name. Should it be "Warren & Brandeis," or "Brandeis & Warren"? The usual test was priority of admission to the Bar. Brandeis had been admitted to practice in Missouri before Warren, but Warren was already a member of the Massachusetts Bar. "I don't give a rap," Warren told his partner in a hastily written note just prior to going off for a week-end, "but I think it worth-while to observe proper etiquette." No examinations for the Bar were scheduled till fall, but Brandeis naturally wished to expedite the matter. "The Committee here," he wrote Nagel, "ordinarily admits attorneys from other states only upon proof of a few years' practice there; but I think I shall be able to slide in anyhow as the Chief Justice [of Massachusetts] intends to submit my case." Leaving the whole matter to Brandeis, Warren suggested: "If you are admitted on the Comity of States, your name, I think, should come first." But it didn't. The firm established itself as "Warren & Brandeis."

Shortly thereafter Brandeis was admitted on motion to the Massachusetts Bar. "We have taken a room," he wrote Nagel, July 12, "No. 60 Devonshire Street (desirable location) in the 3rd story (2 flights) and shall move in soon. The room (No. 5) is only $200 a year—very cheap everybody says." Their greatest extravagance was a messenger boy at three dollars a week.

GETTING ESTABLISHED

The law review editorship did not materialize. Instead, Brandeis took time from his practice to act for nearly two years as law clerk to Chief Justice Horace Gray of the Supreme Judicial Court of Massachusetts (appointed in 1881 Associate Justice of the United States Supreme Court). This work gave Brandeis firsthand experience in writing judicial opinions. Nagel considered this connection with Gray the greatest advantage in his brother-in-law's new situation. On July 5, 1879, Nagel had written: "You seem to me to be splendidly situated. The arrangement with Warren may indeed easily enough turn out a complete success. This chance is worth a great deal. The association with him cannot but be of benefit to you unless a perfect partnership should be followed by an early separation without an apparent good and unexpected reason. The situation with the Chief Justice seems to be the most desirable of all the chances offered you in Boston. It must be in every way instructive and fortifying. Aside from a safe investment of your capital, you seem to have a chance in a lottery, with 50 per cent large rewards. No one can help seeing that such a connection means a chance at every desirable position offered in Boston and even at Cambridge. I presume you still prefer to enter upon active practice and with that in view, the above position is particularly important. You will probably be able to get on the right side of the Justice; although I can imagine that a man of his description might make a pleasant relation impossible for you. You will soon know all about this. . . . From one of your letters I see that you incline somewhat to the idea that teaching is your real talent. It may well be so; and if you turn to it, you seem to have the President and half the corporation for you now. . . . On the whole, your chances seem brilliant; your only trouble will probably be that you will still have some deciding to do before you get married; and it may thus tend to make the choice of the lady easier and safer; and your future decisions from the bench more clear and better balanced."

Brandeis naturally vacillated for a while between optimism over his future in Boston and regret for what he had left behind in St. Louis. A reassuring note came from James Taussig: "I may say now that a longer stay would have resulted in a closer business connection between us. But the prospects and opportunities before you are certainly very flattering and full of good promise." [1] "This was, indeed, a surprise to me," Louis wrote Nagel, "yet queerly enough made me feel rather good than blue. I suppose this feeling is attributable to vanity, but the letter was surely fortifying and gave me courage and hope that I might rise here as well as there." On July 12 he replied in full to Nagel's letter of the fifth:

Dear Charlie:

Your long letter was read with much attention and not a little heart-beating. . . . Still, I do not repent my decision although I feel how much I have lost in losing you all, and to what extent I have been deprived of that which contributes so much to the calm happiness of man.

On the other hand . . . I find much comfort and consolation in the feeling that whatever I have achieved, or may achieve here, is my own, pure and simple, unassisted by the fortuitous circumstances of family influence or social position. There is indeed small comfort in this thought if nothing is achieved, but if anything is accomplished, that thought will give me much satisfaction.

I find my temperament much changed during the past two years. It seemed to me peculiarly equable formerly and I was rarely exultant or depressed. Now I find myself as variable as the atmosphere, as unstable as a barometer. This morning I was boiling over with joy and in such good humor that I could not keep quiet.

His letter continues on a highly enthusiastic note:

At present, everything looks rosy here. My position with the Ch. J. [Gray] is pleasanter than my fondest hopes had pictured. None of the unpleasant peculiarities for which Judge Gray is noted have appeared in my intercourse with him. His arrogance and impatience are apparently the judicial wig and gown, for off the bench, there is no sign of them. On the contrary, he is the most affable of men, patiently listening to suggestions and objections and even contradiction. I have worked with him daily since Tuesday and have enjoyed most of the mornings keenly. Our mode of working is this. He takes out the record and briefs in any case, we read them over, talk about the points raised, examine the authorities and arguments, then he makes up his mind if he can, marks out the line of argument for his opinion, writes it, and then dictates to me. But I am treated in every respect as a person of co-ordinate position. He asks me what I think of his line of argument and I answer candidly. If I think other reasons better, I give them; if I think his language is obscure, I tell him so; if I have any doubts, I express them. And he is very fair in acknowledging a correct suggestion or disabusing one of an erroneous idea.

In these discussions and investigations I shall learn very much. Many beautiful points are raised and must be decided. The Ch. Justice has a marvelous knowledge of Mass[achusetts] decisions and statutes and I expect much advantage in this respect.

GERMAN AND ENGLISH ACADEMY.

QUARTERLY REPORT
of

Louis Brandeis,

From September 1st, to November 15th, 186

Number of times late.	Absence in half days.	Deportment.	Home Study.	Reading.	Orthography.	Grammar.	Reading.	Orthography.	Grammar.	Composition and Rhetoric.	English	German	Object Lessons.	Geometry.	Algebra	Universal	American.	Geography.	Natural History.	Natural Philosophy.	Chemistry.	English Literature.	French.	Latin.	Vocal Music.	Drawing.	Gymnastics.
ATTEND- ANCE.				ENGLISH.			GERMAN.				PENMAN- SHIP.						HISTORY.										
2	6	6	6	6	6	6	6	6	6	5		5		6	6		6	6	6								

EXPLANATION.—*The different grades of deportment and home study, and the progress in the various branches of instruction are indicated by the figures 6, 5, 4, 3, 2, 1, and 0; the figure 6 denoting perfection, the lower ones inferior grades. Studies without any mark are not taught in the class of the respective pupil.*

Respectfully submitted to the Parents,

W. N. HAILMAN,
Principal.

Louis deserves special commendation for conduct and industry.

W. N. Hailman,

FREDERIKA DEMBITZ BRANDEIS

BRANDEIS AT FIFTEEN   AT THIRTY-EIGHT

The only mechanical work is the dictation and of that there is precious little. We have worked about twenty-five hours together and there has not been an hour's dictation.

The prospect of teaching was still in the forefront of his mind:

My connection with Warren promises well also. There are many fine points about the man both in mind and character and it looks to me as if he would be a success. His "push" is great—the same bulldog perseverance and obstinacy which brought me here will, I think, pave a way which he seems determined to make. He is bent now on making clients and getting business and I think he will do it. Already he has quite a number of small claims with a prospect of some larger ones. If matters continue to come in as now, we are safe. . . .

What you say about teaching is undoubtedly sound and I recognize that, when the time comes, I shall have to decide between that and practice. I have not made up my mind yet, because it is not necessary but, as far as I can analyze my feelings, I think it was the prospect of teaching that kept me here. I recognize that my being here would make it easier to get the place—should I want it—and that it would be much easier too, to test my capability and love for such a position—without risking all.

Of course I do not know how I shall feel when an opportunity offers for taking the step—if it ever does, but it seems to me that if my eyes allow, I should make the move. The law as a logical science has very great attractions for me. I see it now again by the almost ridiculous pleasure which the discovery or invention of a legal theory gives me; and I know that such a study of the law cannot be pursued by a successful practitioner nor by a Judge (I speak now from experience). Teaching would mean for me writing as well. However, this is all talk. I may feel differently in three months and the wrangling of the Bar may have the greatest attraction for me. It surely is not distasteful to me now. It is merely a question of selecting between two good things. They are both good enough for me. I question only which I am good for. . . .

A fortnight later he wrote his mother in similar vein, but again his enthusiasm for Boston got the better of a lingering nostalgia for Louisville and St. Louis:

Sunday, July 20, 1879.
Boston, 21 Joy Street.

Dearest Mother:

When I received your letter and those of the others, it seems to me as if I were a fool to have settled here so far away, instead of staying with you and enjoying you and your love. Of course one can live anywhere, but there is also ambition to be satisfied.

But man is strange, at least this one is; he does not enjoy what he has—and he always wants what he does not yet have. That probably is called ambition— the delusion, for which one is always ready to offer a sacrifice.

And so I think that I shall be happier here, in spite of being alone, and if I can write you about success, it will counterbalance all the privations. And, I believe, that you too will enjoy me more from a distance, if you know that I am happy.

We shall see each other quite often and write very often. . . .

The connection with Warren seems to become more and more desirable. He, without doubt, has connections from which something may come, has energy and (at least compared with me) a practical mind. We already have some work, have not collected much money, but we hope for some fees. I am not yet admitted to the practice, but I am expecting a favorable decision this week.

You want to know how I pass my days; then read: I get up shortly after seven o'clock, have breakfast, go for a walk usually until nine o'clock. Then (every day this week) I stayed at the C.J. till 2 o'clock. After lunch I go to our office, talk over our business affairs with Warren, work there or in the Law-library according as business requires, and shortly after six o'clock I have dinner.

The evenings of last week I spent as follows: Monday Bullock and I took a walk to Cambridge and back to fetch my laundry, which was done there tentatively. Tuesday I drove with Warren to Beverly (5 miles from Manchester), where his parents are spending the summer. We left Boston at 5:15 and intended to take a long sailing trip in order to inspect a famous yacht (which belongs to the wealthy Sears). There was no wind, however, therefore we played tennis, rowed a little, swam and enjoyed beautiful nature. Warren's house is situated directly on the lake, the view is marvelous, and it is divine to listen to the rippling of the waves. Near the shores were a few boats, which threw their long black evening shadows over the water. The day had been hot, at five o'clock we were dripping with perspiration. Two hours later we were shouting for joy in the full enjoyment of a bath in the lake.

This is, indeed, an immense advantage of Boston. One can enjoy living (*Man kann das leben lebend geniessen*), and nature is so beautiful. . . . Oh, how beautiful are heaven and earth here, hills and water, nature and art!

Because I have little or no work at all to do for the C.J., I shall devote myself this week to our own affairs, try to collect some debts for a client and probably examine a title for a lot.

The room which I now occupy is fully furnished. In the fall I have to give it up. But I can get a little room in the same house or can move to Warren's.

The house of Mr. Warren is on Mt. Vernon Str. and runs through to Pinkney. In earlier years there were two entirely different houses and the house on Pinkney is entirely divided from the front house. In this back building Sam Warren has his rooms. But there are some rooms still unoccupied, and he wants me to take one of them.

For 10 days I have not seen any of the Cochrans. They invited me to visit them at Manchester for a few days and I probably shall do it sometime during the summer.

If I can I would like to take a walking tour to the mountains again this fall with Philip Marcou or Richards.

If only a man can stay strong and healthy—he will indeed be able to accomplish something. Marcou spends the summer in Magnolia—I would like to go there for a while. If one had nothing to do, one could really live more cheaply in the mountains or at the shore than here. . . .

When you have read my letter to Charles, you will know everything about me that can be written.

Many thanks for having kept your part of the pact.

Good-bye. Love from
Your Louis

THE NEW LEGAL AND SOCIAL LUMINARY

Warren & Brandeis soon began to expand. They acquired some New York clients through the offices of Walter Carter, in later years the father-in-law of Chief Justice Hughes. Carter was accustomed to keeping an eye on bright young Harvard graduates, and naturally couldn't miss Brandeis and Warren. Certain Harvard connections, especially Professor Charles Saunders Bradley, also were helpful. Bradley had important clients in Rhode Island and elsewhere, and once called Brandeis to Providence to argue *Allen* v. *Woonsocket*. The fee was appreciable, but more important, Brandeis's performance made him many friends among Rhode Island lawyers and businessmen. While he was in Providence, Warren gave him moral support from Boston, writing on March 29, 1880:

My dear Old Man:
Your note of Saturday gave me infinite pleasure.
I knew you would come out strong, and the faint praise you allow yourself is, I know, to what you deserve, as dawn to sunrise. I'm sorry I was not there but it was better not as there were matters here which needed my attention. The brief also came, and is a "daisy"—Gray is deep in it. The C.J. wants you, but I write you are engaged before the Supreme Court of Rhode Island (toney, eh?).

Warren went on to tell of several new cases acquired in his partner's absence, one involving an estate of "over half a million," and concluded optimistically: "The success of W. & B. is assured." The assurance was reinforced, November 22, 1880, when Louis's father passed along to his son Chief Justice Gray's remarkable encomium: "I consider Brandeis the most ingenious and most original lawyer I ever met, and he and his partner are among the most promising law firms we have got."

Nevertheless, after more than a year of practice, Brandeis, in a philosophical mood, jotted down these lines in his notebook: "One cannot be pulled up a great height. Only a short distance can you be lifted by your arms. But by climbing with your feet and stepping on the solid ground below, you can climb mountains." [2]

Cases took Louis to New Hampshire also. From there he wrote his sister Amy, January 2, 1881: "Yesterday was a sad day. We buried irretrievably a half dozen of the most beautiful and lucrative lawsuits—and all for the love of our clients. Yes, we settled up the complicated New Hampshire transactions by an agreement wonderfully favorable to our clients. From love of them we did it. But I fear 'The expedition of my violent love outran the power of reason.' No more trips to New Hampshire—no nothing. The only consolation is that we get our opponent for a client."

"All work and no play" was not Brandeis's creed, and as his business developed so did his social life. He delighted in the society of intellectual and cultured people, and frequently dined out or enjoyed a game of whist. In a somewhat frivolous vein he reported his social activities to Amy in the letter of January 2:

You want to know what I am doing. Why, nothing. Were I Othello, I should answer,

> "Little do I know of this great world
> More than pertains to feats of broil and battle."

But don't take that answer for mine. It is not quite true. Like the shellfish which walks backwards and is not a crab, and like our forefathers, I shall begin at the end and tell you of the dissipations of the week. Well, at 8:45 P.M., I called at a certain Mrs. Bush's, a friend of Jessie [Cochran's], where I was invited for Christmas and was constrained to excuse myself. Previously I had been at the Cochrans' for tea. Miss Helen Cochran and I are great friends now and I approach her without fear and trembling. On the contrary, I think she is almost afraid of me now.

The other day when I called, I was telling her about the Illustrated Weekly *Puck* of which she knew nothing, and in praising the tendency of the paper, said quite innocently, "The remarkable fact is that the paper is always on the right side of every question." "How do you know what is the right side?" she said, in an unmistakable tone. "Oh," said I, "the side that I take." The subjugation was complete. Sedan was not a more decisive victory.

Friday evening I dined at the Emertons'. [Philip] Marcou was there and in his honor two Misses Page of Boston were invited. One of them, the elder, a lady I should say of 28 "summers" and quite as many winters, I found extremely interesting. She is tall, has a finely chiseled, half Southern face, with black hair and sparkling jet eyes, and would be very handsome but for a total absence of freshness and health in her appearance. On the other hand, her delicate look gives her the charm, which people of character who have suffered always possess and the appearance of refinement which goes with it.

This very inadequate description of her appearance is given merely in order to lay some kind of foundation for her conversation, which was of unusual character and quality.

She is decidedly an excellent talker but of a different category from most persons possessing that talent. She spoke neither of books, nor of art, nor of the theatre; nor is there a particle of humor in her conversation. I had hardly seated myself next to her when she began to talk about some people whom I slightly know and with these remarkable variations of character-soul-and mind-painting that can be imagined and that cannot be described. Most persons one meets never get beyond the preliminaries of an acquaintance. Like the legendary Autolycus, you drag, at each meeting, your barleycorn of interest up the encircling wall of conventionality; but before you reach the top, you fall exhausted to the ground. Not so with her. Like mercury, she cleared the wall tops with a bound and in a moment I found myself in the deepest conversation, such as George Eliot's characters indulged in.

Brandeis joined clubs and organizations, believing that such contacts enriched his life and contributed directly to professional success. He loved boating and became a member, later a director, of the Union Boat Club.[3] He was an enthusiastic rider and helped organize the Dedham Polo Club. For professional and lunching purposes he joined the Exchange Club and the Union Club. He also lunched occasionally at the Hole-in-the-Ground, the rendezvous of a small literary group.[4] He served as secretary of the Boston Art Club, and frequented also the Turnverein, an athletic club, where he tried to keep fit. After a year and a half in Boston he wrote Amy with remarkable candor: ". . . I must go soon to the Turnverein and try and be captivating . . . and get some clients from their number." [5] Brandeis belonged also to an exclusive law club, formed to dine and "talk shop" at "some pot house." This club counted among its members such Brahmins as Francis C. Lowell, Robert H. Gardiner, Morris Gray, G. Fred Williams, F. J. Stimson, Frederick P. Fish, and his own partner Sam Warren.[6]

Ever since law-school days Brandeis had been in good standing with the "best" people of Cambridge and Boston, such as the Emertons, Shalers, Thayers, and Delands. Now, chiefly through Warren, he extended his social and professional contacts and made a permanent record of them. This record he kept in his notebooks where, during his first years in Boston, he jotted down incredibly long lists of people he had met, who had introduced them to him, where he had met them, and, occasionally, what they were like. One of these people was Oliver Wendell Holmes, Jr., Warren's old boss, in whose room he had had his desk. Naturally when Warren and Brandeis became partners, Holmes was among the first persons Brandeis met. He was invited to spend a week-end with Holmes and his wife at Mattapoisett in the summer of 1879, and from then on they were friends. In those days the Holmeses occupied a second-floor apartment next to the Athenæum, just across from the State House on Beacon Street. They took their dinners at the Parker House and Brandeis occasionally joined them there. Before Holmes was elevated to the Supreme Judicial Court of Massachusetts, he, Warren, and Brandeis often met in a tavern near the Parker House for discussion of legal and other matters.[7] After Holmes became a judge, Brandeis saw him less frequently, until he himself became a judge and "Holmes and Brandeis dissenting" became so typical of Supreme Court decisions.

The esteem in which Holmes held Brandeis is indicated by his soliciting a place for his nephew in the Brandeis firm:

Commonwealth of Massachusetts
Supreme Judicial Court
Court House, Boston

Jan. 16/99

Dear Mr. Brandeis:

When I wrote you last week I did not anticipate the suggestion which I now venture to make. My nephew, Edward T. Holmes, now 3rd year, wants to go into an office on leaving the Law School and I should be delighted if he could get with you. Will you let me know whether there is any chance for him?

Sincerely yours,
O. W. Holmes

And the warmth of this earlier friendship is indicated by Holmes's note acknowledging Brandeis's congratulatory message on his nomination as Associate Justice of the Supreme Court of the United States:

Beverly Farms,
Sept. 4, 1902

Dear Mr. Brandeis,

For many years you have, from time to time, at critical moments, said things that have given me courage—which probably I remember better than you do. You do it again now, with the same effect and always with the same peculiar pleasure to me.

I thank you and am

Always yours,
O. W. Holmes

LAWYER OR PROFESSOR

To teach or not to teach? That question still troubled Brandeis. He could not make up his mind. Against the day when he might finally decide to teach, he kept up his relations with Harvard. Thus, when in his first year of practice Professor Thayer urged him to publicize the Law School's need of additional funds, he responded eagerly. Harvard had received a large gift, and Thayer wanted part of it for a new law building.[8] Brandeis strongly supported the project in a letter to the *Post,* while Warren did likewise in a letter to the *Boston Evening Transcript.* That same year Thayer asked Brandeis's help in collecting material for his course on constitutional law.[9] This help Brandeis was only too glad to give.

Brandeis did another good turn for the Law School in connection with the endowment of a chair for Holmes. The latter had delivered the Lowell Institute lectures in the winter of 1880–81, at least one of which Brandeis attended.[10] These were published in 1881 as *The Common Law.* Response to the lectures and to the book was enthusiastic. Friends of the Law School immediately began to seek funds to endow a Holmes professorship. Thayer was especially anxious to add Holmes to the faculty. For advice as to ways and means of raising the necessary funds, he conferred as usual with Brandeis.

With this on his mind, Brandeis one day strolled across the Boston Common to his office, and chanced to meet William Weld, whom he once had tutored at Law School. Weld's grandfather, a shipbuilder, had just left an estate of sixteen million dollars, of which Weld himself had inherited three million. Brandeis quickly connected Weld's good fortune with the projected Holmes professorship. He told the young millionaire of the excellent opportunity to turn a small portion of his inheritance to good account, suggesting that he take the matter up with Professor Thayer. The sum required was $90,000. Weld contributed all of it on condition that the donor remain anonymous, and Holmes became Professor of Law, January 23, 1882.[11] On February 9 Professor James Barr Ames wrote Brandeis: "We are greatly pleased with the bright outlook for the Law School with its new professorship and new building and library fund. Mr. Thayer tells me that we are under obligation to you for your active interest in our behalf. It is particularly gratifying to know that any benevolence to the school is stimulated by its recent graduates."

But Thayer was not through. He was to get a short leave from the Law School in 1881, and at his suggestion Brandeis was invited to give his course in "Evidence—that neglected product of time and accident." [12] Because of shortage of funds, however, Thayer's leave and Brandeis's teaching debut were postponed.[13] In March 1882, however, President Eliot himself invited Brandeis to give the course in Evidence the following year —two lectures a week at a salary of $1,000. This was a flattering offer to a young lawyer not yet twenty-five and Brandeis accepted it.[14] Apparently his decision was being made for him.

Brandeis promptly sent President Eliot's letter of appointment home. His mother was ecstatic, writing April 2, 1882: "My dearest child, how happy you make me feel! My heart is a prayer of thanksgiving, and at the same time it is filled with the deepest wish that heaven may protect you."

His father wrote on the same day that it was "the greatest honor that can be given to a young man of your age," but he hoped Louis was not accepting it only for his father's sake. "I simply cannot help being aware," he continued, "that the profession of an academic teacher and possibly a writer is the most satisfying and desirable, and it may have been imprudent on my part to have expressed my opinion so unreservedly." His greatest concern was lest Louis overtax his strength: "For I have only *one* scruple about the thing, and that is that you not exert yourself too much in accepting these new and difficult duties. If something must be sacrificed, then sacrifice rather a part of your practice than the smallest bit of your health. For the former sacrifice will be in any case only temporary, while your health must last your whole life, please God. And if your new duties should induce you to overexert yourself even a very little, I would reproach myself terribly for ever having expressed my feeling about it. Promise me, therefore, that you will rather let your practice suffer than your health, if necessary, and this promise to your father will, so help you God, keep you from overexertion."

His uncle, Lewis Dembitz, wrote on April 16: "Last Friday night your mother came to our house near 10 o'clock with President Eliot's letter of appointment in her hand, addressed to you as 'Louis Dembitz Brandeis.' It's the first time that I felt glad at your changing your middle name from 'David' to 'Dembitz.' Your grandfather, if he could know it, would be but too happy in knowing that one bearing his name has achieved an academic office, for none had a greater veneration than he for anything connected with the University."

Winthrop H. Wade, a law student, took notes on Brandeis's course in Evidence. It was so good, or else Wade's notes were so excellent, that Oliver Wendell Holmes got Wade's consent to his keeping them for his own use.[15]

The law faculty also thought well of Brandeis's teaching and he was offered an assistant professorship. At last he had to decide what he was going to be. First he had to consider his health. "I am rather disgusted with myself physically," he wrote to his father, May 30, 1883. "I have taken very good care of myself—worked moderately, and still find myself much below par; that is, I am easily exhausted and worn out, without adequate reason. You and mother seem to think that Warren could relieve me of much work if he wanted. That is not true to any extent. The work which I do could hardly be done for me by another, and he is tending to his own clients now."

Then there was the combativeness of trial work which Brandeis loved and thought he wasn't getting enough of. "I presume," his letter continued, "I shall take another year at Cambridge but I may refuse the Cambridge offer—in the hope that something of the other kind may turn up later—or with a view to working less next year. The decision has not yet been made. What I should prefer is some position that would give me practice in trying cases. I feel I am weak in this experience and think that with practice I could do well at it."

Finally the decision was made—against the professorship. Although the family had indicated a preference toward teaching, they wanted Louis to choose for himself. His father had written on April 17, 1882: "Perhaps I could be called a coward for taking so little pleasure in a struggle, and I probably should congratulate myself that my sons are made out of better metal. I think that I have tried all my life to do my duty, and this sense of duty my sons have inherited from me. Fortunately, the love of a struggle and a little ambition is given to them as their maternal inheritance, and therefore they are so truly every inch men—may God help them!"

Brandeis's decision against the professorship did not end his interest in the Law School. He envisioned Harvard as a truly national institution, and conceived the idea of having prominent alumni in every state in the Union encourage able students to come to Cambridge. In 1886 a voluntary committee of seven was formed to organize the Harvard Law School Association for this purpose. The drive was planned so that announcement of the new association would coincide with the 250th anniversary of the college.[16] Thus on September 23, 1886, the Harvard Law School Association was formally organized "to advance the cause of legal education, to promote the interests and increase the usefulness of the Harvard Law School, and to promote mutual acquaintance and good fellowship among the members of the association." James Coolidge Carter became the Association's first president, and Brandeis the secretary. On Brandeis fell the responsibility of a voluminous correspondence with prominent alumni throughout the country, the organization of meetings and banquets. In recognition of his work Harvard made him Master of Arts in 1891, having a year earlier admitted him to Phi Beta Kappa.

Brandeis was also keenly interested in establishing the *Harvard Law Review,* and in 1887 aided the founders, John J. McKelvey, Julian Mack, and Joseph Beale, with funds and advice. Brandeis himself became a trustee of the *Review* and its first treasurer.[17] He continued as trustee until 1916, when he became Associate Justice of the United States Supreme

Court. In 1890 he became a member of the committee appointed by the University's Board of Overseers to visit the Harvard Law School, and that position he also held until 1916.* At a banquet in 1895 in honor of Dean Langdell's twenty-five years of service, Brandeis brought to Harvard a large group of distinguished lawyers, including the English scholar Sir Frederick Pollock.

Interest in Law School affairs led him to make specific suggestions for enriching the curriculum. As an examiner for admission to the Suffolk Bar, he had noticed that Harvard men were particularly weak in Bay State law and procedure. In 1889 he wrote Dean Langdell proposing a course on the peculiarities of Massachusetts law.[18] Brandeis's suggestion was carried out, but the course from the start proved unsuccessful, owing to misunderstanding of its purpose and to the instructor's inability to raise his teaching above the level of technical detail. When President Eliot asked Brandeis about discontinuing the course, Brandeis replied that he deplored any attempt to "teach details from which the student's mind recoils," yet he maintained that this need not be the case.[19] If properly taught, he was convinced the course would prove to be of great interest and value. It continued in the doldrums for a while longer and was finally abandoned for want of a suitable teacher.

In 1889 the partnership of Warren and Brandeis ended with the death of the former's father. The elder Warren's estate was not distributed at once among the heirs, but for their benefit continued partly undivided in a trust drawn up by Brandeis and Warren. Warren became a trustee of his father's estate. He also became head of the family's paper business. Brandeis continued to advise his former partner on trust and business matters.

The entire relationship between Brandeis and Warren had been one of mutual satisfaction and helpfulness. Warren had made this clear in a letter to Brandeis, written while on vacation in England in 1886: "You overcompliment me on the result of last year's work. I don't think alone, and without your equal, persevering, and courageous character to fall back on, I should not do anything. Certain it is that you without me would make a much better showing than I without you." [20]

Though the partnership was dissolved in 1889, the firm name remained Warren & Brandeis until 1897, and their friendship lasted to the end of Warren's life. A note to Brandeis, January 1, 1890, reveals their close attachment:

---

* His associates on the Committee included Robert Grant, William C. Loring, Joseph B. Warner, Charles P. Greenough, Francis J. Swayze, Langdon P. Marvin, Chandler P. Anderson, Henry L. Stimson.

Dear Louis:

There is no need of wishing you a Happy New Year (tho I do) because a man who well and fearlessly faces every duty without a shirk is bound to have a Happy Year. Open all my letters, and send me those you think I want or ought to see.

Yours affectionately,

S. D.W.

SCHOLARSHIP IN THE LAW

Brandeis had rejected the offer to teach students at Harvard, but he never gave up teaching himself and others. In a rough memorandum on "What the practice of the law includes" he set down certain axioms: "Know thoroughly each fact. Don't believe client witness. Examine documents. Reason; use imagination. Know bookkeeping—the universal language of business: know persons. Far more likely to impress clients by knowledge of facts than by knowledge of law." The memorandum continued: "Know not only specific case, but whole subject. Can't otherwise know the facts. Know not only those facts which bear on direct controversy, but know all the facts and law that surround."

Brandeis not only wrote these maxims, but followed them. "It has been one of the rules of my life," he told a *Boston Globe* reporter, on January 28, 1916, "that no one shall ever trip me on a question of fact," and hardly anyone ever did. Indeed, it was Brandeis who by having strange information at his finger tips often tripped his opponents.

One such instance occurred when he was trying a case for a Boston lady who had rented a house near that city. The owner, a cantankerous person, sued the lady for damage to personal property. As the trial proceeded it became clear that Brandeis's client was being held up for an exorbitant claim. Among the damaged articles listed were pillows. Whimsically, it seemed, Brandeis jumped on these, and quite knowingly began to ask how much they weighed, what they were stuffed with, and how much they cost. Actually he was thoroughly versed in the subject, because a few years earlier, to help cure his insomnia, his mother had gone out and bought him a good horsehair mattress. Brandeis, at the time, examined the bill for the mattress and noted the quality, quantity, and cost of the materials that went into it. One item especially attracted his attention— the charge for horsehair at forty-one cents a pound. From that day on he watched market quotations on horsehair. Thus, after the cantankerous owner had committed himself on the witness stand, Brandeis showed, without any reference to documents, that the pillows had been fabulously overvalued. Then he promptly dismissed the witness. The jury liked Brandeis's dramatics and he won his case.[21]

Not many of his cases were as trivial as this one. Among his more important were those in which the Warren paper interests were involved. Often these cases did not arise from litigation, but simply from the ordinary conduct of the business. Thus in 1887 Brandeis was sent to England to purchase for the firm a patent on an electric bleacher for making pulp.

Though no longer partners in practice, Warren and Brandeis, in 1890, collaborated on an article published in December of that year in the *Harvard Law Review* as "The Right to Privacy." Quite characteristically, for Brandeis, this study grew out of a specific situation. On January 25, 1883, Warren had married Miss Mabel Bayard, daughter of Senator Thomas Francis Bayard, Sr. They set up housekeeping in Boston's exclusive Back Bay section and began to entertain elaborately. The *Saturday Evening Gazette,* which specialized in "blue blood items," naturally reported their activities in lurid detail. This annoyed Warren, who took the matter up with Brandeis. The article was the result.

Brandeis and Warren based their argument for the "right of privacy" not on the law of defamation, which they held did not cover injury to a person's feelings, but upon the individual's right not to have his thoughts, statements, or emotions made public without his consent. "Our hope," Brandeis explained, "is to make more people see that invasions of privacy are not necessarily borne. . . . Of course many desire to be insulted, 'court' the insult as it were. The most, perhaps, that we can accomplish is to start a back-fire, as the woodsmen or prairie-men do." [22]

Years later Brandeis said of the article: "This, like so many of my public activities, I did not volunteer to do." The article was so well done that Dean Roscoe Pound later said it did "nothing less than add a chapter to our law." [23]

As Warren had predicted, his passing from the firm did not slow up its progress. In November 1889 Brandeis argued his (and the firm's) first case before the United States Supreme Court in *Wisconsin R.R.* v. *Price County* (133 U.S. 496). The opportunity came quite by accident. During the previous summer Edwin H. Abbot, President of the Wisconsin Central Railroad, suddenly found he had an important case coming up before the Supreme Court. Judge Jeremiah Smith of New Hampshire, Story Professor of Law at Harvard, was retained as senior counsel, and Abbot invited Brandeis to come in as junior counsel, to assist in preparing the brief. Ordinarily Brandeis would not have argued the case. It happened, however, that their local attorney, who had the matter well in hand, did not turn up. Senator Spooner, nominally counsel for Wisconsin Central, was not conversant with the facts, and when Smith failed to reach Washington in time, Brandeis's admission to the Supreme Court Bar had to be expedited. Conventionally garbed in a borrowed frock coat, Brandeis successfully pleaded his case, which promptly led to a retainer as eastern counsel for the Wisconsin Central Railroad, a relationship which lasted until 1905.

In 1893 the Northern Pacific Railroad leased Wisconsin Central and that September went into receivership carrying Wisconsin Central with it. Extensive litigation and reorganization followed. Brandeis presented a plan of reorganization which was adopted substantially unaltered in 1899. During the whole period he was in close touch with accounting matters, following the road's monthly operating figures in minutest detail. Before all the complicated issues could be resolved, he not only had made important contacts with New York's largest law firms, but also had mastered railroad accountancy and finance so well that in 1911 he stated flatly: "My special field of knowledge is figures"—a subject of which most lawyers know next to nothing.

PERSONAL MATTERS

Brandeis's early professional success was tempered by private misfortune. His favorite sister, Fannie Nagel, whose ill-health since childhood had clouded the life of the entire family, died March 5, 1890. Her death was the more tragic because of the earlier death of her young son Alfred. Knowledge of this had for a time been kept from Fannie, but shortly before she died Louis wrote his father: "I hope you will conclude to let nature take its course with Fannie, whatever that course may be. Don't force her to eat, or even induce her to eat, if she does not desire to do so. If there is a Providence (and I believe there is) he may be offering the great corrective for the suffering which she has borne. We interfered once and have had reason to regret it. I am glad she knows of Alfred's death. I cannot bear to be guilty of untruth with her any more. However, I would not interfere with her action as to herself in regard to eating. I have heard it said that with some patients the desire to refuse food was the one sane wish." [24]

Many years later Brandeis declared that his sister Fannie had the best mind he had ever known—a remarkable tribute from a man who, in sixty years, met so many exceptional people.

Charles Nagel, meanwhile, had been following his brother-in-law's career with keen interest. As early as 1885, before Brandeis was thirty, Nagel had suggested that a career so full might well be shared. On March 18 of that year he wrote to Brandeis: "From all accounts, including your own, you are at least as successful as ever; which is saying a great deal. . . .

You are a fortunate and a deserving man, and there is no one to envy you; unless it is perhaps some noble woman who thinks that she might fairly be included in the halo of your happiness and herself intensify if not enlarge it. However, I do not want to be stopped and so I presume will have to shift my ground." But six years passed before Louis married.

In the spring of 1890, when he was called home by Fannie's death, he visited his uncle Dr. Samuel Brandeis. In the doctor's house he met his second cousin, Alice Goldmark, who, while on a western trip with her engineer brother Henry, had stopped off in Louisville for a two weeks' visit with her Aunt Lotti, Dr. Brandeis's wife.[25]

Alice was the daughter of Dr. Joseph Goldmark, a distinguished scientist who had been a captain in the Academic Legion, an organization of students and professors at the University of Vienna, which took part in the Viennese revolution of 1848. He became a deputy of the Reichstag that year. Then the revolution, instigated by his group, got out of control, and when on October 6, 1848, Baron Latour, a reactionary Minister of War, was assassinated by a mob, Goldmark was indicted for murder. He fled to Switzerland and thence to America, where he arrived in 1850. In 1856, on false evidence, he was condemned to death in absentia for treason and the murder of Latour. In 1868, when a less reactionary regime ordered a general amnesty for political offenses, he returned to Austria, stood trial, and was acquitted.[26]

Alice and Louis had met before when he had occasionally called on the Goldmarks in New York. But their serious interest in each other began with the Louisville meeting, and grew that summer when the Goldmark and Brandeis families spent their vacations in the Adirondacks. Louis arrived on August 26. "Intercourse picked up just where we left it in the spring," Alice noted in her diary of the 28th. The days following, Louis courted his beautiful and accomplished cousin most assiduously. On September 2 Alice noted: "We spent the morning at Mr. Sheldon's retreat, a long, pleasant and thoughtful talk, never to be forgotten. . . . September 3: We are on the water before breakfast. L. takes each of the children out to paddle—always thoughtful of others. . . . September 4: L. appears early to go walking—he is anxious to see the river. His eyes are always upon me. We go down to the river and he tells me his story—we have found each other."

Back in Boston a week later Louis was eager to break the news to his friends. "I wish you could have seen Mrs. Glendower Evans when I told her," Louis wrote Alice, September 15. "She fairly bounded across the room." Charles Townsend Copeland expressed the sentiments of all his Boston friends: "She must like me," he said. "Tell her to—or at least to pretend to."

Sam Warren wrote his partner's fiancée at length:

September 1890

Dear Miss Goldmark:

Louis's is one of the characters (I may almost say the only one) about which I generally keep silence for the unusual reason, that I fear to appear fulsome in my praise of it.

To you, who know at least a part, I shall not be open to this charge.

That you have perceived enough to bring about the engagement, of which he informs me, makes me most anxious to know you.

What you do not know about him, you may trust to the future to develop with absolute confidence in the joy it will bring you.

I know of no one else of whom I should feel like saying so much. I know of him in all ways except the one he is now about to enter with you, but I know that

"The bravest are the tenderest,
The loving are the daring."

I know that his courage is high, his fidelity perfect, and his sense of honor delicate.

For weapons he has an acute and highly trained intellect, and for motive power a high enthusiasm for the right.

I sincerely trust that you may be in Boston before long, and that Mrs. Warren and I may have the *pleasure* of welcoming you to Boston, and to that important part of our lives which we have in common with Louis.

Very sincerely yours,
Samuel D. Warren

To other friends Brandeis announced his news in a very few words:

Boston, October 13, 1890

My dear Walter [Child]:

I am engaged to Miss Alice Goldmark of New York.

Cordially,
Louis D. Brandeis

"Will you be content," Louis had asked Alice, September 29, "to make the day of publication Saturday, October 4? Then I can announce it—flee from my pursuers to your protection and we can have Sunday together before meeting the public."

Louis then began to spend his week-ends at Alice's house, 473 Park Avenue, New York. Only most pressing business could force him to skip the weekly visit. "I long for the time when you will be with me always," he wrote, December 4, 1890. "You have become so large a part of my life that I rattle about sorely when you are absent." He continued: "Is it not strange? For seventeen years I have stood alone—rarely asking—still less frequently caring, for the advice of others. I have walked my way all these years but little influenced by any other individual. And now, Alice, all is changed. I find myself mentally turning to you for advice and approval—indeed, also for support, and I feel my incompleteness more each day. I feel myself each day growing more into your soul, and I am very happy."

Louis bought a house at 114 Mt. Vernon Street, next door to his friends the Delands. "Of course it is not ideal," he wrote Alice, "but all things considered it is the best that could be obtained." Lorin Deland and Louis planned alterations and "humbly submitted" the estimates to Alice for approval:

The estimate of the shades has come—$25.25 for 25 shades. The estimate for the papering has also come:

Hall	$13.50
Reception room	13.50
Dining room	11.45
Library	11.90
Spare room	10.50
Two rooms, 3rd fl.	8.08
Preparing walls	3.50.

All this totaled only $72.43. "You and I are very economical," Louis noted. He agreed that Lorin's ideas were usually excellent, but rejected as many as he could, for "I don't want the cost of alterations to reach too high a figure. I vow we shall compensate for these extra expenses by economies in the time to come." When Alice advised Louis to do whatever seemed best, he demurred: "You must exercise the prerogatives of a partner—to doubt and to criticize."

While Louis struggled with carpenters, plasterers, and paper hangers, Alice spent exhausting hours with dressmakers and in shopping—all of which she found most tiresome. But Louis did not share her lack of concern for dress.

"I don't know whether to be sorry or glad that clothes and the like seem such a nuisance to you," he wrote, February 26, 1891. "I believe in good clothes; it is only the unreasonable accumulation of them which is objectionable, like the other heresies attending weddings. Don't let the abuse of the convention sicken you of the thing; for you know I shall be very exacting about your *dress*."

IN THE ADIRONDACKS, 1890

In the back row, first and second from left are Alice Goldmark and Louis
Brandeis; at the extreme right is Adolph Brandeis. In the middle row at the left
is Mrs. Adolph Brandeis, and third from left is Mrs. Joseph Goldmark.

ALICE GOLDMARK, 1890

BRANDEIS WITH DAUGHTERS AT MANOMET, MASS., 1904

ELIZABETH AND SUSAN BRANDEIS AT FOUR AND SEVEN

He went on: "When a woman happens to be both handsome and artistic a certain obligation rests upon her; there is a call upon her thought and taste. With a woman of mind and of taste, there is the same reason why her dress should be more effective as there is that her house should be more attractive and her table better." [27]

Louis began to share his philosophy of life and work with his future wife even before their wedding day. In late October 1890, Alice had sent him some lines from Longfellow's "A Day of Sunshine":

O Gift of God! A perfect day;
Whereon shall no man work but play;
Whereon it is enough for me,
Not to be doing but to be!

These sentiments struck responsive chords: "Of course, you are right, Alice; at least I think so; for it has been a pet opinion of mine, formed early, and often recurred to. I remember in my Cambridge days talking enthusiastically of Mrs. John Ward of Louisville, a warm friend of ours, who possessed the rare combination of beauty and mind, charm of manner and character. When I had finished my rhapsody, Mrs. Emerton said: 'What has she done?' I answered, somewhat heatedly, 'Done? Nothing. She is!' That conversation defined my ideas on the subject.

"And only as recently as last summer," his letter continued, "Father and I talked over the same subject. He referred to some petty success of mine and remarked, 'You must be proud of that honor.' I told him that I could not recall ever having been proud of anything accomplished or to have deemed any recognition an honor. Indeed, I believe that the little successes I may have had, were due wholly to the pressure from within— proceeding from a deep sense of obligation and in no respect to the allurement of a possible distinction. Our talk the other Sunday touched upon the same ground."

During these rapturous months he saw much of intimate Boston friends, especially Mrs. Glendower Evans and Lorin and Margaret Deland, because with them he could talk freely about his fiancée. Growing impatience overcame him as the wedding day approached. "Occasionally I am oppressed," he wrote, March 15, 1891, "by the multitudinousness of things, and I sigh for the rest and peace which can only come in the thought of your continuous presence. If the twenty-third were not fixed immutably, I should feel like anticipating it, and, like the Barons of old, break away and carry you off."

Louis and Alice were married by her brother-in-law, Felix Adler, at the Goldmarks' house in New York on Brother Alfred's birthday, March

23, 1891. They went off for a two weeks' honeymoon at the Mansion House, Bolton Center, Massachusetts. A note almost as curt as that announcing his engagement to Child gave Samuel D. Warren news of the wedding and evoked warm response next day: "I thought of you on the 23rd and often since, and I got your short note. Life has become so full for you and for me (too full I suggest) that it is only in these resting places that one has a chance to say any small part of what is constantly in mind. To you there can be but one message from me: and that, by way of confirmation of what has gone before. I can think of nothing the years will change less than our friendship and my belief in you."

THE BROADENING POWER OF FRIENDSHIP

Alice's entrance into "cold-roast" Boston society was made easy by the friends Louis had already made. Besides the Warrens, Delands, and Evanses, there were Melvin O. Adams, Arthur Cabot, Albert Otis, Charles G. Loring, Henry Angell, George Wigglesworth, and others—all with impeccable Yankee pedigrees. Louis's most intimate friend was Mrs. Glendower Evans. He had met Mrs. Evans and her husband in the early eighties at the house of Barrett Wendell, the obstreperous literary historian, then assistant professor of English in Harvard College. Mrs. Evans recalls that her husband, a prominent lawyer, rang Wendell's bell just as two young men were departing. "Are those some of your little charges?" she asked Professor Wendell. "No," he replied, "one of them is Louis Brandeis." "Louis Brandeis," said Evans discontentedly, "is a man I have always wanted to know and here he is leaving just as we arrive." "Well," his wife remarked, "why don't we ask him to dinner? We live in a nice house and he presumably lives in lodgings; he might like to come; and if he doesn't, no harm will be done." [28]

Louis quickly formed the habit of dropping in on the Evanses for dinner or just for talk. On Sunday mornings he often went walking or boating with them. Mr. Evans died suddenly in 1886, at the age of thirty, but Brandeis remained a close friend of Mrs. Evans. "He was not content," she wrote later, "that our friendship should drop when Glen died. I can hear him as he said to himself, 'What will happen to that poor girl alone? How will she grow?'" From then on "he just took charge of my life," finding for her "worth-while things to do."

Though she was wealthy, Brandeis fostered and encouraged her interest in labor. On his urgent request she went to England in 1908 "to find out what socialism and the socialist party was like." Later she attended, at his suggestion, the convention of the Women's Trade Union League held at Jane Addams's Hull House in Chicago. From there she visited

Wisconsin, studied LaFollette progressivism at first hand, and called on Milwaukee's Socialist Mayor Emil Seidel. Back in Boston, "Mr. Brandeis had much to ask about [her] experiences." [29]

Naturally, when Louis became engaged, he took Alice to call on Mrs. Evans, and when they were married they sent Mrs. Evans the key to their new house, so that she might unpack their trunks and prepare for their arrival.

CHAPTER FIVE

The Brandeis Way of Life and Law

BRANDEIS and his wife arranged from the beginning to live simply but well. He was determined to become financially independent as early as possible, for, he said, "in this age of millions, the man without some capital can only continue to slave and toil for others to the end of his days." [1] Yet Brandeis had no intention of killing himself to become rich. In his eighty-fourth year he recalled an incident of sixty years before, when he had made an error in judgment because of fatigue. He had resolved that this would never happen again. Thus sufficient rest and frequent vacations were always part of his routine.

Early in his career Brandeis inscribed in his notebook Charles Dalton's comment on long hours: "As soon as I heard that General Frémont worked day and night, I lost my confidence in him." Brandeis himself gave his family a goodly share of each day. From the time his two daughters, Susan, born February 27, 1893, and Elizabeth, born April 25, 1896, were out of the nursery they joined their father in his seven o'clock breakfast. With him they read for an hour, books ranging from Robert Louis Stevenson's *Kidnapped* to Barry's *Later Roman Empire*. Sometimes he would devote the hour to mathematics or to history and even philosophy. Early evenings, after leaving his office at his usual hour—five o'clock—he would go horseback riding or, weather permitting, paddle on the Charles.

Though Brandeis was a charter member of the Dedham Polo Club, where he kept his horse, he did not himself play polo. Indeed, he would never enter a race or join in games involving chance or competition. He preferred to pit his skill against nature, against a strong current or a head wind on the river. It was a common remark among the people of South Yarmouth, observing a man taking apparently foolhardy chances in a canoe—"That must be Mr. Brandeis."

The Brandeis family began early to spend spring and fall week-ends in Dedham near Boston. At first they took rooms at the house of one Emma Hickey. Later they rented, and finally bought, a house of their own. On Saturday afternoon the whole family would drive to Dedham in a sort of open wagon. There, unless business was extraordinarily pressing, in which case he would spend the early morning hours strenuously at work, Brandeis gave all of Sunday to his wife and children. They would ride or skate, play tennis or paddle, as the season allowed. Susan took carpentry lessons in school and with her father's assistance built a big playhouse in their Dedham back yard. This was pleasant when bad weather forced them indoors.

Brandeis took a vacation whenever he felt he needed one. The test was the frame of mind with which he approached the day's work. If he could not look forward to it with pleasure, he knew a vacation was overdue. On this subject, he wrote William H. Dunbar, a brilliant young lawyer in his office, on February 2, 1893: "A bookkeeper can work 8 or 10 hours a day and perhaps 12, year in—year out, and possibly his work may be always good (tho' I doubt it). But a man who practices law, who aspires to the higher places of his profession must keep his mind fresh. It must be alert and be capable of meeting emergencies, must be capable of the *tour de force*. This is not possible for him who works along, not only during the day but much of the night, without change, without turning the mind into new channels, with the mind always at some tension. The bow must be strung and unstrung; work must be measured not merely by time but also by its intensity. There must be time for that unconscious thinking which comes to the busy man in his play."

Actually, Brandeis almost always took his vacation in August. "I soon learned," he said in the summer of 1940, "that I could do twelve months' work in eleven months, but not in twelve." The twelfth month for Brandeis was August. And August was for play.

He spent August of 1885 in "the wilderness of Canada, fleeing from overcivilized Boston for the forest and a few like-minded friends." His most ambitious exploit was a long and arduous journey through the wilds of eastern Canada with Herbert White in 1899. They sailed on White's boat, the *Frolic,* taking much time out for fishing, walking, and canoeing. They visited a coal mine and climbed mountains. Brandeis recorded all of it in a notebook.

RECIPE FOR SUCCESS

In a notebook, too, Brandeis early set down Swift's words: "Who does not provide for his own house, says St. Paul, is worse than an infidel. And I think he who provides only for his own house is just equal to an infidel." Brandeis wanted money to be able "to provide for his own house"—and more. He also wanted time and carefully budgeted every working day. He reached his office regularly at half-past eight or earlier, and disposed of correspondence by ten. Then he saw clients. Every conference was speeded up—so much so that one client remarked that he could not stay in Brandeis's office except by clinging to some substantial object. The office itself was furnished with austerity. There was no rug or easy chair. The temperature was kept so low that in winter the client could be comfortable only by keeping on his overcoat.[2]

Brandeis himself was usually amiable toward his clients. But he was quick to see through ostensible aims to real motives. Early in his career he jotted down, with a slight twist, the Biblical phrase: "Lawsuit—Some clients prosecuting remind one of the man who had no sheep and lost one. Matth. XXVI-12." Nevertheless, he usually would sit quietly and listen intently while a client explained his problem. Then with a simple question or comment he would go to the heart of the matter.

Brandeis was short with people because he understood them quickly. This, he thought, was part of his business. He made this clear for Dunbar's benefit, who, Brandeis believed, was not getting on so well as he should. The letter is worth quoting from at length:

Cultivate the society of men—particularly men of affairs. . . . Lose no opportunity of becoming acquainted with men, of learning to feel instinctively their motivation, of familiarizing yourself with their personal and business habits; use your ability in making opportunities to do this. . . .

The knowledge of men, the ability to handle, to impress them, is needed by you—not only in order that clients may appreciate your advice and that you may be able to apply the law to human affairs—but also that you may more accurately and surely determine what the rules of law are, that is, what the courts will adopt. You are prone in legal investigations to be controlled by logic and to underestimate the logic of facts. Knowledge of the decided cases and of the rules of logic cannot alone make a great lawyer. He must know, must feel "in his bones," the facts to which they apply—must know, too, that if they do not stand the test of such application, the logical result will somehow or other be avoided. You are sometimes inclined to the attitude of "then so much the worse for facts."

If you will recall Jessel's * opinions you will see what I mean. Knowledge of decisions and powers of logic are mere hand maidens—they are servants, not masters. The controlling force is the deep knowledge of human necessities. It was this which made Jessel the great lawyer and the greater judge. The man who does not know intimately human affairs is apt to make of the law a bed of Procrustes. No hermit can be a great lawyer, least of all a commercial lawyer. When from a knowledge of the law, you pass to its application, the need of a full knowledge of men and of their affairs becomes even more apparent. The duty of a lawyer today is not that of a solver of legal conundrums: he is indeed a counsellor at law. Knowledge of the law is of course essential to his efficiency, but the law bears to his profession a relation very similar to that which medicine does to that of the physicians. The apothecary can prepare the dose, the more intelligent one even knows the specific for most common diseases. It requires but a mediocre physician to administer the proper drug for the patient who correctly and fully describes his ailment. The great physicians are those who in addition to that knowledge of therapeutics which is open to all, know not merely the human body but the human mind and emotions, so as to make themselves the proper diagnosis—to know the truth which their patients fail to disclose and who add to this an influence over the patient which is apt to spring from a real understanding of him.

Your law may be perfect, your ability to apply it great, and yet you cannot be a successful adviser unless your advice is followed; it will not be followed unless you can satisfy your clients, unless you impress them with your superior knowledge, and that you cannot do unless you know their affairs better than they do because you see them from a fullness of knowledge. The ability to impress them grows with your own success in advising others, with the confidence which you yourself feel in your powers. That confidence can never come from books; it is gained by human intercourse. . . .

Dunbar replied freely, though a little sadly, to his boss, thus showing the spirit that prevailed in Brandeis's office:

Cambridge
February 7, 1893

Dear Brandeis:

I got the letter you wrote from Washington last night and read it with great interest. I recognize fully the truths that you tell me. I am fully and painfully aware of the shortcomings you refer to and think myself that they have done more, partly consciously and partly unconsciously, to cause a dissatisfaction that I have felt at times than anything else. It necessarily has been apparent to

* Sir George Jessel (1824–1883), eminent English jurist. He was appointed Solicitor-General in 1871, and in 1873 became Master of the Rolls and Privy Councilor. The second Judicature Act of 1881 relieved him of duty in the rolls court and made him president of the first court of appeal, on which he served until his death.

me for a long time that I produce less effect than others who started after me and that my work in certain lines at any rate was in spite of longer experience less successful, and that as a consequence I did not fill, in the external relations of the office, the place that I should naturally have been expected to occupy—in short that George [George R. Nutter] was regarded as your *locum tenens* in your absence instead of myself. The only satisfaction that I have been able to derive from this was the fact, and I candidly believe it to be a fact, that I had succeeded in preventing myself from feeling any unworthy personal rivalry: this has hardly been a virtue, however, considering who the person was and the entire considerateness that has always been shown among us. The only time, I think, in which I allowed myself really to feel or to exhibit any such sentiment remains to this day a thorn in my side: I was on the point of apologizing at the time and have often since wished that I had [not] passed the point.

I am perfectly aware that you did not write with a reference to these things and I only mention them to show that I am not unmindful of the characteristics of temperament or habit that you speak of, and of the untoward effects that they produce.

It is so much easier for me however to recognize the evils than to see how the remedy is to be successfully applied, that I am even yet in doubt as to whether any effectual remedy is possible. The sort of social intercourse that you have in mind has been a difficult undertaking for me during the past ten years. The endeavor to keep up with any general conversation, whether among men or women or both, where the closest attention does not enable you to hear all that is said, is a pretty steady strain and makes what might be a pleasurable recreation become very similar to serious and distasteful work; and undoubtedly the annoyance of failure to keep up assumes an undue magnitude with the person who experiences it. I am not sure that naturally I should have been more of a "hermit" than most men who have engrossing occupations and can get as much pleasure from books as from persons, indeed I used rather to enjoy mixing in public or quasi-public gatherings, but that is a taste I suppose that is soon lost unless one is able to take in some degree a prominent part and fill it to one's own satisfaction at least. At any rate the taste remains with me only as a desire for something that might have been—like desire to try cases of fact. Of course however I appreciate that, the question is not one to be determined by reference to tastes but to needs; and I cannot well doubt that I need the results of the course that you think that I should pursue. Nor am I ready yet to succumb to the effects of their absence. Even though I can hardly feel very confident of accomplishing all that you believe possible, I think it would be unmanly not to make some effort, and I should be ashamed to prove inferior to the opinion which you have expressed as to my having sufficient ambition to try. The most serious difficulty in the way of trying is that the undertaking is one of such an intangible sort as to make not only the first step but every succeeding one very obscure to me at present. I hardly know how to go about the work of cultivating the society of "men of affairs." I suppose I can make a more frequent use of my club membership and by dining there once a week get to see more of men than I do now—and perhaps other things will suggest themselves to me. But I shall stand in need of all the suggestions from you that you are ready to make and I will try to act on them.

At any rate, don't doubt that I am exceedingly grateful—and somewhat gratified.

Yours,
William H. Dunbar

I am afraid this letter sounds very egotistic, but the subject seems to make that unavoidable.

MR. BRANDEIS AND HIS FIRM

Dunbar * and George R. Nutter † were among the first new members Brandeis added to his firm as practice grew. "Nutter is very able and is my first lieutenant," Brandeis wrote in a letter to his fiancée on October 13, 1890. In 1895 Brandeis began to delegate his own work to Nutter, Dunbar, and others. He himself only enjoyed a particular type of case the first time he handled it. So he made it a practice to refer subsequent cases of like nature to others, for he believed they were getting exceptional opportunities, while he became himself a freer man professionally, and freer also to engage in public activities.

His youthful and brilliant colleagues, however, did not entirely agree with him. By 1896 some of the young lawyers in his office—perhaps all of them—began to feel that their status was hardly more elevated than that of hired men; that their professional performance, however brilliant, won no commensurate professional recognition for themselves as individuals; that their best effort seemed only to enhance the reputation and prestige of Brandeis. Dunbar, a highly sensitive person, deeply conscious of his extreme deafness, took the lead in telling Brandeis of this feeling in the office, writing on August 17, 1896:

I suppose that every professional man of ordinary ambition hopes to make for himself some reputation; to have his work, if in any degree successful, count

---

* A.B., 1882; LL.B. and A.M., 1886 (honor degree); Phi Beta Kappa; Secretary to Mr. Justice Gray; Member Executive Committee, Massachusetts Bar Association, 1910, 1911, 1912; Member Grievance Committee, Massachusetts Bar Association, 1913, 1914, 1915; Member special committee of three of Boston Bar Association to confer with committee of Massachusetts Bar Association and agree upon a common code of ethics; Member Council Harvard Law School Association, 1910, 1911, and 1912.

† A.B., 1885; LL.B. and A.M., 1889 (honor degree); Phi Beta Kappa; Editor-in-chief of the *Harvard Law Review;* Member of Council of Massachusetts Bar Association, 1916; Member Committee on Grievances of the Massachusetts Bar Association for three years; Member of committees appointed by the Council of the Boston Bar Association on Amendments of the Law, and Admissions; Member of Committee on English, appointed by the Board of Overseers of Harvard College, 1886–89; Secretary to President Eliot, 1885–86; One of three trustees of the *Harvard Law Review* from 1889.

not only as a source of income but as giving his name some individual value. This result it seems to me he can reach only by having his name known and by working as a principal. Our present arrangement I think does not permit of this. My work yields to me almost literally no return except a pecuniary compensation.

I am aware that for reasons personal to myself I cannot expect under any circumstances to acquire such a reputation as I might wish. It has seemed to me however that as I am now situated it is impossible for me to acquire such reputation as I might otherwise hope for. I cannot disguise from myself that the work I now do is not my work; that for the most part I not only am not known, but am not in fact a principal. So far as I am successful in what I undertake the result benefits me pecuniarily; but whatever reputation comes from the success of all our joint labors reaches me only in a dimly reflected form and only so far as my connection with you is known in a limited circle.

I look upon these results as unsatisfactory both in the practical aspect that my name acquires none of the value which seems to constitute the chief capital of a professional man and in other more sentimental but perhaps to me equally important aspects. The results seem to me the necessary consequence of an organization like ours in which there is not in fact any real partnership between the different persons associated together.

I have endeavored in thinking over the matter to give due weight to my own disabilities and to balance the very real pleasures and advantages of the present arrangement with the difficulties of a more individual career. After doing so the impression remains that all things considered the latter course would in the long run prove more satisfactory, and that I ought seriously to consider the matter and reach a final conclusion as soon as possible. My confidence, so far as I have any, that there may be a solid foundation for this feeling, is strengthened by finding that George [Nutter] and Ezra [R. Thayer] have independently of me and of each other come to similar conclusions and I write to you at this time because after consultation with them it seemed to me probable that you would prefer to have an opportunity of thinking of the matter in a season of leisure.

I do not wish you to suppose that I am doing more than opening my mind to you. The matter is too serious to me to be lightly determined, and my chief wish is that you should give a perfectly frank and candid opinion on the subject and, so far as I can ask it, your advice. In any event you will I hope understand that I have taken a greater satisfaction in the work of the last nine years than would have been possible if I had been similarly associated with any one except yourself.

Two days later Brandeis replied, attempting to justify the existing set-up, and stated his conclusions thus:

First: The organization of large offices is becoming more and more a business —and hence also a professional necessity,—if properly planned and administered—it must result in the greatest efficiency to clients and the greatest success to the individual members both pecuniarily and in reputation.

Second: In such an organization the place of each man must be found—not prescribed. The advantage of the larger field is that every man has the opportunity of trying himself at everything or anything—and by a natural law comes to do those things that on the whole he does most effectively.

Third: As to that class of things which the individual makes his own, he must become in the office in time the principal—for those dealing with the office learn that he is considered the authority there on those things and shortly follow suit; the duration of time required for this public recognition and its extent depend on personal qualities—largely independent of intellectual ability and attainments—namely the ability to impress one's personality upon others—and of creating followers. In other words a reputation in the practical world to which the practice of the law belongs—is determined by a large number of qualities and in a proper organization they have even better scope for effectiveness today than in individuals standing alone.

Fourth: Besides the things as to which the individual becomes the principal— there must be always much as to which he is the associate, the Junior or Senior of the others in the organization and every man must stand ready to give every other man full aid. Every man also must hold himself to a stricter performance of his task—on account of his relations to the others.

That such organizations are the most effective means of doing the law work of this country—so far as clients are concerned—is proven by the success of the great New York firms—the pecuniary success and the professional success or reputation of the individual members. This reputation has in no sense been dependent upon the individual's name appearing in the firm designation. Beaman was known everywhere before Southmayde's retirement gave his name a place in the firm—and Treadwell Cleveland is now reaching the point of reputation which Beaman had a few years ago. In Alexander & Green, John J. McCook reached the pinnacle in 1888.

In other words I think it only essential that the man should have the opportunity. If he has it and has the will—his work tells in the community as in the office in course of time—sometimes soon—sometimes much later.

As to your own case—I had always felt that your own talents and attainments would be most fully utilized in such an organization as ours—that you would do the most effective work there, and achieve there, in the end, the best professional and pecuniary success. You will remember our conversations about the importance of impressing upon others that ability which you have and of making your work stand for as much out of the office, as it does in it. I know you agreed with me—and I doubt not that so far as you may have failed to impress the general public—it has been due not to any lack of will—but to a modesty or sensitiveness—which causes your merits to make themselves known to others far more slowly than like merits would in many men.

My impression is that despite the discontent you may have felt from time to time—you would be less happy standing alone—and obliged to deal with many phases of professional life which are now very distasteful and even painful to you.

But as I said, I do not want to advise definitely without a full discussion with you—and have only stated what lay in my mind from an earlier consideration of the general subject.

I have said nothing of the regret which I should feel in severing a connection which I hoped and still hope may continue through our professional lives—as I have no right to urge or indeed consider my own wishes or sentiment.

Brandeis obviously did not meet Dunbar's points squarely but put him off by rehearsing the conventional arguments for large-scale organization—arguments of which Brandeis himself was to be more than skeptical later. Certainly for him no other arrangement could have been so congenial as the one he had in his office. By having enough lawyers of varying tastes and specialities, he was relieved of much that would have been drudgery to him, though perhaps of interest to others. Nevertheless, the complaints of Dunbar and the others had to be met. In 1897 the firm's name was changed from Warren & Brandeis to Brandeis, Dunbar & Nutter, and the "real partnership" for which Dunbar had asked was in fact created.

From then on the advancement of staff members was never the matter of negotiation. Brandeis worked out a formula with an appropriate factor for the source of the particular matter, whether it was a novel contribution of a particular man or a matter which came to him personally. Then he would estimate the value of the work done by the different members. He went on the principle that men do good work only when there is held out to them the certain prospect of recognition and advancement, the enlargement of their spheres of influence. He quickly rewarded individual worth in his office, gave generous increases in salary, and conferred successively larger responsibilities. No one ever attempted to follow the intricacies of the formula, but everyone always felt fairly and liberally treated in the internal readjustments which he proposed.

Many men and women have occupied places of influence and usefulness because of Brandeis's encouragement. Miss E. Louise Malloch came to his office in 1895, a girl in her 'teens. Within two years she was given responsible work involving his personal investments, and when he went on the Supreme Court in 1916, she was put in full charge of these matters. Under his tutelage Miss Alice H. Grady rose to the office of Deputy Commissioner of Savings Bank Life Insurance in Massachusetts.

With the courts and the outside world there was constant effort to put the younger members forward as fast as they were ready for the task. There is no instance known of Brandeis's seeking personal fame, or even accepting it, for their accomplishments. His pride in them and their achievements was great. The late Joseph B. Eastman had not even been admitted to the Bar, had not, indeed, finished his law course, when, working in Brandeis's office under his close supervision, he wrote and alone signed the brief submitted to the Interstate Commerce Commission in the New Haven case, May 15, 1913. On Brandeis's recommendation Governor David I. Walsh in 1915 appointed Eastman, then in his early thirties, to the Massachusetts Public Service Commission. Four years later President Wilson, at Justice Brandeis's suggestion, appointed him to the Interstate Commerce Commission. "It is always a comfort to be with Eastman," the Justice commented years later. "He is hard and hard-headed—honest, courageous—makes for faith in this crazy world." [3]

Brandeis's active participation in trial cases dropped off sharply after 1895 when Edward F. McClennen joined the office, right out of Harvard Law School. In 1905 Brandeis gave him the Old Dominion Copper Company Case,* the most important the firm had handled up to that time. Mr. McClennen prepared the brief, presented it to the lower court and then to the United States Supreme Court. Had Brandeis followed standard practice, he himself would have presented the brief, arduously prepared by his younger colleague. He chose, rather, to put McClennen forward, not only because McClennen was thoroughly competent to handle the matter and merited the recognition, but because the responsibility involved in a million-dollar dispute would give tremendous stimulus to an ambitious young attorney.

To his own staff Brandeis always seemed aloof. But his high professional standards were infectious. After he gave up practice to join the Supreme Court, his former colleagues, whenever a delicate matter was settled nicely, would often remark, "Even Brandeis would have approved that." [4]

AN EMINENT LAWYER WITH A DIFFERENCE

By 1890 Brandeis was a successful corporation lawyer, vieing with the biggest in Boston and New York. But he differed from the usual corporation lawyer in two ways. First, he dealt only with the heads of corporations as his personal clients and never acted as a mere legal employee of a corporation itself. "I would rather have clients," he said, "than be somebody's lawyer." Among his clients were such astute manufacturers as Charles P. Hall, Charles H. Jones, and W. H. McElwain, all of Massachusetts. These men became his lifelong friends though, as Brandeis later explained, their wives never exchanged visiting cards with Mrs. Brandeis. In the second place, he treated corporate practice in its broader business context, not

* See pages 487 ff.

merely as involving legal issues. Approaching each case in this way, he found that it called for quite as much business judgment as for legal advice. Thus the heads of large corporations called upon him increasingly for counsel on matters both of business and law.

It was this broader view of the lawyer's function that prompted President Francis A. Walker of the Massachusetts Institute of Technology to invite Brandeis to give a course on Business Law. Tentative plans for the course were made for the school year 1891–92, but Brandeis's ill-health forced postponement to the following year, when he gave the course, teaching Saturday mornings from nine to ten o'clock.

From the moment the course was offered to him, Brandeis began collecting cases, illustrative newspaper clippings, and other data. On February 12, 1890, he asked Dunbar to collect cases on specific points. He worked and reworked all this material until he finally had it pounded into more or less popular lecture form. As originally planned, his course was to be a routine defense of the adequacy of the common law to deal with industrial and commercial problems. Before any lectures were given, however, the virtual war between strikers and armed Pinkerton strikebreakers broke out at the Homestead, Pennsylvania, plant of the Carnegie-Illinois Steel Company. Brandeis was deeply affected, especially by the harsh measures taken by the company to destroy the Amalgamated Association of Iron and Steel Workers. Brandeis later considered this a turning point in his career:

I think it was the affair at Homestead which first set me to thinking seriously about the labor problem. It took the shock of that battle, where organized capital hired a private army to shoot at organized labor for resisting an arbitrary cut in wages, to turn my mind definitely toward a searching study of the relations of labor to industry.

I had been asked to give a course on Business Law at the Massachusetts Institute of Technology, and had gone to some pains to prepare my lectures, tracing the evolution of the common law in its relation to industry and commerce, when one morning the newspaper carried the story of the pitched battle between the Pinkertons on the barge and barricaded steel workers on the bank. I saw at once that the common law, built up under simpler conditions of living, gave an inadequate basis for the adjustment of the complex relations of the modern factory system. I threw away my notes and approached my theme from new angles. Those talks at Tech marked an epoch in my own career.[5]

The lectures were undertaken with the understanding that they would be given biannually, but they were not repeated after 1895–96. They were, however, the means by which Brandeis worked out for himself a new understanding of the relation between law and business. Soon he went beyond even that. He began to see that both law and business involved politics. The result was his unique public career.

From law-school days Brandeis had been a Republican in politics. Among his papers is a Republican ticket inscribed in his own handwriting, "Louis D. Brandeis, his ticket, Cambridge, Mass., November 7, 1876." But when, in 1884, James G. Blaine ("the Continental Liar from the State of Maine") and John A. ("Black Jack") Logan were nominated by the Republican National Convention, Brandeis took his first independent stand. With two or three hundred other Boston "mugwumps," as the Republican bolters were called, he signed the following:

THE CALL

We, the undersigned Republican and independent voters of Massachusetts, believing that only men of high character should be elected to high office, and that the nominations just made in Chicago ought not to be supported in any contingency that now seems likely to arise, invite those who think with us on this point to meet in the old dining-room at Young's Hotel, Boston, on Friday, June 13, at 3:30 P.M. to consider what action to take in opposition to these nominations.[6]

This action bothered Brandeis's politically sagacious brother-in-law, Charles Nagel, who wrote: "The *Advertiser* has reached me, and I found your name where I expected it! But I am not able to go with you this time. It is not pleasant to be called a 'Tough' or to differ from the men with whom you are accustomed to go, but I cannot see my way this time!"[7]

After 1884 Brandeis always referred to himself as a "democrat with a small 'd'" but he was not much interested in party politics and supported from time to time candidates of both parties. "A very urgent invitation came today from the Democratic State Central Committee to accept the nomination for Representative to the Legislature from Ward IX," he wrote his fiancée, October 10, 1890. "It would be interesting, but of course I cannot do it. It is one of the many things one must postpone or leave wholly undone. This year would be a great one in politics. The Republicans must yield soon and blows will tell now." A week later he was "so indignant at their [Republican] doings that it requires some self-command not to take the stump." He exercised the necessary "self-command."

A LAW PRACTICE MERGES INTO A PUBLIC CAREER

But party politics was not the only avenue to a public career. There were in Boston in the eighties, various reform movements which a prominent middle-class citizen could foster without rousing the ire of the financial and social elite. These Brandeis began to take up. In 1884 he was elected to the executive committee of the Civil Service Reform Association of the Fifth Congressional District. In 1887 he joined the Boston American Citizenship Committee.

Thus Brandeis started reforming innocuously enough. Gradually he got tougher. The lobbying activities of public utilities were becoming more and more open in the 1880's. Rumor had it that more than $300,000 had been given in bribes to Massachusetts legislators alone. J. P. Morgan, Sr., himself was supposed to be implicated. In 1890 George Fred Williams, an able and courageous Yankee legislator, proposed a thorough investigation. He called upon Brandeis for aid, and this was freely given. On December 27, 1890, Williams wrote to Brandeis: "Recalling your very kind letter, written during my West-End fight, I want to suggest to you that you could do a great deal, if you would, to help some of the reforms, which this winter will be pushed in the legislature by the "Young Democracy." My own fear is that there is not all the talent there, which is necessary to carry through the measures which [Governor William E.] Russell will propose. . . .

"Knowing from your appreciation of my work in the last Legislature how heartily you sympathize with such work, I venture to ask, if you cannot get time to study some particular measure and identify yourself with it: this much for the State. Some of us have given ourselves up to this work, and I believe our participation in politics has done much to steer the people toward Democracy. You belong with us and your influence would help amazingly, if only exercised incidentally. Read this over in your closet and do not throw it aside in your office."

On Williams's urging, Brandeis turned to the liquor lobby. The distillers were represented in Massachusetts by William D. Ellis, Boston agent of a Cincinnati distillery, a Brandeis client, and member of the Executive Committee of the Massachusetts Protective Liquor Dealers' Association. Brandeis had known and liked Ellis for years and one day asked him to come to his office. The visit had not gone far when Brandeis produced the list of Massachusetts legislators which he kept in his roll-top desk. He passed the roster to Ellis and asked him to check all those who could be bribed. Ellis did so and handed it back without a word. Brandeis looked at him and asked, "Ellis, do you realize what you are doing?" Then Brandeis went on at length about the evils of bribery until "tears ran down the liquor agent's face." [8]

The Legislature at this time was discussing temperance measures so restrictive as to threaten the existence of the liquor business. Brandeis disapproved of this and became counsel for the Association on condition that Ellis be made chairman of the Association's Executive Committee, which controlled expenditures. No money was to be spent except on Brandeis's order or approval. Then in a carefully reasoned but unconventional brief in February 1891, he deplored blind and hasty legislative action and asked for a scientific diagnosis of the liquor evil. "All the morning," he wrote Alice on February 19, "I was before the legislative committee fighting the errors and hypocrisies of so-called temperance people."

A few lines on the frontispiece of his printed brief summed up his entire argument:

Liquor drinking is not a wrong; but excessive drinking is.
Liquor will be sold; hence the sale should be licensed.
Liquor is dangerous; hence the business should be regulated.
No regulation can be enforced which is not reasonable.

The better the men who sell liquor, the less the harm done by it.
Hence, strive to secure for the business those who are respectable.
Self-respect and prosperity are the most effective guardians of morals.
Unenforceable or harassing laws tend to make criminals.

For fifteen years an unenforceable law had been on the Massachusetts books, prohibiting the sale of liquor except as part of a meal. Almost every liquor dealer violated the law. This made criminals, Brandeis argued, out of those who were at heart law-abiding. It also bred corruption and made "liquor dealers a potent force in politics." Brandeis went on: "You can make politicians of shoemakers or of farmers; you can make politicians of any class of people, or of those in any occupation if you harass them, if you make it impossible for them to live unless they control, unless they have secured power to determine when, and how, and where they may live. *You can remove liquor dealers from politics by a very simple device— make the liquor laws reasonable.*" [9]

This the Legislature did.

Brandeis turned next to Boston's care of its paupers. This was in 1894 when he became counsel for his philanthropic friend Mrs. Alice N. Lincoln. Long public hearings had revealed many poor-law abuses, and people like Mrs. Lincoln were demanding the dismissal of all responsible officials. Brandeis argued, however, that the officials were incompetent rather than corrupt. He did not join in the cry for dismissal; actually he credited them with two virtues: economy and integrity. He pointed out, however, that they were blind to the real problems of pauperism. Their policy, he said, "has not been directed to the prevention and cure of pauperism, but merely to its care."

Paupers, Brandeis argued, were abnormal and must be studied as such. He emphasized the necessity of research into each applicant's history. He pleaded for classification of inmates, based on this research. He demanded better care of the ill, work for the able. "We have not," he said, "found fault with the commissioners for not making them [the paupers] work, that is a charge against the system. There should be a law passed to provide and compel work, not merely because it will save the city expense, nor only because it will decrease the number of inmates, but because it will improve the character of those who work, making them self-supporting and giving them self-respect." [10]

But more than work was needed. "These people are not machines," he said, "these are human beings . . . they . . . have emotions, feelings, and interests. . . . They should have entertainments, they may be literary, they may be musical, they may perhaps be of a class hardly worthy to be called either. . . . But each one of them, and all of them, can be raised and raised only by holding up before them that which is higher and that which is better than they." [11]

"Men are not bad, men are not degraded, because they desire to be so; they are degraded largely through circumstances, and it is the duty of every man and the main duty of those who are dealing with these unfortunates to help them up and let them feel in one way or another that there is some hope for them in life, and some distinction between them and the worse." [12]

To public-spirited Bostonians he said: "Unless you bring the outer life, the outer sunshine, into the darkness of the lives of these unfortunates, you can never expect to get that moral growth to which this institution should ever strive to bring its inmates. These are the main considerations. All else is subsidiary." [13]

Brandeis moved next to the national stage. Nominally a representative of the New England Free Trade League, he appeared on January 11, 1897, before the House Ways and Means Committee to testify on the Dingley tariff bill. The New England Free Trade League was made up largely of carpet, woolen, paper, and metal goods manufacturers. They were, as the name of their League indicated, free traders. Brandeis was not, but he had his own purposes and testified anyway. "I have not undertaken," he said, "to make a speech for free trade, because I do not understand that this is the time or place to do it. What I have undertaken to do is to appear on behalf of the consumer and a large number of workingmen in New England. I have undertaken to object to a change of conditions which are very far removed from free trade. Where duties are largely over 40 per cent, I think it can hardly be called free trade. What I make an argument for is that we be left undisturbed in business, in order that business may recover."

He continued: "I desire to speak in behalf of those who form, I believe, a far larger part of the people of the United States than any who have found representation here. I appear for those who want to be left alone, those who do not come to Congress and seek the aid of the sovereign powers of the government to bring them prosperity."

Of such people he said: "This asking for help from the government for everything should be deprecated. It destroys the old and worthy sturdy principle of American life which existed in the beginning when men succeeded by their own efforts. That is what has led to the evil of protective tariff and other laws to that end, by which men seek to protect themselves from competition." [14]

Brandeis's testimony was received coldly. "If he had appeared as representative of certain individuals who wished to put hundreds of thousands of dollars of public money into their pockets," a reporter for the *Springfield Republican* observed, "he would have been allowed to state his case uninterruptedly." As it was, the leading Democratic members of the committee had to hold a long conference about him before he was allowed to speak at all. Then Representative McMillin * remarked that "he supposed it would be in order for one man to appear who represented the consumer."

"Mr. Brandeis persevered," declared a news report, "in the face of his Republican critics, and in spite of the side remark of Mr. Dalzell,† 'Oh, let him run down!' His reception was altogether such as to discourage any man of a shrinking disposition who might think proper to make the suggestion that the 70,000,000 consumers of the United States had some interests worth a 10-minute hearing before the Committee." [15]

In a letter to the *Boston Herald,* January 12, 1897, William Lloyd Garrison applauded Brandeis's courage. "With one exception," Garrison wrote, "not one word of public spirit, not one sentiment implying a thought of equal rights and privileges, has relieved the montonous record of corporate and private greed which casts its shame upon popular government. That exception, for which let us be thankful, came from Massachusetts, in the person of one of Boston's most respected lawyers, Louis D. Brandeis."

At first Brandeis gave to charity the fees received for representing good causes. Later he habitually refused pay for any work he considered to be in the public interest. This was accepted by Boston society as perhaps

---

* Benton McMillin (1845–1928), University of Kentucky, Representative, 4th Tennessee Congressional District (1879–99), Democrat.
† John Dalzell (1845–1922), Yale, 1865, Representative, 22nd Congressional District of Pennsylvania, (1887–1913), Republican.

quixotic but on the whole commendable. In later years, however, when Brandeis had become known as the leading opponent of economic privilege, his refusal to take fees for public work was regarded as proof of dark and ulterior motives.

IDEALS AND DOUBTS

During the late eighties and early nineties Brandeis's letters expressed underlying restlessness as well as ingrained moderation. An abiding and ardent desire for reform did not, however, make him favor drastic or revolutionary change. His remark of later years that "my earlier associations were such as to give me greater reverence than I now have for the things that are because they are," [16] may lead one to wonder whether this keen-visioned law student of the late seventies was metamorphosed by successful practice and the amenities of Boston society into a complacent and well-intentioned Tory. In thus evaluating Brandeis's character, his critic falls into two errors. First, he attributes to him a higher degree of malleability than is justifiable and assumes that his environment imposed its own standards upon him; second, such criticism assumes that his later attacks on accepted social and financial abuses were due not so much to experience and insight as to a sudden awakening or conversion, similar to the religious experience of being "saved."

There is no evidence to show either that Brandeis was absorbed into Boston middle-class society, or that he suddenly saw the error of his way and then began systematic war on things formerly approved. Both these views are out of keeping with his character. He was far too critical, too independent in thought and action, to be carried from one extreme to another. He appreciated and valued Boston aristocracy, but his head was never turned by it. Nor, on the other hand, was his mind of the type that accepts or rejects an ideology entire, so that after the middle nineties he could see nothing but evil in the society he had formerly enjoyed, nothing but good in some envisioned utopia.

Brandeis as a reformer was concerned only with the world as it is and *can be*—here and now. That was always his concern—to preserve continuity with the past, to change only that which could be improved. To this effect he wrote his mother on her birthday, November 12, 1888: "I must send you another birthday greeting and tell you how much I love you; that with each day I learn to extol your love and your worth more—and that when I look back over my life, I can find nothing in your treatment of me that I would alter. You often said, dearest mother, that I find fault —but I always told you candidly that I felt and sought to change only that little which appeared to me to be possible of improvement. I believe, most beloved mother, that the improvement of the world, reform, can only arise when mothers like you are increased thousands of times and have more children."

Brandeis believed the world could be improved—if only a little—by improving men's character. He wrote Alice, October 27, 1890:

Of course results are not to be despised. They are evidence of what produces them. But they are not the only evidence. They are often deceptive—and their absence is by no means conclusive. It is only in the Latin sense that talents are to be "admired"; they are to be wondered at. But character only is to be "admired" as we use that word. It is the effort—the attempt—that tells. Man's work is, at best, so insignificant compared with that of the Creator—it is all so Lilliputian, one cannot bow before it.

Feeling this strongly, you can imagine, Alice, what happiness it gave me to find on the fly-leaf of your diary those lines of Matthew Arnold's (which I had, of course, *not* known before):

"Life is not a having and a getting;
but a being and a becoming."

I pour out my innermost thoughts without reserve.

Furthermore Louis believed that character could profit from example. "At times," he wrote Alice, December 9, 1890, "I feel as if there were in me the potential of something; and if it is there, I am sure you will bring it out. . . . You speak my thoughts in what you say about right living. The value of that is surely underestimated by even the good people of the world. I mean the value of an example. We Americans particularly have been so overwhelmed with huge figures that we are apt to underestimate the value of the unit in the great mass. To me the potency of example seems very great. Most people are like the iron pyrites with which the teachers in physics perform their experiments. They lie powerless—motionless—dormant, before the magnet is applied. Then they move wherever they are drawn—and it is a matter of chance whether it be the positive or the negative pole to which they march."

About this same time a number of worth-while causes began to suggest themselves. Into what channels could his energies be most effectively directed? As to this Brandeis felt the need of guidance. To Alice he wrote on February 2, 1891: "Lots of things which are worth doing have occurred to me and among others to write an article on 'The Duty of Publicity.' * You know I have talked to you about the wickedness of people, shielding wrong doers, and passing them off (or at least allowing them to pass themselves off) as honest men. Some instances of that have presented themselves within a few days which have fired my indignation. If

---

* Louis never got around to writing the article, but he did fulfill the duty.

the broad light of day could be let in upon men's actions, it would purify them as the sun disinfects. You see my idea. I leave you to straighten out and complete that sentence."

But this was only a small matter. What he needed was to give some direction to his career. He had already spent over twelve years in practice and had acquired an enviable professional reputation. Yet the prospect of a long life limited to conventional law practice was not enough. He wanted new worlds to conquer, fresh problems to spur him on. He had begun to find a challenge in public activities. A letter of July 28, 1891, from his friend and former partner helped him embark on his true path:

Dear Louis:

It did me good to see you the other day.

When you think of business (affairs I mean) do not concern yourself with the case in hand but with your life policy (not insurance in the technical sense but perhaps in a larger one).

Your life is very largely before you—with a great lead over all contemporaries. It is, I think, no longer a question of doing everything well that comes to your hand but of selecting well the objects to which you will apply your force. Consider whether or not you will direct your course toward public life. I think you are fitted for it. This would not mean to seek office or place, but to command the leisure for public service as opportunity presents.

The life of R. H. Dana goes to you by this mail. Ponder well the lesson of his life.

Your friend,
Samuel D. Warren

Besides the example of Dana's life, Warren had a year earlier sent him some lines from Euripides' tragedy of the Suppliants—*The Bacchae*. This play, wrote Warren, "did more for me last year than anything I found." Later he sent this selection, and from it Brandeis drew enduring inspiration:

> Thou hast heard men scorn the city, call her wild
> Of counsel, mad; thou has seen the fire of morn
> Flash from her eyes in answer to their scorn!
> Come toil on toil, 'tis this that makes her grand.
> Peril on peril! And common states that stand
> In caution, twilight cities, dimly wise—
> Ye know them; for no light is in their eyes!
> *Go forth, my son, and help.*

PART II

New England Battles

CHAPTER SIX

Breaking with Bourbonism

DURING Brandeis's early years as a lawyer a revolutionary era was in progress. Free lands were largely absorbed, the frontier closed; agriculture ceased to be the norm of American life. This new age was industrial. The drift of our population was from rural to urban industrial areas as the corporate form of business organization displaced individual enterprise and copartnership. Railroad consolidations, as well as the integration of small industrial and commercial concerns into larger units, soon became the order of the day. As the pattern of American life underwent this fundamental change, promoters, exploiters, monopolists, and trust magnates pushed aggressively to power in a new and inordinately complicated society.

Many things happened almost at once, and while causes were complicated, results were simple. Technological improvements so speeded up production that markets, however fast they expanded, could not be developed rapidly enough to absorb all the goods of competing companies. Yet manufacturers, geared to the scale of good years, could not easily stop producing; even if they did not make a profit, they must pay interest on money borrowed for new machines, pay taxes or rents on land and buildings. The greater the pressure became to meet these fixed charges (especially in periods of declining demand), the more intense cutthroat competition became. Price wars and violence were common. Industrial leaders realized they could not go on that way, and the strongest merged with their competitors, either buying them out or driving them to the wall.

It was an era of mergers, great combines, trusts, and monopolies. This trend toward aggregation and combination was greatly speeded up after the crash of 1893 and during the ensuing depression. Thousands of weak companies caved in while strong ones consolidated their positions. Among the dominating figures were such magnates as Carnegie in steel, Rockefeller in oil, the Guggenheims in copper, Huntington, Hill, Harriman, Vanderbilt, and others in railroading. Over all stood the bankers who financed great combines, having themselves emerged as the "Money Trust," men like George F. Baker, Charles M. Stillman, Jacob Schiff, Felix Warburg, and, leading all the rest, J. P. Morgan.

Since most great trusts had to exploit natural resources, the trust heads as a matter of course enlisted the politicians on their side. This they did with money and favors—giving corruptible executives and legislators hot market tips and loans with which to use them.

These abuses in American life were notorious. The minority that profited so hugely was blatant and aggressive in lauding the "new age." The majority, however, soon began to protest. "The freest government . . . would not long be acceptable," Daniel Webster had said long before, "if the tendency of the laws were to create a rapid accumulation of property in few hands, and to render the great mass of the population dependent and penniless. In such a case, the popular power must break in on the rights of property, or else the influence of property must limit and control the exercise of popular power." [1] In the eighties and nineties the "influence of property" was used to elect and control the representatives of "popular power." On the farms the people fought back through the Grange, the Farmers' Alliance, the Populist Party, while in the cities Knights of Labor, Socialists, Henry Georgites and the muckrakers, with their horrendous revelations of corporate greed and corruption, megaphoned the popular protest.

Partial results were achieved. As early as 1887 Congress passed the Interstate Commerce Act and set up the Interstate Commerce Commission to regulate the railroads. In 1890 Congress passed the Sherman Anti-Trust Act, avowedly to break up industrial monopolies. In 1894 Congress again enacted a Federal Income Tax Law, to tap this swollen wealth which virtual private governments had seized. State legislatures also passed anti-trust laws, railroad regulation, and income tax laws.

Some of these enactments, both state and federal, were later declared unconstitutional. Practically all proved to be unenforceable, or if enforceable, hardly bothered the corporations under attack. Gradually the people forced adoption of stronger measures. For as Brandeis himself noted, the people have begun "to think, and they show evidences on all sides of a tendency to act"—a determination to "realize the power which lies in them." [2]

BAR AND BENCH IN THE NEW ERA

When the great monopolists saw the protests of the electorate becoming effective, they had recourse to politicians of another stripe; they looked to the long-term and lifetime appointees on the Bench and to the corporation lawyers from whose ranks judges, usually conservative, were drawn. In 1905 Brandeis noted and deplored this tie-up of the Bar with the dominant economic interests.

"The leaders of the Bar," he said, "without any preconceived intent on their part, and rather as an incident to their professional standing, have, with rare exceptions, been ranged on the side of the corporations, and the people have been represented, in the main, by men of very meager legal ability. If these problems [regulations of trusts, fixing of railway rates, the relations of capital and labor, etc.] are to be settled right, this condition cannot continue." [3]

But it did continue. Moreover, the factors that brought this condition about were vigorously defended in the writings of orthodox professors of economics and politics and of like-minded newspaper editors; and were aggressively advanced in briefs and public addresses of constitutional lawyers and in court opinions of pro-corporation judges. Economic activity, they all held, is governed by natural laws of its own; so long as government does not interfere, these basic laws work inevitably for universal human betterment. To these partisans, all movements of dissent were stimulated by "foreign agitators," and had to be ruthlessly suppressed if American institutions were to endure.

This dogma was very clearly stated in 1893, in an address before the American Bar Association, by United States Supreme Court Justice Henry Billings Brown: "While enthusiasts may picture to us an ideal state of society where neither riches nor poverty shall exist, wherein all shall be comfortably housed and clad . . . such a Utopia is utterly inconsistent with human character as at present constituted. . . . Rich men are essential even to the well-being of the poor. . . . One has but to consider for a moment the immediate consequences of the abolition of large private fortunes to appreciate the danger which lurks in any radical disturbance of the present social system." [4]

That same year (1893) Brown's colleague on the Court, Justice David J. Brewer, said in a speech before the New York State Bar Association: "It is the unvarying law that the wealth of the community will be in the hands of the few. . . . It always will be true that the wealth of a nation is in the hands of a few, while the many subsist upon the proceeds of their daily toil." Justice Brewer disliked "a movement of coercion" among wage-earners, and thought "the attempt to give to the many a control over the few—a step toward despotism." He urged lawyers and judges to be on guard against this threat, and also against the "coercive" activity of government in regulating "the charges for the use of property," and subjecting "all property and its uses to the will of the majority." [5]

Those favoring "movements of coercion," Brewer went on, are "unanimous in crying out against judicial interference, and are constantly seeking to minimize the power of the courts," in order to create the belief that "judges are not adapted by their education and training to settle such matters."

Just such an opinion had been expressed in 1891 by the anti-monopoly economist Richard T. Ely, who wrote: "We have, to an extent unknown in any other country in the world, government by judges. What does this mean to the student of social legislation? It means a great deal, and the fact cannot be disguised. It means a force on the whole adverse to the interests of labor. . . . The only practicable remedy in the United States seems to be a broader, more liberal, and more thorough education of the lawyers who are our ruling class. At the present time, the training which our American lawyers receive is, as a rule, woefully deficient, and cannot entitle them, as a whole, to the rank of a liberal profession. The condition of legal education in this country becomes apparent when it is stated that the political and economic science implied and expressed in Blackstone's *Commentaries on the Laws of England* is still regarded as sound doctrine by at least nine American lawyers out of ten." [6]

Certainly Brewer believed in it. Posing for himself the question "whether the functions of the judiciary should be strengthened and enlarged, or weakened and restricted," Justice Brewer said: "The great body of judges are as well versed in the affairs of life as any, and they who unravel all the mysteries of accounting between partners, settle the business of the largest corporations and extract all the truth from the mass of sciolistic verbiage that falls from the lips of expert witnesses in patent cases, will have no difficulty in determining *what is right and wrong between employer and employees, and whether proposed rates of freight and fare are reasonable as between the public and the owners; while as for speed, is there anything quicker than a writ of injunction?"* [7] (Author's italics.)

Justices Brewer and Brown and others on the Court had "one single rule about industry, that it should be free." The threat of organized labor to this freedom loomed so large in the mind of William Howard Taft as to justify "blood-letting." When, for example, the future President and Chief Justice heard, July 7, 1894, that thirty of the Pullman strikers had been killed by federal troops, he remarked hopefully: "Though it is a bloody business, everybody hopes that it is true." The next day, however, he was discouraged: "The Chicago situation is not much improved. They have only killed six of the mob as yet. This is hardly enough to make an impression." [8]

Some months earlier, in denouncing the Income Tax Law, Joseph H.

Choate had bulldozed the Supreme Court with his sulphurous spectacle of government by the "mere force of numbers," of "communism," "socialism," "populism." The judges responded to Choate's witch-hunting by declaring the law unconstitutional. A majority of the judges saw income tax as "but the beginning of an assault upon capital, as communism on the march." [9] Frederick N. Judson, in 1891, had already considered this problem before the American Bar Association. The "duty" to stop it, he had said, "devolves primarily upon our profession." [10]

CONSERVATISM—NEW STYLE

Brandeis saw the role of his profession differently. "There will come a revolt of the people against the capitalists," he warned, "unless the aspirations of the people are given some adequate legal expression; and to this end co-operation of the ablest lawyers is essential." [11]

So far this co-operation had not been given. Brandeis made this clear in an address before the Harvard Ethical Society, May 4, 1905:

The leading lawyers of the United States have been engaged mainly in supporting the claims of the corporations; often in endeavoring to evade or nullify the extremely crude laws by which legislators sought to regulate the power or curb the excesses of corporations. . . . Instead of holding a position of independence, between the wealthy and the people, *prepared to curb the excesses of either,* able lawyers have, to a large extent, allowed themselves to become adjuncts of great corporations and have neglected the obligation to use their powers for the protection of the people. . . .

It is true that at the present time the lawyer does not hold as high a position with the people as he held seventy-five or indeed fifty years ago; but the reason is not lack of opportunity. . . . We hear much of the "corporation lawyer," and far too little of the "people's lawyer." The great opportunity of the American Bar is and will be to stand again as it did in the past, *ready to protect also the interests of the people.*[12]

Brandeis himself was eager to grasp this opportunity. And not because he was in any sense a radical. Indeed, by 1895 he was rapidly becoming a millionaire. He was esteemed in the nation's highest financial and business circles. Big businessmen and heads of great corporations were among his clients and friends. He spent the 4th of July, 1890, on Lake Champlain as a guest of Major H. L. Higginson of Lee, Higginson & Company, "communing," as he later expressed it, "with the great and the good." The first person to call upon his wife after their marriage had been Mrs. Higginson. Many of their wedding presents came from "the leading families." To all appearances he seemed to fit very nicely indeed into the new capitalistic oligarchy.[13]

Why then did he not play the game as others did—and still do? Brandeis was perfectly frank about the reasons. He saw his "great" friends and clients as "naïf, simple-minded men," who were vainly trying to freeze the *status quo*. He saw change as inevitable. In 1905 he said: "The next generation must witness a continuing and ever-increasing contest between those who have and those who have not. The industrial world is in a state of ferment. The ferment is in the main peaceful, and, to a considerable extent, silent; but there is felt today very widely the inconsistency in this condition of political democracy and industrial absolutism. The people are beginning to doubt whether in the long run democracy and absolutism can co-exist in the same community; beginning to doubt whether there is justification for the great inequalities in the distribution of wealth, for the rapid creation of fortunes, more mysterious than the deeds of Aladdin's lamp." [14]

Brandeis saw democracy fatally threatened by the "excesses" of capitalism, by its own "acts of injustice." When, he said, "the great captains of industry and of finance, who profess the greatest horror of the extension of governmental functions ignore these facts, they become the chief makers of socialism." [15] Brandeis knew, as the rank and file of corporation lawyers did not, the futility, the social and political danger, present and future, of trying to create "a kind of order in the midst of wretchedness." "From talking much with laboring men," he knew that they were not impractical, doctrinaire hoodlums. "Many working men," he observed, "otherwise uneducated, talk about the relation of employer and employee far more intelligently than most of the best educated men in the community." [16]

Furthermore, Brandeis anticipated that "immense corporate wealth" would necessarily "develop a hostility from which much trouble will come to us unless the excesses of capital are curbed." "Our country," he warned, "is, after all, not a country of dollars, but of ballots"; the workingmen "must in a comparatively short time realize the power which lies in them." The prevailing unrest was not to be put down by law and force, or even by the "speed . . . of a writ of injunction."

The social turmoil, as he saw it, was but the natural, inevitable by-product of a changing order, of the shift of power from the few to the many. Here lay the signal opportunity for lawyers, "the richest field for those who wish to serve the people." It lay within their power "to say in what lines [social] action is to be expressed; whether it is to be expressed temperately or wildly and intemperately; whether it is to be expressed in lines of *evolution or in lines of revolution*." [17]

That was the nub of Brandeis's urgency; that was the key to his break with the "naïf and simple-minded" Bourbons. He did not hate capitalism; he deplored its abuses. Nor had he any intention of giving up his own lucrative practice of corporation law. As long as it was a matter of defending one corporation against another, where the lawyers were reasonably well matched, he was content to practice law in the conventional manner, confident that "the judge or jury may ordinarily be trusted to make such a decision as justice demands." But when a corporation had achieved power to crush competition, or hold labor, the consumer, and the public helpless in its grip, "a very different question presents itself." In such conflicts between private and public interest, Brandeis recognized that the contending lawyers were usually ill matched. He said in substance: "You have in those cases representing private interests often ability of a high order, while the public interest is not being represented at all, or is inadequately represented. Frequently legislation is put through the legislature or the city council with much effort expended on behalf of the private interests while no one represents the public at all. That presents a condition of great unfairness to the public. As a result of that common practice, a great many bills pass which should not and never would have become law if the public interest had been fairly represented; and many good bills are defeated which if supported by able lawyers would have been enacted. Lawyers have not, as a rule, considered the unfairness, the unethical character of that practice." [18]

Thus it was largely to protect the great private interests from themselves that Brandeis became protector of the public interest. But just as these magnates and their "lawyer adjuncts" did not know where their real interests lay, so too they did not know that Brandeis was also on their side.

"There was a smugness and self-satisfaction in existing conditions manifested by practically all leaders of the American Bar," a well-known New York lawyer recalled in 1944. "Anyone in the profession who had any doubts about the sacredness of existing institutions became an unsafe person and suffered professionally in consequence. The leaders of the Bar Association were mostly self-satisfied economic Pharisees who did nothing but make a good living out of things as they were and who were distinctly opposed to any form of social change. *Brandeis was the only major exception*. He was of great service in taking the respectability out of laissez faire by specific action rather than by 'general shouting.'" [19]

"When I was a young man," this correspondent wrote, "Brandeis was the first great lawyer to break with Bourbonism. He was the first great lawyer I ever knew who had a social conscience and a genuine desire to make a better world. Look at the lawyers who were our leaders—Choate, Parsons, Coudert, and in a smaller way, Austen G. Fox. They were all servants in the House of Rimmon, where they were very comfortable, thank you, and making money. They saw no reason why a state of society of which they were beneficiaries should be disturbed. In any event, they never turned a hand to anything outside the narrowest type of professionalism. None of them made any contribution to the social growth of America. Brandeis did and they hated him for it." [20]

Amid transition marked by conflicting ideas and forces, Brandeis became the great "adviser of men." He did so not solely to battle for "the people," nor to aid and abet any one fixed program of radical social action, nor to undermine "time-honored institutions." In blazing his trail as People's Attorney, he interpreted his function as that of curbing the "excesses of capital," as that of "a brake on democracy." He was "prepared to curb the excesses of either," interpreting the lawyer's function as that of safeguarding society against ignorant change as well as ignorant opposition to change, as that of canalizing dynamic human aspirations for freedom along structural lines of law and order. He emerged full armed as an alert and forward-looking conservative. The independence he had won by responding to the forces of his time he devoted, as we shall see, to helping meet the basic needs of his day and of the years to come.

CHAPTER SEVEN

The Boston Traction Contest, 1897-1911

IN 1893 when the West End Railway attempted to extend its tracks across Boston Common, Brandeis participated in his first traction contest. This, he said many years later, was "my first important public work," [1] and we have an eyewitness account of his effectiveness.

"Never before this morning," Walter H. Reynolds wrote him, February 21, 1893, "has it been my good fortune to hear so logical, clear and convincing an argument on the very important question of street franchises as that made by you at the State House. I wish that your remarks could be printed and sent to every taxpayer in the city. No subject seems to be more misunderstood than this franchise question."

Boston was more fortunate than most American cities where special interests habitually took advantage of public apathy to acquire valuable franchises gratis from councils and legislatures. Until 1897 the people kept the franchises of street-using corporations well under their own control. Then the newly organized Boston Elevated Railway Company stealthily secured from the 1897 Legislature grants of well-nigh permanent franchises in many of the principal streets. The terms also protected the company for a period of twenty-five years from compulsory reduction of fares below five cents.[2] Time for public protest had almost passed when, on April 30, 1897, Brandeis wrote the editor of the *Boston Evening Transcript,* arguing at length against these smuggled charter changes and urging "all good citizens" to rally and protest. "The proposal is," he said, "at odds with the established policy of the Commonwealth and would, if enacted, sacrifice the interests of the public to that of a single corporation."

The Elevated retorted by spreading charges that Brandeis had been hired by hostile interests to defeat their proposal. This stung Brandeis deeply. "I was told today," he wrote Colonel William A. Bancroft, president of the Elevated, "by a common friend that you stated to him that I was retained by the Municipal League to oppose the Boston Elevated Railway Company's bill, and was paid for so doing. The statement is absolutely without foundation. I have been retained by no person, association or corporation, directly or indirectly in this matter, and *I have opposed it solely because I believe that the bill, if passed, would result in great injustice to the people of Massachusetts, and eventually great injustice to the capitalist classes whom you are now representing, and with whom I, as well as you, are in close connection."* [3] (Author's italics.)

AN EARLY AND INSTRUCTIVE DEFEAT

Brandeis's effort to block the Elevated failed. It was now clear that though he and Bancroft had "close connections" with the capitalist classes, their convictions as to how those classes should serve the city had little or nothing in common.

The traction interests had won a great victory. As the first break in the dam, it seemed to ensure the collapse of Boston's established franchise policy. The victory was incomplete, however, because of the city's peculiar traffic situation.[4]

Prior to 1893 congestion in the business center had already become intolerable. Surrounded on three sides by sea and river and partially blocked on the fourth by Beacon Hill and the Common, with narrow and winding streets, the business district could be entered through only two main arteries—Tremont and Washington Streets. High real estate values in this area made it financially impracticable to widen streets, open new thoroughfares, or build an elevated. The city itself therefore constructed a subway under Tremont Street. This duplicated the surface tracks of the West End Railway; the Legislature, to relieve congestion, ordered the latter removed.

The city-owned Tremont Street subway and its control thus became crucial in the struggle of Boston's transportation interests. Gathering up traffic from trolley lines extending miles into the suburbs, the subway provided the one route for surface and elevated cars through the heart of the city. Here, indeed, was the vulnerable spot in the Elevated's monopolistic armor. With the subway in municipal hands and leased to the Elevated on short and reasonable terms, the city still had command and could thereby circumvent, perhaps, the extraordinary charter privileges granted in 1897.

To break city control, the Elevated first sought legislative authorization to put back the Tremont Street surface tracks, thus making the subway no longer essential. Public protest, however, forced a referendum—and the company's proposition was overwhelmingly defeated. In 1900 the Citizens' Association of Boston proposed a bill authorizing the construction of another subway under Washington Street. As originally proposed, this route was to be leased to the Elevated on substantially the same terms as the Tremont. If the Elevated could, in effect, own this new thoroughfare, it would have a substantially complete and independent street railway system.

Brandeis realized, as other public-spirited Bostonians did by this time, that the transportation interests had not been stopped in their drive for long-term franchise monopoly. He saw also that isolated individuals, however zealous, were no match for corporate power. Earlier encounters had proved that in the fight against privilege even the best cause needs organized support. "All law is a dead letter without public opinion behind it," he had commented to Alice Goldmark, December 28, 1890, "but law and public opinion interact and they are both capable of being made. Most of the world is in more or less a hypnotic state, and it is comparatively easy to make people believe anything, particularly right."

The Elevated's own genius for converting public-spirited citizens to its views was demonstrated at the start of the battle when traction company officials got the Citizens' Association to substitute the corporation's measure for the Association's original proposal. Under the amended bill the Elevated was to build and own the new subway. Thirty years after its completion, the city was to have a three-year option to buy at cost.

ORGANIZING FOR VICTORY

By 1900, however, the opposition was effectively organized in the Public Franchise League—a small group of influential citizens formed to guard the people's control of the streets. Besides Brandeis the League membership included Edward A. Filene, head of Boston's largest retail business; Dr. Morton Prince, distinguished specialist and son of a former mayor of the city; James R. Carter and Andrew Webster, prominent leaders in commercial organizations; Robert Treat Paine, Jr., formerly a candidate for governor; George P. Upham and Edward R. Warren, who became interested in the League as an instrument for preserving the beauty of Boston Common. Enemies of the League soon deplored the fact that such "a tiny group of vociferous Bostonians" should have so much influence. The publication *Practical Politics* later said: "It is the mission of the Public Franchise League to do or say things. It is not yet where it can live up to its mission, but it can turn out more language, per capita of its membership, than any other organization in Boston, which is saying a great deal." [5]

Also backing Brandeis in the franchise fight was the Associated Board of Trade, whose membership included other progressive businessmen— John Mason Little, Francis B. Sears, and John T. Boyd. As counsel for the Board of Trade, Brandeis appeared before the legislative Committee on Metropolitan Affairs opposing the now joint Citizens' Association and Elevated Railway bill. In hearing after hearing throughout the spring of 1900, he argued that its passage would surrender to the Elevated for more than a generation the entire control of Boston's street transit. [6] The Board of Trade itself then introduced a bill (not unlike the original proposal of the Citizens' Association) for construction and ownership by the city of the Washington Street subway, and for its lease to the Elevated to run concurrently with that of the Tremont, thus preserving city control.

The Legislature's decision was carried over to the next year, when the Elevated produced a third proposition, offering to build the Washington Street subway at its own expense under the supervision of the Transit Commission. On completion the subway would be owned by the city, but in return the Elevated, under the jurisdiction of the transit commissioners, would have the free and sole use of it for fifty years.

Brandeis anticipated that the Elevated would attempt to jam this measure through just as it had the 1897 bill. In an article published in *Good Government,* he wrote:

The proposition looks fairly well on the face of it, but it is a poor one for the city and it should not be forced on the people or enacted into law without the referendum attached.

The main objection is to the length of term of free use—fifty years. . . . In the rush hours of that previous Legislature (1897) a five-cent fare was fastened on Boston for thirty years. With subway control for fifty years it would mean twenty years additional of the five-cent fare. It is this twenty years, however, that the elevated wants.[7]

But such considerations made little impression on the Committee on Metropolitan Affairs. What did count was the fact that someone other than the city was to foot the bill; beside this the inordinately long-term franchise seemed unimportant. The Committee accepted the Elevated bill unchanged.

Brandeis and his backers—the Board of Trade and the Public Franchise League—were ready for the fight. Success depended primarily on the League's publicity committee, which had a hard row to hoe owing to the Elevated's stranglehold on the press. "It is a shame," Edwin H. Abbot wrote Brandeis, "that the papers were again so muzzled by the Elevated gang. We need a real, *independent* organ, strong in brains and brave in idea and owned by men who will *risk money to support it*." [8] There was no such "independent organ" in Boston. In fact, only one Boston newspaper, the *Post,* fought consistently on the side of the public. Therefore other ways had to be found to crystallize popular protest. Spurring Filene on, Brandeis summarized the steps to be taken at once to defeat the Elevated's bill:

Dear Mr. Filene:

Dr. Prince informs me that you have assumed the obligations of Chairman of the Publicity Bureau.

In my opinion, our success will depend largely upon the thoroughness with which you may succeed in having the following done:

First: Have editorials and similar notices in various papers, particularly the *Springfield Republican,* the *Worcester Spy,* and the Pittsfield papers, advocating the Board of Trade bill. These editorials should appear if possible on Sunday, Monday or Tuesday, the earlier, the better.

Second: Have the labor organizations repeat their protest against the modified Elevated bill as embodied in the Committee's report, and have copy of the resolution sent by special delivery to each of the members from the Metropolitan District. These should reach them not later than Monday morning.

Third: Have personal letters written to members from the Metropolitan District, particularly from Boston, by their constituents, and have these persons ask for seats in the House during the debate. Our greatest danger is from the Boston members, and I think that this can be overcome by a strong showing from their constituents.

Get as many letters into the Boston papers as you can.

We rely upon you for this work.[9]

Filene went into action. Letters by the hundred were sent out—all converging on the legislators—denouncing the bill as in conflict with settled state policy and as giving Elevated stockholders a "large gratuity" and other advantages. The Public Franchise League and the Associated Board of Trade, now joined by the Merchants' Association, appealed to the Governor for a veto if the bill passed the Legislature.[10] As a final safeguard, Brandeis himself wrote Governor Crane pointing out "some serious, perhaps fundamental defects in the Committee's bill." In case the bill reached the chief executive "in any form," he asked for an opportunity to call such defects to his attention.[11]

Brandeis had met Governor Crane a few months before in connection with the notorious Westminster Chambers case,[12] which grew out of the effort of the wealthy Ayers family to build a Copley Square apartment house higher than allowed by state law. A special bill had been hurried through the Legislature permitting such a building. Scandal surrounded the episode and many lawmakers had to explain why they changed their votes, or "flopped" as the press put it. Drawn into the case by Edward R. Warren, Brandeis found himself confronted by Albert E. Pillsbury, who was also counsel for the Elevated. "My only interest in the matter," Brandeis commented years later, "was as a citizen. I induced Governor Crane to veto the bill on the ground that it was condoning a deliberate violation of the law. Crane practically embodied my view in his veto message and that was the beginning of my relations with him as Governor." [13]

Except for this contact with Governor Crane the reformers' worst fears might have been realized when in June 1901 the Legislature passed the Elevated's bill.[14] On June 18 the Governor vetoed it, riddling it "with holes as thickly as a sieve." [15] Crane saw defects in almost every section. Following Brandeis's argument, the Governor pointed out that all other street railways but this one had revocable franchises. "This bill will, if it becomes law," he said, "give to a private corporation a valuable monopoly in a great public thoroughfare and will perpetuate that monopoly for fifty years. It not only binds this generation, it ties the hands of the generation to come. The surrender of rights which belong to the public, even for a brief term of years, should be permitted only after the most careful consideration, and for controlling reasons of public policy; but no exigency has been shown to exist to justify the taking away of such rights from a generation yet unborn." [16]

In the House, Crane's veto was sustained by 135 to 98, and in the Senate by 25 to 11. Brandeis was delighted with the Governor's "very strong, dignified statement of the arguments against the bill." [17] "You have performed a great service for the Commonwealth," he wrote Crane, June 20,

1901. "You have not only defeated a bad measure, but you have done it in such a way as to teach people what to strive for, and what to expect. The message should stand as an addition to our Declaration of Rights."

Brandeis, in turn, was praised for his own part in the struggle. "I want to tell you," F. W. Taussig, the Harvard economist, wrote, May 25, 1901, "how much I value the good work you are doing in this subway business. You are a true tribune of the public and deserve the gratitude of all of us. I wish I knew more about the business myself. . . . As to the details of the legal and industrial situation, I follow your judgment with confidence."

From Edwin H. Abbot, then in London, came a congratulatory message, July 7, 1901. "I have just read your capital 'interview' on Gov. Crane's veto, in *Boston Transcript,*" Abbot wrote. "Another admirable message. Such things encourage much. I congratulate you on your good and skillful work, and am quite enthusiastic over it. You are on your way into public life I see clearly, and you ought to be in it. You are needed."

In the "capital" interview to which Abbot referred, Brandeis had spoken of the way in which the Elevated had extended its control over newspapers, government officials, and voluntary organizations. But most extraordinary of all, he said, was the fact that the railway company should have been able to camouflage its true purpose by inducing the Citizens' Association, and some eminent bankers connected with it, to act for it in presenting to the Legislature the bill which was to give so much to the Elevated. Brandeis continued: "It is especially to be regretted that in this struggle to protect the community against the aggressions of the Elevated, the people were left with no assistance from the municipal authorities, and that they were opposed by the great majority of their representatives in the Board of Aldermen and the Legislature; . . . that a bill so clearly against public interest as to require a veto, a bill which was strongly opposed by a large number of prominent and influential citizens and labor organizations, as depriving the citizens of valuable rights, should have received in the House after days of debate and public discussion, the votes of forty-six out of fifty of those who were elected to represent the interests of the public." [18]

ATTACK SECURES AND EXTENDS VICTORY

Brandeis and his backers saw clearly that any succeeding Legislature might give the Elevated what it wanted. Taking the offensive, therefore, the Associated Board of Trade and the Public Franchise League, in January 1902, sponsored their own bill authorizing a city-owned Washington Street subway, to be leased to the Elevated on strict terms. [19] Meanwhile the Elevated had hatched a new measure of its own—the Matthews-Livermore Terminal Subway bill, which Brandeis, before the Committee on Metropolitan Affairs again, labeled, "An act to surrender to the Boston Elevated Railway Company the control of the Transportation System of Boston without the payment of any compensation therefor." [20] He denounced the bill as "but another step in the persistent attempts of the Elevated Railway Company to acquire a long tenure of the Boston streets."

By the end of February, Brandeis began to fear that the Elevated's bill would pass while the League's bill would be swamped. With a desperation he rarely exhibited, he wrote James R. Carter, president of the Associated Board of Trade, on February 24, 1902:

I am greatly disappointed to find that we do not get better support from the Associated Board of Trade in the fight we are making. You must take this matter up with your associates and see that they are prepared to talk and do talk and do write letters and do work in this matter. After we have brought this cause to the point of victory we should not omit the necessary effort to accomplish what we are aiming at. Please let me know what you can undertake to do.

I realize fully how busy you are, but everybody else who is working in this cause is equally busy, and unless all the work that has been done is to be thrown away, you must put your hand to the wheel now.

I am very anxious that among other things during the next week there should appear in the papers each day proper letters setting forth the advantages of our bill and the great danger of letting control go out of the City's hands, which it would under any bill on the line of the Matthews bill.

That same day he prodded Edward R. Warren, of the Public Franchise League:

I think that our campaign is in a critical condition and that after having brought our cause to the point of success we should certainly not fail of the necessary effort now.

I was sorry you were not at the meeting this morning to see how completely the effort of getting our speakers in line failed. There were only a few there for us and those who came either said they were unprepared to speak or when they spoke showed that they were unprepared. I think it absolutely necessary that you take up this matter yourself now and get things into good shape for the hearing, which is now set for Tuesday evening, March 4.

A matter of first importance was to win the active support of Mayor Patrick A. Collins. Brandeis took upon himself the task of converting Collins and succeeded in obtaining his presence at the legislative hearings. Nevertheless Brandeis still feared defeat. On April 4, 1902, he wrote Filene: "We cannot secure legislation except by a most determined effort, by arousing public opinion, and getting the press, not only of the City but of the State, to take up the matter."

While Brandeis and his allies were pushing their bill for all it was worth, the Elevated seemed lackadaisical about its measure. But the Elevated was only hiding its hand until the final hearings, April 14, 1902.[21] Then Albert E. Pillsbury, the Elevated's counsel, stated that the Company's income failed to match expenses, which were rapidly increasing partly because of overliberal extension of free transfers. Pillsbury therefore asked that action on the subway be postponed till the company's financial condition improved.[22] To establish more firmly his contention that the company could ill afford to lease the proposed subway as suggested in Brandeis's bill, Pillsbury tried to confuse the committee with a "cloud of figures."

The Elevated's counsel had deliberately delayed showing his hand until the opposition had only a few minutes to reply before committee hearings closed. But Brandeis was not to be put off by such strategy. Dissipating Pillsbury's "cloud of figures" in his mind even while Pillsbury recited them, Brandeis retorted that the Elevated's financial position really was strong, its stock having risen from 105 to 170 in less than four years. Even with certain lines out of operation the company had paid $600,000 in dividends. To get rid of its surplus the management, he charged, had raised the dividend rate from 4 per cent to 6 per cent. All this proved that the Elevated was financially able, but unwilling, to lease the subway unless under arrangements which included Elevated ownership of a lucrative and long-term franchise. Brandeis concluded: "It is your business, gentlemen [of the committee], and it is our business, who are not officers and managers of the company, to see that the interests of the community are protected, and to look not merely to the interests of the community today, but to look out for conditions for generations to come. We are here to see that the control rests with the community, that the Elevated Railway Company, or any company that serves us as transporters of passengers, is the servant and not the master of the public; and this company will be the master of the public if you do not reserve this power of control. . . . That, Mr. Chairman, is the broad ground on which you will refuse permanent franchise or leases for a long period." [23]

When committee hearings were reopened, Brandeis was ready to turn the tables on Pillsbury again. Using the Elevated's own financial reports, he dealt point by point with Pillsbury's financial and other statements, prefacing his analysis with carefully worded comments: "This statement is incorrect." "This statement is at least misleading." "This statement is grossly misleading," and so on.[24] Here in fifteen printed pages was foreshadowed the much more ambitious report he made later on the financial condition of the New Haven railroad.

Pillsbury took no specific exception to Brandeis's analysis, but occupied himself in vehemently denouncing his opponents as "impractical and ignorant." On receiving Brandeis's published "comments," he wrote:

Bro. Brandeis:—I acknowledge with thanks the receipt of your statement (which I understand has already been torn to pieces by our auditor). In exchange for your sophistries, I hereby return you the truth.[25]

Others, however, were more favorably impressed, among them Brandeis's nephew, Louis Brandeis Wehle, then a student at Harvard Law School. "I want to express to you my satisfaction with your presentation of the Elevated Railway figures," he wrote on April 20. "Your statement is admirable—and conclusive. Whom the gods wish to destroy they first make mad. You have stuck to them with bull-dog tenacity and deserve the thanks of the Commonwealth. You have mine." Enthusiastic praise came also from a young Boston lawyer, William S. Youngman:

I have read with pleasure your masterly analysis of the Washington St. Subway problem. I am only a young man but my vote counts *one*.

In a conversation with your nephew, Louis B. Wehle, I suggested that you looked like Abraham Lincoln. After reading this brief I should add, you argue like Lincoln. Let the good work go on. When you need a volunteer send for

Yours truly,
Wm. S. Youngman

The Legislature also was won over by Brandeis's "sophistries." In 1902 an act was passed authorizing municipal construction and ownership of a Washington Street subway, to be leased to the Elevated for twenty-five years at a rental of $4\frac{1}{2}$ per cent of cost. The measure was accepted by the Elevated and approved by popular referendum.[26]

Brandeis thought his victory would be a blow to the Elevated's financial backers, Kidder, Peabody & Company, and thus would be welcomed by Kidder, Peabody's archrival, Lee, Higginson & Company. On June 6, 1902, he wrote to Major H. L. Higginson: "I hope you are satisfied with the subway bill. You have been so much interested in the work of the Franchise League that I venture to tell you that the expense of the campaign has been quite large, and to ask whether you care to make a contribution." There is no record of Higginson's reply!

Shortly thereafter the Associated Board of Trade by unanimous vote formally thanked Brandeis "for the very able manner in which you represented the Board before the different committees of the Legislature having in charge the consideration of the bill for the Proposed Subway under Washington Street; also for the very unselfish and generous manner in which you refused to accept any compensation for your valuable services in preparing the so-called Board of Trade bill; advocating the same before said committees at which members of this Board were asked to appear." [27]

Though Brandeis and his allies had made the Boston Elevated realize that its function lay in public service on fair terms, it was only by constant vigilance that the ground thus won could be held. Again in 1905 Brandeis and his League opposed a legislative attempt to incorporate and enfranchise the Boston Transportation Company to build local freight tunnels and conduit systems in Boston, Cambridge, and Somerville, with a charter in perpetuity and without compensation other than ordinary taxes. As to these proposals, Brandeis curtly observed: "The City of Boston cannot afford to have any of its citizens run the risk of this enterprise, and to get that advantage or hold upon it which would appear to be deemed the necessary compensation for running the risk." [28] Within three weeks the bill was killed.[29]

Again in 1906 Brandeis had to warn the Committee on Metropolitan Affairs against another Boston Elevated measure to build a subway in Cambridge connecting with the Boston railway system, because this also would grant the company free locations, irrevocably and in perpetuity.[30] In 1911 the Elevated made a final effort to get long-term franchises and exclusive possession of present and prospective subways, and actually succeeded in persuading the Transit Commission to favor leases of forty-two to fifty years. Once more Brandeis came forward. "Are the people of Massachusetts to be trusted less now than during the last fifty years?" he asked.[31] Being on good terms with Governor Eugene Foss, he conferred with him repeatedly on the subject. At the conference of the Governor and Brandeis with Robert Windsor and F. E. Snow of the Elevated, the company declared it would not press the matter.[32] Later, after further conferences with the Governor, Brandeis drew up another bill, satisfactory to all parties, by which Elevated's consolidation with the West End Railway would take place in 1922 when the lease between the two companies expired, and in the early fall of 1911 the West End voted to consolidate. Also authorized were new subways and tunnels, built and owned by the city, to be leased to the Elevated at $4\frac{1}{2}$ per cent of cost per year, the leases terminable at will by either party after twenty-five years. This bill, approved by the Governor, was passed.

LESSONS LEARNED

From these early encounters Brandeis became closely acquainted with the means, direct and indirect, by which street railway magnates further their ends while evading their responsibilities. He realized that to fight them singlehanded was wasted effort. Utilizing various small dynamic organizations for the fight, he discovered their value in collecting and digesting material, in handling newspapers, and in crystallizing public opinion.

Nor was this all. He had been subjected to stinging personal abuse, and social ostracism loomed over the horizon. Years earlier his old friend Professor Shaler had warned him against going into active public life, saying that he was "too sensitive." He now appreciated Shaler's point and realized "that just as he was prepared to sacrifice the favor of that element in society which would make him the most money, so he must make himself indifferent to misrepresentation and never make any answers which would indicate any sensitiveness to abuse." [33]

The common ties, the "close connections," binding him to the representatives of the capitalistic classes were steadily becoming more tenuous. In seeking to prevent "great injustice to the people" and eventually great injustice to the capitalist classes themselves, he had begun to sense the unbridgeable gulf of interest dividing them—a division that was to grow through the years by geometric progression as he carried the war for the general welfare nearer the citadels of capitalist power.

CHAPTER EIGHT

Setting the Stage for Civic Reform, 1902-1907

THE BOSTON franchise fights incidentally bared the pecuniary affiliations of state and municipal politics. Legislators and councilmen fawned on public service corporations, thus getting jobs for themselves as well as for their political ward heelers. Some aldermen and senators have, Brandeis discovered, "from one to two hundred such persons on the corporate payroll." [1] Legislate, "pass a law," extend the range of public power and authority—the conventional correctives for lobbying and corrupt practices—had first occurred to him. In 1900 he actually drafted two bills to cut the ties between corporations and lawmakers but decided to delay such action rather than complicate the Elevated fight. Furthermore, he knew that the

public had to be waked up and shown the seriousness of the evil, that
dynamic pressure groups had to be organized and led. Brandeis was ready
to press directly for such legislation in 1903. By that time he had set in
motion the machinery necessary to get and keep the people behind his
bills.

PRIVATE POWER VERSUS PUBLIC POWER

Costly experience had taught Brandeis that he alone could not sufficiently arouse the people. Therefore he became in 1902 a member of the
Executive Committee of the Election Laws League, and in 1903 helped to
organize the Good Government Association. Like the Public Franchise
League, these organizations had small but influential memberships, determined "to secure clean, honest, and efficient municipal government." The
primary object of the Good Government Association was "to reform the
citizens of Boston, to secure the election of aggressively honest and capable men." We "have opened a ledger account with every man in public life
or who aspires to be in public life," ran one of the Association's broadsides.
"His good deeds and his bad deeds will be impartially recorded, and whenever a candidate is to be voted for, his record will be published in the newspapers and otherwise, in such a manner as to be conveniently accessible to
every voter in the city." [2]

Public opinion was formed and focused on specific issues. "No one,"
Brandeis said, "can grow enthusiastic over virtue in general and become
indignant over evil in general. It is the particular virtuous or vicious act in
all its details which receives our admiration or excites our condemnation.
You can't be indifferent unless you keep yourself ignorant of the facts." [3]

Brandeis contributed his full share of money to these organizations and
much more than his full share of energy and leadership. He was now experienced in the techniques of mobilizing public opinion, and he knew
well how to teach those techniques to his subordinates. Above all they had
to learn, as Brandeis himself had learned, not to be discouraged by occasional setbacks. "Of course yesterday's [municipal] election is a complete
defeat for the Good Government Association," he wrote the secretary,
Edmund Billings, on December 16, 1903. "Now is the time to make good
your promise that the work for next year would begin today. It is important for your committee to show that it is not even stunned by the defeat."
Seize, he urged, the first dinner of any available business or other association at which afterdinner speaking occurs and make that a Good Government meeting. Get at the individuals and their funds by direct contact.
Printed notices asking people to join or contribute are of little or no value.
Write them personal letters.

Brandeis urged Billings to work systematically and mapped the campaign in detail. His letter of December 16 continued: "There are, I believe, twenty-four business organizations connected with the Associated Board of Trade. There are undoubtedly as many more not connected, and there are a great many subsidiary organizations not called business organizations, but which have meetings, such as the Bank Clerks' Association. By getting into relations with the president and secretary of these associations you could probably arrange that they would, during this season, give up one evening to the Good Government Association . . . and then arrange so that at the meeting Good Government matters can not only be discussed, but that you can enroll members, and perhaps also take up collections. . . . Get the list of the voters at this election, and in that way endeavor to reach the individual."

Brandeis insisted that the same course be followed with other associations, especially those having "a moral tone, or more or less so, like the Congregational Club and Unitarian Club." There would, of course, be some difficulty in getting speakers for the hundred or so meetings resulting from "going about the matter systematically," but this could be overcome. "Men could be developed in the course of the work. The untried ones could be put down for small speeches first, and in due course many would undoubtedly develop considerable power.

"It is important," he told Billings, "to be quick and to be insistent during these months—be persistent and persistent daily. I jot the above down in form hastily," he concluded, "to get this before you at once, but it has not been hastily thought out."

FACTS AS AMMUNITION FOR REFORM

What Brandeis's leagues and associations needed most was to know all about the size of the city payroll, the names and addresses of all employees, and the period of their employment. Such information was basic to any thoroughgoing improvement in city administration, but every effort to secure it had been foiled. Brandeis once had suggested that Dr. Morton Prince go to Mayor Hart and let him know "in your most winning way that we want the city payroll right away." [4] Dr. Prince refused "positively," because he felt Brandeis was "the man for this job."

The city payroll was only one of many secrets politicians withheld from the public. Brandeis had on many occasions solicited city officials for information their reports failed to reveal. In scores of letters from 1902 on, he made specific suggestions as to the form and content of official reports so as to make them of greater public service. But little happened. Brandeis was especially insistent that the city modernize its accounting methods. When a promised investigation into these methods bogged down, he wanted to know why. His query to Mayor John F. Fitzgerald is typical: "In your letter of April 9, 1906, replying to mine of March 21, you stated that you hoped to be able to give attention soon to the matter of accounting. I should be glad to know the results of your investigation, and whether any change in the city's method of accounting has been decided upon." [5]

State reports also failed to disclose essential facts. The Board of Railroad Commissioners, for example, did not publish the amount of capital actually invested by specific companies. Brandeis wrote James F. Jackson, the chairman, on July 24, 1905, suggesting how data so essential for "dealing justly with the companies and the public" could be made "a matter of public record and easily available." Cost accounting practice of the State Board of Charities, the Prison Commissioners, and other state departments was not in accord with "approved business methods and were misleading," Brandeis asserted, and he wrote Governor Curtis Guild, March 21, 1906, suggesting how departmental reports could be made of greater public service. Again his suggestions were not followed.

Brandeis did more than collect factual ammunition, prod government officials, map strategy, and plan work for others. He entered directly into the fight himself. Indeed, he opened the battle for civic reform, March 19, 1903, with a bristling speech before the Boot and Shoe Club. After recounting actual instances of proved larceny, bribery, and fraud among legislators, councilmen, and administrators, he exclaimed: "We should not allow ourselves to be represented in our city government by men who are dishonest and reckless of the great heritage of an honorable and glorious past handed down to us by our fathers." The enormous increase in city expenditures could be attributed to the "high degree of corruption" especially in padded payrolls, "many of whose beneficiaries were paid for work not done and never intended to be done." What the situation demanded, he continued, was a vigilant and fighting public. "The politician can stand any amount of attack, but he cannot stand the opposition of public opinion." [6]

Brandeis's goal was not "perfect" government, but "good" government. Periodic indignation against wrong would not yield that result. For "good" government citizens would have to organize, plan, designate particular persons for particular tasks, and hold each responsible for informing himself and others as to what goes on. Thus only could the "light of truth and honesty and honor" penetrate the darkest civic corners.

In April 1903 Brandeis carried the battle to one of his "associations having a moral tone." "Conviction has come to many minds," he told the

Unitarian Club, "that misgovernment in Boston has reached the danger point." [7] He praised Mayor Collins for employing an expert accountant to investigate finances at City Hall. The accountant's reports, he said, though not all one could wish, were of "inestimable value. They are full of human interest even for those who abhor arithmetic, and contain some matter of which even our antiquarian and historical societies will wish to take note." [8] But much of the mayor's effort was offset, Brandeis pointed out, by those plague spots on the city, the aldermen. "Think," he said, "of the kind of things done by that Board of Aldermen we give the Mayor for a Board of Directors." To free itself from publicity, the Board had set up a Committee on Public Improvements which, Brandeis explained, was but a device whereby "the whole Board of Aldermen, in secret session, talks matters over unconcernedly, and votes in private. The desire for secrecy is not surprising," he commented in an aside, "when the quality of some of the acts is considered which have received the approval of a large majority of the Board." [9]

How, he inquired, can the citizen meet his first obligation—"to know" —unless all matters are discussed in open session. "We want," he said, "a diffusion of knowledge on all these matters, and then we want men who will take office as a sense of duty. We want a government that will represent the laboring man, the professional man, the businessman, and the man of leisure. We want a good government, not because it is good business but because it is dishonorable to submit to a bad government. The great name, the glory of Boston is in our keeping," he concluded. "We are guilty of a shameful breach of trust if we do not, so far as is in our power, preserve that inheritance with glory, and hand it down to those who follow us at least as great and noble as it was when it came to us." [10]

In another address, this time before the Good Government Association, Brandeis pointed out that the waste and theft of public funds by criminals in public office were bad enough, but the resulting demoralization of the community was "a hundred times worse. Think what a heritage we shall leave to our children if corruption is allowed to stalk unstayed. Think of the awful responsibility which rests upon us for the political miseducation we are giving to the new citizens whom we are making in such numbers in the North and West and South Ends. The ships which carry the products of our rich country to other lands come back freighted with thousands of men and women who fleeing from the oppression or the hopelessness of their old homes, seek this as a land of liberty and opportunity. Shall we permit these, our fellow-citizens—perhaps our future rulers—to be taught that in Boston liberty means license to loot the public treasury . . . that in Boston opportunity means the chance for graft?" [11]

THE INTERESTS COUNTERATTACK

Several days later the *Boston Traveler,* under big black headlines, carried a story giving "the particular reason why Louis D. Brandeis" was "so busily engaged in leading the starry-eyed goddess Reform around by the hand." The mystery had at last been solved: Mr. Brandeis was a reform candidate for mayor. Of course he was not out, the *Traveler* explained, packing caucuses or lining up ward leaders. That was not the reformer's way. Brandeis was a "true reform candidate, broader than the ward lines of a municipality, with his little dish, its receptive side uppermost, expecting the prize to land therein at the proper time." [12]

Fearing that Brandeis had set up "a false standard of civic virtue," Alderman Edward J. Bromberg also spoke out. Many things attracted Mr. Bromberg to Brandeis. "He is," the Alderman admitted, "a man of remarkable legal and literary ability, a great scholar, a very influential person and, I am told, he is, or was, my coreligionist." But in spite of all this, Bromberg insisted that Brandeis's moral and civic education had been neglected: "I desire to indicate that his entire life, as counsel for wealthy clients and as an associate of wealthy men, is colored by the greenish-golden light of finance." [13] Bromberg, like the *Traveler,* had divined sinister motives beneath Brandeis's reforming zeal. "My past experiences in politics," he said, "teach me that men do not suddenly engage in joint debates, charge the officials in office with incompetency or worse, and then throw an awkward half-forgotten sop to the laboring classes, without having a more or less personal ambition in mind." [14]

Brandeis did not see the *Traveler* story until a reporter from the *Record* asked him to comment on it. After reading it, Brandeis said: "Nothing could be farther from my thought than to be a candidate for mayor, or for any other public office. What I have desired to do is to make the people of Boston realize that the most important office, and the one which all of us can and should fill, is that of private citizen. The duties of the office of private citizen cannot under a republican form of government be neglected without serious injury to the public." [15]

Bromberg's slurs, particularly those "by way of insinuation and suggestion," Brandeis described as "wholly unfounded in fact." But he endorsed the Alderman's statement that "Bribe takers are bad enough, but bribe givers are far worse, and some corporation directors are bribe givers directly or indirectly, and they know it." [16]

Brandeis was unable to "conceive of anyone being really sensible who was not a reformer, as well as earnest and progressive." [17] He despised the cant of those who, while "speaking with horror" of corrupt politicians, *did* nothing about getting better ones. "Politicians," he said, "even if their motives are not of the purest, come much nearer performing their duties than the so-called 'good' citizens who stay at home." [18] The duties of really good citizens, he said, were exacting; they demanded intelligence, effort, and persistence. It was not enough just to cast a ballot. "It is essential that men vote right and to vote right involves intelligent discrimination as to both men and measures"—discrimination between "what will advance and what will impair the Commonwealth." The voter must "distinguish between the good and the bad, between the genuine and the sham, between the demagogue and the statesman." [19]

Once, three representatives of a group of Harvard undergraduates sought Brandeis's advice on how to work for civic betterment. Brandeis emphasized his formula that "knowledge is the basis of wise public action." As there were some twenty-five departments in the state government, he suggested that for each department the Harvard group appoint a committee whose business it would be to attend all relevant meetings and hearings and to follow through on legislation affecting each particular department. "Above all," he said, "the one thing you must do is to treat this as a fundamental and urgent service. No theater or dinner parties should be allowed to take precedence over it." This was a poser for the young men, and they left Brandeis with their civic zeal somewhat dampened. They would have to defer their decision, they explained, until after conference with their constituents. The final answer might well have been anticipated. Brandeis's program for public service involved too great personal sacrifice.[20]

But it did not involve too much sacrifice for Brandeis himself. In his campaign for anti-bribery legislation on November 24, 1903, he prevailed upon Governor John L. Bates to include in his inaugural message a "strong recommendation" for Brandeis's bills. "I shall be glad," he wrote the Governor, "to call on you if I can be of any service." The chief executive replied courteously on November 26, saying he "heartily approved" the reform legislation, but wanted to be "sure that it can be absolutely enforced." He hoped he and Brandeis could "have a talk later on."

When the Public Franchise League's petition for carrying out the Governor's inaugural recommendation was referred to the next General Court, Brandeis, "much disappointed," wrote Bay State legislator William H. Grove, April 1, 1904: "I should like very much to know the grounds which have induced the Legislative Committee to take this action." Not being able to follow up the matter himself, he asked Charles M. Cox to call upon the lawmaker. "I trust you will talk with him," Brandeis suggested, "as freely as you would with me."

During the fall of 1904 the newspapers again heard the political bee buzzing around Brandeis's head. When he was mentioned along with Henry M. Whitney and William L. Douglas as possible nominees for governor on the Democratic ticket, a reporter asked: "Would you accept the nomination?"

"I have never considered the matter and cannot say; I did not know that I was being considered."

"Isn't it quite probable that you will allow your name to be used?"

"I cannot say anything about it, as I have never given the matter a thought." [21]

Immediately following the election Brandeis reminded Governor-elect Douglas that the Democrats had protested strongly throughout the campaign against contributions to political campaign funds by those who might seek or get favors from the state administration. "I trust you will recognize the importance of prohibiting such contributions and insert in your inaugural message a recommendation to that end." Nothing had been accomplished by the next year, so the same courteous but firm suggestion went out to "My dear Curtis"—Governor Guild.

Key members of the Legislature were also kept on the alert. "I desire particularly to emphasize," he wrote the chairman of the Election Laws Committee, "the importance of requiring absolute publicity as to election expenses, and absolute prohibition of contributions by corporations either for nomination or election." [22] In 1906 the League's bill became law. Persistence had won its reward.

SUPERIOR ABILITY AND INDEPENDENT LEADERSHIP

The job of getting and keeping good government, Brandeis contended, fell chiefly upon those of superior ability. Just as "the rich should contribute most in money to the expense of government," so should those possessing "greatest ability and intelligence" contribute most in responsible leadership.[23] He tried never to miss an opportunity to preach good government and constant vigilance to every professional group that would listen to him. On June 14, 1905, for instance, he grasped the opportunity to address the Annual Convention of the Massachusetts Medical Society.

Brandeis spoke on the close relationship between municipal graft and medical science. He assured the physicians that they could carry their full weight in municipal politics only by organized action. "Despite your numbers and your education, your college and your university degrees, you count for nothing politically," he told the medical men, "when compared with the great leisure class employed by the street department, or indeed the employees of less favored departments." [24]

The physicians were just then beginning to deal systematically with public health, to deal with society as well as the individual. For Brandeis this trend was highly significant. "You are undertaking," he said, "to secure life and health to the individual through governmental action, but you will find that with us success is possible only through good government—that you cannot eradicate disease from the human body unless you eradicate it from the body politic. Your professional success can be attained only through good citizenship. To the great ends for which you are working your own active participation in the government of our community is a necessary condition. You need not, perhaps, go as far as Oliver Cromwell, who, 'seeking the kingdom of heaven took England by the way'; but you must, if you would succeed, join with other forces who are working to make the government of Boston and of other cities worthier of their traditions and of their privileges." [25]

Brandeis was an outstanding reformer in the Boston of his day. But he was not the only man of "superior ability" who was willing to use his ability for the general good. Others were also working; and while they supported Brandeis's reforms, he returned the favor—often many fold. With Harvard's President Eliot he became active in the Public School Association. He helped Henry Beach Needham, journalist and friend of Theodore Roosevelt, to strengthen the People's Lobby. He joined the Citizens' Committee of One Hundred crusading for a new city charter. He became a sustaining member of a group called "All Together for Boston," to promote the civic and commercial interests of the city. When a small group—"Boston-1915"—organized to make theirs the finest city in the world by 1915, Brandeis naturally got on the bandwagon.

In a letter to Needham, September 23, 1907, Brandeis explained once again why he joined public welfare pressure groups. "Private interests," he said, "will always be and should properly be active in presenting to legislators what they deem to be required for the protection of the enterprises they represent. *But it is essential to just and safe legislation that the interests of the public should also be specifically and ably represented.*" (Author's italics.) This idea was so new that however often Brandeis expressed it, he was always suspected of ulterior motives—not the least of which was a high political office for himself.

Yet it was perfectly clear from his actions in attacking or supporting individual Republicans and Democrats alike, that Brandeis was not currying favor with either party. In 1905, for instance, the year following mention of himself as a possible Democratic candidate for governor, he campaigned vigorously for the Republican mayoralty nominee: "I signed with my own hand the request for the Hon. Louis A. Frothingham to become a

candidate for the Republican nomination for Mayor of Boston," he wrote
Henry S. Dewey, November 13, 1905. "Although I am a Democrat, I
earnestly hope that the Republicans will see fit to nominate Mr. Frothingham as their candidate for the mayoralty, and thereby perform a great
public service to all the citizens of Boston without regard to party."

"There is," Brandeis had observed in 1904, "no such thing as a Republican or a Democratic principle in the administration of a city office." As to
candidates for public office, he endorsed Jefferson's criteria. "Is he honest,
is he capable, will he be faithful to the Constitution?" To these, Brandeis
added another: "Will he devote himself to the honor and the best interests
of the community?" [26]

Brandeis felt the same way about his own private "parties," about his
clubs and associations and their leaders. They were to him no more sacrosanct than the political parties themselves. Thus when some members of
the Public Franchise League in their contemporaneous fight to improve
Boston's gas supply proved as ready to wrong capital as monopolists were
to exploit the public, Brandeis condemned them much as he did the corrupt politicians. He must have felt even more strongly about the League's
recalcitrant members, because they were men of "superior ability," shirk-
ing public duties which such men were peculiarly equipped to assume and
bound to fulfill.

CHAPTER NINE

The Sliding-Scale Rate Principle,
1904-1907

IN 1903 eight companies were supplying Boston and neighboring Brookline with artificial gas. It might have been supposed that since the companies were apparently competitive, service would be excellent. Actually
Boston's gas supply had long involved poor service, exorbitant rates, duplication of plants, the preoccupation of management with profits and politics, and numerous other ills.[1] Several of the eight companies were in the

grip of financial and industrial magnates, including J. Edward Addicks, Henry H. Rogers, Thomas W. Lawson, and Henry M. Whitney. When the Boston Elevated's fight for long-term franchises failed, Whitney, fearing that traction profits would slump, threw his great powers, personal and financial, into the illuminating gas interests.[2] Besides Whitney, the leading gas executive in Boston was James L. Richards, a farmer's son who had made a fortune before he was forty and whom the investment house of Kidder, Peabody & Company selected to head its gas interests.

To avoid duplication of facilities, and at the request of the gas companies, the Boston Board of Gas and Electric Light Commissioners, in 1903, sent the Legislature a draft bill to combine the eight companies in Boston and Brookline.[3] Stock in the consolidated company was to be limited to an amount approved by the Commissioners and equal to "fair value" of the combined properties. As Brandeis said several years later, the scheme had many excellent features, but it was "a rather poor consolidation bill" [4]—being drawn primarily in the interest of the gas group themselves. The Public Franchise League opposed the bill, but Brandeis was then occupied with private affairs and did not join in the fight. In 1903 the bill became law.

PRODDING THE PEOPLE'S ATTORNEY

The next year certain members of the League became considerably agitated. On April 30, 1904, Edward R. Warren wrote Brandeis expressing fear lest the Commissioners, yielding to "powerful influence," saddle the consumers with "fair value" of $24,000,000. The Franchise League, Warren thought, had slackened its zeal and was not concerning itself as it "should in the Gas situation." Unless it could now "stand by" and lend moral support as during the subway fight, Warren threatened to interest a "new set of men." He hinted that perhaps the League had "outlived its usefulness." Reversing the usual procedure, Warren had to prod the People's Advocate, reminding him that the gas problem was "of too great importance to be neglected."

Brandeis coolly replied, May 2, 1904, asserting his own leadership:

It does not seem to me advisable that we should make what appears to me to be a quixotic attempt to repeal or amend the bill passed last year authorizing the gas consolidation in order to prevent the capitalization of property which was in part an accumulation of past earnings.

I agree with you, however, that there is a chance for a wide difference of opinion as to what should be considered a fair capitalization under the present bill, based on the valuation of various properties, and that it is important that the Gas Commission should have the moral support and assistance from without which would enable it to resist the pressure and influence which may be brought to increase the capitalization beyond what is proper. . . .

I also agree with you that it is the duty of the League to concern itself with this matter until it is settled, and to impress upon the Mayor the importance of co-operating with the Commission in safeguarding the public interests.

I am not aware that the League has had submitted to it the question whether it should take such action, and I agree with you that the question should be properly submitted to the League for action. . . .

I do not share your fear that the League has outlived its usefulness, but I am of the opinion, which I think I have expressed to you from time to time, that its membership should be strengthened by the introduction to it of new men, preferably younger men.

I think it would be a great mistake to form a separate organization. . . .

And who, by the way, Brandeis pointedly inquired, "are the new men you have in mind?"

For Warren the public interest was identified solely with "fair value." Still others, led by Hearst's *Boston American,* saw the situation as demanding the drastic solution of municipal ownership. Brandeis found neither of these approaches acceptable. "Fair" price and "fair" value were for him but single facets of a much larger problem. As for government ownership, it should by all means be averted.

Massachusetts had long been struggling with the problem, but with indifferent success. Since 1885 all the Bay State gas companies had been subject to the supervision of a commission with broad powers, including that of fixing prices. And yet abuses had grown steadily worse. Anti-stock-watering legislation had, Brandeis recognized, protected the community from certain evils, but experience had not shown it a panacea. Surveying the whole situation, he concluded that in so far as current expert opinion could be reconciled at all, it held that "neither private nor public ownership, as ordinarily practiced, is wholly satisfactory." [5] The problem, in his mind, required a fresh approach.

The companies claimed that their joint properties had "cost" them over $24,000,000 and that "fair" value should be not less than $20,609,989.99. Warren and the Public Franchise League, on the other hand, contended that any figure in excess of $15,124,121 represented not contributions by stockholders, but accumulations from excessive charges previously exacted from gas consumers. Therefore the League insisted that the Consolidated company's capital stock be limited to the aggregate capital of the consolidating companies. It proposed further that the rates set for gas should be such as to promise a satisfactory return on this limited capitalization. The *Boston American* at this time suggested eighty cents per thousand cubic feet as a fair price, but Brandeis considered this low, while the companies tried to hold their current price of a dollar. Three years later the eighty-cent rate was in effect, largely because of Brandeis's work.

Considerable publicity was given the whole matter in the fall of 1904. In 1905 various organizations and individuals urged the Legislature to scale down Consolidated's "fair value." Beside the Gas Commissioners and the Mayor, a central figure in the fight was Boston's corporation counsel, Thomas Babson. He not being "over diligent" or "at all enthusiastic" about fighting for the public, the Public Franchise League decided "to give Babson support" in his fight on valuation.[6] George W. Anderson became paid counsel for the Public Franchise League, carrying the fight for lower capitalization before the Gas Commissioners and the Legislature, while Brandeis, as *unpaid* counsel, represented the Massachusetts State Board of Trade.

Besides their great financial resources, gas companies had political support of a peculiarly insidious and parasitic nature, even for Boston. They had a costly and experienced lobby at the State House and City Hall. Like the traction companies, the gas companies carried on their payrolls an army of ward heelers placed there by state legislators and city aldermen.

Obviously the Public Franchise League and the Board of Trade—that is George Anderson and Brandeis—had set themselves against formidable opponents.

GOING TO THE HEART OF THE PROBLEM

On March 9, 1905, Brandeis appeared before the State Committee on Public Lighting to support the principle of gas company consolidation, but to oppose the Special Consolidation Act of 1903. "It is believed," Brandeis said, "that better results can often be obtained by consolidation under one management of several gas companies or several electric-light companies." But, "shall we undertake to meet this demand by the passage of special acts, and subject the community to all the dangers and injustice attendant upon special legislation? Or shall we look over the field of the law as it exists in Massachusetts and see whether we have not now in Massachusetts some law governing the consolidation of public service corporations which has been tested by experience?"[7]

Brandeis found such a law in the Anti-Stock-Watering Act of 1894. "The law against stock-watering," he said, "rests upon the fact that, in order to determine what a reasonable compensation is and to limit the return on capital to a reasonable compensation, it is essential that there should be before the public a knowledge of the capital originally invested in the enterprise. The devious devices of stock-watering have the inevitable effect of concealing that fact from the public, and by virtue of that concealment tempt the owners of the property to make unreasonable exactions from the public." [8]

This act, he argued, fitted the current gas company consolidation perfectly. Moreover, it was just to the companies and just to the public. It recognized that those who invest their money in public service corporations have a right not only to a fair return on their capital but also to profits, in excess of fair return, commensurate with the risk assumed. It also recognized that those who engage in a business affected with a public interest undertake as trustees to perform a public service and that the public can hold them accountable for doing so. Because this law was designed to restrain companies from inflating their capital, it was attacked as socialistic. Brandeis told the committee this notion was absurd: "To my mind nothing can be farther from the fact. When Massachusetts passed the anti-stock-watering laws, it adopted a measure of a most conservative character—a measure more potent for the protection of individual private property than any other which could have been devised. The greatest factors making for communism, socialism, or anarchy among a free people, are the excesses of capital; because, as Lincoln said of slavery, 'Every drop of blood drawn with the lash shall be requited by another drawn with the sword.' It is certain that among a free people every excess of capital must in time be repaid by the excessive demands of those who have not the capital. Every act of injustice on the part of the rich will be met by another act or many acts of injustice on the part of the people. If the capitalists are wise, they will aid us in the effort to prevent injustice."

Brandeis went on to remind the capitalists: "It is almost as important to legislation as it is to administration of justice in the courts that it [legislation] should not only be pure in itself and just in itself, but that the public should recognize that it is so. There is," he warned, "only one safe course for the community, only one safe course for you and for us who want property rights protected and preserved; and that course is neither to seek nor to grant special privileges. Let us all stand equal before the law, and let the law be so just, so reasonable, so carefully drawn, that it protects alike the rights of all. . . . The conservative classes in the community are not those who wish to leave unrestricted the power of wealth, but those who in economic relations are working for justice to capitalists and to public alike."

As soon as Brandeis ended his argument, questions arose on the whole controversial matter of "fair" value and dividends. He then reiterated that capital should get dividends commensurate with risk, while surplus should not be allowed dividends in excess of the rate at which money could be borrowed, say, 4 or 5 per cent. Dr. Morton Prince of the Public Franchise League made it clear that Brandeis was not speaking for the League, when he testified that he disagreed with Brandeis and did not think the companies should be allowed any dividends on surplus. Brandeis replied: "There is in the community such a thing as vested wrongs as well as vested rights. The community was wrong in allowing the surplus to pile up. There should be some return on the surplus; that fund is one in which the community has an equitable interest, but it has no right to confiscate it." [9]

Though he claimed he was trying to protect the gas companies as well as the public, Brandeis's argument hardly pleased the companies. Indeed bitter disagreement was voiced by their counsel, Frederick E. Snow. Drawing heavily on his imagination, Snow accused Brandeis of demagogy, of making false statements, of holding up the specter of Standard Oil (which Brandeis had not mentioned) to frighten the public. [10]

MAKING ENEMIES—RIGHT AND LEFT

Brandeis, of course, expected objections from the gas companies who wanted to capitalize and pay dividends on their surpluses at the same basis as on their original capital. Nor was he surprised on April 1, 1905, when the magazine *Practical Politics* erroneously connected his stand with that of the Public Franchise League and tried to kill off both by oblique attack:

Louis D. Brandeis, co-operating as counsel with the Public Franchise League, is a very active and successful lawyer. Mr. Brandeis can argue plausibly, and he obtains large fees for arguing. Retained by the gas companies or the promoters of consolidation, he would have argued still more plausibly, and with still greater recognition of external conditions now existing. That Mr. Brandeis was not retained by those who are trying to bring about the consolidation shows that they believed in the uprightness of their aim. . . .

The men, two or ten, who compose the Public Franchise League, have never in their entire lives accomplished one-tenth part for the reputation and welfare of the City of Boston that those men have accomplished who are now trying to end, once and for all, the complications of the gas question in this city. The respectable men who are fighting settlement are doing so, partly because of their own conceit, and partly because they are pushed to it by others who are out for advertising or graft. . . . They have been carried off their feet by the bellowings of noisy newspapers and the methods of a noisy newspaper's paid exploiters, and they, too, are joining in the dance for notoriety and reform—and especially for reform.

After Dr. Prince's testimony, Brandeis must also have anticipated objections from others among his friends who had strongly opposed granting the companies the right to capitalize and eventually pay dividends on their ill-gotten surplus.

What Brandeis did not anticipate was the bitterness of his friends' opposition to his stand. Indeed he had little reason to expect this, since one of the first letters he received after this testimony contained only praise. On March 9, 1905, Edwin L. Sprague of the Massachusetts State Board of Trade wrote: "I want to say that your argument before the Committee on Public Lighting today was a most excellent and forceful presentation of the case of the Massachusetts State Board of Trade as it seemed to me and I think all others must have agreed. Personally, too, I want to thank you."

Sprague, however, soon retracted his praise. He was, as Brandeis said, "a one-idea man," that idea being "the iniquity of stock-watering under any circumstances." Edward R. Warren was apparently the same type. The day after his testimony Brandeis found in his mail a "terrible protest" from Warren:

There seems to have been an unfortunate misunderstanding in regard to your position at the hearing before the Public Lighting Committee, as far as the Public Franchise League is concerned.

In the first place our Executive Committee certainly understood that you had volunteered to represent the League, as well as the State Board of Trade, on behalf of the general bill. Secondly, you advocated to the Committee the desirability of dividends being paid on the surplus earnings of a public service corporation, though I believe at a lower rate than on the paid-in capital. So far as I know this doctrine is not held by the members of the League. . . . Don't you think we should have a clearer understanding in the future? [11]

Brandeis replied immediately:

First: I did not understand that at this hearing I should represent the League, and I feel very certain that a stenographic report would show that I did not mention the Public Franchise League once in any way in the course of my remarks.

Second: The position that I took in respect to paying some return upon the surplus is one that does not directly affect the legislation under consideration. The view which you speak of as the view of the League against paying returns on the surplus was expressed by Mr. Prince fully and effectively. I think it is a view which is not sound, for I believe it to be unjust, and I believe that the insistence upon such a view is prejudicial to the chances of proper legislation. When we meet, I shall be glad to discuss this matter more fully with you.

I entirely agree that it is desirable that the counsel of the League should represent fully the views of the League, and there is no distinction in this prospect whether he is a paid counsel or not. . . .

I am not aware, however, that the principle that no return should be paid upon the surplus has ever been accepted as the principle of the League, and feel that it has not at any meeting at which I have been present.[12]

In a postcript to this letter Brandeis incidentally went into the method by which he thought the price of gas to the consumer and the amount of dividends to the investor could be tied together:

As you were not present at the hearing, I will say to avoid any misunderstanding that the view I expressed was this:

That the amount of dividend to be permitted at any time, whether upon the original investment or upon the surplus, was a matter which should be determined only indirectly, namely, in fixing the price of gas. And that in fixing the price of gas, the Board would determine from time to time, according to circumstances then existing, what it was proper that the company should have, and that the amount the company should have should depend, in my opinion, upon what was given to the community. If they gave, for instance, 75-cent gas, they ought to be allowed to receive more in dividend than if they gave $1.00 gas. But that this question of what the amount of return on the capital should be ought to have nothing whatever to do with fixing the amount of the capitalization which is to be fixed for all time when the consolidation is effected.

Brandeis was now thinking in terms of London's municipal "sliding scale" utility rates. The essence of the "sliding scale" in use there was that it permitted profit-sharing between the utility and the consumer. It was practically a mutual or bilateral bonus for efficiency; as the dividend to stockholders rose, the selling price of gas to the consumer fell. Brandeis eventually got the "sliding scale" adopted in Boston.

These letters, of course, widened the breach between Warren and Brandeis. The latter apparently had few regrets about it. Of Warren he wrote later: "In that [Public Franchise] League, Edward R. Warren was an important member, not by reason of his ability, but mainly because of his energy and the time which he could and did give to it. He is a man essentially narrow-minded and of few ideas." [13]

Brandeis thought of Warren and also of Sprague as fanatics against stock-watering. His opinion of such men he had recorded years before: "Fanatics should be sacrificed when the end is accomplished—like animals which had borne the gods to sacrificial feasts." [14]

Little more was heard from Sprague on the gas matter; but Warren was not yet ready to call quits. He openly attacked Brandeis and the gas companies when the Legislative Committee on Public Lighting asked the Public Franchise League to help prepare the final valuation bill. This came about through a complicated chain of events, leading to a conference, arranged by a mutual friend, Charles P. Hall, between Brandeis and

James L. Richards. Both apparently laid their cards on the table, Richards explaining his plans, which included acceptance of the sliding scale and capitalization of the new company at $15,000,000, with 7 per cent dividends. Writing Dr. Morton Prince, April 24, 1905, Brandeis said:

I told him [Richards] that in my opinion the thing they should do is to accept a consolidation now on the basis of the aggregate capital, issuing stock to pay the debts under the general law, and then let the matter of sliding scale be considered by the community and have it passed upon next year.

I told him further that this was what the community wanted and I was convinced it was the best thing also for the company. Also that if they should get any legislation through this year which gave them any special privileges, no matter what their character, it was practically certain that the community would believe they had obtained their end by bribery and that a victory now under those circumstances would be for them merely the beginning of new trouble; that the only way they could get the good will of the community was by asking no special privileges and by trusting the community. . . .

I think he was at least somewhat shaken in his views after our interview.

This meeting paved the way for workable compromise. After numerous conferences between Brandeis, Richards, and Snow, the two gas company men drew up a bill. Brandeis presented their draft to the Public Franchise League and to representatives of the State Board of Trade, meeting jointly at the Hotel Bellevue, May 3, 1905. Though there was a small minority bitterly opposed, Brandeis won overwhelming support.

The most vociferous objector was Warren, who promptly retired from the League "with loud protests" that were "never silenced." [15] In his mind an important matter of principle was at stake. The League had, he later explained, stood firm during the "whole preceding winter" against stock-watering only to be presented with a compromise measure which for him, as for Sprague, was "treachery to the principle of no stock-watering." [16]

Dr. Morton Prince shared Warren's wrath, and after Brandeis's "wonderful magnetism" had carried all but Warren and himself off their feet, Prince asked whether it would not be possible later to reopen the question. In disgust Brandeis replied in words Warren could never forget: "Don't cry, baby!" [17]

Dissension in the League spread even to Robert Treat Paine, Prescott F. Hall, and E. H. Clement of the *Boston Transcript*. Included also "among the radicals who," as Brandeis said, "could not see the bearing of the whole situation," was the League's counsel, George W. Anderson, who shortly after the Bellevue meeting informed Brandeis in double-edged words:

The more consideration I have given to this so-called compromise, the more desirous I am that you should have the entire credit of having originated and put it through, and also the entire responsibility for its final form, and for the extraction of all colored gentlemen from this very large wood-pile.

I do not believe in the bill and I do not believe in the form that the bill is put in, and I want a record made which will make it clear to everybody who knows anything about the inside of this matter that I am not entitled to any of the credit, and have assumed none of the responsibility for this proposed legislation.[18]

But after the settlement was reached, in accordance with the sliding-scale principle, Anderson, unlike any of the other League dissenters, wrote Brandeis "a very handsome letter" in praise of his achievement.[19] With Warren, on the contrary, the grievance rankled for years, and in 1916, when Brandeis was being considered for the Supreme Court, Warren went to Washington to convince the Senate Judiciary Committee that Brandeis had blinded the League to a most elementary principle of public right.[20] Neither Brandeis nor anyone else, then or later, took Warren's irreconcilable attitude very seriously. "Of course," Brandeis wrote E. A. Filene, May 24, 1905, "Warren's talk about the 'Executive Committee proceeding on a low ethical plane' would be insulting if it were not absurd."

This breach among the reformers marked the second stage in the gas fight. Thereafter Brandeis had to contend not only with gas companies but also with his former allies.

THE FIGHT FOR SLIDING SCALE GOES ON TO VICTORY

The new bill drawn up by the gas companies and the Franchise League fixed consolidated capitalization at not more than $15,124,600. The price of gas was to be reduced to ninety cents per thousand cubic feet within a year after consolidation.[21] Since this compromise settlement was a great improvement over the Act of 1903, Brandeis and others thought it better to stand by it than risk having to keep the old act.

Meanwhile the Governor appointed a committee to investigate and report on the expediency of the London sliding-scale price system. Besides the Gas Commissioners, this committee included private citizens James E. Cotter and Charles P. Hall, a close friend of Brandeis. In August 1905 Cotter and Gas Commissioners Barber and George went to England and Ireland to study the system in action. In a report to the Legislature the Gas Commissioners attacked the London system.[22] Hall and Cotter, however, endorsed the sliding scale and published their own favorable report for which Brandeis was largely responsible.[23]

This division of the Governor's investigating committee was but a reflection of the wide divergence of opinion on the sliding scale. Corporation Counsel Babson thought it would promote efficiency of management and lead to an appreciable reduction in the price of gas.[24] The Consolidated companies, Brandeis, and the Public Franchise League also favored it. George Anderson himself spoke for it before the Committee on Public Lighting.[25] The opposition within the League, on the other hand, held that the sliding scale was academic and unworkable in practice, that by its adoption Massachusetts would admit that commission regulation of corporations had failed; that under it the company could raise prices; that reduction in price might be brought about only by reduction in quality.

The whole issue was complicated by those who held that public ownership was the only solution. Brandeis was much opposed to this and had indeed invoked the sliding scale to avert public ownership.[26] On numerous occasions he had warned "perfectionists" against such cure-all programs. In writing Frank Parsons, July 29, 1905, he had spoken of the importance of not having the Economic Club "committed to the side of extensive municipal ownership." Now, in 1906, he joined up with the Consolidated companies to fight municipal ownership. The sliding-scale plan was his main weapon. Thus, on April 20, 1906, Richards of the Consolidated wrote to Brandeis: "It seems wiser that a bill upon these lines (containing the sliding scale) should be introduced by the Public Franchise League rather than by us and that it will be better also to introduce the bill without saying specifically that we agree to its terms.

"I write this to say that if a bill is passed on these lines, substantially in the form which you and we agree upon, our company will accept the bill within the time provided by the act."

Taking due precaution against possible failure, Richards added that "if this bill should for any reason not pass we are not to be quoted in any way as having assented to 7 per cent as being a proper dividend." He wished to have it understood that the agreement as to a 7 per cent dividend and to an increase of 1 per cent in dividends for every five-cent reduction, was reached "in view of the desirability of securing legislation."

Following Richard's suggestion, the League on April 23 submitted to the Committee on Public Lighting a final draft of its sliding-scale bill.[27] Brandeis spoke briefly in its favor, pointing out that the bill's passage would result in eighty-five-cent gas immediately if the company were to continue its policy of paying 8 per cent dividends; that it would give an incentive to reduce the cost of gas through improvements and particularly through increased output. He said, furthermore, that it would give the company "the assurance that it would be allowed to attend to the business of manufacturing and distributing gas, and not have to attend to the business of hearings before the Commission or the Legislature, and indeed, it seems to me also not of elections."[28]

The sliding-scale bill did not limit the right of the city to enter the gas business, nor did it invite the city to do so. On April 27, 1906, Brandeis wrote to Samuel Bowles what he expected from the bill:

The bill if passed will I am confident bring us at a very early date a further reduction of the rate in Boston, but it will bring us what is far more important even than cheaper gas, the complete withdrawal of the Boston Gas Co. from the field of politics, and if this corporation is able to conduct its business without the necessity of a political department, there is good reason to believe that others of our public service corporations will follow the lead.

The principal evil that has been done by our public service corporations is not excessive charges, but the corruption of our municipal and state governments.

Some one has said that the reason that our municipalities should enter upon the field occupied by the public service corporations is that the latter have invaded the field of government.

If the Public Franchise League can carry through this sliding scale bill and have it accepted by the company, which we think we can, it will be probably the first instance in America of substantially divorcing a public service corporation from the political field.

As soon as the bill was presented to the lower House of the Legislature, May 1906, the fight started all over again. Some condemned the bill as merely a ruse to retard public ownership.[29] The Gas Commissioners attacked it for the old reasons.[30] Commissioner Morris Schaff denounced it as a revolutionary break with Commonwealth policy and contended that the gas interests, desiring guaranteed dividends, were the bill's real promoters. On May 16 Robert L. O'Brien, publisher of the *Boston Transcript*, asked Brandeis for one of his "judicious editorials." He responded immediately, his article being printed May 18. Two days later he sent the *Transcript* a letter in which he noted that the Gas Commission had "apparently without dissent on his [Schaff's] part, permitted, from year to year, other companies to pay 10 or even 12 per cent."

In the meantime, the Consolidated's old enemy, Hearst's *Boston American,* queried Brandeis's connection with the bill and denounced him as author of the Cotter-Hall report. Later the *American* discovered and loudly proclaimed that the League was not entirely united on the bill, and blithely added fuel to the flames, saying that ". . . many members have practically withdrawn from the League because of the action of attorneys representing the executive committee on matters relative to the sliding scale." [31]

One "withdrawing member" was, of course, Edward R. Warren, and it was easy for the *American* to get him to oppose the bill publicly. On May 14, 1906, he wrote for Hearst's paper:

I thought, and still think, that the company was allowed to overcapitalize. In my opinion, it was given at least $2,000,000 more than it was entitled to. When the men representing the Public Franchise League became parties to that compromise I declared that the principles of the League had been betrayed, and said I would get out of the society. I have done so.

If I were not sure that my action was right in that instance, I have found support for it in the attitude that the League has been put in by George W. Anderson and Louis D. Brandeis on the sliding-scale proposition.

In reply, the League made it clear in a letter published May 16 that its members had not been single pawns in the hands of Anderson and Brandeis:

Many members of the League carefully collected and collated statistics bearing upon the price of gas and upon the effect of the sliding scale, and upon the effect of the proposed bill as to the future price of gas and the rate of dividends to be paid by the Consolidated Gas Company. As a final result of all this study, every member of the Executive Committee of the League who had taken any part in the discussion at any of the conferences was in favor of advocating the bill which was finally presented, except Mr. Robert Treat Paine, Jr. Mr. Paine objected not to the sliding scale as such but to certain terms of the bill which he considered fundamental. . . .

Mr. Edward R. Warren and Mr. Prescott F. Hall, who signed the protest against the bill, are not members of the Executive Committee of the League.

James Richard Carter
Chas. M. Cox
Geoffrey B. Lehy
Edward A. Filene
Louis D. Brandeis
Morton Prince
G. W. Anderson
George P. Upham
Andrew G. Webster
Robert A. Woods

Joseph B. Eastman, Sec'y.

Amid all this chaos of publicity, and "in spite of the strenuous opposition of both conservatives and radicals," the sliding-scale bill made its way unamended through the House and Senate. On May 22, 1906, Brandeis wrote of its progress to his brother Alfred: "Our sliding-scale gas fight is on in the Legislature. We have won so far—triumphantly in the House—and the prospects are good in the Senate. But we have many opponents—the most active being some of our own former associates who are, in my opinion, fanatics, *and as ready to do injustice to capital as the capitalists have been ready to do injustice to the people.*" (Author's italics.)

The bill reached Governor Guild on May 25. It was rumored that he might veto it, but after conferences with Brandeis, Anderson, Jerome Jones, J. R. Carter and Andrew G. Webster of the Boston Merchants' Association, and Corporation Counsel Babson, Guild signed the bill next day.[32]

The Governor, too, had had a hard fight, as Brandeis disclosed when on May 27 he relayed the good news to his brother: "The Governor signed our Sliding-Scale Gas Bill—after much heart-rending wrestling—yesterday. The poor man was afraid this action might injure him politically and was sorely distressed and made me lots of work. I consider this a most important step in public economics and government—an alternative for municipal ownership—which will keep the Gas Co. out of politics. If, as I anticipate, this succeeds well in Boston, there will be many followers, also in other lines of public service.

"I succeeded in running this campaign mainly by putting others on the firing line—as your girls would say—'the man behind.' Some of our old allies—now too radical—were our most formidable opponents."

The immediate effect of the new sliding-scale act was reduction of the price of gas from ninety to eighty-five cents.[33] The Consolidated did this to secure the right to continue its 8 per cent dividend. A year later Boston was getting eighty-cent gas.*

Brandeis had been "the largest factor in obtaining so satisfactory a piece of legislation," and George L. Barnes, chairman of the Committee on Public Lighting, thanked him for his "courtesy" and "very valuable assistance."[34] Charles P. Hall also recognized the value of the work Brandeis had done by offering to share with him the $2,000 Hall received from the Commonwealth for his own services. In refusing, Brandeis wrote Hall: "I shall take it as a personal affront if you insist upon paying to me or for me in any form, shape, or manner discernible by man any part of the $2,000 which you are to receive from the Commonwealth for your services on the Special Gas Commission." But, he added, "if it will relieve your mind, I shall not object if a small part of it goes to the Public Franchise League."[35]

THE GROUND WON

To Brandeis the gas fight was not so much for cheap gas (which was of course a factor) as for good government. He said over and over again that he wanted to keep government out of business; but more important, he wanted to keep business out of government. Since he said this so often, we

* In practice the sliding-scale system proved to have one serious drawback—the lack of sufficient elasticity to meet successfully a period of inflation. It was finally abandoned during the First World War, under the stress of rapidly rising operating costs. (James C. Bonbright in his foreword to *Business—A Profession*, p. lxxvii.)

may justly quote him once or twice again. Thus on June 13, 1906, he wrote Clinton Rogers Woodruff of the National Municipal League: "The great gain is not confined to cheaper gas. We expect to get, what is more important, purer politics, because the bill will have the effect of eliminating the Gas Company from the field of politics. For the larger part of twenty years past the Gas Company has been in politics in a most objectionable way. The passage of this act, however, will, I think, prove to be of national significance as providing the first instance in America of a reasonable alternative to municipal ownership."

A year later, in Albert Shaw's *Review of Reviews,* Brandeis wrote again that ". . . The officers and employees of the gas company now devote themselves strictly to the business of making and distributing gas, instead of dissipating their abilities, as heretofore, in lobbying and political intrigue. . . . If the demand for municipal ownership in America can be stayed, it will be by such wise legislation as the Public Franchise League has promoted and by such public service as Mr. Richards and his associates are rendering in the management of a private corporation." [36]

Brandeis's second campaign as unpaid counsel for "The People" ended in victory. But it was a victory that, more than any other up to now, had cost him the friendship of people he had worked with and respected. Genteel reformers, not privilege-seeking capitalists, had now become his most vociferous opponents—such men as Dr. Morton Prince and Edward R. Warren. These men, said Brandeis, had become too zealous, too occupied with their unyielding principles, too autocratic. Of such people—these fanatics—Brandeis felt he could say with Rousseau that "when any one interest lays hold of the sacred name of 'the public good' . . . the general will becomes mute." In line with this, he did say in this struggle that any "who wield a large amount of power always should feel the check of power. The very principle on which the nation exists is that no person shall rise above power." [37]

In the world Brandeis wanted there would have to be room for many interests, and free—if just—competition among all legitimate interests. Certainly Brandeis was engaging in no war against capital. Rather he easily accepted as his own platform that on which Mazzini a century before had hoped to establish the republic of Rome:

No war of classes, no hostility to existing wealth, no wanton or unjust violation of the rights of property; but a constant disposition to ameliorate the material condition of the classes least favored by fortune. [38]

CHAPTER TEN

Justice to Employer and Employee, 1902-1907

INDUSTRIAL workers, even in America, were among "the classes least favored by fortune." As early as the 1880's, Brandeis had become intensely interested in labor. Among his friends he counted John F. O'Sullivan, labor reporter for the *Boston Globe,* and his wife, Mary Kennedy, the first woman trade union organizer. A little later he became closely associated with Henry Demarest Lloyd, whose *Wealth Against Commonwealth* of 1894 impressed him deeply.[1] So did the writings and speeches of Henry George. "I wish you were here," Brandeis wrote his father from Boston, November 21, 1889. "I should tell you about Henry George. . . . Don't fail to hear him if he comes within reach of you." Probably more instructive to Brandeis than books and speeches was actual labor warfare such as he witnessed during the Homestead strike of 1892 and the acute labor troubles of his own industrial clients.

Reading and investigation in the field of employer-employee relations convinced Brandeis that absolutism must be destroyed. "Industrial democracy should ultimately attend political democracy," he said. "We must avoid industrial despotism, even though it is benevolent despotism." [2] As usual, he meant this for both sides—for labor as well as for capital. Capitalists, Brandeis warned, must discard their belief that the only labor contract they could afford to make was with the *individual* worker; they must rid themselves of their hatred of trade union organizations. Collective bargaining, he insisted, was essential to the survival of capitalism against the rising tide of socialism. On the other hand, he advised labor that socialism—much less the despotism of the worker over the capitalist—was no solution for the workers' problem. "Don't assume," he said, "that the interests of employer and employee are necessarily hostile—that what is good for one is necessarily bad for the other. The opposite is more apt to be the case. While they have different interests, they are likely to prosper or suffer together." [3]

Because he was not and could not be committed unqualifiedly to either side, Brandeis's labor views, like his political philosophy, made him an enigma. Here was a successful and aggressive corporation lawyer maintaining that unions were not only legitimate but necessary—necessary even to employers. Here was Brandeis accepting the dominant judicial dictum

that "the right to purchase or to sell labor is a part of the 'liberty' protected
by the Fourteenth Amendment," yet defending and supporting legislation
for hours of labor and minimum wages. Here he was condemning industrial violence yet insisting that blame rested about equally with business
management and labor leadership. Here he was generally opposing the
closed shop, yet, under certain circumstances, defending it; proclaiming his
friendship for unionism, yet advocating one of labor's most hateful buga-
boos—incorporation of trade unions.

UNION INCORPORATION TO PROTECT LABOR

Brandeis's even-handed approach to the whole problem of labor relations was shown in his debate with Samuel Gompers on the question:
"Shall Trade Unions Be Incorporated?" The debate took place at Tremont
Temple, Boston, December 4, 1902, under the auspices of the Economic
Club of Boston. There Brandeis praised labor unions for benefiting the
entire community, including employers. He cited the case of "a very wise
and able railroad president" who said, "I need the labor union to protect
me from my own arbitrariness." There was, Brandeis conceded, a tendency
among labor unions to be impatient with the requirements of civilized
living; their actions sometimes were taken without deliberation; at times
they were arbitrary. Denouncing this, he observed: "A bad act is no worse,
as it is no better, because it has been done by a labor union and not by a
partnership or a business corporation. If unions are lawless, restrain and
punish their lawlessness; if they are arbitrary, repress their arbitrariness;
if their demands are unreasonable or unjust, resist them; but do not oppose
unions as such." The unions, like the railroad president, "need something
to protect them from their own arbitrariness. The employer and the community also require this protection." Incorporation of unions would give
the community, the employers, and the unions themselves the protection
they require.

The fact that unions were not incorporated often made it impracticable for
employers to sue them for damages, since there was no one actually to
pay or to be sued except the usually impoverished workers. Labor leaders
naturally thought this immunity of their funds a great advantage. "To
me," Brandeis argued, "it appears to be just the reverse. It tends to make
officers and members reckless and lawless, and thereby to alienate public
sympathy and bring failure. It creates on the part of the employers a bitter
antagonism, not so much on account of lawless acts as from a deep-rooted
sense of injustice, arising from the feeling that the union holds a position
of legal irresponsibility."

Incorporation was, therefore, urgently needed in the interest of trade unionism itself: "The practical immunity of the labor unions from suit or legal liability is, in my opinion, largely responsible for the existence of the greatest grievances which labor unions consider they have suffered at the hands of the courts, that is, so-called government by injunction." Incorporation of unions, Brandeis believed, would practically eliminate the use of the hated injunction. But the advantage of incorporation would be far greater; it would establish "the position of the union as a responsible agent in the community, ready to abide by the law." [4]

The *Boston Herald* on December 5 described Brandeis's argument as that of a man with no interest in the matter beyond that of the public-spirited citizen properly affected by movements which concern his country. He spoke, the *Herald* reported, in a calm, conversational, dispassionate manner, making no effort at oratorical effect, leaning with his left arm on the desk and with his right hand in his trousers' pocket. No vote was taken, but the preponderance of applause, according to the *Boston Post* of the same day, favored incorporation of the unions.*

INVESTIGATING UNEMPLOYMENT

Brandeis, at this time, had just been drawn into the great Pennsylvania anthracite coal strike of 1902 by Henry Demarest Lloyd. With Lloyd he visited the Scranton coal fields, met John Mitchell, the strikers' chief, and helped Lloyd prepare the case for the miners.[5]

This strike, Brandeis thought, had turned public attention to trade unionism to a degree unprecedented in the country—and not to the disadvantage of the unions. The arbitrary attitude of employers contrasted sharply with the informed leadership of John Mitchell, and furnished a "warning example" to many employers that they could deal with employees otherwise than directly or individually; that "representatives of unions may be recognized without impairment of business honor." [6]

The anthracite coal strike taught Brandeis other lessons. The one he stressed most was that irregularity of employment is one of the worst features of the industrial system. The miners were striking for higher wages, but since they worked, as he discovered, only 181 days a year, even higher wages would not mean an adequate livelihood. The loss of earnings due to lay-off was bad enough; the demoralization caused by periodic

* The burden of Gompers' argument against incorporation was that the workers knew from hard experience that they could not expect to receive fair treatment at the hands of the courts, and his audience responded heartily when he cited the sweeping injunction recently issued against labor in the anthracite coal strike.

Later, in a letter to Roger Sherman Hoar on April 13, 1911, Brandeis himself favored legislation restricting the use of injunctions in labor disputes on the score that the labor injunction encroached on executive functions, that the exercise of police protection by the judiciary undermines public confidence in, and respect for, the courts.

enforced idleness was even worse. Gradually he came to believe that elimination of irregular employment was the most urgent social problem.

Little or no thought had been given to this "chronic evil" even by the unions. Irregularity of employment was then (as now in certain quarters) regarded as a law of nature, a "cross to be borne with resignation." Brandeis could not be so quiescent. On July 14, 1904, he wrote John Graham Brooks, humanitarian and social reformer: "Will you kindly let me know to what extent the question of regularity or steadiness of employment has been investigated; that is, the number of days in the year in which men work in particular employments? Obviously steadiness of employment is as important, perhaps more important, than the rate of wages, and yet I find that subject very rarely referred to. I should also be glad if you could let me know of any articles, though not statistical, in which this subject has been treated." He made many similar requests, but little or no information was forthcoming, even from official sources such as the Department of Commerce and Labor.

How, he wondered, could an evil seemingly so unnecessary be corrected? As usual he must get the facts. The first step was to get responsible official reports prepared in such a way as to make full information easily available. In a long letter to Charles F. Pidgin, Chief of the Bureau of Statistics of Labor for Massachusetts, Brandeis suggested how this might be done: "An accurate diagnosis of the facts should disclose where there has been a failure to work for the whole of the working period, whether this omission to work was voluntary on the part of the laborer or due to causes personal to the workingman as sickness; or whether the failure to work is due to causes for which in a certain sense an employer can be held responsible, namely a failure to provide work; or whether it was due to conditions for which neither employer nor employee can be held responsible—like weather prohibitions." [7]

Brandeis next turned to businessmen themselves. Here he found almost incredible ignorance. To one of his clients, faced at the time with labor trouble, Brandeis almost shouted: "You say your factory cannot continue to pay the wages the employees now earn. But you don't tell me what those earnings are. How much do they lose through irregularities in their work? You don't know? Do you undertake to manage this business and to say what wages it can afford to pay while you are ignorant of facts such as these? Are not these the very things you should know, and should have seen that your men knew too, before you went into this fight?" [8]

Certain of Brandeis's clients co-operated with him by introducing in their own plants methods of determining the number of hours each man worked and whether their unemployment was compulsory or voluntary.

One of his more enlightened clients took the position that "if the amount of time voluntarily not worked is large, my employees must explain; if the amount of compulsory idle time is large, I must explain."

From these investigations Brandeis soon learned that the responsibility for irregular work rested about equally upon employers and employees. The unions had mistakenly emphasized higher wages. They had failed to see that the important question was not how much a man was paid per day, hour, or piece, but how much he was able to earn in a year. Every man, Brandeis argued, should have the opportunity to work every day in the year excepting Sundays, holidays, and vacations. Therefore he urged unions to demand steady work and co-operate with employers in securing it.[9]

Steadiness of work, Brandeis contended, was of equal importance to employers. The manufacturer's purpose, even in the narrow terms of profit, should be to run his factory all the time and thus get the most use out of his machines and the lowest unit cost on his products. He could then operate on a narrower margin of profit per unit. But he may not even have to do that, because the worker, guaranteed year round employment, would be content with a lower wage per day or per piece. All this in turn would keep down the price of the product, increase the demand for it, and thus make more work for more people.

Brandeis had firsthand experience on which to base his neat theory, gained in 1902 when a client, W. H. McElwain, called him in to help break his workers' resistance to a wage cut. McElwain, a prominent shoe manufacturer, pointed out in advance that the workers had little basis for complaint since they were getting relatively high wages and had good working conditions. But Brandeis, seeing that their employment was irregular, immediately asked: "Are you giving me the average pay they receive for fifty-two weeks of the year, or are you giving me the pay they earn while they are working?"[10]

McElwain's "high wages" were unimpressive because almost every worker in his plant, through no fault of his own, lost many working days during so-called "slack" times. Actually his annual wage was miserably low. Brandeis said this was "absolutely unnecessary. It is an outrage that in an intelligent society a great industry should be so managed." "Clients talk to me," he said later, "of seasonal conditions and averages. I abhor averages. I like the individual case. A man may have six meals one day and none the next, making an average of three per day, but that is not a good way to live."[11]

Then Brandeis gave McElwain some advice. Reorganize the selling end of your business, he said. Make the salesmen get their orders early. Accept no orders unless they come in well ahead of the delivery date. Then lay out the work, looking months ahead. Organize the working force to take care of that work, and keep the factory within that limit. Accept no rush orders; they will demoralize your plant.[12]

McElwain did as he was told, and the results were all he and Brandeis could have hoped for. Henceforth there was very little slack time in Mc-Elwain's factory. His workers were contented, not because their daily wages had been increased, but because their annual wages for regular work throughout the year had increased enormously.

There was, as Brandeis saw it, no over-all solution for irregular employment. What worked in McElwain's business might not necessarily work in some other business. Therefore he urged unions to adapt their demands to the conditions of a particular business. "The possibilities of employers' businesses vary like the employees' capacities," he declared. "If you attempt to apply rigidly a uniform rule to all, you may kill the goose that lays the egg; and except in extreme cases, the goose must be kept alive whether the egg be golden or not." [13]

INSTITUTIONALIZING EMPLOYER–EMPLOYEE RELATIONS

From firsthand experience in adjusting labor disputes Brandeis quickly learned the importance of bringing the employer and labor representative face to face. Among employers a dogma often heard was, "This is my business and I shall run it as I please." Similarly, the labor representative, "swaggering in his power to inflict injury by strike and boycott," would tell the employer to run his business to hell. Both attitudes were mutually destructive. The important thing was to get the employer and the union leaders into a mood to talk things over. Even then negotiations sometimes took months.

Brandeis always insisted that the real head of the business participate in these conferences, that he take the labor representatives into his confidence, and even open his books for their inspection. For often it was only from full knowledge of the financial condition of the business that the arbitrary demands of either capital or labor could be tempered and the real interests of industry, labor, and the public be served. Brandeis believed the interests of all would be even better served, if management-worker negotiations were permanently institutionalized instead of arising only at times of crisis.

As in the case of McElwain and irregular employment, Brandeis got a chance to try his theory in a client's business. The client this time was Edward A. Filene, head of a big department store in Boston. The Filenes, though known for their enlightened labor views, did not set out to improve industrial relations throughout the entire country or even in their own state. They attacked the problem in their own store. Brandeis assisted in setting up their system of self-government for employees—the Filene Cooperative Association. He attended meetings and participated in the discussions. He also joined with the Filenes in creating the Industrial League, its "purpose being to promote the investigation and study of economic and industrial questions and aid in improving relations between employers and employees."

The experiments of the Filenes, like that of McElwain, demonstrated that industrial democracy and social justice were consistent with marked financial success. Thus "the so-called 'practical businessman,' the narrow money-maker without either vision or ideals, who hurled against the Filenes, as against McElwain, the silly charge of being 'theorists,' has been answered even on his own low plane of material success." [14]

This plane was too low for Brandeis. Though he was attacked later as "Brandeis—business baiter—destroyer of property values," he actually entertained the highest ideals for business and looked forward to the day when business would rise to a professional level. He thought his friend McElwain, whose death at the age of forty left Brandeis "greatly distressed," had reached this higher level. "He was in my opinion really the greatest man of my acquaintance," Brandeis commented in a letter to Alfred, January 12, 1908, "and the greatest loss to the Commonwealth—possessing the rare combination of great ability, courage, high character, and personal charm. As yet he had devoted these high qualities almost exclusively to building up his business organization so that he was probably the largest shoe manufacturer in the world—having started with nothing. For about five years he had been overworked. But I think—had he lived—he would soon have emerged from business into the field of his higher ideals and become a commanding figure in the Commonwealth. . . . I feel that he was really a sacrifice to overwork, to the perfecting of his business organization, for he had no love or even respect for money as such. . . ."

In judging the Filenes, Brandeis also emphasized not their pecuniary success but their contributions toward the solution "of the greatest problem before the American people in this generation—the problem of reconciling our industrial system with the political democracy in which we live." He saw the Filenes' experiment as capable of exerting nationwide influence. It proved, he said at a meeting of the Filene Co-operative Association, May 9, 1905, that industrial democracy could not fail, if only people put thought to its success:

Thinking is not a heaven-born thing. Intelligence is not a gift that comes merely. It is a gift men make and women make for themselves. It is earned, and it is earned by effort. There is no effort to my mind that is comparable in its qualities, that is so taxing to the individual, as to think, to fundamentally analyze. The brain is like the hand. It grows with using. . . .

One hundred years ago the civilized world did not believe that it was possible that the people could rule themselves; they did not believe that it was possible to have government of the people, by the people, and for the people. America in the last century proved that democracy is a success.

The civilized world today believes that in the industrial world self-government is impossible; that we must adhere to the system which we have known as the monarchical system, the system of master and servant, or, as now more politely called, employer and employee. It rests with this century and perhaps with America to prove that as we have in the political world shown what self-government can do, we are to pursue the same lines in the industrial world.[15]

Brandeis was eager to spread industrial democracy as far as possible, and he became a vice-president of the Civic Federation of New England, a more ambitious organization than Filene's for bettering employer-employee relations. At one of the Federation's dinners, Brandeis noted that all the labor men had been lined up together at a long table. "When we have another dinner," he wrote the secretary, Hayes Robbins, "I think it would be desirable instead of having a long table to use small tables at which six or eight could sit, and then use great care in bringing people together at the same table who ought to meet. . . . It is important that all interests should be well mixed."[16]

Brandeis sought this "mixing process" at all levels. At a meeting of the Economic Club, he and Lincoln Steffens once co-operated in subjecting a friend and prominent labor leader to it. Afterward Steffens, in reporting to Brandeis, described their friend's "sincere wonderment, especially after I told him who the men were he had met: a leading attorney, a leading banker, a leading editor and publisher, the head of the Gas Trust, 'the worst men in town,' as I explained, all interested in anarchy."[17]

Brandeis was always meticulous to obtain representation of varying shades of opinion. One had no right to assume, for example, that representatives of capital and business were identical. When E. A. Filene, in making nominations for committee membership in the Business Men's Association, failed to take this distinction into account, Brandeis protested:

As you know, the general criticism which I have found as to the selection made has been that this business organization has in its officers too much representation of capital as distinguished from business. My conviction is that the interest of the businessman is distinctly local in the city or state; that on the other hand, the capitalist at best is a citizen of the world, and that it is entirely immaterial to him in his business operations whether the particular community in which he lives develops or not.

Our business organization needs at its head businessmen, and therefore I should ordinarily select businessmen even in preference to representatives of capital, although the latter were individually of greater ability.[18]

TRADE UNIONISM: FUNCTIONS AND PRINCIPLES

Among early pronouncements on employer-employee relations, one of the most complete was an address Brandeis delivered at the annual banquet of an employers' organization, the Boston Typothetæ, April 21, 1904. Earlier Brandeis had been called in by the Typothetæ when a Boston Typographical Union struck for higher wages. The pressers and feeders quit work in sympathy, thus violating a contract for arbitration of grievances, as well as an agreement barring sympathetic strikes. As counsel for the employers, Brandeis obtained an injunction and ended the strike. But one would not have suspected that he had done so from the address he delivered to his former clients. He seized this occasion to remind them that responsibility is the counterpart of power.

Employers, he told the Typothetæ, require unions for self-protection— to stay them from "the fall of vanity"; the community at large has to have unions "to raise the level of the citizen." The right of labor to organize is recognized by law, and should be respected by employers, despite admitted abuses and shortcomings. "We believe in democracy," he said, "despite the excesses of the French Revolution." [19]

In an address before the Economic Club of Providence, Brandeis saw trade unions as a force tending "toward conservatism." [20] "The trade unions also stand," he said, "as a strong bulwark against the great wave of socialism. They for the most part stand out for individualism as against the great uprising of socialism on the one hand and of the accumulation of great fortunes on the other." [21] America needs strong unions balanced by strong employers, each able, if necessary, to resist the unjust demands of the other. "I should not rely upon the goodness of heart of anybody," he said years later. "Nobody ought to be absolute; everybody ought to be protected from arbitrariness and wrong decisions by the representations of others who are being affected." [22]

Brandeis's conception of industrial society, and his suggestions as to how industrial liberty and justice may be secured, recall Madison's Federalist papers Numbers 10 and 51. Where Madison in 1788 envisaged checks and balances as correctives of political injustice, so Brandeis in 1904 and 1905 advocated mutual checks and balances to correct the industrial power of both corporate and labor union groups. "Every business," he said, "requires for its continued health the *memento mori* of competition from without. It requires, likewise, a certain competition within, which can exist only where the ownership and management on one hand, and the employees on the other, shall each be alert, hopeful, self-respecting, and free to work out for themselves the best conceivable conditions." [23]

A union controlling each trade, but preferably not by the closed-shop device, was to Brandeis the ideal condition. In any trade it is well, he felt, to have "an appreciable number of men who are non-unionist. . . . Such a nucleus of unorganized labor will check oppression by the union as the union checks oppression by the employer." [24]

Unionism, too, should embrace public employees. To a specific request for comment from the *Boston Globe*, he replied: "In a free country every person, be he an employer or an employee, be he in the public or in private service, should have an opportunity to combine with any other person or persons for the purpose of improving his condition. The right to combine is absolute; but the action of a combination must necessarily be confined to such action as is lawful, and should be confined to such action as is reasonable." [25]

On the whole Brandeis condemned the closed shop; but when President Eliot of Harvard declared categorically in a speech before the National Civic Federation that "the closed shop and the union label will never give us peace with liberty— Never!" the lawyer hastened to add qualifications.[26] In sending his Typothetæ address to F. S. Baldwin of the *Boston Transcript*, suggesting that "you may care to publish it in full," Brandeis explained:

I do this as I think that some antidote is desirable to President Eliot's address. Very much that he says is true, but I am inclined to think that the address is apt to do quite as much harm as good at the present time. The statements which are true are coupled with very important propositions which seem to me unsound, and the general tone is one which I think will impress the reader with hostility to trade unions and the labor cause and tend rather to widen the breach which President Eliot deprecates than to lead to the good-will for which he longs.[27]

The point was elaborated later in Brandeis's address before the National Civic Federation:

The cause of industrial liberty will ordinarily be best subserved by an open shop in which a strong union has a predominating influence. But it is not true that the closed shop—that is, the shop open to all willing to become union men, and to such only—"will never give us peace with liberty." The union shop is not necessarily prejudicial to industrial liberty; its adoption may, at times, be indispensable to the attainment or preservation of liberty . . . ; e.g., where the employer, while pretending to run an open shop, is actually and insidiously discriminating against union men. . . . In such cases, adoption of the union shop becomes proper war measure.[28]

Brandeis abhorred the folly, dishonesty, and waste of restrictive union regulations—soldiering on the job and other techniques reducing production. Above all, he warned labor against lawlessness. On this subject he counseled employers: "You may compromise a matter of wages, you may compromise a matter of hours—if the margin of profit will permit. No man can say with certainty that his opinion is the right one on such a question. But you may not compromise on a question of morals, or where there is lawlessness or even arbitrariness. Industrial liberty, like civil liberty, must rest upon the solid foundation of law." [29]

In an address before the Central Labor Union, February 5, 1905, he advised:

Unions should strive to make the earnings of any business as large as possible.
Unions should not limit the production of individuals.
Should be so faithful and diligent that espionage will not be needed.
Should demand steady work.
Should adapt their demands to the conditions of a particular business.
Labor unions should strive to make labor share all the earnings of a business except what is required for capital and management.[30]

Brandeis heartily endorsed certain union demands, especially those asking additional pay for overtime work. Excessive hours, anything over eight hours a day, he said, are wasteful of our most valuable resources, our manpower, not only directly by causing cumulative fatigue, but in the long run by shortening the worker's productive life. Excessive hours impoverish the entire community. Without leisure time and unless workers are fresh enough to make real use of it, their education cannot be continued, nor can they take their rightful share in public affairs. Leisure is essential, above all, to the successful functioning of democracy:

The welfare of our country demands that leisure be provided for. This is not a plea for indolence. Leisure does not imply idleness. The provision for leisure does not contemplate working less hard. It means ability to work not less, but more—ability to work at something besides bread-winning—ability to work harder while working at bread-winning, and ability to work more years at bread-winning. We need leisure, among other reasons, because with us every man is of the ruling class. Our education and condition of life must be such as become a ruler. . . . The citizen should be able to comprehend among other things the great and difficult problems of industry, commerce, and finance, which with us necessarily become political questions. He must learn about men as well as things. . . . Our great beneficent experiment in democracy will fail unless the people, our rulers, are developed in character and intelligence.[31]

Brandeis was growing more and more accustomed to attacks by both sides on any public problem he dealt with. Certainly in his attempts to solve the most difficult industrial conflicts he could not expect to go unscathed—and he didn't. When he thought he was helping labor by advocating union incorporation, Gompers remarked, "We fear the Greeks even when they bear us gifts." [32] On the other side, George B. Hugo, president of the Employers' Association, denounced Brandeis's Central Labor Union address as revolutionary, as an unwarranted affront to the American employer, as fomenting "class hatred," as "weaving a net of evil about the industries of America which, if not checked, will require a sword to cut its meshes. Does Mr. Brandeis believe," Hugo challenged, "that the hour has come when mind power, with all its acquisitions, is to be subject to the demands of hand power?" [33]

Brandeis had already answered Hugo, a year earlier, in commenting on the recently organized Anti-Boycott Association—formed to preserve "individual initiative and liberty" and to safeguard management's "absolute liberty to manage it [the business] as it sees fit." "The liberty which we seek," he told a meeting of the Economic Club, November 16, 1904, "is the liberty of all regardless of occupations, not of the employer to do as he pleases. . . . Leaders not masters of industry are needed." [34]

Once again he was thought a traitor to his class, but Brandeis could not give in to class. He explained part of his reason in a letter to his brother, June 18, 1907, after settling a strike in Syracuse. "I am experiencing a growing conviction," he wrote, "that the labor men are the most congenial company. The intense materialism and luxuriousness of most of our other people makes their company quite irksome."

CHAPTER ELEVEN

Old Services for New Needs, 1905-1941

BRANDEIS's championship of regularity of employment and trade union-ism helped American workers win larger yearly incomes. His attack on the great insurance companies warned the workers against the nearest thing to a racket ever run by respectable American businessmen—industrial life insurance.

This type of life insurance differs from others in many ways. It is sold by house-to-house solicitors working only in the poorer districts. Its premiums are collected by agents in person, and in cash, sometimes under duress. Being fixed for all ages at five cents or multiples thereof, the premiums seem small. Actually they are so large as compared with the incomes of the insured, that the lapse ratio of industrial policies is extraordinarily high. Nor is this the whole story. In 1905 only one-fourth of the policy was payable in case of death after three months; one-half after six months. Nothing was payable if death occurred within three months. The policy-holder could die and still not win. This was intolerable—not insurance but exploitation. But nothing was done, until, in a roundabout way, Brandeis made one of the greatest insurance exposés in financial history.

In 1905 American insurance companies had in their hands more than twelve billion dollars of the people's savings. These billions were very tempting to the great financiers, so much so that intramural warfare broke out between James Hazen Hyde and James W. Alexander for control of the Equitable Life Assurance Society of New York. The fight got so hot as to endanger disrupting the company. Bostonians, having nearly a mil-lion dollars in premiums at stake in the Equitable, were greatly concerned, and on April 18, 1905, formed the New England Policy-Holders' Protective Committee "for the purpose of advising themselves as to the condition of the Company." Brandeis was retained as counsel.[1] Years later he recalled the "stormy session" with Committeemen William Whitman and Ed-win H. Abbot before they agreed to let him serve without compensation.[2] In a matter of such far-reaching potentialities, as he saw them, Brandeis wanted not only to represent the committee but also to be free to take whatever action he might deem wise in the public interest. The committe-men yielded, and Brandeis became the People's Advocate in life insurance matters.

DEMANDING RADICAL CHANGES IN THE SYSTEM

Brandeis again went on the trail of his precious "facts." And again he got them. In due course he prepared three reports, all of which were published by the committee. So basic were the faults Brandeis found that his first report of May 19, 1905, declared: "The disclosures already made indicate a failure to perform fully the sacred obligation assumed by those who have managed this great trust. Neither the recovery of the profits wrongfully diverted nor mere substitution of other officers, however scrupulous and efficient, can afford an adequate remedy for the evils disclosed. The interests of present and future policyholders demand that there be made radical changes in the system." [3]

In a long address—"Life Insurance, the Abuses and the Remedies," delivered before the Commercial Club of Boston, October 26, 1905, Brandeis went further into the subject. [4] He showed that nearly half the tremendous assets of the ninety legal reserve companies (i.e., $1,247,331,738) were concentrated in the "big three" in Wall Street; that under their prodigally wasteful management exorbitant costs were saddled on the insured. He pointed out further how this system affected directly or indirectly the well-being of half the population, and how it was particularly dangerous for both industry and politics. Insurance throughout the country, he discovered even as early as 1905, "is in the main held by what we term 'the people'—that large class which every system of business and of government should seek to protect." [5]

There had already been much scandal and discontent as to insurance management, and though the lid had not yet been blown off, reforms had been suggested. One of these, which had the support of President Theodore Roosevelt, was for federal rather than state supervision. Indeed Senator John Fairfield Dryden, who was also president of the Prudential, had introduced on February 27, 1905, a bill providing for federal licensing of insurance companies. "Nearly all the presidents of insurance companies all over the country," Senator Dryden said, "desire national supervision. . . . Every company would naturally prefer just one set of regulations, for that would make it so much easier to shape policy." [6] For Brandeis, however, Senator Dryden's remedy was but a demonstration of "frankness which is unusual and an effrontery which is common—among the insurance magnates." [7] "Federal supervision," he said, "would serve only to centralize still further the power of our government and perhaps to increase still further the power of the corporation." [8]

As against federal supervision, Brandeis urged more drastic state supervision and regulation. He did not at this time recommend that savings banks be authorized to sell life insurance, but even in his Commercial Club address he held the savings bank up as a model for insurance companies. He compared what it cost the "big three" insurance companies to manage their funds with the cost of running Massachusetts savings banks, and concluded that "the pro rata cost of conducting the insurance business and taking care of the savings invested in these three insurance companies was *seventeen times* as great as the expense of caring for savings invested in our 188 savings banks. . . ."

"The faithful treasurers of the 188 modest Massachusetts savings banks," he continued, "supervised mainly by obscure but conscientious citizens, earned during the year ending October 31, 1904, 4.40 per cent on the average assets. The return earned by our savings banks is thus 5 per cent greater than that of the three insurance companies, and a comparison of net returns is even more favorable to the savings banks. I do not say that the income returns of the great companies manned by the great financiers were unreasonably low, but merely that the small banks with their low salaried officers earned more." [9]

These savings banks, Brandeis pointed out, employed no solicitors, paid no agents' commissions. Why should insurance companies impose on policyholders an expense so unnecessary? He looked askance at the lavish payments for advertising space. Such practices, he observed, being "common among the promoters of mining enterprises and of patents, have no place in the business of life insurance." [10]

So far, Brandeis had been dealing with life insurance in general. Then he turned to attack the worst of all life insurance abuses—those in industrial insurance. "How many wage-earners would insure in these companies" (Metropolitan and Prudential), he inquired, "if they were told that for every dollar they pay, forty cents will go to the stockholders, officers' and agents' salaries, or for other running expenses? How many wage-earners would assume the burden of premiums if they knew that there is but one chance in twelve that they will carry their policies to maturity?" [11]

Naturally the great insurance executives resented such exposure. They disliked even more Brandeis's contemptuous thrusting aside of the screen of prestige and mystery behind which insurance officers habitually hid their business from public examination. "The business of life insurance is one of extraordinary simplicity," Brandeis announced. "To conduct it successfully requires neither genius nor initiative, and if pursued by the state does not even call for unusual business judgment. The sole requisites would be honesty, accuracy, persistence, and economy." [12]

Brandeis's trembling Bostonians had not been the only ones stirred by the Equitable's Hyde–Alexander duel. On July 20, 1905, Governor Frank W. Higgins of New York recommended the appointment of a legislative committee to investigate the insurance business and propose corrective legislation. Heading the committee was New York State Senator William W. Armstrong. To conduct the investigation Armstrong called in Charles Evans Hughes as counsel.

Committee hearings began September 5 and continued through December 30, 1905. Two months later the committee made its report to the Legislature in a volume of nearly five hundred pages which summarized the evidence and recommended remedial legislation. Many of the suggestions that were made Brandeis had already put forth in his New England Policy-Holders' Committee reports and in his Commercial Club address. The New York Legislature promptly enacted legislation corrective of abuses in regular life insurance, but nothing was done in New York or elsewhere about industrial insurance. And yet the Armstrong committee report had dealt with these abuses rather more fully than had Brandeis.

Discussing the largest industrial insurance company, the Metropolitan, the committee showed that ". . . the Industrial Department furnishes insurance at twice the normal cost to those least able to pay for it; a large proportion, if not the greater number of the insured, permitting their policies to lapse, receive no money return for their payments. Success is made possible by thorough organization on a large scale and by the employment of an army of underpaid solicitors and clerks; and from margins small in individual cases, but large in the aggregate, enormous profits have been realized upon an insignificant investment." [13]

John R. Hegeman, president of the Metropolitan, confessed such extortion. "You might safely assume," he told the Armstrong committee, "that the ordinary man of modest means, working on a week's wages, or day's wages, pays twice for the necessities of life as compared with a man better off." "He pays twice for his insurance," Mr. Hughes suggested affirmatively. "He has to; he is willing to pay it," Hegeman naïvely replied.[14]

". . . We have not expected to make any money out of the ordinary business," explained Haley Fiske, Metropolitan vice-president. "We are satisfied to come out even. . . ."

"That means that all your profits are made out of industrial premiums?" Hughes asked.

"Oh, yes, sir," said Fiske.

"That is what it really means?" said Hughes.

"Oh, yes, sir." [15]

Accepting such practices as beyond remedy, the Armstrong committee frankly stated that it was "not prepared to make recommendations with reference to industrial insurance further than to say that the subject is one deserving of special investigation." [16]

"A great reform could be accomplished," the Armstrong report aptly suggested, "if the expense of solicitation and collection could be avoided by the establishment of branch offices where insurance might be obtained by the thrifty poor who desire it." [17] Yet insurance officials and the Armstrong committee alike assumed that, as a practical matter, the entire intolerable situation was incurable.

Brandeis did not agree. Insurance for persons of small means was (and is) a social safeguard, an economic necessity, and he felt early in 1905 that he simply had to find a way. Industrial insurance posed a challenge, not an impasse. But first he himself had to learn a great deal more about the business. From 1905 through June 1907, night after night, he lugged home suitcases filled with reports of the Commissioner of Insurance, the Commissioner of Banks, and other relevant material. He brought these back to the office next day and then went home with another load. He studied the insurance and banking experience of other states, and religiously followed up every possible lead as to material here and abroad. In the autumn of 1905 he told his secretary, Alice H. Grady, "We've found the answer. The savings bank *can* be adapted to the writing of life insurance."

MAKING THE IDEA WORKABLE

That stated his basic hypothesis. But no such problem could be solved in an ivory tower. His troubles in the real world were just starting. It was one thing to work out a remedy to his own satisfaction, quite another to prove it sound in practice, to frame it as a bill, to pilot the bill through public hearings, through the treacherous shoals of the Great and General Court, and to final signature by the Governor.

On November 24, 1905, Brandeis wrote at length to Walter C. Wright, [18] a leading actuary and son of Elizur Wright, the great insurance reformer. He intended, he told Wright, to submit a savings-bank insurance project to the recently appointed Joint Special Recess Committee on Insurance, and asked Wright's help in perfecting it. Wright was glad to do so, not only because of interest in the idea but also because he needed a job. His first memorandum, however, proved inadequate. "Upon a cursory glance," Brandeis wrote him on December 27, "I felt that the report did not give as full a report upon some of the matters referred to in my letter of November 24 as I expected." Certain points were not "fully covered," he complained, and he wished "to have the actuarial proof of all statements" as well as "the processes by which you reach that conclusion and exactly how it is worked out in figures." These were large and exacting orders, and Wright then suggested an interview, since, as he said, "the points are not as susceptible of such elucidation as you suppose."

The ensuing months were filled with interviews and communications. Wright occasionally offered suggestions, quite outside the actuarial realm, that might well have discouraged almost anyone but Brandeis. Wright's "most decided doubt" as to the "feasibility" of the project centered on "the fact that as the savings banks are so entirely successful in their present operations, their officers might be disinclined to accept new and more complex features in addition to their present function." [19]

Brandeis hardly needed Wright to tell him who and how powerful his opponents would be. His only response was that, given the strength of the opposition, his and Wright's own campaign had to be "very carefully planned, and we must secure for the work all possible support." [20]

The result of this correspondence and discussion was Brandeis's article, "Wage-Earners' Life Insurance," which he was ready to submit to his actuary and to a wide circle of friends on June 8, 1906.

Among others who received and commented on the manuscript were William Whitman, Charles H. Jones, Charles Evans Hughes, Robert F. Herrick, George L. Barnes, Edwin H. Abbot, Judge Warren A. Reed, E. A. Filene, George S. Baldwin, and George Wigglesworth. Hughes described the article as "a strong and unanswerable statement of the evils of industrial insurance as now conducted." But, anticipating that the native conservatism of savings bank officials "would distrust an insurance annex to their business," the future Chief Justice urged Brandeis to show with considerable detail the feasibility of the plan, for "even with such a showing I fear that conservatism would refuse to be convinced." Hughes wished to see the experiment undertaken, believing that "it would be as important a philanthropic work as model tenements, for example." [21]

Robert F. Herrick, the distinguished Boston lawyer, grasped the plan's social philosophy more clearly, commending it warmly as "a scheme whereby the poor can be helped to help themselves." [22]

Brandeis, of course, had written the article not for his friends alone, but for publication, and on June 25, 1906, sent it to Norman Hapgood, editor of *Collier's Weekly*. "It seemed to me," he told Hapgood, "that you might deem it wise to have *Collier's* lead in the movement . . . . to secure our working people life insurance under proper conditions." Hapgood apparently "deemed it wise," for the article appeared in *Collier's* on September 15, 1906. Hundreds of reprints were distributed, and Hapgood agreed to have it appear simultaneously in metropolitan newspapers all over the country. On September 11 the *Boston Evening Transcript* published the article in full, and on September 12 the *Boston Post* began a series of supporting editorials.

This essay [23] repeated in part Brandeis's Commercial Club address of the year before, but was much more specific, centering on the worst of insurance abuses as they affect wage-earners and proposing a remedy. The companies selling industrial policies admitted that these supplied practically all their profits; yet such policies averaged only about $140 and ordinarily provided barely enough to meet the expenses of the wage-earner's last illness and furnish decent burial. How important this form of insurance was to the companies, Brandeis indicated by the fact that of 20,936,565 "level premium life insurance policies outstanding in the ninety American companies on January 1, 1905, 15,678,310 were industrial policies." The premium payable for any given amount of industrial insurance, he pointed out, "is about double that payable on ordinary life . . . policies. . . . About two-thirds of all industrial policies lapse and are forfeited within three years of the date of issue—the premiums paid thereon proving a total loss to the policyholder." Add to this the fact that "the industrial policyholder pays toward expense of management four times as much as even the present expense charge borne by the ordinary life policyholder for the same amount of insurance."

Massachusetts savings banks, Brandeis argued, could easily add this new function. They could sell life insurance in small amounts at cost, without agents or solicitors. There were, he said, only three elements in insurance not common to savings banks: (1) fixing the terms on which insurance shall be provided; (2) examining the insured; (3) verifying the proof of death. The first of these could be done for the banks, Brandeis said, by a state actuary, the second by a state doctor. As for the third, the savings banks were already doing this in the case of deceased depositors.

"The sacrifice incident to the present industrial insurance system," Brandeis said, "can be avoided only by providing an institution for insurance which will recognize that its function is not to induce working people to take insurance regardless of whether they really want it or can afford to carry it, but rather to supply insurance upon proper terms to those who do want it and can carry it—an institution which will recognize that the best method of increasing the demand for life insurance is not eloquent persistent persuasion, but, as in the case of other necessaries of life, is to furnish a good article at a low price."

Adverse comment on Brandeis's article came almost exclusively from vested interests. *Insurance Press* of September 19 saw the savings-bank project as "positively grotesque in its absurdity. It betrays the theorist and indicates an utter ignorance as to the practical workings of industrial insurance or the peculiar make-up of the wage-earning class." The most exhaustive and dogmatic analysis came from Frederick L. Hoffman, Prudential statistician, who wrote in *Insurance Press*, January 30, 1907:

> One might as well attempt to run a car by animal power over a system of electric traction in the hope of developing a better transportation system as to attempt to run a savings bank in connection with an insurance company. . . . To combine the insurance function with that of a savings bank would be a most dangerous experiment with every promise of disastrous failure and permanent injury to the cause of sound investment and insurance. . . .
> Brandeis' various propositions have only been superficially considered, and there is no evidence that he has anything like the necessary knowledge and experience in connection with so vastly important a matter as the safe and permanent conduct of a life insurance business.

The *Insurance Post* of February 2, 1907, summed up the companies' attitude:

> Getting life insurance, like "getting religion," has never been achieved to any appreciable extent by hanging out a sign or distribution of printed exhortations in the one case, nor by the passing around of Bibles and printed tracts in the other case. . . . Nobody need lose any sleep over the dream of the Boston theorist, for the dream has about one chance in a million of ever coming true.

If insurance magnates could have seen Brandeis's plan for what it was—as a design to block the trend toward socialism—they might have accepted it. In his Commercial Club address he had said: "In my opinion the extension of the functions of the State to life insurance is at the present time highly undesirable. Our Government does not grapple successfully with the duties which it has assumed, and should not extend its operations at least until it does. But whatever and however strong our convictions against the extension of governmental functions may be, we shall inevitably be swept farther toward socialism unless we curb the excesses of our financial magnates." [24]

Continuing, he said: "The talk of the agitator alone does not advance socialism a step. . . . The great captains of industry and of finance, who profess the greatest horror of the extension of governmental functions, are the chief makers of socialism. Socialist thinkers smile approvingly at the operations of Morgan, Perkins, and Rockefeller, and the Hydes, McCalls, and McCurdys. They see approaching the glad day when monopoly shall have brought all industry and finance under a single head, so that with the cutting of a single neck, as Nero vainly wished for his Christian subjects, destruction of the enemy may be accomplished." [25]

Brandeis reverted to the same theme in the conclusion to his *Collier's* article, and presented his savings-bank plan as the only alternative to state insurance. "If we fail," he wrote, "to offer to workingmen some opportunity for cheaper insurance through private or quasi-private institutions, the ever-ready remedy of state insurance is certain to be resorted to soon—and there is no other sphere of business now deemed private upon which the state could so easily and justifiably enter as that of life insurance. . . . The question is merely whether the remedy shall be applied through properly regulated private institutions, or whether the state must itself enter upon the business of life insurance."

MOLDING AN AFFIRMATIVE PUBLIC OPINION

From the start Brandeis had seen the correction of insurance wrongs primarily in terms of education, and so far had done most of the educating himself. He studied, investigated, wrote. Speechmaking began at the Commercial Club in October 1905. By January 1906 Brandeis's campaign was in full swing. "This is a pretty busy insurance week," he wrote his brother, January 3, 1906. "Shall speak six times—having had two meetings last evening."

"Our insurance fight proceeds merrily," he wrote two weeks later. "Talked only three times this week. Going to Fitchburg Friday. Next week have four performances."

Though Brandeis often spoke on short notice, and kept dinner clothes in his office for this reason, his meetings usually were carefully planned. If there was more than one speaker on the program Brandeis spoke last. He saw to it that the "key-men" of each community were especially invited to attend: the state senator and representatives, town officials, county commissioners, officers and employees of national, savings, and co-operative banks. He usually gave the press advance copy of his talks, and editors were notified of time and place and asked to have reporters on hand.

To judge by the reaction of savings-bank officials, Brandeis by November 1906 had accomplished nothing. That month the *Boston Post* canvassed such officials on his insurance scheme and on November 14 published some opinions received. J. C. Holmes of the Boston Five Cents Savings Bank said: "We have trouble enough as it is now, from depositors who are hardly able to write their names, and if an insurance department were to be added here I don't see how we could find time or floor space to handle it. Of course, such a plan might be feasible, but Mr. Brandeis has not gone into detail sufficiently for us to pass much of an opinion upon his scheme. Mr. Brandeis is a philanthropist, of course, and undoubtedly is working in the interest of the poorer classes, but a more thorough discussion of the permissive industrial insurance scheme would have to be gone into before savings bank people could take sides for or against it."

Treasurer Thomas Kelly of the Union Institution for Savings thought that Brandeis's plan would be of great benefit to depositors. "But," he said, "it's a little bit early yet for discussion of such a scheme." Joseph Shattuck, Jr., treasurer of the Springfield Institution for Savings, predicted: "I am positive that if a roll were taken among savings bank treasurers throughout the Commonwealth there would be a majority against it. While I am open to conviction, I am opposed to having my bank enter a business for which it is not fitted. It appears to me that the average savings bank cannot well conduct an insurance business because the bank is a local institution only. The machinery of insurance would be costly even if there were a central association to keep us in touch with our policyholders in other parts of the state."

These men naturally had to be brought around before much progress could be made. Brandeis wanted Pierre Jay, newly appointed Bank Commissioner of Massachusetts, to help him with the savings-bank officials. He asked Charles P. Hall to get Jay interested. But Hall replied, "I have no suggestion [in regard to Jay] unless it is to get him in some way under the spell of your magnetic voice." [26]

Brandeis's voice proved effective enough, for on November 26, 1906, Jay arranged a conference between himself and officials of the savings banks, and invited the reformer to speak.

Brandeis didn't get any further with these conservatives than before, and he turned to New York, seeking to get a committee organized to push savings-bank insurance in that state. If interest could be aroused there, the cause would be helped in Massachusetts. "My belief is," he wrote Henry Morgenthau, Sr., November 23, 1906, "that this movement can be advanced best by having presented publicly and with persistency the evils of the present system. If the community is convinced of the evils of the present system, and is driven to the point of finding a remedy, it will, I think, discover that there is no immediate remedy available except through the savings banks. . . . If we should get tomorrow the necessary legislation without having achieved that process of education, we would not make a practical working success of the plan."

This "boring from without" failed. Morgenthau told Brandeis early in December 1906 that none of the large New York banks was favorable to his plan, their attitude being: "Let Massachusetts do the experimenting and we'll see how it works." All these gentlemen ought to understand, Brandeis replied December 5, "that true conservatism involves progress, and that unless our financial leaders are capable of progress, the institutions which they are trying to conserve will lose their foundation."

Undaunted by the lukewarmness among New Yorkers, he accepted an invitation to speak at the state capital. "I spent Tuesday at Albany talking savings-bank insurance to the New York State Bar Association," Brandeis wrote his brother, December 11, 1906. "Dined with Hughes and other potentates in the evening."

Brandeis returned to Massachusetts still fighting. In a letter to Norman H. White, a young client of his, a publisher and candidate for the state Legislature whom Brandeis had converted to his scheme, he outlined the next step in the campaign: "I am convinced that if we are to overcome the ultra-conservative views of the savings-banks treasurers, we must in the main work, not directly upon the treasurers, but through the trustees of the banks, and for this purpose carefully organized personal missionary work must be done with the trustees. Rand, McNally & Co.'s *Bankers' Directory*, of which the latest issue is July 1906, contains a list of all of the trustees of all of our savings banks. I think that, if you would take up that list and study it with your executive committee, you could work out a way of reaching through personal interviews a number of selected trustees, and through them convert other trustees and ultimately the officials of the banks." [27]

White tried this "personal missionary work" but nothing happened. "They are a pretty tough crowd," Charles H. Jones wrote Brandeis about the trustees, "and a few of them have such a strong prejudice against even listening to a proposition for anything new, that they have been held back surprisingly." [28]

Individual missionary work having failed, Brandeis now increased the organized pressure. Earlier he had enlisted Hayes Robbins, secretary of the Civic Federation of New England. At a Federation luncheon on November 26, 1906, the Massachusetts Savings-Bank Insurance League had been organized with Norman White as secretary. In January 1907 the League began its first real membership drive. By March 21 it had over seventy thousand members, and early the next month, in a one hundred-page booklet, quaintly titled "A Few Members of the Massachusetts Savings-Bank Insurance League," it paraded the names of these members. Many were well-known professional and businessmen, and among them were President Eliot of Harvard, Bishop Lawrence, Bishop (later Cardinal) O'Connell, and the Reverend A. A. Berle, Sr. There were more than twenty vice-presidents, a distinguished Executive Committee, a "Committee of One Hundred," and so on.

The million-to-one shot was getting closer home, and the newspapers began to take notice. Much publicity was given the League's imposing list of officials. The non-partisan aspect of the League was made particularly evident, when former Republican Governor John L. Bates, a trustee of the Wildey Savings Bank, became vice-president, and former Democratic Governor William L. Douglas, president of the People's Bank of Brockton, became the League's President.

Douglas was a good front for reasons other than his name. He himself owned the newspaper with the largest circulation in Plymouth County. Moreover, as a big shoe manufacturer, he was famous as a benevolent employer, and was even then considering an insurance scheme for his own workers. Brandeis sought to influence him through Judge Reed of Brockton. On December 3, 1906, Brandeis wrote Reed:

If his [Douglas] purpose is to buy insurance from some existing company, he may possibly get from them a cheaper rate, but his doing so would tend to perpetuate the existing pernicious system. The general injustice to workingmen would continue, while his own favored employees might, through his capacity and generosity, escape. The Commonwealth as a whole would be injured rather than benefited by such notion on his part.

On the other hand, if his idea is to undertake the insurance business himself and pay the death benefit as a gift or as an addition to the men's wages, the men contributing nothing, he would also, it seems to me, be making an unfortunate precedent. *What we want is to have the workingman free; not to have him the beneficiary of a benevolent employer, and freedom demands a development in the employees of that self-control which results in thrift and in adequate provision for the future.* The development of our savings banks and savings-bank insurance will be effective in this direction. . . . (Author's italics.)

Do get Mr. Douglas to commit himself to savings-bank insurance. His support would absolutely insure its success, and if I could have a letter from him advocating the plan and saying that he stood ready to provide the necessary guaranty fund for his savings bank, I think that all the opposition of the insurance companies and the passive resistance of the savings banks would be overcome.

On January 14, 1907, Douglas dispatched precisely the letter thus sought. Brandeis, capitalizing on the millions Douglas had spent familiarizing the United States with his face and his shoes, immediately publicized this letter endorsing savings-bank life insurance.

Through Douglas and Judge Reed, twenty-one of the twenty-four trustees of the People's Bank of Brockton joined the League. On February 1, 1907, the trustees of the Bridgewater Savings Bank all came in, and the Commercial Club of Bridgewater announced that it would procure the guaranty fund of $25,000 required by the plan, as soon as the system was legally in effect. Largely through the efforts of Charles H. Jones, a Brandeis client, the Whitman Savings Bank on March 11, 1907, voted unanimously, with all members present, in approval of the plan. Thus the system was sure to be given a trial once the Legislature authorized it.

BATTLING IN THE LEGISLATIVE MELEE

The first legislative hurdle was the special Joint Recess Committee, appointed by the Massachusetts Legislature in 1906 to investigate insurance evils and propose reforms. Since membership of this committee could determine the fate of Brandeis's scheme, he had written the Speaker of the House, John N. Cole, on June 4, 1906: "Some time at your convenience before you make up the appointments to the Recess Insurance Committee, I should like an opportunity of talking with you." On June 15 Cole invited Brandeis to see him at his office or anywhere convenient.

Of the Recess Committee's fourteen members, none gave Brandeis greater confidence than George L. Barnes, young Weymouth lawyer, who had helped establish the sliding-scale gas principle. An expert strategist with a genius for friendship, Barnes could be depended upon to win over several of the Recess Committeemen. Brandeis appeared before the committee, November 8, 1906, and concluded his remarks with: "The whole insurance business should be reformed, but the part that affects wage-earners should be the main care of the Commonwealth. . . . The only way to meet the socialistic and restless spirit of the times is to meet and remove each individual case of injustice. The present companies should be allowed to work out their scheme as best they can. Either their business will decrease or they will change their system, and the people will get the benefit. The only way to tell whether conditions can be improved is to try." [29]

High insurance officials were on hand, but none thought Brandeis's plan merited even a word. *Insurance Press* dismissed it as merely a "Utopian scheme from the standpoint of practical experience." In the Recess Committee itself, a bitter—and losing—fight took place. Stopping Brandeis in the corridor, Barnes said, "Perhaps you would like to know how the committee voted on your plan."

"Yes," said Brandeis eagerly, "how did it go?"

"Fourteen to one against you."

An adverse committee report seemed inevitable, but not to Brandeis. "The significant feature [of the contest] is the support which Mr. Brandeis is piling up on the outside among labor bodies and at similar gatherings," commented *Practical Politics,* December 29, 1906. "He has already precipitated a campaign into the Recess Committee on insurance with such good effects that the committee is at sixes and sevens on the whole project. They do not want to report it, and a majority are against it, but one or two of the especially active men are threatening minority reports on the subject unless they get what they desire. On top of that the Governor has been having conferences with the chief promoter of the plan, and the committee may be in the position of having a section in the next message [of the Governor] advocating it."

Governor Guild's message to the Legislature, January 3, 1907, showed how completely he had been brought under Brandeis's spell. "Life insurance without agents or collectors is," the Governor observed, "an experiment in which the demands of the people are supplemented by practical plans. I commend for your consideration the study of plans to be submitted to you for cheaper industrial insurance that may rob death of half of its terrors for the worthy poor."

Five days later the Recess Committee unanimously endorsed the savings-bank project.

Brandeis had purposely delayed framing his idea as a bill, fearing that if one were drafted too long before presentation to the Joint Legislative Committee, his opponents would kill it by piling up criticisms on unimportant details. He also considered it sound policy and good tactics to get savings-bank men to present their own suggestions as to its statutory form. "My conviction is," Brandeis told Charles E. Stabrook, November 26, 1906, "that if we can get the savings banks committed to the measure, we may well leave it practically to them to draw the bill."

The only hitch in that scheme was that Brandeis could not get bankers "committed to the measure." He therefore took the initiative and late in February placed his own draft bill in the hands of all institutions whose interests were involved—savings banks, co-operative and national banks, trust companies, labor organizations. Representatives and senators were amply supplied with supporting literature, preparatory to Joint Legislative Committee hearings on the bill which were held on March 21, 1907. Room 204, the biggest in the State House, could not accommodate the crowd that day. Brandeis began his testimony with a devastating attack on the whole industrial insurance business. After three hours Chairman Buttrick asked whether he would finish by one o'clock. "Most certainly not," Brandeis replied. "Even if a small part of the people who favor this measure appeared before the committee each speaking the words—'I favor this bill'—the committee would be unable to hear them in the entire month of April." Brandeis laughed with the amused audience, and the chairman thereupon announced that the hearing would be continued on April 2.

Knowing that his opponents would put the intervening time to hostile use, Brandeis, two days after the first hearing, consulted Judge Reed on the "best course to pursue."

On March 23 Reed replied:

I have been watching the result of our first hearing. What is on the mind of the average legislator could be expressed in one word, "hobby." The average legislator says the banks do not want it; there is no public demand for it. Of course, you and I understand that this means that the insurance companies are using this method to kill our plan. They do not come out boldly, but expect to use the trustees of the savings banks to weaken our efforts. . . .

I consider it absolutely necessary that this movement should be taken up by the legislative committee of organized labor. . . . Until the wage-earners ask for our bill themselves, the Legislature will ignore it, I am afraid. There are so many things in the Legislature where they give and take with each other, that a measure that has no particular friends will fail, no matter how good it is.

At our hearing, we need to make the committee feel that it is a public demand, rather than a private hobby of a few well-meaning gentlemen. We must remember that laws are passed in answer to a public demand, rather than because they are good, and our first object should be to start such a demand.

This Brandeis knew how to do. When the hearings were resumed on April 2, leaders of both political parties, labor leaders and industrialists, ministers and educators, all came forward to back the plan.

In his argument Brandeis again emphasized that his measure had been framed so that savings banks might open the new department or not, as they wished. Even the commercial companies could sell industrial insurance as before, except that they would henceforth meet competition from a far more effective system. The wage-earner, Brandeis explained further, could take out policies with industrial companies or savings banks as he himself chose. In short, the plan did not endanger any existing institutions and certainly would help the wage-earners get insurance at lower rates.

Denouncing the insurance leaders as "the most dangerous of socialists and anarchists, because true conservatism necessarily involves progress," Brandeis continued his plea: "It is clearly for the interest of the community that that trial should be made, and those who have confidence in the intelligence and character of our working people, including the labor leaders themselves, believe that the experiment will succeed. The question is whether the judgment of our leading manufacturers, merchants, and financiers, who have a knowledge both of the financial institutions and of our working people themselves, should be accepted, or whether the opportunity of making the experiment should be denied because of the belief of ultra-conservatives or pessimists, and more particularly whether the views

of the Metropolitan Insurance Company and the officials of other companies should be accepted, whose selfish interests prompt them to oppose the
measure for relief."

At the end of the hearings prospects seemed bright. But those who knew
legislative procedure realized that much remained to be done. "We will
give you some sort of bill—probably," the lawmakers told Judge Reed.[30]
But Reed and Brandeis wanted *their* sort of a bill—and immediately. Beginning early in April, they repeatedly canvassed the legislators to find
where application of pressure would do the most good. Then they got
members of all sorts of groups to drown the wavering legislators in post
cards, letters, and telegrams.

Brandeis himself kept after these supporters to step up the fight. Thus
when the Associated Board of Trade endorsed his plan, he did not consider that enough. "It is important," he wrote John T. Boyd, April 22, 1907,
"for your legislative committee to make known, so far as possible, to the
members of [the Legislature's Insurance] Committee the views of your
Board. . . . It is very important that it should be taken up by them during
this week." Labor organizations by the hundreds had gone on record but
Brandeis knew this would not count unless the legislators knew it. "Certain lawmakers," he wrote Dennis D. Driscoll, secretary-treasurer, State
Branch, A.F. of L., May 1, 1907, "should be much strengthened in their
championship of savings-bank insurance." Enclosing the draft of a letter
to be sent to each of the unions, Brandeis suggested: "If you approve of
sending a letter in this form, and will send me one copy duly signed tomorrow, together with about three hundred A.F. of L. letterheads, I will
see that the letter is mimeographed and sent out to all of these unions at
once."

The main point the opposition had made was that savings-bank men
themselves were against Brandeis's scheme. This had to be counteracted;
the lawmakers had to be convinced of the banks' support of the bill. "If you
see no objection," he told Hamilton Mayo of the Leominster Savings Bank,
April 29, "I think it would be well to write to each member of the Insurance Committee separately."

All the work done since the first hearing in March, however, seemed in
vain. But Brandeis kept on. He explained the nature of the crisis and what
he had done about it in a letter to Norman H. White on April 23, 1907:

Dear Norman:
    First: From two sources apt to be well-informed, I learn that there is at the
State House considerable feeling of doubt as to whether the Insurance Committee will report the savings-bank bill, and I think that every effort must be

made to bring before the members of the Insurance Committee the importance of doing so.

I have not heard from you since the 17th, and I should be glad to know what the situation is.

Second: I talked with Joseph Walker today and endeavored to impress upon him the importance of his attending when the Insurance Committee takes this matter up in executive session. He said he would do so, and would remind the committee of their promise to permit his attendance.

Third: I also talked with Mr. Higgins about this matter and hope to see him further tomorrow.

Fourth: I also talked today with Mr. Wilson of the Henry Siegel Company who has talked with Senator Williams, and with Mr. Robinson, and will take the matter up further with Mr. Lowney, and will also ask Mr. Kramer of the Henry Siegel Company to do what he can in this matter.

Fifth: I also talked today with Mr. George T. Dewey of Worcester, who, unlike most of the Worcester men, is favorable to our measure, and I think he will write to the Worcester County members of the committee.

Sixth: The report that got into the *Advertiser* that the committee would be likely to have our bill go over to the next General Court has been very widely read, and has had a bad effect. I hope that there will be published some other statement which will correct that impression. . . .

> Yours very truly,
> Louis D. Brandeis

Brandeis had done his work thoroughly and well. On May 12 State Representative Robert Luce acknowledged this. "I congratulate you," he wrote, "on the effectiveness of your organization. It ought to win out." And it did win out. On May 16 the Joint Legislative Committee favorably reported the bill, by a vote of 10 to 4.

The same day the measure was referred to the House Ways and Means Committee of which Joseph Walker was chairman, and the fight started all over again. Brandeis wrote scores of letters to the House members. None was more hostile than the Cambridge insurance agent George A. Giles, yet Brandeis wrote to him in his usual vein. Another arch-opponent was William F. Garcelon, and on May 24 Brandeis asked James R. Carter, a director of the Boston Merchants' Association, to work on him: "I am confident you can secure his vote for us." He also wrote Charles P. Hall that "the situation in the Ways and Means Committee is very critical. Could you not see Governor Guild and ask him whether he will not say something to Giles, Kemp, Garcelon, Dean, and Mayhew as to the desirability of passing the bill?"

Brandeis won this round too. The Ways and Means Committee reported favorably on May 28. Next day the bill appeared at last on the House calendar. The contest was intensified on both sides. "A very stubborn fight is being made against the bill by the Metropolitan and by certain savings-bank people who are connected with insurance companies," Brandeis told his lieutenants. "It is important that we should summon all our forces." Letters began to go out again. The one to James R. Carter on May 29 is typical: "I notice that Dennis E. Farley, a paper manufacturer of Erving, has expressed himself as rather hostile to the bill. Do you know him? In any event I wish you would write to him (for he certainly knows you) and try to secure his support for the bill, or at all events to insure his being passive. Will you do this? Awaiting your reply."

The newspapers were also mobilized. "The savings-bank insurance bill comes up," Brandeis reminded E. A. Grozier of the *Boston Post* on June 3, "as the first business in the House tomorrow. Won't you write one of your rousing editorials so that we may carry the bill through the House triumphantly?"

Leadership of the House opposition lay with Representatives Giles and Garcelon. On June 5, 1907, both made impassioned speeches. Giles said: "The opponents of this bill in no sense of the word are opposed to cheap life insurance for any class of people, and I believe that every man in this House would welcome any legislation that would reduce the cost of insurance, particularly to the people of the middle classes. We are not defending the Metropolitan or the John Hancock or any other insurance company, but we do say that this proposed bill is too hasty. It is impractical . . . and our savings banks are too sacred an institution to be used as an experiment. . . ."

Garcelon resorted to sarcasm: "I congratulate the gentleman [Norman H. White] on his method of promotion. I congratulate him because he has carried the influence of this League all over the state. I have tackled every single man I knew or met whom I have seen connected with this League, and the answer I get, with perhaps one exception, has been, 'I don't know anything about it. I believe in cheap insurance.' That is why they joined the League. That is why the labor unions have urged this matter. They have heard the other side of it. They have heard Mr. Brandeis and the gentleman from Brookline [White] explain in a beautiful way about this beneficent scheme." [31]

Neither Giles nor Garcelon could convince the House, however, and the bill passed on June 5, by 126 to 46.

The million-to-one shot was looking better all the time. But there was still the home-stretch, still the Senate and Governor. Brandeis realized this better than anyone. He continued to write letters. "I congratulate you," he wrote John H. Schoonmaker on June 6, "on the result of your work on behalf of the savings-bank insurance and annuity bill. The important thing now is to think seriously of the fight in the Senate." To Joseph Walker he wrote: "Your argument on the savings-bank and annuity bill was most effective. Whom can you get in the Senate to take up the fight there in the same masterly way?"

To Charles H. Jones he wrote on June 5: "I have understood that Senator Wheatley of Abington is favorably disposed towards our savings-bank and annuity bill; but I know that the opposition has been working at him, and I think it is very important that he should be strengthened, not only in his faith in our bill, but that he should take an active part in supporting it."

At the hearing before the Senate Ways and Means Committee on June 12, Brandeis got his men out in full force. Charles W. Hubbard of the Ludlow Manufacturing Company and a trustee of the Franklin Savings Bank, testified. "Our industrial center at Ludlow," he said, "is convinced that it is a fine thing and a magnificent boon for the workingman." Meyer Bloomfield, a distinguished social worker, spoke at greater length, and with some bitterness: "The antiquated system of chasing up industrial insurance in tenements of the North and West Ends of Boston, as is practiced now and has been practiced for years, is a disgrace to this Commonwealth. This measure is safe and proper, and no one has argued, not even the opposition, that it would be bad for the poor people."

By June 13 the Senate committee was convinced and reported that the bill ought to pass without dissenting vote. It did pass on June 17 by a vote of 23 to 3. "Delighted to know," Reed wrote Brandeis June 18, "that we were strongest where we thought we were weakest. The Senate did nobly. I congratulate you on the wonderful success of your plan, and hope that your endeavor to help those who cannot help themselves will be a continual comfort to you."

But Brandeis knew that the victory was not his alone. For him "the most helpful feature of the whole campaign" was the fact that "the enlightened representatives of labor and capital were co-operating so fully to secure the desired end." "The success of the bill was not wonderful," Brandeis wrote Reed, June 19, "when one considers the admirable work which has been done by those whom I was fortunate enough to interest in its career."

The Senate victory was heartening, but as Brandeis wrote F. F. Baldwin on June 20, "Our opponents are still active and the bill has yet to pass the . . . Governor." On June 24 Brandeis wrote John Golden, a labor leader, that he had been informed "that the Governor would sign the bill." This the Governor did on June 26.

GREAT OAKS FROM LITTLE ACORNS GROW

Some might have thought that the time for celebration had come. But not Brandeis. He had his bill. Now he had to get into operation the system his bill made possible, and he had to get it going under the auspices of the very men who had fought it hardest—the savings-bank officials themselves. Nevertheless his optimism persisted. Within a year he could write: "All indications point to our experiment meeting with complete success. Every problem seems to be settled except that which only experience must settle, namely, whether people can be educated to take the necessary article which is offered them on exceptionally favorable terms." [32]

Nothing at all was left to chance. On June 25, 1907, Brandeis sent Governor Guild a list of names as trustees of the forthcoming system. "It is important, my dear Curtis," he wrote, that the "trustees should be not only men of standing and business experience who are strong believers in the work, but that they should also be men whose business experience would enable them to meet readily such difficulties of detail as will necessarily arise in putting a whole new plan into successful operation. I have therefore considered carefully whom I should recommend to you as the first board of trustees. . . ."

"If you have any doubts," he concluded, "in regard to the selection of any one of these, or have in mind the selection of any other person for the position, I shall be greatly obliged if you will give me the opportunity of talking with you before acting."

Brandeis guarded against the Governor turning down his recommendations. The same list went out on July 1 to Charles P. Hall, with this note: "So far as you agree with me on these recommendations, I wish you would promptly take up the matter with Governor Guild. It is important that he shall not make the wrong appointments." Governor Guild reacted as suggested, save in the case of W. B. Jackson, and Brandeis promptly recommended another supporter, Hamilton Mayo of the Leominster Savings Bank.

Substantial victory, so far, had been won. "The Trustees of the General Insurance Guaranty Fund will probably be appointed by the Governor today," he wrote Alfred, July 10. "Then another stage will pass and I shall get a step nearer vacation, which begins to become a welcome change."

Soon, however, things began to look worse than ever. At least three banks—the People's of Brockton, the Whitman, and the Bridgewater Savings Banks—had indicated their purpose to establish insurance and annuity departments when the law was enacted. But almost a year after the laws had passed, none had begun business. Announcements that the system was about to begin were repeated so often that even its friends became skeptical and cynical. "The deliberation with which its preliminaries are arranged," ran the sardonic comment of the *Boston Transcript,* May 14, 1908, "recalls the saying that when the Almighty wants to grow an oak tree he takes forty years, while a single summer suffices for a cabbage. If beginning slowly affords any test, the savings-bank insurance plan has certainly made for itself a place in the oak-tree class."

"The insurance fraternity," *Practical Politics* remarked, August 15, 1908, "is indulging in quiet chuckles at the difficulties their amateur competitors are encountering and are now more certain than ever as to the final outcome of the experiment."

There were good reasons for this delay. The savings banks had to raise the $25,000 special expense and guaranty fund. They had to get the approval of the Banking and Insurance Commissioners. These steps took time, but needn't have taken a year or more, if the bankers had been really anxious to give the plan a trial. The first break came in June 1908, when the Whitman bank at last opened its insurance department. In November Douglas's Brockton bank got started. These beginnings gave Brandeis an opportunity to chant his new theme. Dozens of letters went out saying: "You were so much interested in our campaign last year to secure legislation authorizing the extension of the functions of our Massachusetts savings banks to the issuing of life insurance and old-age annuities to wage-earners, that I know you will be glad that the plan has finally been put into practical operation. . . ." He wrote particularly to labor leaders "to consider a plan for developing the work." He himself wrote many articles for labor, trade, charitable, and other magazines, describing the plan and emphasizing its social advantages. He continued to shower editors with material for editorials and news items.

Still the system showed no marked tendency to grow. But even in this Brandeis found some good. "It was a pioneer business," he remarked at a Workers' Conference, September 23, 1910, "and one in which it was easy to make mistakes, and I have thought that it was very fortunate that the growth of the business was not more rapid than it was. If it had been, we would have got into pitfalls. But we have had now two years' experience, and we have learned a great deal. . . . I am sure that time is an important element in getting the movement going. People have got to see that it is here to stay, and because it is here to stay, it depends very largely upon you who are here to make that success rapid." [33]

The insurance companies realized now that eventually the banks would get going. If Brandeis had accomplished nothing else, he threatened the gouging companies with new competition. And like smart businessmen they responded in the most convincing way. On January 1, 1907, they cut their charges 10 per cent. On July 1, 1909, they cut another 10 per cent. Even before Massachusetts savings-bank insurance really got started, it effected economies amounting, in 1910, to more than one hundred millions annually for insured wage-earners throughout the United States. "Industrial companies have imitated our system in many of its particulars," Brandeis wrote to Judge Reed, October 15, 1907, "as well as endeavoring to approach us on rates, and although the Metropolitan social department may be largely hypocrisy, it is to be borne in mind that imitation is the sincerest form of flattery, and hypocrisy the tribute which vice pays to virtue."

PERSISTENT GROWTH VERSUS VESTED HOSTILITY

The industrial insurance companies did not keep up the good work. Instead, they persisted in an effort to destroy their competitor. In April 1915 they tried to have discontinued the small appropriation in support of the system. Judd Dewey, however, unpaid counsel for savings-bank life insurance, learned of this. About one-thirty on the day the bill was to come up, Dewey went to see Calvin Coolidge, then president of the Massachusetts Senate, and told him of the opposition's plan, explaining briefly what savings-bank life insurance had accomplished, the purposes for which the appropriation would be used, and the reasons why the bill should be passed. As was his custom, Mr. Coolidge expressed no opinion and gave no indication as to what he would do, if anything, beyond remarking, "What you say sounds reasonable."

As Mr. Dewey emerged from Coolidge's office a senator inquired, "What did Mr. Coolidge say?"

"He didn't say anything," replied Mr. Dewey, "except 'it sounds reasonable.'"

"My God," exclaimed the senator, "did he say that? Then you're all right."

When the bill was reached after the Senate came in at two o'clock, the president repeated the formula, "Those in favor say 'Aye.'"

Nobody responded, but as the Senate's president called for "Those opposed," a loud chorus of "Nays" went up that seemed to include three-quarters of the Senate.

With the expression on the Coolidge countenance absolutely unchanged, the president ruled: "The yeas have it, and the bill is ordered to a third hearing." [34]

This was but one of several occasions on which Calvin Coolidge helped savings-bank life insurance while president of the Senate and later as Governor.

A major objective of enemy companies and their agents has been to have the Legislature limit the amount of savings-bank life insurance which an individual can buy. In 1927 they proposed a $2,000 limit, but the Legislature threw their bill out. A $5,000 limit was proposed in 1929, and when the Legislature seemed uninterested this was raised to $10,000, but the schemes were rejected. In 1930 the insurance interests again tried a $5,000 limit and again the General Court said no.

In 1938, as a provision of its law, New York set a $3,000 limit. Immediately a similar proposal was introduced in Massachusetts and referred to a special Recess Commission which held public hearings on all phases of the long smoldering controversy. Justice Brandeis was consulted as to ways and means for combating the attack. "I am glad you wrote me," he replied to Clyde S. Casady, executive vice-president of the Massachusetts Savings-Bank Life Insurance Council, April 16, 1938. "Throughout the long years when the companies sought to suppress or curb Savings-Bank Life Insurance by legislation, their record of failure was unbroken; and we rose from each struggle strengthened. I trust the 1938 experience will be no different. But we must do everything possible to make impressive the victory for which we hope. We have made friends and all should have the opportunity of showing that they value our work."

After months of study the Massachusetts Commission issued a comprehensive report rejecting the proposal.

The insurance companies' determination to block savings-bank life insurance is still unabated, although in 1939, after exhaustive hearings, the Temporary National Economic Committee [35] reported that "industrial insurance continues to exhibit the same inherent evils. . . . In fact the situation has not radically changed since 1905." [36] The same report in turn applauded "safe, low-cost" savings-bank insurance. "It has been pre-eminently successful in serving its purpose," [37] the T.N.E.C. concluded. The average net cost is today about one-fourth less than that of "ordinary" commercial insurance and about 50 per cent less than weekly premium "industrial" policies.*

* Not only was cost less, but income from invested funds was greater. Judd Dewey told the T.N.E.C. in 1939 why this was so: "A perfectly natural reason is that the trustees of savings banks, say, the little Whitman Savings Bank with assets of five or six million and with premium income of a few hundred thousand, can do a better job investing that sum of money than anybody can do with two or three or four million a day. . . . They can devote more time and attention to the particular investments; they can make sure of the quality of them. . . . The persons in that savings bank who consider the application, in a great majority of cases, will know the man applying for the mortgage; they will know what kind of person

"Also of importance," the T.N.E.C. observed, "is the fact that the savings banks experience a very low lapse rate. . . . In 1936 industrial lapsed 34.52 per cent; ordinary, 29.9 per cent; and savings banks, 1.25 per cent." [38]

Savings-banks insurance has proved its worth so abundantly that one may well wonder why more wage-earners have not taken advantage of it, why no other states, except New York in 1938, and Connecticut in 1941, have seen fit to adopt the system.* There are of course many answers. Probably the most important was supplied by the T.N.E.C. in 1939: "In Massachusetts, savings-bank life insurance has met constant opposition from insurance agents. Both the Association of Life Insurance Presidents and the Life Underwriters Association have vigorously combated savings-bank insurance bills when introduced in other states."

Brandeis himself told what happened to an officer of one of the largest national banks in Boston who merely was seen in public one day with supporters of savings-bank life insurance like George Wigglesworth, James L. Richards, Charles H. Jones, Lincoln Filene, and other leading citizens. A few days later a life insurance executive asked him whether he favored savings-bank life insurance, to which he replied in the affirmative. Within a few hours the insurance company withdrew deposits of about $2,000,000 from the bank. The bank officer did not at once withdraw his support from savings-bank insurance, but within a few days he had to do so, because several life insurance companies were taking steps to compel so many resignations from his board of directors that he would have to rebuild his bank. The situation became so disturbing that friends of savings-bank life insurance advised this man to withdraw his public approval in order that he might avert such changes in his bank as would disturb public confidence and react unfavorably upon the bank itself. [39]

Savings-banks life insurance continues to play its part as alternative to the agency system, as the competitive yardstick, the object lesson showing

he is; they will go and look at his house, they know whether he pays his bills or keeps his cellar clean; they know what kind of person they are dealing with." (Hearings before the Temporary National Economic Committee, "Investigation of Concentration of Economic Power," 76th Cong., 1st Sess., Part 10, pp. 4475–76.)

* One reason for slow progress is that until recent years those who led the fight in Massachusetts did not encourage other states to follow. When, on March 2, 1910, Senator G. L. Meade of New York consulted Brandeis as to introducing a bill, Brandeis advised that such effort be postponed until "an effective campaign of education should be undertaken."

Again, on December 20, 1911, Brandeis wrote S. H. Wolfe: "I have not myself urged the adoption in other states because I felt that the movement might develop most satisfactorily in the long run if we in Massachusetts who inaugurated the movement should work it out to a practical success with perfected methods and machinery before it should be taken up by those who might not fully appreciate the spirit, who lack the practical experience which comes with surmounting the difficulties which necessarily arise from time to time in the early stages of any pioneer institution."

what wage-earners' insurance should be and should cost. But when Brandeis rated this service as his "greatest achievement," he had something in mind other than the economic betterment resulting, great as this is. He saw in the system *moral* advantages of greater significance than the workers' cash savings. "What we want," he had told Judge Reed early in the struggle, "is to have the workingman free; not to have him the beneficiary of a benevolent employer [or a benevolent state], and freedom demands a development in employees of that self-control which results in thrift and in adequate provision for the future."

Savings-bank insurance fortified that kind of freedom and gave Brandeis's favorite "little fellows" the opportunity to participate in, to share responsibility for, matters involving their own well-being. Thus the addition of the insurance function to local savings banks not only served as a safeguard against money-power "bigness," but also created in "small men" that vital sense of contributing to the success of something that transcends the bounds of self.

Brandeis felt deeply that "what America needs is not that we do anything for these our fellow-citizens, but that we keep open the path of opportunity to enable them to do for themselves." [40]

Savings-bank life insurance is a concrete symbol of his creed.

CHAPTER TWELVE

The New Haven Railway Building an Empire, 1905-1909

So far Brandeis, both as lawyer and as citizen, had dealt with great financial empires: the huge traction interests, their cousins in the local utility field—the gas-electric groups—and finally the insurance interests whose assets ran into billions. Indeed, Brandeis had engaged these opponents almost simultaneously. But there were still bigger foes ahead, and biggest of all was J. P. Morgan, Sr., although Brandeis never really tangled with

Morgan personally. In the New Haven Railway contests he fought with the New Haven's president, Charles Sanger Mellen, and, as Mellen himself admitted, Morgan had "had the directors elect me." [1]

Brandeis's encounters with Mellen began as indirectly as most of his fights, and more mildly than usual, in 1905. It wasn't until 1907, however, that the two actually locked horns, and it wasn't until one warm May day in 1913 that Mellen inadvertently let out of the bag exactly what he thought the fight was about.

That day, in a crowded courtroom in Boston, Mellen was telling the story of the New Haven's merger with the Boston & Maine Railroad. "May I stand up?" Mellen asked. "I'd rather." The tall, spare man behind the desk agreed that he might. For three hours President Mellen stood up, walked around, or leaned on Interstate Commerce Commissioner Charles A. Prouty's desk, explaining—explaining miraculous achievements in railroad expansion, grandiose projects of corporate finance, fantastic transactions running into astronomical figures. Then came the dramatic conclusion. This merger, Mellen declared, "gives the New Haven absolute control of the rate situation in New England, as far West as Duluth, Chicago, Milwaukee, and all intermediate rate-making points, and it will enable the New Haven to be absolutely independent during the season of navigation of any other connection in the naming of such rates."

Mellen's attorney, Charles F. Choate, Jr., was shocked that the New Haven's monopolistic purpose should be exposed so bluntly: "You mean the control as with reference to business outside of New England? You mean you could get your share of through business without being subjected to their dictation?" But Mellen could not be stopped. "I don't know that I care so much," he replied, "for the enormous business that might be brought to us, as I do for the regulation of the rates on which we should do the business." [2]

It was to block this monopolistic purpose that Brandeis had declared war on the New Haven in 1905. By 1913 it looked as if he had been defeated, that Mellen—and New York—had wrested "absolute control." There was still one battle left, however, and this Brandeis won. The New Haven never recovered from it.

But that is far ahead of our story. Let's start at the beginning.

In the year 1874 the Massachusetts Legislature passed a law forbidding railroads, unless expressly authorized by the Legislature, to hold "directly or indirectly" the stock of another corporation. In 1905 the Boston & Maine Railroad had a bill introduced in the Legislature permitting it to acquire street railways. The B & M people pointed out in support that they were simply trying to get legislative sanction for what the New Haven was actually doing—and in defiance of the law of 1874. The New Haven, through holding companies, had thus acquired about one-third of Massachusetts street railway mileage.

To Brandeis and to his friends in the Legislature the B & M bill seemed an attempt to make two wrongs a right—an attempt to legalize wrongs done by the New Haven, so that the B & M could legally do the same. Therefore, in an address on April 19, 1905, at what the *Boston Globe* described as "one of the longest sessions ever held by the Massachusetts State Board of Trade," Brandeis denounced the B & M measure, and the Legislature rejected it. Left unsettled was the question of the legality of the New Haven's prior acquisitions. As the *Boston Post* queried: Now that the New Haven has demonstrated how "to drive the devil around the stump" by resort to holding companies, what is to prevent Massachusetts corporations from evading the law of 1874 by the same device? Discussion of the B & M proposal had reopened the basic matter of principle—"Whether it is yet desirable," as Brandeis put it, "to allow such a combination of railways as will put the transportation business of the state virtually under monopolistic control." [3]

ABSORBING THE BOSTON & MAINE

In response to public demand Governor Guild sent a special message to the Legislature on June 23, 1906, urging legislation to clarify the entire transportation situation. He said: "Slowly, surely, the control of our own railroads, the control of the passage to market of every Massachusetts product, the control of the transportation to and from his work of every Massachusetts citizen is passing from our hands to those of aliens. . . . Let Massachusetts announce that transportation within her borders is in the future to be controlled by the people of Massachusetts, and not by men beyond the reach of her law and the inspiration of her ideals."

Nothing happened; indeed, things got worse rather than better. The New Haven, far from divesting itself of Massachusetts Street Railways, was actually acquiring a controlling interest in the B & M itself.[4] When rumors of this reached Governor Guild, he asked Mellen for a statement of intentions. Mellen simply replied: "Interests identified with my company have acquired a large stock interest in the Boston and Maine Railroad." Such "interests" had in fact stealthily acquired more than one-third of B & M stock.

This was tantamount to a merger; but Mellen's opponents contended that the New Haven's purchases required legislative sanction. Certain large stockholders of the B & M, led by General Samuel C. Lawrence and his son William, retained Brandeis as counsel to fight the merger. Brandeis explained why, once again, he worked without a fee.

When Mr. Lawrence came in to get me to act as counsel for him in the matter of the Boston and Maine merger, he intended to retain me in the ordinary manner, and has undoubtedly supposed that I would make charges to him as in any professional matter.

I feel, however, that this being a matter of great public interest in which I am undertaking to influence the opinion of others, I do not want to accept any compensation for my services.

Under the peculiar circumstances of the retainer, I do not think that my partners and others interested in the profits of the firm [Brandeis, Dunbar & Nutter] ought to be affected by my own feeling in this matter, and I therefore wish to substitute myself as the client of the firm in this matter so far as charges for my own services are concerned.[5]

Under this arrangement Brandeis, in six years, actually paid his own firm $25,167.32 for services in connection with the merger controversy.[6]

As his first step, in June 1907, Brandeis prepared a sweeping anti-merger bill, making it a penal offense for the New Haven to acquire any more B & M stock, and, further, requiring disposal of all its B & M holdings before April 1, 1908. "I have endeavored to draft an act," he explained optimistically, "so clear in its terms that it would not need the interpretation of the highest court in the state to tell what it means, so that even Mr. Mellen and his counsel might not be in doubt as to what it means."[7] Addressing the legislative committee, Brandeis spoke of the merger as "the most important economic question that has come before the Legislature in a generation. There is for a community," he said, "a general limit where efficiency can be reached by consolidation. To that point I am in favor of it, but I am now, and always have been, directly opposed to distinct monopoly. The matter we are considering is an attempt to consolidate the entire railroad transportation of the country." He denied the value to the country of the consolidation even under "proper safeguards." "I do not believe," he said, "it is possible to create a power strong enough to 'properly safeguard' it."[8]

Mellen himself testified before the same body, June 11, 1907, in the imperial manner of the man who held New England's "traffic destinies within his grasp."[9] Interests identified with the New Haven corporation, he explained, made the B & M purchase, but "I do not want to spin any nice technical threads about it. . . . The way it has been done is immaterial. The corporation stands here before the committee, to all intents and purposes, as if it had done it itself. I do not dodge one bit. I defy any man to show that I have not kept my pledges to the State." [10]

One inquisitor asked whether he had read the Brandeis bill. "I have," Mellen replied. "I could see but one objection to it—it wasn't strong enough. I would amend the bill by requiring the New Haven road to sell the stock and prohibit anyone from buying it. . . . And I'd put anybody in prison who discussed the subject." [11]

As the day's hearing was about to close, Brandeis broke in, "I would like to ask a few questions."

"Of course," said the committee's chairman, but promptly added, "You don't have to answer Mr. Brandeis unless you desire to, Mr. Mellen. Nobody is compelled to answer questions." Mellen took the cue, saying that he would not give ammunition to the enemy.

"Then, Mr. Chairman," Brandeis coolly suggested, "if Mr. Mellen will not answer any questions, I would like to have him present while I make certain statements." Whereupon Mellen ran for the door, saying, as the crowd made way for him, "I will read your questions in the newspapers in the morning, if you please." [12]

Telling Mark Sullivan of this episode some months later, Brandeis remarked: "It was really very fortunate for our side, and very effective; in fact, he [Mellen] had sort of mesmerized the people, and I had had grave doubts as to whether I should not be the sufferer from cross-examining him." [13]

Despite Mellen's hasty exit, the House killed Brandeis's bill, and passed a last-minute measure, introduced by Speaker John N. Cole, which allowed New Haven to hold its B & M stock until July 1, 1908.

In a full-page interview in the *Boston American*, Brandeis strenuously opposed the Cole act. "It is not," he said, "a question merely of monopoly in railroads but monopoly of the whole transportation system. . . . No system of regulation can safely be substituted for the operation of individual liberty as expressed in competition. It would be like attempting to substitute a regulated monarchy for our republic. Human nature is such that monopolies, however well intentioned, and however well regulated, inevitably become, in course of time, oppressive, arbitrary, unprogressive, and inefficient." [14]

But no one listened. The New Haven's prestige was at its height, and Mellen considered the issue closed. "The road is freer today from attack than at any time in its history," he declared, October 30, 1907, "except the possibility of government attack, to which every railroad in the country is now subject." [15] And he was right. Municipal Corporation Counsel Thomas Babson, speaking for Mayor Fitzgerald, ruled that the merger was legal. The Boston Merchants' Association, through its representative, Jerome Jones, asked only that "Boston" be not removed from the Boston & Maine cars. Even Governor Guild accepted the consolidation. Like many others, he had come to think that "merger was inevitable." [16] After seeing the Governor, Mellen told a friend: "I did the best day's business yesterday that I ever did. I had an hour and a half talk with the Governor, and I am not only going to overcome the objection to the merger, but I am going to get the seal of the Commonwealth on it." [17]

FACTS AS AMMUNITION

Mellen had underrated the persistence of the "chronic howler," as Brandeis came to be called by his enemies. "I had a chance for the mayoralty," the anti-merger leader wrote Alfred, October 19, 1907. "The Republican City Committee and the Good Government Association jointly requested me to make the run. . . . I concluded that on the whole it was best to decline. I have the merger on hand—and shouldn't like to have that job interfered with. . . . My course in knocking heads right and left is not exactly such as to create an 'available' candidate."

The reader knows by now how Brandeis would go about killing the "merger job." Step one: Get the facts. And it was at this time that he "began to be filled with doubt as to the financial condition of the New Haven; it had bought so much and there was so much current talk about high prices paid that it seemed . . . that they might be overbought, and that even the rich New Haven could be brought down to a low financial level. . . ." [18]

On October 19, 1907, he also wrote Alfred that "I think, before we get through, the estimable gentlemen who scrambled for the chance of exchanging their B & M stock for New Haven will find that they have been served a gold brick. At the present stage of investigation it looks as if Mellen had gone ahead like other Napoleons of finance—joyously as long as borrowing was easy and that he will run up against a stone wall as soon as his borrowing capacity ends. There are some indications that it has ended (with his stock at 139) and that he is resorting to all kinds of devices to get money. I have not been able to figure out yet from data available what he has done with all the money he raised and should not be at all surprised to find that some had already gone into dividends."

Brandeis eagerly awaited the New Haven's annual report to its stockholders. When it appeared in the fall of 1907, he was very surprised. He knew the company's fixed charges had increased tremendously, yet the report failed to reveal this. The balance sheet listing contingent liabilities did not include certain items which he knew existed. What startled him most was the absence of a full statement of resources—a conspicuous departure from accounting practice.

To fill in gaps in the company's report, he wrote the Statistical Department of Moody's Corporation for details about assets, liabilities, profits, and losses of known New Haven subsidiaries, such as the New England Investment and Securities Company, the Springfield Railways, and the Providence Securities Company. Moody's replied that the New Haven had refused to supply the information requested. Brandeis then turned to the Massachusetts Board of Railroad Commissioners, but with no more success. To Board Chairman James F. Jackson he wrote on October 19, 1907: "One might study the report filed with your board from end to end and never know that the New Haven held any interest in the Boston & Maine railroad stock, or in the Rhode Island Railway System, or in any of the Massachusetts Street Railways controlled by the New England Investment Security Company."

Jackson sent Brandeis's comment to Mellen. Mellen replied: "Quite probably the foregoing does not cover all the information that certain parties are desirous of obtaining through the agency of your commission, so anticipating further inquiries, I beg to state that the 109,948 shares of Boston and Maine stock which are owned in the interest of our company were on June 30, 1907, at the time of filing this report, in the treasury of the New England Navigation Company which was at that time the owner of the same."

Brandeis thereupon suggested to Mellen on November 18, 1907: "As it appears to me important that the exact facts in regard to the financial condition and operations of these companies should be laid before the Massachusetts Commission on Commerce and Industry and others considering this so-called merger question, I respectfully request that you furnish me copies of the financial reports of the companies above named."

Mellen replied with characteristic bluntness on November 19: "Before deciding whether or no I should comply with your request for information, it would seem to me proper that I should have some knowledge of whom you represent in this matter and the purpose to which the information is to be put."

Brandeis countered on November 20: "In making the application to you I represent only myself, but I am co-operating with others who like myself believe that the proposed merger of the Boston and Maine and the New Haven system would be a calamity to the Commonwealth, and for that reason are endeavoring to prevent it. In making this effort to prevent a merger, I am acting as a citizen and not in a professional capacity. . . .

"The purpose to which the information is to be put is this: It is of the utmost importance that the people of Massachusetts and of other states who are called upon to determine whether the merger shall be permitted should have accurate information concerning the financial and other facts bearing upon the question. The reports of the New York, New Haven and Hartford Railroad issued to stockholders, and those filed with the Massachusetts Railroad Commissioners and the Interstate Commerce Commission all fail to disclose fully the facts bearing upon the financial condition, investments, and operations of your company."

In his reply of the same day Mellen also declared himself: "My company has no intention of seeking any legislation whatever to permit a merger of the Boston and Maine and the New Haven Railroads. I do not and none of my directors desire such a merger unless it is the expression of public opinion that such a measure is wise public policy. The request should come from the representatives of the public, rather than from the company with which I am connected." Mellen then called an abrupt halt: "I have furnished all proper information sought by any public authority, and I shall always do so, but I do not think it necessary to supply materials to advocates of either side of this question."

Public agitation had already begun to fret the New Haven president. Speaking before the National Grange, November 13, 1907, he likened the attack on corporations to a drunken man's debauch; he condemned "brass band methods," and charged that the anti-merger investigation of his road was instigated by stock gamblers for purposes of blackmail.[19]

Brandeis had to get along as best he could without Mellen's help. He got along well, too: "Pretty soon I got the Railroad Commissioners' [of Massachusetts] reports and later I got from Washington the Interstate Commerce Commission's report and some others, and it became perfectly clear to me that Mellen was putting out reports for the purpose of misleading the public and the stockholders as to the New Haven's condition. Then I worked this thing up and continued working it up and with this result: I found that the New Haven didn't earn the dividend which it paid last year."[20] That was good enough for a start.

Late in December 1907 Brandeis published an impressive pamphlet, suggestive in format and appearance of the annual reports of large railroad companies, entitled "Financial Condition of the New York, New Haven & Hartford Railroad and of the Boston & Maine Railroad." In a talk with the *Boston Journal*, January 8, 1908, he stated the reasons for the pamphlet:

A year ago I appeared before the legislative committee in opposition to the expansion policy of Mr. Mellen, and his associates, in connection with the absorption of the trolley lines, as I felt that the methods being pursued were dangerous. . . .

After that fight had been temporarily settled, I resolved upon making a full and thorough investigation of the whole business in its every phase. . . . I entered the investigation—an investigation that has consumed several months of diligent effort, and that has likewise encountered obstacles that at times seemed to be well-nigh insurmountable. I have, however, kept steadily at work, and I believe that the statement which I have completed, and which I intend shall be placed in the hands of legislators, and given also as wide a distribution as possible among the stock and bondholders of the two roads, is absolutely correct, so far as its figures are concerned. And the deductions therefrom are the only reasonable and proper ones that can be made. Although in a sense an analysis of this sort is necessarily technical, and intended primarily for financial and railroad men, the facts given are so clear that its chief points can be readily understood by anyone, and I am satisfied that they will carry weight with any unprejudiced man who studies them.

Brandeis's chief point in his pamphlet was that the New Haven's "change from financial strength to weakness has been accomplished in an extraordinarily short period of time; the published reports of the company have been so framed as not to disclose its real condition." For example, Brandeis could find no provision for maintenance. On the other hand, he found the ordinary expenditure of about ten million dollars for rolling stock, repairs, etc., charged not to operating expenses in the regular way but to profit and loss. If the amount had been charged in the conventional way, he pointed out, the New Haven would have fallen $1,171,550.82 short of paying its 8 per cent dividend.

Brandeis turned next to the Boston & Maine—improvement of which had been the main argument in favor of the merger. But Brandeis stated bluntly that instead of the Boston & Maine needing financial assistance from the New Haven, the reverse was true. The pamphlet fired its heaviest shot last: "If the New Haven's solvency is to be maintained, A LARGE REDUCTION IN THE DIVIDEND RATE IS INEVITABLE."

SMOKING OUT THE MERGERITES

New Haven officials, asserting that the Brandeis pamphlet would "fall by the weight of its own falsities and half truths," declined even to discuss it. The Boston News Bureau branded it as "one almost continuous and unbroken string of errors, misstatements and fabrications"; to consider its facts and figures seriously would be a "useless waste of time."

Throughout New England the New Haven had been regarded as the Gibraltar of Yankee financial strength. It had paid dividends of 8 per cent or more since 1872. It was the trust investment of New England, carried in the portfolios of countless estates, of schools and colleges and universities, widows and orphans. Yet here was a Boston lawyer, untrained in accountancy, who had never had, as one banker declared, "any business experience, particularly in railroading," who dared to question the judgment of J. P. Morgan, Charles S. Mellen, William Rockefeller, Nathaniel Thayer, and George F. Baker—all "pre-eminently successful" men who had made "enviable marks in the business world." [21] Without taking sides the *Boston Traveler,* January 8, 1908, had this to say: "It is a curious commentary on financial skill and official astuteness that a lawyer who says he is not working for a fee and strictly *pro bono publico* should succeed where they failed."

The *Springfield Republican,* hitherto one of Brandeis's stanch supporters, seemed somewhat uncertain on this subject on January 8:

If this examination of the New Haven's finances does grave injustice to the company, Mr. Mellen and his board of directors have only themselves to blame, for they have so deeply hidden the facts of the company's situation in subsidiary enterprises and companies and associations as to compel resort to inferences where no room should have been left to infer anything.

The most lurid comment had come from the *Boston Herald* on December 20, 1907:

The merger has got into Mr. Brandeis' head again, and it rouses his stern soul. He sees the state destroyed, the republic gasping its last breath, and humankind swept from the starry watches of the night, all humankind save Brandeis, who, bestriding New England like a colossus, exudes righteousness and brave texts over a desert world. . . .

In him Pure Patriotism sings. Undaunted and alone he defies Octopus and Malefactor alike. Memory hath its portraits of him. Behold him, in the right-hand gallery, with bared breast, a charter member of the Public Franchise League. Under the central dome, where the limelight plays tenderly, perceive him supporting the holy right of savings banks to adventure in life insurance while their ungrateful officers stand around the pedestal and make faces. Wherever you look you behold Brandeis wrestling with the oppressor. His conscience and his mind alike are sleepless. He lies awake at night devising new engines for the death of wrong. . . .

There is promise of a new heaven and a new earth—but alas, not of a new Brandeis.

The pamphlet "has created quite a stir," Brandeis wrote Alfred, January 2, 1908. "The New Haven people have supported the stock and I am told their bankers advise them not to answer it. If they don't Mellen is doomed —and I don't believe they can. Nothing but a miracle of good times could make their way smooth. . . . I have made a larger camp of enemies than in all my previous fights together, but I think I have also made a large break in the serried ranks of the merger phalanx. The policy of silence under such attacks won't work nowadays in our community and they are still afraid to come out in debate."

On February 10 he wrote Alfred again: "I think the company is educating the public now to a reduction of dividend. I should not be surprised to see its March 31 dividend 1 per cent instead of 2 per cent. But, perhaps, they will persist rather than have my prediction verified. The fight goes merrily on."

When Mellen was invited, as New Haven's head, to address a meeting of the Boston Fruit and Produce Exchange, where Brandeis also was to speak, he declined. "If I were to do so," he explained, "it might be urged, and with some show of reason, that the matter is one of great importance to myself and my company, which is far from being the fact; . . . I do not care to agitate the matter in any way." [22]

But Brandeis did care to agitate the matter. In fact, he liked nothing better. He arranged to speak to organizations all over the state, including the Boston City Club, the Boston Credit Men's Association, the New England Dry Goods Association, the Sheet Metal Workers' Union, the Boston Art Club, the Economic Club, and many others. He told the secretaries of each organization how crucial the merger issue was and named New Haven officials who might be invited to oppose him in debate. When they refused to be smoked out, Brandeis attacked their secrecy. He had felt all along "that the only thing to do was to make public opinion by letting people hear and reason out the arguments in reference to the merger. . . . The New Haven evidently recognized the force and strength [of] that argument . . . and set upon the deliberate purpose of not having any discussion." [23]

To crystallize popular sentiment, Brandeis again resorted to organized action and helped form, in December 1907, the Massachusetts Anti-Merger League, an organization modeled on the Savings-Bank Insurance League —in fact, "practically the same outfit." Writing Alfred of the League's activities, Brandeis commented, February 16, 1908: "We are at least harrying the enemy. They take it out on me when they can, publicly and privately, but I am used to that."

Leading the attack on Brandeis and his followers was a brand-new Business Men's Merger League, formed in January 1908. "Just why," Brandeis commented sarcastically, "thirty-eight businessmen of Boston and other cities of the Commonwealth have banded together to form what they have been pleased to style 'The Business Men's Merger League' which they brought into being at the Exchange Club, is revealed by a short glance into their commercial and family relations."

The situation favored Mellen in January 1908 when Governor Guild, in his address to the Legislature, declared himself in favor of "some union of railroad interests, provided adequate safeguards for protecting the public are made." The New Haven's program at this time also had the backing of Wall Street operators, railroad experts, and college professors, including William Z. Ripley and Bruce Wyman of Harvard and Jacob Gould Schurman, president of Cornell. "We have got to have a monopoly," declared Professor Ripley, "or we cannot have service." "Monopoly is inevitable," said Schurman, and "the only way of dealing with it is by sane and effective regulation."

THE MERGERITES OFFICIALLY VINDICATED

The New Haven, the Business Men's Merger League, and other Brandeis opponents were rescued in March 1908 by the state government. Although none of them could answer Brandeis's pamphlet or the speeches he based thereon, the Massachusetts Commission on Commerce and Industry published its own report on the merger that seemed to vindicate the New Haven at every point.

This report has its own little history. At the end of the 1907 legislative session Governor Guild had quietly referred the merger question to this official body and on July 25 had written Chairman Charles Francis Adams (1835–1915): "It is my earnest request that even if it be the only topic treated in your report, the best policy to be adopted by the Commonwealth in regard to transportation should be considered and investigated."

On November 22 Brandeis appeared before the Commission, but it turned out to be merely a private conference with subcommittee members Joseph B. Warner, George G. Crocker, and Charles Francis Adams. Brandeis instructed them, saying: "To put yourselves in a position to justify you in making an official recommendation requires, in the first place, a thorough examination into the finances and operations of the New Haven Company. That investigation, in view of the way in which the accounts have been kept, and in which information has been withheld from the public, and been handed to the public in a misleading form, cannot be made except by a body which has the power of enforcing attendance of witnesses, the compelling of answers, and the production of documents. . . . The broad question whether we shall have monopoly or not, independently of the question of government ownership as a desirable thing, is something that the public is entitled to decide. It is in a high degree a political question in the best sense of the word 'political.' I believe that public discussion is fundamental. . . ." [24]

But the Commission continued to work behind a smoke screen, and on November 27 Brandeis wrote Warner: "As I stated to your Commission, I requested Mr. Mellen to appear at the hearing in order that your Commission might have the benefit of any denials or criticisms which he might make of my statements. Unfortunately, Mr. Mellen did not avail himself of this opportunity and I therefore venture to request your committee to permit me to see any statement of Mr. Mellen on this general subject."

When his request was declined, he kept in touch with the Commission's doings through Garrett Droppers, its secretary. [25]

The Commission's report was a thoroughgoing vindication of the New Haven's entire consolidation policy. Through economies in administration and by easier exchange of freight, the report said, the merged New Haven and Boston & Maine would give New England a strong, unified railroad system. The Commissioners thought the legality of the New Haven's purchase of B & M stock debatable but irrelevant: "It is to be remembered that if the company has acted unlawfully, it is not to be punished by compelling it to undo the unlawful act unless it is for the interest of the state to have it undone—otherwise we should be punishing the state itself." [26]

Hearst's *Boston American* suspected the Commission's too solid endorsement and began at once to investigate the investigators. It identified Warner as an owner of some New Haven stock and as attorney for H. L. Higginson, whose firm had sold B & M stock to the New Haven. It forced Crocker, a well-known politician and lawyer, to admit he owned a "few hundred shares of New Haven." It showed that Chairman Adams also held New Haven stock, as did Harvard College, of which he was treasurer.

Two Commissioners, not members of the subcommittee, issued dissenting reports. That of former Governor William L. Douglas, representative of business on the Commission, had a most Brandeisian tone. "I am convinced," Douglas said, "that this merger would strengthen the power of special privilege in this Commonwealth. . . . I am certain that it would place the people of this Commonwealth in a position of servility to a foreign corporation. . . ." James R. Crozier, the Commission's labor representative, declared that capitalists, corporation lawyers, and public service corporation personnel were heard eagerly by the Commission but that it did not listen to a single representative of organized labor or of salaried employees and heard only a few merchants and manufacturers.

Mellen, of course, considered only the majority report, and that as final.

On March 20 a letter written by him to Governor Guild was published in part by the *Boston News Bureau:*

The financial condition of the New Haven and wisdom of its expansion policy would seem to have been sufficiently passed upon to be no longer a subject of serious doubt or comment.

Brandeis kept up the fight. On April 12 the *Lawrence Leader* congratulated him:

If the fight against the New York, New Haven & Hartford "grabbing" of the Boston & Maine proves successful, not a small share of the honors will fall to Louis D. Brandeis, Esq., of Boston, whose campaign has been a remarkable one. Day after day, before committees of the Legislature, commercial bodies, meetings of all kinds, wherever he can get a hearing, Mr. Brandeis is spreading his anti-merger doctrines and administering staggering blows to the New Haven interests.

On the whole, though, Mellen was pleased. The Cole Act would automatically lapse July 1, 1908, and unless restrictive legislation were enacted before then, the New Haven would be free to press its aggrandizement. To be sure this would be so, the New Haven's counsel, Charles F. Choate, Jr., submitted a bill to the Legislature on May 2, authorizing the New Haven to hold and vote its B & M stock indefinitely and to acquire at its discretion additional stock and securities. And although the legality of the New Haven's trolley purchases was still under fire in Massachusetts courts, eminent counsel assured the New Haven management that no danger need be feared from that quarter.

IN THE TOILS OF THE LAW

Eminent counsel turned out to be wrong. The fight took a new and aggressive turn, and within a week the New Haven's situation was not quite so bright. On May 8 the Massachusetts Supreme Court unanimously sustained the interlocutory decree handed down by Judge Arthur Prentice Rugg, which required the New Haven to dispose of its trolley lines.

Brandeis at once made the implications plain: "The prompt and unanimous declaration by the Supreme Court that the New Haven's acquisition of stock in trolley corporations is a violation of our law . . . absolutely decides, also, that the acquisition and holding of the Boston & Maine stock by the New Haven is a violation of the Massachusetts law. This decision has completely changed the position of the parties in the merger controversy. Up to the present, the New Haven and its supporters have been saying to the anti-merger men, 'What are you going to do about it?' It seems to us now that the New Haven and its friends are called upon to say what they will do about it." [27]

Capitalizing further on the decision, Brandeis wrote Henry J. Skeffington, May 13: "It seems to me that this is the opportunity of the Democratic party. Let it come out now, not merely as an anti-monopoly party, but as a party which stands for the enforcement of the laws against the rich as well as against the poor, and let them write upon their banner that they stand for equal enforcement of the law."

Next day Brandeis sent a seven-page letter to President Eliot of Harvard, reviewing the merger controversy and stressing that the Supreme Court's decision of May 8 had "transferred the merger question from the sphere of economics to that of morals and good citizenship."

On May 17 the *Boston Post* concurred in a ringing editorial, DON'T CONDONE THE CRIME, of which Brandeis owned authorship. The editorial ended:

> *Defiance of Massachusetts law by a great corporation should not be condoned. The New Haven road has been convicted by the Supreme Court of the essential theft of the trolleys and the Boston & Maine stock. To permit the New Haven road to retain the stolen goods on any pretense whatever is to encourage lawlessness and invite anarchy. . . .*

Mellen was "never more surprised in his life than by the adverse decision," [28] and he had more surprises coming. On May 19 the full and favorable report of the Commission on Commerce and Industry was discredited when the Legislature's Railroad Committee produced a letter of February 2 from Choate to Joseph B. Warner, a member of the Commission, making suggestions which were practically identical with the recommendations in the Commission report.[29]

Mellen's political and legal woes were severely aggravated by the New Haven's financial condition, which was steadily growing worse. "I suppose you noticed the March 31 statement of the New Haven," Brandeis wrote his brother, May 3, 1908. "It shows for the nine months over $2,700,000 deficit after paying dividends—and it does not show all the deficit there is. The July 1 dividend will give them some thinking; i.e., whether to reduce or not and if so how much. . . . What they ought to do is pass it altogether but that would bring disaster."

In the midst of these accumulating problems Choate's bill sanctioning the merger was ready for Railroad Committee action. "The army of the merger is camped in State House Park," the *Boston American* had observed on April 30. "You can almost see the tents. Turned down by the people, slammed by the Supreme Court of the Commonwealth, the mergerites have drawn on their last hope—the lobby. The lobby is at work."

Of equal importance in mergerite strategy was smearing Brandeis. Joseph B. Warner pictured him as a secret emissary of E. H. Harriman, who sought to get the B & M stock for himself. But the accusation backfired. The *Transcript* on May 23 observed caustically: "It would have been suicidal for him to permit representatives of his office to go about openly and above board collecting proxies for Mr. Harriman, as they have done. No critic of Mr. Brandeis has ever yet charged him with being a fool. . . ."

"You needn't worry," the anti-merger leader reassured Alfred, "I have not suffered in mind or body, and the only effect upon my estate is to leave me more time to pound the enemy. No amount of pounding of me can, however, increase the New Haven's earnings and I think their follies will bring them to book in due time."

Since sincere men were honestly puzzled by Brandeis's tactics, E. A. Filene at this time prepared an article in which he explained:

If a man were to give $50,000 a year for some public cause, and many of our men do give such an amount, or a larger one, that would not create astonishment. If Mr. Brandeis gives, as he does give, his professional services for a cause which he believes he ought to assist in the public interest, the action is yet so uncommon as to lend itself to the arousing of suspicion of his motives, even as all uncommon things may be so used.[30]

George W. Wigglesworth, an old friend, on reading Filene's article, wrote a friendly word to Brandeis on May 24: "It seems to me he [Filene] expressed what every right-minded person must feel. At such a time it cannot be amiss to say frankly what one feels and I want to say that the public spirit and generous devotion which your life so well exemplifies makes the lives of many of us seem despicably mean, sordid, and narrow. For its own sake I hope the community will appreciate as it should the example you have set us."

Meantime the fight went on. "Last week," Brandeis wrote Alfred on May 18, "was a very busy one on merger. The New Haven forces are fighting for their lives, fighting more vigorously than ever, and have injected several new perils into the situation. . . . The hearings before the [Railroad] committee closed Friday and that body is pondering over their report. . . . The New Haven put up a fine array of witnesses; but I still think we shall whip them."

The *East Boston Free Press* thought so too. On May 23, 1908, it commented:

Mr. Brandeis is giving Charles F. Choate, Jr., the biggest fight he ever had and Choate's ingenuity is taxed to the utmost to find ways of stopping the various moves that are made so skillfully and rapidly that everyone is dazzled with the brilliancy with which the anti-merger general builds up his case and tears down the structure that Mr. Choate so skillfully and laboriously builds.

Nevertheless, the Railroad Committee reported favorably on the New Haven's bill which would allow the company to hold its B & M stock until July 1, 1910. This postponed the final issue for two years, giving the New Haven plenty of time to get legislative approval of its illegal acquisitions.

Brandeis suggested an opposing bill of his own, which specifically required the New Haven to sell, or otherwise dispose of, its B & M stock, whether held directly or indirectly, before January 1, 1910. His bill also enjoined stock control of any other concern. "Would you at any future time consider the merging of these two roads?" inquired Representative O'Connell. "Deal today with what you know today," Brandeis replied. "You know today that you ought not to condone the offense against the state law. If in the future it is shown to be advantageous for the state to allow the New Haven to hold the stock of the Boston & Maine, then you or your successors can authorize the New Haven to take it."

The New Haven bill passed the Senate, 17 to 4, but the anti-mergerites had succeeded in holding it up long enough to consolidate their strength in the House, where, under the leadership of Representative Norman H. White, they were in command of the situation and won an amendment incorporating the essence of the Brandeis bill. Instead of being allowed to hold the stock until July 1, 1910, the New Haven would be required to sell it before that date.

Brandeis was jubilant. "We got the New Haven in a beautiful fix," he wrote his brother, June 4, 1908. "Either . . . our House bill, or no bill would put them in a hole. Each course had advantages for us. We could calmly sit by and poke the animals and let Nature take its course. I think nothing remains now but to bury the corpse. . . . I had expected two years of agony for the New Haven, or of labor for us. But death came quickly as a relief to all."

Brandeis in triumph told Mark Sullivan, June 16, 1908: "Our victory is complete. . . . The legislative experts had declared that the combination we were opposing—of corporate interests and financiers, with the large backing of respectability—was invincible, but I think our bitterest opponents will admit that citizen soldiery has a considerable advantage over mercenaries."

For once the leader of "citizen soldiery" had underestimated his opponent.

BILLARD'S MAGIC WAND TURNS THE TRICK

Early in July 1908 the press noted quite innocently that New Haven's B & M stock, as required by the lapsing Cole Act, had been sold—to one John A. Billard, an obscure coal operator of Meriden, Connecticut.

". . . 110,000 shares have been sold to Mr. Billard, and the stock has been paid for and delivered to him," Mellen commented serenely. "That is all I have to say on the subject, except that Mr. Billard's ownership and control of the stock is absolute." [31]

Brandeis was equally noncombative when he told reporters on July 10: "I have no right to assume that the road has not sold its Boston & Maine shares in good faith. I do not wish to assume that there is any further disposition on the part of the New Haven to defy or evade the Law of the Commonwealth. If anything of that sort is involved in this latest transaction, I have no doubt it will be so much the worse for the road a little later. . . . When the Legislature adjourned without taking any action on the matter, the merger was dead. What the New Haven has been doing since then is to give the thing as decent burial as possible." [32]

Three days later Brandeis was more alert. "I suppose you have read in your metropolitan dailies," he wrote his brother, "that the New Haven has sold its B & M stock—all of it momentarily to one Billard—presumably for a syndicate. That suits me entirely. If it is genuine it is what we want. If it is not genuine, the New Haven must be even more of a fool than I have found the present management. Double dealing again would give us a handle most potent. If they should by this means end the federal suit, they would practically bar themselves from attempting to get even a permissive merger in the future, as long as the anti-trust laws stands, because any such merger would be in the face of an undecided claim by the government that a merger is a violation of the law."

The federal government, through the Anti-Trust Division of the Department of Justice, had also come into the picture. In the spring of 1908 Brandeis had supplied United States District Attorney Asa P. French with the information necessary to start the wheels of justice under the Anti-Trust Act, but Mellen was on exceptionally good terms with the "little White Father," as he called Theodore Roosevelt. Surely T. R. would not now turn a deaf ear to "reason" and sound business judgment." Federal Attorney-General Charles J. Bonaparte, however, filed a petition on May 22 perpetually enjoining the New Haven "from the enjoyment and use of the stock and franchise of interstate trolley lines which it indirectly held and of the Boston & Maine Railroad." On October 2 the government requested that the petition be given "precedence over others and in every way expedited and be assigned for hearing at the earliest practical day." The day hadn't come by January 15, 1909, when the *New York Evening Telegram* reported "a long conference of Louis D. Brandeis with officials of the Interstate Commerce Commission in relation to the New York, New Haven & Hartford absorption of the Boston & Maine."

In January 1909, too, state Attorney-General Malone sought to invoke the 1874 statute requiring revocation of the charters of lawbreaking railroads. Mellen didn't seem to care. "The Attorney-General has expressed his opinion," he said. "Massachusetts, however, as yet has not spoken." [33] Mellen's sudden confidence in Massachusetts became somewhat clearer after he and his vice-president, Timothy Byrnes, emerged from a conference with the new governor, Eben S. Draper. "I have nothing to say," Draper remarked. "Mr. Mellen called as any gentleman may call at any time." Mellen added: "We are just studying that new beatitude—blessed are they that expect nothing, for that's what they'll get." [34]

A truly Oriental mood was coming over these Americans. On April 20 Governor Draper sent this special and peculiarly cryptic message to the Legislature:

> At the present time, there is a large amount of stock in the Boston and Maine railroad which is generally understood to be owned by foreign corporations or by gentlemen who are not citizens of the Commonwealth of Massachusetts. . . . I, therefore, suggest that you consider the advisability of creating a commission which, under such limitations as you prescribe, shall have the right to purchase and hold stock in the Boston and Maine Railroad, giving to any railroad corporation incorporated under the laws of this Commonwealth, if necessary, the power temporarily or otherwise to finance said corporation, and I would suggest that if a charter is granted to such corporation its powers be strictly limited.

Even Brandeis failed to see the plot. "Until some carefully worded message explanatory of his recommendations is forthcoming from the Governor," he told a *Boston Post* reporter, "I fear that I cannot take an intelligent position on either side of the question." [35]

No "carefully worded explanation" came. Instead, on May 13, a carefully worded bill, fully approved, if not drafted, by Mellen's group and embodying Draper's recommendations, was submitted to the Railroad Committee. The bill authorized chartering a holding company for the sole purpose of acquiring the whole or any part of the capital stock and bonds of the B & M.

Brandeis now began to see the light. But he was still optimistic in writing Alfred, May 22: "The merger situation is acute. The Governor's message has been followed by his putting in a merger bill which is pernicious. We had beaten out the New Haven and its 'businessmen' friends; but this new merger proposition with all the power of the gubernatorial position and party whip, is very threatening. . . .

"A just cause and Norman White's strong hold in the House is our only reliance. It looks now as if we should still be able to beat the enemy; and if we do it will be extraordinary, for the press, reptile and otherwise, is also agin us. But I know that our enemies are badly scared—they look it; and we are of good cheer."

Brandeis, having kept his finger on the New Haven's pulse all the while, had the right to feel fairly confident. On Washington's Birthday he had written Alfred from Dedham: "I have just come from studying the New Haven figures for the calendar year 1908. They fully justify my prophecies. . . . The deficit, after paying dividends is, according to their own figures, nearly $4,000,000—i.e., they paid 8 per cent and earned little over 4 per cent. But their figures don't tell all. The equipment depreciation, about $1,500,000, they charged to P. & L., instead of to operating expense, so that their net distributable income (of 1908) was only about 2½ per cent on the stock. The last six months, of course the best in any R.R. year, show a deficit of $1,115,000, after paying the dividend."

A month later, March 20, 1909, he had written again: "For lack of foreign travel, I am amusing myself with the New Haven—a battle again. Their lot is not an easy one . . . They are just now negotiating a $5,000,000 one-year note issue. I had supposed they had money enough to last them until next Fall; but it costs something to pay unearned dividends."

Now the Washington front grew active again. On March 4, 1909, after the new Taft administration had taken office, Attorney-General Bonaparte was succeeded by Wall Street's George W. Wickersham. Two days after Governor Draper's message, the newspapers reported a conference between Wickersham and E. D. Robbins, counsel for the New Haven. "It is understood," the *Transcript* declared on April 23, "that Mr. Robbins asked for a speedy trial of the case or its prompt discontinuance."

It seemed odd that the New Haven, which, up to this point, had thrown every possible obstacle in the path of the federal anti-trust suit, should now ask for a "speedy trial," final action. A clue to what lay back of the New Haven's eagerness is provided when we return to Massachusetts, where all weapons were brought into play to gain command of the state house and push through the Draper holding company bill. The New Haven's supporting argument soon got so badly out of hand that the railroad claimed monopoly as inevitable, as the "manifest destiny" of American business. The *Springfield Republican,* May 1, 1909, remarked:

It [the Draper holding company bill] is the cataleptic merger striving to come forth from its long trance and enter upon the natural life for which we are solemnly assured, from time to time, is its unescapable [sic] destiny. If so, why legislate or worry? Why not let Nature take her course? If all the New England railroads must infallibly be run by one man or set of men, according to the immutable divine decrees, why all this fuss, year after year?

But Mellen was not content to "let Nature take her course." Instead, as the *Pittsfield Journal* of May 24, 1909, reported, he gave a party for the legislators:

The lawmakers were invited to look over Mellen's great estate, Council Grove Farm. They inspected the lakes, the goats, the prize swans, peacocks, ducks, pheasants, and fancy fowl of all kinds, many of which are worth $500 apiece. Most of the solons had never before seen such high-priced birds and just a sight of them was a rare treat. . . .

Mr. Mellen's visit to the [Red Lion] Inn at the same time as the legislative committee's was merely a coincidence, not arranged beforehand by either party. . . . One of the representatives said after the inspection that mergers, street railways, railroads, and politics were not mentioned during the visit to Council Grove.

Capitulation to the New Haven both in Boston and Washington seemed imminent on May 19, 1909, when Brandeis pleaded with the Railroad Committee to reject the Draper bill: "I say to you gentlemen—don't trifle with the law; don't trifle with these rich lawbreakers; but insist upon dignity; insist upon observing the law; insist upon what every man in Massachusetts regards as the right and duty of the Commonwealth. Start fair. Start on a legal basis." [36]

He introduced the Anti-Merger League countermeasure, limiting the holding company to acquisition of the 109,948 shares of stock owned by Billard, forbidding railroad companies from acquiring stocks or bonds of the holding company, and reserving the right of the Commonwealth to take the B & M stock by eminent domain. This move failed. The Railroad Committee reported the Governor's bill, and it rolled through the Senate where no amendments were even considered.

Reporting to Alfred, June 6, the anti-merger leader admitted that "Our situation is pretty desperate. Only a miracle can land us safely. We could handle the New Haven and their money and their moneyed friends well enough; but the Governor and the Republican machine have joined forces with them unreservedly. There appears to be a resurgence of McKinleyistic materialism and I think that worsens our chances much. But we are making a glorious fight and are full of courage."

"The expected happened today in the merger fight," Brandeis wrote again, June 15. "We got unmercifully licked amidst innumerable broken promises of support; but it took all the power of the Republican machine and of the bankers' money to do it, and I am well content with the fight made. The aftermath of fighting continues."

The New Haven had won in Massachusetts. In Washington the anti-trust suit was still pending but at the hearings on the holding company bill in Boston, Harold J. Coolidge, a lawyer closely affiliated with the New Haven, had stated: "I have certain information from Washington which would tend to the belief that the merger suit is not likely to be pressed." [37] Coolidge proved right. Less than one week after Governor Draper signed the holding company bill, the Department of Justice announced: "The Attorney-General received today a certified copy of the act passed by the Legislature of Massachusetts and approved last Friday by the Governor of that state creating the Boston Railroad Holding Company. . . ." Two days later this entry on the New Haven case was recorded in the docket: "Discontinuance by the United States filed." [38]

This was done by the United States District Attorney in Boston, Asa P. French. He had long sided with Brandeis, but now he had his orders. "I hated to do it," he commented a few years later, "but the Massachusetts Legislature had passed its holding bill and evidently the department at Washington thought that as long as the Legislature had made itself responsible by blocking matters our inquiry should end. . . . I had spent nearly two years in working up our case and believed there was ample ground for criminal prosecution, but orders are orders. Mine came from Mr. Wickersham. . . . We had many startling facts to present. But we could not do so. I was very sorry." [39]

Brandeis's disgust was unrestrained. "I am rapidly becoming a Socialist," he wrote his brother, August 19, 1909. "What the bankers leave undone their lawyer minions supply."

Actions formerly devious now became crystal clear. "The New Haven railroad found itself," the *Boston Transcript* observed, July 10, 1909, "through the legislative and judicial activities of the State of Massachusetts in an uncomfortable position as owner of a controlling interest in the Boston & Maine Railroad. It got Mr. Billard to take this elephant off its hands until such time as it could itself provide the bulky animal with comfortable housing and suitable provender. . . ."

Clear also were the interrelated movements in Washington. The prompt transmission of the Holding Company Act to the federal Attorney-General, his even more prompt dismissal of the suit without investigation or consultation with his District Attorney in charge of the case, the conference at the Department of Justice with New Haven officials immediately after the Governor's holding company message, H. J. Coolidge's peculiar confidence that federal action would not be pressed, Robbins's plea for a "speedy disposition of the case"—all mystifying developments considered independently and as they occurred, now fitted together and pointed to one conclusion—the capitulation of federal authorities to New Haven monopolists, not on June 26, but two months earlier in Massachusetts, when the Government of the United States had acted merely to support the play on New Haven's political chessboard.

CHAPTER THIRTEEN

The New Haven Railway An Empire Crumbles, 1909-1914

THE NEW HAVEN now had authoritative grip on New England's transportation. For the time being Brandeis's onslaughts subsided. Since January 1910 he had been going to Washington for long periods at a time to track down big game in President Taft's Interior Department. There he became acquainted with Senator Robert M. La Follette, Sr., who, like Brandeis, was deeply concerned with railroads, monopolies, and trusts. They talked long and often of the New Haven, of bringing its activities into the open and finally to trial. The results became apparent on April 12, 1910, when La Follette rose in the Senate presumably to talk about the Mann–Elkins amendments to the Interstate Commerce Act. It soon became clear, however, that with facts and figures only Brandeis could have supplied, La Follette was reopening the New Haven merger issue.

"I suppose you marked La Follette's New Haven merger speech yesterday," Brandeis wrote his brother, April 14, 1910. "You must read it in full. It tells well the merger story and the flaying of the Attorney-General is something he will remember (against me) and which is fully deserved. Wickersham will get his innings now. . . . And he is sure to be W.H.T.'s principal adviser—the Blind leading the Blind."

ANOTHER OFFICIAL CLEAN BILL OF HEALTH

Massachusetts was erupting too. Early in 1909 state Attorney-General Malone had reported to the Legislature that the New Haven's violation of Massachusetts laws made its franchise subject to forfeiture. But Malone was disinclined to take the next step. The Legislature then turned the matter over to a special commission headed by George F. Swain of Harvard's Engineering Department and made up of the three railroad commissioners, the tax commissioner, and the bank commissioner. This body was given broad powers and aided by legal experts from the investment house of Stone & Webster. Known as the Validation Commission, it had all the appearance of impartiality and solid authority. On December 18, 1912, the *Boston News Bureau* hailed its report as "a verdict of admirable financial and physical integrity—a clean bill of health for the Mellen regime." Earlier the *News Bureau* had gloated:

> In view of the magnificent credit of the New Haven—never higher than now —it is instructive to recall the reckless onslaught upon the finances of that company and the integrity of its management made a little over three years ago by Louis D. Brandeis, Esq., of Boston. . . . This remarkable concoction [Brandeis's pamphlet] is practically forgotten. Even its author might now blush to read it. . . .
>
> Three years have passed and dividends have been steadily maintained. It is now 1911—and who says "insolvency"? [1]

The anti-merger leader nevertheless had stuck to his guns and on September 25, 1911, had written Norman Hapgood:

> When the New Haven reduces its dividend and Mellen resigns, the "Decline of the New Haven and the Fall of Mellen" will make a dramatic story of human interest with a moral—or two—including the evils of monopoly. Events cannot long be deferred and possibly you may want to prepare for their coming. Anticipating the future a little, I suggest the following as an epitaph or obituary notice:
>
> Mellen was a masterful man, resourceful, courageous, broad of view. He fired the imagination of New England, but being oblique of vision merely distorted its judgment and silenced its conscience. For a while he triumphed with impunity over laws human and divine, but as he was obsessed with the delusion that two and two make five he fell at last a victim of the relentless rules of humble arithmetic.
>
> Remember, O Stranger!
>
> Arithmetic is the first of the sciences and the mother of safety.

Mellen's storm-tossed empire flew distress signals late in 1911 when New Haven stock slumped sharply. Rumors were rife of a reduction in dividends, but Mellen promptly branded all such talk as "the vaporings of a disordered mind." [2] He assured stockholders that Mr. Morgan wished "the New Haven to be recognized as a permanent 8 per cent stock." Even if not earned, he implied that investors and management preferred to maintain regular dividends lest hardship be inflicted on countless small investors, and "serious distrust" arise.[3]

But as a safeguard the management did order drastic economies. Men were laid off, improvements discontinued, train service curtailed. Still the slump continued. In the fall of 1911 a newly formed efficiency committee was given instructions as to the "importance of cutting out everything that can be dispensed with that means money." Economy produced results, but not those anticipated. Shippers complained of delays and inadequate facilities. Serious and expensive wrecks occurred.

As criticism intensified, the company sought other lines of escape. On April 10, 1912, Governor Eugene Foss, after conference with the president and vice-president of the New Haven, recommended electrification in Greater Boston, a tunnel between the South and North stations in Boston, and other such measures. Brandeis opposed this new move as an act of "supreme unwisdom. Let us have a diagnosis . . . in advance of action," he urged. Failure to ascertain where the defect lies "would be like applying a quack medicine to a sick man without attempting to diagnose his illness, and the results undoubtedly would be the same in both instances." [4] Furthermore, the Interstate Commerce Commission, he said, would soon investigate service and rate complaints against the New Haven management. Why not await its report?

BRANDEIS STEPS UP THE ATTACK

The Mellen–Brandeis war was now almost seven years old. Through most of it, Mellen had been the aggressor, Brandeis the counterfighter. Up to now the aggressor had usually won, though never decisively. Now, the aggressor was ready for a decisive victory. But this time Brandeis took the offensive.

It came about in this way. Back in 1910, despite strong opposition from the New Haven, the Massachusetts Legislature had invited the Canadian Grand Trunk Railroad to extend its lines to Boston. Construction started soon thereafter, and as the New Haven's financial condition deteriorated, Mellen grew more restive over this new rival. Apparently he found a way to stop the Canadian line, for suddenly, on November 8, 1912, it was announced out of a clear sky that construction on the extension would be abandoned. Almost immediately Gilson Gardner, a journalist, brought out a special article on "King Morgan Slips Invaders $4,000,000 to Stay Out." [5]

In rapid succession it was announced that the irrepressible Brandeis was in Washington urging the Pujo Banking and Currency Committee to look into the Grand Trunk episode; that Attorney-General Wickersham would order a probe of the incident to determine whether there had been violation of the Sherman Act in the suspected collusion; that a federal grand jury was beginning an investigation; and that Representative O'Shaughnessy of Rhode Island had introduced a resolution in the House providing for congressional investigation into the deal with the ominous possibility of Brandeis as counsel.[6]

Brandeis had still other strings to his bow. In July 1912 he induced Interstate Commerce Commissioner Charles A. Prouty to begin a broad investigation of railroad rates, service, and financial management. I.C.C. hearings were resumed that fall at Portland, Maine. "We had three successful days," Brandeis wrote his brother, October 4, 1912, "and it looks as if we should make some real progress in getting from the I.C.C. a real show up of the situation, and an honest report on the results of monopoly."

Brandeis was determined to make the railroads—including the New Haven—toe the mark of public responsibility. As usual, publicity was the device he trusted most. On December 8, 1912, he told his brother how he had taken advantage of an interruption in his professional activities caused by "a sort of inflammation in my right eye": "During the interval I was confined to dictating interviews for various papers on the New Haven— some few of which have doubtless reached you. Have just finished a more careful screed for Wednesday's *Boston Journal* and *N.Y. Press,* entitled 'The New Haven—an Unregulatable Monopoly'—or something on that line. The *N.Y. Post, N.Y. World, Morning and Evening, N. Y. Journal* and *American* and *N.Y. Press* are with us this time and the *Boston Journal.* With the Washington end lively, Messrs. Mellen *et al.* have their hands pretty full."

On December 13, 1912, the *Boston Journal* gave a whole page to Brandeis's diagnosis of the New Haven's ills. The trouble, he said, was twofold: monopoly and bigness. These evils, he pointed out, are not necessarily twins: "The evils of bigness are something different from and additional to the evils of monopoly. A business may be too big to be efficient without being a monopoly; and it may be a monopoly and yet (so far as size is concerned) may be well within the limits of efficiency. Unfortunately the so-called New Haven system suffers from both excessive bigness and from monopoly."

And what was the remedy? For Brandeis that was drastic but simple: Break up the unholy, illegal alliance, the railroad-trolley-steamship monopoly; restore competition. This could be done, he said, either "under the

BRANDEIS (RIGHT) WITH NORMAN HAPGOOD, 1910

BRANDEIS'S "DREAM OF EMPIRE"

Truth, May 17, 1913

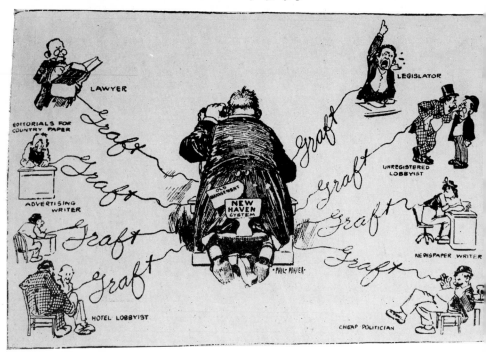

MERGER "PUBLIC OPINION IN THE MAKING"

Boston Journal, September 29, 1913

Sherman Anti-Trust Law, or by the states exercising sovereign powers to take away a part of the New Haven's property, as the Boston & Maine." [7]

THE NEW HAVEN COUNTERATTACKS

To Mellen—and to Morgan—who now entered the fight directly—the New Haven's difficulties were due neither to bigness nor to monopoly. They were due to Brandeis alone. They made this clear in a vigorous advertising campaign which ran a series of statements signed by Mellen himself, labeled "Truth No. 1," "Truth No. 2," and so on. And on December 20, 1912, Mellen and Morgan signed a long statement to the press:

Every one of these attacks defaming New England and its railroad system, so far as I have learned, traces back to Brandeis, his associates or organization. . . . When, for ulterior purposes, the integrity of the management is assailed by underground campaigns and publicly by irresponsible mouthpieces, and when accidents, still beyond the reach of human invention, have carried trusted employees and those in their charge to their death, and such misfortunes are used to frighten, and to demoralize the transportation and traffic of New England, I ask the public, who have the most at stake in this matter, if the time has not now arrived when, in their own interest, they should call "Halt." [8]

This joint statement was highly praised by the *Boston News Bureau:*

The country has been given two masterly expositions of statesmanship in business—each by an authority and exemplar. Mr. Morgan discussed banking and the nation, Mr. Mellen railroading and New England. . . . Both are confutations of traducers, as well as revelations of the authors' ideals and policies. . . .
The time has come for all the great business organizations, for organized labor, and for the people generally to recognize that there is a concerted movement, engineered from outside of New England, to damage the trade, the credit, the commerce of this whole section, in every possible way.[9]

A magazine bearing the seductive name *Truth,* edited by George R. Conroy, made subtle hints as to the nature of this force from "outside New England":

Mr. Schiff is the head of the great private banking house of Kuhn, Loeb and Company, which represents the Rothschild system on this side of the Atlantic. He has been described as a "financial strategist" and has been for years the financial minister to the great impersonal power known as Standard Oil. He was hand-in-glove with Harriman, the Goulds, and the Rockefellers in all their railroad enterprises and . . . has become the dominant power in the railroad and financial world of America. . . .
Brandeis, because of his great ability as a lawyer and for other reasons which

will appear later, was selected by Schiff as the instrument through which Schiff hoped to achieve his ambitions in New England. His job was to carry on an agitation which would undermine public confidence in the New Haven system and cause a depreciation in the price of its securities, thus forcing them on the market for the wreckers to buy. . . .

We do not say this, remember, in order to criticize, but simply in the interest of truth. The New England railroad fight is simply part of a world movement. It is the age-long struggle for supremacy between Jew and Gentile. Schiff is known to his people as "a prince in Israel." He has given millions to Jewish charities, and keeping in mind always the Yiddish proverb, "He who has the money has the authority," is ever solicitous for the progress of his race along financial lines, confident that in the end it will control the world.[10]

Brandeis had noted the growing intensity of the smear campaign in writing his brother, December 20, 1912, from the Hotel Sherman in Chicago: "New Haven matters seem lively in my absence. Mellen continues his fire on me—the root of all offending—and I carefully refrain from attacking Mellen personally, or answering personalities. . . . The New York papers have been on the job and there is little need for me to hammer now; but I have still some rods in pickle."

One of his "rods" was in the form of a full-length speech, on March 6, 1913, before the Boston Chamber of Commerce, where he denounced as "unworthy of the Commonwealth" the drift of Massachusetts policy since the enactment of Draper's Holding Company Act. The proper course was clear: the New Haven should voluntarily relinquish its hold on the Boston & Maine, or the state should take the road and operate it. "The fact that we are here today," he said, "is due to the inexorable law that nothing is settled until it is settled right. . . . Time enough has elapsed since the consolidation of the roads to warrant judgment of the results upon the principle of 'By your faults shall we know you.' . . . The first remedy for this situation is to go backward to the place where you lost your way and start on again from that point." [11] In less than a week after this speech was delivered Boston & Maine stock was selling at a new low.[12] As usual, the New Haven's journalists blamed "hysterical assaults." Brandeis replied: "It is all nonsense for anyone to claim that the drop in the Boston and Maine stock is due to the knockers. The knockers have not brought about the reduction in market value any more than they have the accidents on the New Haven. The trouble is due to the New Haven methods. It's merely a matter of arithmetic, that's all." [13]

Brandeis still made little headway. The Chamber of Commerce voted against the state taking over the Boston & Maine and recommended "co-operation" with the railroads. It was a setback for Brandeis—a complete surrender to monopoly. Brandeis kept on. "I talked with Marble" (of the I.C.C.), he told James L. Richards, March 20, 1913, "and later I went to see Clark, who is [I.C.C.] chairman. I spent three-quarters of an hour with Clark and got him very much interested in the situation. I told him what I also had told Prouty—that it was extremely important that we should get to the bottom of all the facts. . . . He also felt that if the period since July 1, 1907, disclosed any such bookkeeping as the period previous, we ought to have criminal proceedings started."

Clark acted quickly; new hearings on the New Haven began in April and continued through May 1913. Representing the Boston Fruit and Produce Exchange, Brandeis elicited from I.C.C. Examiner David E. Brown a neat story of dubious New Haven transactions buried under a mass of phony accounting. Brown's testimony showed that John L. Billard made a profit of $2,700,000 from his flyer in B & M stock without risking a dollar of his own money. Brown also showed that in 1911 the New Haven entered in its "general expenses" account, the sum of $514,000, an amount eight times as large as usual for Class A railroads. He further indicated that if the New Haven had followed the standard ratio for railway depreciation, the deficit on the books of the company would have swelled from $1,267,000 to $3,600,000 in 1911 and from $900,000 to $2,800,000 in 1912. Finally he showed that two vessels written up on the books as worth over $900,000 were sold as junk for $44,000.

Here then was something to go on. In the I.C.C. hearings, Brandeis's "worthless" ammunition suddenly exploded with deadly effect. New Haven Vice-President Buckland tried to muffle the blasts by asking that future hearings be private. Commissioner Prouty refused. *"Sub rosa* investigations," he said, "never achieved anything." So the New Haven press itself got to work. The *Boston News Bureau* said, April 23:

> President Mellen is the one man who can make clear these transactions. He has never yet failed when called upon to make explanation. But this is the one thing that was apparently not wanted—neither explanation by Mr. Mellen nor anybody else—except Brandeis! What is wanted is agitation, public confusion, startling headlines in the newspapers with the biggest black ink and Brandeis waving hands in the air and exclaiming "I told you so."

The New Haven again turned on the "agitator" in a series of Mellen-signed advertisements. Back in 1892, said the first of these, Brandeis had acted for Austin Corbin in raiding the New York and New England Railroad's stock. "Who is the Corbin behind Mr. Brandeis's present activities?" [14] Next day "Another Chapter of Brandeis's Record" appeared, containing Joseph B. Warner's statement that Brandeis's old pamphlet on the New Haven being "completely discredited and shown to be replete with errors and false conclusions, is sufficient assurance that his present accusations will not bear analysis, nor deserve credit." This second installment of biography concluded on the same sinister note: "Who is paying Brandeis? Who is the Corbin in this case?"

The *Boston Journal*, supporting Brandeis, answered on April 25:

> Mr. Charles S. Mellen does not commend himself to the public by his intemperate and twenty-year belated attack on Mr. Brandeis. We hold no brief for Mr. Brandeis but we are frank to say that Mr. Mellen's twenty-year search for a flaw seems to make a pretty good case for the man he seeks to vilify.

Brandeis received scores of letters which denounced Mellen and encouraged "the wrecker." "Please accept my sincere congratulations for the enemies you are making," one correspondent wrote. "Mellen's morals need medicine, and I hope you will continue to administer the proper doses daily," said another. A handsome message came from Federal District Judge Charles F. Amidon, April 24, 1913, after an evening with Brandeis. Judge Amidon wrote: "Lincoln could think of a subject longer without permitting his mind to shift or waver than any other man I ever knew. This is Herndon's most important contribution to an understanding of Lincoln. . . . It describes your method of looking at our business problems and I suppose that is the reason why your thinking on these subjects is so fruitful. . . . To think straight all that our big businessmen have thought crooked during the last fifty years is not the work of a lawyer but a statesman. The man who can unsnarl one snarl like the New Haven from the beginning to the end will lay bare all the other snarls. . . . It is this patient, thorough, firsthand knowledge which distinguishes your work from that of all the other trust-busters. . . ."

Brandeis refused, as usual, to reply personally to his vilifiers. He explained his reasons in a letter to Mark Sullivan, May 10, 1913: "I determined many years ago not to make any denials of any kind or any explanation of any of the vile charges which the interests whom I am fighting put out. I did this partly because a denial would dignify the attack, and partly because if I once began to make denials or explanations, it would easily be in their power to occupy me in this way eight hours a day, and divert my attention from the more important business of attacking their methods."

THE IRREPRESSIBLE CONFLICT

In the meantime the New Haven was apparently at work elsewhere, getting the "agitator" kicked out of the forum which he had himself so skillfully devised. On April 24, 1913, Alton E. Briggs, executive secretary of the Boston Fruit and Produce Exchange, wrote Brandeis: "We find to-day that the present turn which the investigation has taken does not meet with approval of a considerable portion of our members and it is the expression of our directors that further representation on your part for the Exchange be not continued."

Next day, however, Brandeis appeared at the hearings "as a citizen." Choate asked, "Are you still putting up the same old bluff?"

"Well," replied Brandeis, laughing, "I have no occasion to answer that. If I did, it might be unpleasant to you." [15]

New Haven's chief counsel then announced that he too would like to appear "as a citizen. I represent the people, the same as my dear brother Brandeis."

"But, Mr. Choate," brother Brandeis smilingly inquired, "you have been continously employed by the New York, New Haven & Hartford Railroad?"

"That is not true," replied Mr. Choate.

Brandeis persisted. "Or by the New England Navigation Company [subsidiary of the New Haven]?"

There was laughter as Choate replied, "That also is not true. When I acted as counsel I did so openly."

Brandeis then asked Examiner Brown if any payments to Choate had been made by the New Haven. Referring to the record, Brown testified: "I found that the New England Navigation Company paid Charles F. Choate, Jr., on May 31, $13,918.82. . . . By vouchers, it appears that $7,032.82 was for services to the Navigation Company and $6,950 for services to the New York, New Haven & Hartford Railroad." [16]

The next week "citizen" Choate appeared as personal counsel for President Mellen.

The extent to which I.C.C. findings shook the New Haven was indicated by Choate's brief filed with the Commission. Unless the road were allowed to raise rates on the Boston & Maine and thereby secure needed income, the New Haven attorneys argued, no material improvements could be made in New England transportation. Brandeis, of course, opposed the suggestion: "To increase the rates of railroads that have been managed as these have been managed would be like increasing the income of a spend-thrift to meet the deficiencies he is up against at the end of the year." [17]

A still more significant confession was Choate's attempt to explain away all difficulties by attacking Brandeis's accounting methods: "That these matters [financial condition of the New Haven] should have formed the principal subject of Mr. Brown's examination is more than a coincidence.

The facts tend strongly to the inference that the accountant's course was guided and directed by Mr. Brandeis and that that gentleman has succeeded in making use of the powers of the Commission to again exploit those features of his former attack which had already been answered and many of the fallacies which had already been pointed out. . . ." [18]

Choate urged the Commission to rely on the amiable findings of the Commission on Commerce and Industry: "This Commission [Commerce and Industry] had before it the pamphlet issued by Mr. Brandeis in December 1907, and listened to his arguments. They gave careful consideration to his charges and employed skillful accountants to examine his figures. Their report to the Legislature of that year, which report is made a part of the record in this case, was a complete refutation of the charges made by Mr. Brandeis.

"Here, then, you have the issue," Choate's argument concluded. "Shall Mr. Brandeis, acting for himself, his theory and contentions being disproved again and again by impartial commissions and tribunals [Commission on Commerce and Industry and the Validation Commission] be permitted to set up and maintain his opinion against the opinion of men appointed by the stockholders of these roads to conduct their affairs?" [19]

Within a week after the arguments before the I.C.C. closed, New Haven's dividend was cut to 6 per cent. The *Boston News Bureau*, May 9, 1913, had already pointed out cause and effect:

That anti-railroad agitator, Louis D. Brandeis, now bobs up in Washington. . . . Before anybody could answer him he had not only alarmed all New England, and made still further progress in his undermining of railroad credit, but his reiterated declarations so demoralized the operating forces of the New Haven road that the flutter of a bird on the track would cause the setting of an air-brake, and the efficiency of the New Haven, which had been at the highest in the country, dropped from 95 per cent to 45 per cent in sixty days.

But the Interstate Commerce Commission's report of July 9 refused to believe that Brandeis's "agitations" were responsible for the road's difficulties: "Had the stockholders of the New Haven, instead of vilifying the Road's critics, given some attention to the charges made, their property would today be of greater value and the problem an easier one." [20]

Brandeis hailed the report as a source of "great encouragement to all well-wishers of New England and its railroads. It will help our people," he said, "to know the truth, the truth which they might have known throughout the last six years but for the misstatements of the New Haven management. But at last the truth has come. We may look to it to make us free!" [21]

On July 8 Mellen resigned as president of the Boston & Maine. "It has been found impossible," an official statement explained, "for one man to handle satisfactorily the . . . three roads and do justice to each, and the New Haven being the larger and more important, Mr. Mellen will hereafter devote his attention to the affairs of that road." [22]

Brandeis wasted no time celebrating. "Standing alone, it [Mellen's resignation] does not mean much," he said. "Absolute separation of the systems must follow. As I am an optimist, I expect that result later." It was brought a little nearer, when on July 17, 1913, Mellen also resigned from the New Haven.

THE PROVED FAILURE OF FINANCIAL CONTROL

"Mellen's resignation looks as if the seven year war were drawing to a close," Brandeis wrote his brother on July 19. "Of course there is much to be done besides getting a new man—if one man must be overlord again, and I think our Commission is settling down pretty well to that idea. The real disgrace to our country," he added, "is the past attitude of our Pillars of Society—Higginsons *et al.*"

To a *Boston Journal* reporter, on July 18, 1913, Brandeis said: "Mr. Mellen's resignation should be accompanied by the retirement of the board of directors whose policies Mr. Mellen has carried out faithfully for nearly ten years. The directors . . . are obviously not to be trusted to introduce those radical changes which the Interstate Commerce Commission recommended and which are essential to a restoration of the railroads to their former prosperity."

This was no time to sit back and await developments. "Howard Elliott [the new President]," he wrote Alfred, July 28, 1913, "is reputed personally honest, and is likely to prevent graft upon the railroad. I am led to doubt whether he would be equally solicitous of the interests of the public and feel sure that he is not an unenlightened R.R. man and that the power of the government and aroused public opinion will be needed to secure his changing the monopoly policy of the company. There is no rest yet for us."

To Brandeis an important cause of the New Haven disaster was banker-management. As fiscal agent of the road, J. P. Morgan and Company had long dominated its board of directors. "Bankers are credited with being a conservative force in the community," Brandeis observed. "The tradition lingers that they are pre-eminently 'safe and sane.' And yet, the most grievous fault of this banker-managed railroad has already brought heavy losses to many thousands of small investors throughout New England for whom bankers are supposed to be natural guardians. In a community where its railroad stocks have for generations been deemed absolutely safe investments, the reduction of the New Haven dividend and the passing of the Boston and Maine dividend after an unbroken dividend record of seventy-two years comes as a disaster." This failure was no accident—"it was the natural result of confusing the functions of banker and business-man.

"The banker should be detached from the business for which he per-forms the banking service," he maintained. "This detachment is desirable, in the first place, in order to avoid conflict of interest. When a banker-director of a railroad decides as railroad man that it shall issue securities, and then sells them to himself as banker, fixing the price at which they are to be taken, there is necessarily grave danger that the interests of the rail-road may suffer—suffer both through issuing of securities which ought not to be issued, and from selling them at a price less favorable to the com-pany than should have been obtained." [23]

Toward the end of the summer of 1913 the New Haven requested ap-proval from the Public Service Commission (revamped successor of the Board of Railroad Commissioners) for an issue of more than $67,000,000 of debenture bonds.

Brandeis insisted that the Commissioners show up all disbursements of the New Haven and its subsidiaries during the entire Mellen era before authorizing the bond issue. "When that statement shall have been fur-nished for the whole period, the people of New England will be better able to understand why the ruinous management of our great railroad proper-ties was, from time to time, sanctioned by legislative action and why it received commendation from men from whom the community had the right to expect protection instead of exploitation." [24]

The Public Service Commission's findings again proved Brandeis cor-rect. Investigation of the New Haven's "Other Expenses" showed expendi-tures of $337,469.71, from December 1, 1912, to June 30, 1913, to State House lobbyists, newspapermen, newspapers and magazines, former members of the Legislature, political bosses, and lawyers for work not covered by their usual fees. George R. Conroy of *Truth* magazine had felt the New Haven's golden shower. Bruce Wyman, Harvard Law professor, had a retainer of $10,000 per annum to deliver "scholarly" lectures on current transportation problems. Clarence W. Barron of the *Boston News Bureau* received $133,000 in seven months, for thirty-seven columns of "stories" favorable to the New Haven and its interests, and nine columns of attack on Brandeis.

Nevertheless the Public Service Commission voted on October 14 to approve the New Haven's bond issue. In a scorching dissent Commissioner George W. Anderson excoriated his fellow-members for their "supremest arrogance," for their "attempt to repeal by fiat" Massachusetts anti-stock-watering laws.

"I think," Brandeis wrote Norman Hapgood, October 15, 1913, "the decision of the Commission indicates the financial concentration of our community. I am told that there never was more lobbying at the State House than was practiced about the Public Service Commission's office during the last six weeks; and that Governor Foss has been using all his influence to sway the Commission."

Attacks on the Commission's decision led Howard Elliott, in September 1913, to ask a friendly Boston Chamber of Commerce audience for public co-operation—and increased freight rates. Brandeis was incredulous. "Yes, I see," he said, "Mr. Mellen asked for the same thing and got it. Let the consumer beware of the vicious circle of ever-increasing cost of living. . . . Instead of dangerous makeshift we offer a constructive policy—scientific management under which as costs fall, wages rise." [25]

If Brandeis was incredulous then, the public was more incredulous a little later. On December 10, 1913, the New Haven at last passed its dividend for the first time in forty years. Brandeis quickly pointed "a moral, a lesson worth remembering, that observance of law and the truth are necessary to lasting financial success." The broken dividend record, he said, was "but a final confession of ten years' mismanagement of the lines under banker-control." [26]

This action of the New Haven quickly aroused the nation. Brandeis used this excitement to prod Senator George W. Norris, in January 1914, to introduce a resolution calling for another I.C.C. investigation. Henry Cabot Lodge, strongly opposing Norris, was confident that "the passage of the resolution would have nothing but bad effect. . . . I should like the Senate to permit the Attorney-General and the Governor of Massachusetts to effect a reorganization and rescue the road for the good of the stock-holders." [27] Lodge went unheard in the newly elected Democratic and Wilsonian Senate, and the Commission began public hearings again on April 9, 1914.

For the first time the public was given a glimpse of the New Haven's board meetings where the company's "colossal feats" were charted and where J. P. Morgan's control of policy went unchallenged. "I regarded Mr. Morgan," Mellen testified, "and I think we all did on the board, as a man of very great experience, very great energy, very great capacity, and we naturally looked up to him. I think I was no different from the rest in that respect. There were strong men in the New Haven board other than Mr. Morgan. But I do not recall anything where Mr. Morgan was determined, emphatic, insistent—I recall no case in which he did not have his way." [28]

In a more whimsical moment Mellen described Morgan's role in rural terms: "I think the record of the New Haven's transactions with the elimination of Mr. Morgan would have been as tame and uneventful, as devoid of interest and incident, as would the record of a herd of cows deprived of the association of a bull." [29]

Some years after Morgan's death on March 31, 1913, when New Haven affairs were stagnant, Brandeis met Thomas W. Lamont in Washington. After the matter which brought them together had been concluded, Brandeis asked: "I have always been curious to know, Mr. Lamont, what attitude Mr. Morgan took as to my pamphlet on the financial condition of the New Haven; what, if anything, he did about it?" "I have no firsthand information," Lamont replied, "as I was not present when the matter came up. But I have heard that at a meeting soon after the publication of your findings, Mr. Morgan turned to Mellen with the query: 'Charlie, what is there in the report which this man Brandeis has gotten up?' 'Not a God damn thing,' Mellen replied curtly." Pressing his inquiry, Brandeis asked: "Didn't he refer it to a competent accountant for examination and audit?" "Not so far as I know," Lamont said. "It would not have been at all like Morgan to have done so." [30]

The Interstate Commerce Commission report, released July 14, 1914, is a story of "reckless and profligate" financial operations—one of the most remarkable chapters in American railroading and finance: "It has been clearly proven how public opinion was distorted; how officials who were needed and who could be bought were bought; how newspapers that could be subsidized were subsidized; how a college professor and a publicist secretly accepted money from the New Haven while masking as a representative of a great American university and as the guardian of the interests of the people; how agencies of information to the public were prostituted wherever they could be prostituted in order to carry out a scheme of private transportation monopoly imperial in its scope." [31]

Brandeis at last got definite action from the Department of Justice, now headed by Attorney-General James C. McReynolds, later a Supreme Court Justice. In June 1914 the Attorney-General demanded that the New Haven relinquish its control over the Boston & Maine and dispose of its trolley and steamship lines. He also served notice that if the New Haven refused to comply, proceedings under the Sherman Act would begin.[32] When the company hedged, McReynolds, acting on orders from President Wilson, filed a bill for dissolution of the system.[33] On August 11, 1914, the company capitulated.

So far as Brandeis was concerned the government's action dismembering the monopoly brought the fight to an end, and when Norman Hapgood suggested that he write an article on "what the New Haven directors might have done," he declined, saying, "The important thing now is the future, not the past; and the story of the future should be largely the uninteresting one of patience, virtue, and attention to details." [34]

The New Haven paid no dividends from 1913 through 1927. At the height of the Coolidge-Hoover boom it paid one dollar in 1928 and five in 1929.[35] Brandeis's statement that his "special field of knowledge" was "figures," and that " by taking a few published figures of the New Haven and working backward," he had built up "their complete system of bookkeeping," [36] was amply justified.

To Brandeis the "decline of the New Haven was due to a disregard of inexorable laws: first, the fundamental law of business which has recognized the need of competition as an incentive to efficient action; second, that fundamental law of human nature which recognizes the limitations of man, namely, that there is a limit to the amount or number of things which any man or body of men can accomplish or do well; third, the law of arithmetic by which two and two will always make four, despite reports of presidents and financial advisers who insist on stretching it into five." [37]

Brandeis's summary of the New Haven's difficulties continued to be applicable through the years. In 1937 the I.C.C. accounted for the New Haven's continuing maladies merely by reaffirming his diagnosis and its own early reports: "No student of the railroad problem can doubt that a most prolific source of financial disaster and complication to railroads in the past has been the desire and ability of railroad managers to engage in enterprises outside the legitimate operation of their railroads and their securities."

A LESSON OF NATIONAL IMPORTANCE

"The decline of the New Haven is of more than local significance," Brandeis commented in August 1913. "It teaches a lesson of national importance." [38] "The American people," he wrote, "have as little need of oligarchy in business as in politics. There are thousands of men in America who could have performed for the New Haven stockholders the task of one 'who guides, superintends, governs, and manages,' better than did Mr. Morgan, Mr. Baker, and Mr. Rockefeller. For though possessing less native ability, even the average businessman would have done better than they, because working under proper conditions. There is great strength in serving with singleness of purpose one master only. There is great strength in having time to give to a business the attention which its difficult problems demand. And tens of thousands more Americans could be rendered competent to guide our important businesses. Liberty is the greatest developer." [39]

CHAPTER FOURTEEN

The United Shoe Machinery Conflict, 1899-1912

THROUGHOUT the New Haven struggle Brandeis opposed monopoly as repugnant to the American way of life. And yet in the midst of that railroad contest, at the peak of his dynamism as People's Attorney, he found himself in a most compromising position. Admitting that there were *good* monopolies as well as bad ones, he defended the United Shoe Company at the same time that he attacked the New Haven railroad.

Brandeis thus embarrassed himself because at least once he broke a personal and professional rule which he meant to keep hard and fast. This rule had to do with his personal investments and his professional attitude thereto: "My idea is . . . to treat investments as a necessary evil, indulging in the operation as rarely as possible. Buy only the thing you consider very good and stick to it—unless you have come to doubt the wisdom of the purchase. And when you buy, buy the thing which you think is safe, and will yield a fair return, but don't try to make your money out of investments. Make it out of your business. Take in that all the risks you think it prudent to take, but risk only there." [1]

Under this principle Brandeis's savings went into "the best railroad, utility, municipal or government bonds. There was never any deviation," according to his secretary, Miss Malloch, "from his fixed conviction as to what constituted proper investment of his savings." [2] Clients often asked him to put money into their business, but just as often he refused, explaining that he did not wish to share their risks and profits, their enthusiasms and their fears. For if he did, he could not keep his mind clear and free to serve them. [3]

DEFENDING THE SHOE MONOPOLY

In 1899 Brandeis was both an investor, a director, and one of counsel in the newly organized United Shoe Machinery Company.* He joined the board of directors at the request of Rudolph Matz, who felt that Brandeis, as counsel for the Henderson family which had large holdings in one of the constituent companies consolidating to form the United, should continue as a director of their interests. This relationship, though consonant with his position as a corporation lawyer, was discordant with the principles noted above, and perhaps out of key with his growing repute as People's Attorney. The United, through consolidation, had practically gained monopoly, reinforced by patents held on essential machinery. In its leases the so-called "tying clause" was inserted, under which the company could cancel the lease of, say, its stitching machine, if the lessee should rent the cutting machine from a competitor. This clause had the effect of forcing a shoe manufacturer to use United's entire line if he wanted to use any of it. To break this grip, rival shoe machinery companies introduced a bill in the 1906 Massachusetts Legislature to outlaw tying clauses so that a manufacturer could use a United machine for one operation and machines of United's competitors for other operations. President Sidney Winslow then asked Brandeis to join James J. Storrow in opposing the measure, and he agreed to do so.

Some years later Brandeis stated his reasons: "In 1906 there came a clamor against the form of our leases, and a bill came up before the Legislature. It happened to be at a time when Mr. Louis A. Coolidge [United's counsel] was ill and he was not able to attend to legislative matters, and Mr. Winslow asked me if I would go. I had a great deal of hesitation, and finally decided to go. I say a great deal of hesitation, as I did not like particularly to put myself in the position of testifying on the subject. But I felt that the company was being attacked by this bill in the interest of certain shoe machinery manufacturers and not of the public. There were certain shoe machinery manufacturers who had undertaken to have passed a law which I believed inconsiderate and unfair against this company, without taking into their council at all the men who really ought to be consulted— the shoe manufacturers." [4]

Brandeis revealed his embarrassment at the 1906 hearings by stating that he appeared not as counsel but as one of United's directors, and as one of the 4500 stockholders.[5] Yet he submitted a brief and received payment

---

* In 1899 he invested $10,000 in preferred stock and bought five shares of common to qualify him as director. He accumulated further common stock as rights were distributed, the total par value being $2,475. He sold the common stock on April 2, 1910, and the preferred in the summer and fall of 1911.

just as if he had been acting as counsel. His argument also showed appreciation of his dilemma: "The United Shoe Machinery Company is undoubtedly a large and powerful corporation, supplying a large part of the shoe machinery used in this country. But such control of the business it has is exercised in the interest, not only of the stockholders, but of the manufacturers of shoes, and ultimately of the wearers of shoes." [6]

Brandeis explained that the United leased machinery to small manufacturers on the same terms as to large ones, and he argued that this allowed men to engage in shoe manufacturing with a minimum of capital, thus making the newest mechanical improvements available to all manufacturers, large and small.[7] Through this benevolent policy, the United, though practically a monopoly in the shoe machinery business, became "the greatest promoter of competition among the *shoe manufacturers* that there is. . . . There is not a manufacturing business in the United States, unless it be the clothing manufacturing business . . . in which there is the same freedom of competition that there is in the shoe manufacturing business; and that happy result is due largely to the methods adopted by this shoe machinery company." [8]

Pressing this special plea, he said: "Now I say, therefore, that this cry against this company is absolutely indiscriminative, because there is talk against monopoly, and there are recognized monopolies which everybody knows. But we have found in Massachusetts that in certain things we have got to have a monopoly. We have to have a monopoly in electric light, we have to have a monopoly in gas, we have to have monopolies in telephones, and this business stands more even than some of the others just on that basis." [9]

Brandeis went even further with this strange line when he asked: "What is this so-called monopoly? It is nothing more than that control which to a greater or less extent any successful business acquires by virtue of being successful, and therefore of expanding. If this company has machines which are deemed to be desirable by shoe manufacturers, why should not this company be allowed to increase its own business by refusing to let manufacturers have these machines unless they will purchase also from the same concern other machines which they require? . . . Many attempts have been made in trade to secure that result. . . . Great corporations have resorted to it from time to time as a means of increasing their already large business." [10]

The United's monopoly, he said, was therefore morally and economically unobjectionable. But even if it were not, this particular monopoly, being based largely on patents, could not be broken by state interference: "I say constitutionally you cannot do it. These machines are practically patented, all the important ones are, and the decisions of the Supreme Court of the United States, particularly the decision in *National Harrow Company* v. *Bement,* in the 186th U.S. Reports, says absolutely that a man who holds a patent can hold it as he pleases. And our own status is just as good. You cannot limit the right to do business except by the requirements of safety, of health, or of morals. The *O'Keefe* v. *Sullivan* case, a recent case in the Supreme Court, establishes this. I think it certainly would be a great stretch of the imagination to say that either the morals, health, or safety of the community is threatened every time a man leases his machinery at so low a price that another man cannot compete with him. And that is just what this bill says—that you shall not in selling or leasing your machinery, offer such inducements that another man cannot compete with you." [11]

Finally Brandeis told the legislative committee that he had "infinitely greater interest in the shoe manufacturing business as counsel for a large number of shoe manufacturers" than in the United which he represented as director.* These clients were not protesting, he said, against "excessive charges by this company, which has so large a hold on the machinery business." The bill could not, therefore, be regarded as corrective of evils from which the users of the United's products suffered. Its apparent purpose was to protect from competition other concerns engaged in the manufacture of shoe machinery, and might, therefore, be "more appropriately entitled 'an act to prevent the lowering of prices by means of competition in the sale or leasing of shoe machinery.'" [12]

Then, on May 12, 1906, Brandeis turned from defense to attack. He drafted a letter for President Winslow to be sent the shoe manufacturers, pointing out how the proposed legislation imperiled "the exceptionally advantageous terms" of the United leases and urging them to get busy with the lawmakers.[13] The shoe men were told that they would be "far more seriously affected" by the proposed bill than the United and therefore "effort to defeat it should be made by you rather than by us." The bill attacking the United was killed.

DOUBTS AND EXPLANATIONS

Actually the shoe manufacturers were not nearly so impressed as was Brandeis with the "exceptionally advantageous" terms of the United leases. Indeed, he had won their aid in killing the bill in exchange for a clear

* In 1906 his clients, among others, were W. E. Arnold, Brockton Shoe Manufacturers' Association; E. J. Bliss, Churchill & Alden Co.; Commonwealth Shoe & Leather Co.; Fred Drew (of Brockton Last Co.); Dunham Bros. (Brattleboro); Fred F. Feld Co.; R. B. Grover Co.; International Shoe Co.; Geo. E. Keith Co.; P. B. Keith; W. H. McElwain Co.; A. E. Nettleton; Pacherd & Field; Regal Shoe Co.; S. Rosenberg Co.; A. W. Tedcastle & Co.; Endicott. (Memorandum enclosed in letter from Brandeis to McClennen, February 24, 1916.)

understanding that their grievances against United would be considered with a view to remedy before the next session of the Legislature. Speaking for other manufacturers, W. H. McElwain wrote Brandeis, May 21, 1906: "The present leases between the United Shoe Machinery Company and the manufacturers are in some respects unsatisfactory to shoe manufacturers, but we understand that the company is ready and willing to take this matter up with the shoe manufacturers and their representatives, and it seems to us that any ground of dissatisfaction which exists should be taken up for adjustment between the parties directly in interest instead of seeking new legislative action." [14]

These grievances were promptly brought to Winslow's attention, but as he was soon to go abroad he preferred to postpone their consideration until his return in September.[15] Meanwhile Brandeis's conviction as to the invulnerability of the United's legal position was severely shaken. In August 1906 the United States Circuit Court ruled that a monopoly in a certain case involving patents * was referable not to the patents but to combination. Bringing this case to Brandeis's attention, September 14, 1906, Charles Quarles † observed: "The decision is very important, and if sustained will not only deprive the trusts of their last refuge but will deprive the reformers of a great deal of ammunition." [16] Brandeis sent the decision to Elmer P. Howe, the United's general counsel, commenting: "This case was very thoroughly argued, and Judge Seaman, as you know, is an uncommonly able judge. This limit which he places upon monopoly of patents seems to me of great significance." [17]

Yet, on October 5, 1906, Brandeis still insisted that there was nothing "morally objectionable" to the United's methods of doing business. In reply to a query from Erving Winslow (no relation of Sidney) he summarized his legislative argument of April 18 and characterized Erving Winslow's derogatory statements as "grossly misrepresented." [18] But if one may judge from Brandeis's other statements, considerable doubt stirred in his mind.

By this time Sidney Winslow had returned and the question of lease modifications was reopened. But "when it got near December, not one step had been taken in the way of an advance toward removing the difficulties of which the manufacturers complained." [19]

The next legislative session was soon to start and another attack on United's lease was imminent. To meet it, Winslow naturally looked to Brandeis, who now found himself cornered. The shoe manufacturers, his clients in other matters, were again demanding modification of the

---

* *Indiana Manufacturing Co.* v. *J. I. Case Threshing Machine Co., Federal Reporter*, Vol. 148, pp. 21–31.
† Charles Quarles (1846–1908) of the Milwaukee Bar; specialist in Chancery and Corporation law; member of the firm of Quarles, Spence and Quarles.

United's leases, as had been agreed upon when they assisted in blocking the 1906 restrictive legislation. On the other hand, Winslow, his client in *this case*, much impressed by Brandeis's earlier commendation of United as "the greatest promoter of competition that there is," held out against making any change in the leases. Winslow considered Brandeis bound to United indefinitely by his argument of April 18, 1906. But Brandeis, because of the ruling of that "uncommonly able Judge" Seaman, now had grave doubts about the legality of United's leases. He took the only step that was open to him: he resigned as a United director.

In a polite letter to Winslow on December 6, 1906, Brandeis explained that now, with the company firmly established, he and Matz were agreed that the Henderson family no longer needed representation. His own interest in the company was so small as not to justify his presence on the board, and furthermore he felt he "ought not to continue an exception to my general rule of not holding the office of director in any corporation for which I act as counsel." [20]

Later Brandeis made two more realistic explanations for his action. On March 18, 1908, he wrote Henry Beach Needham: "I don't think anything he [Winslow] says about me needs any answer or explanation, except that possibly you may not be familiar with my connection with and severance from the United Shoe Machinery Company. I was counsel and director of one of the original companies that went into consolidation and through that became one of the counsel and directors of the United Shoe Machinery Company, which was professionally a very valuable connection.* This connection I gave up because I was unable to induce the management to adopt the views which I held from a public standpoint in respect to the operations of the Company. . . . The past and present operations of the Shoe Machinery Company have in my opinion on the whole been beneficial to the trade. The grave objection which I had to it was to the principles on which it was operated, and their effect in the future, and to a certain extent incidental methods employed."

Brandeis elaborated on his resignation some years later: "In consequence of the objections raised by these shoe manufacturers the subject was further investigated in the fall of 1906. I then ascertained facts in addition to those which had been previously furnished me by Mr. Winslow and other officials of the company, and to some extent inconsistent with statements made by them, and new considerations bearing upon the matter were brought to my attention. I was not yet, however, fully convinced that the Shoe Ma-

* The connection was not so valuable in terms of fees. During the years 1900–1907 the Brandeis firm received fees from the United as follows: 1900, $1,370; 1901, $1,809; 1902, $2,605; 1903, $1,720; 1904, $3,085; 1905, $1,748; 1906, $4,540.50; 1907, $1,975—a total of $18,852.50.

chinery Co.'s policy was unsound or its methods improper, but so serious a doubt had been raised in my mind as to the soundness of their general policy, and particularly as to the propriety of some of their methods, that I was unwilling to assume responsibility for the company's actions, and having reason to believe that Mr. Winslow was not likely to make any change in policy or methods, and having as one of the nineteen directors no real control, I therefore concluded, without undertaking to decide definitely whether the criticisms made were sound or not, to quietly retire (without raising the question) from the board of directors. . . . I tendered my resignation on December 6, 1906, and it was immediately accepted." [21]

Though Brandeis was no longer a director in January 1907, when legislative action threatened, Winslow asked him, as counsel, to sit in on conferences with the shoe manufacturers. This Brandeis did.[22] But now he "urged most strenuously upon Mr. Winslow and other officials . . . that the policy of monopoly be abandoned, and particularly that the tying clauses be eliminated from the leases." [23] "We discussed it at very great length at several conferences and Mr. Winslow showed that patience for which he is more than remarkable; on one occasion he listened to me for five hours without my making the slightest impression, and I felt that I had done all I could do in the matter and that was the last I did in the way of acting for the company." [24]

STRICTLY NEUTRAL

On January 7, 1907, Brandeis also resigned as counsel for United. From then on he and his law firm had nothing to do with the company except to complete a few minor suits.[25] Winslow soon had cause to regret this, for on June 1, 1907, the Legislature passed an act resembling the defeated measure of 1906 to regulate the sale and lease of shoe-making machinery. Brandeis had nothing to do with this in any way. "For three and a half years," he said later, "I took no part whatever in the questions relating to the policy and methods of the shoe machinery company, and specifically refused to act professionally for those who had adverse interests." [26]

To circumvent the law of 1907 the United added to its leases a proviso that any clause held unlawful should not be deemed a part of the lease, and another proviso that enabled the company to terminate the lease on thirty-days' notice. The legality proviso, Brandeis declared years later, was but a device for evading the law with impunity. On the thirty-days' notice clause, he had this to say: "Practically every shoe manufacturer—with perhaps two or three exceptions—in Massachusetts was absolutely in the power of this company, because if the shoe machinery company did give notice to any man whose action it did not like, why under the thirty-day clause it could pull out his machines, and it would mean that the manufacturer faced bankruptcy. . . . That was in 1907, and nobody could move because there was not another competing system." [27]

By 1910 things had changed. Some years earlier Thomas G. Plant had begun to develop his own shoe-making machines. Around 1907 he had his company set up and asked Brandeis to act as counsel. But Brandeis was then in his neutral mood and declined.[28] Charles H. Jones, one of Brandeis's clients, later declared: "Although after this, to my knowledge, Mr. Brandeis was urged in 1908 or 1909 to act as counsel for Mr. Plant, who was developing an independent system of shoe machinery, Mr. Brandeis firmly declined to do so, and when I suggested to Mr. Brandeis that he was leaning over backward in his desire to do the correct thing, he insisted that he preferred not to do so, in view of his former friendly relations with the United interests." [29]

By the summer of 1910 Plant was ready to place his machines in some of the large shoe factories. Leading men in the trade declared his machinery superior to United's and looked to Plant as an avenue of escape from United's grip. Yet they were wary. In July 1910 Charles H. Jones, president of the Commonwealth Shoe & Leather Company, consulted Brandeis's firm on the legality of United's leases, and for the first time Brandeis acted openly in opposition.[30] His firm's opinion, largely prepared by William H. Dunbar, now was that the leases were probably legal under Massachusetts law, but illegal under the revived Sherman Act, and Jones was told that he might safely use Plant's machines. Dunbar believed that the recent Supreme Court decision [31] in *Continental Wall Paper Co.* v. *Louis Voight and Sons Co.* supported this interpretation.[32] Jones sent the Brandeis firm's opinion * in memorandum form to Plant, who, without the consent of Jones or the firm, published it in July 1910 as an advertisement in Boston newspapers.

Instead of leasing his machines, as the United did, Plant wanted to sell

---

* The firm's opinion was as follows:

"First: The United Shoe Machinery Company is a combination in restraint of trade, and all contracts made by it, as essential parts of the combination or to carry out the purpose of monopolizing and perpetuating its monopoly of the shoe machinery trade, are unlawful. The leases used are such contracts and are unlawful.

"Second: The leases are in themselves, aside from the unlawful combinations embodied in the United Shoe Machinery Company, restraints on interstate trade within the Sherman Act.

"Third: The fact that the United Shoe Machinery Company was formed to deal in patented articles does not prevent the illegality of the combination, nor does the fact that the leases are of patented machines render them legal, since the purpose of the combination and the provisions of the leases are designed to create a monopoly beyond that conferred by the patent laws.

"Fourth: The leases being invalid, you cannot be held liable for failure to perform." (Reprinted in *Nomination Hearings*, p. 163.)

them at a comparatively small profit. This would have cut the ground from under United. If any one large manufacturer of shoes had the courage to deal with Plant, the others would flock to him, or co-operate to force more reasonable terms from United. The easiest solution for United—to buy Plant out—was dangerous, for, as Brandeis pointed out to William Barbour of United's executive committee, it would be an impertinent violation of the anti-trust law. He added that anyone who made such a purchase "would look jail in the face." [33]

That the United found other means to eliminate Plant became clear after October 1, 1910. On that date Plant's obligations of $1,500,000 fell due. A time extension had seemed only a matter of course, but a few days earlier Plant suddenly discovered that his notes would not be renewed. In desperation he ransacked New York and Boston for money, to no avail. The reason was, as Brandeis believed, that the United was the ruling power in the First National Bank of Boston, whose directors had great influence in New York. Brandeis considered the Plant episode as a specific example of the Money Trust backing up the Shoe Trust. This act of piracy roused Brandeis to write to Senator Robert La Follette, May 5, 1911: "It has seemed to me that the United Company's purchase of Plant's business, practically the only competitor in shoe machinery, was the most flagrant instance of violating the anti-trust law that I have known, coming as it did in the midst of the greatest legal agitation against trusts. I have been told that the Department of Justice has had the Shoe Machinery matters under consideration for a long time. Under the old administration considerable investigation was made, and that investigation had been pursued with more or less diligence, I am told, by Wickersham. Louis A. Coolidge, who is now treasurer of the United Shoe Machinery Company, was until about two years ago Assistant Secretary of the Treasury."

There was nothing left for Plant but to surrender. He sold out to United just before October 1. A year later Charles H. Jones described the end of the fight: "Mr. Plant told me that his agreement with the United Company was made during the night preceding the maturity of certain large obligations; that as he left the meeting with the Western Shoe Manufacturers, who were not then ready with all of the cash which was necessary, he went to the office of the counsel of the Shoe Machinery Company, Mr. Robert Herrick. This was after 8:00 o'clock in the evening. Herrick then sent for the officers and some of the Directors of the United Company, and they were engaged in drafting papers until the early morning of the following day—that is, the day on which Plant's notes were coming due, and that the deal was consummated before they left Herrick's office.[34]

The destruction of Plant removed the last hope of shoe manufacturers for forcing more lenient terms from United. Restless under the prospect, some Westerners organized the Shoe Manufacturers' Alliance. The United yielded a little, declaring that it had always been willing to give leases without tying clauses and without demanding additional royalties, if the lessee would make an initial payment.[35] But this hardly satisfied the Alliance which, in May 1911, appealed to Brandeis for aid. He was reluctant to give it and explained: ". . . when the Plant business was bought out and Mr. Endicott came upon the Board of Directors [of the United] the suggestion was made to him by somebody (I think it was made by Mr. Jones) that the shoe manufacturers standing absolutely quiet in the face of an act which was so clearly and flagrantly a violation, of the spirit certainly, of the Sherman Anti-Trust Law was something which free men ought not to submit to. I told Mr. Jones generally I thought that to be true, but as a matter of fact I did not think that with the other burdens resting upon him it was necessarily up to him to take up this fight, and I gave him about the same advice that I took to myself about five years before, when I made up my mind I would not fight the shoe machinery company for a change in its policy." [36]

Besides, Brandeis felt that the Alliance's interest was merely to make money for its members. However, if the Alliance would agree to pass on to the public some of the advantages gained by weakening United's position, then he might be interested. The Alliance promised to do this,[37] and Brandeis agreed to help. To free himself for the fight, he sold his United stock (except for one share).[38] To compensate his law partners for time he spent on a non-paying case, he accepted a fee of $2500 and then himself returned the same amount to the Alliance.[39]

The United, in the meantime, found that it had not swallowed Plant with impunity. The federal government brought suit in January 1911 for United's dissolution, and criminal proceedings were also instituted. A little later the Governor of Massachusetts joined in condemning United's practices. Brandeis, by now an ogre to businessmen because of the New Haven case, was credited with inspiring these actions. But he wrote his brother, July 18: "You probably noticed that Governor Foss has thrown a message at the United Shoe Machinery Company. That didn't come from me. The message was written before I knew he was considering the matter. He showed it to me before he sent it in, but, of course, my old friends will think I am at the bottom of it, as they do that I am responsible for the government investigation, a belief which is groundless."

Soon there were happenings for which Brandeis was responsible. But before the above proceedings and investigations had begun, he attended the meeting of United's directors on July 12, 1911, at their request. The only result was that he got into the records (which later stood him in good stead) the details of how he left the company when it became clear that no change would be made in its leasing policy, how afterward he declined to act for Plant, and how he had finally agreed to assist the Manufacturers' Alliance. He censured the company for altering its leases to evade restrictive legislation, and for its shameless extinction of Plant.[40]

CORPORATION LAWYER AND PEOPLE'S ATTORNEY

In 1911 congressional committees and federal agencies began to interest themselves in patents and monopoly generally, and particularly in United's sharp practices.[41] Brandeis testified before practically all these committees and agencies, showing at length and repeatedly how United's acts proved the need for federal legislation. He had completely changed his tune from the time he had warmly defended United in 1906: "As a matter of fact this shoe machinery corporation is a financial power as much as it is an industrial power. The managers of the shoe machinery corporation are practically the controlling influence in the First National Bank of Boston. They are a very large influence in our leading trust company, and have important influence in the Hanover National Bank and other banks of New York. It has been the steady policy of the United Shoe Machinery Corporation to keep at all times a huge cash balance which was deposited in these various banks, evidently not so much for current use in the business as for the financial control which they exercised through being large depositors in important banks. . . .

"In Massachusetts the allegiance of the shoe manufacturers to the United Shoe Machinery Co. is due in many cases to the financial power. The United Shoe Machinery Corporation may be very helpful by their influence in securing to a shoe manufacturer credit from the banks—and may also cause credit to be withheld. It is only the man who is independent of such influences, who has so much financial abilty that he does not have to ask aid, and does not have to disclose his situation, who can safely take a position of hostility to the United Shoe Machinery Corporation's methods." [42]

In the face of such an attack, it became imperative for the United and its allies to silence, or at least discredit, the People's Attorney. Brandeis's own course in shifting from side to side of this controversy made him particularly vulnerable. Thus (with considerable disregard for the facts, however), on January 19, 1912, Winslow wrote Senator Moses E. Clapp, Chairman of the Senate Committee on Interstate Commerce, before which Brandeis had recently testified, denying that United had forced Plant out of business and terming Brandeis's statements on this matter "grossly in-

accurate and wilfully untrue." Brandeis had contradicted, Winslow told
Clapp, his own earlier statements in regard to the company: "In his present role of an expounder of public morals, he seeks to hold this company
up to public contumely because it opposed a law which he had himself
denounced publicly as unconstitutional."

Making "inconsistency" his theme, Winslow continued: "I have analyzed the arguments which Mr. Brandeis presented with so much force in
1906, because they apply with equal force to the situation today. The policy
of the United Shoe Machinery Company has not changed. Its organization,
principles, and methods of doing business are the same as those with which
Mr. Brandeis was entirely satisfied during the time he was a director of the
company and when he argued in support of them before the committee of
the Massachusetts Legislature, at the same time advising his personal
friends that they were not only legal and moral but economically necessary
and beneficial.

"Only one thing has happened since 1906 to explain his change of mind.
He has been retained by the Western Alliance of Shoe Manufacturers,
organized at the instigation of large manufacturers in St. Louis, who, after
trying unsuccessfully to force special rates from the United Shoe Machinery Company to the disadvantage of small manufacturers, are now attacking the company through various channels." [43]

Thereupon Brandeis obtained permission from Rudolph Matz, a United
director friendly to him, to send Senator Clapp the record of his meeting
with United's directors in July 1911. This he did on February 24, 1912,
when he also wrote a long letter to Clapp in reply to Winslow's charges.
"Amidst some truths," he wrote, "Mr. Winslow presents half-truths and
statements, some false, others grossly misleading." He continued: "It is entirely true that in April 1906 I believed the policies and methods of the
United Shoe Machinery Company were legally and morally unobjectionable and that its activities were beneficial to the public, and as a director
of the company I appeared before the Massachusetts Legislature to oppose
a bill seeking to compel a change in these methods. I was then of the
opinion that under some conditions monopoly in industry could operate
beneficially to the public; or, in other words, that there were 'good trusts'
as well as 'bad trusts.' I believed, not unnaturally, that this company, which
was managed by men in whose ability and judgment I then had confidence
and with which I was myself connected, was such a 'good trust.' The particular ground upon which I based my opinion that the shoe machinery
monopoly operated beneficially was that it appeared to help the small
manufacturer and thus, while itself a monopoly, promoted competition in
shoe manufacturing. . . ." [44]

Brandeis then recalled his interviews with the shoe manufacturers, his unsuccessful attempts to adjust the disputed lease clauses, and noted the severance of his connection with the company: "By the summer of 1910 the situation had entirely changed from what it was in 1906. In the first place the United Shoe Machinery Company had shown a determined purpose to ignore or evade the act prohibiting tying clauses in leases passed in 1907 by the Legislature of Massachusetts and declared by its Supreme Court to be constitutional. In the second place the federal government had shown its purpose of enforcing the Sherman Anti-Trust Law as evidenced by the Standard Oil and Tobacco cases, and the Supreme Court of the United States in 1909 laid down in the Continental Wall Paper Company case a rule applicable to the United Shoe Machinery Company business. But the trust's methods remained unchanged. In the third place, and most important of all, Mr. Thomas G. Plant had developed a complete system of shoe machinery, in which the United Shoe Machinery Company had previously enjoyed a monopoly." [45]

Then, describing Plant's efforts and the methods by which United crushed him, he concluded that ". . . the time had come when I could no longer properly remain passive in the shoe-machinery controversy, and that I ought, if called upon, to lend aid in any effort that might be made to restore competitive conditions in the industry. . . . It should be noted, however, that my criticism of the shoe machinery company's course was not in its contesting the constitutionality of the Massachusetts Act of 1907, but in its so conducting its business as to make it practically impossible for any person to test the act, or, indeed, attempt to enforce it. For the company added to its leases a rider, by which it reserved the right to terminate the lease in thirty days, with or without cause. This put the Massachusetts manufacturer absolutely within its power. He had to be 'good' since no substitute machinery was available to him." [46]

Brandeis published this letter in the *Boston American*. Winslow promptly wrote Clapp on February 29: "Like other gentlemen who have changed their attitude when they thought it for their interest to do so, Mr. Brandeis's actions need a good deal of explanation." He picked flaws in Brandeis's arguments and, referring to Brandeis's statement at the July 1911 meeting between him and United's directors, maintained: "That statement was nothing more nor less than an endeavor at a very late date to justify a change of attitude which has always been unjustifiable." [47]

Winslow followed this up. Early in 1912 United attacked with a disingenuous pamphlet entitled, "Brandeis and Brandeis, The Reversible Mind of Louis D. Brandeis, 'The People's Lawyer'—as it stands revealed in his public utterances, briefs and correspondence." [48] The authorship of this brochure is not known,[49] but Brandeis suspected that someone very high in the counsels of the United Shoe Company's management was responsible.[50] The effectiveness of the pamphlet lay in its almost exclusive reliance on Brandeis's own statements to discredit him. Much was left to the reader's imagination, but a fatal lack of professional integrity was skillfully insinuated by clever selection and arrangement, by putting his original against his later views. The United's operations were neither explained nor dwelt upon, and the reader was apt to conclude that Brandeis, for no good reason, perhaps for some evil motive, had suddenly and bitterly turned hostile to the company he had willingly served as counsel and director, and with whose policies he had expressly sympathized. It ended: "Inasmuch as the Company's methods and policies are the same today as then, the reversed attitude of Mr. Brandeis is open to but one interpretation."

Using United's artful pamphlet, Elbert Hubbard devoted several pages in the July 1913 issue of his magazine to a scurrilous attack, on which George M. Crocker commented in a letter to G. W. Anderson, February 13, 1916, as follows: "I have good reason for believing (without legal proof) that Winslow hired Elbert Hubbard to write a most scandalous article in *The Philistine* about Brandeis a few years ago. It was awful. . . . Elmer Howe and Winslow were active in circulating it. . . . It was so raw that they did not dare to send it around openly as they did their other attacks."

Brandeis had this to say: "Anderson talked about the price that Elbert Hubbard got from the United Shoe Machinery Company for publishing the pamphlet against me. I know nothing about this. My guess is that the way he was paid was by their buying at a high price, and getting him to circulate a very large edition of the number containing that article." [51]

In later years Brandeis was sure that his campaign against the shoe machinery monopoly constituted a contribution to public enlightenment comparable to his seven years' war against the New Haven. To others, however, his action raises questions not easily answered. What light does this episode shed on Brandeis as a lawyer, as People's Attorney?

The facts seem to be that Brandeis before 1906 had shoe manufacturing clients who were using United machines under leases containing the "tying clause," but who were content if the United would relax its monopolistic advantage by fixing lower rentals and making other concessions; that Brandeis accepted employment from United to oppose the 1906 bill on an all-round understanding between United and the shoe manufacturers that the former would lower its prices and put the other concessions into effect; that Brandeis in emphasizing before the Legislature the beneficent use made by United of its monopolistic position was relying upon United's promises as if they had already been carried out; that after the bill had been defeated, largely through Brandeis's efforts, United disregarded this agreement, maintained and strengthened its monopolistic hold on the shoe manufacturers, and within five years thereafter had shut them off from all hope of rescue by killing Plant's competition. Brandeis had relied upon his arrangement with United without obtaining its written promise to make concessions to the shoe men, some of whom had been and still were his clients. Apparently the only course open to him was to withdraw as United's counsel and director.

Then, as United erected an ever greater structure of monopoly upon the foundation he had helped them build, Brandeis began, in 1911, a long fight for the rescue of his original clients, the shoe manufacturers. The same astuteness by which United ensnared Brandeis into the 1906 retainer was now employed to lay a smoke screen and to spread a barrage of innuendo discrediting the one man in New England they really feared. By constantly reiterating that United had in no respect changed its position after 1906, a wholly untrue statement, it sought to make plausible its accusation that Brandeis had been inconsistent and "unethical."

As a corporation lawyer, Brandeis's earlier role in all this is understandable, but it is not clear how one so gifted as People's Attorney, so skilled in factual exploration, could unknowingly have become deeply involved with a corporation designed and operated primarily to achieve monopolistic ends. This is the more baffling in view of his emphatic pronouncements, stated in terms of basic principles, against "irresponsible power," as such, and in all its various fields. On April 21, 1904, Brandeis had told the Boston Typothetæ that "it is essential that neither [employer nor employee] should feel that he stands in power—at the mercy—of the other. . . . Neither our intelligence nor our characters," he said, "can long stand the strain of unrestricted power. Every business requires for continued health the *memento mori* of competition from without." [52] On October 26, 1905, he had analyzed the evils of monopolistic power as manifest in financier control over our great insurance companies. "How," he asked, "has it been exercised? Substantially as all irresponsible power since the beginning of the world," was his all-encompassing answer. "Selfishly, dishonestly, and, in the long run, inefficiently." [53] Earlier that same year, on May 4, before the Harvard Ethical Society, he pointed to the "inconsistency of political democracy and industrial absolutism"; he warned lawyers against becoming "adjuncts of great corporations" and exhorted them to become the "people's lawyer," "the adviser of men." [54]

But in this instance Brandeis himself was as convincing in support of a particular monopoly as he had been only one or two years earlier in arguing against privilege-seeking traction and transportation interests, monopolistic insurance, autocratic employers and domineering trade unionists. Surely Brandeis's course in the shoe machinery episode raises grave questions. Can a lawyer, pledged and enlisted in *pro bono publico* causes, consistently defend monopoly under any circumstances whatever? Having become of counsel, a director, and an investor, could a People's Attorney of the sort he commended, "get out in a perfectly quiet way without raising any trouble at all?" His attempt to do so made trouble, serious and long-continued.*

Inevitably the truce between Brandeis and United Shoe must end. As the 1907-12 combatants parted company on their sharply divergent ways, their inherent hostility banked hidden fires which flared hotly in the nomination battle of 1916.

CHAPTER FIFTEEN

Munitions for Bourbonism, 1892-1910

As BRANDEIS's activities were making him noted as a public benefactor, his enemies were seeking to make him notorious as a shyster lawyer. Throughout these New England battles his opponents and their allies, fearing his abilities and fearing his principles even more, were limelighting those aspects of his professional career on which suspicion might be cast, and thus stocking their arsenals against him. Their apparent aim was to crush him on the score of professional ethics; their weapons were propaganda and misrepresentation. The three main episodes emphasized for attack, besides that of United Shoe already considered, were analyzed in detail and described with venom.

THE NEW YORK & NEW ENGLAND RAILROAD

In 1892 Brandeis was retained by persons later shown to be merely figurehead stockholders for the New Haven Railroad interests seeking to crip-

* Brandeis renewed his attack on United Shoe in 1913. See "Steering With the Wilson Tide," pp. 407-408.

ple the New York & New England's attempt to finance itself. Aggravated competition existed between the two roads. Their lines duplicated each other at many points, both railroads serving New York, Boston, Worcester, Springfield, Providence, New London, Hartford, and other cities. By 1891 the New Haven had set about harassing the New England by whatever methods seemed useful.[1] The New England being in dire financial straits, its president, Jabez A. Bostwick interested Austin Corbin in its rehabilitation. Bostwick retired in 1891, and Corbin was elected president. But internal strife among the board of directors caused him to resign after a few months.

Because of Corbin's personal resentment and his conviction that the directors themselves had wrecked the road financially, he decided to put it in the hands of a receiver for the protection of stockholders and second mortgage bondholders.[2] But he was unwilling to appear publicly against the railroad, although his connection with the suits against it was well known.[3] On the understanding that he would indemnify them for expenses incurred,[4] N. F. Goldsmith and Walter H. Keith of Boston, and Edwin F. Knowlton of New York [who held small amounts of the New England's preferred and common stocks], brought proceedings against the road in 1892, with Brandeis acting as their counsel.[5] He had been drawn into the case by William Kelly, New York lawyer and Corbin's counsel, whom Brandeis had often represented in Boston legal matters.[6] In praying the court that the company be restrained from paying a 3½ per cent dividend on about $3,600,000 of preferred stock, the petitioners maintained that the dividend had not been earned; in fact, it had netted a loss the preceding year. The railroad did not contest the injunction, and indeed its own sworn statement of financial condition during a part of the half-year covered by the proposed dividend showed a loss even greater than the plaintiff alleged.[7]

Seeking ways of financing itself, the New England decided to issue $25,000,000 worth of bonds. Brandeis, for Goldsmith, Keith, and Knowlton, brought suit in several states to enjoin this issue on the ground that the company had exhausted its legal capacity to float bonds under the laws of Massachusetts, Connecticut, Rhode Island, and New York, where it was incorporated.[8] In Connecticut, where the case was most actively pressed, the Superior Court decided that the railroad had no right to issue such bonds and appointed a master to inquire into all the facts and report to the Court.[9]

The New England in defense charged that the plaintiffs were not bringing the action in good faith but as tools of a third party interested in depressing the New England's credit. Hatred of the New Haven was alleged to be inspiring Brandeis's clients. The court, however, held this immaterial—that in seeking restraint of a corporation's *ultra vires* act, a stockholder might not be denied relief by reason of his motives.[10] The New England was still further hampered when Brandeis, acting for the same "stockholders," brought other suits to set aside leases made by the New England of two smaller roads, on the ground that these were illegal and improper since some of the New England directors controlled the two roads. Finally, for the same clients, he brought suit to prevent the consummation of a voting trust by the company, as being undesirable considering the other acts of its management.[11]

It was at this point that Brandeis came perilously near acting for the New Haven and against the New England. Corbin, weary of bearing the expenses of the litigation, considered retiring from it.[12] But in January 1893, while Brandeis was still acting against the New Haven, Lucius Tuttle, William Rockefeller, J. P. Morgan, and Charles P. Clark of the New Haven wrote Corbin, disclosing New Haven's interest in the suits brought against the New England. Rather ingenuously they indicated that they would be only too happy to bear the expenses of prosecuting these suits.[13] As a result of their interposing, Corbin continued the Goldsmith suits, as they were called, apparently being reimbursed by the New Haven.[14] Brandeis's relation to the Goldsmith suits continued, however, until June 1893,[15] and for some time thereafter his firm remained counsel of record.[16]

The New Haven's policy toward the New England was now so obvious that the Joint Standing Committee on Railroads of the Massachusetts Legislature held hearings to investigate the alleged attempt of the New Haven to monopolize transportation between Boston and New York.[17] Representatives of the New England charged that the New Haven, acting indirectly through other parties, was trying to cripple it by injuring its credit, and that the Goldsmith suits were brought with that purpose.[18] Furthermore, Moorfield Storey, counsel for the New England, implied that Brandeis, while acting nominally for Goldsmith, Keith, and Knowlton, was in fact acting for, and in the pay of, the New Haven.[19] Testifying at length before the Joint Standing Committee, Brandeis denied this categorically: "I have had nothing whatever to do with the New York & New Haven Railroad Company, from the first day to the last day. I have never had a conference with any officer or director, or any person in any way connected with the New York & New Haven Company." [20]

Later on Brandeis reiterated that he had had no connection with the New Haven. "The statement which has been made at times that we were acting for the New Haven is absolutely false," he wrote McClennen, February 12, 1916; but he then admitted that he was aware of Corbin, not

Goldsmith, Keith, and Knowlton, as the motivating force in these proceedings.

The fact that the New Haven appeared on the scene in January 1893, and Brandeis continued acting in the case until the following June, on first consideration tends to support the charge brought up again years later that Brandeis had had a deliberate part in "wrecking" the New England for the New Haven's benefit.[21] But it is not certain that Brandeis knew of the New Haven's financial and other interest in the cases he was prosecuting. Indeed it would have been much to the New Haven's advantage to keep in the shade as far as possible, and while matters stood thus, it certainly had no reason for enlightening Brandeis as to its assumption of the financial end of the litigation. On the other hand, Brandeis might have surmised what was going on. He was too well informed and too astute not to have guessed that such suits against the New England would be of absorbing concern to its rival—therefore that the New Haven might be helping Corbin finance the suits. In any case, Brandeis, as we have seen, withdrew from active participation in these matters in June 1893.

The last bill of Brandeis's firm, in April 1894,[22] was paid after legislative investigation had brought to light the New Haven's nefarious practices. The fee, paid as usual through Kelly, might have been New Haven money. Brandeis and his firm were accepting payment for valuable services rendered Goldsmith, Keith, and Knowlton. In this he was following the normal legal practice, but later on it was ammunition for his foes.

The end of the New York & New England, undoubtedly hastened by the Goldsmith suits, was not slow in coming. On July 9, 1895, its property was sold under foreclosure decree and acquired by the New England Railroad Company (chartered August 25, 1895), practically all of whose stock was purchased by the New Haven by 1898, as one more step in monopolizing New England transportation.[23] All this, distorted for hostile purposes, was advertised in full detail by Brandeis's enemies in 1912 and again in 1916.

THE LENNOX CASE

During the New Haven battle Clarence W. Barron, of the *Boston News Bureau* had, as he put it, "employed a Boston lawyer to examine Court's records." This man, William S. Youngman, ferreted through various sources for weapons against Brandeis. The deadliest bomb found was his participation in the affairs of the Lennox firm and family. The undisputed facts were these: In September 1907 James T. Lennox, representing P. Lennox & Company, a Massachusetts tanning concern then on the verge of bankruptcy, called in Brandeis to discuss the company's faltering financial condition. Lennox was accompanied by Moses J. Stroock, counsel for Abe Stein & Company, a Lennox creditor. They came to Brandeis knowing that his firm had from time to time represented another Lennox creditor, Weil, Farrel & Company. There were two conferences of which full stenographic record was made. Having canvassed the company's financial situation, Brandeis observed: "I think there is very little doubt under all the circumstances but that it will be necessary to make an assignment to trustees for the benefit of creditors. I should think that that was one of the things that would have to be done."

But later on he suggested: "Well, I don't think it is necessary to decide at this minute what is best. . . . I think the thing for you to do is to go out and talk the matter over with your father [then past eighty] and then let us talk together again. . . . I think it is entirely possible that your father may have some preference in the matter of counsel." [24]

The next day Lennox reported that his father had authorized him to do all that he "saw fit in the matter. He wants to pay a hundred cents on the dollar."

"Well now, Mr. Stroock," said Brandeis, "I should think the question that we ought to decide now is as to whether I should act for Mr. Lennox in this matter or not. I, of course, understand you came to me after conference with Mr. Lennox to ask me whether I would act for Mr. Lennox."

"May I ask you this question, Mr. Brandeis?" Stroock asked in turn. "From all that you know, do you believe that you could remain in the case in view of your firm's position with Weil, Farrell & Company?"

"Yes, I think I could," Brandeis answered. "The position that I should take if I remained in the case for Mr. Lennox would be to give everybody, to the very best of my ability, a square deal."

"That is what we want," said Stroock.

"Mr. Lennox . . . is in a very serious position," said Brandeis. "Whatever he has done is done, but he wants to pay, just as his father says, a hundred cents on the dollar, or whatever there is to go to creditors. . . . I should, if I acted for Mr. Lennox, see that he [Abe Stein & Co.] got his legal rights—no more, no less. I should feel that I could say to Mr. Nutter who handles particularly Weil, Farrell's business: 'This is the position— Mr. Lennox wants to give up his property for the benefit of his creditors according to their legal and fair rights. Weil, Farrell are entitled to their legal and equitable share—no more or less.' Now they shall get it, and I think that it would undoubtedly be advisable to make an assignment, individual and firm, for the benefit of creditors, to somebody whom we agree upon, so that you will know that everything that is done here is done openly and above board." [25]

Pressing for a clearer understanding as to the role Brandeis should play in the situation, Stroock inquired: "Do you think that the interests of all would be better subserved by Mr. Brandeis appearing as attorney for trustee of the Lennox family or as attorney for the Stein Company, so that if need be some strong man will be in a position to assert that right, and then have some other person attorney for Lennox & Company?"

"I am inclined to think," Brandeis answered, "that if we all agree that what we want to do is to distribute this property according to the legal rights of creditors, I could be more useful to that end by acting for Mr. Lennox instead of for Mr. Stein. . . ."

"I should feel that *if I were acting for Mr. Lennox as trustee,* that it was the duty of the trustee to see that everybody got his legal rights as nearly as we could make it, and if we could not determine actually the question of law and of fact, that ought to be determined by proper settlement, and I should feel that we ought to have a committee of the creditors with whom the trustees could confer, and if there are any questions of doubt in adjustment, that we get the advice of that committee and through them make the proper settlement." (Author's italics.)

"I can appreciate your position," Stroock said, "and undoubtedly under most circumstances your theory would work out all right; . . . but I do not want you to think I am overzealous, nor am I attempting in this way to sacrifice Mr. Lennox or any other creditor as against Mr. Stein's interests."

Lennox then expressed his desire to escape notoriety and safeguard his equity. "The course that I should pursue," Brandeis suggested, "if it were decided I should act for you [Lennox], would be to prepare at once and complete an assignment so that it could be used at a moment's notice, getting your father's signature as well as your own and having it here so that it could be recorded at a moment's notice."

"Well," inquired Lennox, "in what kind of a position does that leave my father and myself in the meantime?"

"You would have transferred your property," Brandeis replied. "The trustee would be in a position where he could employ you to assist him and could make you a reasonable allowance. . . . My own feeling is that the best thing for you to do is not to be thinking too much of yourself, but thinking of the best interests of your creditors." [26]

Stroock said he agreed "absolutely," and added, "I think that Mr. Brandeis's suggestion is the best." Lennox joined in, "I think it is."

"Without in any way being a flatterer," Stroock concluded, "I think Mr. Brandeis's reputation in the community would best work this out. We will start out substantially under Mr. Brandeis's reputation for a square deal, and in the second place he will virtually represent the large interest to start with."

"You are speaking now of Mr. Brandeis acting as my counsel?" Lennox asked.

"Not altogether as your counsel," Brandeis intervened, *"but as trustee of your property."* (Author's italics.)

"I came to you," said Lennox, "and I shall certainly do whatever you say; that is why I came to you."

Stroock and Lennox having apparently accepted the suggestions, Brandeis conferred briefly with his partner Nutter, whom he had mentioned as assignee. "Now, I think," he said, resuming the conference, "that the thing to do is for Mr. Nutter to prepare with Mr. Lennox an assignment or transfer to trustee; to have it executed so it can be delivered at any time."

No further question might ever have been raised had not Patrick Lennox refused to turn over substantial real estate holdings, alleging that he, an old man, had not understood the import of the assignment when affixing his signature to it, and, further, that he and his son were not actually partners. His son, James T. Lennox, withheld information from the assignee, and when his demand for $500 as weekly compensation for assisting in the administration of the trust was refused, he declined to give Nutter any further co-operation. The Lennoxes then brought criminal action, contending that the assignment had been obtained by fraud. They retained Sherman L. Whipple, prominent Boston trial lawyer, who immediately took up the tangled issues with Brandeis himself.

Recalling the substance of their interview, Whipple later quoted himself as telling Brandeis: "They [the Lennoxes] say you advised an assignment to your partner, Mr. Nutter, and took all Mr. Lennox's property, and that you now claim that you are not and never have been his counsel, and I thought, Mr. Brandeis, it would be better for me to come right to you and talk over a situation which seemed to me to be serious, because if you did agree with the Lennoxes that you would act as their counsel, and now are acting in a position hostile to them, through this assignment, you will agree with me that a rather serious situation is presented." [27]

"Of course that would be a serious situation," Whipple quoted Brandeis as rejoining, "but it is not the situation at all; I did not agree to act for Mr. Lennox when he came to me. When a man is bankrupt and cannot pay his debts, Mr. Whipple, he is a trustee for his creditors; he has no individual interest; he finds himself with a trust, imposed upon him by law, to see that all his property is distributed honestly and fairly and equitably among all his creditors, and he has no further interest in the matter. Such was Mr. Lennox's situation when he came to me, and he consulted me merely as the trustee for his creditors, as to how best to discharge that trust, and I advised him in that way. *I did not intend to act personally for Mr. Lennox, nor did I agree to.*" (Author's italics.)

"Yes," Whipple countered, "but you advised him to make the assignment. For whom were you counsel when you advised him to do that, if not for the Lennoxes?"

"I should say that I was counsel for the situation."

This answer did not satisfy Whipple at all. Acting for "the situation" was unlawyer-like, unconventional, perhaps a subterfuge.

"I must say, Mr. Brandeis," Whipple commented sharply, "it looks to me very much, according to your principles, as if when a man was bankrupt, and went to a lawyer, and the lawyer advises him to make an assignment for the benefit of his creditors, he assigns his lawyer with it, very much in the way a covenant runs with the land."

Brandeis was deeply hurt: "Mr. Whipple, I think that is a very unkind and very ungenerous statement for you to make. It impugns my motives, and I can only assure you that I had no such motive in doing it." [28]

Brandeis then went on to explain that he had occupied himself "with seeing that this property . . . was equitably and fairly distributed among the creditors, and I was looking after the interests of everyone; I was looking after any interests that Mr. Lennox had, if any, . . . but in the first place, looking after the interests of creditors."

Brandeis pointed up his position more sharply in writing Stroock, December 4, 1907: "I undertook to act in this matter . . . as counsel for the trustee, for the creditors and debtors under the assignment." [29]

Pursuing the matter further, Whipple told Brandeis how both Lennox and Stroock had said that "there was no suggestion of your acting for anybody except the Lennoxes; that you were employed for nothing else, and that you would look after them."

But Brandeis pointed out, "I received no retainer from them." Nor had he asked for one.

"You got all the property in your firm, did you not?" Whipple went on.

"Only in the trust relation," Brandeis persisted.

Still incredulous, Whipple commented sharply: "Mr. Brandeis, I do not see how you are going to escape the suggestion that if you had remained as counsel for the Lennoxes, under the bankruptcy law you would have gotten a very moderate fee, while going with the assignee, and following the property in that way, your firm is likely to get a very large fee."

Again Brandeis was hurt. "That is impugning my motive, and if you think I was influenced in what I did by any such mercenary considerations, why, you must think so; I can just assure you that I was not." [30]

The situation was further complicated by the fact that Brandeis had chosen one of his own partners as trustee. But here Whipple found no substantial ground for censure. To advise an assignment to one's self or one's partner was not unusual among lawyers. Though Whipple did not himself follow the practice, it was, as he put it years later, a "matter of taste," and became less blameworthy in this instance when one took into account Brandeis's "broader view"—"the paramount duty of seeing to an equitable distribution of this large estate."

Whipple believed that Brandeis erred chiefly in not making his position more clear, "so that a layman would understand just what he was talking about." [31] But Brandeis's sin of omission in this instance was not to be measured merely by the fact that he failed to make his position altogether plain to laymen. He had not made himself clear even to Stroock, a competent lawyer.

A compromise settlement of the case was eventually reached in the bankruptcy proceedings, and the Lennoxes' criminal suit was dismissed. Nevertheless, Brandeis's position was complex and not easily explicable to others.

Brandeis had been "misunderstood," in part perhaps, because of his failure to observe those requisites he had himself stated and underscored in writing William H. Dunbar many years earlier. "Cultivate the society of men, particularly men of affairs," he had advised Dunbar; "lose no opportunity of becoming acquainted with them." As Brandeis became more deeply involved in public activities, the purely legal work of his office was handled by others. No longer trying cases, his contact with Boston lawyers began to diminish in 1893, and by 1907 it had reached the vanishing point. From then on he had little contact with members of the Boston Bar except in matters of public concern.[32] And when friends and club members sharply criticized his stand on public issues, he lunched less frequently at the Exchange and Union Clubs, thus further diminishing his association with members of the local Bar. These unforeseen developments made it extremely difficult for him to follow the sage counsel he had given Dunbar back in 1893.

"In the twenty years before 1916," Edward F. McClennen has recalled, "Brandeis's contacts in practice with other lawyers was confined very largely to matters of advice and negotiation. Many of the active trial lawyers of this period rarely if ever met him. This had its effect upon his comradeship at the Bar. His long and frequent absences in response to calls elsewhere had its effect. He had always been engaged on serious pursuits which left little time or strength for the jovial meetings of the lawyers of Boston." [33]

THE WARREN CASE

Numerous charges were also made against Brandeis for the part he played in framing the arrangements for conduct of the Warren family's paper-mill business after the death of his partner's father. The facts in this case are not in dispute, nor is there any problem of interpreting the written word, as in the Lennox litigation. The issue was similar, however, in that here again Brandeis was "counsel for the situation," "adviser" to members of a family originally harmonious, who later drew apart. Then when disagreement arose, his firm acted for one of the disputing parties—his former partner Samuel D. Warren.

The elder Warren had died in 1888, leaving a valuable business to his family, a widow and five children, all of age. Warren and Brandeis had acted as counsel for S. D. Warren & Company before the elder Warren's death, and after Sam's retirement to take over management of the business, the Brandeis firm continued in this capacity. Warren, with Brandeis's advice, created the plan whereby three trustees—Samuel D. Warren, Mortimer B. Mason, and Mrs. Warren, Sr.—leased the property to Samuel D. Warren, Mr. Mason, and Mr. Fiske Warren as individual operators. All members of the family living in or near Boston actively participated in these arrangements, except Edward P. Warren, who resided in England. But his brother, Samuel D., submitted to him an outline of the plan together with the papers for his signature, advising him that competition was then setting in which would probably mean that the earnings of 1888 would represent the high-water mark in years ahead. A connoisseur of antiques, Edward signed and settled back to receive his share of the profits which he promptly invested in non-income-producing works of art.

No dissension arose until after the death of Mrs. Warren in 1901, which left a vacancy in the board of trustees. Henry Warren, next in age to Sam, had also died. This limited the choice to Edward or his sister Cornelia. Both Mason and Sam believed Edward unqualified to be a trustee quite apart from his residence abroad. They favored Cornelia, but Edward opposed this. Meanwhile earnings fell off and Edward asked for an advance. When this was not forthcoming he retained William S. Youngman to look into the property arrangements made after his father's death. A protracted family quarrel ensued which terminated miserably with Sam Warren's untimely death early in 1910.

Hollis R. Bailey, whom Brandeis had known at Harvard Law School, was also one of counsel in the case, having prepared a bill in equity in behalf of Edward against his brother in which he [Bailey] alleged that Samuel D. Warren, assisted by Brandeis, framed and carried out a plan for disposition of the family property under which his client suffered financially to the tune of hundreds of thousands of dollars.

Another and more fundamental point in Bailey's criticism was the now familiar charge that Brandeis had ignored professional ethics by purporting to act for all the Warrens, when, as Bailey assumed, diversified interests were necessarily involved.[34] But his view on this point was later repudiated by two distinguished members of the Boston Bar, Sherman L. Whipple and Moorfield Storey, although the latter was among Brandeis's severest critics. Storey had been in the case as counsel for Fiske Warren.

"The arrangement which was made seemed to me, as I examined it," Storey testified, "a perfectly fair arrangement. It probably, in view of what happened afterwards, would have been better if Mr. Edward P. Warren had had independent advisers to counsel him. But the thing was submitted to him and agreed to by him, and I saw nothing in the arrangement as to which he could complain. . . . I should have done perhaps very much as Mr. Brandeis did if I had been in his place."[35]

For his part Whipple contradicted Bailey's contention that Brandeis deliberately prepared the lease to his former partner's advantage. "This belief I do not share with Mr. Bailey," Whipple observed. "I cross-examined Mr. Warren at length, and I was then impressed, and so expressed myself, . . . that the entire transaction was free from any taint of dishonest motives or intentional fraud."[36]

But Whipple also "had the feeling that Brandeis was possibly careless in not making very, very clear to Mr. Edward P. Warren the whole transaction and its possible effects upon his rights."[37]

The full measure of Brandeis's alleged wrongdoing in this case did not come to light, however, until years later. While Bailey contended that the Brandeis firm ought not to have acted as counsel for Samuel D. Warren in 1909–10 at all, inasmuch as the firm had been counsel for Edward P. Warren in the transactions under investigation, others bitterly condemned Brandeis for having failed personally to conduct the trial in Warren's behalf. Being occupied at the time with the Ballinger-Pinchot case in Washington, Brandeis left the Warren affair in the hands of the firm's trial lawyer, Edward F. McClennen.

As to this alleged neglect, the late Richard W. Hale of the Boston Bar wrote: "Warren's immediate and other family and most of the intimates upon whom he lavished his talent for friendship believe that Warren's death was hastened by the ingratitude of Brandeis's desertion of Warren at a critical moment because Brandeis thought his duty to public matters had priority over the claim of Warren to be defended by him against unhappy attack. . . . I believe it to be true that when Warren, the soul of honor—in bad health—was accused of being a rascal for doing things Brandeis planned, he desired that Brandeis should defend him, and that Brandeis was more interested in various public causes and left Warren in lesser hands." [38]

·When this charge was brought in 1913, Brandeis reminded Norman Hapgood that he had hesitated to take full charge of the Ballinger case. "He told me," Hapgood wrote President-elect Wilson, February 21, 1913, "how much he disliked to leave this Warren case to his partners on account of his own personal feeling for Warren, although he felt that his partners were as able to conduct it as he was." *

After Sam's death the other Warrens bought Edward's interest in the business, which was the only payment made to him. "Brandeis wished to fight the case through but the family had no desire for further exhibition of their brother's [Edward's] character." [39]

As in the New England Railroad and Lennox litigations, the Warren case involved almost solely an issue of professional ethics, and was revived for hostile advantage in subsequent controversies.

The intensity of the anti-Brandeis hostility as it developed in later years, centering around these well-known cases, may have had its origin quite early in Brandeis's career. From the very outset he had demonstrated willingness to sacrifice personal popularity among fellow-members of the Bar "out of consideration for the rightful interest of his client." In 1941 Edward F. McClennen, Brandeis's former law partner, recalled one such incident:

Some fifty or more years ago he [Brandeis] became convinced that his client had been much overcharged. . . . There were provisions in the law that a successful litigant was entitled to recover not merely his claim and interest, but also costs at a rate defined by set statutory rules. These costs were not fixed by actual disbursements, and they were small in amount. It was the practice among some lawyers for the lawyer for the successful party to retain these costs as a part of his compensation for the services rendered. . . . In the case in hand, many suits, substantially identical in form and substance, had been brought against many defendants for a single plaintiff. The successful result in one of

---

* Mr. McClennen was himself an extremely able lawyer. Like Brandeis before him, he had led his class at Harvard Law School. Professor James Barr Ames had considered him "among his best pupils." (James Barr Ames to Edward F. McClennen, June 29, 1895.)

On hearing him in court for the first time, Oliver Wendell Holmes had written Brandeis, January 13, 1899: "I have just been listening to your McClennen and he fully justifies your praises of him. Some of these young chaps contrast very agreeably in brevity, style and point with a good many of those to whom I once looked to be leaders."

That Mr. McClennen's conduct of the case was eminently satisfactory to the Warren family is evidenced by letters to him from Mrs. Mabel Bayard Warren dated October 24, 1910, and from Miss Cornelia Warren, November 25, 1910.

the cases was a virtual demonstration that the plaintiff was entitled to recover in all of them. The costs in all of them were retained by the plaintiff's lawyer. The plaintiff was convinced, and convinced Mr. Brandeis, that this resulted in giving to the lawyer much more than just compensation for his work. This presented the issue whether it was right to retain all these costs. In the contest which ensued some leading members of the Boston Bar, fully a generation older than this young man from Kentucky, testified to the prevalence of this course of treatment of costs. The client's interest dictated the vigorous pursuit of the client's rights without any craven subservience either to the comradery of the Bar or the austere dignity of these leaders of it. . . . Brandeis would not compromise for his personal benefit on what he thought his duty to his client required. Accordingly, he conducted a cross-examination which offended the dignity of these elders and left an impression on them unfavorable to this young man. That impression circulated beyond the particular men involved and created an attitude in some groups which lasted years after the cause of it was forgotten. This planted germs of a wholly unwarranted dislike of him, the extent of the growth of which can never be known. . . .

According to McClennen, this "disloyalty" inflamed hatred of Brandeis among lawyers entirely ignorant of the incident itself. One of Brandeis's supporters in 1916, for example, though probably unaware of this old grudge, accounted for the opposition in this way: "By way of explanation, may I say that we have what I may call an aristocracy of the Boston Bar. I do not use the word at all offensively; on the contrary, they are high-minded, able, distinguished men. But they can not, I think, consider with equanimity the selection of anybody for a position on the great court of the country from that community who is not a typical, hereditary Bostonian." [40]

PART III

On the National Stage

CHAPTER SIXTEEN

More Life in the Law, 1908-1914

BRANDEIS's methods inevitably carried him on to the national stage. As the tentacles of industry, transportation, and finance took hold beyond state and regional lines, Washington rather than Boston became the center of his activity. The national spotlight had first fallen on him in 1897 when he spoke on behalf of consumers amid the jeers of tariff-supporting legislators. But the next time he commanded national attention even the reactionaries applauded. This was in 1908 when he presented to the United States Supreme Court his brief in *Muller* v. *Oregon,* a case involving a state statute limiting the hours of women in industry.[1]

Brandeis's triumph in the Muller case was truly epoch-making. But the grounds on which he won his victory were even more important. For the first time, argument in a Supreme Court case was based not on dead legal precedents, but on the living facts of industrial America. Brandeis brought law and life together. Fitting eighteenth-century concepts to twentieth-century conditions, he made the law grow a hundred years in a day. To judge that achievement, we don't have to go to the dusty books. We have only to look about us to see how law (though not by all lawyers) is practiced today.

BLIND LEADERS OF THE LAW

In *Muller* v. *Oregon,* Brandeis applied concepts which he had been urging on lawyers for some time. A little later he elaborated these ideas in a notable address before the Chicago Bar Association, entitled "The Living Law." [2] Here he described how conditions had changed in the United States in recent years—how independent small businessmen had fallen before the trusts and monopolies; how entrepreneurs had been forced to become workers for someone else; how the workers themselves had become mere cogs in an industrial machine which depended on sharp division of labor for mass production and upon mass production for its profits. No longer could all men reasonably expect to become independent business-men; workers now depended on big companies for jobs; responsibility for their welfare shifted necessarily from themselves to their big employers or ultimately to the state.

The law had not been altered to fit the new conditions of American life but "our longing shifted," he said, "from legal justice to social justice." It was realized that government must "keep order not only physically but socially," that "the law must protect a man from the things that rob him of his freedom, whether the oppressing force be physical or of a subtler kind." Yet the law was doing none of these things.

As a consequence, Brandeis noted with much concern the waning public respect for law, for lawyers, and for judges. This had happened many times before in history. The lawyers' failure to keep up with social and economic progress, Brandeis said, was as old as the profession itself—it was inherent in the very process of erecting a working law for today upon the precedents of yesterday and the day before. It was not heavenly inspiration alone which made the physician Luke proclaim: "Woe unto you, lawyers! for ye have taken away the key of knowledge: ye entered not in yourselves, and them that were entering in ye hindered." [3]

Brandeis saw this divorce of law from life as peculiarly dangerous in America, where constitutional limitations were invoked "to stop the natural vent of legislation. Where statutes giving expression to the new social spirit were clearly constitutional, judges, imbued with the relentless spirit of individualism, often construed them away." Where social science recognized revolutionary change, he continued, "legal science—the unwritten or judge-made law as distinguished from legislation—was largely deaf and blind." No wonder that during the first decade of the twentieth century demand arose for the popular recall of judges, for radical amendments to the Constitution, and even for its abolition. Dissatisfaction with the law was clear evidence that "it had not kept pace with the rapid development of our political, economic, and social ideals."

Brandeis thought he knew the reason for all of this: "The judge came to the bench unequipped with the necessary knowledge of economic and social science, and his judgment suffered likewise through lack of equipment in the lawyers who presented the cases to him. One can hardly escape the conclusion," Brandeis remarked * "that a lawyer who has not studied economics and sociology is very apt to become a public enemy." [4]

Brandeis did not condemn lawyers and judges personally. "What we need," he wrote, "is not to displace the courts, but to make them efficient instruments of justice; not to displace the lawyer, but to fit him for his

* Quoting Charles R. Henderson, Professor of Practical Psychology, University of Chicago.

official or judicial task." Since modern practice has to be specialized, he would "correct its distorting effects by broader education—by study undertaken preparatory to practice—and continued by lawyer and judge throughout life: study of economics and sociology and politics which embody the fact and present problems of today."

Nor did Brandeis condemn the Constitution. "It was not obsolete," he said. Rather the judges, in ignorance of modern industrial life, had erected their own economic prejudices into impassible legal barriers, and made these part and parcel of the Constitution itself. "A judge," he observed, "rarely performs his functions adequately unless the case before him is adequately presented. Thus were the blind led by the blind. It is not surprising that under such conditions the laws as administered failed to meet contemporary economic and social demands."

"In constitutional cases," Brandeis pointed out, "the traditional policy of the Supreme Court had been to presume in favor of its [legislative action] validity, until its violation of the Constitution is proved beyond all reasonable doubt." [5] But recently, he said, the Court had transferred responsibility so that anyone attacking a state law did not have to prove it unconstitutional; the state itself, in such a case, had to prove the law constitutional. This was practically impossible where judges and legislators did not see eye to eye on the social needs of the nation.

Brandeis illustrated the point with specific cases. In 1895, he said, "freedom of contract had justified the Illinois Supreme Court in declaring invalid an eight-hour law for women. The judges could see no "fair, just, and reasonable connection between such legislation and the public health, safety or welfare proposed to be secured by it." [6]

In 1905 the United States Supreme Court by a narrow margin of 5 to 4 had set aside New York's ten-hour law for bakers as "mere meddlesome interference with the rights of individuals." The Court dared those favorable to the legislation to show "that there is material danger to the public health or the employee, if the hours of labor are not curtailed." The judges then noted that legislative interference "with the ordinary trades seems to be on the increase" and frankly said they did "not believe in the soundness of the views" supporting this policy. "Clean and wholesome bread," Justice Peckham said, "does not depend on whether a baker works but ten hours per day or only sixty hours a week," and the Constitution, he held, guaranteed workers "the right" to labor even for injuriously long hours and at substandard wages, if they so "desired." [7] The Constitution did it, he said, not the Court.

In 1907 the New York Court of Appeals, in a case involving restrictions on hours for women, was just as obtuse. "When it is sought," Judge Gray observed, "under the guise of a labor law, arbitrarily as here, to prevent an adult female citizen from working any time of day that suits her, I think it is time to call a halt." [8]

HOURS OF LABOR

For Brandeis, on the other hand, when judges rendered such decisions it was the very time to begin. His opportunity came in 1907, when Mrs. Florence Kelley, the Chief Factory Inspector of Illinois, and Miss Josephine Goldmark, of the National Consumers' League, learned that the Oregon ten-hour law for women was to be contested before the United States Supreme Court. To defend the law, these women wanted the most competent legal talent in the land. They turned first to Joseph H. Choate. They knew, of course, that Choate had no knowledge of, nor sympathy for, labor. Nevertheless they asked him to defend the act. He declined. He could see no reason why "a big husky Irishwoman should not work more than ten hours a day in a laundry if she and her employer so desired." The next day they asked Brandeis, who accepted at once, provided an official invitation were sent him by the State of Oregon. He was unwilling to appear as *amicus curiae,* believing official participation essential.

The invitation was gladly extended. Brandeis then outlined the material needed for his brief. The legal part he would himself cover in a few pages. For the economic and social data showing the evil of long hours and the possible benefits from legislative limitation, he would look to his sister-in-law. It was on these materials, not on the legal argument, that he would base his case.

This was a bold innovation. No one knew whether or not the Court would notice a brief so unconventional. But, Brandeis noted, in all the cases in which social legislation had been set aside, the judges, by recourse to abstract logic, had confidently denied any "reasonable" relation between the legislation and the stated objective of improved public health. Sometimes the Court more modestly suggested that if any such "reasonable" relation did exist, it had not in fact been shown. The inference was, therefore, that if the reasonable relation could be proved, the Court would be forced to accept it. So far no lawyer had dared to furnish the requisite social and economic statistics, to demonstrate this "reasonable" relation. No lawyer had confidence that the judges would see it even if it were shown; no lawyer had confidence in his ability to *make* the judges see the "reasonable" relation, whether they wanted to see it or not. That is, no lawyer had this confidence in the judges or in himself—except Brandeis.

Many years earlier he had recorded in his *Index Rerum:* "A judge is presumed to know the elements of law, but there is no presumption that he knows the facts." In this spirit he drew up his revolutionary social and economic brief.

The first step was to bring the judges around to seeing how they had practically asked for such a brief—for a "reasonable" demonstration of the needs of public health, not merely a "logical" array of legal precedents. Included in his brief was a detailed list of the Court's holdings in the New York ten-hour law case, and with the judge's rules to guide them, he showed that his brief was not so revolutionary after all. What were these rules?

The legal rules applicable to this case are few and well established, namely:

First: The right to purchase or to sell labor is a part of the "liberty" protected by the Fourteenth Amendment of the Federal Constitution.

Second: This right to "liberty" is, however, subject to such reasonable restraint of action as the State may impose in the exercise of the police power for the protection of health, safety, morals, and the general welfare.

Third: The mere assertion that a statute restricting "liberty" relates, though in a remote degree, to the public health, safety, or welfare does not render it valid. The act must have a "real or substantial relation to the protection of the public health and the public safety." It must have "a more direct relation, as a means to an end, and the end itself must be appropriate and legitimate."

Fourth: Such a law will not be sustained if the Court can see that it has no real or substantial relation to public health, safety, or welfare, or that it is "an unreasonable, unnecessary, and arbitrary interference with the right of the individual to his personal liberty or to enter into those contracts in relation to labor which may seem to him appropriate or necessary for the support of himself and his family."

But "If the end which the Legislature seeks to accomplish be one to which its power extends, and if the means employed to that end, although not the wisest or best, are yet not plainly and palpably unauthorized by law, then the Court cannot interfere. In other words, when the validity of a statute is questioned, the burden of proof, so to speak, is upon those" who assail it.

Fifth: The validity of the Oregon statute must therefore be sustained unless the Court can find that there is no "fair ground, reasonable in and of itself, to say that there is material danger to the public health (or safety), or to the health (or safety) of the employees (or to the general welfare) if the hours of labor are not curtailed."

For all this *Lochner* v. *New York* was cited as authority. Brandeis apparently agreed with Justice Peckham that "no law limiting the liberty of contract ought to go beyond necessity." He diverged from Peckham, however, in his next step. To determine "necessity," he said, logic is not enough. "There is no logic that is properly applicable to these laws except the logic of facts." [9] And in the "logic of facts" he went on, "common knowledge" is not enough. Common knowledge is "equivalent" only to "popular ignorance and fallacy." All the facts are needed, not merely the common facts; [10] and Brandeis set out to furnish them.

Brandeis's brief-making enormously extended the bounds of common knowledge and compelled the Court to "take judicial notice" of this extension. In the Muller brief only two scant pages were given to conventional legal arguments. Over one hundred pages were devoted to the new kind of evidence drawn from hundreds of reports, both domestic and foreign, of committees, statistical bureaus, commissioners of hygiene, and factory inspectors—all proving that long hours are *as a matter of fact* dangerous to women's health, safety, and morals, that short hours result in social and economic benefits.

Brandeis appeared in oral argument in January 1908, before a Court dominated by superannuated legalists, including Chief Justice Fuller, Justices Peckham, Brewer, and Day. The "dry bones of legalism rattled" [11] as opposing counsel argued that women were endowed, equally with men, with the fundamental right of free contract; that woman's "freedom" to bargain with employers must not be impaired. This time, however, the Court could not be screened from all knowledge of the living world.

"The distinguishing mark of Mr. Brandeis's argument," Miss Goldmark recorded, "was his complete mastery of the details of his subject and the marshaling of the evidence. Slowly, deliberately, without seeming to refer to a note, he built up his case from the particular to the general, describing conditions authoritatively reported, turning the pages of history, country by country, state by state, weaving in with artistic skill the human facts—all to prove the evil of long hours and the benefit that accrued when these were abolished by law. It was the result of intense preparation and concentration of thought. In hours of preparation beforehand, submerging himself first in the source material, he was determining the exclusion or inclusion of detail, the order, the selectiveness, the emphasis which marked his method. Once determined upon, it had all the spontaneity of a great address because he had so mastered the details that they fell into place, as it were, in a consummate whole." [12]

To this approach the elderly jurists on the bench were responsive. The Oregon ten-hour law was upheld, and the Court, speaking through Justice Brewer, approved Brandeis's technique and, most unusually, mentioned him by name. The Court's spokesman, Justice Brewer, said: "It may not be amiss, in the present case, before examining the constitutional question, to notice the course of legislation as well as expressions of opinion from other than judicial sources. In the brief filed by Mr. Louis D. Brandeis . . . is a very copious collection of all these matters. . . .

"The legislation and opinions referred to in the margin may not be, technically speaking, authorities, and in them is little or no discussion of the constitutional question presented to us for determination, yet they are significant of a widespread belief that woman's physical structure, and the functions she performs in consequence thereof, justify special legislation restricting or qualifying the conditions under which she should be permitted to toil." [13]

Here for the first time the Supreme Court was recognizing the need for facts to establish the reasonableness or unreasonableness of social legislation. For the time being the Court had rejected its own freedom-of-contract fiction as regards working women. Brandeis followed up this advantage immediately. After the Muller case he appeared for oral argument in defense of other labor laws and sent briefs to some fourteen different courts.

In 1909 an Illinois statute similar to that involved in the Muller case was contested before the state Supreme Court. Here a manufacturer claimed that a woman, thirty-five years in his employ, could not earn a living wage unless she worked over ten hours a day. Brandeis went to Illinois and saved the ten-hour law there. Some years later he explained how he used the technique of the Muller case to do it:

In 1895 the Illinois court held in the first Ritchie case that the eight-hour law for women engaged in manufacturing was unconstitutional. In 1908 the United States Supreme Court held in *Muller* v. *Oregon* that the Women's Ten-Hour Law was constitutional. In 1910 the Illinois court held the same in the second Ritchie case. The difference in decision in the two Ritchie cases was not due to the difference between a ten-hour day and an eight-hour day. . . . In the two Ritchie cases the same broad principles of constitutional law were applied. In each the right of a Legislature to limit (in the exercise of the police power) both liberty of contract and use of property was fully recognized. But in the first Ritchie case the court, reasoning from abstract conceptions, held a limitation of working hours to be arbitrary and unreasonable; while in the second Ritchie case, reasoning from life, it held the limitation of hours not to be arbitrary and unreasonable. In other words—in the second Ritchie case it took notice of those facts of general knowledge embraced in the world's experience with unrestricted working hours, which the court had in the earlier case ignored. It considered the evils which had flowed from unrestricted hours, and the social and industrial benefit which had attended curtailed working hours. . . . In the light of this evidence as to the world's experience and beliefs it proved impossible for reasonable judges to say that the Legislature of Illinois had acted unreasonably and arbitrarily in limiting the hours of labor. . . .* [14]

* The Illinois Act was again under attack in 1912 when Brandeis successfully defended it in *People* v. *Eldering*, 254 Ill. 579 (1912).

In 1911 he was invited by the Attorney-General of Ohio to assist in defense of a statute

Brandeis's technique later proved successful in New York state. There the Court of Appeals had declared invalid a statute prohibiting night work for women as "discriminative against female citizens, in denying to them equal rights with men in the same pursuit." [15] Prior to enacting a second measure the Legislature surveyed the facts on which the new statute was based. In 1915 the constitutionality of the new statute was questioned, and Brandeis defended it. Again he won. In sustaining the new law the Court of Appeals commented: "While theoretically we may [in 1907] have been able to take judicial notice of some of the facts and of some of the legislation now called to our attention as sustaining the belief and opinion that night work in factories is widely and substantially injurious to the health of women, actually very few of these facts were called to our attention, and the argument to uphold the law on that ground was brief and inconsequential. . . ." [16]

THE MINIMUM WAGE

In 1913 the Oregon Legislature set up an Industrial Welfare Commission to regulate wages, hours, and the safety, health, and welfare of employees. The commission at once promulgated a minimum wage requirement for women employed in factories and stores. The validity of the act under which these orders were issued was contested, and at the commission's request Brandeis filed a brief.[17] The statute was unanimously sustained by the Oregon Supreme Court on grounds previously urged in support of hours of labor for women. When the case came before the United States Supreme Court, on December 17, 1914, Brandeis appeared in oral argument: [18] "No proposition in economics is better established than that low wages are not cheap wages. On the contrary, the best in wages is the cheapest. . . . Why should the proposition be doubted, that wages insufficient to sustain the worker properly are uneconomical? Does anybody doubt that the only way you can get work out of a horse is to feed the horse properly? Does anyone doubt that the only way you can get hens to lay, is to feed the hens properly? Regarding cows we know now that even proper feeding is not enough, or proper material living conditions. . . . Experience has taught us that harsh language addressed to a cow impairs her usefulness. Are women less sensitive than beasts in these respects?" [19]

Four Justices were impressed, as was Judge William Hitz of the District

regulating hours of labor for women. He prepared the brief and successfully presented it to the Supreme Court of Ohio. *Ex parte Anna Hawley,* 85 Ohio 495 (1911).

This case was carried on appeal to the U.S. Supreme Court where Brandeis filed a brief and took part in the oral argument. The act was sustained in *Hawley* v. *Walker,* 232 U.S. 718 (1914).

of Columbia Supreme Court, who wrote Felix Frankfurter, December 17, 1914:

I have just heard Mr. Brandeis make one of the greatest arguments I have ever listened to. . . . He spoke on the minimum wage cases in the Supreme Court, and the reception which he wrested from that citadel of the past was very moving and impressive to one who knows the Court. . . . When Brandeis began to speak, the Court showed all the inertia and elemental hostility which courts cherish for a new thought, or a new right, or even a new remedy for an old wrong, but he visibly lifted all this burden, and without orationizing or chewing of the rag he reached them all and held even Pitney quiet.

He not only *reached* the Court, but he *dwarfed the Court,* because it was clear that here stood a man who knew infinitely more, and who cared infinitely more, for the vital daily rights of the people than the men who sat there sworn to protect them. It was so clear that something had happened in the Court today that even Charles Henry Butler * saw it and he stopped me afterwards on the coldest corner in town to say that no man this winter had received such close attention from the Court as Brandeis got today, while one of the oldest members of the Clerk's office remarked to me that "that fellow Brandeez has got the impudence of the Devil to bring his socialism into the Supreme Court."

THE GROUND WON

Despite the remarkable encouragement from both state and federal courts, Brandeis realized in 1916 that "the struggle for the living law has not been fully won." Even when social facts were furnished by counsel, the Court did not always find these either important or acceptable. Direct contact with reality was still cut off by the "potency of mental prepossessions." When "stubborn facts were confronted with stubborn theory," the latter often won.[20] Facts proved to be a double-edged weapon. By resort to their own preferred facts the judges continued to find social legislation based on the police power arbitrary and unreasonable and therefore in violation of "due process."

Nevertheless, Brandeis had unfailing confidence in our basic institutions and in their power, wisely administered, to satisfy the demands of a changing civilization. To those who doubted the capacity of our legal system to cope with the needs of the time, he observed cheerfully: "The law will catch up. It will adequately meet modern conditions." [21] His brief in *Muller* v. *Oregon* had shown lawyers and judges the way to catch up.

---

* Charles Henry Butler (1859–1940) was a distinguished lawyer and author, specializing in International Law. Reporter of United States Supreme Court decisions, 1902–16, and editor of Volumes 187–242 of the U.S. Supreme Court Reports.

CHAPTER SEVENTEEN

The Ballinger-Pinchot Conservation Feud, 1910

THE MULLER case brought Brandeis to the national stage, and the Ballinger–Pinchot controversy kept him there. This controversy involved the whole problem of conservation of our natural resources. Brandeis did not come on the scene, however, until preliminary skirmishes had been fought.

Theodore Roosevelt made the American public very much aware of the tremendous natural wealth with which the United States had been endowed, and the prodigal way in which much of that wealth had been exploited by private corporations. He made a vigorous fight for conservation, and in this was warmly supported by James R. Garfield, Secretary of the Interior, and Chief Forester Gifford Pinchot of the Department of Agriculture.

In March 1909 William Howard Taft succeeded Roosevelt. During the campaign leading to his election, Taft pledged himself to continue Roosevelt's conservation policies. One of Taft's first steps upon entering office was to appoint Richard A. Ballinger Secretary of the Interior. A lawyer and once reform mayor of Seattle, Ballinger had represented private corporations in suits involving public lands, and Pinchot was fearful lest the Roosevelt–Garfield policies be overturned. The Chief Forester thought he saw confirmation of his fears in August 1909, when Ballinger reopened for sale certain valuable coal lands in Alaska, known as the "Cunningham Claims," which Roosevelt had withdrawn from the market.

THE FEUD BEGINS

From the moment he took office, Ballinger was openly critical of the methods used by Roosevelt's "whoop 'er up boys" to publicize the need for conservation. By midsummer 1909 the press was commenting regularly on the "strained relations" between Ballinger and Pinchot. In August the simmering pot came to a boil. Early that month Louis R. Glavis, Chief of the General Land Office Field Agents (in the Interior Department), realized that something was afoot between certain Interior officials and the Guggenheims, particularly as to the Cunningham coal claims. He suspected all sorts of law evasion schemes in regard to Alaskan lands, and he reported these directly to Ballinger. Taft's Secretary seemed uninterested, so on

August 5 Glavis turned to Pinchot. Glavis said he wanted to resign and make public the whole record showing misconduct on the part of high Interior officials. Pinchot, however, advised against anything so drastic until Glavis had reported the facts to Taft himself.

Glavis spent the next two weeks preparing his formal charges against Ballinger and his staff, and on August 18 presented them to Taft at the summer White House in Beverly, Massachusetts. At Taft's request Glavis stayed on call in Boston. After four or five days he was told that the President did not wish to see him again and that he could return to his Portland, Oregon, office. On August 22 Taft officially apprised Ballinger (then in the West) and the others of Glavis's charges and asked that their replies be made "as full as possible."

Ballinger returned to Washington on September 3 to put the finishing touches on his formal answer to the President. He was in a bellicose mood. Next day, after telling reporters of his various activities, he added: "Incidentally I propose to kill some snakes." [1] Three days later Ballinger was on his way to Beverly, accompanied by Oscar W. Lawler, an Assistant Attorney-General assigned to the Interior Department. With them they took supporting records which, as subsequently printed, ran to 730 pages.

The President conferred with Ballinger and Lawler on the evenings of September 6 and 7 and sat up September 6 until three o'clock in the morning "studying the record." He also discussed the matter on two or three occasions with Attorney-General Wickersham. Finding Wickersham's views in substantial agreement with his own, Taft on September 13 wrote a lengthy letter to Ballinger exonerating him and authorizing dismissal of "L. R. Glavis from the service of the government for filing a disingenuous statement, unjustly impeaching the official integrity of his superior officers." The President assured Ballinger that "the case attempted to be made by Mr. Glavis embraces only shreds of suspicion without any substantial evidence to sustain his attack." [2]

Taft hoped that this would put an end to an annoying, but not very serious, issue. So did Ballinger, who promptly told reporters: "You may say for me that I am greatly delighted over the manner in which this affair has come to a close. I have never had any doubt as to what the President's review of the coal-land cases would disclose, as we have always understood one another on matters of conservation." [3]

Taft apparently realized this, for on September 13, the same day he exonerated Ballinger, he also wrote to Pinchot: "I urge that you do not make Glavis's case yours. . . . I write this letter in order to prevent hasty action on your part in taking up Glavis's cause, or in objecting to my sustaining Ballinger and his subordinates within the Interior Department, as a reason for your withdrawing from the public service. I should consider it one of the greatest losses my administration could sustain if you were to leave it." [4]

Taft also warned Ballinger in a second letter on September 13: "Please . . . advise your subordinates to be very particular not to involve Mr. Pinchot in this matter and to rest silent in view of the complete acquittal they received from my letter. . . . Should it be necessary, as is not unlikely, to submit all this record and evidence to Congress, I shall be glad *to have your authority and that of* your subordinates to leave out of your answers any *reference to Pinchot* or the part he took in bringing Glavis's report to my attention." [5] (Author's italics.)

But Pinchot could not be won over. Conservation, he wrote Taft on November 4, 1909, is "the most critical and far-reaching problem this nation has faced since the Civil War." And Ballinger is "the most effective opponent the conservation policies have yet had." [6] Certain circumstances indicate that Pinchot was trying to force the President to request Ballinger's resignation and thus bring the fight into the open.[7] Before Taft could move, however, the fight became a tremendous public issue by the publication of Glavis's original report in *Collier's* on November 13. Norman Hapgood, the editor, had received this report from John Bass, a journalist and brother of Robert P. Bass, Governor and Republican boss of New Hampshire. In presenting the report to Hapgood, Bass said: "As Secretary Ballinger, Attorney-General Wickersham, and President Taft have all turned down Glavis's report on the stealing of the public domain that is going on, we have decided to go straight to the public. . . ." [8]

Collier's cover carried a picture of Ballinger framed in a clutching hand and a huge question mark, with the query: "Are the Guggenheims in charge of the Department of the Interior?" Inside, the story was titled "The Whitewashing of Ballinger." Such muckraking captions do not convey the real quality or the content of the article, which is a simple, factual account showing how Glavis's demand for an impartial investigation of the contested coal claims had been repeatedly frustrated, how the President had sustained Ballinger and discharged Glavis without a hearing and on inadequate evidence.

The result of the article was a nationwide demand for a congressional investigation. In this Ballinger himself concurred. He wrote Senator Wesley L. Jones on December 21, 1909: "The best interests of the Interior Department require a broad and thoroughgoing investigation, and I assure you it cannot be made too broad in its scope to suit me. I shall hope that there will be no delay in the offering of a proper resolution of investigation."

Collier's knew early in December that such an investigation would soon be undertaken. Through Payne Whitney,* an old college friend of Robert J. Collier, the latter also learned how the Taft men were aiming to manipulate the investigation. Whitney said he had reliable information that the investigating committee, the majority of whom would be Republicans, would almost certainly whitewash Ballinger, and, on the basis of this whitewash, administration leaders were planning to teach "radical" *Collier's* a lesson by starting a million-dollar libel suit.

During Christmas week of 1909 *Collier's* called an emergency war council of those involved at the house of Henry L. Stimson, a New York lawyer. Present were Gifford Pinchot, his brother Amos, George Wharton Pepper, James R. Garfield, Robert J. Collier, and Norman Hapgood. Their main work was to line up legal talent to counsel Glavis and Pinchot at the forthcoming investigation. Stimson and Pepper agreed to handle the legal work, and at the insistence of Hapgood, Brandeis was also retained at a fee of $25,000, plus expenses.

With his precise role still undetermined, Brandeis came to New York on January 12, 1910, and worked in seclusion at the Harvard Club, seeing no one but Hapgood. After a few days he had acquired a working knowledge of the Interior Department, public land laws, conservation, and other relevant matters. By that time each lawyer's task had been decided. Stimson, it turned out, could not find time to take any major role at all.[9] George Wharton Pepper of Philadelphia and Nathaniel A. Smyth of the New York Bar were to represent Pinchot. Brandeis, Joseph P. Cotton, Jr. (who later served as Undersecretary of State in the Hoover cabinet), and George Rublee of New York were to act for Glavis.

Early in January 1910 the press announced the names of the six senators and six representatives who were likely to make up the Joint Investigating Committee. But the press calculated without insurgent Representative George W. Norris of Nebraska. Norris had no intention of letting Speaker Joe Cannon pack the committee with Taft men. He arose on the floor of the House, January 6, and said: "Mr. Speaker, I am not in favor of narrowing this investigation. . . . I believe the committee ought to be elected by the House of Representatives and not appointed by the Speaker, and in accordance with the idea, I offer, Mr. Speaker, the following amendment: . . . that the committee will be elected by the House of Representatives from members of that body." [10]

"If it had not been for my motion amending the Resolution," Senator Norris explained years later, "there would have been nothing but a white-

* The son of William C. Whitney, the traction magnate and Cleveland's first-term Secretary of the Navy.

wash, pure and simple. . . . The fact that there was one insurgent [E. H. Madison of Kansas] on the committee, together with two Democrats [Ollie M. James of Kentucky and James Graham of Illinois], from the House made it possible for a fight to be made." [11]

The fight began at the Joint Committee's first hearing on January 26, 1910.

PATRIOTS AND PARTISANS IN SEARCH OF A VILLAIN

The committee tried to run its hearings like a court, but the effect was more theatrical than judicial.[12] At the head of a long table in Room 210 of the Senate Office Building, Senator Knute Nelson of Minnesota presided as chairman. At Nelson's left were the Senate members of the committee, to his right were the House members. At the opposite end of the table, in an elevated chair, squirmed the witness. And before all of them sat the daily audience. Ninety per cent of the "regulars" at the hearings were women, the most violent of partisans, who expressed their opinions freely and audibly.

Ballinger's wife, herself a fairly regular attendant, occupied a seat in the front row next to the press table. Pinchot's mother usually sat just behind Mrs. Ballinger. Each of these ladies had her own outspoken supporters. One day Mrs. William E. Humphrey, wife of the congressman from Seattle, complained to Chairman Nelson that the comments of the Pinchot ladies were "perfectly disgusting and dreadfully annoying" to Mrs. Ballinger. Less than fifteen minutes later one of Mrs. Pinchot's friends complained that the comments of the ladies with Mrs. Ballinger were "abhorrent and annoying" to the mother of the former Chief Forester.[13]

Throughout, Senator Nelson was bitterly anti-Pinchot, anti-Glavis, anti-Brandeis. He missed no opportunity to cast ugly reflections on the latter. Once he carried this so far that the committee considered making a formal disavowal of his remarks. It was decided, however, that the record should stand to show the bias and prejudice of such a chairman. After Brandeis had repeatedly charged that essential papers were being held back "for reasons satisfactory to the Interior Department," Chairman Nelson allowed him partial opportunity to examine these documents under the critical eye of the committee's clerk. Baffled and outraged by such obstructive tactics within the committee itself, Brandeis finally went to Senator Nelson's private office, demanding explanation. "I had a private tussle with Senator Nelson," Louis wrote Alfred, February 10, "about withholding the documents of the Interior Department which we had called for, but won my point and relations are diplomatically friendly."

Another time Brandeis requested Ballinger to furnish a list of land cases in which he or his firm had acted as counsel during the year between his retirement as Land Office Commissioner and his appointment as Secretary of the Interior. Chairman Nelson ruled that such information was irrelevant. "Mr. Chairman," said Brandeis with emphasis, "I think it is important." Apparently his tone irritated the chairman: "You need not snap at me!" Nelson shouted. "You can insult witnesses, but you cannot insult the committee." Before the attorney could reply a woman spectator shouted: "The committee has no right to insult him either." The committeemen maintained a painful silence; Brandeis offered no apology; the sergeant-at-arms called order, and the moment passed.[14]

Especially annoying to certain committeemen was Brandeis's obvious effort to get his evidence out to the public. On one occasion, as Brandeis's line of inquiry evoked more than the usual protest, Nelson interjected: "It might help senators to understand that counsel is trying this case for the other table, the press table, and not this one"; whereupon Senator Fletcher pertinently reminded the chairman: "I want to say that this case is not only being tried for this committee and Congress, but for the country."

Senator Frank Putnam Flint of California, seated on the chairman's left, specialized in calling Counsel Brandeis to account for alleged derelictions in procedure. Senator George Sutherland, next in order, objected to Brandeis's calls for documents, objected to his examination of witnesses, and, in short, objected to "nine-tenths of the testimony." Senator Elihu Root, seated next, shared Sutherland's impatience with the proceedings, which to his legalistic mind were a "perfectly frivolous waste of time. Let us go on with the testimony," he would say. "What we want, Mr. Brandeis, is to go on with extraordinary swiftness." [15] "We have been here forty days," he complained, "and it is time the children of Israel should get out of the wilderness." [16] Senator Root joined Senators Flint and Sutherland and Chairman Nelson in placing every ballot in the Republican box.

The two Democratic senators, Fletcher and Purcell, played appropriate roles as members of the opposition. On the other side of the table sat Representative Samuel W. McCall of Massachusetts, vice-chairman. Unlike his more distinguished Republican colleagues, Root and Sutherland, he was able occasionally to think and vote independently. Representative Olmstead quietly, Representative Denby vociferously, joined Root and Sutherland in extricating Ballinger whenever he became badly entangled in Brandeis's traps.

Representative Ollie James of Kentucky, his torso generously draped over a goodly portion of the chair specially constructed for his use, shared honors with Brandeis for annoying the G.O.P. stalwarts. "I saw your friend Ollie James when I was in Washington," Mrs. Brandeis wrote Alfred, April 11. "He certainly is doing all he can for Louis."

Representative Graham, an able lawyer, never tired of objecting to Chairman Nelson's prejudicial decisions on disputed points of procedure or on the admissibility of evidence. Once, when Nelson accused him of wanting a scrap, Graham sharply replied: "I do not want a scrap. But I will tell you, Mr. Chairman, what I do want. I want fair play here." [17]

Representative Madison, insurgent Republican, came nearer to having an open mind than anyone else. He repeatedly broke deadlocks and restored to the embattled committee the semblance of objectivity befitting the investigation.

Committee hearings would have been much less theatrical—and much less fair—had Chairman Nelson's idea on how to conduct the investigation prevailed. Nelson's view was that committee members alone should put all questions on the basis of memoranda submitted by counsel. This would have denied Brandeis any opportunity to examine witnesses. He protested vigorously, pointing out that in view of the mass and complexity of the record, the only way the evidence could be properly brought out was by oral examination by counsel who had familiarized themselves with the record.

Nelson's proposal was rejected, and Glavis, whom the administration had cast as the villain, opened the hearings. "Glavis has proved an extraordinary witness," Brandeis wrote his brother, January 31, 1910. "I have never seen his equal. *Der junge Mensch* is only 26."

Glavis's uncanny memory for dates and details forced a change in Ballinger's tactics. At first he would have no counsel, but after Glavis's testimony and Brandeis's introduction of supporting documents, Ballinger realized that the administration's committee members would need some expert help to keep the investigation in line. Senator Sutherland proposed that the Attorney-General act for Ballinger, and when this was rejected, Mr. John J. Vertrees, a soft-spoken Tennessee lawyer, President Taft's intimate friend and personal choice, entered the fray.[18] Aiding him, indeed often taking the case right out of his hands, was Edward Finney, the land-law expert and Ballinger's confidential man. As Brandeis remarked many years later, Finney was "perfectly cast in the role of Mephistopheles."

George Wharton Pepper has described Vertrees as "a lawyer of the old school, a fire-eating southerner. . . . Though experienced in combat of various sorts," he was "quite helpless when called upon to meet the more subtle strategy of Brandeis." Pepper tells of an incident one day when Vertrees suddenly rose from his chair to interrupt Brandeis. Addressing the chairman with emphasis and deliberation, Vertrees observed: " 'The gentleman says what is untrue and what he knows to be untrue.' Brandeis gave him a beaming smile and waited. 'The gentleman,' repeated the colonel, 'states an untruth, and he states it knowing it to be an untruth.' This time surely there will be an explosion, perhaps a challenge and possibly an old-fashioned free-for-all. Not a bit of it. Brandeis with arms folded and wearing an indulgent smile, looked silently at the old gentleman for a few seconds and then asked with an air of deference: 'Anything further, Mr. Vertrees?' The colonel, literally speechless with rage, sank into his chair, and Brandeis resumed his argument at the point at which he had been interrupted." * 19

Long before the investigation ended, Senators Root, Sutherland, and Nelson despaired of subduing Brandeis. "After each attempt," the *Boston Journal* observed on May 19, "Mr. Brandeis bobs to the surface with a smile that is the most exasperating facial expression ever encountered by a discontented body of men. Instead of soothing the ruffled feelings of the men before whom he is trying his case, Brandeis deliberately continues to rub the fur the wrong way. . . . Mr. Ballinger will be no happier to be rid of the Boston attorney than will a majority of the members of the committee."

BRANDEIS STATES AN INCREDIBLE HYPOTHESIS

Early in March, as the investigation dragged along, a startling idea occurred to Brandeis, and he wired Norman Hapgood to come to Washington. When Hapgood arrived Brandeis asked him whether he had noticed anything suspicious in the Wickersham "Summary and Report" to Taft, dated September 11, 1909, which the President later submitted as part of the record to support his firing of Glavis. Hapgood said he had noticed nothing. Brandeis, using his favorite tool, simple arithmetic, showed Hapgood what he meant.

The problem concerned two dates—September 6 and September 11, 1909. Accepting the dates as stated, Wickersham would have had less than a week to study the record of the case, which was more than half a million words, and then write a well-documented opinion covering seventy-four closely printed pages. Brandeis knew only one man who could have done that job in that time, and his name was not Wickersham. But even if Wickersham could prove he was that fast, Brandeis could prove Wicker-

* Mr. Pepper saw this episode in terms of a conflict between "two philosophies of life." In a letter to the author on February 10, 1945, Pepper wrote in elaboration: "Vertrees had the spirit and method of one whose ultimate appeal was to force—duel and a pistol, if necessary. Brandeis was the embodiment of an Oriental philosophy of non-resistance—such as Gandhi has effectively demonstrated in more recent times. Of course I do not mean that Brandeis lacked physical courage; I simply mean that he perceived the futility of the sort of demonstration which Vertrees ineffectively staged."

sham still couldn't have done it, because he had not spent all his time on it. Among other things, Wickersham had then been preparing important amendments to the Interstate Commerce Act. Brandeis believed that actually less than half of Wickersham's time had been given to the Glavis charges. This checked with what Brandeis learned from his brother-in-law, Charles Nagel, Secretary of Commerce and Labor, and a close friend of Wickersham's.[20]

Hapgood was therefore asked to consider the possibility that the Wickersham report might have been prepared much later than September 11 and then predated, perhaps to create in the public mind the belief that Taft's exoneration of September 13 was based upon and amply supported by the "Summary and Report"; that the President's action therefore was not merely a whitewash.

As yet all this was mere hypothesis. Brandeis busied himself to get irrefutable evidence. Pondering the Wickersham document for internal clues, he noted at one point that the Attorney-General's report cited a charge which Glavis had not made until after the date of the report. This seemed conclusive enough to Hapgood but not to Brandeis. Error in speculation on so delicate and crucial a matter would bring his whole case down like a house of cards, just as proof would cave the roof in on Taft.

Brandeis moved cautiously. When Edward Finney took the stand for Ballinger on April 22, Brandeis asked Hapgood to sit among the reporters. "I want you to be present when I cross-examine Mr. Finney. I will lead up to the Wickersham report about twenty minutes after I begin the cross-examination. Watch very carefully the witness's reaction and those of Ballinger's aides, and report to me later."

Accordingly Brandeis began leading up to the Attorney-General's report.

BRANDEIS: You saw that statement of the Attorney-General?

FINNEY: I saw it after it was printed in this document.

BRANDEIS: That is the first time you saw it?

FINNEY: That is the first time I ever saw the Attorney-General's statement. . . .

BRANDEIS: When did you first hear that someone else in the Interior Department . . . had seen the report of the Attorney-General?

FINNEY: I do not think that any one of them ever told me about reading it. Someone told me that he had made some sort of a report to the President.[21]

The luncheon recess followed these questions and Brandeis conferred with Hapgood. Both had noted uneasiness among Ballinger's lieutenants. They were now ready for frontal attack.

BRANDEIS: I would like to ask you one other question, Mr. Finney. Is it not a fact that this summary of the Attorney-General, which purports to have been made September 11, 1909, bearing date September 11, 1909, was, as a matter of fact, not completed for more than two months after that time?

FINNEY: I do not know when it was written, Mr. Brandeis.[22]

Next day, April 23, Brandeis wrote to Chairman Nelson requesting that the Attorney-General be directed to submit "all letters, telegrams, memoranda, and any other papers relating to, or used in connection with, the preparation of said 'Report and Summary' or of said 'Summary,' received or sent by any person who assisted the Attorney-General in connection with said 'Summary' or said 'Report and Summary,' including, among others, any member of the Department of Interior." This legalistic dragnet caused heated controversy. "It is simply a question," Senator Root protested, "whether we shall proceed with an investigation of the Attorney-General and the Attorney-General's office." [23] The committee turned Brandeis down by the usual vote of 7 to 5.

"Wickersham and White House continue their silence, which confirms our conclusions," Brandeis reported to his brother, April 24. "I am making another call on Wickersham for 'papers.' "

"I sent Nelson for transmittal a heavy call for papers from the Attorney-General," he wrote his brother two days later. "Nelson has held it since yesterday A.M. without transmittal. We may have a fight at all events. It appears to hurt."

Brandeis returned to the matter April 30, asking the committee for a statement of the grounds on which his request of April 23 had been denied. None was forthcoming, but the committee did vote the attorney fifteen minutes in which to state his position: "I had some reason to believe, pendent upon bits of evidence which came to me from many sources, that this report of the Attorney-General, which is dated September 11, 1909, two days before the President's letter exonerating Secretary Ballinger and condemning Mr. Glavis, had actually been prepared months subsequently. . . . I asked for them [the papers] . . . for the purpose of having the documents themselves in the various stages, with a view to showing the chronology of the making of that report—not merely as bearing upon the Attorney-General's action, but as bearing upon the action of the Secretary of Interior. . . . It is the question not merely whether Mr. Ballinger was properly exonerated, or whether Mr. Glavis was properly condemned, but whether, after the events which occurred on September 13, steps were taken with the idea of making that appear proper which was not proper when done. The question is of far more importance than the question of the correctness or the error in the original proceedings.[24]

Brandeis's argument seemed logical enough, but not for Representative McCall, who said that he "did not see how it was at all material . . . to call on the Attorney-General to furnish the different drafts that he made of his summary. I do not see how the operation of his mind is at all material." [25] Vertrees seconded McCall and added: "Of course we have been treated morning after morning to these usual plays here to the press reporters; for that, in the last analysis, is all this application and its predecessors are." [26]

Vertrees went on to say that the Interior Department had no information concerning Wickersham's summary. Expanding on "the conspiracy which puts him [Brandeis] here and keeps him here," Vertrees explained: "It is no longer a question of Secretary Ballinger, but is also directed at persons connected with the President and others, and was prompted by the resentment of the former Secretary of the Interior [Garfield] who was not retained in the cabinet." They [Garfield, Pinchot, Brandeis] "represent the miserable spirit that will tear down and destroy any man of respectability; they endeavor now to reach out and lay their hands on the Attorney-General . . . and all because he stands as one of the advisers of the President who is distasteful to certain persons." [27]

Ollie James rose to defend Brandeis's request: "Here is a finding of the Attorney-General bearing date of September 11, in which he charges Glavis with certain conduct in office which is not in keeping with his duties. Now if it turns out as a matter of fact that he was discharged before this finding, do you not think it would be important to Glavis, or at least to his defense?" At this point the discussion was abruptly ended by Senator Root's reminder: "Mr. Chairman, I understand the fifteen minutes are up and I think we have spent altogether too much time already on this matter." [28]

The motion was put and again Brandeis lost 7 to 5. From this time on the prediction was freely made that by 7 to 5 Ballinger would be whitewashed once more.

Back in Louisville, Alfred Brandeis had been observing Louis's "unmerciful" strategy in carrying the investigation beyond the Interior Department to the Attorney-General's office and even to the White House. He expressed concern that Louis might be pressing his case too hard. Louis replied on May 1, 1910: "Your remarks are entirely pertinent but I think not sound. There is nothing for me to do but to follow the trail of evil wherever it extends. *Fiat iustitia.** In the fight against special interests we shall receive no quarter and may as well make up our minds to give none. It is a hard fight. The man with the hatchet is the only one who has a chance of winning in the end. This chance is none too good. There is a chance—but a

* Let justice be done.

chance merely—that the people will now reverse all history and be able to control. The chance is worth taking, because there is nothing left for the self-respecting man to do. But every attempt to deal mercifully with the special interests DURING THE FIGHT simply results in their taking advantage of the merciful. . . .

"I think Wickersham and his acts are a fair sample of the product of our special interest activities—what Wall Street and high finance make of a finely gifted and no doubt originally honorable man."

In his drive toward the Attorney-General's office and the White House, Brandeis had, for the moment, been blocked. But he had badly frightened the enemy, and now he pressed the attack from a new angle. While Ballinger was on the stand Brandeis extracted from him an admission that his official counsel, Oscar W. Lawler, had prepared for the President "a sort of résumé of the facts." So on May 7 Brandeis wrote again to Chairman Nelson, requesting that Lawler be ordered to produce a copy of his memorandum. Lawler replied to Nelson's inquiry by saying that he had, at the request of the President, "prepared a memorandum of the facts shown by the records, which was delivered by me to the Attorney-General. I considered it manifestly improper to retain any copy of said document and did not do so." [29]

Lawler's admission showed that the Attorney-General was, or had been, in possession of a document not yet submitted in answer to the committee's calls. This was ominous for Wickersham and for Taft because each had already been requested, once by the joint committee and earlier by Senate resolution, "to transmit to Congress any reports, statements, papers, or documents upon which he had acted in reaching his conclusions with reference to said [Glavis's] charges." Encouraged by this, Brandeis pressed for the document, saying: "I believe everybody will realize, and must realize, that under the circumstances that memorandum is an extremely important one in the consideration of this case."

"You must except me, Mr. Brandeis," Senator Root broke in, "I consider it of no importance whatever." [30]

While these events were taking place in the committee, in the House itself, after a conference with Committeeman Graham, Representative Francis Burton Harrison of New York on May 2 introduced the following resolution:

Resolved, That the Attorney-General be and he is hereby directed to furnish to the House of Representatives the following named documents and the information herewith requested:

A. The original—or if the original be unavailable the letter-press copy of the

original—letter transmitting to the President the Attorney-General's summary
or review of the evidence in the so-called Glavis charges against the Secretary
of the Interior.

B. The original final draft of said summary or review as it was sent to the
Public Printer.

C. All earlier drafts or parts of drafts of said summary or review.

D. All documents and memoranda used in the compilation of said summary
or review, with a statement of their origins.

E. Originals, or copies where originals are unavailable, of all communications between the Attorney-General and any and all other officers of the government, relative to said summary or review.

F. A list of the names of those assisting in the preparation of said summary
or review, whether as attorneys, stenographers, copyists, or otherwise.

G. A statement of the dates upon which said assistants worked, together
with a statement of the work done by each in the preparation of said summary
or review.[31]

Wickersham remained adamant. Writing Richard Wayne Parker, House
Judiciary Committee Chairman, May 9, 1910, he said that while "there is
no mystery about the matter and nothing which may not be freely stated
. . . due regard for the constitutional authority of the Executive forbids
that the action of the President and his adviser shall be called into question
by a co-ordinate branch of the government in this way."[32]

This resort to constitutional and official immunity impeded Brandeis,
but such subterfuges aroused strong public suspicion that the administration was bent on a conspiracy of suppression.

BALLINGER DEFENDS AN "UNSULLIED" CHARACTER

On April 29 the chief figure in the investigation, Secretary Ballinger,
took the stand. From the start he was vituperative, standing with one hand
held jauntily in his pocket, and denouncing "lies" and "liars." As Ballinger's
cross-examination was about to begin, Brandeis felt great emotional tension. Turning to his colleague, George Rublee, he said, "Hold my hand."[33]

Brandeis began the attack on Ballinger with a strategic diversion, apropos the Secretary's strong insistence that the Taft administration's sole
guide was *the law.* He drew the Secretary's attention to a letter he had
written to a subordinate, directing that all appointments in the Interior Department not filled by the President himself be made only after consultation with the administration's political broker, Postmaster-General Frank
H. Hitchcock. Brandeis then inquired whether Mr. Ballinger or his legal
advisers had ever found any act of Congress giving such supervisory power
over Interior Department appointments to the Postmaster-General.

BALLINGER: No, sir; and I did not have to look to that for any such power.

BRANDEIS: Then this was not one of the instances where a scrupulous regard for the law required a reversal of the Garfield policy?

BALLINGER: This was a disposition and a securing of appointments, and it seemed to me that was the proper thing to do. . . .

BRANDEIS: Well, will you explain to the committee why Postmaster-General Hitchcock should have been consulted in regard to the selection of these coal experts and mineral experts who, by special exemption of the President, were to be selected for these important positions? . . .

BALLINGER: It was a matter of my own concern which I do not propose to state anything further about.

BRANDEIS: I ask you, Mr. Secretary, is it not a matter of the country's concern? [34]

Brandeis pressed his questioning while Ballinger squirmed and evaded. Finally he snapped: "I have given you all the reasons you are going to get. You may pursue as long as you please." Senator Nelson relieved the tenseness by suggesting that Postmaster-General Hitchcock might have been consulted because he "got acquainted with a large number of experts in his political work. (Laughter.)"

Having shown that Ballinger had no particular respect for law, Brandeis went a step further. Earlier the Secretary had testified that under T.R. he had headed the Land Office in the Department of the Interior, only to resign a little later to resume private law practice in Seattle. There, he said, he was besieged by persons interested in public lands who wanted some grievance righted. He did all in his power to discourage this sort of clientele. When he did allow himself to render assistance, he did so out of friendship, to help Mr. Conover's mother-in-law, or one Mrs. Burns, widow of an old soldier. Fees for such services were out of the question.[35]

Such generosity puzzled Brandeis. "Well, Mr. Secretary," he said, "if you had that strong disinclination to perform any service in connection with the Land Office, why did you consent to perform this service in connection with the Cunningham claims in drafting that affidavit and making the appeal to Secretary Garfield and to Commissioner Dennett?"

"That was a matter of accommodation more than anything else," Ballinger returned.[36]

Ballinger repeatedly denied that he had been counsel for the Cunningham claimants and had led President Taft to believe that he had been consulted by only one of them. But the former Governor of Washington, Miles C. Moore, had understood that Ballinger was acting as counsel for the Cunningham claimants as a group. He made this clear in a letter to Secretary Ballinger on May 24, 1909, when he said: "Owing to the fact that you were at one time counsel for our people, you cannot consistently act [in the Cunningham case]. . . ." Brandeis made much of this point as the examination proceeded.

BRANDEIS: How should he [Moore] have gotten the idea that you did not know that you were counsel for him, as well as others, if it was not the fact?

BALLINGER: . . . I do not see that it cuts any figure how he considers it. . . . How they may construe it is a matter that I am not in any sense bound by nor concerned regarding.[37]

BRANDEIS: Well, why should you have spent your valuable time in accommodating these Cunningham claimants?

BALLINGER: There wasn't any reason why I should accommodate them any more than I did a great many other people. It was sometimes easier to accommodate them, to get rid of them in that way, than it was to be pestered by them.

BRANDEIS: But recognizing, as President Roosevelt put it, that here was a $20,000-man who had returned to practice in order to earn what his services entitled him to, why should you have spent your time with the Cunninghams?

BALLINGER: There is no attorney practicing law that does not do a great deal of work that he does not expect any compensation for and does not get compensation for. . . .

BRANDEIS: Now, Mr. Secretary, that might be natural enough with those poor rainbow-chasing claimants and poor persons whom you referred to generally, but why should that be true when you are dealing with great businessmen, accustomed to large affairs, like C. J. Smith and Horace C. Henry and men of that character, whose interests are large, and who certainly must be accustomed to paying for legal services in the important matters with which they are connected?

BALLINGER: . . . So far as these people are concerned, I had no legal connection with them at any time. I did not expect to represent them as their attorney—did not desire to represent them as their attorney. Here was an incidental matter that came in in which they desired my assistance.[38]

BRANDEIS: Is there any service that counsel could have performed that would have been more important than the services which you undertook, providing they had been successful?

BALLINGER: Why, that same service might have been performed by a dentist or a doctor or anybody else that knew Mr. Garfield and Mr. Dennett and asked them about the matter, just as I asked them.

BRANDEIS: Well, would the dentist or the doctor have been competent to have drafted the affidavit which you drafted, and the purpose of which was to overcome a difficulty in which apparently the claimants found themselves by reason of an affidavit which had been previously presented? . . .

BALLINGER: Anybody could have done that.[39]

Confronted with evidence that at least half a dozen of the Cunningham claimants were prominent businessmen and politicians in Seattle, and that Ballinger was on intimate terms with them, Ballinger still denied that such acquaintance affected in the slightest degree his action as Commissioner of the Land Office in clear-listing * the Cunningham claims for patent. Yet when he was asked to explain coincidences between various actions of the Cunningham claimants and similar actions by his own office, he could give no satisfactory answer.

Brandeis particularly questioned Ballinger on the telegram he had sent former Governor Moore, February 28, 1908: "Temporary delay caused by report of Field Agent." Brandeis wanted to know whether this delay affected the Cunningham claims and whether those claims were specifically in Ballinger's mind when he appeared before a congressional committee, March 3, 1908, in support of the Cale bill.†

BALLINGER: So far as having any consideration or any thought of the Cunningham claims, I deny that anything like that was in my mind or thought in regard to the matter.

BRANDEIS: Well, Mr. Secretary, I want to see if I cannot refresh your recollection as to whether they were in your mind on March 3, 1908. Is it not a fact that as shortly before March 3 as the twenty-eighth day of February you had personally considered the status of these Cunningham claims?

BALLINGER: In what way?

BRANDEIS: I want to know whether you had not in some way personally considered the status of the Cunningham claims?

BALLINGER: You refer to a telegram?

BRANDEIS: That is what I had in mind.

BALLINGER: I suppose it was.

BRANDEIS: Yes?

BALLINGER: It was just in answer to former Governor Moore to the effect that the claims were still under investigation.

BRANDEIS: And that telegram happens to have been dated as recently before your appearance before that committee as the twenty-eighth day of February?

---

* Clear-listing, by the General Land Office, was prerequisite to the transfer of title in public land from the government to the claimant.
† If enacted, the Cale bill would have validated the disputed Cunningham coal claims. *See* my *Bureaucracy Convicts Itself,* pp. 48–52.

BALLINGER: Probably it was prepared by someone for my signature.

BRANDEIS: Well, let us see whether that is the fact.

BALLINGER: I do not know whether it was; it might have been prepared by me.

BRANDEIS: I understand; I want just to see whether it was or not.

BALLINGER: I recall having seen the original recently where there were some pencil memoranda put on the telegram by me; yes, sir.

BRANDEIS: Yes; that indicates that you personally—

BALLINGER: Yes; I personally.

BRANDEIS: Did you dictate that telegram?

BALLINGER: I dictated—I wrote that telegram, if you want it, and I assume all of the responsibility. And all the awful responsibility connected with that telegram I assume.

BRANDEIS: Now, that is just what I wanted to bring to your attention.[40]

A point on which Ballinger was peculiarly evasive, and on which Brandeis continued to harp, concerned the precise role played by the Secretary's special counsel, Oscar W. Lawler, Assistant Attorney-General.

BRANDEIS: Mr. Secretary, why did you not mention on your direct examination, when you told of going to Beverly to see the President [on September 6, 1909], the fact that Assistant Attorney-General Lawler went with you?

BALLINGER: I did not consider it a matter of any material moment.

BRANDEIS: Is it not a matter of moment, in view of the part that he subsequently played?

BALLINGER: What part do you refer to?

BRANDEIS: Well, any part within your knowledge that he subsequently played.

BALLINGER: My answer is no.[41]

BRANDEIS: Now, why did Mr. Lawler go to Beverly?

BALLINGER: At the request of the President.

BRANDEIS: Why did he go?

BALLINGER: I decline to state any conversation with the President in connection with the matter.

BRANDEIS: I did not ask you to state any conversation. . . . What did Mr. Lawler take with him when he went to Beverly the latter part of the week?

BALLINGER: A grip with some clothes in it. I do not know what else he took.

BRANDEIS: You know that he did have something else?

BALLINGER: And some records. I know that he had other things; yes.

BRANDEIS: What were they particularly, bearing on the Glavis–Pinchot controversy?

BALLINGER: He had some records of the case or memoranda.

BRANDEIS: What?

BALLINGER: I cannot definitely define just what he had in his portfolio or what he took with him. . . . He had certain memoranda that he made up himself; that is, I know of some memoranda. I do not know what else he had."

Lawler, in drawing up the memoranda referred to, apparently had had some help. Brandeis now explored that alley.

BRANDEIS: And who were the . . . persons with whom he consulted?

BALLINGER: I think possibly he consulted—I do not know this of my own knowledge—but I think he consulted with Mr. Schwartz [Chief of Field Service].

BRANDEIS: And with Mr. Finney, did he not?

BALLINGER: I do not know. I say of my own knowledge.

BRANDEIS: You have heard that he consulted with Mr. Finney, have you not?

BALLINGER: I could not say that I ever heard that he consulted with Mr. Finney.

BRANDEIS: And with Mr. Carr [Ballinger's private secretary]?

BALLINGER: I cannot say that I even heard that he consulted with Mr. Carr.

BRANDEIS: Did he consult with you?

BALLINGER: I would not say that he consulted with me, but I went over his memorandum. . . .

BRANDEIS: Where did he leave the copies of that memorandum?

BALLINGER: Your question implies that he did leave a copy with somebody. I do not know whether he did or not.

BRANDEIS: How many copies of that memorandum were prepared?

BALLINGER: Your question implies that I know. I do not know anything about it.

BRANDEIS: Will you state to the committee what you do know?

BALLINGER: I have stated.

BRANDEIS: What became of the copy or copies of that memorandum?

BALLINGER: I know nothing about the copy or copies of that memorandum.[42]

All this grilling, probing, and prodding finally got from the reluctant Ballinger that Lawler had had in his grip containing clothes, "a sort of résumé of the facts as set forth in the records." Further inquiry showed that this "sort of résumé" had in fact been prepared at the request of the President, and that Ballinger himself had gone over and approved it.

Brandeis then, in another question, implied that in Lawler's memorandum not everything relating to the Cunningham claims was shown to Taft. "That question implies an insult . . . that we made a selection to suit our convenience," Ballinger retorted hotly.[43] "I have stated heretofore . . . that all of the facts were stated, and not by way of selection. Gentlemen of the committee, I appeal to this committee for protection against the insolence of this man who is attempting to cross-examine me. He appears here . . . by sufferance of the committee—not by any right under the resolution that called this committee into existence . . . I have invited this investigation and have asked that [it] should be searching . . . but . . . I think I am entitled to be free from the continued imputations that the gentleman is placing in his various questions." [44]

One looks in vain for anything in the Secretary's performance which even suggests Taft's glowing eulogy of October 9, 1909: "Richard Ballinger's character is as unsullied as the snow of your mountain ranges. As well attempt to shake the foundations of the great Mount Rainier as to assail the character of the Secretary." [45]

Under Brandeis's cross-examination Ballinger's psychology was in fact that of a man on edge, fearing the worst. As some apparently innocuous question inflamed a grievance, he would burst forth in angry harangue. Brandeis did little or nothing to relieve this altogether natural tension, save occasionally to caution him: "Mr. Secretary, if I may be allowed to suggest, I think the committee is more desirous of light than of heat." [46] When Ballinger's memory lapsed, when he made misstatements, or refused to make direct replies, Brandeis added to the Secretary's discomfiture by merely asking the stenographer to repeat the question. When Brandeis referred to the Secretary's unofficially announced intention to "kill some snakes" in the wilds of the Interior Department, Ballinger rose to the lure with obvious relish: "When it comes to snake-killing I want to say that if I stay at the head of the Department they are going to be killed, and I am going to administer that Department as I consider it should be administered, with loyal support from every man in it, and I want it understood that I am serving notice in that respect." [47]

The Secretary's belligerence abated somewhat, however, as Brandeis inquired: "Well, now, did it ever occur to you, Mr. Secretary, that this supposed lack of loyalty, or, putting it another way, that the personal loyalty of one in public service to a superior or to an associate might involve disloyalty to 99,000,000 people?"

"I will not argue that question," Ballinger replied.[48]

THE INCREDIBLE HYPOTHESIS CLEARED AND PROVED

On May 13, 1910, Brandeis wrote his brother: "The situation is pretty tense and my disgust with the administration is now unbounded. Yesterday's performance added to the store of lies. If our newspaper statesmen were allowed to tell all they know and think there would be no doubt in people's minds. . . . After all, the Ballinger episode is dwarfed by the awfulness of the President–Wickersham–Lawler frauds. . . . If only there were a Democratic party, what havoc would be wrought!"

Few realized that the "havoc" Brandeis hoped for was about to break out within the committee itself. Day by day, week by week, he had kept up the monotonous chant: "Mr. Chairman, I would like to renew my daily complaint in reference to the papers not produced which have been called for. I suggest that the committee address a special communication calling for the production of the papers not yet delivered." [49] But nothing seemed to happen.

From his obscure corner in the Interior Department, Frederick M. Kerby, twenty-four-year-old stenographer, had been watching the play for documents between Brandeis and his chief, the one determined to get them, the other bent on withholding them. Since early March, Kerby had noted that Brandeis was seeking Lawler's memorandum on the basis of which Taft had apparently exonerated Ballinger. Kerby knew the circumstances under which this memorandum had been prepared. Furthermore he had, on his own initiative, told the entire story to his former chief, as early as the middle of February, when Garfield visited at the house of Gifford Pinchot. At Garfield's request Kerby repeated his statement to Brandeis. None of these gentlemen advised the stenographer what course to pursue. All realized that to disclose this information meant certain loss of his job and possible injury to his reputation.

So long as it was still possible that the Lawler document might be produced in the regular way, Kerby kept silent. But when the committee, after heated debate, decided by the usual 7-to-5 vote not to call on the Attorney-General for the Lawler opinion, he felt increasingly the burden and responsibility of his knowledge. He asked his wife what he should do. A newspaper syndicate wanted the story, and the newspapermen told him his patriotic duty was to divulge the facts. At last, recalling that Ballinger himself had asked that "all the facts" be disclosed, and feeling that his obligation to the public was greater than his obligation to Ballinger, Kerby, on promise of a job from a newspaper syndicate, prepared a long statement for the press.

Kerby told how Lawler had closeted himself in Ballinger's own private office, where he worked furiously, and in constant consultation with Ballinger and his handymen, Dennett, Finney, and Pierce, on draft after draft of a letter. The letter was written in the first person, "as if he [Lawler] were President," addressed to Ballinger, triple-spaced to facilitate corrections and revisions in case the President wished to make them. Throughout Ballinger was referred to as "you" and the personal pronoun "I" was used in such a way as to show that the letter could be signed by no one save President Taft himself. The document was evidently prepared, according to Kerby, as a draft or model for the President's exoneration of Ballinger and dismissal of Glavis. Kerby himself at Lawler's dictation had typed a part of this document, knew what was involved, that Ballinger himself had been consulted throughout its preparation, and had approved the final version. The stenographer also told of the secrecy surrounding both the preparation and transmission of the letter to the President. He told how the rough drafts were carefully guarded and of Mr. Lawler's warning not to consign them to wastepaper baskets. Every scrap was gathered up, taken to another room, and burned, as Kerby and certain of Ballinger's subordinates looked on.

"The papers blazed up," runs Kerby's dramatic statement, "and burned furiously. We stood around the fireplace and watched the smoke curl around the pages and the fire lick up line after line of typewriting. We didn't leave until every bit of paper had been consumed and the drafts were reduced to an unrecognizable mass of black ashes." [50]

It was near midnight on a Friday when the final document—an original and three carbons—was completed. One copy was placed in the confidential files of Secretary Ballinger, one was kept by Schwartz, the original and a carbon were taken by Lawler to Beverly.

Kerby's story appeared in the afternoon papers on May 14. That same day Attorney-General Wickersham himself produced Lawler's letter. To Chairman Nelson, Wickersham explained: "I caused a further careful search to be made in the files of the Department, and have found a paper which I transmit to you herewith, and which is either the original or a copy of the memorandum prepared by Mr. Lawler . . . on September 11, 1909. To the best of my recollection I left the memorandum with other papers at the President's house in Beverly on September 12, and received it in New York about a week later, together with other documents and memoranda relating to the Glavis matter. Since that time, to the best of my information it has been in the possession of my secretary or among the papers in this department, although it seems to have been overlooked in collecting papers in answer to your previous communications." [51]

When the news of Kerby's statement became public, Ballinger, unadvised of the Attorney-General's discovery that day, hurried to the White House, only to find that the President was at the Chevy Chase golf links. However, the President's secretary, Fred W. Carpenter, succeeded in reaching him, and Secretary Ballinger had a long telephone conversation with Taft. Upon telephone order from the President, Ballinger prepared a statement which was immediately released to the press:

"With reference to the published affidavit of Mr. F. M. Kerby, the stenographer in the office-of the Secretary of the Interior, to the effect that the President's letter of September 13, 1909, exonerating Secretary Ballinger was substantially prepared for the President's signature by Assistant Attorney-General Lawler, it was said at the White House today that there is absolutely no foundation for any such statement. The President dictated his letter personally as the result of his own investigation of the record and in consideration of documents and papers in his possession at the time and upon the general report to him." [52]

Apparently Taft, as well as Ballinger, was ignorant of the Attorney-General's successful "search" of the day before. But within twenty-four hours they were aware that the Lawler memorandum had been delivered to the committee. The falsity of the White House statement was now apparent. This "worst lying," as Brandeis called it some years later, indicating "a ruling passion, strong in death," demanded a long cabinet meeting on Sunday, the 15th. [53] That same day Taft wrote a letter to Chairman Nelson embodying a more complete and considered statement of the facts.

The President gravely explained how he had "requested Mr. Lawler to prepare an opinion as if he were President," the reason being that he [Taft] was about to leave on a long western journey; that he had some six or seven set speeches to deliver early in the trip and therefore could not give time to such a detailed statement as the matter demanded. Mr. Lawler's draft letter, according to Taft, was not altogether satisfactory. The President adopted only a few paragraphs of it, notably those in which Mr. Lawler, writing "as if he were President," heaped praise on his chief, Ballinger. [54]

The last paragraph of Taft's confessional fully confirmed the hypothesis on which Brandeis had been working since March 5, namely, that Attorney-General Wickersham's "Summary and Report," on which the President had purported to rely, was predated. Taft explained that on September 12 he delivered the whole record to Wickersham. After studying the voluminous documents all that day, Wickersham returned to Beverly in the evening with rough notes and reported orally the conclusions reached. The President then set himself to rephrasing Lawler's memorandum, using the Attorney-General's notes. The consideration he gave the matter, Taft admitted, was not all that could be desired: "I was very sorry not to be able to embody this analysis [that of the Attorney-General] in my opinion, but time did not permit. I therefore directed him [the Attorney-General] to embody in a written statement such analysis and conclusions as he had given me, file it with the record, and date it prior to the date of my opinion, so as to show that my decision was fortified by his summary of the evidence and his conclusions therefrom." [55]

From Vicksburg, Mississippi, October 28, 1909, while the President was still on tour, he acknowledged receipt of Wickersham's additional report which Wickersham had just completed and predated September 11, 1909.

Brandeis's tactics in squeezing this confession from Taft troubled George Wharton Pepper: "I thought what had been done 'was not cricket,' whereas Brandeis took the view that no public official had any right to have a private file and that as he was to give his whole time to the public, there was nothing which was beyond the reach of whatever strategy could be invoked to get possession of it. I found myself unable to argue the question effectively with Brandeis. It was a question of original apprehension. He felt thoroughly justified in doing what he did and I had a sporting instinct which condemned it." [56]

As Brandeis pressed the investigation still further, others also condemned his tactics. Brandeis now sought to direct his questioning of Kerby so as to get into the record the White House release of May 14 declaring that there was "no foundation" for the stenographer's statement. This Brandeis wanted to set against the qualified explanation made by the President the next day. Senator Root became so indignant that he thumped the table vigorously in denouncing Brandeis's efforts to draw the President further into the controversy.[57] "We are not here to investigate the President of the United States!" Root shouted angrily. "We are here to investigate the Department of the Interior. Counsel has been endeavoring assiduously and not altogether ingeniously to lead the investigation into a trial of the President."

In the debate that ensued Root contended that the Lawler memorandum was irrelevant inasmuch as it related solely to an act of the President, and he nodded warm approval of Senator Sutherland's outburst. "To inquire into this," snapped Sutherland, "is an insult to the President, and I, for one, do not propose to be a party to it." Representative James and Senator Purcell, on the other hand, defended Brandeis's inquiries because the "attempted suppression" of the Lawler document reflected on Ballinger's credibility as a witness. On roll-call the committee sustained Root's objections by 7 to 5. However, Brandeis was allowed to make an extended statement during which he got into the record all that Senator Root had objected to so strenuously, and a good deal more besides.

All that took place after May 15 was anticlimactic, except the appearance of Lawler. On the stand at last, his violent and irascible testimony served to measure the effectiveness with which Brandeis had waged his "war of nerves" against the administration cabal. Lawler was confident that "gum-shoe men" had been after him for months, following him "hither and thither in the city of Washington and elsewhere. I knew," he told the committee, "that there was absolutely no depth of degradation to which these despicable scoundrels who were on my trail would not stoop."

Ollie James interrupted to inquire: "Would you mind telling us . . . just who they were?"

"There is one," said Lawler, indicating Brandeis. "The man Hapgood, who has been sitting next to him for weeks, is another one. . . ."

"Well, now, was that before the memorandum was prepared by you?" James asked.

"Some of those things were. The following of me was before."

"And Mr. Brandeis?" queried James.

"He [referring to Mr. Brandeis] is a subsequent development and is simply the flower of this foul flock." [58]

Not only did Lawler believe that these men were "on his trail," but he testified that they had engaged in "corruption of the foulest sort," inducing men, especially Kerby, to testify falsely. "Would you tell the committee," Mr. Graham inquired, "whom you know to be the corrupter?"

"I do not know, but I believe that James R. Garfield and Mr. Gifford Pinchot and Mr. Brandeis are the parties."

Lawler's accusations brought hisses from the "prosecution's" women supporters, whereupon the Assistant Attorney-General, much irritated, turned upon them with the remark: "Geese and snakes make noises like that." [59]

Nor was Lawler alone in casting Brandeis in the role of an unscrupulous detective. Elihu Root had earlier entertained similar suspicions. Brandeis's cross-examination of Ballinger had revealed an amazing, almost uncanny, knowledge of the Secretary's comings and goings down to the minutest detail—what day and hour he arrived in Washington to prepare his reply to the President, and on what train, the precise day and hour he started the journey to Beverly, the name of the hotel where he stopped, the names of the gentlemen with whom the President was playing golf as the Secretary arrived, and so on.

No longer able to withhold his curiosity, Senator Root inquired: "Mr. Brandeis, I am merely curious to know, but did you have a detective shadowing Mr. Ballinger?"

278 BRANDEIS: A FREE MAN'S LIFE

"No."

"I am very glad to hear it."

"I will be very glad later, or now if you like," Brandeis said, "to tell you the source from which I received the information."

"No; your word is enough," Root rejoined.[60]

But when Lawler openly accused Brandeis as well as Hapgood of shadowing him, Sutherland interrupted to say that Lawler's suspicions were by no means groundless: "I want to remind Mr. James that during the cross-examination of the Secretary, Mr. Brandeis disclosed a surprising knowledge of the movements of Mr. Lawler and of everybody else. . . ."[61]

To forestall any further spread of Lawler's persecution mania, James insisted that Brandeis explain the sources of his information: "Senator Root said he was satisfied with Brandeis's statement, but Senator Sutherland seems not to be."

Brandeis then told in detail how and where he got his facts, concluding: "Every step in regard to the action of the President (and of others) appears by the collation of the Washington and New York papers, the *Tribune* and the Boston papers, the *Boston Transcript,* covering that period, except such facts, perhaps, as appeared from the hotel register at the Hotel Touraine. Now, that is open to anybody. It is a perfectly simple way, but when you put those in sequence, one upon the other, you have what appears to be very extraordinary intimate knowledge—"

"Of gum shoeing," Senator Purcell interrupted.

"Yes; of gum shoeing," Brandeis confirmed.[62]

Even after Brandeis had revealed the Ballinger–Wickersham cabal in all its nakedness a discouraging lack of knowledge of the facts prevailed. "New York is in dense ignorance of the subject," Brandeis wrote Alfred, May 23, 1910. "Even [Chas. C.] Burlingham * hasn't gotten the point that the President represented the Attorney-General's report as one on which he acted in reaching his conclusions."

Harvard also was "in dense ignorance," as indicated by President Lowell's letter of June 13, asking for information. "Your inquiry," Brandeis replied, "taken in connection with the selection of the Attorney-General to deliver the address at the Harvard Law School Association celebration, leads me to think that you may not be entirely familiar with certain facts affecting the Attorney-General developed in the course of the investigation. . . . As you appear to be making some investigation into the matter,

---

* New York lawyer. Member of the firm of Burlingham, Montgomery & Beecher. L.D.B.'s friend since 1878, when they first met at the Harvard Law School.

I think the following brief statement, giving dates, may be of assistance to you."

Brandeis then proceeded to give Lowell a point by point statement (ten in all) of the facts. The real punch was in nine and ten:

Ninth: It thus appears that the President, with the co-operation of the Attorney-General, sent to Congress in response to the Senate resolution, an important paper on which in fact, he had not relied, because it was not in existence; and also that the President omitted to send to Congress in response to the resolution another important paper on which he did rely; from which he copied portions, and a number of other statements in which he adopted the substance.

Tenth: It should be noted that neither the President nor the Attorney-General gave this information to Congress or to the committee until the facts had been otherwise established.

Finding absolutely nothing in Brandeis's communication with which to embellish the citation of Wickersham for an honorary degree, then apparently under consideration, the Harvard President replied curtly: "Thank you very much for your letter of June 16. I had not meant to give you so much trouble." Wickersham did not get a Harvard honorary degree until 1921.*

TOWARD THE GENERAL WELFARE

As anticipated all along, the investigating committee voted 7 to 5 to sustain Ballinger. The final report said: "Neither any fact proved nor all the facts put together exhibit Mr. Ballinger as being anything but a competent and honorable gentleman, honestly and faithfully performing the duties of his high office, with an eye single to the public interest. . . . No ground whatever has been shown justifying the opinion that he is not a faithful and efficient public officer." [63]

The report was signed by Knute Nelson, chairman, Frank P. Flint, George Sutherland, Elihu Root, Samuel W. McCall, Marlin E. Olmstead, and Edwin Denby—all Republicans.

There were two impressive minority reports. In one, the four dissenting Democrats (Duncan U. Fletcher, William E. Purcell, Ollie M. James, and James M. Graham) indicted Ballinger as "an unfit man to hold the office of Secretary of the Interior. . . . His conduct and association, his charac-

---

* Commenting on this episode, Brandeis wrote Norman Hapgood, March 14, 1916: "I was at the time horrified at Wickersham's making the address for the Law School Association. The inquiry which Lowell made of my office gave me the opportunity of writing him fully. His letter in reply showed how disgruntled he was at getting my letter, but the result of that letter was that Harvard refrained from giving Wickersham the LL.D. which it was expected that he would get."

ter and conception are such as to make it unwise and improper to continue him in charge of the public service . . . that he is not sufficiently devoted to the interests of the common people, or sufficiently diligent and resolute in resisting the insidious aggression of special interests." [64]

In the second (the one least colored by prejudice), E. H. Madison, insurgent Kansas Republican, also held that Secretary Ballinger's administration of the Cunningham coal claims was not in the public interest, and recommended that the Pinchot–Glavis charges be sustained and that the Secretary not be retained in office.

Congress took no action upon either the majority or minority reports,* Collier's was not sued, the Cunningham claims were canceled, the Republicans lost their House majority in the fall elections, and the press continued to demand Ballinger's dismissal as persistently as if the committee's majority had voted the other way. The whole episode contributed to the downfall of Taft's administration, and for this Taft had himself, not Ballinger, to blame.

As Brandeis said, the wounds the administration suffered were largely self-inflicted. It was the lying, he explained later, that undermined both Ballinger and Taft in the public confidence. Had they brazened it out, told everything frankly, stood by their policy, whatever its defects, as the one they honestly believed to be in the public interest, they might have withstood the attacks of Glavis and Pinchot, Brandeis and Collier's.

The Ballinger affair was more than an episode or interlude in Brandeis's career. From it he learned once more how important a free press can be in a democracy. Without the courage of a few newspapers and magazines, a faithful, though minor, public servant would have been fatally wronged and a major battle for decency in government lost. In his closing argument Vertrees indignantly stated that "in this inquiry the press has been more in evidence than I have been accustomed to . . . and in a way that has not pleased me at all." This indeed was largely Brandeis's doing.

In almost daily conferences with newspapermen, he gave them the high points of the proceedings. The editors of Collier's consulted him frequently, followed his advice implicitly as to topics to be singled out for publicity, and sent him their editorial proofs for correction and approval.

---

* George Wharton Pepper explains and justifies Congressional inaction thus: "Everybody was so busy talking about the case and about the prominent people whom it involved, that few took the trouble to analyze the proceeding on its constitutional side and to consider what the function of the committee really was. . . . Neither the Senate nor the House has, in my judgment, the right to pass resolutions condemning the conduct of executive officials. As I see the situation, it is impeachment, executive discipline, or nothing."

But Pepper's views are neither popular nor acceptable in certain quarters. See E. S. Corwin, The President, Office and Powers, pp. 226–28, 442–45.

The activity was mutual, for newspapermen like C. P. Connolly and Jerry A. Mathews from time to time furnished Brandeis with facts of great value.

After the hearings were concluded, Brandeis wanted the newspapers and magazines to keep up the fight. Thus he wrote Benjamin B. Hampton, June 4, 1910: "I hope the excellent work which *Hampton's* magazine has done in arousing public opinion to an appreciation of the Alaskan situation will be followed by some comprehensive article on the Ballinger investigation. The investigation has been so protracted, the questions involved are so intricate, and the reports, particularly in the eastern papers, so inadequate, that I am sure that only a very small portion of the people know what was developed. On the other hand, I am led to believe that there is a great desire to know, and to have stated in a clear and accurate form, what was developed in the investigation."

Brandeis conducted his own educational campaign by sending out hundreds of copies of the Glavis brief (largely the work of his assistant counsel, George Rublee) to newspapers, editors, and other persons who might possibly exert influence. The results of this campaign were indicated by Henry L. Stimson, who wrote Brandeis on June 17, 1910: "I wish very much I could have heard your closing argument in the investigation, and I am rejoiced to see the way in which sober second considerations of the matters therein involved—by the public and the press—tend more and more to vindicate Mr. Glavis and to substantiate the justice of his position."

Brandeis's closing argument summarized his feelings about the case:

We are not dealing here with a question of the conservation of natural resources merely; it is the conservation and development of the individual; it is the conservation of democracy; it is the conservation of manhood. That is what this fight into which Glavis entered most unwillingly means. . . .

With this great government building up, ever creating new functions, getting an ever-increasing number of employees who are attending to the people's business, the one thing we need is men in subordinate places who will think for themselves and who will think and act in full recognition of the obligations as a part of the governing body. . . . We want men to think. We want every man in the service, of the three or four hundred thousand who are there, to recognize that he is a part of the governing body, and that on him rests responsibility within the limits of his employment just as much as upon the man on top. They cannot escape such responsibility. . . . They cannot be worthy of the respect and admiration of the people unless they add to the virtue of obedience some other virtues—the virtues of manliness, of truth, of courage, of willingness to risk positions, of the willingness to risk criticisms, of the willingness to risk the misunderstandings that so often come when people do the heroic thing.[65]

So much for the larger meaning of the case to Brandeis. The more immediate practical result was that severe criticism and public resentment finally forced Ballinger's resignation on March 7, 1911, and Taft had to accept it. The embattled Secretary was succeeded by one of Brandeis's friends, Walter L. Fisher, a public-spirited Chicago lawyer. When about to assume his official duties, Fisher wrote Brandeis substantially thus: Because of your profound knowledge of the Interior Department and its problems, I wish your counsel and advice on matters of administration. Brandeis replied: I have but two suggestions to offer—approve no documents the contents of which you do not understand; sign no letters which you have not read. Fisher retorted tersely: You ask the impossible.

CHAPTER EIGHTEEN

The Controller Bay Fiasco, 1911

"If they had searched the nation over," Brandeis said of the new Secretary of the Interior, "they could have found no better man than Fisher. . . . I think that his ideas of loyalty will differ from those of Mr. Ballinger." [1] Fisher might have been different, but the Interior Department seemed to be the same. Early in 1911 newspapermen again smelled something cooking in the Department, and on April 20 the *Philadelphia North American* took the lid off the pot. "TAFT SECRETLY GIVES CONTROL OF ALASKA COAL TO GUGGENHEIMS," ran an ominous headline. The story, written by Angus McSween, declared that on October 28, 1910, President Taft had signed an executive order granting the Morgan–Guggenheim syndicate the only outlet from the Alaskan coal fields to tidewater not already in its control. Actually McSween was guilty of overstatement, as the order on its face merely withdrew from the Chugach National Forest, 12,800 acres of land on the shores of Controller Bay. Nevertheless, circumstances lent plausibility to his charge, for Controller Bay was of supreme importance to any group interested in exploiting the Bering coal fields, which included the

Cunningham claims. According to McSween, there was only one other feasible outlet for these coal fields—Cordova Bay—and that was already under the domination of Morgan and Guggenheim.

As soon as McSween's story appeared, Senator La Follette introduced a congressional resolution, which was passed without objection, calling on the Secretary of the Interior for complete information on Controller Bay.[2] Fisher promised to investigate and to halt any monopolization schemes.[3]

On May 17 Miss Myrtle Abbott, a young graduate of Radcliffe College, called at Fisher's office, armed with a letter from Norman Hapgood. She also wanted information on the Controller Bay affair. "What bee has Norman got in his bonnet now?" Fisher wanted to know. "Or perhaps it is a bee in your bonnet." [4] He assured her that nothing was wrong and as proof offered her the entire record. That was just what she wanted; she sat down in Fisher's office and took copious notes on Interior Department paper. Then she went home and wrote a sensational article.

Hapgood, from a low opinion of the merits of Miss Abbott's story, or from journalistic policy, or for personal reasons, refused to publish her piece. But John E. Lathrop, correspondent of the *Portland Evening Journal*, valued her findings more highly. After a vain attempt to interest Hapgood, he advised Miss Abbott to syndicate the article; as a result, her materials appeared in several papers connected with the Newspaper Enterprise Association and the United Press.[5] Miss Abbott charged the administration and the Morgan–Guggenheim syndicate with conspiracy to despoil Alaskan riches. She maintained that Probst-Wetzler and Company, a commission banking firm for which Richard S. Ryan had acted in the deal, was a dummy for the syndicate. She further contended that since surveys of the Controller Bay lands had begun only three days after the signing of the executive order by President Taft, Ryan and his associates must have had advance information that the order would be signed.

The part of her story which fascinated the public most was a postscript to a letter from Richard S. Ryan to Richard A. Ballinger, dated July 13, 1910: [6]

Dear Dick:

I went to see the President the other day about this Controller Bay affair. The President asked me whom I represented. I told him, according to our agreement, that I represented myself. But that didn't seem to satisfy him. So I sent for Charlie Taft and asked him to tell his brother who it was I really represented. The President made no further objection to my claim.

Yours,

Dick.

Miss Abbott did not hesitate to conclude from this that the President's own brother, Charles P. Taft, had acted as contact man in negotiations between the President and the Morgan–Guggenheim syndicate. The implication of scandal in high places, of intimacy between Ryan and Ballinger as indicated by the "Dick to Dick" relationship, and the strong suggestion of double-dealing in the tone of the note, immediately caught the popular imagination. Interest doubled when a search was made in the files of the Interior Department—and the postscript could not be found!

President Taft indignantly denied that Charles P. Taft had ever discussed Controller Bay with him. He ordered a search of his correspondence with his brother, and absolutely nothing could be found on the subject of Alaska. A search of Charles P. Taft's letter files also disclosed nothing to connect him with Controller Bay or Richard S. Ryan.[7] Were there no letters? Or was this another Ballinger affair—with mysterious juggling of Interior Department files, disappearance of records, charges against the President, denials from the White House, and devious operations by the Morgan–Guggenheim syndicate? As muckrakers and anti-muckrakers, conservationists and anti-conservationists, girded for action, Representative Cox of Indiana introduced a resolution calling on the President for all information in connection with his executive order opening the Controller Bay lands to entry. At the same time announcement was made that a House committee would immediately begin an investigation.[8]

James M. Graham, chairman of the House Investigating Committee, wanted Brandeis as committee counsel but hesitated about asking him to take the job. The matter was broached to Brandeis by W. B. Colver of the Newspaper Enterprise Association, who conveyed this apologetic letter from Graham: "I had not the 'nerve' to ask your assistance in our committee inquiry as I am not in a position to promise compensation, but I have thought of you and wished for you ardently when I think of the opportunity we have to render popular government a great and lasting service." [9] Graham's embarrassment proved unwarranted, for Brandeis wrote back: ". . . The fact that your committee is not in a position to pay counsel fees will not in any way alter my decision. . . . I am very glad that Mr. Colver undertook to call upon me on your behalf in this matter. . . ." [10]

Brandeis did not want to make a final decision, however, until he could talk to Hapgood. He wanted most of all to know why Hapgood had turned down Miss Abbott's article. Some newspapers hinted that he had done so merely on personal grounds. The *Boston Transcript,* for instance, reported that shortly before Hapgood's rejection of Miss Abbott's story "Mr. Fisher ate a meal with the editor of *Collier's Weekly,* and told him that her story was no good." [11] And the *Philadelphia North American* said: "We are confident that certain publishers of newspapers and magazines who have unbounded faith in Secretary Fisher are deferring publication of important facts in their possession out of deference to his wishes." [12] Hapgood's own correspondence with Miss Abbott indicated that the papers were right. [13] "I am still firm," he wrote her, "in the opinion that *Collier's* should give Mr. Fisher a chance. We are perfectly willing to sail in later if it turns out to be necessary, but personally I believe that he will do well, and I do not wish to add to his difficulties." [14]

This wasn't good enough for Brandeis, but since Hapgood was in England and could not return before August, Brandeis had to decide without him. After conferences with Graham, Gifford and Amos Pinchot, John E. Lathrop, and Mark Sullivan, Brandeis accepted Graham's invitation.

Again the first step was to get every bit of information from those who had discovered the story of Taft's secret order releasing Controller Bay to entry. For that purpose a conference was called in the offices of the Newspaper Enterprise Association in Washington. [15] In attendance were Brandeis, Amos Pinchot (who had volunteered to act as Brandeis's assistant in the investigation), Miss Abbott, Gilson Gardner, John E. Lathrop, Overton W. Price, and James Wickersham, delegate from Alaska. For three days they studied the subject.

Having gained command of the principal facts, Brandeis indicated the lines on which the investigation should proceed. It was necessary, among other things, to trace the movements of Richard S. Ryan and Charles P. Taft for the past year or more, to investigate thoroughly Ryan's business affiliations, to find out the nature and extent of the friendship between Ryan and Ballinger, to obtain a comprehensive record of the activities of the Morgan–Guggenheim syndicate in Alaska, and to make a survey of the ownership of all properties in Alaska. Brandeis set his corps of investigators—Gardner, Colver, the Newspaper Enterprise staff, Miss Abbott, Amos Pinchot, Lathrop, and Wickersham—to work on these projects. To give them time for a thorough job, he advised Graham to postpone hearings until September or October. Then he left for his vacation at Chocorua, New Hampshire. [16]

Meanwhile the controversy grew in scope and intensity. President Taft sent a special message to the Senate saying he would take full responsibility for opening the Chugach National Forest Reserve to settlement and development. He branded the "Dick to Dick" postscript a "wicked fabrication." As for any connection between his brother and the affair, he was vehement: "He has no interest in Alaska, never had, and knows nothing of the circumstances connected with this transaction. He does not remem-

ber that he ever met Richard S. Ryan, he never heard of the Controller
Bay Railroad until my cablegram of inquiry reached him. . . ." [17]

The President further declared that the Controller Bay Railway and
Navigation Company was an independent enterprise, unconnected with
Messrs. Morgan and Guggenheim, and that no evidence to the contrary
had been brought to his attention. In conclusion, Taft spoke feelingly of
"the wanton recklessness and eagerness with which attempts have been
made to besmirch the characters of high officials. . . ."

T.R., now editor of *The Outlook*, did not take kindly to Taft's message:

Whether there was or was not impropriety in the way in which the elimination was brought about, whether or not there was impropriety in the action
which resulted in the instant filing of claims by Mr. Ryan and others, does not
go to the root of the matter. The root of the matter is that no such elimination
should have been made by the Interior Department. The public interest demanded that this land should be kept under public control. . . . [18]

Backing up T.R., Gifford Pinchot declared that Taft's defense simply
showed "how hard it is to make a good excuse for a bad mistake." [19]

Brandeis, however, felt differently. "The President's message on the
Controller Bay subject is an able document . . ." he wrote Alfred on
July 26, 1911; "none of the slipshod work of Ballinger days. I guess Walter
Fisher is on the job. There will be some fun, if it proves vulnerable.
W.H.T. has played his hand."

More vulnerable than Taft's speech, at the moment, was Brandeis's advice to Graham to postpone the investigation. When Graham tried to delay committee action, it was charged that, after stirring up unfounded
slander against the administration, the committee was deliberately trying
to hush up the whole matter. "What has happened that the truth is no
longer desirable to those who are so eager to investigate these irresponsible
charges?" fumed Representative William E. Humphrey of Washington.
"Is the famous and infamous 'Dick to Dick' letter an ordinary and stupid
forgery, misshapen and untimely, born of the distorted and distempered
imagination of an irresponsible, hysterical, petticoated muckraker, or was
she [Myrtle Abbott] only the unsuspecting and innocent tool of designing
enemies of the President who were too cowardly to strike except from the
dark and from behind?" [20]

Similar accusations appeared in the press. The *Seattle Times* summarily
declared that the committee, finding that it had discovered a "mare's nest,"
was waiting for Brandeis to save it from its predicament. Phrases such as
"infamous unfairness," "deliberate scandal-mongering," and "playing the

sneak" were current among the newspapers which deplored the committee's "sinister accusations." [21]

Brandeis returned from vacation at the end of August and went right
ahead studying the material. There appeared to be several possible explanations for the "Dick to Dick" postscript. If it were a genuine letter
from Ryan to Ballinger, its presence in the files of the Interior Department
could be accounted for as accidental—that is, as having been among Ballinger's private letters and slipped into the file through inadvertence. On
the other hand, it might have been purposely put into the file by someone who might have wanted to create trouble for the President out of vindictiveness because Ballinger had in effect been dismissed, and who himself
perhaps was expecting to retire shortly from the Department.[22] Assuming the letter to have been a forgery, it could be accounted for either on
the ground of animus against the President or of "a plan to catch *Collier's.*" [23]

Actually the postscript, while it made exciting newspaper copy, was of
no great significance to the real question at hand—whether or not the
President had connived to turn over to the syndicate control of the Bering
River coal fields. The question really went further even than that. Brandeis
saw in this affair, as in the Ballinger case, the need for a clear policy in
regard to the whole development of Alaska.[24] He therefore extended his
researches. He asked the Library of Congress for a bibliography on Alaska.
He obtained government reports, maps, and personal observations, sought
information on Alaska's railroads, on wagon roads, trails, telegraph, soil
characteristics, and every other item that might possibly have a bearing
on the solution of the problem. He based his researches on a program he
had outlined in July, and which he had sent to Gifford Pinchot: "It seems
to me most important that when the plan [for Alaska] is presented, it
should be broad, bold, and comprehensive. It should deal with the whole
problem in a way to make clear: first, that Alaska is to be developed; second, that the development of its resources is for the people of the United
States; third, that the opportunities of earnings of the settlers in Alaska
will be the most liberal conceivable, not only through giving them the
opportunity to work for the public lands under favorable conditions, but
to provide favorable external conditions of opening Alaska through giving
transportation and other facilities at the lowest possible cost. . . ." [25]

Specifically Brandeis recommended public ownership of railroads, a
leasing plan for mineral lands, settlement of other lands under public land
laws, government ownership and development of public utilities, and
management of Alaska's resources by a government commission, directly

under the President.[26] Such a program seemed essential if the resources of Alaska were to be developed and at the same time protected from exploitation. Hitherto the only way to protect any part of the territory had been to withdraw it from use, but the American people were entitled to gain the benefits that would flow from utilizing the territory's unexplored treasures. Merely hoarding public resources to protect them from private monopolists was not enough; the government must take positive steps to insure proper use of them.[27]

Brandeis submitted these ideas to Senator La Follette, who presented them in a speech in the Senate on August 21, 1911.[28] Finally, early in September Amos Pinchot was put to work drafting a bill which would embody these proposals.[29]

While Brandeis was becoming a student of Alaska and champion of its development, the specific Controller Bay investigation was getting nearer. To get firsthand information, Secretary Fisher himself early in August began a tour of the entire ground concerned in the controversy. He inspected Controller Bay, ascended Bering River in a canoe, mushed over long trails to the coal fields, and talked with Alaskans. John E. Lathrop, believing that Brandeis should have on-the-spot information of his own, followed Fisher on his tour and sent Gifford Pinchot on August 19, 1911, an urgent appeal to join him: ". . . The other side has a horde of men up here, officials not less than fifty, newspapermen in great number. They will be able to flood the country with their side of the fight. So far as I know, I am the only one on our side. I shall do the best I can; but we need you here."

Pinchot was only too glad to go. "I hope this trip of mine to Alaska will result in some material valuable to you," he wrote Brandeis, August 31. "At any rate, I shall try to keep my eyes open." He left for Alaska early in September.[30]

All this expenditure of energy went to waste, however, when the Controller Bay affair collapsed as suddenly as it had begun. On October 27 Secretary Fisher, in an address at Chicago before the American Mining Congress, revealed the results of his inquiry into the Alaskan situation and made public his recommendations, which were very similar to Brandeis's. Moreover, Fisher hinted that one of Mr. Ryan's entries on Controller Bay, on which a railroad terminal had been located, was illegal, and Ryan, with commendable alacrity, promptly withdrew his claim.[31]

Meanwhile Brandeis had discovered several inaccuracies in the charges made by Miss Abbott and Angus McSween. The evidence indicated that the administration had acted unwisely, but not improperly, and shortly after Fisher's Chicago speech, Brandeis himself bowed out of the Controller Bay picture. In a letter to Representative Graham, he wrote: "The elimination from the Chugach National Forest of a large tract of land on Controller Bay in aid of the Controller Railway and Navigation Company was, in my opinion, opposed to the best interests of the people, but I find no evidence of illegality or bad faith on the part of any government official. . . .

"The policy and method pursued by the President, under which private individuals were afforded an opportunity to control the transportation of the Bering River coal field, appears now to be recognized as mistaken. Substantial agreement having thus been reached upon the principles which should govern the immediate development and safeguarding of the resources of Alaska, in the interest of the people, the main object of the proposed inquiry has been attained. . . ."[32]

The committee accordingly discontinued investigation, and the "Dick to Dick" postscript, whether it ever existed or not, was soon forgotten.

The *Boston Transcript* put the proper finish to the whole affair when it commented on December 4, 1911:

Friends of conservation should rejoice that Mr. Brandeis is broad-minded enough to see that it is much better to accept in good faith a reversal of the administration's policy as showing that it is turning to the light than it is to try to drag into publicity the scandals and disagreements of a repudiated department head.

CHAPTER NINETEEN

Democracy in the Garment Trades, 1910-1916

IN THE Ballinger and Controller Bay affairs Brandeis had shown no more respect for the White House than he had had for the House of Morgan in the New Haven case. He had gone about, as he said, "knocking heads right and left," relentlessly following what he chose to call the "trail of evil." This had begun to cost him many friends, notably his brother-in-law

Charles Nagel, who once had written him how difficult it was "to differ from the men with whom you are accustomed to go."

By not differing with such men, Nagel had done very well for himself in the law and in politics. Brandeis had commented on this back in March 1908, when he wrote to Alfred: "Charlie's appointment to the Republican National Committee means, I suppose, a cabinet position if Taft is elected. Charlie has certainly worked long and hard for the party."

On May 3, 1908, Louis wrote Alfred again: "He [Nagel] looks fine— rather stouter and apparently entirely easy of mind. He says he doesn't want an office—prefers to influence public opinion by speaking, etc. . . . His call on me was rather formal. He also called on Alice and was charming and oratorical, but hardly *herzlich*."

Whether he wanted an office or not, Nagel in March 1909 became Taft's Secretary of Commerce and Labor. This connection with the administration naturally made him all the more sensitive to his brother-in-law's activities. Brandeis noted this in a letter to Alfred, March 27, 1910: "My meeting with Charles N. occurred Friday. He was walking on Pennsylvania Avenue 9:30 A.M. from 10th toward the New Willard, as I went to the Capitol. (Why he should have been there at that hour, moving in that direction, I can't imagine.) But we met, and he couldn't escape—talked a few moments about Hildegarde [Nagel's daughter] and from a remark dropped I see he is 'taking notice,' widow-like, of the Ballinger inquiry. Charlie was pleasant enough; but he looks worn and troubled as compared with last summer—just as you found him recently."

For all the unpleasantness this weakening of old friendship may have caused Brandeis, he seemed to thrive. Just after the nasty Ballinger business, he wrote to Alfred from Boston on June 14, 1910: "I am in excellent shape. Everyone seems to say: *Was der lebt noch?* But with a man who would rather fight than eat, the surprise is unwarranted. There is not over much work devastating me. If a fellow will stay away long enough leisure comes easy. 161 Devonshire Street seems rather quiet after Washington, D.C."

Later that month he went on vacation with his family to the Mount Pleasant Hotel in Bretton Woods in the White Mountains. Within a week, however, he wrote Alfred of his move from the Mount Pleasant to humbler accommodations: "This little hotel [The Glen] is the former servants' quarters of the Old Glen House and is as simple and remote from twentieth-century uncivilization as anything we saw in Switzerland or the Tyrol. Alice, Pauline [Goldmark], Elizabeth [his daughter], are delighted with it after the horrors of Bretton Woods grandeur." After New Hampshire, the family planned to complete the summer at South Yarmouth where, as Brandeis said, "the opportunities for loafing in various ways were good."

Things seemed quiet for a change in the Brandeis household. But it couldn't last. While they were all still in New Hampshire, word had come from A. Lincoln Filene, telling of a general strike in that most sweated and anarchistic of industries—the New York garment industry. The walk-out had become something like the "gigantic uprising of a whole people against their oppressors." [1] Millions of dollars were tied up; thousands of workers were idle; hundreds of shops were closed; riots and evictions occurred daily. What could Brandeis do about it?

THE STRUGGLE FOR THE PROTOCOL

The garment industry, operated by hundreds of individual proprietors who lived largely by their successful sensitivity to shifting styles and fashions, had long resisted consolidation. Any enterprising man with a couple of hundred dollars, a few rented machines, and half a dozen workers could break in among the established and reputable firms. Competition was cutthroat. Bankruptcies and strikes were frequent. Employers and workers alike were predominantly Jewish immigrants from Germany, Austria, Hungary, Poland, and Russia. Neither side had formed any stable organization. The International Garment Workers' Union had existed since 1900, but the locals, organized for unified action as the Joint Board of the Cloak, Suit & Skirt Makers' Union of New York, spent most of their energy fighting the International's leadership as too conservative. Between the editors of the *New Post,* mouthpiece of the Joint Board, and of the *Garment Worker,* the International's monthly magazine, factional-political controversy raged, with advantage accruing to the *New Post,* a cheap weekly reaching practically all members of the union. The vociferous dominance of the Joint Board only agitated antagonism in the manufacturers who saw unionism embarked on a Marxist conspiracy to destroy capitalism. This internal strife left employers free to discriminate against all unionists, to keep wages down and working conditions bad. The weakness of the union meant also that the employers themselves did not have to organize. It was not until July 7, 1910, when they were faced with the general strike, endorsed by both International and Joint Board leaders, that the employers formed their Cloak, Suit & Skirt Manufacturers' Protective Association.

All attempts even to bring the contestants together had failed, the major obstacle being the union demand for closed shop. Production was at a standstill. As a large retail distributor of wearing apparel, A. Lincoln Filene of Boston was much concerned. "I think," he told Brandeis, "I will go over and look into this thing. I think you had better come too." Brandeis did not go. "Then and there," he recalled some years later, "I told him that I would have nothing to do with any settlement of the strike involving the closed shop. That I did not believe in it, and that I thought it was un-American and unfair to both sides." [2]

Filene went to New York and talked first with one group and then with the other. Associated with him in these peace efforts were Henry Moskowitz, later adviser to Governor Alfred E. Smith, and Meyer Bloomfield, lawyer, social worker, and member of the Civic Federation of New England. They found the situation deadlocked, the General Strike Committee holding out stubbornly for the closed shop, the Manufacturers' Protective Association refusing even to recognize the union. Finally, on July 21, 1910, the indefatigable Bloomfield emerged from another session with the strike committee. A hopeful idea had been suggested which he promptly reported by wire to Brandeis:

Said to Lennon * and Dyche † that there was only one open door—to take a big man like Brandeis and empower him . . . to confer with both sides and draw up a fair basis of negotiations. Both responded heartily and suggested that I invite Mr. B. and come with him for a private talk. Am convinced that in final conference fundamental injustices will be righted, the union not be smashed, and an open shop prevail.

Brandeis agreed to come. "I was called to New York last night," he wrote Alfred, July 24, "to try to settle the New York garment workers' strike. About 50,000 men are out. I am trying to bring the parties into conference. It remains to be seen whether my journey will be as futile as that of the French King and his 40,000 men."

Brandeis's first step was to persuade the General Strike Committee to waive the closed shop. On July 24 he had the Joint Board of the local unions draw up their demands and authorize him to present them to the Manufacturers' Protective Association. The same day Brandeis wrote to Julius Henry Cohen, counsel for the Association: "All of these officers understand fully that under this proposal the closed shop is not a subject which can be discussed at the conference."

The following day the manufacturers formally accepted the terms on which the peace conference would take place.

The conference was almost wrecked, however, even before it began, when on July 26, the day sessions were to start, the Manufacturers' Association published in the *New York Call* this premature claim of victory:

* John Lennon, co-chairman of the strike committee.
† John Dyche, International Union representative.

Louis D. Brandeis . . . came here from Boston on Saturday and consented to act for the strikers without compensation. Mr. Brandeis has acted as attorney in more than a score of strikes, in the majority of instances, acting for the employers. His opposition to the closed-shop idea is well known, and in retaining him, the strikers tacitly waived their demand for the closed shop in the cloak, suit and skirt trade. The complete withdrawal of the demand was made later upon the advice of Brandeis as a preliminary step to the arrangement of the conference.[3]

Adding fuel to the flames, J. H. Cohen said the same day:

It gratifies me beyond expression that Brandeis has consented to act as attorney for the union in this strike. His presence in the situation expresses more emphatically than any words the complete elimination of the demand for the "closed shop." This is no longer a matter for discussion.[4]

The unions were up in arms. President Abraham C. Rosenberg of the International proclaimed vehemently:

The [employers'] statement is a misstatement from top to bottom. In the first place, we have not retained Brandeis as our attorney. Brandeis was in New York. . . . He visited us, and asked if we were not willing to meet the manufacturers in a conference. We told Brandeis that we were ready to meet the bosses ever since the strike was called, and that we were ready to meet them now, too.

With this the matter ended. We have not asked Brandeis to act as our attorney, and we have not waived our demand for the closed shop. Our position remains the same. Rather than waive this demand our people will be out on strike twenty weeks yet, and then they will rather lose it than submit to such a compromise.[5]

Rosenberg's action widened the breach between the radicals and the more conciliatory workers on the closed-shop issue. The crisis became so acute that Samuel Gompers, A.F. of L. president, had to come from Washington as peacemaker. A semblance of amity was established when Benjamin Schlesinger, vociferous opponent of compromise and editor of the radical labor journal *Vorwarts,* was added to the strike committee to counterbalance John Dyche's conservatives.[6]

With the split in union ranks momentarily healed, and the parties brought closer together, Meyer London, union counsel, and J. H. Cohen, for the employers, finally sent a joint telegram to Brandeis on July 27, asking him to act as chairman of the meeting. The next day he consented.[7]

From July 28 to the evening of July 30 the contestants were in session, Cohen leading for the employers and London for the employees. Each was supported by ten representatives.* The Manufacturers' Association presented a united front. With the closed shop banned from discussion, however, the union delegation was in no such accord. Rosenberg and Lennon remained violently opposed to the very conditions on which the conference had agreed to assemble. Yet Brandeis never indicated that he doubted the sincerity of the conferees or questioned the possibility of a successful conference. Opening the sessions, he said: "Gentlemen, we have come together in a matter which we must all recognize is very serious, and an important business, not only to settle this strike, but to create a relation which will prevent similar strikes in the future. That work is one which it seems to me is approached in a spirit which makes the situation a very hopeful one, and I am sure from my conferences with counsel of both parties, and with individual members whom they represent, that those who are here are all here with that desire." [8]

Brandeis earlier had arranged with opposing counsel the order in which topics were to be considered—the least disputed matters heading the list, the more controversial topics being placed at the end. When dissension arose, his method was to let the disputants "talk it and themselves out." Often the parties would take stands so much alike that Brandeis could point to fundamental agreement and hurry them along to the next topic. Other times the "talking out" process resulted only in greater obstinacy. When Brandeis saw this, he cast aside his noninterventionist role and appealed first to one side and then the other. By much questioning he often checked rising tempers and cleared the air.

In this way the less contentious issues were so readily disposed of that optimism rose daily. Gompers, who had kept in close touch with proceedings, returned to Washington, July 29, "confident that the garment workers' strike would be settled speedily." [9] The New York Globe on July 28 anticipated agreement within a few days, while the New York World on the same day reported more cautiously that the conference might end in a week or a little more.

All were wrong. The conference crashed on its third day—because of the closed shop.

CLOSED SHOP VERSUS PREFERENTIAL SHOP

On several occasions Rosenberg had come perilously close to broaching the forbidden subject; each time Brandeis had steered him from it. But on July 30, shortly after opposing lawyers had made eloquent speeches

* Representatives for the manufacturers were E. A. Lefcourt, M. Silverman, M. M. Schwarcz, Max Meyer, Joseph Jonasson, Max Rubin, William Fishman, I. Stern, Max Solomon, and R. Sadowsky. For the unions: A. C. Rosenberg, J. A. Dyche, J. B. Lennon, Benjamin Schlesinger, J. Greenberger, S. Polakoff, H. Kleinman, Alexander Bloch, A. Baffa, and Morris Siegman.

emphasizing their eagerness for peace and good-will,[10] Lennon suddenly loosed a thunderbolt too swift even for Brandeis to handle.

LENNON: I am not going to appeal to the chairman for any views upon any subject, but I want to call attention to something that I know to be a fact. There is absolutely no such thing as the open shop. . . . They are either union shops or they are non-union shops. . . . Just as soon as there is anyone employed in the factory that is not union, the shop is a non-union shop. . . . Now, I say that the first step toward making co-operation effective is the union shop.

COHEN: What do you mean by "the union shop," Mr. Lennon?

LENNON: I mean . . . that the employees shall all belong to the union.

CHAIRMAN: I do not understand that Mr. Lennon is at all discussing a closed shop proposition. Mr. Lennon understands [what] the whole proceeding here is—the whole conference proceeds upon the agreement that the closed shop shall not be one of the subjects discussed. I have assumed that what Mr. Lennon meant, and I think I am right in that assumption, from my knowledge of union—general union—phraseology, that he refers by a "union shop" to a shop which has reached that high degree of perfection in organization that everybody in it is a union man, and not by agreement with the employer, but as a result of those processes of persuasion that have been so effective in extending the union body. I think that that obviously is what Mr. Lennon means, because it would be a distinct breach of the terms on which our meeting and conference has proceeded, if what we commonly call the "closed shop" were a subject before us.

LONDON: . . . I would say that the subject of the closed shop can be taken up under the subject of remedies, if we reach the conclusion that there can be no remedies suggested other than the closed shop.

CHAIRMAN: I think, Mr. London, that the subject of the closed shop—I should rule that the subject of the closed shop could not be discussed at all, except with the absolute consent of everyone who has entered here into the conference, because it was expressly understood, and I gave my assurance upon my own understanding of the written document which I received, that that was a subject which could not be brought up, and we proceeded wholly on that.

LONDON: Was it your understanding, Mr. Chairman, that it could not be brought up under the subject of remedies?

CHAIRMAN: It was my understanding that it could not be discussed at all.

LONDON: Even under the subject of remedies?

CHAIRMAN: Under any circumstances: that it was one of the tabooed subjects, so far as this conference was concerned. . . . On the other hand, of course, the subject of approaching perfection in this and in other respects, is a subject that is open, and I conceive that to be but a general step in the movement of strengthening the union. . . . That is a question of degree, but I consider the question of a closed shop an entirely different proposition from any other, and that different proposition I assume to be excluded by our agreement. I should certainly myself, and I am a party with you in that, because I acted for the unions in arranging this conference—I should consider myself precluded from even discussing in conference—

LONDON: Unless as a remedy—if we reach the conclusion that it is a remedy?

CHAIRMAN: No. . . .

LONDON: That does not exclude the discussion of the question of a union shop?

CHAIRMAN: Certainly not, because, as I say, union is merely a degree. It is an end which everybody who favors a union must long for, as we long for perfection in other things. . . . And as that high perfection . . . is something that everybody here is agreed on, I think we can talk about reaching perfection.[11]

Brandeis did not succeed in convincing the more radical leaders that what they really wanted was the "union," not the closed shop. When he finished, Lennon abruptly asked for a recess to confer privately with his delegates.[12] In granting the request, Brandeis sensed impending disaster. He tried to avert it with flattery: "I want to say that I have never had the opportunity of participating in a conference on labor matters which has been conducted, on the whole, with such intelligence and fairness and consideration as this one. I have never had the opportunity of attending at any conference where I felt that the progress made in the interests of a better condition of the trade, and, specifically, a better condition of the working people, has advanced as rapidly as here. Now, I think both of you were right in the suggestions that there is the hope of doing something that is really great and epoch-making in the movement of co-operation, and in the movement, specifically, of the organization of labor, as a necessary instrument toward the improvement of the condition of labor."[13]

When the conference reconvened, Brandeis, who before this had not spoken more than a few sentences here and there, tried again to get around the closed shop issue. In an eloquent plea covering five pages of the record, he now presented his famous compromise—the preferential union shop, which he had tried to introduce back in 1907 when he appeared as counsel for the manufacturers in the Boston cloakmakers' strike.

In part Brandeis said:

I realize that in the ordinary open shop . . . there is great difficulty in building up the union. . . . It seems to me . . . that aid could be effectively and properly given by providing that the manufacturers should, in the employment of labor hereafter, give the preference to union men, where the union men are equal in efficiency to any non-union applicants. . . . Your men would be in control, and even if it should happen that in individual shops a small percentage of other men should be in, owing to particular conditions, that would not interfere with the union. Now, that is the basic idea which I have to present to the manufacturers on the one side, and to the unions on the other. It involves, of course, this as a consideration. In the first place, that the decision in regard to who is a competent person to admit and to retain in the employ must rest with the employer . . . but that if anyone should be guilty of discrimination . . . it would be decided by the appropriate board. . . . I feel that that would accomplish, and probably that alone would accomplish, everything that is desired in results. I feel that it would be infinitely more effective in result than a closed shop agreement entered into under the duress of a strike and entered into, as it would be, with reservations. . . . Such an arrangement as I have proposed rests for its efficacy, necessarily, upon good faith. . . . I realize equally that if the manufacturers on the one hand, and the union leaders on the other hand . . . should approve of such an agreement, that it would require very considerable effort on their part to induce their associates who have not had the benefit of conferring for days, each with the other here, of the wisdom—of the possibility of doing this. And while I consider that too to be a difficult task, I am convinced that it is a possible task, and that if you gentlemen would undertake on each side courageously to present the advantages that would be gained by such a course . . . you can educate them to an understanding of it, and an adoption of it. I think that if such an arrangement as we have discussed can be accomplished, it would be the greatest advance, not only that unionism has ever made in this country, but it would be one of the greatest advances that has generally been made in improving the condition of the working man, for which unionism is merely an instrument.[14]

The manufacturers, against the "better judgment of counsel," favored the preferential shop. But union men were cold to it. The conference, Lennon said, has been "grievously disappointing. Ill rather than good" has been accomplished. At the direction of the union delegates he asked that the discussions be terminated.[15] Cohen remarked that the reason for breaking up "is not the issue of wages nor the issue of hours, but the fact that the intelligent men at this table are not confident of their ability to secure the approval of what they themselves have been willing to recognize as just and reasonable." [16] Going further, he charged that union delegates lacked the courage to face their own men.

To avoid a free-for-all Brandeis promptly introduced several less explosive topics. For a moment the crisis abated. Then he brought up his preferential shop idea under a less offensive name—the union shop. He explained that it was "something that was very hopeful as compared with the alternative of continuing the fight with all the disaster and suffering that would be with it, and particularly, in my mind, with a setback to unionism, as I see it, which would be very serious." [17]

Certain delegates sided with Brandeis, but the extremists prevailed. "The employment of union men only," they said, "is the only proposition that can be accepted by our organization. . . . We will keep up this strike, whether we like it or not; whether it will do us good or not. We have to; we will." [18] Then Dyche told the union men that the preferential shop would destroy unionism: "For the sake of self-preservation, you would be committing suicide to go into an agreement where such a condition prevailed. Give us a chance for half a year, and let us see if we can make good."

CHAIRMAN: That is what *we* say.

DYCHE: But I have no faith in it, Mr. Chairman.

CHAIRMAN: I have no faith in yours.

DYCHE: It is something too new. It cannot be done at this crisis. [19]

With this, the conference broke up. It was agreed that Brandeis, Cohen, and London should meet the following day, to work out a solution to be presented in writing to both sides. Thereafter the conference might be resumed. Brandeis now considered the prospect as almost hopeless. "The outcome," he wrote Alfred on July 31, "is doubtful, with probabilities that there will be no settlement because of the union demand of an all-union shop."

On August 1, however, things were brightened considerably by the written agreement Cohen had drawn up. Among other things, this proposed the establishment of a Joint Board of Sanitary Control with power to enforce sanitary conditions, and a Joint Board of Arbitration. The manufacturers were to stipulate the importance of unionism and to declare their willingness to strengthen it "if it be well organized and wisely led." They would be obligated to employ union men wherever possible, but would not surrender control of their own factories. The statement went on to say that the unions did not seek the closed shop, but rather the union shop, defined as one where the majority of the men employed are union men and the employer known to be a union sympathizer. No strikes or lockouts could take place until grievances had been submitted to arbitration. [20]

Brandeis approved the Cohen draft but added a clarifying amendment on the preferential union shop: "They [the workers] seek the union shop, by which they mean a shop in which union standards prevail and the union man is entitled to the preference." [21] Cohen agreed and sent the amended statement to London, who refused to commit himself, saying he could take no further action until he consulted the executive board of the unions.

This was not very promising since even before he had seen the employers' statement Rosenberg had said belligerently: "If the draft looks to us like a union agreement, then we will consider it. If not, further conferences would be only a waste of time." [22] Schlesinger's *Vorwarts* at the same time denounced the preferential shop as "the open shop with honey." [23] Cohen's "agreement" got nowhere, and negotiations were discontinued.

On August 3 Brandeis resumed his vacation at South Yarmouth. Apparently he had washed his hands of the whole affair. But that same day the Manufacturers' Association telegraphed him, asking for a photograph of the document empowering him in "the situation," and also the statement concerning waiver of the closed shop.[24] On August 4 Max Meyer, secretary of the Association, repeated the request, saying that many "well-meaning employees" were distressed that their leaders had repudiated their signed pledge. Brandeis directed his office on August 5 to send Meyer's letter and everything else on the case to Filene, and suggested that Filene and Bloomfield act as they saw fit. "The document which seems to me more important," he wrote, "is my letter to Cohen of July 24 enclosing the other documents, which recites that all those who signed the authorization understood that the closed shop could not be discussed at the conference. This letter was approved in writing by Dyche. My copy bears his approval."

Before the photographs of the documents were delivered, Cohen brought the equity courts into the controversy on the employers' side by securing a temporary injunction restraining strikers from in any way interfering with men wishing to return to work. Filene now began to wonder whether the request for the photographs had been made in good faith. Writing Brandeis on August 9, he said: "My first thought was that the employers had some justice in their claim for this demand upon you, and that probably their object was to put themselves straight with the public; but I find, as per clipping enclosed, that they have secured an injunction against the union, which makes me feel that they want to use this as evidence."

Filene therefore denied the request, explaining to Max Meyer on August 9 that "It would very largely handicap any future negotiations and his possible good offices if Mr. Brandeis acceded to your request without first securing the sanction for doing so both from Mr. Cohen and Mr. London. . . . As chairman of the conference, it is important to keep neutral the position Mr. Brandeis has maintained, and any use of his own notes or original papers ought to come only through mutual consent."

Henry Moskowitz also urged Bloomfield to keep Brandeis aloof: "He has made a profound impression on both sides. He will kill his standing with the workers if the judicial silence is broken. I have no doubt he feels the same way. His capital importance to the labor movement in America

is more essential than a statement at the present juncture, which may help
to misrepresent his purity of motive." [25]

Meanwhile peacemakers Filene, Bloomfield, and Moskowitz had enlisted Jacob H. Schiff, New York financier, and Louis Marshall, well-
known constitutional lawyer and leader of American Jewry.[26] Schiff and
Marshall arranged a conference with Cohen and London. They discussed
at length Cohen's earlier agreement which had been accepted by Brandeis.
Some changes were made, and on August 30, in a revised form, it was
agreed upon by Cohen and London.

Things looked promising again when Filene wrote Brandeis on August
31: "We, Dr. Moskowitz and myself, were on the East Side until one
o'clock this morning, talking to a group of East Siders. . . . They all feel
that if the *Vorwarts* could be brought around the strike would be over. . . .
I haven't much hope but I feel that if the mass could be gotten at somehow
and explained what this agreement means, it would bring about a reaction,
for we are told by these East Siders that we met last night that, 1st, the
people do not understand and, 2nd, if the leaders or the *Vorwarts* would
say the word the strikers would settle. We do not feel that the leaders
want to face the manufacturers. We do feel that they haven't the courage
to do and dare."

In order to make the new agreement acceptable to the rank and file, an
appropriate label had to be found for it. London suggested "this collective
agreement." Fearful that such a phrase might encourage rather than abate
"the war spirit of the radicals in the union," Cohen suggested "treaty of
peace." Louis Marshall then came forward. "Why not call it 'protocol'—
neither group will know what that means and it will achieve the result." [27]
"Protocol" it became.

On September 1 the protocol was submitted to the executive board of
the General Strike Committee, and the next day some two hundred shop
chairmen met and after long discussion voted to accept it. The agreement
was signed on September 2, 1910.[28]

The protocol was designed to establish self-government in industry—
thus forestalling any outside interference. At a time when there was little
or no factory inspection, the protocol set up a seven-member Joint Board
of Sanitary Control to standardize working conditions. It also set up a
Board of Grievances to settle disputes that could not be handled by union-
management shop committees. If the Board of Grievances failed, no lock-
out or strike could be called until the dispute had been submitted to the
highest authority under the protocol—an unpaid, three-man Board of
Arbitration. Above all, the protocol proclaimed and endorsed the union

shop; "a shop where union standards as to working conditions, hours of labor, and rates of wages as herein stipulated prevail, and where, when hiring help, union men are preferred; it being recognized that, since there are differences in degree of skill among those employed in the trade, employers shall have freedom of selection as between one union man and another, and shall not be confined to any list, nor bound to follow any prescribed order whatever." [29] This was, of course, the preferential shop under a less controversial name.

PROGRESS UNDER THE PROTOCOL

Enthusiastic letters poured in on Brandeis and he replied in kind. "I think we are all to be congratulated," he wrote Max Meyer, September 6, "and it is a satisfaction to know that there are so many who have contributed to the happy result." His letter to Jane Addams noted that "the success obtained in New York was due in very large measure to the admirable team work of A. Lincoln Filene, Meyer Bloomfield, and Dr. Henry W. Moskowitz. Without their careful work of preparation, their patient watchfulness and excellent judgment it would have been impossible for me to accomplish anything. Indeed, they are entitled to far more credit than I am." [30] Yet thereafter Brandeis seized every opportunity to publicize his own contribution—the preferential shop—as marking a new epoch in American trade unionism.

Thus on September 6, 1910, he wrote to Lawrence Abbott of *The Outlook:* "The objections, legal, economic, and social, against the closed shop are so strong, and the ideas of the closed shop so antagonistic to the American spirit, that the insistence upon it has been a serious obstacle to union progress. On the other hand, the open shop, as ordinarily practiced, has tended to disintegrate union membership, and has in it inherent injustice— namely, that the burden of obtaining satisfactory wages, hours, and conditions is borne by but a fraction of those who enjoy the benefits. The preferential union shop seems to offer a solution consistent with American spirit and traditions as well as with justice and with the necessity of strengthening the unions."

All sides agreed that the fulfillment of such high hopes would depend largely on the personnel of the Board of Arbitration. The chairmanship was most important, and Brandeis seemed the only choice. Cohen wrote him on October 10: "I had not the courage to face you with the appointment as chief arbitrator under the protocol. I was confident, however, that the scheme once more was likely to fail unless you would help to work it out, and while you were entitled to have the best kind of a trial made, I was confident that such a trial could not be had without you. On the other hand, it seemed to me that I was sacrificing your own personal interests to those of my clients. The call to you, therefore, should come—I reasoned— from the public, and as Filene in this particular instance was very much of 'the public,' I put the matter before him. I was glad, indeed, to get this morning his letter indicating that you had accepted."

Even with Brandeis as chief arbitrator, however, the protocol soon ran into trouble. Neither side welcomed it as a new "charter of industrial states-manship." The workers saw it only as a favorable settlement of the general strike. The employers saw it as a protection against strikes. They also thought it would check cutthroat competition by equalizing working con-ditions in all plants, and thus give the whole industry a more respectable position in the community—which some employers were very anxious to attain.

The consequences of this partisan view of the protocol were soon appar-ent. As chairman of the Board of Arbitration, Brandeis resisted all de-mands for a meeting of that body. He hoped by these tactics to have all disputes settled on the spot by shop stewards or at least by the Board of Grievances.

As Brandeis saw it, the protocol's success depended, primarily, upon conciliation, on the give-and-take of discussion; arbitration was a last resort, to be used only in case of a deadlock on the most important matters of policy. The only result of Brandeis's tactics was that grievances accu-mulated. Ultimately both sides became so restless that Brandeis was forced to call the Board of Arbitration on March 4, 1911. He acted as chairman; Hamilton Holt represented the manufacturers, Morris Hillquit the unions. In opening the session Brandeis said: "What I desire is not to go into a hearing on controverted questions, but to get down to the real facts. I have myself a conviction that until you get down to the specific facts, outside of general statements, and until you try to put them down in black and white, you really do not know what has happened." [31]

When the facts were produced, they showed, as Brandeis had expected, that most of the complaints were due to faulty functioning of the Board of Grievances. Brandeis requested that the two lawyers draw up a plan for strengthening the board.[32] This they did by March 14. For a time the protocol worked more smoothly.

Indeed, the protocol was so successful in bringing order into one of the most disorganized industries, that under Brandeis's prodding, newspapers, magazines, even governmental reports, spread the fame of the preferential shop.[33] Brandeis himself, in 1911 and 1912, received and answered count-less requests for information on the subject from civic organizations, social workers, high school and college debating clubs, newspapermen, and scholars.

Moreover, agreements similar to the protocol were readily adopted in other branches of the New York garment trade. Early in September 1911 a protocol was set up in the Ladies' Tailors and Dress Makers' trade, following a whirlwind strike called by Local 38 of the I.L.G.W.U.[34] Cohen, again representing the employers, wrote Brandeis, begging him to accept chairmanship of the new arbitration board. "The mere presence of a permanent Board, of public standing and influence," Cohen now believed, "does more to prevent a raising of issues than any other single institution."[35] With so many heavy obligations still unfulfilled Brandeis hesitated, but finally accepted.[36] In January 1913 he became impartial chairman in a third trade when a protocol agreement followed a strike called by the Waist and Dress Makers' Union.

Though busy much of the time in Washington with congressional committee hearings, Brandeis kept "talking up" protocolism. In September 1911 the *American Cloak and Suit Review* published his article, "The Spirit of Get-Together," in which he praised the original agreement and added "that whatever is found to be wrong is not to be borne, but is to be removed, and that it can be remedied—by careful study, in an uplifting spirit, by patient striving in the spirit of get-together." On February 26, 1912, in a letter to Lincoln Steffens (copies of which went to other editors and newspapermen), Brandeis wrote at great length on the whole subject of unions and employee–employer relations:

In my opinion the time is ripe for a great advance in the scope and influence, and the quality of trade unionism.

On the one hand, the disclosures incident to the labor policies of the strong trusts and particularly the hours of labor, wages, and conditions in the steel industry are making many Americans recognize that unions and collective bargaining are essential to industrial liberty and social justice.

On the other hand, the abuses of trade unionism as we have known them during the last twenty years with their violence, restriction of output, and their lack of constructive policy, are in large part the result of the fact that they have been engaged in a bitter struggle for existence. When public opinion is brought actively to the support of labor unions these abuses will, I believe, tend rapidly to disappear. But the American people should not, and will not, accept unionism if it involves the closed shop. They will not consent to the exchange of the tyranny of the employer for the tyranny of the employee. Unionism therefore cannot make a great advance until it abandons the closed shop; and it cannot accept the open shop as an alternative. The open shop means the destruction of the union.

The advance of unionism demands therefore some relation between the employer and the employee other than either the closed or open shop, and I feel confident that we have found a solution in the preferential union shop.

> This seems to be the time to commence the campaign of education. Much hammering will be necessary; for the employers will be loath to enter into so comprehensive an agreement with unions; and unions will be loath to give up the closed shop. But the preferential shop seems to be a way out of our present serious difficulty; and we must pursue it unless a better can be found.

Good feeling prevailed throughout the garment industry for a time. Trade was brisk. Working conditions were improved. Over 90 per cent of the workers were organized, and even the Cloakmakers' Joint Board was happy.[37] Writing to Brandeis, June 5, 1911, Henry Moskowitz, now clerk of the Board of Arbitration, passed along these tidings: ". . . Substantial progress has been made by both sides; . . . they are getting together more and more; . . . they are developing efficient modes of negotiation; good feeling seems to be strengthening on both sides; . . . I believe that the leaders of the unions are actually losing a little of their suspicion."

DISTRESS SIGNALS

It was not long, however, before both sides began to hammer away at the agreement. With protocolism being used in three of the garment trades, trouble spots multiplied and became increasingly difficult to settle. On December 7, 1911, Moskowitz wrote Brandeis that he believed that "both sides have made a mistake in the settlement of the dispute . . . that a protocol similar to that of the Cloak and Suit industry has been indiscriminately applied without taking cognizance of the state of the industry and the state of the union."

The protocol proved a failure first in the ladies' tailoring and dressmaking trade, and this failure marked the beginning of a series of crises. On July 9, 1912, Moskowitz wrote Brandeis: "We must put our heads together to prevent a serious break. . . . I fear that the good-will which is at the basis of our protocol is being subjected to a severe strain. . . . The atmosphere is charged with tension and we must provide some outlet else something will break."

By the end of 1912 hundreds of sub-manufacturers were beyond the protocols' reach.[38] At that time too, strife between the conservatism of the I.L.G.W.U. and the radicalism of the Cloakmakers' Joint Board was worse than ever. The *New Post* harped more and more on the class struggle. This attack on capitalism root and branch increasingly irritated Cohen and the employers, and in the end seemed to confirm their belief that Brandeis's "appeasement" policy had been a tragic blunder from the start.[39]

The storm broke in January 1913, when the Grievance Board machinery came to a standstill. On January 29 Moskowitz wrote Brandeis: "The situation is critical and needs handling. Your presence here will help. I do not know what position you must take as arbitrator; I hope you will be able to interpret the instrument so as to make the International the responsible body."

Brandeis arrived in New York on February 2, but owing to Hillquit's absence a regular meeting of the Arbitration Board could not be held. On February 3 and 4 Brandeis and Hamilton Holt met the representatives of the unions and the manufacturers in informal conference to investigate the grievance machinery, stalled because of sharp differences as to whether authority to speak for the unions was vested in the Joint Board or in the International.[40] Dr. Isaac Hourwich, newly elected union chief clerk of the Board of Grievances, attended the conference and held that supreme power lay in the New York locals, of which the Joint Board was the qualified representative. But the Manufacturers' Association insisted that it would "have absolutely no dealings with the Joint Board of the Cloak & Suit Makers Union," and would "deal only with the International." Hourwich retorted vehemently: "We are the men whom you must listen to. The International is one organization—a federal organization of officers. If you desire to deal with the shadow instead of the body, it is your privilege, but you must be aware of the fact that they cannot deliver the goods." [41]

The employers stubbornly refused to do business with the Joint Board on the ground of its irresponsibility in carrying out its obligations under the protocol and threatened: "If we cannot have the stoppages of work stopped, then the protocol is at an end automatically." [42]

Brandeis remained inconspicuous during this debate, but at its close tried hard to restore peace. The *New Post's* articles, of which the manufacturers had bitterly complained, he cast lightly aside as "more or less philosophic discussions of government between the parties," and entirely proper as an exercise of free speech. Nevertheless he suggested that in the future all *Post* articles be passed upon by Hourwich, as chief clerk, so that nothing would get in to discredit the protocol. He then emphasized the need for strong action by the Manufacturers' Association and the unions, to avert all violations of the protocol. The protocol was entered into, Brandeis said, by the locals of the Joint Board, through the officers of the International; and however strongly he may have disapproved of the belligerence of the Joint Board, Brandeis upheld it as being the organization with which the manufacturers would have to deal.[43]

Brandeis then approached the stoppage of grievance machinery by the manufacturers' clerks with the utmost tact and gentleness: "If the facts were as stated, and they certainly were believed to be such, it is not at all unnatural that Mr. Morris Silberman should have taken the law into his own hands. Men do that frequently in life when they haven't got the right to do it, and their moral guilt is not perhaps very great, but it seems to us entirely clear that the action of the stopping of the machinery was an action which was in violation of the protocol. . . . It seems to us that while Mr. Silberman's action as a layman was not unnatural under the provocation as he understood it, it cannot be legally justified. . . ."

With undaunted optimism, Brandeis concluded: "We appreciate very much, and I think fully, the difficulties under which the manufacturers have labored, and the difficulties of the situation which are inherent in the position of the union officials. The suffering, and the difficulties, and all that has been disclosed here, has made us feel that you gentlemen have performed the work which you have been called upon to perform as members of your Grievance Committee and Executive Committee on the whole with very extraordinary discretion and patience and skill, and that the progress which has been made in the operation of the protocol since the arbitrators were called in in March 1911, seems to us very great, and extremely encouraging, and that we look upon this new method of dealing with differences between employers and employees with far more hope than when you called us here, or at any other time before, and we are greatly obliged to you for letting us come in and take some part in the settlement of your troubles." [44]

L'AFFAIRE HOURWICH

Though Brandeis tided over this crisis he failed to check the disputes among divergent elements in the unions. The split between the International and the Joint Board grew more tense as time passed, and kept the protocol under constant fire.

Keeping the fire hottest was Dr. Hourwich. As a writer, economist, lawyer, and a man of recognized integrity, Hourwich seemed admirably qualified for his post on the Board of Grievances. But his highly inflammable personality soon got the better of him and he became the center around which the bitterly contested issues of the garment industry swirled—arbitration versus conciliation; protocolism versus class war; radicalism of the New York locals versus conservatism of the International.

Hourwich precipitated a new crisis in April 1913 when he seized upon a minor dispute to call a meeting of the Board of Arbitration. When Moskowitz, as clerk of the board, dismissed the issue as unworthy of the board's consideration, Hourwich hurried to Washington to see Brandeis. "Hourwich appears considerably worked up," Brandeis wrote Moskowitz on

May 10, 1913; ". . . I think you ought . . . to talk over this situation very fully with Hourwich, and also with others, to get him into line. His main point seems to be that, without constant resort to the decisions of a court, the protocol will not work. I have considered the best feature of the protocol that we did not resort to courts, and that we dealt by proper discussions of the questions as they arise."

Soon Hourwich furnished Brandeis with a statement, labeled "proposed amendents to the protocol," denouncing conciliation and demanding "arbitration with teeth." Brandeis presented this statement to the Manufacturers' Association, suggesting a conference, but the Association urged postponement. On May 27 Hourwich wrote Brandeis: "If the Association will then persist in its unyielding attitude, I do not want to foretell the consequences."

In the meantime, the *New Post* published an article culled from Hourwich's speeches and interviews, in which it said:

There are two sorts of capitalists. One is the capitalist of the old Frankish style, who looks upon the workingmen as upon slaves. . . . The second capitalist is a modern one—more up-to-date. He concedes that the workers also have rights, as the horse of a truckman has. He may demand light and a dry stall and enough oats, but when the driver says "get up," the horse must go and ask no questions. The liberal capitalist may listen more or less patiently to a demand for wages, but he cannot listen to the rights of the workingmen in the shop; there, in the shop, the boss is absolute dictator.

In the protocol which we have, there is embodied the principle of this modern capitalist. . . . The justice which the protocol promises is interpreted by the manufacturers to their benefit, and the machinery which has been created to enforce the protocol in actual life—the Board of Grievances and the Arbitration Committee—work so that we can seldom get justice.[45]

Brandeis naturally was disturbed by Hourwich's stand and the *New Post's* article. On May 28 he wrote to Moskowitz: "The attitude of ominous threats disclosed by Hourwich is rather disconcerting. I think you and some of our other friends ought to get in touch with him at once." Moskowitz replied: "The editors of the *New Post* are no diplomats, they speak in forte tones. They are so accustomed to the bass-drum method of appeal that they constantly make a noise even when a soft pedal is necessary. In this case the noise is significant." Cohen and London are fair-minded, Moskowitz continued, but "the minor leaders on both sides need cracked ice treatment." For the moment, he thought it best for Brandeis to keep hands off lest "Mr. Brandeis the mediator interfere with Mr. Brandeis the arbitrator."

The conference which Hourwich so eagerly sought between the Joint

Board and the Manufacturers' Association began July 8 and lasted until July 30. In these proceedings, he, not Meyer London, was the idol of the garment workers. "The protocol," Hourwich contended, "gives the union the right to submit every grievance we have, small or big, to the Board of Arbitration." [46] He boldly took this stand in opposition to the manufacturers, the arbitrators, and the International—who were all against such extensive arbitration. As chief spokesman for the Joint Board, Hourwich was "uncompromising and unelastic," as "adamantine as the Rock of Gibraltar." [47]

The employers were equally stony. "Even if the employers think of making any concessions, they will not grant them to Hourwich. They are afraid that if they do so they will enhance his prestige. If some way can be devised by which the concession could be made to the International and not to Hourwich, the employers would show a readier responsiveness to some of the demands." [48]

Following the conference on Hourwich's proposed amendment, the Board of Arbitration (Brandeis, Holt, and Walter E. Weyl) conferred from August 3 to August 6. The meeting opened with consideration of Hourwich's demand for an increase in their number. The arbitrators said no. Brandeis freely admitted that six additional men might well be superior to the present three arbitrators in judgment but, he explained: "We have difficulty enough in educating ourselves. We are finding at all times that it is the facts that we want to know, and we are gathering gradually a knowledge of those facts through you. . . . And it seems to us that any interposition of other persons deciding certain questions which come up from time to time, whether their decisions be as good or better than ours would, at all events, defeat the main purpose, because it would prevent continuity of thought and continuity of effort, and would come to substitute sporadic and individual opinions for some continuous constructive line of work." [49]

Back of Hourwich's request for enlarging the Board was the desire to make its members more accessible to disputants. "With all due respect to you, gentlemen," he said, "our Board of Arbitration is something like the Council of the Dalai Lama of Tibet; it is too invisible. We have all the respect in the world for you gentlemen, but we have got to have a Justice of the Peace a great deal more often than a session of the Supreme Court, and unless we have it, I do not see how this protocol can live." [50]

The Board took no official notice of Hourwich's outburst, but proceeded to the wage increases demanded by the unions. There were no reliable statistics on garment industry wages, but one thing was clear—the industry was marked by extreme seasonality, which caused great irregularity of employment. Brandeis found himself back to his old theme, that year-round, regular employment was much more important than high hourly wages. He found himself practically alone in believing that garment industry employment could be spread evenly over the year: "I, for one, have been wholly unable to accept the idea that whatever is, is inevitable, even under the capitalistic theory and system. I know in certain industries, with which I have come in contact, which are capitalistic in their nature, and where irregularity has been considered inevitable, it has yielded. . . . I only feel convinced of two propositions: . . . that much which seems impossible is possible; and that most of the things worth doing in the world have been declared to be impossible, before they were done; and necessity has proven itself the mother of invention."

He added cheerfully: "I have no thought whatever of philanthropy, and I have not thought that it is possible for the gentlemen here to find any device which is going to meet this situation completely, but in other lines of industry it has been found possible to stimulate the invention and enterprise of individual manufacturers. . . . That is . . . you could devise a system by which each individual manufacturer could have an incentive so that he and each one of his confreres would be driven to strive, with the aid of his employees, to make work more regular. . . . I consider this a joint responsibility of employer and employee." [51]

At the final session on August 6 Brandeis paid high tribute to the chief clerks: They could not have attained their "high record of performance unless they had gone forward on this work with that determination of recognizing the frailties of man, the impossibility of perfection on this earth, and of trying to get a sort of workable arrangement between man and man. And the utmost, which is absolutely essential in that, and to that end, is mutual respect and confidence." [52]

Hourwich (who had earlier denounced the chairman's "paternalism" and "dictatorial attitude") rejected Brandeis's alluring words and became more determined than ever to force his resignation. [53] Hourwich's disruptive foray stirred the Manufacturers' Association to demand a follow-up meeting of the Arbitration Board. This took place on October 3 and 4, when the Board censured Hourwich's action as "insurrection and rebellion" and denounced the New Post as subversive of the protocol.

By this time Brandeis considered Hourwich "an inveterate trouble maker." "We shall have no peace," he wrote Weyl, December 3, 1913, "with him in position." Hourwich, however, knew his own strength. A referendum on his re-election, December 13–15, resulted in an overwhelming vote in his favor. The employers, however, refused to accept this decision, and called upon the International to remove him. Until this was done, they would decline to participate in any discussions under the protocol.

The next meeting of the Arbitration Board, on January 18, 1914, centered on the "trouble maker." Brandeis conceded that the parties to the protocol —the union and the employers—had the right to choose their own representatives and without interference, yet he pointed out that "it is of the essence of the protocol that the parties thereto shall work together in harmony." Furthermore, the manufacturers had declared "their firm intention to terminate the protocol forthwith because of their conviction that its purposes cannot be carried out so long as the Union is represented by Dr. Hourwich." Leaving room for Hourwich to retire gracefully, Brandeis concluded: "While the manufacturers have no right to compel his withdrawal, he himself has the right to withdraw, and if in his loyalty to the Union and to the protocol he should voluntarily decide to do so, a continuance of the protocol would in our opinion be assured, and a dangerous and anomalous crisis, involving the certainty of great suffering for tens of thousands of men, women, and children would be averted. Each side to the protocol has the right to terminate its existence at a moment's notice. In the present crisis, however, where feeling has been aroused by months of acrimonious discussion, a short time should be allowed to elapse before any action is taken which may lead to a permanent destruction of this great protocol of peace.

"We therefore suggest a truce of eight days. We suggest that the Protective Association, the International Ladies' Garment Workers' Union, and the Joint Board, each agree that they will not, before noon Monday, January 26th, take action terminating the protocol." [54]

Cohen accepted the recommendation for the employers, but Hourwich blew off steam in a long, fiery speech. Brandeis pressed him for a definite understanding that no rank-and-file union meeting on terminating the protocol would be held before the proposed cooling-off period ended. Hourwich reluctantly agreed to this. He went even further—he resigned as clerk.

THE PROTOCOL IN DECLINE

The Hourwich affair led to an important change in the machinery for settling disputes under the protocol—the creation of an arbitration committee, the Committee of Immediate Action, made up of the two clerks of the Grievance Board and a full-time impartial chairman, chosen by the employers and the union. This committee would act when the Grievance Board failed. When either party was dissatisfied with the committee's award, it could then appeal to the Board of Arbitration.

The "impartial chairman" was a new and important development in labor relations machinery. But Brandeis warned that this innovation, like the protocol itself, would prove valueless without good faith. He was soon proved right. The bitterness of the Hourwich affair destroyed whatever was left of the "spirit of get-together" that Brandeis had tried to instill from the start. Many of Hourwich's followers became outright opponents of protocolism. Soon the employers also split on the issue. The depression of 1913 and the outbreak of the war in 1914 made the whole problem seem of secondary importance, and when in December 1914 the Board of Arbitration convened to consider a particular controversy, "the very life and existence of the protocol" was at stake.[55]

This session of the Board eventually took up such subjects as the right of discharge, cause of incompetency, misconduct, and the whole gamut of labor–employer problems. The meetings dragged on from December 19, 1914, to January 21, 1915. The trial of strength was at hand, and the victor most likely would be the side which was most stubborn. Unions and employers alike had drifted far from their original determination not to insist upon narrow legal rights, "but to do those things, so far as they could do them consistently with the conduct of the business, which should make the living arrangements between them practicable and reasonable."[56]

The Board rendered its decisions on January 21, 1915, but within a few weeks the parties were again at each others' throats. This time the manufacturers were the complaining party. They were threatening to break with the unions over the issue of "what they call economic freedom." Again Brandeis heeded Moskowitz's call for a "healing conference."[57] And again Brandeis offered only his tiresome incantation: "We think that the paternal advice we should give is, 'Children, love one another,' that you ought, in any possible way, as we have said—in every proper way—each aid in strengthening the other's organization; the success of the protocol demands it."[58]

The days of the protocol were now numbered. The March issue of the Manufacturers' Association's official publication carried an inflammatory article laying all the blame for the protocol's declining prestige on "radical" union leadership. At the same time, the manufacturers trumpeted their own declaration of independence: "For four and a half years the manufacturers have been chained to the protocol and have been denied the economic freedom which they should have and must have in order to continue their business." The manufacturers claimed that they had done "more than their part" to carry out both the letter and the spirit of the protocol, while the unions had stood back, alert only to enforce their own demands with their own "big stick"—the general strike. The article continued: "There has been much of the spirit of the Industrial Workers of the World in the workers of the union in their attempt to carry out the protocol. . . . Sabotage and direct action and force have meant more to them than mediation and arbitration." [59]

John A. Dyche, former secretary of the International, endorsed the manufacturers' indictment. Writing Brandeis on February 9, 1915, he scored the New York garment workers as an "undisciplined *kampflustige* mass whose power can only be a powerful evil." The unions needed, he said, to be made into a democracy instead of a class-struggling mass.[60] The Arbitration Board, by its leniency, was only spoiling them. Dyche added: "I wonder if anything could be done in this inevitable collapse of the protocol idea, which is becoming utterly discredited and hated both by the employers and the employees, that the whole idea of trade unionism should not be discredited with it."

In his reply on February 11 Brandeis tried to dispel Dyche's pessimism. He admitted lack of discipline in the unions, but pointed out that "discipline is not common in democracies, and it is particularly difficult to introduce it where the ranks of the privates are largely composed of thinkers." The protocol was subjected to a severe test, he said, not so much by lack of discipline as by the serious industrial situation. "The bad business condition puts a strain upon every business relation, and upon the temper of the individual; and the friends of the protocol and of unionism should lend all possible aid. I am convinced that this is not a time when criticism is useful. What we need particularly is encouragement and tact. Criticism, however well founded, if allowed at this time, will do harm, and may prove fatal. The protocol needs nursing, and those who are like yourself, with wide experience, should lend so far as possible a gentle, sympathetic helping hand."

On April 25 the Board of Arbitration was again called in session. It met for a brief time only, as Brandeis was occupied in Washington. With the parties at the breaking point, he again pleaded with them "to avoid acrimony and to endeavor to live, while we are waiting for an opportunity of settling the difficulties that exist." [61] On this tired note the Board of Arbitration adjourned, never to convene again in formal session.

At this time, the unions' radical element, which had always opposed Brandeis, was in power. The employers too now became outspoken enemies of protocolism. In an article in *Women's Wear* on May 4, 1915, Henry Gordon, of counsel for the employers, wrote the protocol's epitaph:

The relationship between the employers and the employees in the cloak industry has been built upon sophistry, casuistry and ethereal concepts. One must go back to the writings of the Greek philosophers to find such metaphysics and mental gymnastics as make up the record of the deliberations between the cloak maker and the cloak manufacturer during the last four and one-half years, and all this, because certain settlement workers, social uplifters, and reformers have been tolerated to formulate the rules for the making of cloaks in this city, and because the relationship between employer and employee has been controlled, not by economics and business principles, but by theoretical precepts which were often communicated over the long distance telephone. . . .

The time has come, Gordon said, when both manufacturer and worker must "extricate themselves from this labyrinth." The first step was to banish "alleged conciliators, legislators, and industrial Napoleons," to "cast into the rubbish heap all their records and precedents." Gordon would revert to that "natural and rational relationship between employer and employee," in which the manufacturers will "proceed to make their own rules for the making of cloaks in this city."

Chaos faced the garment industry, and Moskowitz tried to call the arbitrators together. The manufacturers, however, said that they had "lost all faith in the unions' ability to join in any rational enforcement" of the agreement.[62] On May 20 the Association broke off relations with the Joint Board and openly repudiated the protocol. The tireless Moskowitz tried to rally Max Meyer, Association counsel, and Morris Hillquit, Union counsel. From both he got the same story: they were sick of the protocol and for the same reason—it had proved to be a mechanism of joint frustration.

Moskowitz turned again to Brandeis, who on June 1 sent word that he would gladly confer with the manufacturers in Boston. They refused, explaining that a conference would be "susceptible of misunderstanding," and "would not help the situation at the present juncture." [63] After a meeting with London and Meyer in New York a few days later, Brandeis accepted this view.

An armed truce continued for weeks. Then, on June 28, the International and the Joint Board suggested to the Manufacturers' Association that a committee under the chairmanship of Brandeis or Mayor John Purroy Mitchel try to save the protocol. This was agreed to, and on July 9 the Mayor appointed a council made up of Dr. Felix Adler, chairman, Brandeis, Henry Bruère (later President of Bowery Savings Bank), Dean George W. Kirchwey of the Columbia Law School, Charles L. Bernheimer of the New York Chamber of Commerce, and Federal Circuit Court Judge Walter Noyes. The committee began its work on July 13 and adjourned July 23. Though present at all twenty sessions, Brandeis was conspicuously silent.

The purpose of the committee, as Dr. Adler stated it, was "to rescue a valuable instrument of social progress, to suggest modifications, needed revision, but to save that which was precious in it, and prepare the way for its further enlargement." [64] Accordingly the committee upheld the right of the employer to discharge workers without consulting the union, and agreed that the workers had an "inalienable right" to organize and to be free of discrimination because of union membership.

That was as far as the committee went. It wasn't nearly far enough. That the committee had solved nothing was made tragically clear on April 28, 1916, when the Manufacturers' Association locked out about 25,000 workers. The International retaliated May 3, calling out 60,000 workers in a general strike.

When peace was restored on August 4, 1916, the system of the preferential shop was swept away, and the whole protocol went with it. The workers regained their right to strike, the employers their right to fire.

Still Brandeis was not convinced. On October 3, 1916, he wrote to Judge Julian Mack: "I dare say either of us, if we could have been constantly on the job in New York, might have made things move more smoothly. But it was never contemplated that the Chairman of the Board of Arbitration should be always in attendance, and indeed the whole purpose was to make resort to the Board of most infrequent occurrence. We believed that that was the only way in which this essay in industrial democracy should proceed."

TOWARD MORE ENDURING INSTITUTIONS

The preferential union shop suffered from the defects of its qualities. As long as a shop was never either strictly "closed" or strictly "open," the Manufacturers' Association and the unions alike were tempted to use any opportunity to increase their own power and thereby undermine that of the opponent. Brandeis himself did not think of the preferential union shop as "the final solution of the labor problem." One would "hardly be justified," he had said, "in making such a claim for any man-made plan." [65] At most it was but a halfway measure, a temporary expedient, a steppingstone to the establishment of those institutions which he considered prerequisite to industrial peace—strong organization on both sides. In urging this expedient, he had in mind a long-range educative policy promoting industrial welfare.

With the abandonment of the protocol, the industry sank into a welter of economic warfare. But this semi-anarchy differed from that abysmal chaos for which Brandeis had originally offered the preferential union shop as a corrective. The anarchy of 1910 was worsened by absolutist, authoritarian tendencies on both sides. The manufacturers habitually denounced trade-union leadership as "irreconcilable," as bent on making a "deliberate and planned attack on capitalism." The extreme unionist goal was, they said, "domination of the industry by a socialist labor union." But even as Cohen and others deplored such Marxist tendencies, they professed and applauded their own absolutist utopia. For them this struggle should have been prosecuted as a "war to end war"; it should have been seen as an opportunity to establish "law and order," to "lift the industry to a higher plane." Cohen asserted that Brandeis, being "new to the situation," was guilty of a "tendency to compromise rather than fight it out"; that he had not foreseen the dreadful consequences of union-dominated industry.[66]

The truth appears to be that Brandeis did foresee the actual consequences, in terms of injury to democracy and to law and order, if the industry were dominated by absolutists, either employers or employees. The preferential union shop thus became not only prerequisite to fair negotiation but also a step toward stable, responsible unionism.

CHAPTER TWENTY

Explaining Science to the Railroads, 1910-1911

WHEN the garment industry conflict arose, Brandeis was still entangled in the Ballinger affair. And even while he was occupied with both these matters, a third contest of tremendous national importance was upon him. This new struggle began in June 1910, when the railroads asked the Interstate Commerce Commission for a general advance of freight rates east of the Mississippi and north of the Potomac and Ohio Rivers. If granted, the shippers in this territory would be saddled with extra costs running into millions of dollars annually. They organized to fight, setting up a Committee of Commercial Organizations, headed by David O. Ives. As manager of the Transportation Department of the Boston Chamber of Commerce, Ives had been closely associated with Brandeis in the New Haven antimerger campaigns. Ives thought Brandeis was just the man for counsel of his new committee. "Dave Ives is here again," Brandeis wrote Alfred,

August 20, 1910, "and there is considerable talk *re* rate advance hearings."
The People's Attorney agreed to embark on another crusade.

THE RAILROADS PRESENT THEIR CASE

Hearings on rate increases began at the Waldorf-Astoria in New York
on August 15, 1910, before Special I.C.C. Examiners George N. Brown and
C. R. Hillyer. Lawyers gathered in such numbers as to tax the Waldorf's
accommodations. The *New York World* on September 7 called it "the
most extraordinary aggregation of legal talent ever assembled together to
battle for varied interests." Besides Brandeis, there were Francis B. James
and John Atwood for the Shippers' Association, Clifford Thorne for the
Corn Belt Meat Producers' Association, and others. Brandeis was their
acknowledged leader. "From the moment the hearing opened," a *New
York World* reporter observed, September 25, "it became patent that Mr.
Brandeis was the dominating factor at the hearing and the one who probed
deepest into the affairs of the corporations."

Railroad witnesses brought quantities of facts and figures, attempting
to swamp the shippers with a "mass of intricate and hazy figures." Yet they
were, with one or two exceptions, minor officials "entirely at sea in analyzing causes." "Time and again," the *New York Evening Post* observed,
September 8, "the shippers' lawyers, Louis Brandeis, Clifford Thorne,
Francis B. James, Frank Lyon [counsel for the I.C.C.], and others, took
up the testimony and secured admissions from the witnesses that they did
not know how the figures they presented had been arrived at. They knew
certain things but they did not know the causes of the things." Their
testimony was thus limited to the obvious facts that there had been a wage
increase, and that the railroads wanted to meet it with a general advance
in freight rates. They could not be forced to tell more because Brown and
Hillyer of the I.C.C. were not legally empowered to force them. Then
Brandeis stepped in. " 'Dilatory' progress of the freight rates hearing was
rudely interrupted today by Louis D. Brandeis," the *Evening Post* commented, September 9. "Soon after the session opened . . . he addressed
himself to ex-Judge G. N. Brown, Chief Examiner of the I.C.C., and to the
railroads' counsel, pleading with all to give up repetition and evasion and
stick to the facts. After Mr. Brandeis's appeal . . . it was noticeable that
the hearing moved much smoother and more rapidly."

These preliminary hearings ended in late September, and on October 12,
1910, counsel for railroads and shippers met in Washington before the
Interstate Commerce Commission—Chairman Martin A. Knapp, Judson C.
Clements, B. H. Meyer, C. C. McChord, Charles A. Prouty, Franklin K.
Lane, E. E. Clark, and James S. Harlan. Here the Advance Rate Case as-

sumed major importance and demanded the attention of top railroad executives. Appearing as witnesses were James McCrea, President of the Pennsylvania, Daniel Willard of the Baltimore & Ohio, W. C. Brown of the New York Central, W. H. Truesdale of the Lackawanna, John C. Stuart of the Erie, and others of equal rank. Each said essentially the same thing: that the recent wage increases would in 1910 cost the railroads $34,000,000 more than they paid to labor in 1909. Besides wages, they said, the cost of materials was also going up. Moreover, Stuart of the Erie told the Commission, ". . . in the process of regulation within the past two or three years there have been a great many things introduced that all cost money." [1]

Other things had also cost money. The roads, they said, had extended and improved their service—many times at the demand of the shippers. They talked of improved terminals, better cars, and increased speed. Because of these improvements, operating expenses were increasing more rapidly than operating revenues.[2] And despite an ever-mounting volume of freight, earnings showed a pronounced tendency to fall off. McCrea of the Pennsylvania demonstrated this contention with statistics from his own "standard railroad of the world."

The railroad men went on to tell what this trend meant to themselves as managers, to their stockholders, and to the general public. Either the railroads would have to increase their revenues by advanced freight rates, or they would have to curtail expenses drastically. Indeed, they had cut expenses almost to the bone; still net earnings and surplus dwindled to such a point that railroad credit was badly shaken. "I have stated very distinctly," McCrea observed, "that I am not advocating an advance in these rates so that we can earn money for the purpose of paying interest or paying a return on some investment that we have made in the past and have not capitalized. I am asking it so that we may be enabled ourselves to recoup our income sufficiently to be able to continue doing that which we have done, and which the record of twenty-five years shows has been our policy." [3]

Allied with the railroad officials were the Railway Brotherhoods, 300,000 strong, requesting that the Commission grant the advance. Officers of the Brotherhoods were to appear before the Commission, but none actually testified.[4] In January of 1911, however, P. H. Morrissey of the American Railroad Employees and Investors' Association presented a written statement to the Commission endorsing the railroads' contentions.[5]

GIVING CROSS-EXAMINATION THE FORCE OF ARGUMENT

When Brandeis cross-examined the eminent railroad witnesses, he did not exhibit that deferential politeness to which they were accustomed. He seemed bent on wringing out of them all the facts, instead of just those they wished to present. Running through all his questions was the insistence that the railroads had not been operated efficiently, that veteran railroad officials did not understand their own business. Naturally, McCrea, Willard, Truesdale, and the others resented the imputation. Resentful also were a miscellany of traffic vice-president, financial vice-presidents, and operating vice-presidents, as well as the eminent railroad lawyers who had so often demonstrated their ability to tell the railroads how to do exactly what they wanted to do. All such veterans looked at first with amusement upon this "outsider" who came into court to tell them how to run their businesses.[6]

Brandeis quickly saw that the railroad heads did not understand their changed legal position under the Mann–Elkins Act, passed June 18, 1910.* Brandeis understood it perfectly well and was determined to make the most of it. "Mr. Brandeis," the *Philadelphia North American* had commented on September 15, "has a remarkable talent for framing questions so as to give them the force of an argument in the case." It appeared, for example, that prior to petitioning for rate increases, the railroads had consulted no "judgment" but their own. "Where can you show," Brandeis asked New York Central's Charles F. Daly, "that you have exercised in regard to each individual rate, I mean each individual article—"

"We have not professed to," Daly broke in.

Brandeis continued, "The same judgment, for instance, that you exercised when you dealt with the matters of steel or the matters of cement?"

"Impossible, Mr. Brandeis. There are hundreds of articles in each class. . . . From the best of our knowledge and belief, based on great experience, we do not feel that the rate which it is proposed to inaugurate in the classes is unduly high, or that it will have any serious effect on the manufacturers."

Brandeis sought the evidence that lay back of this "knowledge and belief." Daly tried to evade him: "I know it in the same way you know the things that make you such a clever lawyer." "I thank you for the compliment," Brandeis replied, "but whatever knowledge I may have has come from the particular study of specific facts, and so I am seeking to find out from you what the specific facts are upon which you base your judgment in this matter."[7] More sparring followed, and finally Brandeis challenged: "I don't care to spend time, but I want to know, Mr. Daly, just as clearly as you can state it, whether you can give a single reason based on anything

---

* This Act, amending Section 15 of the original I.C.C. Act of February 4, 1887, provides: "At any hearing . . . on a rate sought to be increased after the passage of this Act, the burden of proof to show that the . . . proposed increased rate is just and reasonable shall be upon the common carrier. . . ."

more than your arbitrary judgment, as you have expressed it." Daly replied, "None whatever."

This frank admission made it clear that Daly had not grasped the railroads' rate-making responsibility under the Mann–Elkins Act. "We have stated why and what we did," Daly observed fretfully. "We haven't anything from you or from your clients, except your statement which is not in our judgment worth any more than mine, and in this particular instance, I don't think it is worth as much."

"I am not undertaking, Mr. Daly, to set up my statement," said Brandeis. "Fortunately, counsel have only to present the evidence. You understand, of course, that under this new law the burden rests upon you . . . to show that the change you propose making is reasonable? . . ."

"Well, in order for you to disprove my statement you must show to the Commission that what we have done has injured your industry," Daly answered.

"I submit that there is no such obligation resting upon me or my clients . . . ," Brandeis stated.[8]

Brandeis's point was that if the rates which the railroads proposed were proved "just and reasonable," it would be pure accident, since the railroad men had not consulted the shippers. "Do not make any advances on any of those articles," Ives had requested the railroads, "without giving us a chance to argue the matter with you." "And what," Brandeis wanted to know, "was the attitude of the railroads?" "A courteous and positive refusal to consider any change," Ives replied.

Brandeis then stated his own views on carrier–shipper relations: "What we say is this: That intelligent consideration of the problem necessarily involves that the shippers should have an opportunity of considering—just as you admit they do in certain commodity rates—and taking up with the railroads each problem to be affected. . . . The persons who are to be considered and ought to be consulted before and not after the raise is made are the shipper and the consumer, who are directly to be affected by it." [9]

This closing statement was obviously more extended than is usual while witnesses are being called. Clyde Brown, New York Central attorney, therefore suggested that the place for argument was before the Commission when the hearings were over. "I thank the gentleman for his suggestion," Brandeis said with a bow. "I should have been glad to avail myself of the information he imparts if he had made it before I was done."

Through all this questioning Brandeis kept to the fore his argument for improving railroad efficiency. President Brown of the New York Central told the Commission his railroad must have the rate advances or it would not be able to earn enough money to sustain its credit or to make the improvements which were absolutely necessary.[10] President Willard added that railroad credit was already suffering from the situation. "The market was considered somewhat shaky in January," he said. "It fell off very rapidly in the following two or three months; and in April and May it became practically impossible to sell securities. Good bonds, guaranteed by the Baltimore & Ohio Railroad, could not find a purchaser." [11]

To round out their story the railroads produced George E. Ide, of the Association of Life Insurance Presidents. He testified that railroad bonds were held by insurance companies representing thousands of small investors. All these people, Ide said, were vitally interested in the railroads' financial safety. All favored rate increases.[12]

But Brandeis was incredulous. It amazed him to find the railroads willing to discredit their own credit, for no other purpose than that of winning the rate advance. In cross-examining McCrea, Brandeis began at once to educate him as to the prosperity of his own company. McCrea had estimated the Pennsylvania's regular common stock dividend as only 6 per cent, but Brandeis informed him that, if salable rights and additions to surplus were included, they amounted to at least 12 per cent. "If so," McCrea commented, "I am very much surprised. I only know, as a stockholder, what I have been getting, what returns came to me, and what there is any likelihood of my being able to secure. . . ."

"Let us see whether you have not misunderstood my question," said Brandeis.

"I think likely I have. I do not follow the drift of a good deal of what you are saying," McCrea countered.

"I think it may be, if I am permitted to say so, Mr. McCrea, that you are thinking of arguing the question with me instead of simply answering yes or no. . . ."

"All right," McCrea retorted. "My answer to your question is that I cannot say; I have never had the matter presented in that way; I have never thought of it in that way." [13]

Brandeis went on to point out that the New York Central's dividend had averaged over 7 per cent in the aggregate, and the company had raised cash payments from 5 to 6 per cent at the very time when the wage increase was to go into effect.[14] The railroads generally were better off financially than almost any other industry in the nation. Why, then, should they resort to this fiction of "shaky credit"? "When you were making your inquiries," Brandeis asked Willard, "among the bankers in regard to the financing of this question and finding out the views that were held here and there and the trepidation in regard to railroad investments, did it occur to you as possible that this attitude in regard to the railroads was due to some concerted action, more or less concerted action, on the part of those eminent financiers, very few in number, who actually control the operations of the financial world, and of the railroads among other things?"

"What action have you in mind? What is the character of the concerted action?" Willard asked.

"Concerted action to make it appear that unless the railroads get what those who actually control them—namely, the financiers—want, the people of this country cannot get the money with which to make the desired improvements?"

"Oh, no," said Willard; "I saw no evidence of that."

"Well, did you in the course of your investigation or of your recent inquiries find that there was in the community such a view?"

"No," Willard replied shortly.[15]

Brandeis put the same questions to McCrea and Brown, and elicited the same reply. This suggestion of financial control, like so many of Brandeis's ideas, seemed to them entirely new. All were frankly innocent of any "concerted effort" to control railroad credit.

Brandeis, however, succeeded in showing not only that the railroads were controlled by great financiers, but also that the same financiers controlled the steel companies. This was a very interesting relation, for the steel companies were the biggest suppliers of materials to the railroads—they supplied tracks, parts for freight and passenger cars, locomotives, station and yard equipment. Now, what if the railroads sought to meet their higher operating costs not by increasing rates, but by better bargaining to reduce the price of materials? Naturally the financiers wouldn't like that. Yet, Brandeis argued, the shippers should not be expected to pay higher freight rates because railroads were paying unnecessarily high prices for materials.[16] If the railroads could co-operate to secure rate advances, could they not work together to secure lower steel prices? The shippers, he said, failed to see reasonableness in rate advances which would result in increased returns, not to railroad stockholders, but to the United States Steel Corporation.

In his final argument Brandeis made this point clearer still:

In cross-examining President Brown of the New York Central, I called attention to the fact that Mr. J. P. Morgan was a member of their executive committee, J. P. Morgan & Co. the financial agents of the road, J. P. Morgan & Co. of course the influential people in the steel corporation; and I asked Mr. Brown and the other presidents whether, during that long period of years, when they were considering the question of increase of rates, they had at all considered undertaking to secure from the steel companies a reduction of the price of that most important article of traffic, and most important article of use by the rail-roads. No.

And I asked the same question of President McCrea, and he answered no; that it had not been considered. Now, why? Why had they not undertaken by co-operation to produce that result? I think there is probably a very simple answer to that question. It is because these steel companies are working to-gether, are controlled by the men who control the railroads. Of the sixty-five directors in these steel corporations, forty are directors in the railroads. . . .

I do not call attention to that by way of criticism of the forty directors of the steel companies. . . . If there is any bargain to be made, if the interests of the railroads are to be looked after and to be protected, how can you hope to get full protection when the man who ought to protect the railroads is in a position which is necessarily not a disinterested one, so far as this other relation is con-cerned?

I say that if the railroads would show the same zeal in co-operating to reduce costs as they have shown in co-operating to increase rates . . . we should have a reduction in operating costs that would far exceed the 3 per cent equivalent of the proposed raise on other merchandise. . . .[17]

Brandeis had still another point to make. The New York Central had, he said, recently acquired the Boston & Albany Railroad, which netted the company an annual loss of $1,000,000. When President Brown found it hard to show the wisdom of the transaction, Brandeis suggested that the acquisition might have been part of a policy of "unsatiated aggrandize-ment."[18] To this Brown could only give an unconvincing "no." Brandeis turned next to President McCrea and the Pennsylvania's contemplated acquisition of the Northern Central, to demonstrate a general tendency among railroads to get control of properties for power rather than effi-ciency. And how, he asked, could there be justice and reason in rates which required the public to pay for the railroad managers' imperial dreams and aggrandizing mistakes? The whole trouble, as he saw it, was this itch for giantism:

Everyone has called attention to this fact, that while the great systems—I mean great in mileage and great in earnings—have been suffering from in-creased operating expenses, certain other railroads have not. The Delaware and Lackawanna, the Lehigh, the Central of New Jersey, the Philadelphia & Read-ing, and even the Erie, have shown a tendency to greater net returns and pros-perity.

Is that a fact of significance?

I ask the Commission to consider whether there is not a causal connection between the fact of bigness, the fact of this extraordinary gross, and the fact of reduced net; whether it is not a fact that the Pennsylvania System, and the New

York Central System, and . . , the Baltimore & Ohio System have not exceeded what may be called the limit of greatest efficiency, . . . where by reason of the multiplicity of problems and the distance of the circumference, looseness of administration arises that overcomes any advantage from size, overcomes it so far as to make it a relatively losing proposition.[19]

FINDING AN INTERNAL REMEDY: SCIENTIFIC MANAGEMENT

In his cross-examination Brandeis had made three main points: the railroads did not need increased funds; the proposed rates were, in any event, unjust and unreasonable; and even if increased revenue were needed, the railroads could secure it through economy and efficiency without burdening the shippers and the consuming public. Brandeis struggled to make this third point clear. He had made a thorough study of industrial engineering and the new scientific management. The leaders in this science—Frederick W. Taylor, Harrington Emerson, F. B. Gilbreth, H. L. Gantt, and F. A. Halsey—were among his friends. His office diary shows he was often in conference with them as the hearings proceeded. Thus Brandeis knew what he was getting into.

BRANDEIS: You stated, Mr. McCrea, that you thought the limit of increase in efficiency and resultant economy was practically reached?

McCREA: I did, sir.

BRANDEIS: Instancing that you had made practically all the improvements in roadbed—

McCREA: I said growing out of reduced grades, enlarged locomotives, and increased capacity of cars.

BRANDEIS: Yes; and that those methods of increasing efficiency had, so far as you were aware, exhausted the improvements in the line of efficiency that you deemed possible?

McCREA: In the line of economies. . . . You said "efficiency"; I say "economies." That is about true. I said, "practically so"; that is my belief.[20]

Taking up the Brandeis line, Commissioner Lane inquired of Willard: "Do you think that there should be an increase in rates every time there is a considerable increase in wages?

WILLARD: . . . In my opinion the two things will be found to be very closely related to each other in the future, and for the reason stated by Mr. McCrea yesterday. I think the possibilities of further operating economies have been pretty well exhausted. . . . I must confess that I am unable to see very much more that can be done in the way of reducing the cost of operation."[21]

Even where they thought they might be more efficient, the railroads said large expenditures would have to be made for improved technical devices. Brandeis made it plain that he was talking about a different kind of efficiency—the efficiency of men.

BRANDEIS: What economies have been instituted in the past ten years on the Pennsylvania Railroad resulting in what I should call increased efficiency, which were not brought about through the expenditure of money but through improvement of method or development of the individuals performing the work?

McCREA: Oh, there are too many of them for me to undertake to make a list. They go into every detail of your operation.

BRANDEIS: Will you be so good as to have a list of those prepared?

McCREA: Such a thing is impossible. I do not know. I will make a try at it." [22]

Brandeis's questions became more pointed. He wanted to know just how much was spent for maintenance, repair of cars, locomotive renewals, etc.

BRANDEIS: . . . Take the question, for instance, that we were talking of, about the repair of a locomotive. Is it not a fact that it [the lump statement as to cost] does not give you any idea as to whether you are getting that article at what it ought to be, at cost, if you estimate that you are getting it at a certain per cent per locomotive mile? That does not give it, does it?

WILLARD: I think it is worth something. It does not determine it, but it is a factor to be considered.

BRANDEIS: It is a factor, but it does not give it to you with accuracy, because conditions may govern it altogether. It was pointed out yesterday by Mr. McCrea that 10 cents per locomotive mile on one road and in one year may be more efficient work than 5 cents per locomotive mile on another road because the engines may be different and all the conditions may be different. Now in the manufacture of something other than transportation men have come to know—for instance, in the shoe business—the cost of each one of the 100 operations or 150 different operations which enter into the single article of a shoe, by which they can test themselves, and predetermine what the cost ought to be. Why can not that be done? Why can you not do what they have found so necessary to do in competitive businesses?

WILLIARD: It can be done and is done.

BRANDEIS: Is it done?

WILLARD: Yes. . . . Take the repair of freight cars. . . . It costs on various roads from $30 to as high as $80 or $90 per car per year, depending on the character of the road, the kind of car, the prices paid for labor in various parts of the country, the miles of service, etc.

BRANDEIS: Just see how uncertain that factor is. . . . You are taking the average. The only way you could tell whether the work on any one of those cars was efficiently done, is it not, would be for you to know the particular thing that was done on that particular car? [23]

This is perhaps the most important page of testimony in the hearings, for it pictures the railroads' obsolete accounting and managerial methods, and gives the nub of Brandeis's criticism of them. Railroad operations had not been analyzed as units but as summations of whole series of units. Railroad managers did not know what maintenance costs actually were in terms of unit costs. To correct this, Brandeis prescribed that each unit of operation be reduced to its lowest terms and then compared with a standard or normal operation of the same kind. Then, and only then, could it be known whether each operation in an entire process was or was not efficient.

As Brandeis went into more and more detail, the Commission, prodded by lawyers, became impatient. It was one thing to upbraid the railroads as inefficient, quite another to produce facts that would help settle the rate issue. Brandeis was ready with his answer. The railroads, he explained, were no longer competitive. But that didn't mean they could deny the public the advantages of competition. "I think the Commission should find," Brandeis observed, "that it would be a most serious danger to the country to establish the principle that if, according to present conditions, they need more money they raise rates instead of doing what in every competitive business it is necessary to do, namely, to consider whether you can not make more money by reducing your cost. . . . If we are to travel in the vicious circle of meeting higher costs by ever higher costs, if the burden of increased rates and other burdens are to come upon the community, then where is the limit?" [24]

Brandeis had set the stage by November 1 for showing how the railroads might solve their dilemma by the introduction of scientific management. It had, he said, been successfully applied in various lines from the manufacture of locks to the shoveling of coal: "From the days of Adam it has been supposed that everybody knew how to shovel. But it occurred to the scientists that there might be very great differences; that just as in the case of carrying pig iron, there was an amount of coal which a man might carry on his shovel without tiring him; that is, that he should carry throughout the day. If he carried too much, he would wear out. If he carried too little, he would not get the full benefit of what he did, because he goes through the motion of throwing his shovel up and carries the shovel, which has considerable weight, and he is wasting effort. So the scientists put onto that operation the study incident to ordinary science, in every department of life, and with what result? . . . When science demeaned

itself, as some would think for the purpose of doing the humble work of
the unskilled workman, it was found that without more effort he could
also do two or three times the amount he did before. He could earn from
30 to 60 per cent more than the regular wages paid in the trade." [25]

Thus the employer received two or three times as much for only 30 to
60 per cent more wages paid; the laborer earned extra wages without ex-
pending any extra effort. It was all a result of applying science, of doing
things in the best possible way. "We will show you, may it please your
honors," Brandeis went on, "that these principles, applicable to all businesses, are applicable to practically all departments of all businesses, and
that the estimate which has been made that in the railroad operation of
this country an economy of a million dollars a day is possible is an estimate
which is by no means extravagant: and you will see as we develop the
science and develop its application in varied businesses that that estimate is,
if anything, an underestimate instead of an overestimate." [26]

THE PROOF OF THE PUDDING

Brandeis's claim that scientific management could save the railroads a
million dollars a day got spectacular publicity but it was no mere advertising stunt. He proceeded to put on witnesses—ten in all—to show how
equivalent savings had been effected in other industries. Horace K. Hathaway, vice-president of the Tabor Manufacturing Company, told how scientific management had, without additional labor force, plant, or machines,
increased his company's dollar production from 200 per cent to 300 per cent.
Henry R. Towne, president of Yale & Towne Company, makers of Yale
locks, told how the new science had saved his company when it had been
faced with rising costs and falling prices in the panic of 1893.

Brandeis's first two witnesses were not, they said, qualified to say that
scientific management could be applied to the railroads. James Mapes
Dodge, Brandeis's third expert witness, expressed greater confidence. Addressing himself directly to the Commission, he said: "I must call your
honors' attention to this, that all manufacturers who start with a raw material and change its shape by the removal of some of that material are in the
same business. . . . There is no business I have ever heard of—that is,
theoretically at all events, and I am sure in most cases practically—where
the same fundamental systems may not be absolutely applicable and the
workman helped to increase his feeling of independence and manhood
and to make additional wages by doing his full duty." [27]

Counsel for the railroads cross-examined Brandeis's earlier witnesses at
length, but later their questions became few, and the Commission decided

that scientific management had been explained. Commissioner Prouty observed: "Mr. Brandeis, you can hardly add anything to your case by calling the representative of some other industry and showing these same principles have been applied there. It is perfectly evident that if they have been applied in one case they can be applied in another analogous case. If the railroads were to show, in answer, some facts which tended to prove that they could not be applied to railroad operations, then you might desire to go further; but it seems to me that you have made out your case now, as far as it can be made out. If you have anybody who can show this method has been applied to railroad operation he will be a material witness." [28]

Brandeis then called Charles B. Going, editor of *The Engineering Magazine*. He testified that Harrington Emerson had applied scientific management in the repair shops of the Atchison, Topeka & Santa Fe Railroad, saving in excess of $1,000,000 a year in locomotive repairs alone.[29] Later on Brandeis called on Emerson to tell the Commission in detail just how he had arrived at that figure. Under Brandeis's lead, Emerson went further, suggesting that scientific management could be of untold value not only in meeting the problem in hand but in future operation of the railroads. To aid them in seeking efficiency he recommended that the Commission undertake thorough study of railroad operating methods and costs, such information to be available for the use of all.[30] As to this Brandeis remarked:

We have had combinations to increase prices, of which the proposed rate increase is an instance. What we need to reduce the cost of living is a combination to reduce the costs of production. As a first step to accomplishing this it is necessary (a) that unit costs be determined; (2) that these unit costs of all the railroads be published through the Interstate Commerce Commission so as to be available to each road. In this way we hope, as a first step toward scientific management and increased efficiency, to learn the lowest cost at which each operation is produced by any road so that each company may reach the lowest then existing record in that department. After such unit costs are ascertained, there may then be an advance in the science by elimination of waste and by improvement of method, to secure a still lower cost.[31]

The railroads offered little or no criticism of what Brandeis's witnesses had said. They had not contended that they were using these modern methods. Many witnesses, in fact, had said that they were not. At first they were amused but later somewhat sober. As the *New York Evening Post* put it on November 26: "The railway cross-examination may be said to have begun in a spirit of flippancy and ended in rather awkward silence."

CALLING THE BLIND MEN'S BLUFF

On November 23, 1910, even before Harrington Emerson had testified, the railroads tried in an oblique way to discredit Brandeis. Several Western railroad presidents * informed newspapermen that day that they had sent him this telegram, signed by O. L. Dickinson of the Burlington:

It is reported you have stated before the Interstate Commerce Commission that American railways are wasting $1,000,000 daily. If you can point out a practical way by which a substantial portion of this amount may be saved several western railways would be pleased to tender you employment, allowing you to name your own salary. This proposition is made to you in the same spirit of sincerity in which you rendered your statement to the Commission.[32]

According to the *Chicago Examiner,* November 24, 1910, this offer was the direct result of a statement by that elder railroad statesman, James J. Hill. "If Mr. Brandeis's intemperate utterance contained a modicum of fact," Hill had remarked, "he might name his own price for his services to any American railroad." The railroad men had not committed themselves; they had in fact only queried Brandeis's good faith by making their offer in "the same spirit of sincerity" as that which they believed had motivated him.

Brandeis refused at first to comment, telling newspapermen that, because of the Thanksgiving holiday, he had not been to his office; as far as he knew no such offer had been made. On November 29 he gave his answer to the press:

Your telegram of the 23rd, sent on behalf of the Western railroad presidents to me, care of Interstate Commerce Commission, was not delivered until this morning, owing to my absence in Boston.

You refer to the estimate quoted by me that a million dollars a day could be saved in operating American railroads by the introduction of scientific management and say that if I can point out a practical way by which a substantial portion of this amount can be saved several Western railroads would be pleased to tender me employment, allowing me to name my own salary. I am convinced that such saving is possible through the introduction of scientific management and shall be glad, as a public service, to arrange for conferences with these Western presidents at an early date and point out how scientific management will accomplish these results. I suggest that the Eastern presidents be also invited to attend the conferences.

I must decline to accept any salary or other compensation from the railroads for the same reason that I have declined compensation from the shipping organizations whom I represent—namely, that the burden of increased rates,

* Darius Miller, B. L. Mitchell, H. E. Mudge, and F. A. Delano. O. L. Dickinson of the Burlington was authorized to speak for the Western railroad presidents.

"THEY ALL WANT MR. BRANDEIS NOW"
Boston Post, February 25, 1911

"THE BRANDEIS BREAD LINE"
Truth, April 4, 1914

BRANDEIS AT FIFTY-EIGHT

"The most liked and the most hated man at the Bar in America."
—L. S. Richard, *The Independent,* July 27, 1914

while primarily affecting the Eastern manufacturers and merchants, will ultimately be borne in large part by the consumer through increasing the cost of living, mainly of those least able to bear added burdens. I desire that any aid I can render in preventing such added burdens should be unpaid services. Kindly suggest date and place for conference.[33]

The railroad men never answered Brandeis's telegram.

Prior to his million-dollars-a-day thunderbolt, the newspapers carried quiet inner page discussions. Now the subject leaped to the front page, and when Brandeis squarely called the railroaders' bluff, the press featured his retort in blazing headlines. Ears pricked up all over the country. A dozen or more metropolitan papers published feature articles, all in answer to the nationwide question: "Who is this man Brandeis?" Some of those favorable in content he had himself inspired. "I have been very pleasantly surprised at the support which we have had here in the East," he wrote Alfred, December 5, 1910. "I rather expected support from the West, and worked hard with some of the New York papers myself, but we have had solid support from many which I did not approach, and from which I only had expected to have sneers and abuse."

The *New York World* called Brandeis a "modern Hercules," and added this thumbnail sketch:

Personally, he is a medium-sized, wiry man, rather uncouth in appearance, with piercing gray eyes and a mass of black hair streaked with gray that is always more or less tousled. He doesn't run much to clothes. He wears queer forlorn glasses and puckers his forehead when thinking deeply—which is most of the time. He can laugh infectiously, however, and tells a good story. If it weren't for the fact that he was born in Kentucky he would be a typical Boston practitioner—green bag included. Even with Southern birth he has the Yankee accent as a result of early transplanting to Massachusetts soil. He talks with emphasis and to the point, with a trick of gesturing when he is particularly engrossed in developing an idea.[34]

A *Philadelphia Public Ledger* reporter quoted him in answer to questions about his serving without fee:

Some men buy diamonds and rare works of art, others delight in automobiles and yachts. My luxury is to invest my surplus effort, beyond that required for the proper support of my family, in the pleasure of taking up a problem and solving, or helping to solve it, for the people without receiving any compensation. Your yachtsman or automobilist would lose much of his enjoyment if he were obliged to do for pay what he is doing for the love of the thing itself. So I should lose much of my satisfaction if I were paid in connection with public service of this kind.[35]

The highest praise came from Louisville, where the *Courier-Journal* said:

This is not the first time Mr. Brandeis has entered the lists to fight for the cause of the people at his own charges. He is an example of the better citizenship that we are developing out of the chaos and strife of our political and social systems. While such men are produced in the republic we need not despond. They are the hope of tomorrow.[36]

A few critics thought the whole thing a farcical bid for publicity or an effort to confuse the Commission. The *New York Sun*, voicing the old distrust of New Yorkers for Bostonians, said:

Mr. Brandeis is something of an Admirable Crichton, perhaps, but he is thought by some people to be more of a Boston idealist and regulator. We are afraid that this is what the railroad presidents will find him.[37]

But even the *New York Times* which had accused him of impractical idealism now decided that the railroads should have known better than to make such an offer:

Those somewhat too humorous gentlemen will probably regret the levity, not to say the impudence that characterized their communication. They saw fit in their irritation and rashness, it will be remembered, to impugn the sincerity of Mr. Brandeis by declaring that their own sincerity in making this offer equalled his.

Their hilarious incredulity revealed a surprising ignorance of Mr. Brandeis's record and reputation as a man honestly and disinterestedly devoted to the public service. Many could have told them, including not a few who have disagreed with him, . . . that his beliefs and his actions invariably went together.[38]

The *Chicago Tribune* added this:

Let the railroads drop their tone of conscious superiority and deep disdain in discussing Mr. Brandeis. They do not understand the situation. They do not realize the impression he has made on the public mind. Otherwise they would not be so tactless in their methods.[39]

The *Louisville Evening Post* denounced the railroaders for refusing to listen to Brandeis:

President Elliott, of the Northern Pacific, says that he resents outside interference, and railroad lawyers ridicule Mr. Brandeis for intimating that railroads could possibly be better managed. Yet it was outside interference that abolished rebates, abolished passes, forced the adoption of air brakes and patent couplers and grade crossings. It is outsiders who are expected to buy railroad stocks and bonds, and it was outsiders who voted bond subsidies and land subsidies for the railroads.[40]

Even the *New York Tribune* commented:

Whatever the possibility of scientific business management may be, it is only through new economies that there can be any escape from the vicious circle of higher rates to meet higher wages and higher costs, followed, inevitably, by still higher costs in response to higher rates.[41]

RAILROADS AND LABOR PRESENT THEIR CASE

Railroad officials now frankly stated their views. Of nine railroad heads interviewed, none had a favorable word for scientific management or for its proponent. Some used ridicule. "Brandeis?" Vice-President W. L. Park of the Illinois Central commented. "Why he's a joke—doesn't know what he's talking about—is a fool. He's going to spring that old piecework chestnut which has been proved a failure already. The United States couldn't make a success of the system in its navy yards: the Union Pacific abandoned the scheme some time ago, after spending $2,000,000 for the experience." [42]

Naturally the railroad trade papers joined in. Said the *Railroad Herald*: There is so little of true information in support of his assertion that railroads are wasting a million dollars a day in shop and operating deficiencies that it is difficult to credit him with other than a sensational motive. He did the cause of his clients no good, and he gave the railroad side not facts, but newspaper headlines, to refute. Truly Mr. Brandeis' love of sensation clearly exceeds his information.[43]

The *Railway Age Gazette,* then, as now, the most authoritative railroad trade publication, admitted the possibilities of further economies, but denounced Brandeis's calculations as "the merest moonshine." The *Gazette* thought the obstructive attitude of labor the real obstacle to economies and had no doubt that a general strike would follow any large-scale effort to introduce scientific management.[44]

President W. C. Brown of New York Central also underlined the labor obstacle:

Mr. Brandeis, as I understand it, suggests that if the railroads have increased their expenses by increasing wages, they may now decrease their working force and let the men they retain do the work they have done before and also the work of the men who have been dismissed. I don't think that he takes the labor unions into consideration.[45]

Labor spokesmen themselves seemed to go along with Brown, but for other reasons. John Mitchell, of the United Mine Workers of America, who expressed "highest esteem for Mr. Brandeis as a valued friend of labor," observed: "I do not believe that anything can be safely saved on them [the railroads]; if there is a waste of $300,000,000 a year it lies outside the sphere of costs occupied by the workmen. And I am against the premium or bonus system and against too much specializing." [46]

Samuel Gompers, president of the American Federation of Labor, several months later expressed agreement with Mitchell. Scientific managers had defended the bonus system as differing from piecework, but Gompers was unconvinced. [47]

The unions in general saw in scientific management chiefly, if not exclusively, two devices most feared by labor—piecework and its relative, the "speed-up." As soon as some workers in a plant had demonstrated that they could do more pieces of work in an hour or in a day than was expected of them, management more often than not reduced the piece wage so that all workers would have to speed up production in order to make as much money as they had received before. Scientific management seemed to labor a way to speed up this "speeding up" trend; naturally workers hated the thought of it. Frederick Taylor, the exponent of scientific management, denied that this would happen; and he pointed to Hathaway, Towne, Dodge, and Gilbreth, who had testified that they had never cut a piece rate once it was established. [48] This hardly convinced the workers' spokesmen. What would happen, they asked, when all competitors had adopted scientific management and competition was fierce? Surely so long as unions were not strong enough to make certain that wages would be maintained, Gompers and the others had good reason to suspect scientific management.

There was another danger—that scientific management might create unemployment. If a given amount of goods were produced each year, and it suddenly became possible for fewer employees to produce them, less would be hired. The railroads were a case in point. Once the railroads stopped expanding (as they did within a few years) and the skill of labor increased, some railroad men would have to find work elsewhere. Of course no harm would be done if employment could be found. But other employment would be available only if the productivity of business as a whole expanded as rapidly as the efficiency of labor. The union leaders saw little hope for this.

Nevertheless, scientific management captured the public's imagination. The *American Metal Market* suggested that there was immediate need for it in the steel and coal industries. [49] The *Chicago Tribune* wanted to apply it to reform Chicago's water company. [50] The head of the Chicago Civil Service Reform Association saw that it could be ideally applied to city government.[51] A lecturer at Simmons College near Boston told his audience of young ladies that it could and would be used by future house-wives to abolish kitchen drudgery.[52]

Much of this was just talk. Some railroads, however, began to do something about it. Joseph Ramsey, Jr., president of the Ann Arbor Railroad, became so interested in what Hathaway, Towne, and Dodge were saying that he missed two trains back to Michigan. "Like a number of other railway men he was seen bending forward in his chair with his hand to his ear." [53] T. DeWitt Cuyler of the Pennsylvania and E. T. Stotesbury of the Reading and the Lehigh Valley left on a trip west to study the accomplishments of Emerson on the Santa Fe.[54] Soon after, James R. Wood, Passenger Traffic Manager of the Pennsylvania, remarked: "Brandeis said what is more or less true when he declared that we are in one measure or another inefficient. Every one of us should seek to avoid waste. I believe we are not doing all that we ought to do. Our passenger business has been keeping abreast of a good standard so far, but I think we can do better." And it was announced that the Rock Island had begun eliminating waste by scientific methods.[55]

THE FIRST DECISION

All this took place before the Commission reached its decision on the rate advance. Brandeis filed his brief on January 3, 1911. On January 11 he argued for three hours, ending with this statement: "This investigation has developed clearly that the railroads to meet any existing needs should look not without but within. If their net income is insufficient, the proper remedy is not higher rates, resulting in higher costs and lessened business, but scientific management, resulting in lower costs, in higher wages, and increased business. If their credit is impaired, the proper remedy is not to apply the delusive stimulant of higher rates, but to strengthen their organizations by introducing advanced methods and eliminating questionable practices. Thus they will maintain credit by deserving it." [56]

On February 23, 1911, the Commission handed down its decision, unanimously rejecting the rate advances. Though Commissioner Prouty did not base his opinion squarely on the principles of scientific management, he declared: "Before any general advance can be permitted it must appear with reasonable certainty that carriers have exercised proper economy in the purchase of their supplies, in the payment of wages, and in the general management of the business." [57]

The shippers were elated. They estimated that the decision would save them $190,000,000 per annum. Brandeis was still their spokesman. When newspapers asked for his comment, he recalled Park's harsh words, saying:

"I am accustomed to be called a fool, nor do I blame the railroad men for what they have said about me." Their arrogance is due to the fact that they represent "absolute monarchy." Until a few years ago the local freight agent was "one of our great American moguls and would have felt quite as free as a railroad president to call me names if I had tried to tell him anything about his business." [58]

Now things were different. Brandeis had won, as he said, a decision "in favor of the great mass of people as against the aggregation of capital. . . . It will tend to convince the people that there is power in our government to create a body which can successfully resist the demands of great corporations, and it must therefore tend to allay not only hostility and suspicion, but the demand for government ownership of national monopolies. It tends therefore in the direction of popular contentment and peace." [59]

Brandeis had, for the moment, failed to take into account the determined resistance of railroad leaders, backed by the great financiers. They weren't ready to admit that a government body "can successfully resist the demands of great corporations." The day after the Commission announced its decision the Stock Exchange opened with a bear drive on railroad stocks; 464,566 shares were sold in the first hour, including large blocks of Union Pacific and Reading. The average price fell four points in a few minutes. But the great banking houses were able to check the bears quickly, and before the Exchange closed, prices had returned almost to their opening levels. [60]

Wall Street had refused to get panicky; but Wall Street, of course, was not pleased. The *Commercial and Financial Chronicle,* alleged to be the personal property, and at times the oracle, of Mr. Morgan, stormed:

. . . So permeated with radicalism is the Commission as recently reorganized, that out of the seven members of the board not a single one had the spirit of equity, the sense of decency, to stand out against such harsh treatment of the carrying interests, the largest single industry in the country. [61]

Other railroad men all over the country were "disappointed," "shocked," "stunned." They "voiced either open or implied criticism of the ruling," the *New York Evening Post* reported. "How they would oppose it, if at all, was not indicated; but it was plain that they wanted to make a fight if they could see an opening." [62] President Gardner of the Chicago & Northwestern confirmed the *Post* when he said: "We shall keep right on in our endeavor to secure permission to raise our freight tariffs." [63]

CHAPTER TWENTY-ONE

All Sides and Angles of the Railroad Rate Situation, 1913-1914

THE RAILROADS made their new bid for increased rates on May 14, 1913, when fifty-two lines in so-called "official classification territory" * petitioned the I.C.C. for a rehearing of the 1910 case. Alleging increased capital charges, wages, taxes, and other burdens, they asked for a 5 per cent horizontal rate advance.†

Two days before this official petition Brandeis had written Alfred: "I don't know whether I shall actively take part in Rate Advance matters, but I have inspired some editorials the country over demanding efficiency and abolishing interlocking directorates first." By mid-July Brandeis was back in the case. His first act was to draw up for Commissioner J. Russell Marble a list of questions on freight cars, steel rails, interlocking directorates, and "so-called legal and public expenses" of the railroads. "If full answers are given to these inquiries," he wrote Marble, July 18, "some light will be thrown upon efficiency in operation, and the comparative data collected should at least serve to show the insufficiency of present accounting, and the necessity of scientific cost keeping, and the ultimate establishment of a Federal Bureau of Railroad Costs." ‡

AN EQUIVOCAL ASSIGNMENT

Brandeis wasn't sure that he was going to do more than this on the current case, but on August 15 Commissioner James S. Harlan invited him to aid the Commission. Harlan wrote at great length about the capacity in

---

* In the railroad world this expression is used to describe the territory bounded by Canada and the Great Lakes on the north, by the Atlantic Ocean on the east, by the Mississippi on the west, and by the Ohio and Potomac rivers on the south. This classification territory is divided into three rate areas, known as New England, Trunk Line, and Central Freight Association territory. (I.C.C. Reports, Vol. XXXI, June 1914 to October 1914, p. 353. For map, showing the subdivisions, see p. 350.)

† Though the proposed increase in tariffs averaged about 5 per cent higher than the existing rates, the increase in some instances was below 3 per cent, and in others rose as high as 50 per cent. The increases were not general as to commodities or as to territories, there being many exceptions. (I.C.C. Reports, Vol. XXXI, June 1914 to October 1914, pp. 355-56.)

‡ Following the line taken in the 1910 case, Brandeis suggested that the Commission might wish to employ F. Lincoln Hutchins, who had done some work for Harrington Emerson, and called attention to Hutchins's articles in *The Engineering Magazine*: "The Railroad Problem: Rates, Unit Costs and Efficiency," January 1912; "The Railroad Problem: Capitalization and Regulation; The Deduction from Unit Costs of 20 American Railways, February 1912.

which he wanted Brandeis to serve: "We are of course aware that the carriers will not fail fully to present their side of the case, and the Commission has felt that every effort should be made in the public interest *adequately to present the other side*." Harlan went on to explain that in a number of cases of large importance and wide interest special counsel had been retained "not as advocates or to support any special theory of the issues involved, but as a means by which the Commission might be advised of all the facts and not have to decide the issue upon a record made up largely in one interest.

"I have been asked," the Commissioner continued, "to ascertain whether your engagements and inclinations are such as to permit you to undertake the task of *seeing that all sides and angles* of the case are presented of record, without advocating any particular theory for its disposition. In making this last observation you will of course understand that you will be expected to emphasize any aspect of the case which in your judgment, after an examination of the whole situation, may require emphasis. The Commission however wishes to avoid a record based solely on a particular view or theory. . . . My personal feeling is that your participation in the case will give to the public at large the assurance that the whole case will be fully presented. . . . (Author's italics.)

Though Harlan had obviously intended to be explicit, his letter was in fact very ambiguous. The role of special counsel in presenting "the other side" from that of the carriers was not necessarily identical with the role of "seeing all sides and angles." From the beginning Brandeis and the Commission interpreted his position as expressed in the latter phrase. Others, understandably enough, supposed him employed merely to combat the roads, or to represent the interest of "the other side"—that is, the shippers. This difference of opinion was soon to cause trouble.

On August 21 Brandeis accepted the I.C.C.'s invitation, and Harlan announced the appointment on October 9, again describing Brandeis's status in such language as to make it uncertain whether he would represent "all sides" or "the other side": "His [Brandeis] selection for this duty has no other significance, except as it may be regarded as a recognition by the Commission of his standing as a lawyer, and of his well-understood ability in analyzing and broadly treating questions of large importance and public interest. Doubtless certain protestants will have their own attorneys, but Mr. Brandeis will be the general channel through whom the view of others opposing the proposed advance may be presented of record." [1]

The press generally assumed that Brandeis had been retained to oppose the railroads' petition. In an editorial, "The Railroads' Nemesis," the *New*

York Times on October 10 said flatly that his appointment on "the ship-pers' side weakened the hopes of railroad managers."

". . . Mr. Brandeis has been a consistent foe of the railroads," the *Washington Post* editorialized, October 11, "having frequently volunteered his services in the anomalous capacity of 'citizen' in anti-railroad litigation. If Mr. Brandeis is to enliven the proceedings as a free lance, carrying a feeless brief,* why should the Commission not take the public into its confidence?" The *New York Times Annalist,* October 13, dubbed him "propagandist"; the *Capitalist,* October 25, spoke of him as "the bitterest and most inveterate foe the railroads have in this country."

Attorneys for shipper interests also assumed Brandeis was on their side, and they promptly expressed their satisfaction in his appointment and their desire to help. "I think this method of procedure is wise," Clifford Thorne, chairman of the Iowa Board of Railroad Commissioners, wrote Brandeis on October 27. "There should be a head to the *public's* presentation." But Professor Ernst Freund warned: "I venture to express the hope that you will set a precedent of importance in Administrative Law, and make it clear, whatever your conclusions, that a counsel of a quasi-judicial commission, as distinguished from counsel employed by a prosecuting department, represents not one side or the other of the controversy, but purely the *public* interest, which is the interest of justice to all concerned." [2] (Author's italics.)

The *Philadelphia Inquirer* again complained on November 26: "Why should the Interstate Commerce Commission, which as a quasi-judicial body is supposed to maintain, and which certainly ought to maintain, an attitude of entire impartiality, need to be represented by counsel whose only business must be to furnish it with some reason or with some pretext for refusing to comply with the railroad companies' request? How does it happen that Mr. Brandeis, whose hostility to the railroads is notorious, is chosen for its adviser?"

Clearly, Commissioner Harlan's assumption that Brandeis's participation would reassure the public was not entirely justified. Speculation was rife on all sides as to Brandeis's status, and Chairman E. E. Clark felt obliged to make this statement: "Mr. Brandeis is not employed as an advocate for any special interests, but is employed to assist the Commission in analysis of the big general question which underlies this proposal by the railroads. We see no reason why anyone should assume that his employment can disadvantageously affect any interest." [3]

Still Brandeis's impartiality continued to be questioned because of his

---

* As a matter of fact, his services were not uncompensated. For the original hearings the I.C.C. paid him $12,500, and an additional $1,250 for the supplementary hearings.

earlier campaigns against the New Haven and his current attacks in
Harper's on the "Money Trust." Even the *Boston Evening Transcript,*
his stanch supporter in the 1910 case, said somewhat dubiously, November 29, 1913:

The railroads see in the person of Louis D. Brandeis, employed as special
counsel for the Commission, a man with whom they will have to reckon. Mr.
Brandeis's attitude on the New England transportation system is familiar to
everyone, and it is this attitude of his which is giving the railroads their greatest
cause for uneasiness today. Mr. Brandeis has a desk in one of the offices of the
Commission; legally he represents them; actually, it is felt, he will represent
the kind of opposition to the railroads for which he has long stood. His appearance, then, in what amounts to a governmental capacity, indicates to the most
casual observer that the Commission, by availing itself of Mr. Brandeis, has in
effect given notice to the transportation interests it trusts Mr. Brandeis's judgment in these matters.

THE TANGLED RAILWAY WEB

Unperturbed by the rising hostility, Brandeis threw himself into the
fight with the eager spirit of a scientist. He was off again on his favorite
tack—investigating, analyzing, dissecting. To get their rate advance the
railroads had to justify it. To do that they would have to answer the Commission's or Brandeis's questions. These Brandeis tried to make as pointed
as possible. From the Forest Service of the Department of Agriculture he
obtained a set of questions on railroad ties; [4] from the Department of
Commerce, similar questions on methods employed by the roads in buying,
testing, and distributing supplies. [5] From I.C.C. Attorney James W. Carmalt,
he obtained information about the effect of industrial combination on
the prices of materials and supplies. [6] He prepared his own detailed questions on "the economic and efficient use of equipment." [7] He sent a hastily
written note to Joseph B. Eastman, requesting that he "pick out at once
from his and our papers all those items bearing on Diamond Jim Brady's
relations and contracts with the New Haven." [8] Shippers, investors, workers, and reformers, harboring real or fancied grievances against the railroads, bombarded Brandeis with gratuitous information.

Meanwhile the railroads, under the skillful direction of their new publicity man, Ivy L. Lee, were working up their case. Daniel Willard, their
chief spokesman, after enumerating for the press the sources of increased
burdens, fell back on the old plea that only higher rates could secure the
new capital the railroads needed to carry their increasing load. "Railroad rates," he declared, "have been practically stationary in the United
States over a considerable period of time. . . . The proposed increase

is very moderate and will bear but lightly upon any particular unit of traffic." [9] Some of the commissioners were favorably inclined toward Willard. "No one can deny," Chairman E. E. Clark of the Commission wrote moderately, "that there has been extravagance in financing and in management in years gone by. . . . The railroads are arteries through which all our commerce must move, and without them commerce would be paralyzed. It seems to me, therefore, impossible to eradicate all these wrongs at one time without doing irreparable injury to many and innocent businessmen and interests." [10]

Preliminary hearings began on November 24, 1913, before six commissioners, with Brandeis, Charles W. Needham, and James W. Carmalt appearing for the Commission, a host of eminent lawyers and officials for the railroads, and others for the protestants, mostly shippers. The *New York Times Annalist,* December 1, 1913, described the opening scene:

Promptly at 10 o'clock the person corresponding to court crier or bailiff rapped for respectful attention. Everybody rose. The Commissioners filed in and took their seats. The bentwood chairs creaked, papers rattled, and Louis D. Brandeis, representing all those who consume the commodity called transportation, began to comb his hair with his fingers. He ought not to do that. It is a distraction and tends to create uneasiness on the other side. He was not going to cross-question the witnesses at all, as the railroads were to be allowed to put in their direct case without interruption, but the witnesses did not know that, and when he volunteered from time to time to help them with their own facts, to make them stronger and even more favorable, they were visibly agitated.

President Willard led for the carriers. It was the same old story—ever-increasing financial burdens that must be met by advanced rates. After other rail officials had given more specific reasons for rate increases, the preliminary hearing closed. The Commission and Special Counsel Brandeis then set about studying the voluminous material they had accumulated.

A great variety of issues now clamored for Brandeis's attention. In January 1914 Congressman James M. Curley, the mayor-elect of Boston, offered him the post of city auditor of Boston and pleaded with him to accept: "I only want you to serve as auditor six months, for I realize that you would be making a great sacrifice in accepting the offer, but the methods in the auditor's office are so antiquated and the waste is so great in the buying of supplies and the like, that I am sure with you introducing an up-to-date and adequate system, Boston will be saved $300,000 a year at the least. I hope you will be able to make the sacrifice." Though Brandeis offered to co-operate in every way possible, he was then too busy in Washington to do more.

"Lectured the Industrial Commission two hours yesterday and House

Committee on Interstate Foreign Commerce a like quantity today," he wrote his wife, February 4, 1914. "For tomorrow I have a conference with the Attorney-General on trust bills. I wish they were all on the other side of the world and they would let me study the railroad problem undisturbed." On February 24 he wrote Alfred: "The I.C.C. matters are so interesting, that I greatly begrudge the time which trust and kindred legislation are taking. *Zu fragmentarisch ist Welt und Leben.* I long for the days of Ballinger isolation."

THE RAILROADS TURN ON HEAT

From late November 1913 on through 1914 there was a great deal of press comment on the railroad freight issue, inspired in part by Ivy Lee's campaign. On November 29 both the *Washington Post* and the *Boston Evening Transcript* brandished the dread spectacle of public ownership, and on December 4 the *New York Times* emphasized the disastrous effect of rate controversy on foreign investors' confidence. One *Washington Post* article was so ill-tempered as to warrant a disclaimer of authorship from George Stuart Patterson, general counsel for the Pennsylvania.[11] Elbert Hubbard in *The Philistine,* March 1914, once more denounced "Brandeis, the Boss Business Baiter": "The wholesale condemnation and disparagement of railroadmen and railroad interests by Mr. Brandeis has tended to kill credit, until America is no longer buying railroad bonds, and railroads often have difficulty in getting money to meet current expenses. . . ."

In much of the pro-railroad propaganda Brandeis was featured as the villain who had somehow gotten the I.C.C. under his insidious thumb. Having, as his critics asserted, "Brandeized the Commission," [12] he would certainly take advantage of his position to repay "the interests for the damage they had done him less than a year previously." * "It is the irony of fate," the *Boston Evening Record* commented, May 26, 1914, "that Mr. Brandeis should have become the boss, so to speak, of the railroads. They have hated him and high finance had arranged quite a fall for the lawyer, but here he is on top in Washington, and where are they? They got mightily together in February of 1913 and succeeded in making it impossible for President Wilson to appoint Mr. Brandeis Secretary of Commerce. . . . Mr. Brandeis was dreaded as such, and some people wanted to get even. They did."

In similar vein Frederick W. Whitridge, president of the New York Third Avenue Elevated Company, in a letter to the *New York Times,* July 15, 1914, exclaimed: "The Interstate Commerce Commission! They seem to be a clumsy, inarticulate lot, with a penchant for shady lawyers."

---

* In the fight against his appointment to Wilson's cabinet. *See* Chap. XXV.

While the *Boston News Bureau* reported Hubbard's entire blast, the strongly pro-railroad *New York Times Annalist* pleaded that the railroad managers must be "saved from their friends."

With the weight of propaganda heavily against the Commission and its counsel, the *Philadelphia North American* on April 6, 1914, denounced editorially "the deliberate campaign of misrepresentation and coercion," and called attention to "three vital facts: first, that the Commission is a judicial body, with a dual function—it represents the interests of the public and the interests of the railroads; second, that the companies which clamor for higher rates have been wasting or diverting millions of dollars of revenue annually in wrongful allowances and free services for favored shippers; and, third, that the railroad presidents themselves have been compelled to admit on the witness stand that they are predicting a crisis and demanding more revenue from the public at the close of a year which has been one of the most successful in their history."

"It is because of this astonishing propaganda," this same paper commented, May 5, "carried on by the predatory interests and their organs, that we foresee a rapid growth of the sentiment for government ownership of railroads."

NEW EVIDENCE AND NEW ENEMIES

In addition to the hearings, the I.C.C. had to examine the mountains of documentary evidence it received from the roads in answer to its seventy-eight questions. Throughout the Commission emphasized two issues: first, whether existing rates yielded adequate revenues; second, assuming inadequacy of revenues, what course should the carriers follow to meet the situation.[13] The railroads and the shippers centered on the first question. The Commission and Brandeis clung tenaciously to the second. In search of ways whereby the roads could cut their costs so that rate increases would not be needed, the Commission unearthed a complexity of free services and special privileges which the railroads were granting as favors. With ill-concealed zest Brandeis presented evidence showing that such gratuities sometimes ran as high as 25 per cent or more of the total revenue on the freight involved. Certain roads loaded and unloaded carload lots, reimbursing their favored customers when the latter did their own loading. "Why not let the big shippers, notably the trusts, pay for the special services which they now get free from the roads?" he suggested.[14] Taking Brandeis's cue, Gilson Gardner commented: "The bigger the shipper, the more he is favored by the carriers, and the more the big shipper is favored, the harder it is for the small shipper to compete with him. Why not put the increase on those best able to bear it? Why don't you collect $50,000,000 from these big shippers who are now getting all kinds of special favors that the little shipper does not get?"[15]

The shippers hardly expected such queries and suggestions from Brandeis. "I guess I am raising up several new crops of disgruntled critics in the I.C.C., among the big shippers," he commented in a letter to Alfred, February 24, 1914. The shippers, hitherto his allies, now rose in arms against him; nor were they appeased by Brandeis's assurance that there was no intention of destroying this "system," but only to see to it that the carriers had adequate compensation for all the services they rendered.

"You would not wish to be understood as claiming that there was a vested right to free switching service in the future?" he asked one representative of shipper interests. "That is a legal matter," the witness hedged. "I mean as a moral matter. Considering the economic and social feature of it, you would not claim that?" Brandeis pressed him. At once the witness ducked: "I could not discuss the legal rights."[16] Later, however, another witness asserted that shippers equipped with sidings did have a "moral" right to free service, and if the I.C.C. imposed charges it would be a breach of faith on the part of the railroads.[17]

It became perfectly clear that shippers were not to profit by any bias in their favor when Brandeis proclaimed: "The shippers in every conceivable line of industry have come here, and I cannot recall any in which we have not heard that this margin [of profit] is so small that a slight charge added on to them—it is all right for other people—would spell bankruptcy."[18]

BRANDEIS VERSUS THORNE

Oral arguments were scheduled for April 22, 1914. Clifford Thorne, who had been associated with Brandeis in the Advance Rate Case as counsel for the shippers, was anxious and somewhat meticulous as to the order in which counsel would appear. He wrote Brandeis on April 9: "I trust you will notify me as soon as possible the amount of time that is to be allotted either side, the order in which you will direct the oral argument in behalf of the public, and how much time you will allot to my argument. I will abide absolutely by what you prescribe and will content myself entirely with the same." Thorne hoped to conclude the argument, Brandeis having preceded him, as he recalled, in the 1910 case.

"I firmly believe," Thorne continued confidingly, "that the success of our case is now going to rest with you. I know of no man in the country more able to present this subject to the Commission than yourself. I most sincerely hope that I have not disappointed you in the further presentation of the facts requested by the Commission, and in the cross-examination, and if you firmly believe that we are right I know that we will succeed.

Please understand that anything and everything which I have made of record is for your use absolutely if you deem it worthy of the same."

Thorne soon discovered, however, that Brandeis, not he, had closed the 1910 case, and he wrote again on April 11 to say that he would be perfectly willing to continue that arrangement.

He apparently entertained some doubt as to what position Brandeis would take. He looked anxiously through Brandeis's brief for a statement holding that the rates in general were adequate, and found none. From Carmalt, the Commission's attorney, he learned that Brandeis planned to argue that certain rates were inadequate. Thorne himself then questioned Brandeis, who replied that he felt that the rates of railroads in Central Freight Association territory were too low. This fully satisfied Thorne at the time.

Brandeis began his argument, saying:

May it please your honors, it may be helpful if at the outset I state the conclusions which a review of the record in these cases has brought to me. They are these:

First, that on the whole, the net income, the net operating revenues of the carriers in official classification territory, are smaller than is consistent with their assured prosperity and the welfare of the community.

In view of this, it is desirable that steps should be taken as promptly as reasonably may be to increase these net revenues.

Second, that the method proposed by the carriers for increasing these net revenues is essentially unsound; that it is, except as to a small part of the tariffs that have been submitted, entirely too low, and would, if approved, involve the exceeding of the powers vested by Congress in this Commission; and as to that small part of the tariffs as to which it would be legal to approve them, it would be extremely unwise both for the carriers and for the community to grant that approval.

Third . . . that there exist, as has been indicated on this record, adequate means of increasing those revenues without resort to the unsound, largely illegal, and undesirable method of the alleged horizontal increase.[19]

Continuing his argument, Brandeis denied that there had been any increase in the cost of railroad supplies. He emphasized the serious burden of underpaid mail and passenger service and characterized free services as "leeches upon the revenue, growing and eating into the vitals of these railroads." He denied that the proposed advance in rates was in proportion to proved increase in operating costs and censured the carriers for waste of credit, singling out the nefarious operations of the New Haven, Frisco, Père Marquette, and the Cincinnati, Hamilton & Dayton as imperiling the credit of all. "Nothing," he concluded, "could bring on government ownership so rapidly as to grant the rate advance." The railroads "must not be stampeded by their friends in the financial district," he said, "but they must look at the matter as operating men and handle the problems manfully, as they have been manfully handled, and as operating men live up to the great possibilities of the noble profession to which they have dedicated themselves." [20]

One special point of difference between Brandeis and Thorne concerned the amount of surplus which railroads should be allowed to earn. Brandeis contended that if rates were reasonable, the railroads should be allowed to earn as large a surplus as they could by efficient and economical management. Thorne, on the other hand, held that surplus should be definitely limited. Inasmuch as Brandeis's views, particularly his remark as to surplus, moved Thorne to attack bitterly Brandeis's confirmation as Associate Justice in 1916, it is of interest to quote that part of Brandeis's argument.

We must give to those of our railroads that are managed well, where the judgment is good, and where the roads are managed with integrity and skill, and with a special effort and desire to advance the interests of the railroad as well as the community, an opportunity to earn. I myself care little for the laying down of any specific rule as to the percentage, because I never would stick to any limit at all. If the per cent is such as will yield just and reasonable rates, but which will yield to those who manage well, and who have exercised good judgment as ample reward for their efforts and for the risks of the stockholders as if they had engaged in some other similar business involving similar risks, they should earn it. Of course, that involves the earning of surplus, and you need a surplus, not only to provide for the lean years which must come—and which ought not to drive us into a panic when they do come—but in order that there may be such stability to the property as will assure to the investor a sense of safety and induce him to take securities at a relatively low rate. . . .

The point made by Mr. Thorne is sound, that we ought not to be building up a surplus taken out of the community, and then have the community pay for it again, thereby making an undue return upon that surplus and ultimately, if the railroad is taken by eminent domain, paying for what has been accumulated in addition to a handsome return paid out to the stockholders.

I think proper provisions could be made by which that question of surplus could be determined. I for one think it very much better to run the risk in the court of protecting the community against injustice in respect to the surplus, when that question comes up, rather than to deny the surplus which is essential to good business, and essential to obtaining capital at reasonable rates. . . .

While I would much rather it were possible to remove a fact—that fact that Mr. Thorne suggests as being such a peril to the community—I myself would rather look with hope to the ultimate working out of this problem by the Supreme Court of the United States, with the aid of the Commission and other courts, instead of denying to the railroads today that which, in good business judgment in looking to the immediate future with which we have to deal, is an essential of the health of the railroad.[21]

Thorne then asked Brandeis, "Did you understand me to deny any surplus?"

"I thought you were rather niggardly as to surplus," Brandeis returned.

"I allowed the same surplus," said Thorne, "that the Commission did in 1910, and if your remark applies to my allowance, it applies to the other."

In great mental turmoil Thorne filed, with the Commission's consent, a supplementary brief, saying in conclusion: "I did not anticipate the vicious attack on the surplus I had allowed as being 'niggardly.' As an honest public servant, seeking simply to do justice by all, with a record of fairness in office in which I take great pride, I resent most bitterly the unpardonable attack made by Mr. Brandeis."

Thorne also released a scathing statement to the press: "Had I known that Mr. Brandeis was actually going to take the railroad side of the particular question up for discussion as to the adequacy of the railroad revenues as a whole, I should certainly have asked that he be heard along with the railroad counsel before I made my argument. . . ."

Having misunderstood Brandeis's function, Thorne had no recourse but to denounce his argument. "What a most delightful and pretty bit of argument from the railroad standpoint," Thorne fumed. "A second Daniel, indeed a second Daniel, well worthy that distinguished ancestor of our modern advocate for the people's side in the greatest controversy of the present generation." [22]

EXPOSING MONEY-TRUST TACTICS

The oral arguments closed on May 1, but Brandeis had yet to lay bare the relationship between the Baltimore & Ohio and the Cincinnati, Hamilton & Dayton. He spent a good part of May poring over the records, mortgages, agreements, and financial statements of the B & O. When hearings were reopened on May 29 he put President Willard on the stand and elicited from him a reluctant account of the machinations of the House of Morgan and other financial powers, showing how the B & O, undefended by its own eminent directors, had been saddled with the bankrupt C, H & D, under which burden it still labored. Lest confidence be shaken the company had scrupulously avoided informing stockholders of the ugly facts and blithely continued paying the regular 6 per cent dividend. As of May 29 Willard persisted in his belief that the B & O's policy was perfectly sound.[23]

"Do you mean, Mr. Willard," Brandeis inquired incredulously, "that with that history back of the C, H & D you believed that this investment was an investment that would pay a return in money directly to the Baltimore & Ohio, a return upon these securities?"

"I believe exactly what I have already said," the witness answered. "I will say it again. Up until the advent of the Dayton flood [of 1913] I believed that this whole arrangement would work out, that the Baltimore & Ohio in the end would not be a loser." Willard held out obstinately to the very end: "So far as I am concerned I can see no reason to suggest that the Baltimore & Ohio's dividend should be reduced." [24]

Special Counsel continued in pursuit. "You have asked me that question several times," the witness complained. "I have asked that question several times," said the lawyer, "because I cannot believe that a man of your experience, and a man who has asserted again and again the importance of preserving a surplus and of protecting the property, should be willing to assert, when the matter is specifically called to his attention, that it is good railroad financing to continue to pay that dividend with a loss of $25,000,000 to $40,000,000 impending to your railroad." [25]

After Brandeis got from Willard a confession that even when he realized the danger the stockholders had not been informed of it, he lectured him: "Here is a very important investment; a very important connection. You go into a great number of things in your statement [annual report] which are perfectly clear and which give to the reader, or should give to the reader, full knowledge as to what the Baltimore & Ohio is doing, but there is nowhere in the report anything that would give the holders of the Baltimore & Ohio securities any knowledge of this precarious enterprise that I can find." [26]

On May 30 Brandeis wrote Alfred: "I am afraid Dan Willard didn't like my enquiry of yesterday into the C, H & D. The financial end put a terrible strain on the operating men."

Brandeis had stumbled into the B & O's tangled web of intercorporate finance quite by chance,* and yet it looked to an outsider as if hearings on the matter had been carefully timed to occur after the arguments and briefs were in. It was a serious setback for the railroads' case as newspapers gave full publicity to the disclosures. Brandeis himself added fuel to the flame in rehashing the story to magazine editors, pointing to it as a "striking example of the power and bad habits of the money trust." "They preach conservation," he wrote Norman Hapgood, June 1, "and are reckless in financial management. They complain of the public's having a lack

* Brandeis evidently got some of his information on the C, H & D from an article by Charles Edward Russell. (Theresa H. Russell to L.D.B., May 15, 1914.)

of confidence, and almost every important matter which one investigates should convince us that the people have far more confidence than the facts justify. It seems to me that this extraordinary suppression of information, amounting to ingenuity and misrepresentation, is a great disgrace to those who have been charged with management, and among them as bankers is Kuhn, Loeb & Company, who are represented on the Baltimore & Ohio Board of Directors by Paul Warburg, Speyer & Company, represented on the Board by James Speyer, and the New York City Bank, who are represented on the Board by James Stillman. The Board of Directors contains the names of such other estimable citizens as Norman B. Ream, Robert S. Lovett, and Robert Garrett."

In view of Brandeis's spectacular claims for scientific management as the answer to the railroads' proposal of increased rates in 1910, one may well wonder why that same solution was apparently less strongly pressed in 1914. In his brief of 1914 Brandeis did not neglect scientific management. Under the heads "Conservation of Revenues," and "Economy and Efficiency," it was still stressed as a corrective, but relatively more space was given to factors brought to light since the 1910 case, such as "unremunerative services" straining credit by "undue expansion" and the various ramifications of the Money Trust as it affected railroad finances.*

THE VERDICT

The Commission handed down its decision on July 29, 1914, Commissioners Daniels and McChord dissenting. The 5 per cent advance was allowed only in the Central Freight Association territory.† Elsewhere the increase was denied. The majority opinion bore the stamp of Brandeis throughout. Chairman Harlan declared: ". . . We are of opinion that the net operating income of the railroads in official classification territory, taken as a whole, is smaller than is demanded in the interest of both the general public and the railroads; and it is our duty and our purpose to aid, so far as we legally may, in the solution of the problem as to the course that the carriers may pursue to meet the situation." [27]

The report then went on to suggest, again following Brandeis, specific ways whereby the railroads might recoup much needed revenues. In all this there was not a little evidence that the Commission had, as his critics said, been "Brandeized."

* In his brief of January 3, 1911, on behalf of Traffic Committee of Commercial Organizations of the Atlantic Seaboard, 99 of his 180 pages were given to scientific management; in his brief of April 27, 1914, as special counsel for the I.C.C., scientific management claimed only 50 of his 199 pages.

† Including such important cities as Cleveland, Detroit, Cincinnati, Buffalo, Indianapolis, Toledo, Chicago, and St. Louis. (For a map showing the three areas comprising the official classification territory, see I.C.C. Reports, Vol. XXXI, p. 350.)

Friend and foe alike practically credited him with authorship of the report. "Although your name does not appear attached to the opinion," Frank Lyon, I.C.C. attorney, wrote in a congratulatory message on August 13, "I think I know to whom should be addressed a letter commending it." "In the original decision," Clifford Thorne commented bitterly, "the Commission practically adopted the language of Mr. Brandeis as to the inadequacy of revenues as a whole. But they did not grant the general advance. In that respect they also followed out Mr. Brandeis's theory as to the disposition of the case." [28] The *Boston Traveler* called it "a Brandeised decision" and sarcastically suggested that "instead of fighting for their rights, the railroads should get down on their knees to Mr. Brandeis and beg for mercy."

Brandeis had hoped that the roads would respond to the Commission's offer "to aid" them and undertake complete revision of their rates, believing that it would be a great misfortune both to themselves and the public if they did not do so.[29] But the auspices for revision were highly unfavorable. The World War, as Harlan wrote Brandeis, "seems completely to have overshadowed the conclusions of the Commission," precluding rational consideration of the problem either by the public or the railroads.[30]

Before the end of August the railroads found in the World War itself new excuses for the advance, and on September 9 the heads of six roads appealed to President Wilson, suggesting an era of good feeling toward the carriers.[31] A week later they filed formal application with the I.C.C. for reopening the case. The shippers strongly protested further hearings, and the Commission ordered the case postponed thirty days.[32] Opposing this, the *Boston Traveler* stormed: "Is this to give Brandeis another opportunity to place sand in the gear-box?" [33] The *Philadelphia Press* inquired:

Is he again to be the dominating influence and the final arbiter of a question that is vital to the well-being of the United States? . . . What the country wishes to know, and what it has a right to know is whether it is necessary to convince and satisfy Mr. Brandeis as to the necessity for more railroad revenue before the Commission will grant the relief that is asked. . . . Is the Commission powerless to give the aid that the circumstances justify without the permission of Mr. Brandeis? [34]

The case was reopened on October 19, 1914, amid clamorous protest, Brandeis again appearing as special counsel. It was essentially the same case all over again—the same contestants, the same spokesmen and counsel, the same arguments pro and con. Brandeis saw this battling of the roads for higher rates as undermining both government regulation and private enterprise. He wrote Alfred, October 24: "The railroads and bankers did not do themselves much credit. If they have their way they will utterly break down the Commission and even if they are beaten they will have succeeded in greatly impairing its standing and their own defense against lawlessness and public ownership." *

In the final arguments Brandeis, as special counsel, had expected to conclude the case, but Thorne, still harboring bruised feelings, strongly objected. "I hardly knew on which side he was," Thorne explained later. "I took it up with the counsel for the shippers. All but one of these gentlemen . . . combined in asking Mr. Brandeis to speak first, so that we would have a chance to answer what he might have to say. He declined to agree to it. I then went to Commissioner Clements in regard to it. He said that he would bring it up at the open hearing. At the time of the rehearing we had had the experience of the original case, and we did not—or at least I did not—propose to see that the *public side* should be thrown again." [35]

Brandeis yielded, and when the carriers' lawyers had finished he said: "Your honors, counsel for some of the shippers have expressed a desire that they should follow me, in order that they might have an opportunity of answering what I say as well as what the carriers have said; and, if there is no objection on the part of the Commission, I will address the Commission now." Again opposing a general advance, Brandeis questioned the Commission's authority to raise rates without proof that the increase was "just and reasonable. Does mere need," he asked, "force the decision of your honors so as to compel a finding that rates are just and reasonable, because only with such increases can the necessary amount of money be raised?" [36]

Brandeis was far from optimistic as to the outcome. Harlan's ill health and his frequent absences did not augur well. In a last minute effort to reinforce his argument, he submitted to Harlan a detailed memorandum covering the entire situation. The Commission was, as he saw it, "at the parting of the ways." One of three courses was open: to affirm the decision of July 29, 1914, and immediately take the initiative in carrying out a vigorous policy of co-operation to make effective its "suggestions" of that date; to affirm the decision of July 29, 1914, but refrain from affirmative

* While the rate decision was still pending Brandeis appeared before the Senate Interstate Commerce Committee in opposition to the Rayburn bill, which would have extended the I.C.C.'s power to include supervision of the issue of railroad securities. The Commission, he argued, was already overburdened and there was the additional danger that its approval of security issues might be construed as a governmental guarantee. He offered an amendment prohibiting railroads from engaging in any business other than that of a carrier, and to prevent them from growing into huge transportation trusts, forbidding them to acquire by purchase, lease, or otherwise any stock or interest in other transportation enterprises, except with the approval and under the close supervision of the Commission. (*New York Times,* June 20, 1914.)

co-operation in carrying out its suggestions; to reverse its decision of July 29 in whole or in part. Brandeis urged the first course not only from the point of view of the community, but also in the long-run interests of the roads. What they needed in additional revenue was nearer $150,000,000 than the fifty they hoped to get from the 5 per cent increase. He saw the roads suffering depletion of revenues from a great variety of sources. Besides widespread inefficiency of operation and management there were unremunerative rates and unjustifiable burdens imposed by the state; unremunerative rates on federal mail service; unremunerative rates due to pressure of powerful shippers, etc. "The granting of the 5 per cent would," he told Harlan, "be disastrous to the railroads themselves, because the abuses are of such a character that the depletions must grow rapidly, and the Commission could not, if it would, counteract the depletion by horizontal increases in freight rates. In other words, if the Commission continued to apply the stimulant of horizontal increases, their burden would curtail traffic."

The Commission had endorsed Brandeis's argument in its decision of July 29, and had followed him closely in the formulation of "suggestions" for meeting the railroads' problem. "There is literally nothing in the new evidence submitted on rehearing," Brandeis argued, "which . . . can form the basis for a decision different from that reached [on July 29]." The intensified need for revenue brought on by the World War makes it all the more imperative that the Commission's "suggestions" of July 29 be affirmed and vigorously executed. "If the Commission is unwilling to take the positive, courageous, energetic, constructive course," his memorandum concluded, "its own destruction and that of private ownership in railroads is inevitable. It has under the law now all the power that is necessary to remedy the situation. It has declared that it is 'our duty and our purpose to aid, so far as we legally may, in the solution of the problem as to the course that carriers may pursue to meet the situation.' It should live up to its resolution. A doubting or halfway course is fatal." [37]

Nevertheless, some subtle intimations that the advance would be granted were in his mind as he wrote Alfred, December 12, 1914: "Am confirmed in views expressed to you in October about I.C.C." The blow fell December 16 when the Commission voted 5 to 2, granting the twice-contested advance.

The reasons for the Commission's complete about-face can only be surmised. The shift is the more puzzling since little or no additional evidence was presented to warrant it. A very important factor, no doubt, was the psychological effect of the World War—the check it gave reform effort and progressive measures generally and the need for unity in the face of national emergency. Changes of personnel within the Commission coupled with the decline in Harlan's power due to ill health—all this may have helped produce the change. Last but not least was the effective propaganda campaign, organized and carried on by the railroads and their organs against the Commissioners' striking at them through President Wilson. In any event, the decision called a halt to Brandeis's persistent drive for intelligent revision of rates and for broad consideration of the entire railroad problem. He was profoundly pessimistic, his usual calm in the face of untoward happenings conspicuously absent.

"The I.C.C. decision," he wrote Alfred on December 23, "will prove a misfortune to both the railroads and the I.C.C. and will do much to hasten government ownership." His effort to have "all sides and angles" of the railroad problem considered and the findings put into effect had been repudiated even by those he had been appointed to guide.

CHAPTER TWENTY-TWO

Spotlighting the Trusts, 1911-1912

MUCKRAKING publicists and political agitators had long been harping on social and political wrongs. Thus far nothing very constructive had been done, but signs were now multiplying that action impended. Congress, reflecting the public's impatient temper, began a series of committee investigations. "What is wrong in American industry?" they wanted to know. What is the basic cause of such widespread labor unrest? And what is the remedy? For answers they turned to men of prominence in business, law, and politics.

"Since 1890 we have learned much about trusts," Brandeis declared in December 1911, "and to my mind we have been learning the last few years at an accelerated pace." [1] As counsel for independent tobacco associations, he had seen how anti-trust prosecutions, even when affirmative judgments were obtained, might be completely nullified. He opposed the Tobacco Trust Disintegration plan worked out by government counsel, and prepared a brief showing in detail the plan's ineffectiveness. The Circuit Court of Appeals, however, rejected practically all his suggestions; the whole proceeding simply gave the trust an "immunity bath" by legalizing an illegal monopoly. Testifying before the Committee on Interstate Commerce in December 1911, he suggested that the Court had practically declared: "What man had illegally joined together let no court put asunder. . . . You have left these rich breakers of the laws of God and of man in undisturbed enjoyment of all their ill-gotten wealth." [2]

J. P. Morgan, Sr., exhibited the attitude of financial oligarchy when he angrily informed a lawyer who expressed doubt as to the legality of a proposed transaction, "Well, I don't know as I want a lawyer to tell me what I cannot do. I hire him to tell me how to do what I want to do." [3] When the merger of the Great Northern and Northern Pacific Railroads into the Northern Securities Company was under federal prosecution, Morgan saw the conflict between government and business enterprise only as a disagreement between rival potentates. "If we have done anything wrong," he told President Roosevelt, "send your man [the Attorney-General] to my man and they can fix it up." [4]

Thus, despite the Sherman Act, combination and consolidation proceeded apace, steadily narrowing the zone of competition. Independent business was driven to the wall, slaughtered, or bought out. But Brandeis's experience showed him how the Sherman Act might be clarified, strengthened, and made effective. "I take it that it is not a problem that the American people are unable to meet, and to meet readily. We have been hearing constantly that the tendency to combinations is a natural economic law, that it is useless to attempt to stem the tide, that we ought to accept the Trust and undertake to regulate it. I believe that position to be absolutely unfounded. . . . Combination is not natural any more than any of the other things in life are natural which it is easier to do if you have no occasion to count the cost. The law may be made, to my mind, perfectly adequate to stem the growth of these organizations, and to say that it cannot be made adequate is to declare the lawmaking power bankrupt. . . ." [5]

The Sherman Act, even without the corrective amendments he advocated, was less faulty than generally supposed. "I think your lawyers or anyone else can tell you where a fairly safe course lies," Brandeis told one puzzled executive. "If you are walking along a precipice no human being can tell you how near you can go to that precipice without falling over, because you may stumble on a loose stone, you may slip, and go over; but anybody can tell you where you can walk perfectly safely within convenient distance of that precipice." The trouble was that businessmen "wanted to go the limit" rather than "go safely." [6] It was necessary that the practices which had proved conducive to monopoly, such as tying clauses, agreements to divide territory or trade, various types of railroad discrimination, and different forms of cutthroat competition, as utilized to great advantage by the Standard Oil and American Tobacco Companies, be expressly forbidden as restraints of trade, and the legal machinery strengthened, so that businessmen would not be tempted by the possibility of "going ahead."

THE BANEFUL BLIGHT OF BIGNESS

Early in 1911 Senator La Follette had decided to do something about trusts, particularly the Money Trust. On February 17 he wrote Brandeis: "I want you to give me as many cases as you can of business coercion and business assassination, attempted and accomplished by the System, cases within your personal experience, each exact, complete, brief—each definite as to locality, character of business, and detail of System method. I do so want to have such instances as have come under your observation, with the names of the firms or corporations involved. This will enable me to state that I have all the facts in each case, but withholding names for obvious reasons, when I make use of the data in the Senate, or in my magazine articles on the Money Power."

Brandeis replied February 24, 1911, and after numerous memoranda to and from the Senator, "Fighting Bob" introduced on August 19 a measure known as the La Follette-Stanley Anti-Trust bill. This bill embodied three main features: It undertook to remove existing uncertainty as to which combinations were reasonable and which were in restraint of trade —that is, it provided a danger light beyond which businessmen could not "go safely." It dealt with the difficulty experienced by the government when it had to prove a combination unreasonable and placed the burden of proof on the trusts (just as the Mann–Elkins Act of 1910 required railroads to prove their case when wishing to raise rates). And it sought to make the law effective in execution—that is, to avoid decisions as preposterous as those in the Standard Oil and American Tobacco cases.

"After these trusts had taken millions of dollars from the people and crushed thousands of competitors," Brandeis observed, "the utmost the court could decree was that they don't do it again. The proposed bill provides that the moment formal decree is entered against a trust, competitors need only prove damages and every fellow will get triple awards for whatever he has lost by competition." [7]

A little earlier another anti-trust bill had been proposed by Senator Francis G. Newlands, and Brandeis, suspicious of it, had prodded Moses

E. Clapp, Chairman of the Senate Committee on Interstate Commerce, to begin immediate investigation of federal policy toward business. "It seems to me particularly important," he had written Clapp on June 22, 1911, "to take up this subject now, before Senator Newlands' project gains much momentum. I have seen only some newspaper comments, but if I understand correctly what he has in mind, it appears to me to be a measure of very doubtful expediency."

Before the Clapp Committee, where hearings began August 4, two sharply conflicting views were presented. One, forcefully expounded by George W. Perkins of the Morgan interests, the Steel and Harvester Trusts, held that these industrial giants had grown because of superior efficiency, that their existence was in any event inevitable, that they should be made to behave by the simple device of government regulation. December 14 to 16 Brandeis presented the opposite view—"that trusts, that monopoly, is not only not more efficient than competitive business, but that monopoly is inefficient as compared with competition; inefficient both economically and socially. There used to be a certain glamour about big things," Brandeis commented. "Anything big, simply because it was big, seemed to be good and great. We are now coming to see that big things may be very bad and mean." [8]

Perkins and other apostles of bigness had not come around to this position, Brandeis argued, because they had erroneously assumed that "with the increase of size comes increase of efficiency." While recognizing that a business unit may be too small to be efficient, the current danger, as Brandeis saw it, was the tendency to create too large units. The businessman yields to this "temptation" because he "may make a great deal more money if he increases the volume of his business tenfold, even if the unit of profit is in the process reduced one-half." [9]

The inefficiency which inevitably attends bigness became even more obvious, Brandeis told the committee, when one considers that "success or failure of an enterprise depends usually upon one man; upon the quality of one man's judgment, and, above all things, his capacity to see what is needed and his capacity to direct others." Nor did modern business organizations—new methods of communication, the telephone, the stenographer, etc.—refute his basic maxim that "there is a limit to what one man can do well." For if judgment is to be exercised wisely, the facts on which it is based must be "both known and carefully weighed." Brandeis elaborated his point, saying: "When . . . you increase your business to a very great extent, and the multitude of problems increase with its growth, you will find, in the first place, that the man at the head has a diminishing knowledge of the facts, and, in the second place, a diminishing opportunity of exercising a careful judgment upon them. Furthermore—and this is one of the most important grounds of the inefficiency of large institutions —there develops a centrifugal force greater than the centripetal force. De- moralization sets in; a condition of lessened efficiency presents itself. . . . These are disadvantages that attend bigness." [10]

Examination of the trust record showed that those having size but lack- ing control of the industry and hence of prices, either failed or achieved no marked success. The annals of the Whisky Trust, the Cordage Trust, and the Malting Trust were unimpressive as compared with Standard Oil, Shoe Machinery, and Tobacco. The latter, Brandeis explained, dominated their trades. "To this monopolistic power, in the main, and not to effi- ciency in management, are their great profits to be ascribed." [11]

For the special edification of "Steel man" Perkins, and to confirm his own stand, Brandeis dug up some disconcerting facts. If the trusts were more efficient, as Mr. Perkins maintained, why was it that the Steel Trust had not been able to hold its own against competitors, as was shown by its declining percentage of business? Why was it that the I.C.C. had had to investigate a great increase in derailments because of defective rails? Why was it that farmers had made so many complaints about deterioration in the quality of fence wire that the Department of Agriculture had had to investigate? Why was it that the United States had been sinking to lower rank in the steel markets of the world? [12]

More important than the desire for greater efficiency were "the thirst of promoters and bankers for huge commissions," the urge to eliminate "what those interested deem destructive, or at least very annoying, competition." The creation of such monsters as the Steel Trust, he went on to say, often represented "the desire to capitalize failures." Steel men, for example, see- ing that competition with Andrew Carnegie was impossible, had capital- ized their inability, bribed him to go out of business, so their own less efficient concerns could survive. "I am so convinced of the economic fal- lacy in a huge unit," Brandeis concluded, "that if we make competition possible, if we create conditions where there could be reasonable competi- tion, that these monsters would fall to the ground." [13]

Besides the failure of the trusts to produce evidence of their vaunted efficiency, Brandeis noted still other shortcomings. They had discouraged invention. Once secure in their position, the reasons for effort to reduce cost were less urgent. "Men have not made inventions in business," he told the committee, "men have not made economies in business to any great extent because they wanted to. They have made them because they had to, and the proposition that 'necessity is the mother of inventions' is just as true today in the time of the trusts, in the era of the trusts, as it was hundreds of years before." [14] Nor had the trusts, as sometimes supposed, benefited consumers by giving them lower prices: "So far as prices have been reduced, it has been in spite of the trusts." [15]

Brandeis urged the committee to weigh well all the "by-products of big business. For by their by-products shall you know the trusts." He cited first the Money Trust, which means, he said, "nothing more than that a few men affiliated with Wall Street are able by their control of the liquid capital of the country to say practically what may or may not be done in all important financial affairs. Before the advent of these trusts," he observed, "the Wall Street money power was practically confined to railroad securities. This advent of trusts, the mobilizing of that huge capital, was like pouring oil into the rising flame of the Money Trust." [16]

The La Follette–Stanley bill, Brandeis admitted, constituted only a beginning, but it would "reduce the favored position of industrial trusts" and thus make some headway "toward grappling with that most difficult subject, the control of capital. I do not think," he said, "that the reduction of the power of the industrial trust will cure the ills attending the Money Trust. It is merely one of many things that would have to be done to make an appreciable advance in that direction. . . . There are so many things that we want to accomplish that we have got to do things in the order of their importance. . . ." [17]

Perkins, on the other hand, disregarding all such "baneful by-products," pointed out that these great corporations were no longer private; they were public enterprises, with innumerable stockholders, all partners in business along with J. P. Morgan & Company—"a consummation devoutly to be wished." But for Brandeis these "partners" and their "partnership" was rather to be regretted than welcomed. "Their only desire is dividends," he said. "Their demand upon the managers is at most to maintain or increase the dividends. They have no power or responsibility; they have no relations to the employees; they are remote. . . . Thus we have reproduced in industry the precise conditions which brought all the misery upon Ireland and upon the other countries where absentee landlordism has prevailed. Large dividends," Brandeis concluded, "are the bribes which managers tender the small investor for the power conferred to use other people's money." [18]

Brandeis was not unaware of how stock-market booming and statistical hosannas could be used to glorify the entire litany of evils that attend bigness and monopoly—the shrinkage of purchasing power, the multiplication of "yes men," the minimizing of the state—in short, a condition that makes individual magnates tyrants and working men serfs. Therefore he warned the committee:

The trust problem can never be settled right for the American people by looking at it through the spectacles of bonds and stocks. You must study it through the spectacles of people's rights and people's interests; must consider the effect upon the development of the American democracy. When you do that you will realize the extraordinary perils to our institutions which attend the trusts; you will realize the danger of letting the people learn that our sacred Constitution protects not only vested rights but vested wrongs.[19]

Brandeis emphasized the seriousness of the situation, but the La Follette-Stanley bill failed to pass.

EXPOSING THE STEEL TRUST

In testifying before the Clapp Committee, Brandeis had used the Steel Trust to show that evils flourished despite the Sherman Act. Soon he was to look more thoroughly into that great monopoly. His chance came in January 1912, when a congressional committee, headed by Representative Augustus O. Stanley of Kentucky, undertook a thorough probe of United States Steel. Robert W. Woolley, a newspaperman (later Interstate Commerce Commissioner in the Wilson administration), was the chief investigator. Largely through the aid of independent companies, such as Jones–Laughlin and Youngstown Steel, Woolley collected a formidable mass of data. So voluminous were his findings that he was at a loss to know what to do next. When he complained of his difficulties, Chairman Stanley advised him to go to Boston and seek the aid of Brandeis. This Woolley did, broaching the question of a fee with some hesitation. "A million dollars is what my services will cost you, Mr. Woolley," Brandeis retorted with eyes twinkling. He then went on to explain his usual custom of serving public causes without compensation. In due course he plunged wholeheartedly into mountains of steel trust materials, particularly as to its industrial relations policy and practice.[20]

Meanwhile Judge Elbert H. Gary of United States Steel had explained in detail to the Stanley Committee his liberal labor policies: "I believe, taking everything into account, the treatment accorded by our corporation to its employees compares favorably with that of any line of industry in this country or any other country at the present time or any period in the history of the world." [21]

Brandeis was unimpressed. "Gentlemen," he commented, January 29, 1912, "that [Gary's claim] is a great challenge, and I want to consider with you to what extent it is true, and, indeed, what the actual facts are as to the treatment of labor." His "facts" showed that the "iron master" employed many men who worked twelve hours a day, seven days a week, at wages little above starvation level; 65 per cent of the workers earned less than the minimum cost of living. "The system" meant workers old at forty, whose "children and, to a certain extent, their children's children, would be degenerates." [22] Far from "comparing favorably" with labor conditions in other industries, Brandeis maintained that the life of steel workers was "so inhuman as to make our former negro slavery infinitely preferable, for the master owned the slave, and tried to keep his property in working order for his own interest." [23]

The Steel Trust, he told the Stanley Committee, looks on its slaves as something to be worked out and thrown aside. Nor is it true that the burden is borne wholly by their families. This "parasitic industry" flourishes at the expense of the community: "We are protecting this corporation by a tariff, by a duty, supposed to be in the interests of the American workingmen. We are bearing a part of its burdens also, the rest of the community, by paying now and paying hereafter the taxes which go to support those who have been made paupers thereby." [24]

Men may reasonably differ as to wages and hours, Brandeis observed, going to the heart of the matter. The crucial question "is whether any men in the United States, be they directors of the Steel Corporation or anyone else, are entitled and can safely determine the conditions under which a large portion of the American [workmen] shall live; whether it is not absolutely essential to fairness, for results in an American democracy, to say that the great mass of working people should have an opportunity to combine, and by their collective bargaining secure for themselves what may be a fair return for their labor." [25]

Welfare work, pensions, and profit-sharing, as proudly cited by Judge Gary, were being forced on the trust by social workers and others, but these did not and could not make up for starvation wages and the absence of collective bargaining. Under pretense of granting pensions, the corporation was actually binding its workers to long service and conduct pleasing to the management. A better name for this device would be "pensioned peonage." * [26]

---

* Acting on behalf of the Boston & Maine Railroad employees, Brandeis secured a pension bill (Ch. 435, Acts of 1909), signed by Governor E. S. Draper, which embodies the feature he deemed vital. The keynote of this pension plan is co-operation. The system is co-operative first in contributions, the funds being supplied in equal amounts by employer and employees, subject only to the employer's making up any deficiency so that the minimum pension shall not be less than $200 per annum. To meet the hardships of those already advanced in years and service, the employer undertakes additional contribution, the precise amount being left to his discretion. With a view to encouraging a reasonably large old-age income, provision is also made whereby the regular pensions may be supplemented by annuities voluntarily purchased by the men themselves through current contributions from wages.

Second, the system is co-operative as to its establishment and management. The vote of both the railroad and the employees is required for adoption, and two-thirds of the employees participating must vote affirmatively. The rules governing the system are made by a Board of Trustees in which the railroad and the employees have equal representation.

Under "profit-sharing" or employer-stock ownership, $12,000,000 had been distributed among employees during the ten years that scheme existed. But Brandeis pointed out that these benefits were in fact inconsequential. The average share of profit due each employee during this period was only six dollars a year as compared with $435,000,000 added to assets, $220,000,000 paid out in dividends on watered stock, and $62,500,000 paid Mr. Perkins's firm of J. P. Morgan for a few months' work as managers of the syndicate creating United States Steel. "Is that," Brandeis inquired, "Mr. Perkins's idea of justice to be attained through these great corporations by applying profit-sharing?" [27] Profit-sharing, like the pension scheme, was but "another of the chains to rivet employees to their employer and deprive them of the liberty of American citizens." [28]

How, in America, Brandeis asked, can anybody explain such conditions of work and "living"? There was but one answer—the employers' successful elimination of trade unionism:

All the power of capital and all the ability and intelligence of the men who wield and who serve the capital have been used to make practically slaves of these operatives, because it does not mean merely in respect to the way in which they have lived, but the very worst part of all this is the repression. It is a condition of repression, of slavery in the real sense of the word, which is alien to American conditions.[29]

The situation was indefensible even in terms of the industrial magnates' own selfish interest. In thwarting trade unionism they sincerely believed they were forestalling the rise of socialism. Actually their hated system of repression and espionage, "the like of which you cannot find this side of [Czarist] Russia," only provided the best kind of seed-bed for socialism. That is why Brandeis could say: "Socialism has been developed largely by the power of individual trusts." [30]

To block socialism, industrial management must share with labor the responsibility of running the business. Then only would management get a full return for labor's hire. The pension and profit-sharing plan, he said, "must be their own business and they must get all the fruit of what is

---

Third, the system creates a body of specific legal rights. If the worker ceases to be an employee of the company, he loses the pension proper, but is then entitled to receive an amount equal to that which he has paid in.

Fourth, the Boston and Maine Act contains a so-called elective obligatory clause, then a new feature in pension legislation. That is, the system when established by the vote of the railroad and the employees becomes obligatory upon all persons thereafter entering the employment, and upon all persons in the employ of the railroad at the time the system was established, unless such person both voted against adoption of the system, and recorded within three months his individual objection to it. Finally, this pension system is placed under state supervision; both the insurance commissioner and the state actuary join in guarding it so as to secure the greatest possible stability and social benefit.

earned over a fair return on capital. . . . Profit-sharing is co-operative work." He offered this theory of employer-employee relations in support of the one "principle by which lasting success can be obtained. . . . Those who do the work shall get in some fair proportion what they produce. The share to which capital is entitled is small. All the rest should go to those, high and low, who do the work." [31]

These and other pronouncements led not a few to regard Brandeis as biased in favor of labor and ignoring its misdeeds. After a speech noting that the oppressions of big business quite naturally produced labor violence, Alfred, January 2, 1912, expressed disapproval of his brother's stand in strong terms: "I must say that if the *Cincinnati Enquirer* of this morning quoted you correctly in your Canton and Columbus, Ohio, speech, I am afraid you are too radical for me to follow. I do not believe that I can subscribe to any justification of the Los Angeles dynamiting, or in any way excuse what the McNamaras or their friends have done. I am afraid it is too much of an arraying of Labor against Capital, for me to follow in your footsteps."

What his brother had not understood was that Brandeis had tried to explain, not justify, such lawlessness. Men of the McNamara stripe were, to him, "like miserable, stupid children, undertaking to solve a difficult problem by the commission of unpardonable crimes. But we should be wise enough to see that their act was the horrible expression of that unrest which arises from injustice." [32]

Unionism was, in fact, fighting for its very existence; and the overwhelming power of industrial corporations had to be curbed, not the insufficient power of labor unions: ". . . I should not think that the necessities of the situation were such as to require the same protection against the union which we now require against trusts," he had remarked before the Clapp Committee. "I mean we are dealing here with a condition and not a theory." In terms of basic principle, Brandeis's attitude toward autocratic trade unionism and autocratic industrialism was the same. "I think there is no man or body of men," he told the committee, "whose character will stand absolute power, and I should no more think of giving absolute power to unions than I should of giving it to capital monopoly power." [33]

His quarrel with United States Steel and similar trusts was twofold; first, that they were too large to be the most effective instrument of production and distribution; and second, even in those instances where size had not been carried beyond the point of greatest economic efficiency, the trusts were often "too large to be tolerated among the people who desire to be free." [34] He was convinced that such a state of things could not long continue. "Either our people will lose their political independence, or they will acquire industrial independence. We cannot exist half free and half slave." [35]

In the course of his statement before the Clapp Committee, Brandeis had produced a clipping stating that Judge Elbert H. Gary, chairman of the Board of Directors of the United States Steel Corporation, had given his wife a $500,000 pearl necklace for Christmas. This to Brandeis was dangerous in view of social discontent prevalent in the country. "Is it not," he inquired, "just the same sort of thing which brought on the French Revolution?" [36] This query elicited from the press a storm of opprobrium. It was called "demagogic appeal to class prejudice," "cheap bid for sensationalism," "breach of good taste." Gary, in grief, declared: "I am surprised that Mr. Brandeis should be the author of such an attack. I did not think he would make such unsupportable statements. I thought he was a bigger man." [37]

But in citing this extravagance Brandeis had a serious purpose. "Social unrest," he said, "is largely caused by industrial oppression on one side and ostentatious extravagance on the other. The extravagance attributed to Schwab, Gary, and others could not have other than a bad effect. There have been stories of trained nurses and special chefs for puppy dogs. How do you suppose this strikes a man making less than or at most a bare living wage for his family?" [38] The conservative *Boston Transcript* now applauded: ". . . It is dangerous to flaunt luxury in the face of the unwashed and underfed. Some of our cavaliers of high finance have not learned this simple lesson. They needed a shock, and Mr. Brandeis administered it." [39]

In January 1912 the industrial storm broke in the textile town of Lawrence, Massachusetts, where a polyglot pool of immigrant labor—Poles, Italians, Lithuanians, Germans, Armenians, French-Canadians—went on strike. The Industrial Workers of the World, a body dedicated to relentless prosecution of the "class struggle," sent Joseph Ettor and William D. ("Big Bill") Haywood to lead the unorganized uprising. Violence and bitter conflict followed. Militia armed with guns and bayonets were marched into town; riots ensued; police were pelted with rocks, and strikers clubbed.

At the height of the Lawrence struggle Marlen E. Pew induced Senator Miles Poindexter to study conditions there with the idea of exposing the situation on the floor of the Senate. While gathering information, the Senator conferred with Brandeis, and after their discussion wrote to Pew: "I wish I could talk longer with Mr. Brandeis tonight—then I would feel prepared to make a speech tomorrow. I do not feel quite prepared now." [40] At Pew's suggestion Brandeis gave Senator Poindexter the strategy for his speech: "Probably the most effective order of presentation would be to set

forth the facts showing reason to believe that citizens and aliens have, under the guise of administering or enforcing the law, been denied civil
rights. Then, develop terrible dangers to the whole country from any
weakening of respect for the law arising from wresting it to suppress the
strike. Describe the condition of workers in the industry, where, as in the
steel industry, tariff and combinations have protected the producer and
left the workers without protection. Then point out existing conditions,
the natural result of denying the worker the right of combination; and
that through unions alone can rights be protected and social justice
done. . . ." [41]

The Senate proved singularly unreceptive to such rationally conservative notions. "The Senate of the United States," Poindexter reported after
giving his speech, "is probably the most discouraging place in the world,
unless it be some such body as the House of Lords of England, to which
to make an appeal of this kind. It certainly is not enthusing to see a lot of
self-satisfied old fossils quibbling and pettifogging over forms and precedents, and chuckling or jeering over the unfortunate condition of these
mill workers." [42]

To Brandeis, however, the inevitable conflict at Lawrence served as an
object lesson, as substantial proof for much that he had maintained before
the Clapp and Stanley Committees. This outburst showed growing doubt
as to the impartiality of local police and civil authorities, and a consequent
decline in respect for law throughout the nation, not only on the part of
workingmen, but among employers, among prominent and "conservative"
citizens. Such was Brandeis's view of the crisis confronting America on
the eve of the 1912 presidential election.

PART IV

In National Politics

CHAPTER TWENTY-THREE

Progressive Politics and La Follette,
1911-1912

DURING 1910 and 1911 the American political barometer was steadily falling. Occasional thunderclaps, like the bitter strike at Lawrence, Massachusetts, foretold approaching storm. The Taft administration, drifting aimlessly, battered by the Ballinger investigation, crippled by popular hatred of the Payne–Aldrich Tariff, saw breakers ahead, especially after the 1910 elections, when Democrats and Progressives gained control of Congress and of many states. That disheartened star boarder of Republicanism observed with alarm: "There is so much demagoguery these days and the people seem to like it. . . . Intelligent men have lost their heads and are leaning toward fool, radical views in a way I never thought possible. . . . The day of the demagogue, the liar, and the silly is on." [1]

Dynamic publicists and political agitators had long been clamoring for public attention. An extraordinary galaxy of talent had embarked on the people's crusade: literary devotees of exposure, such as Lincoln Steffens and Ida M. Tarbell; such investigators of specific corruption in high places as Charles Evans Hughes; political champions such as William Jennings Bryan, Theodore Roosevelt, and Robert M. La Follette had challenged the dominance of our financial–political oligarchy and had roused the American people for social and institutional reform. But little had been accomplished at the national level as compared with what Brandeis, had achieved in New England. This was due in large measure to the fact that his method and purpose differed sharply from theirs.

For fifteen years, since the beginning of his career as the People's Attorney in the Boston Traction case of 1897, Brandeis had been trying to get business to stop buying political favors and politicians to stop selling them. He had also tried to get trade unions to assume more social responsibility in order to forestall government regulation, believing that encroachment of business on politics and politics on business only hastened the coming of socialism. Brandeis would not have paid *any* price to avoid socialism; but he would have paid a good price. Part of that price for business would have been the maintenance of competition, even if it meant allowing someone else to have part of the coveted market. For labor, part of that price would have been the sacrifice of the closed shop, so that no one, in order to earn his daily bread, would be forced to join and pay dues to a union. Business, thought Brandeis, must voluntarily give up its attempt to monopolize markets; unions must voluntarily give up their attempt to monopolize jobs. Only by keeping markets free and jobs open to all could America keep its other freedoms as well.

Brandeis had been fighting monopolies of one kind or another for a long time, but the trend toward monopoly was probably stronger in 1912 than ever before. He was beginning to think that perhaps self-regulation by business and labor was not working so well; he was beginning to think that government must intervene to maintain free competition for markets and for jobs. Like so many reformers (even as far back as 1904 when T.R. first ran for President), he was leaning more and more toward a well-rounded program of federal legislation to keep business from swallowing up freedom in America.

Now was the time to translate constructive ideas into such a program of national legislation. The trumpets of reform had long been blaring, and yet the reign of T.R. and the incumbency of Taft had produced surprisingly little. It had been an era of big pretensions and small achievements.

By 1912—or more accurately, 1911, when the presidential campaign was getting under way—Brandeis was ready to support any candidate whose program seemed to promise what he had been fighting for. It mattered little which party rode in on the popular demand for action, so long as it carried the banner of Progressivism to fruitful victory. He saw then what is now clear to all: that modern social and economic issues cut across traditional party frontiers. A new political alignment was necessary, dividing on the issues which actually do separate reactionaries from progressives.

LA FOLLETTE EMERGES

As far as Brandeis was concerned, two of the more likely presidential candidates had already eliminated themselves. Brandeis had voted for Taft in 1908; * but whatever optimism he may have felt about Taft's progres-

---

* Brandeis wrote Alfred, November 4, 1908: "I voted for Taft, but am sorry he won by so large a majority. I wish he had had a margin of not over 10 [electoral votes].

"As it is, I am glad the Republicans have the whole administration. There will be no divided responsibility.

"Taft is admirably qualified for the position and doubtless will, if he lives, prove a fine President, rather of the Cleveland type; but I fear the Republican party will be less manageable

sivism had vanished by 1910.[2] Brandeis now regarded Taft as a "wobbler," with "no firm convictions." Having associated all his life with men of wealth and privilege, Taft had "incorrigibly aristocratic leanings." [3] The Ballinger investigation had displayed the President's real political character all too clearly. Moreover, Brandeis felt, even if Taft were the right man, the Ballinger case had made it probable that, if renominated, the President would be defeated.[4]

Nor was Theodore Roosevelt, recently returned from a lion hunt in the African wilds, the man of the emerging hour. Beyond adherence to Progressivism, the People's Attorney and the Rough Rider had, in fact, little or nothing in common. The Colonel had served a useful function, Brandeis conceded, in the period of "agitation." His colorful moral crusading had awakened the American conscience to the existence of abuses and had given momentum to the demand for reform.[5]

But Roosevelt was "not objective in his thinking" on the trust issue; he had never really struck the evils at which he had shaken his big stick. T.R.'s fervid call for "the moral regeneration of business" and his habit of punitive verbal onslaught against "the plundering rich," counterbalanced by a similar attack on "demagogues" and "radicals," was not likely to devise the correctives necessary to set business free.[6] La Follette had best expressed the reformers' opinion of Roosevelt when he said that his "cannonading, first in one direction and then in another, filled the air with noise and smoke, which confused and obscured the line of action, but, when the battle cloud drifted by and quiet was restored, it was always a matter of surprise that so little had been accomplished." [7]

Writing about the political situation to Norman Hapgood on April 9, 1912, Brandeis sent along these lines from Lowell:

> New times demand new issues and new men,
>   The world advances, and in time outgrows the laws
>   That in our fathers' time were best;
>   And, doubtless, after us some purer scheme
>   Will be shaped out by wiser men than we,—
>   Made wiser by the steady growth of truth.

The one man who could be trusted to fight for the new issues was La Follette—"The Little Giant of Wisconsin." Brandeis had first met him in Washington in 1910, during the Ballinger case. Their acquaintance quickly ripened into friendship. Mrs. La Follette wrote Brandeis, June 15, 1910:

Every day since you left Washington I have thought I would write you— not just to thank you for the roses which were indeed lovely and lasted a long,

than under Roosevelt and that we shall see much of the money bags we abhor, and whom the V.P. [James S. Sherman] properly represents."

long time, but to tell you how much we thought of you, how much we missed you, and how glad we were that this year had brought you to us. The other day Robert said: "Mother, I believe I like Mr. Brandeis the best of any one we know." Then he qualified it—"Of course not better than Mr. Steffens but better than almost any one else." And that is the way we all feel.

You have done a great work for the nation these past few months. I know that your philosophy and temperament will always keep you busy in the public interest. Probably you can accomplish more as a free lance than in any other way. But I can't help thinking how fine it would be to have you instead of Lodge in the Senate.

Beginning with the Ballinger days the Boston lawyer had a standing invitation to the La Follettes' for a "cold potato" supper. What these meetings lacked in culinary interest was compensated for in the stimulating exchange of constructive ideas. On questions of conservation, railroads, and trusts, these zealous insurgents conversed, exchanged ideas, co-operated, with an eye single to specific and constructive betterment. On fundamentals they were in accord; as to details they were not always agreed.

La Follette's program involved a strong and more direct control of government by the people through such measures as judicial recall, direct nominations, the initiative, and the referendum. He would assault the citadels of corporate power by the devices of income and inheritance taxes, railroad regulation, and more drastic anti-trust laws. Brandeis was in full sympathy with this latter strategy but not with the Senator's ideas on direct government. He had little interest in plans for tinkering with federal machinery. But the strong personal attachment between them served to allay minor differences. Brandeis had the highest admiration for "Fighting Bob's" grit, persistence, and unswerving adherence to his convictions.

But could La Follette be elected President? His forthright, uncompromising nature was not an asset for a would-be national leader who must win all sorts of opinion. He belonged to that rare political species, willing to lose again and again rather than stoop to vote-getting opportunism. Brandeis realized this, but once more he had no choice. Nevertheless it may serve to explain why Brandeis, in spite of unfailing friendship, entertained grave misgivings when La Follette decided to enter the presidential race.[8]

The nucleus of a La Follette-for-President movement was the National Progressive Republican League, organized in December 1910. With La Follette as its leading spirit, the League included prominent Progressives such as Brandeis, Charles R. Crane, Frederic C. Howe, William Allen White, James R. Garfield, Gifford Pinchot, and several Progressive Republican Senators.[9] The League was formed ostensibly for the purpose of attaining more direct popular government; but its real aim, which soon became clear, was to establish Progressive control of the Republican party and put over the nomination of La Follette.[10]

In April 1911 congressional insurgents formally invited La Follette to become the Progressive candidate for President, and soon thereafter he appointed a manager, collected funds, and began a vigorous campaign. During the summer of 1911, as he stumped the country spreading the Progressive gospel, the ranks of his adherents grew steadily. A political "prairie fire" was reported to be sweeping on from the West, and Old Guard Republicanism seemed in imminent danger of being burned out by Wisconsin "radicalism." [11]

The La Follette boom was about at its zenith when two of the Senator's leading supporters—Rudolph Spreckels, the California Sugar King, and Medill McCormick, the radical Chicago publisher—appeared in Boston and visited Brandeis. After what was described as a very satisfactory conference, Brandeis announced that he would support La Follette for the Republican nomination. The La Follette emissaries had come to Massachusetts principally to size up the strength of Progressive Republicanism there, but it was suspected that in making their survey they had asked Brandeis to lead the campaign in Massachusetts. When Brandeis was asked whether he had been invited to undertake such a task, he replied evasively, "That is not possible. I am not a political man and could hardly assume such a responsibility, but I am ready outside of that to co-operate in every way." [12] He did not pretend to know how much support La Follette had in Massachusetts, but personally he was all for him: "I consider him the best statesman we have for the accomplishment of the reforms that are needed at this time. . . ." [13]

ALARM AND CONFUSION

Brandeis's support of La Follette was disturbing to Massachusetts Democratic leaders. The rank and file of that party, as well as Democratic Governor Eugene Foss, had counted on Brandeis in their campaign, and it had been expected that he would write the platform. "The Democrats want a Democratic platform," observed the *Boston Journal,* "and they want a Democrat to write it; and one, no matter how well written, when prepared by a La Follette Republican insurgent, is not to their taste." [14]

The confusion was confounded shortly after when Brandeis came out in support of Foss in the state campaign. While Democrats were somewhat embarrassed by his support, the Republicans attempted to ridicule the apparent inconsistency of his position. Foss's Republican rival, Louis A. Frothingham, had received hearty endorsement from the People's Attorney in the campaign of 1905 for mayor of Boston, and the Republican state committee now made the most of it. The party's state headquarters issued copies of his 1905 speeches declaring that Frothingham was the only one of five candidates fit to be mayor. Pro-Frothingham statements, calculated to embarrass Brandeis, were dug up and published. Sharp contrasts were drawn between his support of Frothingham in 1905 as a "great public service," and his denunciation of him in 1911 as "undeniably . . . a conservative, if not indeed a reactionary."[15]

For the "leading Progressive in Massachusetts" to be a Democrat in that state and a Republican in the nation, was especially disconcerting in view of his political influence. "Make no mistake about it," a "prominent Republican" was quoted in the Boston American, "the active support of Foss by Brandeis means the votes of at least 10,000 Republican Progressives. The people believe in Brandeis. . . ."[16]

Confusion of one kind in Massachusetts was matched by confusion of another kind in the nation. While the Progressive Republicans were backing La Follette, the regular Republican machine was organizing for Taft. In the middle was the colorful and still enormously popular T.R., and for once he was saying absolutely nothing.[17]

On June 25, 1910, after attending R. J. Collier's dinner at Sherry's in honor of T.R., Brandeis had written his brother: "I had a few moments' talk with Roosevelt and also some talk in the afternoon with Pinchot. I feel sure T.R. will not help Taft." But would he help La Follette? Brandeis thought not. On September 23, 1910, he had written journalist Judson Welliver: ". . . One of my ingenious friends asserts that there is no occasion to be exercised on the question as to whether Roosevelt will be the 1912 candidate. He asserts that Roosevelt, talking in parables, has already declared that he would not, and refers to a letter Roosevelt wrote to some English lord, in which he refers to Timoleon as the character he most admired in history. Pull out your encyclopedia and read up Timoleon unless, unlike myself, you are already fully equipped with knowledge on the subject."

Timoleon, Brandeis had discovered, was a Greek statesman and general who, after becoming master of the city of Syracuse and winning a great victory over the Carthaginians, retired to private life without title or office. Significantly, perhaps, he remained powerful both in Syracuse and in Sicily because of his prestige.

Roosevelt was doing nothing to sustain or correct these impressions. His silence was making many Progressives uneasy, but they held their convention in Chicago on October 16, 1911, and endorsed La Follette's candidacy. On October 21 the Boston Transcript called the La Follette candidacy "a premature explosion" and hinted that Progressives who were neither Taft men nor La Follette men were "evidently playing a waiting game" with the idea that if La Follette could block Taft's nomination, the situation might be "turned to the account of somebody else." As late as November 26, 1911, Roosevelt declared he was not a candidate. The more frequently he said it, however, the less people believed him.

ON THE STUMP

In spite of growing signs that Roosevelt would push La Follette out of the presidential contest, Brandeis rallied to the fighting Wisconsinite's support. He consented, though somewhat reluctantly, to go on a speaking tour through the Middle West, beginning January first. He wrote Walter L. Houser, La Follette's campaign manager, on December 21, remarking that he had no experience in political campaigning and inquiring whether it was still important for him to speak. At La Follette's insistence he went ahead, but requested that because of his inexperience he should appear only after one or more other speakers, so that he might "get the feel in an unfamiliar situation." [18] To Columbus, Chicago, Minneapolis, and St. Paul he went gathering "new experience." He spoke mainly on the trust issue, repeating the ideas expressed earlier in articles and before congressional committees, and especially praising the La Follette–Stanley Anti-Trust bill, of which he was himself the author.[19] His was not the customary variety of campaign speech. "I am no politician," he insisted, and stuck usually to measures rather than men. He refused to discuss the politics of the campaign or commit himself as to La Follette's chances. "Is the anti-Taft sentiment of the East for La Follette?" he was asked in Minneapolis, "or is it looking toward Roosevelt?" His reply was adroit: "The anti-Taft sentiment in the East is just beginning to find expression. Interest in national politics has been slower to arouse there than in the West. The people of the East are naturally conservative. . . ." [20] Occasionally, however, he departed from even-tempered discussion of policies and came out with a strong personal appeal for Fighting Bob.

Brandeis's speeches, while quiet and restrained, often carried great emotional intensity. Describing his address at a Progressive meeting in Columbus, the *Cleveland Plain Dealer* said: ". . . In the quiet but highly remarkable speech of Mr. Brandeis there was a gripping, throbbing appeal for the strongest support the delegates could give 'the man whose fight for many years was made alone but always for the people.' " [21]

"Making political speeches is a new thing for me," Brandeis told a St. Paul audience "but I want to tell what I think of La Follette." In Chicago he showed the depth of his admiration for his candidate by declaring that

La Follette understood the needs of the American people as no man had since Abraham Lincoln.[22] There he said: "The real fight today is against the inhuman, relentless exercise of capitalistic power. First we had the struggle for independence, and the second great struggle in our history was to keep the nation whole and abolish slavery. The present struggle in which we are engaged is for social and industrial justice. A few years ago we needed education so that the workers could exercise their right at the ballot box. But reading and writing is not enough. We must have right living conditions. . . . The fight for direct primaries, the initiative, referendum, and recall is good, but they are only means to the real end, which is the declaration of the rights of man." [23]

Although Brandeis was no natural campaigner, newspaper reports indicate that he was well received. Arriving in Minneapolis with the temperature at eighteen degrees below zero, he won the hearts of the Minnesotans when he remarked, shivering all the while: "The Minnesota air is so dry and invigorating that you don't feel the cold." [24]

BATTLE BOB SLIPS, BRANDEIS STICKS

Meanwhile Roosevelt's position was getting clearer—he was going to be a candidate, and some of La Follette's strongest supporters were about to switch to T.R. La Follette and the leading Progressives, including Brandeis, met in Washington on January 29, 1912. Several of La Follette's lieutenants, who first and foremost were Roosevelt men, demanded that the Progressive candidate abandon the contest to the Colonel. The redoubtable Little Giant, however, had never intended to be "a political minute man," and refused to withdraw. Accordingly, Medill McCormick, Gifford Pinchot, and Amos Pinchot, major backers of the La Follette boom, moved over to the Roosevelt camp.

The stage was set for wholesale desertion to T.R. by the chronic Teddy-worshipers when La Follette made his ill-fated speech before the Magazine Publishers' Association in Philadelphia on February 2. Worn out by illness in his family and bitter at what he considered bad faith on the part of certain of his followers, he launched an attack before the magnates of the publishing business against the perversion of the press by money power, repeating himself over and over in a long and confused speech. He gave way momentarily to his tightened emotions, giving rise to the false report that he had suffered a "breakdown" and was withdrawing from the fight.

"The news from La Follette is, of course, distressing," Brandeis wrote Alfred on February 7, "but if the smash is not a bad one, it may be all for the best to have him completely out of the presidential race. I was sorry when he concluded to enter it. Personally, I shall be glad to have no political obligations."

But La Follette was not yet ready to quit, and Brandeis, almost alone among his chief advisers, continued to support him. Shortly after the Philadelphia fiasco, Amos Pinchot issued a public statement announcing that La Follette's withdrawal made it necessary for Progressives to unite behind Roosevelt. When La Follette continued to be a candidate, Pinchot was considerably disconcerted. "I think that you have more influence over the Senator than anyone else at this juncture," he wrote Brandeis on February 9. "He has lost confidence and is unwilling to talk to most of the crowd." Brandeis answered rather curtly on February 13 that he had not seen La Follette nor heard from him since the meeting on January 29, when the rupture among his chief supporters had taken place.

Still La Follette's position was collapsing. On February 21 Roosevelt practically put an end to La Follette's candidacy when he finally announced: "My hat is in the ring." Brandeis was urged to rally behind the Rough Rider's candidacy. His old friend George Rublee wrote him that T.R. had spoken highly of him and solicited a conference at Oyster Bay. Rublee felt—and he was seconded by Felix Frankfurter—that Brandeis, better than anybody else, could give T.R. a deeper understanding of the real issues.[25] But Brandeis remained loyal to La Follette: "No man in public life expresses the ideals of American Democracy so fully as does La Follette in his thought, his acts, his living. No man in public life today has done so much toward the attainment of those ideals. He is farseeing, of deep convictions and indomitable will; straightforward, able, hardworking, persistent and courageous. His character is simple. He is patient, save only of wrongs done the people."[26]

To the voters of Nebraska, Brandeis wired on April 15: "Nebraska's endorsement of La Follette as Republican candidate for President would go far to assure to the American people the triumph of progressive principles; . . . America needs now a great constructive statesman, a leader with deep and passionate sympathy for the common people. La Follette possesses those qualities. He should be the choice of the Republican voters."[27]

Brandeis's loyalty kept the La Follette campaign alive. "This is a real Macedonian cry," W. L. Houser wired Brandeis from California, April 22. "You must come and help carry California. You can do more here than any other man we know. It will be a great sacrifice for you to make but do come if you possibly can. We lost Nebraska and Oregon on account of lack of help." William E. Smythe, who was attempting to halt the Roosevelt tide in the Far West, wired Brandeis on April 30: "Have gone into fight for La Follette, whose desertion by leaders is deeply resented by progressive masses. Tide rising amazingly. Believe carry state. Hope you come out in strong statement. . . . One blast upon your bugle horn worth ten thousand men."

Smythe used Brandeis's name to advantage with the voters of California. There was great significance, he pointed out, in the fact that Brandeis, "who knows more about the trusts than any other man in the country today, is opposed to Roosevelt, because he knows that he is the unblushing candidate of the steel trust. . . . Brandeis is stumping Massachusetts tonight for La Follette because Roosevelt, the man who dared to face the lions in Africa, surrendered to the lions of Wall Street." [28] But they could not win back the thousands enchanted by the rough-riding Colonel. On May 16 the *Boston Herald,* reporting funds contributed to the La Follette campaign in Massachusetts, indicated how abandoned and isolated was the team of La Follette and Brandeis. The total amount was five hundred and ten dollars. Two gentlemen had given five dollars apiece. The rest was listed under the name of Louis D. Brandeis.

The La Follette cause, with slim chance of success from the beginning, had long since become hopeless. When the Republican National Convention met in June 1912, La Follette's boom was officially over. Roosevelt had seen to that; but now he had another fight on his hands—a fight against the Republican machine. Roosevelt had stumped the country in an uproarious campaign and was at his colorful best during the weeks before the convention. His speeches electrified great masses of average Americans; and he had the powerful support of George W. Perkins of United States Steel and International Harvester, Frank Munsey the newspaper publisher, and other leading industrialists and financiers. The Republican party organization, however, remained doggedly behind Taft, and no amount of Rooseveltian histrionics could split it. In spite of the Rough Rider's famous thunderbolt, "We stand at Armageddon, and we battle for the Lord," the nomination was nailed to the mast for Taft. Roosevelt then decided to run on his own party.

CHAPTER TWENTY-FOUR

Finding His Captain, 1912

BRANDEIS could accept neither the Old Guard Republicanism of Taft, nor the pseudo-Progressivism of Roosevelt. He felt keenly the need for a united Progressive party, of members drawn from the ranks of both older parties, so as to reflect the real issues. The chance that such a party would emerge to carry through the measures for which he had long been agitating appeared now to have been thwarted by the loyalties of practical politics and the fascination of political rhetoric. If only there could be a clear-cut division between reaction and progress instead of "the issue of T.R.!" [1]

That clear-cut division did not exist in the Republican party; if it existed in the nation at all, it was only between Republicans and Democrats—especially after the Democrats at their convention in Baltimore on July 2, 1912, nominated Woodrow Wilson, the Governor of New Jersey, for President. The next day Brandeis wrote La Follette: "I know that you will be delighted with the action of Bryan and the Baltimore Convention, as you think so well of both Bryan and Wilson. It seems to me that those Progressives who do not consider themselves bound by party affiliations ought to give Wilson thorough support, not only to insure his election, but to give him all the aid and comfort which he will need to maintain the Progressive position which he has assumed and to carry out the Progressive policies. I wish I might have a chance to talk this over with you soon."

Here was a new chance. The Progressives had lost the Republican nomination; they could still win the election with a Democrat.

Brandeis had never met or even seen the Democratic candidate, but from all he had heard of Wilson, he seemed to have the qualities of a Progressive leader. The Democratic party, moreover, had taken a strong stand for Progressive principles. In a resolution introduced by William Jennings Bryan the party had renounced any affiliation with "the privilege-hunting and favor-seeking class," and with any Democrats in that class. The resolution practically read out of the party by name such financiers as Thomas Fortune Ryan and August Belmont. [2] For Brandeis, this confirmed the party's determination to "drive the money lenders out of the temple." [3] His fervent hope of 1910 seemed now to be fulfilled: "If only there were a Democratic party. What havoc would be wrought!" [4]

Brandeis urged all good Progressives to rally to Wilson's banner. That seemed to him the only course for Progressives—for La Follette men, Roosevelt men, Democrats, and even some Taft men. [5] If Progressives

fought Wilson, there was the chance of a two-term reactionary Taft administration, a noisy but futile Roosevelt administration, or a Wilson administration made impotent by lack of support. But if Progressives rallied
behind Wilson and conservative Democrats went over to Taft, party lines
would be drawn realistically and Brandeis's hope of a clear issue between
Conservatism and Progressivism would be realized. Accordingly, Brandeis
publicly came out for Wilson:

His nomination ranks among the most encouraging events in American history . . . for he possesses in a high degree the qualities of an effective progressive leader. . . . He understands the dangers incident to the control of a
few of our industries and finance. He sees that true democracy and social justice
are unattainable unless the power of the few be curbed, and our democracy become industrial as well as political. . . . But the struggle of privilege for privilege is unending and omnipresent. That struggle is as subtle as it is determined.
The struggle will not close when Wilson is elected. We may be sure that every
effort he may make as President to carry out the Progressive policies will meet
the stubborn resistance from the possessors and apostles of privilege. . . .
The progressive cause can succeed only if it has loyal support from the progressives. It can fail only if the progressives fail in their duty of giving Wilson their
full support.[6]

In taking his stand with Wilson, Brandeis parted company with many
old friends and colleagues. Both Gifford Pinchot and George Rublee expressed their regret at his decision. Rublee wrote him on July 18: "I grieve
that you are not to be in the new [Roosevelt] party, because I think it
needs you more than perhaps any other man."

"T.R. is pretty near irresistible," Brandeis commented on reading that
his friend Henry Moskowitz had joined the Progressive party.[7] But Brandeis stood firm, believing that T.R. was leading "not the Progressive party
but a Roosevelt party."[8]

Brandeis's shifts in political allegiance from Taft to La Follette, and then
to Wilson, were later used to discredit him. Actually he was entirely consistent in the terms of his one dominating purpose—to put through essential reforms. He was not interested in political sectarianism and evangelism.
He wanted things done progressively and objectively. He had no concern
with partisanship. Parties, groups, and individual political figures were to
him but tools for putting constructive ideas into effect. In the shifting cur-
rents of politics, men and political organizations had to be used and dis-
carded as conditions of the moment demanded. His frequent statements
that he was not a political man were in a sense true. When he took part in
campaign fights and put his influence behind one candidate or another, it
was only as a means to an end, and the personalities involved were only

incidentally important. This attitude was, of course, modified sometimes by personal loyalties, as in the case of his faithful adherence to La Follette. The campaign of 1912, however, was for him chiefly a search for the best vehicle by which to put his economic proposals into effect.

THE CAMPAIGN BEGINS

Brandeis's direct relation with Wilson began on August 1, 1912, when he wrote the candidate: "This morning's news that you will suggest dealing with the tariff by reducing the duties gradually at the rate of 5 per cent a year is further evidence that the country may expect from you a wisely progressive administration. The simple plan which you suggest is true statesmanship; and the real tariff reformers should rally to your support."

To this letter Wilson replied: "Your letter of August first has given me a great deal of pleasure. I have been very much cheered and reassured by the knowledge of your approval and support. I sincerely hope that the months to come will draw us together and give me the benefit of many conferences with you."

Late in August, Brandeis received a telegram from Charles R. Crane, saying that Wilson would like to see him. Accordingly, on August 27, he took a night boat to New York, ate breakfast at the Albemarle Hotel, visited the Democratic Headquarters in New York, and rode down to Sea Girt, New Jersey.[9] There, on the afternoon of the 28th, the People's Attorney and the Democratic presidential nominee had lunch and a three-hour talk. They discussed social and industrial problems, chiefly the trust question, which promised to be the leading issue of the campaign.[10] Apparently each man was impressed with the other. After the meeting Brandeis wrote of Wilson: "It seems to me that he has the qualities for an ideal President— strong, simple, and truthful, able, open-minded, eager to learn and deliberate." [11]

A major part of the Sea Girt conference was given to exploring the weaknesses of Roosevelt's party (Brandeis and Wilson conceded Taft the conservatives) and planning how to exploit those weaknesses in the campaign. This was not hard to do. The principles of Roosevelt's party as enunciated at Chicago were the antithesis of those Brandeis had been advocating. Under Roosevelt, industrial problems were to be resolved by having business "be good"; the "inevitable" trend toward monopoly was not to be interfered with; attacks on business under the Sherman Anti-Trust Act would cease; wicked practices in business would be restrained or punished; labor would be aided by "welfare" measures. In short, the Bull Moose platform was the gospel of gentility in politics. Dominant in its administration would be corporation executives like Perkins [12] and

Munsey, who were Roosevelt's chief lieutenants, aided by such assorted gentlemen and ladies as Harold L. Ickes, Boss Bill Flinn, Professor Charles E. Merriam, and Jane Addams. They had great hopes, but first they would have to get in.

Roosevelt's spokesmen tried to becloud the campaign by defining the issues between T.R. and Wilson as regulation versus destructive, wasteful competition. Brandeis, however, dissipated the confusion with a question which summed up the real difference between the two parties: "Shall we regulate competition or monopoly?"[13] His work was creating some trouble for the enemy, and there was more trouble ahead.

Soon after his August vacation began, Norman Hapgood invited him to define the campaign issues for *Collier's*. He finally consented, though Hapgood found it "hard work" persuading him to give up any part of his vacation.[14] *"Entre nous,* I have Norman supplied with editorials through the October 19 number," he wrote Alfred, September 15, "and shall probably add two more to make the full measure." In these editorials as well as in articles published under his own name, he directed public attention to flaws in the Roosevelt–Perkins scheme for "domesticating" the modern industrial monsters. In proposing not only to legalize monopoly as the future policy, but also to condone past violations of law, the New Party, he maintained, was advocating a course which must seriously undermine respect for law. Already the failure of proceedings against the Oil and Tobacco Trusts gave substance to his belief that the law did not operate with equal effect on rich and poor, and if "flagrant violations of law and ethics" as practiced by the trusts were thus to be given legal sanction, it would shake the legal foundations of the community.[15]

Aside from pointing out the economic and social disadvantages of monopoly, which he had so long expounded, Brandeis called attention to certain practical difficulties in the New Party's program. He knew from experience the limits of regulation. Any pious hope that trusts could be harnessed to the general welfare by helpfully regulatory commissions was certain to be disappointed. The I.C.C., which dealt mainly with one type of industry, and that practically uniform throughout the country, was overworked and ineffective. What supermen would be required to understand the details of thousands of totally different businesses in America! He pointed out, moreover, that the I.C.C. had been unable to control power monopolies, notably the New Haven. Its greatest success had been as regulator of competition.[16]

While lambasting the New Party's program, Brandeis also struck at its sponsors. His major target was Perkins, whose Progressive professions contrasted awkwardly with his business affiliations. In fact, Perkins's presence as chairman of the executive committee and financial mainstay of the Roosevelt party perhaps aroused more suspicion than anything else. His dominant influence in the party embarrassed and disillusioned intelligent Progressives such as Amos Pinchot, who wrote Brandeis, October 8, in the middle of the campaign: "I regret more than I can tell you that George Perkins and Frank Munsey are taking so prominent a place in our party. Munsey is painting us, as he has no right to do, as the party of protection, while Perkins is giving people an opportunity to assume that we are the defenders of the trusts. This makes me pretty sick, for I feel that the great majority of the people who have gone in with us are right-thinking and unselfish."

Privately Brandeis described Perkins as a "menace to the country." [17] In an editorial prepared for *Collier's* he released such a barrage against him that Mark Sullivan objected to it strongly and Hapgood had to soften it.[18] "Isn't the Progressive party trying to serve both God and Mammon?" Brandeis was fond of saying. "Think of Jane Addams on the one hand and George Perkins on the other—'two props of virtue for a Christian prince to stay him from the fall of vanity.'" [19]

While most of the fire was concentrated on the "prime minister" of the New Party, Brandeis did not spare its monarch. He resented T.R.'s decision to run and believed that in taking that course Roosevelt himself became the major obstacle to Progressive triumph. He was convinced that but for the overweening vanity of the Rough Rider, Republican Progressives would have joined Democratic Progressives and captured the Democratic party. As time went on, his feeling became more and more intense. "The more I think of T.R.'s performances, the angrier I get," he had written Alfred on August 31. "It will be an interesting test of the American people to see whether he gains on them this trip." He was inclined to agree with the *New York World* that there were "two overwhelming reasons" for the election of Wilson—Roosevelt and Taft.[20] Gleefully he adopted Clark Howell's paraphrase of Teddy's famous peroration: "We meet at Armageddon to battle for the trusts." [21]

Brandeis's contrasts of Roosevelt and Wilson were particularly effective. The Progressive movement had been fortunate, he agreed, in having T.R. as its leader when it was in the stage of "agitation." The Rough Rider possessed exactly the qualities then needed—"the qualities of the great preacher—emotion, imagination, the dramatic sense and dash . . . not only to arouse men but to create a following." [22] In 1912, however, these qualities were outmoded. A large majority of the American people were aware of existing abuses and the Progressives had become powerful enough to compel the adoption of remedies. Not the warrior, but the constructive statesman was now needed: "We need, in addition to the manly virtues and a quick intelligence, that student quality of diligent, patient inquiry; that true open-mindedness which makes one willing to listen, as well as to speak; and that calm, careful, hard thinking which is essential to sound judgment on legislation. . . . We need the will to labor, as well as the power to achieve." [23] The press, he contended, was under a peculiar obligation in this campaign, to draw the clear distinction between "a man of substance" and "a man of noise." [24]

Though aware that the success of Progressive reform in coming years depended much on the personality of the Chief Executive, Brandeis's attention, as usual, was centered on measures and policies. Wilson relied heavily on him for a definition of the Democratic party's stand on major economic issues, wiring him on September 28: "Please set forth as explicitly as possible the actual measures by which competition can be effectively regulated. The more explicit we are on this point the more completely will the enemies' guns be spiked." In his reply of September 30 Brandeis outlined the "fundamental and irreconcilable" difference between the economic policy of Democrats and of Bull Moosers. The two parties were agreed as to a government commission to regulate business, but the policies which such a commission would administer under the two parties were at opposite poles. The issue between them, as he defined it, was the "difference between industrial liberty and industrial absolutism, tempered by government (that is, party) supervision." The Democrats would maintain competition where it existed and restore it where it had been crushed. They believed that "no methods of regulation ever have been or can be devised to remove the menace in private monopoly and overweening commercial power." The New Party, on the other hand, "does not fear commercial power, however great, if only methods for regulation are provided." Furthermore, it insisted that private monopoly might in many cases be desirable, or in any case, was inevitable, and that trusts should not be dismembered, but should be made "good" by regulation.[25]

Specifically, the Democratic program, while applauding the Sherman Act as embodying a declaration of sound economic policy, called for utilizing twenty-two years' experience under the act to improve the effectiveness of its enforcement. A bill drawn up by Brandeis had been, as we have seen, introduced in Congress by Senator La Follette and Representative A. O. Stanley, and this pointed the line of action. The necessary steps consisted in removing the uncertainties of the Sherman Act by defining practices which unreasonably restrained trade, facilitating its enforcement by the courts, and creating a commission to aid in administering the law.

Brandeis's detailed memorandum went on to tell Wilson how these things could be accomplished.[26]

STUMPING FOR WILSON

Brandeis did not confine himself to writing, counseling, and serving as "idea man." The Democratic National Committee arranged a speaking tour for him, covering New England, New York, Ohio, Illinois, Michigan, and Pennsylvania, and in mid-September he once again took the stump.[27] He spoke mostly before economic clubs and Chambers of Commerce, on his favorite subject—the trusts. He attacked the New Party's platform, and elaborated specific measures of reform. Of T.R.'s platform he was accustomed to observe: "The superstructure is beautiful; but the foundations are fatally defective." [28]

Before the state A.F. of L. at Fitchburg, Massachusetts, September 18, 1912, he thoroughly dissected T.R.'s labor plank. He expressed great admiration for its broad scope and clear language, but observed that the very care with which it had been constructed emphasized its glaring weakness. It pledged the party to social justice and to fourteen measures for improving the condition of the working man. These Brandeis himself heartily approved. But it omitted the one thing without which all else was worthless. Nowhere could he find a hint of the party's unqualified endorsement of labor's *right to organize*. This omission, he pointed out, was the more significant, because the party accepted and defended the trusts, whose labor policy had but one objective—"extermination of organized labor." The mere promise that the trusts would be regulated was no guarantee that their labor policy would be liberalized. Brandeis concluded: "Legislation and commissions—like God—help only 'him who helps himself'; and a social program which accepts these things as a substitute for industrial liberty, instead of using them as a means of securing industrial liberty, is fundamentally unsound. You know perfectly well that no legislation, even when sustained by the court—and no commission, though able and honest —will effectually protect labor, unless the workingmen and public opinion are behind them." [29]

Brandeis's analysis was challenged on September 23 by the *Boston Journal,* which charged him with "misrepresentation of the facts." The paper asserted that he "could not have read the platform," and insisted that he correct his statement. He must have made a mistake, the *Journal* maintained, because the New Party's platform said plainly enough: "We favor the organization of the workers, men and women, as a means of protecting their interests and of promoting their progress." Brandeis in a letter to the editor on September 26 replied that nowhere in that carefully phrased plank was the *right* to organize mentioned. He explained that a right means "something that the law protects," and he showed how a recent decision of the United States Supreme Court (*Adair* v. *U.S.,* 208 U.S. 161) upheld the right of corporations to discharge workers for joining a union. How, therefore, could the trusts complacently "favor the organization of the workers" and at the same time rely on the prevailing law, and on their own strength, to prevent it? What the New Party's attitude amounted to, he said, was: "I am in favor of the law but against its enforcement."

Brandeis concluded his rebuke to the editor of the *Journal* with a pithy expression of his own attitude on labor: "The New Party with its program of a few specific and desirable measures which would mitigate some of the evils of existing industrial conditions, is purposing only to take a certain paternal care of the American workingman, who, if given a fair field, could, in the main, take care of himself."

The argument most frequently used to defend monopoly was the so-called wastefulness of competition. But, said Brandeis, the wastefulness of competition is like the wastefulness of democracy. In a speech at Providence he elaborated this theme:

The wastes of democracy are among the greatest obvious wastes, but we have compensations in democracy which far outweigh that waste, and make it more efficient than absolutism. So it is with competition. Incentive and development which are incident to the freer system of business result in so much greater achievement that the waste is relatively insignificant. The margin between that which men naturally do, and that which they can do, is so great that a system which urges men on to action and develops individual enterprise and initiative is preferable, in spite of the wastes that necessarily attend that process.[30]

Besides, Brandeis pointed out, Wilson proposed to eliminate many of the wastes of competition by regulating it. This would not mean fostering artificial conditions in industry; on the contrary, it was the suppression of competition by the great trusts that had created artificial conditions. To regulate competition meant to remove those spurious competitive practices which destroyed it—the methods of the prize ring, he called them.[31] "Competition should be regulated so that it may be protected," and he compared his position to that of the man "who loved peace so much that he was willing to fight for it."[32]

Brandeis's campaign speeches were so hard-hitting that he was urged for his own political interest to soften his blows. Some Progressives were considering him for the Senate, and he was therefore cautioned that "the leaders of the present Progressive party may be led to believe that the difference between your trust policy and that of most Progressives . . . is more vital than in fact is . . . the case." [33] To this Brandeis replied:

I have been disposed to think that the path of duty for me does not lead to any public office, and I as yet see no reason for changing that opinion. On the other hand, I feel that the duty is very clear that I should utilize that insight which participation in practical affairs has given me to prevent well-meaning Progressives from being led into the belief that private monopoly is desirable or permissible, provided it be regulated.

That issue seems to me to be a fundamental one—one on which the New Party is radically wrong, and so long as it stands for private monopoly and privilege, it cannot be the true means of real progress in this country.[34]

Perhaps Brandeis's most effective campaign speech was before the Cleveland Chamber of Commerce on October 15. The day before, Roosevelt had been shot and slightly wounded by a fanatic in Milwaukee, and Brandeis promptly turned the incident to advantage. The attempted assassination was a symptom, he observed, of the declining respect for law in the United States. And what were the reasons for the decline? One was the fact that the law, as administered, did not express the will of the American people. He went on:

See what the effect would be upon the American people, to find . . . that in the year 1912, a political party and a large number of people standing for the best interests of America come forward and declare, "Let us legalize the trust, let us legalize that which under existing law has grown up illegally, because it is impossible, or possibly undesirable, to prevent private monopoly."

If that position, gentlemen, became the accepted policy of America, we would declare, in substance, that not only vested rights but vested wrongs were to be supreme in this country. And there could be nothing to my mind which would so threaten the welfare of America and imperil everything that we are working for, that we prize today, as the solemn declaration of the inability of this government to carry out the will which the people have registered in an act of Congress. . . .

. . . We have been trifling with the people. . . . Jeeringly, jokingly, year after year, we have smiled over the inefficiency of that expression of the people's will, which there [in the Sherman Act] and elsewhere has gone upon the statute books to satisfy a popular demand.

It is, gentlemen, that sort of thing which is bringing on the Los Angeles and Lawrence and Milwaukee incidents, and which, if not corrected and corrected in the right manner, will endanger all our institutions. To secure respect for law, we must make the law respectable.

Brandeis was proud of the speech, thought it was a great success. He wrote Alfred about it: "I gave them a real sermon on respect for law apropos the T.R. incident, working it around to the trusts and I think I rather held them."

Besides the effort of actual speaking, Brandeis felt the constant strain of meeting and talking with people. He welcomed a chance to rest at the Cleveland Athletic Club. "Had a great night's sleep and have had three hours' walking despite numerous callers and interviews," he wrote. ". . . This Club is one of those disgustingly comfortable places which you talk about." [35] In Minneapolis he encountered one of the exasperations of a public speaker: ". . . there was a fiendish noise adjoining which spoiled the fun," he complained. [36] As the tour ended he felt relieved: "Am glad to have the talkfest over and to get down to some other affairs for a while." [37]

VICTORY

The Wilson cause seemed to be going well as election day drew near, but T.R.'s spectacular oratory and personal charm still commanded a large following. The attempted assassination in Milwaukee had helped him, Brandeis observed, "by stopping his talking. There seemed to be very strong evidence of an ebbing tide before. . . ." [38] A few days prior to the election when he had finished his "talkfest," Brandeis wrote: "It looks pretty certain Wilsonway now, but I shall feel relieved when the vote is in. The redoubtable Colonel is too formidable an opponent. That shooting stopped the waning tide, if it didn't help him positively." [39]

Neither the Colonel nor Taft proved formidable enough. When the ballots were counted, Wilson, though he had only a plurality of the popular vote, was found to have carried all the states except T.R.'s six and Taft's two. The Progressives had not united in as solid a front as Brandeis had hoped, but that was no great matter. What pleased him most was T.R.'s defeat in the really progressive strongholds. Progressivism itself was triumphant. On November 13, 1912, he wrote Alfred jubilantly:

". . . Republicans and Progressives have all grounds for congratulation —the Republicans that T.R. was beaten and the Progressives that Taft was. So we may enter upon one of those perilous eras of good feeling. . . . They are both talking about Wilson being a 'minority' President. Your historical study will confirm Ma in saying, so was the blessed Lincoln they talk so much about."

Brandeis's faith in Wilson grew steadily, and with it his confidence in the future. After hearing the President-elect speak at a Southern Society dinner in Chicago on December 12, he wrote Alfred: "It was a noble utterance—worthy of the man and the cause. A declaration of purpose—not a speech or even a sermon. It could leave no man in doubt that he proposes to carry out his promises in letter and spirit—without fear or favor. It was all simple and conversational, as if he were talking to his intimates, the people of the U.S."

CHAPTER TWENTY-FIVE

Marooned, 1912-1913

WILSON's first task was cabinet-making. And the election returns were hardly in when rumor had Brandeis the new head of the Department of Justice. Lincoln Steffens, a shrewd political observer, wrote early in November: "I think Wilson will take him as attorney-general. If he does, some fur will fly. . . ." [1]

But public office held little attraction for Brandeis. As early as 1908 Steffens had said he "would make a corking cabinet officer," [2] and in 1911 Collier's had suggested Taft might show a forgive-and-forget broadmindedness worthy of Lincoln by appointing Ballinger's critic to the next cabinet vacancy. [3] Nothing came of these suggestions, and when in 1911 rumor had him slated as attorney-general of Massachusetts, he said: "I have never been a candidate for political honors, and I don't expect to be. . . ." [4] Brandeis had been urged to run for governor or United States senator on the Republican ticket in 1912, but by coming out for Wilson he had "ended that agony." [5] In response to suggestions that the Socialists nominate him for President, he stated his attitude emphatically: "Aside from all other considerations, I am quite sure that the little I can do to better American conditions can best be performed as a private citizen, and as one who has no aspirations of any kind for any public office." [6]

Still his name kept coming up. [7] Indeed his appointment as Wilson's attorney-general once seemed so certain that congratulatory letters from friends and admirers began to pour in. He dismissed them, saying, "Don't believe all you hear." [8]

SMEARING BRANDEIS

Another kind of letter began to pour in on Wilson. In certain quarters the mere mention of Brandeis as attorney-general caused consternation and even panic. Certain business groups looked upon this idea as a major catastrophe. Bostonians in particular were upset. "The best men here," wrote the financially independent historian, James Ford Rhodes, "men of affairs as well as lawyers, all of whom voted for you or President Taft, will regard the appointment of Mr. Brandeis as a member of your cabinet, should it be made, with profound regret." [9]

Since Brandeis's most bitter enemies could not deny his extraordinary talent, they brought ugly charges against his motives, his integrity, and, in particular, his professional ethics. Fierce attacks on his character were launched. William S. Youngman, Brandeis's legal opponent in the Warren case, now charged that Brandeis had forced Samuel D. Warren into illegal transactions in his management of the Warren family estate and that in acting throughout "for all parties in the case" Brandeis had committed a flagrant breach of legal ethics. "It is worth noting," Youngman said, "that when the scheme of trust management and of rendering trust accounts devised by Mr. Brandeis was called into question and being investigated before the special master in equity, Mr. Brandeis failed to make his appearance for one moment in the hearing room and left the defense of the case to one of his partners." [10] Youngman hinted that Brandeis's treachery was chiefly responsible for Warren's sudden death, suggesting that Warren's belated knowledge of his partner's betrayal had driven him to commit suicide.

Edward R. Warren, formerly a co-worker in the Public Franchise League, warned Wilson:

> Repeated rumor to the effect that Mr. Louis D. Brandeis is being considered by you for membership in your Cabinet, for the office of Attorney-General of the United States, has to my knowledge caused serious apprehension in the minds of many people in Boston.
>
> I felt that I should be remiss in my duty as a citizen, were I to neglect to respectfully urge upon you the importance of examining his record very carefully, if it is true that you have him in mind for this position. [11]

In the van of the anti-Brandeis crusade were the New Haven Railroad and the United Shoe Machinery Company. [12] Through the *Boston News Bureau* and *Truth,* both vociferous hired boosters of the New Haven, they launched their verbal onslaughts. *Truth* said on November 30:

> *Truth* has no hesitation in expressing the hope that Mr. Brandeis may enter the cabinet, since then he will have to come out in the open and be where his

actions and not his explanations will be the basis of his reputation and where the serving of two causes, the one illuminated, the other obscured, will be too perilous even for one so clever and adroit.

This deadly innuendo was reinforced a week later. Said *Truth*:

The average New Englander never sees Brandeis; he hears of him afar off somewhere; he is as nebulous as Prester John; distance lends a curious enchantment to him; there is siren music in his voice; he is said to be battling for human rights; he is pictured with the hero's pose and the martyr's smile; but he is not visible to the naked eye; the gullible Yankee is not close enough at hand to hear his crafty chuckle, to catch his whispered confidences, to see his well-feathered nest, to note that the features of the down-trodden client he is battling for, are those of some interested and sophisticated millionaire.

The *Boston News Bureau* harped continually on the huge fees Brandeis received, and on the difficulty of locating him "on any side for any length of time, either in politics or law." [13] It warned that "the ability of Louis D. Brandeis to appear and disappear and to play both sides and to appear in all parties and all branches of all parties ought to be generally recognized if he is to go into President Wilson's cabinet. . . ." [14] The United Shoe case provided especially hot fuel. Here seemed to be the best evidence of Brandeis's duplicity. He had served as counsel for the company, accepting allegedly large fees; he had even defended the company's leasing system. Then, for no apparent reason, he turned right around and joined the other side. The *News Bureau's* explanation was perfectly simple—Brandeis could always be found on the side of the largest retainer.[15] Echoing these views, Elbert Hubbard said: "He works both ends against the middle. He gets them coming and going"; and he appended this description: "The Honorable Louis D. Brandeis, of Boston, Business-Baiter, stirrer-up of strife, litigious lurer on of hate and unrest, destroyer of confidence, killer of values, commercial coyote, spoiler of pay envelopes." [16]

Racial and religious feeling, though kept in the background, was not entirely absent in this smear campaign. *Life* in opinions on his character noted a "perplexity . . . about the Jewish mind when its operations are complicated by altruism; how it works; whether it is constructive or merely combative; whether it is duly tempered with compunctions; whether it duly respects the *status quo* of a so-called Christian civilization and would use a decent moderation in improving it." As *Life* saw it, "altruistic, radical innovators scare people," and the effect is intensified if they happen to be Jews.[17] Hubbard put it more robustly: "Brandeis is Gompers, Goldman, and Gyp the Blood rolled into one, and given a degree from Harvard. . . . Brandeis does not represent America." [18]

On the other hand, some of Brandeis's most violent detractors were among Jewish representatives of privilege. "A very concerted effort is being made," Henry Moskowitz reported to Norman Hapgood, by "Jewish bankers and Jewish corporate interests" to eliminate him from cabinet consideration on the ground that he is "not a representative Jew." Moskowitz diagnosed the objection to his lack of orthodoxy as "a transparent pretext concealing the non-sectarian fear of all the reactionary interests, Jewish and non-Jewish, of Mr. Brandeis." [19] Some measure of the intensity of this hate among influential Jews is indicated in Rabbi E. B. M. Browne's letter to Joseph Tumulty, Wilson's secretary: "Brandeis, aside from his 'Religious' delinquency, is regarded as a legal quack, travelling throughout the country for the good of the people to dream up cases for about a dozen lawyers associated with him in Boston in an immense show place." [20]

WILSON ASSAYS BRANDEIS

Apparently Wilson was seriously considering Brandeis, for on January 3, 1913, he wrote his Boston friend and Brandeis's client, A. W. Tedcastle: "I want to get all the disinterested opinion I can collect about Mr. Louis D. Brandeis. He is a man of such originality and force and might be made so serviceable to the public that I want to know just what his neighbors whom he has not prejudiced by his action with regard to them personally think about him. Of course I know how some of the best men in Boston hate him, but I think I know the reason for that feeling, and I want to get outside of that circle." *

At Wilson's request Norman Hapgood also gathered opinion on Brandeis, and in addition offered his own. On January 30 Hapgood wrote Wilson: "One thing that brought home to me his [Brandeis's] nature was that nobody except Crane [Charles R.] has been as devoted to me since I left Collier's. Brandeis has been much more affectionate, and has put himself out much more for me, since I have had no power to help him, than he did before."

Hapgood cited this personal item to refute the charge that Brandeis "is difficult and exacting" in his personal relations. Hapgood continued: "It is true that lawyers who have been on the opposite side of cases have criticized him for lack of professional courtesy. There is much nonsense in legal ethics and the point seems to me of minor importance. . . . Mainly I think the men who are making up the feeling against Brandeis are the men who will oppose you anyway, as soon as the first serious struggle is on." [21]

* Tedcastle's report to Wilson must have been verbal. The Wilson papers afford no clue to his verdict.

Edward A. Filene assisted Hapgood by digging up the facts as to Brandeis's activity in certain law cases, including the Warren will matter on which Hapgood wrote: "It was highly significant that the only one of the whole Warren family who objected to anything that was done as to settlement of the estate was Edward." Hapgood pointed out that Brandeis and his firm continued even after the family row to act as counsel for Fiske Warren and Miss Cornelia Warren, and added: "Brandeis thinks that nothing can excuse his [E. P. Warren's] acts except the theory that he was insane." As to Youngman's contention that Samuel D. Warren, "fond of playing polo and seeking other diversions," had been duped by his partner into wrongdoing, Hapgood commented: "E. S. Martin, Colonel House's friend, knew Sam Warren well and Brandeis thinks he would laugh if he were told that S.W. were the tool of Brandeis or of anyone else. 'He was masterful to the highest degree . . . the noblest character he has ever known,' says B." [22]

What is more to the point, Youngman had grossly misrepresented the Warren–Brandeis relationship, making it appear that this crafty outsider had come into Boston, professionally and socially, on Warren's coat tails. Warren himself, more than once, gave an altogether different picture. He had written Brandeis, September 7, 1901:

My dear Old Man:

The best thing I ever did was done in 1879—when I induced you to come to us in Boston. You have been, I think, inexpressibly valuable in all our lives beginning with father's—"a very present help in time of trouble" and a sure adviser at all times. I cannot think of the family and its doings since that time without including you as a most influential part. You have encouraged our right impulses and criticized our faults with an unbiased discernment which could only come from outside. In many ways you are a better example of New England virtues than the natives.

"The more I study charges against Brandeis," Hapgood's report to the President-elect continued, "the more highly I think of him. . . . I traced each one to its source, and in every case it turned out to be made out of whole cloth, or, when understood, to be to the credit of Brandeis." He turned up only one reliable criticism—that of Ezra R. Thayer who had been for a time in Brandeis's office. "Lots of the talk which is going about concerning him," Thayer wrote Hapgood, February 3, 1913, "is rubbish, or worse. The most serious criticism to which he is open, me judice, would refer to unfair fighting. It is the adversary who has most to complain of." Thayer "is honest and intelligent," Hapgood commented in a note to Wilson, "and what he says represents the outside of what can be said against Brandeis without misrepresentation or extreme narrowness."

In turning over detailed memoranda to Hapgood, E. A. Filene had warned him to "be careful in handling any defense of Brandeis," since he "would surely decline any position that he thought came to him because of solicitation or even influence or defense by his friends." [23] Filene himself wrote Wilson, denying what was perhaps the most persistent complaint against Brandeis—that he used unfair methods against his opponents: ". . . never in my experience with him has he allowed any personal assault on him to distract him from considering the just rights of his opponents, however slanderous they may have been. This has been true even when the victory was his and he had in his hands the power to dictate the conditions which his opponents must accept." [24]

A powerful tribute to Brandeis's influence among the country's leading Progressives was contributed by Felix Frankfurter: "To us he has been one of the most commanding leaders in the regenerating movement in our political and social life. . . . To a unique degree, he has pointed out for us definite directions for the realization of those aspirations. . . . His intellectual powers are undisputed—they have been so effective only because they are charged by a burning moral fiber, by an aggressive sense of service." [25]

Senator La Follette put in strong words through Charles R. Crane. "La Follette . . . has worked with Brandeis for several years," said Crane, "and greatly prizes Brandeis's wisdom, patience, and sympathy. He also believes that Brandeis, more than anyone else in Washington and in authority, can pull together the Progressives—whether La Follette, Democratic or Bull Mooser—and harmonize progressive legislation." [26]

Dickinson S. Miller, who had gone on canoeing trips with Brandeis and his wife, had spent Sundays in the Brandeis household, and had seen much of his private life, wrote Wilson his impressions:

1—I asked a Boston lawyer the other day, an intimate friend, who were the first lawyers in Boston if one reckoned by practical effectiveness and the demand for their services? He answered unhesitatingly "Herrick and Brandeis." But to this practical success Brandeis adds larger views as to industrial and civic matters than any other man of business I have known. And through all these years of hard work he has kept up reading on historical, industrial, and political subjects.

2—In council he shines as one of the most reasonable and quietly sensible of men.

3—I have been most struck by his management of his own life, and his skillful husbanding of his great power of work. I know no one whose life has been to any degree under my observation who has struck me as so wise in this respect.

4—Connected with the last is the unostentatious quietness of his life. Welcome as he has been until lately in a rich and artistic circle, it is all the more striking. He earns a large income, but his city house is small and very simple; his country house is, or used to be, an extremely modest roadside cottage.

5—Though ever since his youth when he was at Harvard Law School he was received in influential Boston social circles, he has deliberately held his own course in public affairs, though that has more and more alienated these circles from him, and finally infuriated them. It is a fine example of devotion to principle, to the disadvantage, not only of himself, but of his wife and children.[27]

George W. Anderson, who had worked closely with Brandeis in the Public Franchise League and in the New Haven struggles, at first advised Wilson against the appointment: ". . . his appointment would stir up a good many animosities—not only in the Democratic ranks, but that it would tend to alienate the affections of a great many who now think very well of you and of the Democratic party under your leadership." [28]

Two months later, however, Anderson changed his mind, and wrote Wilson: "So far as I am now able to learn, the general feeling in New England, among both Democrats and Progressives, is that Mr. Brandeis in your cabinet would add intellectual, moral, and political strength—all three—to the administration. As this view is, to a degree at least, inconsistent with the views that I expressed of the political situation in December, it seems to me that I ought to say so." [29]

Brandeis knew he was under cold surveillance. "I feel very lonesome in our little provincial town and long to see our good friends in the Capitol. . . ." [30] As usual, he ignored the slanderous reports. Several of his friends, however, did not intend to permit such loose and unsupported defamation of his character to go by default. When the *Boston News Bureau* attempted to show shady double-dealing, Charles H. Jones, his old client and co-worker in many public battles, indignantly sprang to the defense. Jones prepared an article for the Boston press, refuting the *News Bureau's* charges, point by point. Later on he wrote Wilson: "The fact that these malignant attacks continue to appear, based wholly on falsehoods and innuendo, seems to prove conclusively two propositions. One is that these people fear Mr. Brandeis far more than any other man now prominent in the public life of our city. They know full well that he is subject to no improper influence, and that in the causes which he undertakes, he cannot be defeated. The baseless nature of the slander shows most satisfactorily the exceptional uprightness of character which even under the searchlight of their hatred, has revealed no defect." [31]

HATE FINDS REASONS

Even if Wilson were himself convinced that Brandeis was an honorable man, there were still other objections to be considered. These were voiced largely by Democratic politicians. Quite naturally the Massachusetts Democratic organization regarded with disfavor the idea of appointing to the cabinet a man who had stumped for La Follette and had maintained close relations with leading Republicans. An inquiry addressed to John M. Minton, Chairman of the Boston Board of Election Commissioners, elicited the response that "Mr. Brandeis has neither changed nor canceled his enrollment as a Republican." [32] Thus those who hated and feared Brandeis for reasons they could not make stick now turned to party politics to thwart his entrance into the government.

Early in February this strategy was brought into the open when William F. Fitzgerald, treasurer of the Wilson Campaign Committee in Massachusetts, who had not been kindly disposed toward Brandeis since the Old Dominion case,* appeared in Washington on a mysterious mission.[33] Ostensibly investigating the tariff situation, he was "carrying the anti-Brandeis fight in his suitcase." [34] Doubt as to his mission evaporated when he sent dinner invitations to New England congressmen for the avowed purpose of discussing New England's representation in the Wilson cabinet. It was expected that those present would remove Brandeis from consideration and unite in support of some substitute New Englander. There was no agreement on any candidate, however, and the evening was occupied principally with statements from Fitzgerald and Representative James M. Curley as to the undesirability of Brandeis.[35] In any case, Curley was quoted as saying that Brandeis had been "knocked hard and plenty." [36]

As inauguration day approached, the Brandeis issue became hotter. The *Transcript* reported that he was being more strenuously opposed than any other candidate, and that Wilson's final decision would have important effects on administration support. If the People's Attorney were turned down, it would be regarded as a surrender to the transportation interests of the country, and to the New Haven in particular. If he were appointed, it would be concluded that Wilson had swallowed Brandeis's "radical" economic theories. What would Wilson do?

The issue had become a little more complicated now, for besides the attorney-generalship, Brandeis was also being listed in newspaper cabinet slates as Secretary of Commerce or of Labor.† Toward the end of Febru-

---

* Fitzgerald's grudge is considered on pp. 487–88.
† The Department of Commerce and Labor was separated into two departments on March 4, 1913.

ary his appointment to the latter post was regarded by the press as assured.[37] The *Boston Post* on February 19 even reported that the portfolio had been definitely offered and accepted. Congratulatory messages arrived, one a telegram from Erich A. Brand*ies*, of the Oakland office of the *San Francisco Examiner,* addressed to Louis D. Brand*ies*:

My best wishes for your success as our new Secretary of Commerce and Labor. Although myself only a newspaperman I am proud that the name of Brand*ies* has reached such prominence in the United States.[38]

The opposition made one final drive to get him off the slate. Thomas P. Riley, Chairman of the Democratic State Committee, even while calling Brandeis "the ablest man in New England," saw the President-elect in Trenton, presented a certificate from the Boston Board of Election Commissioners to show that Brandeis was not a Democrat, and formally objected to the appointment.[39] Protests were also submitted to Wilson by Governor Eugene Foss, Charles F. Choate, and other prominent New Englanders.[40]

THUMBS DOWN

What originally had been a transparent smear in the scavenger press was now rendered respectable by the endorsement of highly influential Bostonians. Eventually they got Wilson on their side. James Kerney, Trenton newspaper editor and publisher, tells how this was accomplished: "Dodge [Cleveland H.], Princeton classmate and friend of Wilson, was used by the New England financiers in undermining Brandeis. Dodge was a somewhat unconscious figure in the situation. His purpose was rather to prevent Wilson from making grave blunders than to influence the appointment of anyone to office. Henry L. Higginson of Boston was on terms of intimacy with Dodge. . . . Higginson had been a supporter of Wilson in the election, and he had much to do in convincing Wilson that Brandeis was a dangerous man. . . . He was the medium who filtered the onslaughts through Dodge to Wilson. The attacks on Brandeis included serious charges, and Richard Olney, for whom Wilson had a considerable regard, was drawn in to settle the matter." Kerney thought it was "the personal affection existing between Dodge and Wilson" that was "an influential factor in keeping Brandeis out of the cabinet." [41]

It is more likely, however, that purely political consideration weighed most heavily with Wilson. Having been convinced that the case urged against the Bostonian was groundless, Wilson told Brandeis's opponents "that they could not use charges against Brandeis's character without forcing him to name him regardless of other considerations," but he added that they were free to use argument of availability. "I was told," Hapgood recalled in 1928, "that [Governor] Foss and [William F.] McCombs headed the delegation that persuaded Wilson to change his mind at the end, on grounds of party harmony—an argument, of course, that he believed in, as shown by the Bryan appointment." [42]

At the last minute Brandeis's name was dropped; James C. McReynolds was nominated for Attorney-General and William C. Redfield for Secretary of Commerce. Elbert Hubbard gloated: "Happily, President Wilson was not to be deceived. He allowed the illusion and delusion to be carried along a certain distance, and then he gently dropped Brandeis out of the favorite list." [43] The *News Bureau* crowed jubilantly: "Sentiment has been improved by the fact that President-elect Wilson has eliminated Mr. Brandeis from his cabinet, and that his cabinet selections will now be generally acceptable." [44]

REPERCUSSIONS AND PROSPECTS

Brandeis's friends, and Progressives generally, were outraged. J. Frank McElwain, Charles H. Jones, John H. Fahey, Charles P. Hall, Elmer J. Bliss, and Edward A. Filene jointly sent Wilson an indignant telegram on March 2:

The publications today . . . represent that Mr. Brandeis will be rejected as a concession to influences which have for years sought undue privileges at the expense of our people and that a question of integrity raised by these interests will be decided against him. That such a verdict should be rendered following these outrageous slanders we regard not only as a setback to progress in New England but as disheartening to every man who dares oppose such interests as Mr. Brandeis has offended. If there is any foundation for the press statements we respectfully beg to suggest that in justice, Mr. Brandeis should be asked to answer these attacks direct to you. We believe firmly that the great mass of men who voted for you in Massachusetts are wholeheartedly in favor of Mr. Brandeis as representing the fundamentals on which you were elected.

It was reported that La Follette and Bryan objected strenuously to the loss of Brandeis from the cabinet and had taken up the cudgels in his behalf.[45] Rudolph Spreckels informed Wilson that he had made a great mistake. Gifford Pinchot, writing Brandeis on March 5, the day after Wilson's inauguration, expressed the feelings of many others when he said: "My whole satisfaction with Wilson's Inaugural, his article in *Collier's,* and the general high level of his cabinet is clouded by the absence of your own name among his advisers. It is the one dark spot in an Inauguration which surely begins well. I had counted tremendously on your being here in Washington, not only for the personal satisfaction that would have flowed from it, but because I counted on your influence more than that of any other man to keep the administration straight in certain great fundamentals. It is too bad, and especially too bad because of the influences which are responsible for your being kept out. I am profoundly sorry."

Editorial comment, somewhat excited and quite superficial, displayed varying shades of indignation, disillusionment, and trepidation. Many newspapers thought Brandeis's exclusion from the cabinet much less damaging to him than to the Wilson administration. The President stood to lose not merely the services of the People's Attorney, but a goodly amount of prestige as well. Sections of the press friendly to Brandeis, instead of wasting tears in his behalf, cited Wilson's apparent surrender to the "Interests" as ground for questioning the administration's "Progressivism." The *Malden Evening News* on March 5 saw in the Boston lawyer a coming Disraeli, and was confident that he could not long be excluded from the seats of power. "It is sad," commented the *Boston American* on March 7, "that the first act of the new President seems to have been a timorous rejection of a good man because such a railroad as the New Haven and such a corporation as the United Shoe Company dislike him. If Mr. Wilson fears the hostility of such influences as are represented by Mr. Brandeis's enemies, his administration is bound to disappoint the country." The Boston *Common* on March 8 regarded the absence of Brandeis from the President's circle of advisers as "one dark cloud of evil omen across the dawn of this bright and promising inauguration day." Charles Edward Russell fumed in *The Coming Nation* of March 22 that the People's Attorney had been "crowded out" by "an enormous, lawless, over-capitalized, top-heavy, New Haven."

Brandeis took the news with entire calm. "Probably he is the least perturbed man in the country over not getting a seat in the cabinet," commented the *Malden Evening News*. Ostensibly he had been barred for political reasons, but he knew better. The opposition to him was not "in its essence political." [46] This became clear in July 1913 when George W. Anderson and Henry J. Skeffington, independently, on behalf of the Democratic machine, urged him to run for the Massachusetts attorney-generalship. The "Interests" rather than the politicians, had scored a victory, but it was no defeat for Brandeis, since he had never been in the fight. He kept scrupulously quiet during the whole controversy and at the end wrote: "I am inclined to think that the situation as it is, is best. There is a wide field of usefulness for a public private citizen." [47]

To Alfred he wrote on March 2: "Today's papers will have removed the mystery as to the cabinet. As you know I had great doubts as to its being desirable for me, so I concluded to literally let nature take its course and to do nothing either to get called or to stop the talk, although some of my friends were quite active. State Street, Wall Street, and the local Democratic bosses did six months' unremitting work; but seem not to have prevailed until the last moment. The local Democratic bosses were swayed partly by their connections in the financial district—partly by the fear of being opposed in job-seeking. It is almost, or indeed, quite amusing how much they fear me—attributing to me power and influence which I in no respect possess."

To McReynolds and Redfield, who filled the positions for which he had been considered, Brandeis wrote congratulatory messages on March 5. He looked forward to the "new industrial day" when Redfield's enlightened policies would pervade the business world. His felicitations to McReynolds were inexplicably effusive:

March 5, 1913

Hon. James C. McReynolds
Department of Justice
Washington, D.C.

My dear Mr. McReynolds:

In deciding upon you for Attorney-General, President Wilson has made the wisest possible choice.

Your record in trust prosecutions will assure the country that the President's trust policy will be carried out promptly and efficiently, and business be freed at last. We are indeed to be congratulated.

I intend to call upon you soon and hope you will have time to talk over our special New England needs.

With best wishes,

Very sincerely yours,
Louis D. Brandeis

The New Haven and United Shoe breathed easier now that the Department of Justice had been saved from "radical agitator" leadership. But the rescue of the cabinet from the wolfish Brandeis was not a finished episode; it was only a prelude to the bigger drama. The charges against him had yet to be fought out in the open. Brandeis could not be halted merely by placing one obstacle in his path, and President Wilson was determined to find a place in his official family for him. It was first rumored that he would be made Indian Commissioner, but he promptly and emphatically announced that he did not intend to accept that or any other public office.[48] A little later Wilson urged him to take the Chairmanship of the Commission on Industrial Relations. "There is no one in the United States," the President wrote him, May 19, 1913, "who could preside over and direct such an inquiry so well as you could, and I wonder if it is possible for you to strengthen the whole thing by assuming direction of it." [49] Brandeis hesitated for a while and then finally declined.[50]

Three years later the same men who had saved the cabinet from Brandeis attempted the rescue of the highest judicial body in the land.

CHAPTER TWENTY-SIX

Steering with the Wilson Tide,
1913-1915

DURING the winter and spring of 1913 Brandeis was too busy in the New Haven fight to have much time for anything else. The first week after Wilson's inauguration, however, he conferred with the President on general administration policy. He also talked with Secretary of the Interior Lane, Secretary of State Bryan, Secretary of Commerce Redfield, and Attorney-General McReynolds.[1] ". . . I have been engaged largely in promoting the *entente cordiale* with the administration," he wrote Alfred, March 18, 1913. This naturally helped him in pushing along government action against the New Haven and the United Shoe Machinery Company.

In April he was at the White House again along with John Purroy Mitchel and Henry Bruère—this time for a conference on government economy and efficiency. Brandeis, extraordinarily well informed on scientific management, spoke with confidence. He advised the President not to aim at reducing the amount of money spent, but at getting more for what was spent. The first step, as he saw it, was to adopt a federal budget, under which some legislative or legislative–executive committee would coordinate and regulate expenditures.[2]

THE FEDERAL RESERVE BATTLE

In June, Brandeis was again drawn informally into administration councils when he was asked to join the spirited discussions that preceded passage of the Federal Reserve Act. Up to now he had devoted his attention largely to trusts, labor, conservation, and railroad regulation. He had never made a thorough investigation of banking and currency as such, though in his insurance and New Haven studies he had seen at first hand how the control of money and credit was concentrated in the hands of a few great financiers united by "community of interest." He had observed, as few others had done, the operations of the Money Trust. From May 1912 to January 1913 the evils of the banking system had been the subject of hearings before the House Committee on Banking and Currency (the Pujo Committee); and Representative Carter Glass was patiently gathering information, mapping out a program of constructive banking reform.

Soon after his inauguration Wilson began pressing for action. Immediately a fierce controversy broke out among his advisers—Glass, Bryan, Professor H. Parker Willis, Secretary of the Treasury William G. McAdoo, Senator Robert L. Owen, Samuel Untermyer, who had conducted the Pujo and other investigations, and several prominent bankers. An apparently unbridgeable rift developed between more conservative advisers, headed by Representative Glass, and "extremists," headed by Secretary Bryan. They divided on the question: should the new system be controlled by the government or by the bankers? Bryan would never consent to any program which placed the money supply of the country under the thumb of Eastern financiers, and the loss of his powerful Midwestern support in Congress and in the nation would imperil Wilson politically. Glass, on the contrary, was adamant against subjecting "the banking business of the country to political control." [3] Wilson's position was made even more difficult by warning signals from New York, that government tampering with the financial structure would produce a panic.[4] The situation was critical, involving as it did not merely one pillar but the entire legislative structure of his New Freedom.

Brandeis was sensitive to these dangers. He wrote his brother on June 11, 1913: "The administration is having pretty hard nuts to crack, with the crumbling stock market." He conferred with the President, June 11, and on June 14 presented these opinions: "The power to issue currency should be vested exclusively in government officials, even when the currency is issued against commercial paper. The American people will not be content to have the discretion necessarily involved vested in a Board composed wholly or in part of bankers; for their judgment may be biased by private interest or affiliation. The function of the bankers should be limited strictly to that of an advisory council. Merely placing in the government the ultimate supervision and control over the currency issues would not afford the public adequate protection." [5]

While there was no serious economic depression in 1913, business was rather dormant and confidence in the future was lacking. The election and inauguration of Wilson was not calculated to improve this condition. Some were urging upon the President, therefore, that quick passage of a safe currency bill would go far toward allaying business unrest. Brandeis scouted this idea: "The effect which the enactment of an improved currency law would have in preventing or allaying financial disturbances has, I believe, been greatly exaggerated. The beneficent effect of the best conceivable currency bill will be relatively slight unless we are able to curb the Money Trust, and to remove the uneasiness among businessmen due to its power. Nothing would go so far in establishing confidence among businessmen as the assurance that the government will control the currency issues and the conviction that whatever money is available, will be available for business generally, and not be subject to the control of a favored few." [6]

Brandeis then urged Wilson to be bold in dealing with the money power: "The conflict between the policies of the administration and the desires of the financiers and of big business is an irreconcilable one. Concessions to the big business interests must in the end prove futile. The administration can at best have only their seeming or temporary co-operation. In essentials they must be hostile. While we must give the most careful consideration to their recommendations and avail ourselves of their expert knowledge, it is extremely dangerous to follow their advice even in a field technically their own." [7]

These arguments convinced Wilson. He called Glass, McAdoo, and Owen into conference and announced that he was definitely and finally opposed to any bankers' participation whatever in the control of the Federal Reserve System. When a delegation of bankers came to the White House to object, he threw them into confusion by asking: "Which of you gentlemen thinks the railroads should select members of the Interstate Commerce Commission?" [8] This broke the deadlock and averted a threatened rupture in administration councils. Glass, won over to Wilson's side, gave full support to changes in the measure he had formerly opposed and under heavy critical fire steered the bill through the House of Representatives. It passed the Senate and on December 23 went to the President for his signature.

THE ANTI-TRUST DRIVE

The passage of the Federal Reserve Act was an extraordinary achievement for an administration not yet one year in power. But a far more important part of the Wilson program had still to be enacted. In the struggle between Progressivism and Privilege, trust policy was the crucial issue. It was the campaign issue on which Wilson and Roosevelt had fought. It was the one proposal of the New Freedom which struck directly at the feudal irresponsibility of big business.

During the campaign Brandeis had been the chief exponent of the administration's anti-trust program and he became the President's chief adviser in putting the program into legislative form. But first some issues remained to be settled. Wilson and Brandeis had been in accord on most trust issues since their 1912 conference at Sea Girt, and Wilson had given close attention to Brandeis's articles in Collier's.[9] Wilson's approach, however, was that of a political moralist: he wanted most to punish individuals guilty of monopoly practices. Brandeis's approach, on the other hand, was that of the economist and social engineer; he did not condemn monopolists for immoral behavior but rather saw their actions as symptoms of a faulty system; the system, not the men, must be changed. Then, too, Wilson was not clearly aware of the evils of bigness; Brandeis saw that corporations in many cases were not only inefficient because of excessive size but were also a social and political menace from their overweening power. As in the Federal Reserve issue, Wilson came around to Brandeis's ideas. Together they decided that the Sherman Act had to be clarified and strengthened, the provisions for its enforcement improved, and a fact-finding commission created to administer it.

Brandeis once again urged Wilson to be bold—to act at once. Having enacted his tariff and currency programs, the President was being urged to slow up, to give business a breathing spell. Signs of a coming depression, it was argued, gave special reason for prudence and caution. But Brandeis urged that the administration ignore all such warnings and push ahead. He believed anti-trust legislation not only essential to the New Freedom program, but also "politically necessary to satisfy the demands of the very large number of progressive Democrats and the near Democrats who are already beginning to express some doubt whether the administration will have the courage (in view of the indicated business depression) to carry out the policy which it has hitherto declared." He saw no reason to slow up: "The depression cannot be ended or lessened by any course which the administration may take. Neither the tariff act nor the currency bill have materially contributed to it. Nor will it be appreciably augmented by the administration pursuing undeterred its policy of New Freedom. The fearless course is the wise one." [10]

Brandeis had ready a comprehensive legislative plan to push along the "fearless course." If the government was going to regulate competition, it must know from day to day just what business was doing to check competition. Detailed information on trade agreements must be obtained. For this purpose Brandeis proposed an interstate trade commission. Building on his pet theory that business is, or should become, a profession, he insisted that industry and commerce be aided in the same way as agriculture —through industrial experiment stations and bureaus of research for the dissemination of business information. Free competition requires equal access to information among all competitors; this Brandeis hoped to supply through his new commission. To deal with those who still encroached on the free market, the Sherman Act must be revamped. Its application must be made easier and its enforcement more certain and more drastic. Interlocking directorates allowing the same men to be on both sides of specific business transactions must be abolished. The Interstate Commerce Act must be supplemented to limit the railroads to transportation and thus sever their connection with industrial concerns.

Following Brandeis's advice, Wilson went ahead with this program. Even before it was enacted it had good results, for on January 3, 1914, J. P. Morgan, Jr., George F. Baker, and other great financial leaders issued the sensational announcement that they were withdrawing from directorships in a large number of corporations. Morgan, the foremost figure in Wall Street, made a remarkable public statement: "An apparent change in public sentiment in regard to directorships seems now to warrant us in seeking to resign from some of these connections. Indeed it may be, in view of the change in sentiment upon this subject, that we shall be in a better position to serve such properties and their security holders if we are not directors." [11]

Whether this was a sincere indication of Wall Street's willingness to co-operate with the administration or a mere gesture calculated to stay anti-trust action, it was indeed a triumph for Wilson. The Titans of High Finance, who had once disdainfully regarded Presidents of the United States as lesser potentates, had at last bowed to the bold resolve of a Progressive administration. Wilson was now in the driver's seat, and he began to drive harder.

In his message to Congress on January 20 the President outlined a comprehensive anti-trust program, including the prohibition of interlocking directorates, enlarged powers for the I.C.C. to regulate financial operations of railroads, provisions clarifying the Sherman Act, and the creation of a Federal Trade Commission to advise and inform business.[12] Brandeis was satisfied with these recommendations. "He has paved the way for about all I have asked for," he wrote Alfred, January 23, 1914, "and some of the provisions specifically are what I got into his mind at my first interview."

At the same time Wilson warmly praised the financial leaders for withdrawing from their directorships as a first step toward accord between government and business, the beginning of an era of good feeling: "The

antagonism between business and government is over. . . . The government and businessmen are ready to meet each other halfway in a common
effort to square business methods with both public opinion and law." [13]
Brandeis's attitude was good-humored skepticism: "Confidentially, I think
he rather overdid the era of good feeling." [14]

THE FEDERAL TRADE COMMISSION

Brandeis now gave freely of his time and energy to the bills, of which
he, more than any other man, was the begetter. He consulted with Wilson
and Attorney-General McReynolds. He gave comment, criticism, and suggestions to Senator Newlands, Chairman of the Committee on Interstate
Commerce and chief supporter of this legislation in the Senate. At the
request of Chairman William C. Adamson he appeared before the House
Committee on Interstate and Foreign Commerce and explained his views
on the purposes of trust legislation and the functions of the proposed
trade commission.

Legislation, he believed, should prevent rather than punish, should aim
"to create conditions which will render less likely the existence of restraint
of trade and monopolies rather than merely correct them when they are
discovered." In spite of his reasoned opposition to concentration in industry,
he believed that anti-trust policy should be constructive rather than destructive: ". . . we should approach this subject from the point of view
of regulation rather than of restriction; because industrial crime is not a
cause, it is an effect—the effect of a bad system." [15]

The Federal Trade Commission, as he saw it, should, at least for a time,
be simply a fact-finding body. As usual, he saw the practical impossibility
of "reforming the world in a day," recognized that progress is slow and
demands persistent, painstaking effort. The regulation of practices in thousands of different types of business was, as he realized, a tremendous undertaking, and before anything else could be done effectively, there must be a
vast accumulation of facts. His own I.C.C. investigations had shown the
difficulties encountered in regulating even the railroads, and the variety of
problems confronting the I.C.C. was small indeed compared with those
which the new Commission would face. For this reason he was opposed
to giving the Commission any mandatory powers except to require information and to demand the keeping of books so that information would
be available.

That was a key problem underlying most other regulatory problems. On
this subject of bookkeeping Brandeis liked to quote Colbert: "Accountancy
—that is government." On his own Brandeis added: ". . . In order to
determine results you must be able not only to get at facts, but to get at

facts comparatively, and you can not get at any possible basis of comparison without a most enormous investigation in each individual case unless you establish a standard of accounting. . . . The first essential of wise and just action is knowledge." Without it we shall not "be able to deal intelligently with the problem of the extent to which trade agreements among competitors should be permitted." [16]

Anti-trust policy, Brandeis was convinced, could not be carried out according to some one all-embracing theoretical principle or plan. It must be designed to regulate actual conditions and practices in business, and before regulation could even be considered, these conditions and practices must be known. While the government, through the Bureau of Corporations and the work of various congressional committees, had acquired much information about the biggest industrial giants, such as the Oil, Tobacco, Steel, Sugar, and Beef Trusts, comparatively little was known about the thousand-and-one smaller lines of business. In many competitive types of enterprise, for example, restrictive agreements between producers concerning prices, output, or trade rules and practices, had grown up. Some of them were undoubtedly "reasonable and beneficent restraints upon trade"; others were undoubtedly vicious. But without detailed knowledge, it was impossible to legislate intelligently on the subject.[17]

The accumulation of trade data, he argued, was not only a necessary step to aid government in formulating policies, but also one of tremendous value to the individual corporations and to industry as a whole. Trade information, he believed, should be the common possession of every firm in the industry. Without the aid of the government in publicizing conditions and trends in the industry, the big manufacturer had a considerable advantage over smaller competitors through his ability to collect information and to conduct laboratory and other experiments. Once again, he was thinking of business in factual and professional terms.

Publicity, it had been argued, would limit competition and destroy confidence. Both of these contentions, Brandeis maintained, were untrue or at least shortsighted. Lack of knowledge breeds suspicion, undermines confidence; and publicity, by removing suspicion, does not destroy but rather creates confidence in business. Nor was there any ground for believing that competition would disappear when trade secrets became common property. ". . . As business develops," Brandeis said, "men will talk as freely about the details of advances in business efficiency as physicians now talk about their new discoveries in aid of health. The fact that medical knowledge is open to all does not prevent different physicians from advancing in competition with one another—competition in the larger sense. The fact that the law and the decisions of the courts are public and that we lawyers or any one of us have all the opportunity possible of knowing all that has been decided does not prevent an honorable competition among lawyers." [18]

After much debate Wilson's trust legislation was passed. One bill created the Federal Trade Commission, another became the Clayton Act. Embodied in these measures were certain proposals for which Brandeis had long been clamoring as necessary for clarifying and strengthening the Sherman Act.

STRENGTHENING APPOINTMENTS

Brandeis had good reason to be pleased with the outcome of his long campaign but he realized that many more steps were yet to be taken. He knew that much of the effectiveness of the new legislation would depend on the personnel of the agencies charged with its administration, and he was in a position to do something about this personnel. On his first trip to Washington after Wilson's inauguration Brandeis had been told by members of the cabinet that they lacked good assistants.[19] Later on he was frequently consulted by Wilson and high-ranking officials as to appointments. In declining the chairmanship of the Commission on Industrial Relations, he had recommended Charles R. Van Hise, president of the University of Wisconsin, for the post; [20] he also advised Wilson on the Commission's labor representative.[21] He gave a hand on appointments to McAdoo, Wilson's hard-working Secretary of the Treasury, who complained that he was like a submarine because he was "always running submerged." [22]

Ordinarily Brandeis waited for his opinion to be asked, but when Judge Prouty resigned from the Interstate Commerce Commission, he tried to have the vacancy filled by David O. Ives, his able and faithful aide in the New Haven fight and the Advance Rate Case. Ives was not only an experienced railroad man, but also had firsthand knowledge of the most serious problem facing the Commission at the time—the New England railroad situation. Even before Prouty's resignation was announced, Brandeis wrote Wilson in high praise of Ives: "No man in New England is better qualified by character or ability; and I know of no other man anywhere who possesses the unique experience which would enable him pre-eminently to aid in solving our serious transportation problems." [23] To Secretary of the Interior Lane he wrote: "It would be a calamity if Ives were not appointed. . . ." [24]

In co-operation with George W. Anderson, Brandeis promoted Ives's candidacy. Anderson insisted that they remain behind the scenes because

of the opposition which their support would arouse in certain quarters. "I
have said to the people who are active in this matter that I thought your
name and mine should be mentioned as little as possible; that our activities
should be quiet—subterranean. Subterranean activities, you know, befit a
Public Service Commissioner in Massachusetts. There are some people who
don't like either of us." [25] A movement was organized in New England
for concerted action to determine Prouty's successor, and at a meeting of
representatives of New England business organizations, Ives was unanimously endorsed.[26] A resolution supporting him was presented to the
President, but strong opposition developed, and Ives failed of confirmation in the Senate.[27]

Both Attorney-General McReynolds and his successor, T. W. Gregory,
consulted Brandeis frequently on appointments in the Department of
Justice. He encountered some difficulty in finding men satisfactory on political grounds as well as in character and ability. In connection with the
appointment of a United States District Attorney for Massachusetts, Brandeis wrote McReynolds: "The fact is that no man who has been active in
public or private life and does his duty would be acceptable to most of the
Democratic leaders in Massachusetts." [28] He was much pleased when Gregory named Anderson as District Attorney. And when Governor David I.
Walsh promptly responded to his suggestion that Joseph B. Eastman be
appointed to the post vacated by Anderson on the Massachusetts Public
Service Commission, he asked Norman Hapgood to write an editorial in
Harper's commending the Governor's appointment. "Eastman is a man
of ability," he wrote Hapgood, "a hard worker, of high character, and fine
public spirit. It is particularly gratifying that a man who has in all the
time I have known him never shown the slightest thought of his own interest when that of the public was concerned, should have had the success of
attaining at the age of thirty-three a position of distinction, with a very
good salary. It ought to prove to be great encouragement to others." [29]

Although Brandeis took an active hand in behalf of Eastman and Ives,
he did not see fit, in certain other cases, to do anything to aid the political
success of men with whom he had been associated. Late in 1914 Louis R.
Glavis wired him that his application for admission to legal practice before
the Interior Department had not been acted on because of his dismissal
by Taft and asked him to bring the matter to Secretary Lane's attention.
In reply Brandeis said that he did not think it would be wise for him to
see Secretary Lane personally and suggested that the matter had better be
presented to Lane by a congressman.[30]

Brandeis felt similarly about jobs he himself, in a sense, had created.

The personnel of the Federal Trade Commission was of special interest and importance to him, for he believed that the success or failure of the Commission would depend largely upon the quality of men selected. Since it was expected that he would have a significant voice in the selection, he received many letters from would-be commissioners asking for recommendations. His answer to most of them was that he had made it a rule not to initiate recommendations, but merely to express such opinion as he might have when his advice was sought.[31]

But there were significant exceptions to the above rule. When Representative Ray Stevens of New Hampshire was defeated for the Senate in 1914, Brandeis urged his appointment to the Federal Trade Commission. There was a legal obstacle, however, which prohibited any member of Congress from holding an office created by the Congress of which he was a member.[32] After his failure to get Stevens appointed, Brandeis wrote Colonel House, occasionally the President's alter ego, recommending Joseph P. Cotton, Jr., who had aided him in the Ballinger Case. Finally Brandeis's friend George Rublee was named to the Commission. Through Rublee and Brandeis, Lame Duck Stevens was made counsel.

THE FEDERAL TRADE COMMISSION BOGS DOWN

Apparently good personnel did not solve the Federal Trade Commission's problems. Difficulties were soon encountered, and Rublee and Stevens kept Brandeis in close touch with all their woes. "I don't see how the Commission is going to get along on the funds available," Rublee reported, March 6, 1915. "They are to have practically only what the Bureau of Corporations had had and without freedom in the use of that amount. . . . It looks as if [Chairman Jacob E.] Davies was fast asleep while the appropriation bill was going through."

Before long, there were reports that the Commission was lapsing into premature desuetude. "The work of the Commission is going rather slowly," Stevens wrote, June 22. ". . . Apparently not much will be done this summer on any line." Criticisms of inaction began to appear in the press. On August 23, 1915, Gilson Gardner of the Newspaper Enterprise Association wrote Brandeis: "From the enclosed clippings you will see I ventured a little comment on the activities of the Federal Trade Commission. How about it? This was a creature of your creating. Is this what you intended it to do?" One clipping from the *Memphis Press* of August 20 said:

The Federal Trade Commission has been in existence six months, without having entered a single order for the correction of any unfair business practice.

Which indicates one of two things: Either business is much more virtuous than it used to be, or the Federal Trade Commission is doing something different from what was expected by its promoters. . . .

In replying to Gardner's letter on September 7, Brandeis admitted that the activities of the Commission were not what he had contemplated. With his usual optimism, however, he wrote that the presence of Rublee and Stevens led him to believe that it would still prove to be a valuable government instrument. He had foreseen the difficulties that would beset it, and although he was disappointed in its unpromising start, he did not lose hope. Its work, like most reform, must be slow and painstaking with success often built upon failure.

THE CLAYTON ACT VERSUS UNITED SHOE

While exercising paternal solicitude for the Commission, Brandeis also kept a watchful eye on that other legislative offspring—the Clayton Act. For Brandeis this act was closely tied in with the United Shoe Machinery case. After the election of Wilson, the United was thrown into a panic of fear lest Brandeis be given the power and influence of a cabinet post, and it played, as we have seen, a major part in having him sidetracked. The troublesome attorney was not, however, to be disposed of so easily. The United soon found that on matters connected with monopoly Brandeis was closer to the administration's ear than anyone else. The magnates of the company had cause for dismay when the Clayton Anti-Trust Act was found to include one major section pointing directly at the tying clauses on which the life of United's monopoly largely depended. Worse still, Brandeis was in close contact with Attorney-General Gregory, and now that George W. Anderson was Massachusetts' District Attorney, the company was confronted by a hostile and formidable triumvirate.

During the Taft administration's late-hour display of anti-trust activity, a suit had been filed against the monopoly, but in March 1915 the Federal District Court decided against the government. Charles H. Jones, on behalf of the shoe manufacturers, pleaded with Brandeis to take an active hand in the case: ". . . I feel very strongly that you or your office ought to undertake this appeal to the Supreme Court. I don't believe that we will get anybody anywhere that is nearly as competent to handle it, and the situation is, in my judgment, so desperate that nothing but the most skillful possible handling of the case from now on will save the day." [33]

Though Brandeis was too busy to take the case, he felt sure the shoe machinery monopoly offered an excellent test for the Clayton Act and therefore urged Attorney-General Gregory to begin proceedings at the earliest possible moment. In October 1915 a petition was filed under the Clayton Act asking that the tying clauses be declared illegal.* Brandeis was still harassing United—making suggestions for strengthening the government's petition and advising the Department of Justice in its strategy of prosecution. Even outside the cabinet he was dangerous to monopoly. A showdown was not far off.

CHAPTER TWENTY-SEVEN

Other People's Money, 1913-1914

PROGRESSIVE legislation during the first Wilson administration exceeded that passed in nearly twelve years under Roosevelt and Taft. These new measures embodied many of Brandeis's suggestions, yet were far from being all that he thought necessary. Before the anti-trust and other acts he had fathered were through the mill, he was urging legislation on more fronts. Here he was too early; it was not until twenty years later that his theories came alive in such New Deal measures as the Securities Act of 1933 and the Holding Company Act of 1935.

GENESIS OF OTHER PEOPLE'S MONEY

Brandeis's fame as publicist and prophet rests, probably more than anything else, on a series of articles called "Breaking the Money Trust," † which appeared in *Harper's Weekly* and later was published in book form under the title *Other People's Money—and How the Bankers Use It.* Hapgood announced the series on October 8, 1913, and the first article

* The Massachusetts court dismissed the suit to dissolve United Shoe, and the case came before the United States Supreme Court on appeal in 1917. On May 20, 1918, the Court affirmed the decree of the District Court. In a sweeping opinion Justice McKenna ruled that the United's tying clauses did not violate the anti-trust acts.

† Wilson "gave careful attention," R. S. Baker wrote in his biography of Wilson, "to a series of articles then appearing in *Harper's Weekly*. . . . Some of these articles with Wilson's marginal scorings remain still in his files."

appeared on November 8. Others followed periodically through early 1914. "There will be cries of 'Holy Murder' if the legislation I propose ever gets passed," Brandeis wrote Alfred about the series, "but less than that will do little good."

Years before, Brandeis's New England campaigns against predatory wealth, especially his study of railroad finances and subsequent trust investigations, had shown him that behind all such monopolies stood a greater power, unseen but far-reaching, dominating American enterprise. He knew that money had become concentrated in the hands of financial overlords, and had seen power used to make or break business ventures. His theories were based on knowledge won by factual case studies of the Money Trust in action. Early in 1911 he had projected in a letter to Norman Hapgood the broad outlines of an analysis:

"The honest financiers who are using, as bankers and insurance company managers, etc., the money of others, realize that they hold the money in trust for its owners and must be fair to the beneficiaries. They do not realize, however, that the power which the control of other people's money gives them to grant or to withdraw credit, is a trust for the public—a power to be exercised impartially as the applicant for credit is entitled to it. They exercise their power regardless of that trust, ignoring the square deal, and it amounts practically to their playing the industrial game with loaded dice. . . . By controlling the money of other people at the same time that they are engaged in industrial and other occupations, they suppress competition and get other advantages by means that are illegal. . . . Won't the illegal use of the control of other people's money ultimately force the thought of governmental control of money in order to insure the square deal?"

Prophetic words! But in December 1911 there were not many who agreed with him when he declared: "No economic problem in America is as important today as that presented by the Money Trust—the control which a few financiers exercise over the capital of America. That problem is more fundamental, more serious, than the problem of the industrial trust, more serious than the problem of currency. The control of capital is, as to business, what the control of water supply is to life. The economic menace of past ages was the dead hand which gradually acquired a large part of all available lands. The greatest economic menace of today is a very live hand—these few able financiers who are gradually acquiring control over our quick capital." [1]

Brandeis saw the Money Trust as the biggest problem that American statesmanship must face, but realized that the public had not yet sufficient knowledge to deal with it effectively. In 1910 the heads of great railroad systems, such as McCrea, Willard, and Brown, had testified under oath that they were entirely unaware of any concerted effort to circumscribe their affairs. It had required many investigations and much public agitation over a long period of years to show the dangers of industrial trusts and to produce a public demand for action, and with the Money Trust a similar process of exposure and enlightenment was assuredly necessary. Brandeis's effort in the campaign of 1912 had been largely devoted to a discussion of the evil ramifications of industrial trusts. He now turned to their master and creator—the Money Trust.

"Financial oligarchy," as he characterized it, gathered the golden eggs laid by someone else's goose. The Astor wealth, though too great to be tolerated in a democracy, was relatively harmless. It was "static"; its owners had only the income from their wealth. The wealth of the Morgan associates, on the other hand, was dynamic. Their power came from wielding the savings and capital of others. "The fetters which bind the people are forged from the people's own gold." [2] These fetters Brandeis endeavored to break.

FRIEND AND CONCILIATOR

Collier's Weekly had been Brandeis's chief mouthpiece in the 1912 Wilson–Roosevelt fight. Soon after Wilson's nomination he and Norman Hapgood discussed at some length the stand which *Collier's* would take in the campaign. Hapgood, who predicted that T.R.'s tariff plank would be "slush" and his trust plank "N.G.," decided he would come out for Wilson but refrain from attacking T.R.[3] But his associates, Mark Sullivan and Robert J. Collier, were both Roosevelt enthusiasts. When Brandeis, in preparing editorials for Hapgood, failed to maintain anything even approaching neutrality toward T.R., personal relations in *Collier's* editorial room became strained to the breaking point.

In August, Hapgood reported: "The position the paper is taking on the fight between the Democrats and the Bull Moose is rather hard on Sullivan." [4] Trouble over policies between Hapgood and others on the magazine had long been brewing, and the 1912 campaign finally brought matters to a head. Hapgood and *Collier's* parted company.

After Roosevelt's near assassination in Milwaukee, Collier himself took pen in hand and announced his support of the Rough Rider. Just before the election, a statement from T.R. appeared in the magazine, lashing out against the previous unfairness of its editorial policy toward him. In the issue of November 9 Collier relieved himself of that responsibility by revealing that Brandeis, not Hapgood, had written the campaign editorials.

While he spoke highly of his unofficial editorial writer, he felt that Brandeis's relations with Governor Wilson were somewhat too close.

Recrimination ensued. The impulsive Hapgood wrote irate letters indicating that he had been stabbed in the back.[5] Brandeis's friendship for Hapgood, going back to the epoch-making "Wage-Earners' Insurance" article, published in Collier's, September 15, 1906, prompted him to take a hand. The situation was delicate and required diplomacy. First of all, he disabused Collier of the idea that he had used the editorial pages for political purposes, informing him that when he prepared the controverted editorials, he had had no "relations" with Wilson whatsoever, had never met or even seen him, and had not communicated with him on the trust issue. ". . . I was not only an avowed, but an enthusiastic supporter of Governor Wilson," he wrote, "but I refrained from what would ordinarily be termed 'political campaigning' with the possible exception of my speech before the Social Workers in New York; otherwise than that my speeches, like my articles in Collier's, were directed to the trust issue." [6]

Tactfully he tried to banish acrimony from both sides. Using a most cordial tone, he wrote Collier: "I hope you will, upon further consideration, conclude that the character of Collier's can be sustained without an attack upon Norman personally. Such an attack would, of course, be answered; and from the controversies of this nature both parties usually emerge as losers." He enclosed a copy of his Brown University address, "Business— the New Profession," suggesting that Mr. Collier give his readers the ideal of service for business instead of the motives of profit or power. "I believe that Americans are the most idealistic people in the world," he wrote, "and that nothing better can be done than to suggest to our businessmen a high ideal toward which they may work." [7]

This diplomacy was successful; Collier decided to "consider the incident with Norman closed." Brandeis then made sure of future accord by warning Hapgood against any impulsiveness which might renew hostilities: "It seems to me important . . . that you should so far as possible avoid any discussion with anyone of your past relations with Collier. Anything you say is liable to be repeated in inaccurate form, and ultimately to reach him in much distorted shape. I think you ought to give him no possible ground for withdrawing from the position which he has taken of considering the incident closed." [8]

Brandeis was not satisfied, however, merely to stop the controversy. He immediately undertook to find Hapgood a new position. With the disgruntled editor he visited Charles R. Crane at Hot Springs and obtained his aid in financing a publication for Hapgood to edit. In February 1913 Hapgood had lunch with Thomas W. Lamont, who offered to sell Harper's

Weekly for $100,000.[9] With Brandeis carrying on negotiations, and Crane providing the backing, the deal was put through.[10] After Hapgood assumed his editorial post in June, Brandeis did everything possible to help put *Harper's* on its feet, giving freely of his time, effort, and money. A check for $100 which he received for an article on price maintenance was promptly returned.[11] Quite characteristically he conceived the idea that the best way to get Hapgood and his new magazine successfully launched was to make sure all public libraries were supplied. He himself took the necessary steps for New England and arranged with others to do so in other sections of the country.[12] It was in connection with boosting Hapgood and *Harper's* that he wrote many of his articles, particularly those on the Money Trust.

One of his readers wrote asking why he did not have his articles published where they would reach a much larger audience. "Many have suggested to me, as you did," he replied, "that perhaps it might have been better had my articles been published in the *Saturday Evening Post* or possibly *Collier's,* in view of their large circulation, than in *Harper's Weekly*. But I regard Mr. Hapgood as so important a factor in the American advance movement that if I have been of any service in helping *Harper's Weekly,* as his instrument, I shall feel well content with the decision made." [13]

THE FIGHTING FORCE OF FACTS

Public assault on the great financial monopoly had begun back in May 1912 when the House Banking and Currency Committee (the Pujo Committee), with Samuel Untermyer firing the questions, launched its inquiry into the ways of high finance. Despite stubborn insistence by J. P. Morgan and others that no such thing as a Money Trust existed, the findings of the committee indicated otherwise; and its hearings were no sooner over than financial circles uneasily wondered what Brandeis might do with such incendiary materials. Wall Street was "very uneasy over the intimation that the Pujo Committee will be succeeded by another committee, so much stronger, so much less approachable, and so much more intelligent, as to be almost beyond comparison"; in fact, it was "plunged into a cold perspiration at the thought of an intelligent committee with Louis D. Brandeis as counsel. . . ." [14]

As soon as the Pujo Committee published its report, Brandeis wired Untermyer for a copy, and when he had read it over, commented: "It is admirable, and most of your recommendations I should heartily approve. In some respects it seems to me that the recommendations do not go far enough. . . ." [15] Such a statement from Brandeis meant that further disclosures and more advanced proposals would shortly be forthcoming. The need for further investigation was in fact impressed upon the People's Attorney by Untermyer's admission that he had been "unable to get half through" with the testimony when the session ended, that he had a list of about forty uncalled witnesses, that he himself had prepared the report "at Palm Beach in less than ten days." [16] Little wonder that Brandeis, though approving the recommendations of the committee, considered them "entirely inadequate." [17]

It was soon known that Brandeis intended to begin where Pujo, Untermyer and Company left off. He undertook the same painstaking research that had preceded his study of wage-earners insurance and his report on the financial condition of the New Haven and Boston & Maine Railroads. His heavy correspondence indicates the scope and thoroughness of his work. A letter written to Clinton Rogers Woodruff of the National Municipal League is typical:

I am considering the question of direct issues of bonds by municipalities to investors without the intervention of the bankers; and, in this connection also the question of selling the bonds from time to time "over-the-counter," rather than selling large lots on public bidding. There is waste involved in the methods of selling bonds in large issues, whether through bankers or on public bidding, because large sums of money are received by the cities before they are required, and are then deposited by the city in banks at low rates of interest.

Has the League, or any of its members, to your knowledge made an investigation of marketing city bonds; and if so, will you send me any literature that you may have? Also, will you let me know all such instances, as have come to your knowledge, of sales by municipalities of bonds "over-the-counter"? [18]

As he relentlessly ran facts to earth he sometimes encountered resistance reminiscent of New Haven days. Thus when he wrote Robert S. Lovett, president of the Union Pacific Railroad, asking the amounts of the underwriting commissions in the Union Pacific–Southern Pacific dissolution, the reply was decidedly curt: "Referring to letters which I understand you have addressed to me in New York and to the secretary of the company requesting certain information from Union Pacific R.R. Co., our rule is to give no information respecting our business transactions to unofficial persons except as published for information of all alike, and I know of no reason for departing from that rule in this instance. If there is anything in your relations to the subject, officially or otherwise, making our practice inapplicable or justifying departure from it, I should be very glad to be advised for further consideration." [19]

When he asked for the same information from Jacob Schiff, President of Kuhn, Loeb & Company, investment bankers, who had managed the transaction, he got a more diplomatic rebuff: "I am personally not a member of the Directorate of the Union Pacific Railroad Company, but I can appreciate the position Judge Lovett takes, as chairman of a public corporation, in his reply to the request you have made for certain information. For myself, I can only say that as far as my firm is concerned, there is absolutely nothing regarding this which we would not be perfectly willing to have made public, but I hope you will understand that it would not be good faith toward those we deal with, if we gave information which they, for their own reasons, have declined to furnish." [20]

Through Garet Garret of the *New York Times Annalist,* he eventually tracked down the figure to his own satisfaction,[21] but for purposes of the article he had to content himself with a hint as to its magnitude: "How large the two underwriting commissions were which the Union Pacific paid in effecting the severance of this illegal merger, both the company and the bankers have declined to disclose." [22]

The facts he sought were strangely assorted, sometimes apparently irrelevant. From the president of the Pennsylvania, for example, he wanted to know the number of stockholders of the road, the number who were women, and the number of stations on the Pennsylvania system.[23] From Secretary of the Treasury McAdoo, he wanted to know the number of business corporations in the country, grouped in categories according to size of capitalization. McAdoo replied that no such information was available and that the work of getting it would "involve the labor of five clerks for a period of ten days." Brandeis conceded that the articles for *Harper's* would not justify the effort, but told the Secretary he would like to have the information for use in drafting bills on monopolies and the Money Trust.[24]

In this way, seemingly miscellaneous facts were assembled to form a concise, unified description of the Money Trust and used to set forth a comprehensive program for dealing with it. Control of American business, he showed, had become concentrated in the hands of a few great investment bankers. The core of the financial oligarchy consisted of J. P. Morgan & Company, the National City Bank, and the First National Bank of New York, which together controlled corporations having total resources of over $22,000,000,000. Under the three great masters were a number of "provincial allies" and "satellites," such as Kidder, Peabody and Lee, Higginson of Boston, closely knit with them by joint ownerships, interlocking directorates, and community of interest. Through this integrated system the great bankers held sway over economic operations to such an extent that practically no enterprise of any importance could be undertaken without their approval and participation.

The system had grown up through the gradual assumption by the investment bankers of separate and distinct economic functions. The industrial corporations—"the makers of bonds and stocks"—the life insurance companies—the buyers of bonds and stocks—the banks and trust companies—the depositaries of the quick capital of the country—had all been brought under control by the investment bankers. The process was exactly comparable, in Brandeis's mind, with the growth of political despotism:

The development of our financial oligarchy followed . . . lines with which the history of political despotism has familiarized us—usurpation, proceeding by gradual encroachment rather than by violent acts; subtle and often long-concealed concentration of distinct functions, which are beneficent when separately administered, and dangerous only when combined in the same persons. It was by processes such as these that Caesar Augustus became master of Rome.[25]

Such a system produced many evils. By combining separate functions in the same hands, it gave rise to divided loyalties and violated the principle that "no man can serve two masters." It produced inefficiency by destroying soundness of judgment. Inherent in it was a concentration of wealth and power that grew ever larger by feeding on itself. It fostered industrial combination and suppressed business enterprise.

To break up the system Brandeis saw the need for a variety of attacks. He proposed a thorough and effective prohibition of interlocking directorates; publicity as to bankers' commission, profits, and operations; elimination, wherever possible, of the banker as a middleman in sale of securities; the prevention of all connection between railroads and companies with which they deal; and a great growth of co-operatives.

THE MONEY TRUST STRIKES BACK

The clarity of his exposé and the boldness of his proposals produced serious Wall Street jitters. The Investment Bankers' Association, among others, indignantly protested. On behalf of the Association, Lawrence Chamberlain, their general counsel, wrote in *Harper's* for January 17, 1914, that the Association was "neither partial to the abuses that exist in the financial world, nor opposed to constructive reforms." To emphasize his point, the counsel presented an interesting analogy: "Though Mr. Brandeis is a lawyer, the Association will not hold the legal profession responsible for his mistakes." [26] Later Chamberlain charged that in stating that a few people controlled business and in pointing out the exhorbitant commissions charged for handling securities, Brandeis had "misrepresented" the business of investment banking.[27]

In 1914 Brandeis sounded a warning to which our latest financial tragedies give back a grim, gigantic echo. And yet in 1914 certain newspapers and commentators, valuing the tenets of J. P. Morgan more highly than Brandeis's facts, took no pains to restrain their displeasure. The *San Francisco Chronicle,* reviewing the book, commented caustically: "Here are the famous efficiency and financial expert essays in permanent form, and if you are open to deception they will enable you to understand all about the evils of interlocking directorates said to be responsible for that modern myth, the Money Trust. That there is not, never has been, and never could be a complete monopoly of money, matters nothing to one who has given financial literature many of the graces of romance." [28]

How could the country's financial leaders cheat and defraud the public and still retain the public's confidence? Such a notion, the critics asserted, was obviously absurd and preposterous. In dismissing his charges with complacent assurance, they ignored the point of Brandeis's analysis. He was not presenting a moral indictment against any group of financiers who had robbed and plundered the American people behind a mask of respectability. Neither a muckraking exposé nor a crusading sermon, his book was hardly more personal than that of an engineer who tells a manufacturer that he is using the wrong process for making steel. He was pointing out flaws in the American financial structure—flaws which, if uncorrected, would some day bring national disaster. And when the debacle came the public would not be the sole sufferer. The trusted leaders, demanding to be left alone, would likewise be engulfed.

The glaring weakness of the critics' argument was their easy assumption that because financial leaders had won the confidence of the public, such confidence must be deserved. An uninformed public was easily led to its own undoing; a public conscious of the facts would not be fooled. It was for this reason that Brandeis wrote about the Money Trust. Given the facts, the American people could decide for themselves whether they would entrust their pocketbooks to a few financial overlords. Brandeis was convinced that a small group of men, however virtuous and wise, merited no such perilous confidence. As early as 1904 he had said: "Neither our intelligence nor our characters can long stand the strain of unrestricted power." [29] In spite of the New Haven's fabulous feats of finance, his own previous investigation of that monopoly had proved that J. P. Morgan was not a superman, and the myth of his infallibility should have been well exploded by the New Haven disaster. One of the chief points in Brandeis's argument was that under the existing system financial experts would tend more and more to go wrong. By assuming varied functions, by acting simultaneously in different but interrelated capacities, the banker-experts themselves had created conditions under which it was difficult, if not impossible, to make the right decisions.

Even former friends were now incredulous. Henry B. Joy, president of the Packard Motor Car Company, wrote bewailing what the prohibition of interlocking directorates would do to his business: "All the directors of the Packard Company are directors in other industries, banks, etc., which would require me to lose their services as directors of the Packard Company or require them, under the intent of the law, to give up the supervision of their financial interests in other corporations. The warfare against interlocking directorates is totally, absolutely, and entirely unnecessary. . . . I am a director in a coal mine and a director in several railroads. I cannot sell my interest in those properties; I shall have to appoint dummies to represent me. There can be nothing more evil than that sort of thing, to my mind." [30]

Brandeis replied calmly: "I have thought long and hard on the subject of interlocking directorates. The result of my thought is embodied in the articles in *Harper's Weekly* beginning November 22nd, which I hope you have had time to read. I am convinced that, subject to the possible limitations therein stated, the system of interlocking directorates is an inevitable breeder of evil. The fundamental law that no man can serve two masters cannot be safely ignored as a general working rule, however great the merits or virtues of particular individuals or enterprises."

He then directed Joy's attention to his description of the variety of conflicting positions one man might occupy: "J. P. Morgan (or a partner), a director of the New York, New Haven & Hartford Railroad, causes that company to sell to J. P. Morgan & Co. an issue of bonds; J. P. Morgan & Co. borrow the money with which to pay for the bonds from the Guaranty Trust Company, of which Mr. Morgan (or a partner) is a director. J. P. Morgan & Co. sell the bonds to the Penn Mutual Life Insurance Company, of which Mr. Morgan (or a partner) is a director. The New Haven spends the proceeds of the bonds in purchasing steel rails from the United States Steel Corporation, of which Mr. Morgan (or a partner) is a director. The United States Steel Corporation spends the proceeds of the rails in purchasing electrical supplies from the General Electric Company, of which Mr. Morgan (or a partner) is a director . . ." and so on *ad infinitum*. A man in such a position could not possibly reach an unbiased decision as to the interests of the various companies in which he was active.

There was still another reason for distrusting decisions of the financial oligarchy: Obviously the only justification for the director's existence is that he should direct. . . . For the proper exercise of the functions of director, it is essential that he be distinterested; that is, be free from any conflicting interest. But it is also essential that he have knowledge. Facts, facts, facts, are the only basis on which he can properly exercise his judgment. It is as necessary that he know intimately the facts concerning the business, as that he have only one interest to subserve. Now, no man can have such detailed knowledge of the facts of many enterprises. This is due to the limitations of time and place and to those other limits set by nature upon human intelligence." [31]

This was no ranting against malefactors of great wealth, but practical talk from a man who had himself been a director of corporations, who had engaged simultaneously in varied activities, who knew from his own experience the limits on a man's capacities.

REBUTTAL AND VERDICT

While irate complaints greeted the articles and the book, there was also applause from various directions. One enthusiastic reader wrote: "No man ever did so much to enlighten the people, by a single article, as you have in your contribution which was published in the last *Harper's Weekly*. I have sent for a dozen extra copies, which I propose to mail. I wish that five hundred thousand extra copies could be distributed." [32] Judge Charles F. Amidon wrote Hapgood: "I have been buying *Harper's Weekly* at the news-stands since you took charge of the paper, but I cannot take the chance of missing any of Mr. Brandeis's articles. I therefore enclose annual subscription of five dollars." [33]

La Follette hailed the publication of *Other People's Money* as "epoch-making." The *Washington Star* called it "concrete and amazingly circumstantial, clear and forceful." The *St. Paul Pioneer Press* heartily recommended it to "the reader who is not attracted to long and abstruse financial reports on the one side, or to careless and unsupported generalizations on the other." A lady from Wyoming, New York, wrote: "I am passing your book around and giving copies to friends and to our library. By virtue of my ninety-six years I make no apology for writing you. If you should come to our part of Western New York, mid-way between Rochester and Buffalo, it would give me great pleasure to welcome you to our home. I believe in serious-minded people meeting and talking about the things that interest them." B. H. Meyer of the Interstate Commerce Commission lauded its simplicity: "I had never before seen these matters focused so intensively and brought within the range of understanding of the average intelligent citizen." [34]

A most satisfying tribute came from Judge Kenesaw Mountain Landis: "I feel personally grateful to you for the work you are doing. The strength of your 'Money Trust' articles lies in the fact that the blacksmith, the shoe-maker, the farmer, and even the federal judge can understand the matter as they do the A. B. C.'s. . . . You do not appreciate it but the fact is the atoms that go to make up the great mass of folks in this country know that you are fighting for them." [35]

MORE FUEL FOR THE FLAME

In an address before the Academy of Political and Social Sciences, the Boston lawyer again invaded the stronghold of financial complacency. On the platform with him were Frank A. Vanderlip, president of the National City Bank of New York, George E. Roberts, director of the Mint, and C. J. Rhoads, president of the Girard Trust Company. Brandeis cut an odd figure in such company. "Money and the credit are the life blood of business," he declared, "and the concentration of money and credit has proceeded to such an extent that no large enterprise can be successfully undertaken or pursued without the consent of a few men to whom tribute must be paid." In his conclusion he threw down the gauntlet to financial oligarchy:

Travelers tell how amid the mighty Himalayas, man is cowed.
You will find nearer home a like effect of overwhelming power. . . .
In a democracy it is the part of statesmanship to prevent the development of power which overawes the ordinary forces of man. Where such power exists, it must be broken. The privilege which begets it must be destroyed.[36]

Banker Vanderlip, appalled by Brandeis's grim speech, denounced the notion of a Money Trust as "moonshine," damned the Pujo Committee as that "bureau of misinformation," and concluded: "The Pujo Committee was an outrage to the average intelligence, and its figures were astronomi-cal." His reply to Brandeis's statement that the individual was stunted by such concentration of power was: "Today I head the biggest bank in New York; and I began as a farmer's boy." [37]

The debate was vehement against Brandeis, but from letters he later received he more than held his own. One correspondent said: ". . . I con-sidered Mr. Vanderlip's uncalled-for comment on your address weak and evasive. . . . I thank you for the pleasure your address gave me. It was courageous to make your speech in one of the chief centers of Bourbon-ism." [38] Marlen E. Pew gave him a vivid picture of how the tiff between the banker and himself looked to a bystander: "I have just heard the 'debate' and hasten to congratulate you and thank you for the refreshment. As you were speaking I observed the great banker . . . smarting under the whip of fact and logic and it was funny when he essayed to relieve the pain by an application of the old reliable 'moonshine'! . . . There's a mighty host of individuals who supinely permit the lords to 'get away with' their moonshine talk, but once in a while they meet up with a man who knows and dares. . . ." [39]

Brandeis had further opportunity to hit the Money Trust in 1914, when the National Bureau of Public Utilities Research was organized and his name appeared on the board of trustees. Other leading lights were Charles R. Van Hise, president of the University of Wisconsin, Frederick W. Taylor, the great exponent of scientific management, and Felix Frankfurter of the Harvard Law School.

On November 7, 1914, Morris L. Cooke wrote Brandeis that his attendance at their initial conference would be most important because of the crucial issues between corporation interests and the public interest: "From our correspondence we take it that it is your remarks more than all the other things put together that make the corporation crowd tremble. . . . I have personally been threatened from a very high quarter unless I saw to it that you withdrew, and from another quarter have been asked to give assurances as to what you were going to say."

Carl Kelsey, acting president of the American Academy of Political and Social Science, and Samuel B. Fels of Fels-Naptha Soap joined in the clamor for his presence.[40] He finally gave in, attended the conference, and delivered an address on interlocking directorates.

THE MONEY TRUST GOES ON

Nevertheless, financial oligarchy kept on its course, extending its tentacles further over the economic life, and grew at a vastly accelerated pace during World War I. A provision prohibiting interlocking directorates, included in the Clayton Act of 1914, proved inadequate. This financial evil came to full bloom in the early thirties when Samuel Insull served on more than eighty boards, Richard B. Mellon on nearly fifty, Percy A. Rockefeller on sixty-eight, Albert A. Wiggin on about fifty, Charles E. Mitchell on thirty-two, though two decades earlier Brandeis had warned: "I doubt whether anybody who is himself engaged in any important business has time to be a director in more than one large corporation." [41]

During the decade of the twenties the dreary history of the New Haven monopoly was repeated in almost every phase of our economic life. Concentration of financial power and the intricate union of diverse functions in the hands of an irresponsible few grew apace and finally brought destruction to the oligarchs themselves as well as to those whose confidence they betrayed. The ensuing financial disaster brought confirmation of Brandeis's prediction. At the height of the Coolidge boom and two years before

Herbert Hoover, Republican candidate for President, foresaw the day
when poverty would be banished from the earth, Brandeis made an altogether different reading of the signs of the times. On October 18, 1926, in
telling of a visit from old Louisville friends, the Flexners, he wrote his
brother: "Ben and Min Flexner were in this morning. He is quite as flab-
bergasted as we are by the manifestations of business and says that, never
in his life, has he felt himself so helpless—so unable to cope with the tides
about him. And like some others of his generation, he doesn't like it at all.
Unlike most of his business associates he does not think that the prosperity
will last."

With the acquiescence, even the assistance, of government, federal and
state, the lords of inflation finance led the nation on an endless upward
spiral of sham prosperity. The flaws of the New Economic Era, long detected by Brandeis, suddenly cracked wide open. The Great Depression and
the subsequent collapse of our whole banking system merely underscored
the wisdom embodied two decades earlier in *Other People's Money*. The
probe undertaken in the spring of 1933 by the Senate Banking and Currency Committee, with Ferdinand Pecora as counsel, found nothing new.
In fact, Mr. Pecora's portrait of the financial overlords of the 1920's merely
retouched Brandeis's picture of the Morgan–Mellon combine two decades
earlier. Said Mr. Pecora:

The prestige and reputation of these institutions were enormous. They stood,
in the mind of the financially unsophisticated public, for safety, strength, prudence, and high-mindedness, and they were supposed to be captained by men
of unimpeachable integrity, possessing almost mythical business genius and
foresight. Yet from the very mouths of these trusted leaders, there came forth
an amazing recital of practices, to which the catastrophic collapse of the entire
banking structure of the country seemed but the natural climax. . . .
Even in 1914, Mr. Justice Brandeis had noted the beginnings of this process.
But its proportions then were embryonic compared with the growth that came
with the ensuing years.[42]

Thus did events bear eloquent testimony to Brandeis's views that financial oligarchy is the most serious menace to freedom in modern society;
that the line of greatest advance lies in the direction of public control.
Twenty years before the Securities Act, he had said:

Break the control so exercised by the investment bankers over railroad, public
service, and industrial corporations over banks, life insurance, and trust companies, and a long step will have been taken toward attainment of the New
Freedom.[43]

Yet the Money Trust went its way substantially undisturbed. The New
Freedom was yet to be won.

CHAPTER TWENTY-EIGHT

Political Shoals and Progressive Horizons, 1912-1915

THE YEARS 1910 to 1915 were the fullest of Brandeis's public life. Included among his activities were conservation, industrial relations, scientific management, railroad regulation, banking and currency, government policy toward business, and, above all else, the new politics of power. With equal zest he undertook trust-busting, brain-trusting, publicizing, political maneuvering. Many letters to his brother attest the great multiplicity and significance of his work. "Had two-and-a-half busy and, I think, very profitable days in Washington," he wrote, June 11, 1913, "seeing the President twice and spending much time with Redfield, McAdoo, and McReynolds, and the Commissioner of Corporations, aside from my New Haven activities. . . . Saw Marble and talked with him a bit about rate advance."

"I am off for New York tonight," he commented, February 24, 1915, "after more than a fortnight here, my longest stay since—well, it must be more than a year."

"Have been supplementing Zionist activities by Woman Suffrage, Gubernatorial, Garment Workers Arbitration, and public franchise excursions," he wrote, October 22, 1915. "Am going to Philadelphia today for Frederick Winslow Taylor Memorial. Thus is the honest practice of a profession interfered with."

So varied were the pressures on him that he sometimes lamented inability to center attention on one problem. In addition to major undertakings that ran into months or years, the ubiquitous People's Attorney gave thought to innumerable lesser matters. "There's one of the busiest men in the country," Addison L. Winship, civic secretary of the Boston City Club, remarked one day as Brandeis left his office, Winship having just tried in vain to get him to address the club.[1]

About the same time, he presided over a woman suffrage meeting. Earlier he had opposed giving the ballot to women, but experience had shown him that on many social issues women had clearer understanding than men. Jane Addams told the gathering that the women might have to "throw things" to get the ballot, but Brandeis quietly remarked: "For the solution of these problems we must look to the many, not to the few. We need all the people, women as much as men. The insight women have shown in problems which often men could not understand has convinced me that women not only should have the suffrage, but that we really need the women in politics." [2]

Following his argument in the Five Per Cent Rate Case he was off to New Hampshire, having accepted, on February 22, 1911, an invitation from that state's House of Representatives to conduct an investigation of unauthorized freight rates imposed by the Boston & Maine.* In June 1911 he was back in Boston fighting an "omnibus" bill introduced in the Massachusetts General Court which provided for new tunnels and subways, with leases on a fifty-year basis.

Shortly thereafter he was before a committee of the Massachusetts Legislature in support of Governor Foss's recommendation to amend the constitution so as to provide for a tax on intangible personal property and a state income tax. ". . . Our present tax laws not only permit tax dodging; they encourage it; nay, they even compel it . . . ," he said. [3]

In 1912 Brandeis was giving Franklinlike advice to the "little man" and his wife on the rising cost of living. "More families are ruined through the faults and extravagances of the woman of the household than through the husband's failure to increase his earning capacity," he contended. High prices and moderate incomes necessitate the housewife's training herself in domestic science and learning to save the pennies. He urged that ". . . the model housewife must arise in her might and do that which is necessary to curb the greed of the butcher, the baker, and the candlestick maker, who after all are only trying to get back that which was wrung out of them by the wholesaler or the middleman." He had no sympathy for the flippant wife who refused to take seriously the duties of household management: "The woman who spends the bulk of her time running to this or that club or card meeting will soon bankrupt her husband, unless he is a Croesus, if indeed she doesn't kill him with indigestion beforehand." [4]

He dissented from the great twentieth-century American mania of "keeping up with the Joneses": "We are living in an artificial age, and artificiality is ruining many of those just starting out in life. . . . Seeing others far better off in this world's goods, enjoying the luxuries and good things of life, they deem it necessary to do likewise, for fear, I suppose, that they might be ridiculed for their thrift or sufficient strength of char-

* In recognition of his services the House of Representatives, State of New Hampshire, adopted the following Resolutions.

"Resolved, That the thanks of this House are due and hereby are extended to Louis D. Brandeis, Esq., of Boston, Mass., for his distinguished and disinterested services, rendered without compensation for the Special Rate Committee of this House appointed to investigate the matter of steam railroad rates for fares and freight, and

"Resolved, that the Clerk of the House be and hereby is instructed to transmit to Louis D. Brandeis, Esq., a suitable engrossed copy of this Resolution, signed by the Speaker and Clerk of the House."

acter to say no. . . . The little struggling clerk must bedeck his wife with bizarre clothes so that he can take her out and impress upon those who behold her in all her magnificence that he is making big money, that this excursion is nothing out of the ordinary in his life, and that he is a 'big spender.' That's the rock on which domesticity so often founders." [5]

He looked with distaste on the extravagance that characterized American life. On a trip West in 1914 he stopped in Detroit, and after an evening at a hotel wrote Alfred: "At this hotel, I was introduced to the modernist stunt of having not only an orchestra at dinner and singers, but also dancers. Pompeii and Alexandria are being emulated. I guess a heavy batch of adversity wouldn't hurt American morals." [6]

IN ADVOCACY OF PRICE MAINTENANCE

Brandeis saw the problem of monopoly and eventually rising costs as vitally related to price maintenance. When in May 1913 the Supreme Court held that manufacturers of patented articles could not fix the price at which retailers sold their product to the consumer,[7] he wrote Alfred: "The Supreme Court is all wrong and I want to set machinery in motion to get this straightened out." "When a court decides a case upon grounds of public policy," he maintained, "the judges become, in effect, legislators. The question then involved is no longer one for lawyers only. It seems fitting, therefore, to inquire whether this judicial legislation is sound." [8]

His self-assigned task "to get this straightened out" was the more difficult because the Court's ruling met with considerable support. It was widely applauded by consumers, who felt that price maintenance was a device of monopoly, born of desire to make them pay more; by merchants, who felt they had a right to set their own selling price on articles they bought; and by anti-monopolists, who considered price-fixing a tool of monopolistic oppression. Brandeis was certain that both Court and people were unwittingly fostering the thing they wanted abolished—monopoly. Confusion had resulted, he believed, from inadequate knowledge of the facts.

Brandeis, the country's foremost defender of competition, the champion of the consumer and of "the little man," attacking the Supreme Court's apparently liberal decision and vigorously upholding the principle of price maintenance seemed strangely inconsistent. Yet his stand was taken only after painstaking research. Following his usual method, he inquired of A. W. Shaw, editor of *System:*

1: What, in staple articles of production—like flour, sugar, shoes, cottons, woolens, hardware, ready-made clothing, eggs, poultry, vegetables—is the

mark-up or difference between the producers' selling price and the price paid
by the consumer?

2: To what extent has there been progress in reducing the percentage of cost
of distribution?

3: Can you give me any figures which show what part of the total cost of
distribution is absorbed by the retail selling? [9]

From E. J. Frost of Filene's he wanted to know whether the unit cost
of distribution by retail stores had increased in the previous ten or twenty
years and to what extent the ordinary prices of goods to the purchaser are
increased by the extra amount which the seller must charge to cover the loss
on non-standard goods.[10] Of J. Frank McElwain, the shoe manufacturer,
he asked how the retail selling price of shoes compared with the manufacturer's price and what percentage of the price paid by the consumer represented the net profits of the retailer.[11] He went to the Bureau of Labor
Statistics to find out whether the cost of distributing merchandise at retail
was higher than it had been from 1890 to 1899.[12]

Convinced finally as to the wisdom of his position, he sought support
from editors and businessmen: "It is very important that we, who believe
in competition, should undertake to remove the restriction which the
Court's decision has imposed upon legitimate business practice. . . . We
must afford protection to those agreements between competitors which
preserve and make continued competition possible; and we must protect
also those agreements which the individual engaged in competitive business develops for the prevention of 'cutthroat' competition—so long as
there is nothing in them against the public welfare. The denial of this
right would inevitably further capitalistic combinations. . . . Ultimately,
we must get an express legislative recognition of the right of the individual manufacturer engaged in competitive business to market his goods
through retail channels at a uniform price. It is good morals and is essential
to the existence of the smallest business concerns." [13]

Price maintenance found no more favor with Wilson's Department of
Justice than among Supreme Court judges. Though he firmly believed the
administration's policy unwise, prudence dictated that it be not attacked
directly. "Occurrences . . . have confirmed my conviction that with the
proper campaign of education, our cause will win," he wrote Henry B. Joy,
June 6, 1913. "It is, however, very important that nothing should appear
in public or private literature or communications which could be construed
as criticism either of the Department of Justice or of Mr. Oldfield. All of
the gentlemen concerned have the highest motives and are seeking the
public good. Like the majority of the Supreme Court, they lack, in this

instance, the necessary knowledge of business practices and conditions."
The administration, the Court, and the public alike needed to have the
entire subject canvassed and illuminated. Through his usual formula of
articles, speeches, and statements to congressional committees, he put the
wheels in motion.

When the retailer can cut prices at will on trade-marked articles, he
argued, injury redounds not only to the manufacturer but to the dealer
and to the consuming public. The use of a "leader" sold at less than standard price to attract customers—or, as he termed it, a "misleader"—demoral-
izes trade in that article to the disadvantage of all concerned. But more than
that, price-cutting paves the way for monopoly. It was among the most
effective methods used by the Standard Oil and American Tobacco Trusts
in exterminating the small independent producers and retailers. In the end
the public was the loser: "Farseeing organized capital secures by this means
the co-operation of the shortsighted unorganized consumer to his own undoing. Thoughtless or weak, he yields to the temptation of trifling immediate gain; and, selling his birthright for a mess of pottage, becomes himself
an instrument of monopoly." [14]

In condemning price-fixing, the unthinking failed to distinguish between
"the independent manufacturer who fixes the price on his own particular
product and the monopoly or combination which fixes the price on a
common article of trade." Price maintenance was not a device of monopoly
but a method by which competition could be regulated and protected. But,
as in other phases of his public activity, it was not enough to evolve and
urge a constructive idea; he went further and campaigned for its imple-
mentation. Throughout 1913, 1914, and well into 1915, he continued to give
active support to the American Fair Trade League, addressing the Association of National Advertising Managers, writing articles for *Harper's,*
and advising legislators and others as to strategy. In 1913 the League joined
him in a campaign to win popular support and force legislative action. A
bill, drawn up under his direction, was introduced in Congress by Representative Raymond B. Stevens, and in January 1915 he appeared in support
of this measure before the House Committee on Interstate and Foreign
Commerce. The right of the manufacturer to maintain a price on trade-
marked goods in their original package was, he contended, a fundamental
principle of economic life. That right the Supreme Court had failed to protect. "There would not have been any occasion to introduce the Stevens
bill," he told the House Committee, "but for misapprehension by the Supreme Court of the trade condition and facts necessary to determine what
the public interest demands. What is being asked for here is not any privilege at all; it is a measure to restore a right commonly enjoyed in the

leading commercial states of this country, and the leading commercial countries of the world . . . and which was abridged in respect to interstate commerce by certain decisions of the Supreme Court." [15]

"But we may say," Brandeis continued, "to those men who come here and ask for protection in establishing standard prices, but which the Supreme Court has inadvertently denied them, that we are willing now—"

"We are not authorized now, I think, to assume the Supreme Court inadvertently does anything," Alben W. Barkley (now a senator) interposed.

"Why not?" asked Brandeis.

"Because it is the supreme judicial body of this land, and we are supposed to recognize it as the highest legal authority, and we have no right to presume the Supreme Court, in passing upon this question, acted inadvertently; because if we have that right, we might presume they acted that way in handing down other of their decisions."

"I am very glad of the opportunity of pointing out to Mr. Barkley more clearly what I mean," Brandeis said. "The Supreme Court is a court which, when it is construing the Constitution of the United States, is supposed to lay down the final law. But we amended the Constitution in respect to the income tax because we believed that the rule laid down by the Supreme Court was not consistent with the public interest."

"It was not erroneous with respect to its interpretation of the Constitution, as it turned out later, because we had to amend the Constitution," Barkley retorted.

"The rule laid down was not in harmony with public policy," Brandeis said. "In a very large number of cases where questions of strict law are before the Court we have to accept the decision of the Court as the highest authority. But on a question of public policy it is no disrespect to the Supreme Court to say that the majority of the Court were mistaken. There is no reason why five gentlemen of the Supreme Court should know better what public policy demands than five gentlemen of Congress . . . and if Congress does not agree with the Supreme Court in this respect it should declare so by enacting the Stevens bill." [16]

The bill encountered many obstacles; bickering among its supporters finally led to the introduction of a substitute measure of doubtful constitutionality. When one of the leading members of the Fair Trade League, William H. Ingersoll, manufacturer of the famous watch, supported the substitute bill, Brandeis wrote a sharp letter to dissuade him. Changing horses in midstream, he warned, especially changing to "a horse that was apt to break down before . . . the journey's end," endangers the whole cause.[17] The chief difficulty was widespread prejudice, caused principally by ignorance, against the idea of allowing a manufacturer to "fix" prices.

"I find," wrote Brandeis, that "men of ability and intelligence who are inclined to take the same view of things that I do, approach this subject with prejudice against the principles of the Stevens bill, and it requires even from them considerable study to overcome a natural disinclination at permitting the establishment of standard prices." [18]

Yet Brandeis maintained his customary optimism. It would take time and a great deal of work to "educate Congress and the public" to the need for a price maintenance bill, but eventually it would be accomplished: "I have such confidence in my fellow citizens that I cannot doubt ultimate success in securing this legislation." [19]

Success, however, was long in coming. Like most measures of reform, price maintenance was shelved during the first World War; it was revived without success in the Kelly–Stephens bill of 1924 and in the Capper–Kelly bill of 1931. Still, the process of education made headway, for Brandeis was informed in 1931 that "many of your critics [of 1913] are now enthusiastically supporting your viewpoint." [20] In 1937, twenty-four years after Brandeis took up the cause, victory finally came with the passage of the Miller-Tydings Act.

THE PRINCIPLES OF INDUSTRIAL DEMOCRACY

Brandeis did not, as we have seen, accept President Wilson's offer of the chairmanship of the Industrial Relations Commission. But during April 1914 and January 1915 he spent several days testifying before the Commission. There was then much talk of "overproduction." Experts spun out schemes for reducing production as the sole way of warding off hard times. Brandeis saw this as but the surface indication of a much deeper problem. "It seems to me," he observed, "that we are so far away in this country, and probably in any country, from satisfying the possible wants of the community, that there is no fear of overproduction in its proper sense. It all comes to the question of what people can afford to buy," that is, of effective demand. Analyzing the economic blockade in terms of cause rather than of effect, he saw the real problem as one of "underconsumption, or maladjustment in distribution. There is plenty of consumptive power," he said, "but not enough ability to buy things." [21]

The real trouble lay in the fact that, in the transition from handicraft to machine production, "labor did not get the share to which it was entitled." [22] Nor was successful elimination of trade unionism by employers the only reason for that failure. Labor leaders themselves had not properly appraised their role in modern industrial society. Not a few unions had prevented the introduction of scientific management, ignorantly believing that any increase in production would have the effect of robbing workers of employment. But Brandeis pointed out that labor, the employers, and the community generally—all stood to win by a vastly increased production. "A condition might well arise," Brandeis remarked before the Industrial Commission, "where it might be to my individual benefit to restrict production, but the benefit to labor as a whole would be immensely advanced by increasing production." [23]

Furthermore, unions still considered higher wages in terms of higher pay per hour or per day. But for Brandeis the time had come when regular employment "should be one of the specific demands of society and of labor unions. . . . When we once get to a point where workingmen are paid throughout the year, as the officers of a corporation are paid throughout the year, and the higher employees are paid throughout the year, everyone will recognize that a business can not be run profitably unless you keep it running, because if you have to pay, whether your men are working or not, your men will work." [24]

Vested interests, deep-seated prejudice, and ignorance on both sides, blocked the changes he then urged. Brandeis told the Commission on Industrial Relations how one of the ablest businessmen of his acquaintance, a man of liberal labor views, once remarked to him: "I want to take up the labor question when I get around to it." The highest motives often produced the most unfortunate results. Not a few employers refused to deal with the union because they thought it would be submitting to "union dictation." Their attitude was likely to be: "This is my business and the American has the right of liberty of contract." [25]

What the employer failed to realize, Brandeis observed, was that the exercise of one's rights must be consistent with the exercise of similar rights by others. The representative of a large, successful industry, who had done everything possible, he thought, to improve the condition of his 6,000 employees, once told Brandeis that he would not allow any unionism. "We have this property here," the employer insisted. "We can't run the risk of our property being destroyed by these 6,000 men." "Well," Brandeis had replied, giving his view in a nutshell, "how can the 6,000 men run the risk of their lives being destroyed by you?" [26]

But even if all such prejudice could be overcome and the usual corrective devices of trade unionism, social insurance, hour and wage regulations, and scientific management be recognized and applied, we still would not have struck at the basic cause of social unrest, Brandeis told the Industrial Commission. Men must be properly fed and housed; they must have education and recreation. "We cannot reach our goal without these things. But we may have all those things, and have a nation of slaves. . . . We must have industrial liberty as well as good wages." [27]

"We must bear in mind all the time," he insisted, "that . . . the United States is a democracy, and that we must have, above all things, men. It is the development of manhood to which any industrial and social system should be directed. We Americans are committed . . . primarily to democracy. The social justice for which we are striving is an incident of our democracy, not the main end. It is rather the result of democracy—perhaps its finest expression—but it rests upon democracy, which implies the rule by the people. And therefore the end for which we must strive is the attainment of rule by the people, and that involves industrial democracy as well as political democracy."

Over and over again Brandeis stressed the conflict between our political democracy and our industrial absolutism as basic, as the crux of our labor problem. Said he: "We are as free politically, perhaps, as free as it is possible for us to be. Every male has his voice and vote; and the law has endeavored to enable, and has succeeded practically, in enabling him to exercise his political franchise without fear. He therefore has his part; and certainly can secure an adequate part in the government of the country in all of its political relations. . . ." In the industrial realm "the position of the ordinary worker is exactly the reverse. The individual employee has no effective voice or vote. . . ." [28] Therefore no real solution of industrial unrest, nor even an approximation thereto, could be reached "as long as there exists in this country any juxtaposition of political democracy and industrial absolutism." [29] The fundamental issue is not hours, wages, and working conditions, but whether the position of labor in American industry is consistent with our ideal of democracy. Therefore the only solution that really goes to the root of social unrest is industrial democracy—a policy, not a measure. This means much more than a division of profits. It means that "the employees must have the opportunity of participating in the decisions as to what shall be their condition and how the business shall be run." It means that the worker has "not only a voice but a vote; not merely a right to be heard, but a position through which labor may participate in management." [30] "This participation in and eventual control of industry," Brandeis contended, is "essential for obtaining justice in distributing the fruits of industry." [31]

The arrangement Brandeis visualized was one of strong employers' associations balanced by strong unions, co-operating in the management of industry, in the settlement of day-to-day conflicts. For "the problems of a trade should be no longer the problems of the employer alone. The problems of his business, and it is not the employer's business alone, are the problems of all in it. The union cannot shift upon the employer the responsibility for conditions, nor can the employer insist upon determining, according to his will, the conditions which shall exist. . . . There must be a division not only of profits, but a division also of responsibilities." In this way only could labor learn that in sharing such responsibility it must suffer the consequences along with the employer. "But the right to assist in making the decision," he insisted, "the right of making their own mistakes, if mistakes there must be, is a privilege which should not be denied to labor." [32]

Industrial democracy in such terms was and is revolutionary, and Brandeis recognized that it could not be won without struggle. "All of our human experience," he observed, "shows that no one with absolute power can be trusted to give it up even in part." Thus collective bargaining would have to be fought for and won by those who passionately desire it. It neither could nor should be conferred as a gift on a legislative platter. Government intervention was in order only if corporate power continued to root out trade unionism. Then "the state must in some way come to the aid of the workingman if democratization is to be secured." [33]

The need, as he saw it, was education; the great task was to develop institutions of industrial self-government. There must be created a relation of employer and employee similar to that which existed in the garment trades of New York City under the protocol of September 2, 1910, something in the nature of a constitutional government, the problems of the trade being settled in parliamentary and juridical fashion. His experience in the garment trades had demonstrated that when opponents in a labor struggle confronted each other over a conference table, they developed mutual understanding, learned to adjust and compromise.*

Brandeis warned the unions that sharing the responsibilities of management would carry with it the added responsibility for controlling the actions of individual members. "There is no possible way of bringing about justice in the protection of classes, except the assumption by the class of the obligation of making the members of that class conform to proper moral standards." [34]

While he urged labor to keep its own house in order, he exhorted capital to consider its own interest in dealing, and dealing fairly, with unions, pointing out that in a period of social unrest the most conservative force in the community is the well-regulated union. Union organization was a "safety valve," and the employer would do most to prevent violence and lawlessness by giving the unions justice and demanding the same from

*. . . Most of the difficulties between employers and employees . . . can be adjusted by discussion rather than by arbitration, and . . . up to the present time in the most serious disputes persons other than a state board, the officially appointed individuals, have been more effective in securing the proper adjustment than constituted officials." (*Hearings before the Senate Committee on Interstate Commerce*, 62nd Cong., Pt. XVI, p. 1251.)

them. "The slightest concession to fear, as distinguished from a concession to a just demand" was, he advised, a menace to the community.

Employers should, moreover, realize that democratization of industry would increase greatly the efficiency of employees. The psychological effects of freedom and responsibility are tremendous. "I am working much harder than any of my employees," many employers remarked. For Brandeis the reason was clear: they were assuming responsibility for their business and were getting the consequent satisfaction out of their work. That satisfaction, among employees, Brandeis was convinced, could come only through freedom and responsibility. Much of the discontent of employees, he believed, was the result of the suppression of their individuality:

. . . there are few things so interesting in life as work, under proper conditions; and the way that employers generally work establishes the truth of this. They complain because their employees do not work similarly, do not feel the responsibility of the business. Let them give the employees a chance to bear responsibility, and the response will come. . . . Unrest means ordinarily unused faculties, and there will be labor unrest until the faculties of the laboring man are fully utilized, and they cannot be without a share in the responsibility for the results of the business in which they are engaged.[35]

HOW HE DID IT

How he was able to carry on so many activities at once, to follow so many complicated subjects with precise grasp of detail, was a constant cause of wonder. Railroad men were nonplused as he discussed with authority the most technical questions of rates and traffic. Businessmen who had thought him an "impractical reformer" gasped as he showed them precisely how to improve their methods of organization. Social workers and jurists were amazed by his scientific analysis as to the effect of long working hours. Financial men were awed by his expert mastery of figures. Journalists envied the number, scope, and quality of his clear, vigorous articles. Politicians respected his political strategy. All these talents combined in one of the most masterful legal minds in the country!

How could one find time for all this? If the man on the street had seen his desk piled with work-materials, the stupendous array of his correspondence, his prolific output of manuscript, memoranda, and printed page, he would have been even more astounded. Actually the explanation is quite simple—the key is that he applied scientific management to his own life and work. His day ran according to steady routine, in which hours, even minutes, were carefully scheduled. By planning, personal efficiency could be doubled or trebled. "Between what we do and what we are capable of doing there is a difference of 100 per cent," he maintained.[36]

Another secret of his extraordinary achievement was skillful manage-ment of men. Edward F. McClennen, present head of the Brandeis firm, speaks of his "predilection for getting other people to do and to have credit for doing what he felt they could do as well as he could." This en-abled him, after 1897, practically to withdraw from trial practice. "In the twenty years preceding 1916," Mr. McClennen writes, "so well had he knit together this firm that it is difficult to speak of his practice in that twenty years. It was the firm that was practicing in that period. There were many things in that practice which he came to believe could be handled better by one or another of his partners. He acted on this belief. During the latter half of this period [1896–1916] the court activities of the firm had passed largely into the hands of his partners." [37]

Brandeis preached the virtue of thrift and exemplified it in his own life; the principles of saving could be applied to time and human energy as well as to money. This was easy for him because he profoundly disliked the things of this world that are too much with us, the cumbering incidentals that engross man's thought and care and slay his independence. Nothing in his living quarters could be called pretentious. In 1880 he had sent Alfred "two bits of advice" on furnishing his room: "Buy nothing that is not irre-sistibly handsome. Buy nothing which your grandchildren cannot use."

Almost none of Brandeis's time was given to household details. Domes-tic affairs were entirely in the hands of Mrs. Brandeis. In 1940 the Justice recalled buying only one article of household furnishing—a new-fangled thermometer, purchased soon after his marriage. It proved a failure and thereafter he left all such matters wholly to his wife. He never went shop-ping, even for his own clothes. Having once found the type of attire suitable to his desires and needs, he merely reordered.

At the height of his career he rose at five-thirty. When some pressing question occupied him, he would begin the day at four. Until his seven o'clock breakfast he reviewed the previous day or did preliminary ground-work on new matters. While riding to the office after breakfast, he read the morning papers. Arriving at eight-twenty, he worked at top speed until one, and according to those who saw him in action, his top speed was an extraordinarily fast clip. He usually ate lunch at either the Union, Ex-change, or Boston City Club, and finished his formal day promptly at five.

The happiest hour of the day for him was dinner, to which he fre-quently invited a few friends for discussion of public problems, the one requirement being their ability to participate intelligently. Dinner guests found an evening with the Brandeises a highly stimulating experience. One writer noted that it was an occasion for satisfying more than physical appetite: "Today a dinner with Mr. Brandeis, if not literally a feast of reason, is an affair of assimilation. One understands—what some of the trust magnates have failed to grasp—that this man has for fifty years past been building up within himself a big mind trust. In his friendly, courteous way he seems all the while not merely to be partaking of food; his very active mentality is absorbing you." [38]

Generally he spent other evenings either talking with his family, reading, conferring with men who had been unable to see him during the day, or giving a public speech. He went to bed at ten.

As public activities took him more and more to New York and Washington, the daily routine had to be adapted to changed surroundings, but his orderly arrangement for all waking hours remained the secret of his ability to maintain high efficiency. There were, to be sure, other factors—freedom from worry and knowledge of his own physical limitation being among the most important. Even when a cherished cause failed, or events took an untoward turn, he was likely to observe: "We are of good cheer. The fight goes merrily on." "Did you ever worry?" he was once asked. "No, never—not even when I had the trouble with my eyes." [39]

He heeded promptly any sign that a vacation was due, and thus avoided periodic breakdown, the wastes of involuntary rest and recuperation, so usual among sensitively organized public figures, such as Woodrow Wilson. His favorite playmate was Herbert White, owner of the Harvard University Press, a client since 1896. White had inherited a large fortune, some seven millions, from his grandfather. Though himself a person of considerable ability, he lacked most of the qualities that had made his grandfather financially important. About fifteen years younger than Brandeis, he was addicted to the leisurely, playful life—and averse, as Brandeis fondly twitted him, to "anything useful and in accordance with law." Yet this man of qualities sharply contrasting with his own was the one Brandeis usually chose to accompany him on vacation. These two, the luxurious playboy and the Spartan lawyer, went off on long and venturesome trips on White's schooner, the *Frolic,* to Nova Scotia, Cape Breton, Ontario, Buzzard's Bay, the Florida coast, and through the Panama Canal. In November 1909 they went west by train to San Francisco and Los Angeles, taking in the Grand Canyon and other points of special interest en route. For Brandeis it was an unusual vacation full of new experience and he enjoyed it all immensely. 'We have had a trip exceeding far in interest even my expectations," he wrote Alfred as the California Limited was entering Kansas. "I feel that I have overcome much of my lamentable ignorance of the United States and have now seen its most wonderful parts. West of Lincoln [Nebraska], my previous *Ultima Thule,* the remarkable

America really begins." Brandeis commented approvingly on the free and easy manners of the West, noting that the women especially were much less reserved, more sociable, than in the East.

Though he entered into White's enjoyments with good-natured abandon the trip did not quite supply the relaxation he needed. He wrote Alfred, December 4, 1909, of a short trip he had taken "to get over my western debauch and to be 'gentle in harness again.' "

Brandeis's friendship with White continued through the years, though their ways diverged ever more sharply. "Herbert White blew in the other evening," the Justice commented in a note to his brother, March 28, 1926. "He was south with Storrow [James J.] this winter—a part of the time at a small rich-man's club in North Carolina (60,000 acres), and then visiting a friend in South Carolina (30,000 acres). . . . It is evident you and I are relics of a past world—which I prefer. Herbert is quite his old good self— not visibly affected by his rich associations (and no riches himself). But he is quite the same unregenerate boy whom I first met thirty years ago."

THE COURTS, THE LAW, AND THE LAWYERS

The varied labors of these years were closely co-ordinated with the development of Progressivism. One major peril still loomed ahead—progressive measures must, of course, be interpreted and applied by the courts. Once when asked why he did not undertake to reform the defects and abuses of the law, Brandeis replied: "No lawyer can do that." [40] Nevertheless, from about 1912 on he devoted attention to making the administration of justice more consonant with twentieth-century needs.

Since 1905 public dissatisfaction with the law had become increasingly evident; distrust of courts and legal procedures was more prevalent. The lawyer's influence in the community had lessened. Controversies in increasing number were settled out of court. Lynching indicated a dire breakdown in criminal law—"a monument of inefficiency," he called it. Commercial disputes were increasingly adjusted by voluntary boards of arbitration. Businessmen often renounced their rights rather than engage in long, costly, and indecisive litigation. "One might almost say," Brandeis commented "that at one time or another most of the best lawyers of the country have been engaged in efforts to prevent the enforcement of the law." He cited the anti-trust law as a glaring illustration. The first thought with respect to any unwelcome statute was, "Can't it be held unconstitutional?" Legislation in the mind of not a few eminent lawyers was looked upon "rather as an intrusion upon the domain of the law." Brandeis characterized this attitude as "a most serious charge" against his profession, and stressed the place of legislation in modern society. An economic policy, embodied in legislation (e.g., that stated in the anti-trust act), "may or may not be wise, but it seems clear that it is wise in a democracy to endeavor to carry out the will of the people." [41]

As he saw it, lawyers and judges had failed to keep in touch with the new social and industrial development of America: "It cannot be successfully controverted that the law has been, in the last fifty years, a singularly unprogressive profession." Judges did not understand that "when property is used to interfere with that fundamental freedom of life for which property is *only a means,* then property must be controlled. . . . It has been a frequent error of our courts that they have made the means an end. Once correct that error, put property back in its right place, and the whole social-legal conception becomes consistent. . . . All judges should be made to feel, as many judges already feel, that the things needed to protect liberty are radically different from what they were fifty years back. In some courts the judges' conceptions of their own powers must also change. Some judges have decided a law unconstitutional simply because they considered the law unwise. These judges should be made to feel, that their business is not to decide whether the view taken by the legislature is a wise view, but whether a body of men could reasonably hold such a view. . . ." [42]

It was not that he opposed private property as such. On the contrary, Brandeis believed so strongly in private property that he wanted to see it more equitably diffused among the masses of men. He valued capital so highly that he would make it more easily available to the independent entrepreneur, rather than have it monopolized and controlled by a Money Trust. He had such respect for profits that he desired to enlarge them by scientific management so that the share of both management and labor could be increased and the standard of living raised for all. Indeed, he thought of private enterprise not only as an instrument of gain but also as a means of raising the individual to creative personality.

Much disrespect for law was due to technical deficiencies in legislation. Statutes sincerely intended to carry out the will of the people were so poorly drafted as not to accomplish their purpose. Brandeis therefore recommended Law School instruction in legislative drafting so that the lawmakers (most of them lawyers) would come to their task better equipped. [43] Replying to a letter from Charles Freeman Johnson of the National Legal Reform League, he wrote: "The 'cultivation of respect for the law and the dignity of the courts' will not come until the administration of the law and its creation are made deserving of respect. The present lack of respect for the law and criticism of the judiciary is due largely to the inefficiency of the system. It does not seem to me that the teaching of Ethics and the other admirable subjects of human thought and activity which you propose are apt to be effective in enhancing the respect for the law, except so far as they would advance good citizenship." [44]

Nor could improvement come from a small group of experts aiming to remodel the social system. A proposal for the organization of such a group, elicited the comment: "To secure social advance we must regard the field of sociology and social legislation as a field for discovery and invention. Research is necessary as in the field of mechanical and other arts. . . . And the successes are rarely one man's work, or the work of a number of men consciously co-operating. The successes come very often by one man building upon another's apparent failure. I should have little faith, therefore, in a small group of men evolving a social system or important elements of such a system. We must rely upon all America (and the rest of the world) for our social inventions and discoveries; and the value of the inventions and alleged discoveries can best be tested by current public discussion." [45]

Regarding education as the remedy for many defects in the administration of justice, Brandeis strongly opposed short-circuiting the judicial process by such devices as the popular recall of judges and of decisions. Nor did he consider constitutional amendment necessary. His solution was to bring the judges down from the rarefied clouds of judicial abstraction, to modernize their social and economic outlook by education. Lawyers "should not merely learn rules of law but their purposes and effects when applied in human affairs"—in other words, "a study of the facts, human, industrial, social, to which they are to be applied." [46]

In earlier days the general legal practitioner had clients from all walks of life; he participated in church affairs, politics, society, and sport. With industrial development a new type of lawyer grew up—the narrow specialist, the "corporation lawyer." He learned one small corner of legal science, perhaps learned it well, but his knowledge of things social and economic suffered; he lost the breadth of view which came from active participation in community life; his judgment was therefore distorted. With leading lawyers more and more in this class, judges went to the bench ill-equipped to handle social and economic questions.

Brandeis recognized the necessity for specialization, but he would "correct its distorting effects by broader education," preparatory to practice and continued by lawyer and judge throughout life. Otherwise legal justice could never be in accord with contemporary conceptions of social justice. For "Justice," he wrote, "is but truth in action, and we cannot hope to attain justice until we have the proper respect for truth." [47]

AMERICANISM AND THE ROAD TO PEACE

Brandeis was too deeply immersed in American domestic problems to give foreign affairs much attention. But he was not unaffected when Europe plunged into the 1914 conflict. He was profoundly American, his deepest value being his unshakable faith in our democracy. For him, as for Jefferson, the democratic tradition must be vital in day-to-day living. He almost never spoke or wrote in terms of social or political abstractions unrelated to specific problems which actively engaged him. There was one scintillating exception.

In 1915 the municipal authorities of Boston invited him to give the Fourth of July oration. It was a confused and anxious time; Europe was ending the first year of World War I. President Wilson had enjoined strict neutrality as the nation was increasingly beset by propagandists both of the allied and of the central powers. The authorities deemed it advisable to reaffirm the meaning of Americanism. Newcomers no less than native-born needed to rediscover the ideals of America, and Brandeis chose as his theme "True Americanism." [48]

An eyewitness has described the occasion thus:

I well remember the hot afternoon in Faneuil Hall on which he delivered the oration; the stratified audience—Beacon Hill and the Back Bay; the West and North Ends; South Boston and East Boston; distributed duly and in good order according to cash, caste, and sect; the stuffy smell of the hall, the gaunt figure and the Lincolnlike mask of the orator, his vibrant voice and the measured yet passionate delivery. Reading the address twenty-one years after, what most impresses me is what might be called, after the analogy of the expression "Primitive Christianity," its primitive Americanism.[49]

In simple, human terms Brandeis put into words the ideals of the American common man. In brief, "they are the development of the individual for his own and the common good; the development of the individual through liberty, and the attainment of the common good through democracy and social justice." The development of the individual demanded that the physical conditions under which he worked and lived should be such as would permit him to develop; that every citizen have education, not merely formal schooling but mental improvement continuing throughout life; that he be free from economic oppression; that he be financially independent for such contingencies as sickness, accident, superannuation, and unemployment. He redefined the American way in terms of the Declaration's rights of life, liberty, and the pursuit of happiness. To him these were more than abstract phrases:

Life, in this connection, means living, not existing; liberty, freedom in things industrial as well as political; happiness includes, among other things, that satisfaction which can come only through the full development and utilization of one's faculties.

What was there peculiarly American in these ideals? Other nations prided themselves on liberty, democracy, or social justice—or a combination thereof. The unique feature of Americanism was what he called "inclusive brotherhood."

"Other countries, while developing the individual man, have assumed that their common good would be attained only if the privileges of their citizenship could be limited practically to natives or to persons of a particular nationality. America, on the other hand, has always declared herself for equality of nationalities as well as for equality of individuals. It recognizes racial equality as an essential of full human liberty and true brotherhood, and that racial equality is the complement of democracy."

The opposed principles of democracy and aristocracy, applied to peoples as well as to individuals, had been in conflict for centuries: "Democracy rests upon two pillars: one, the principle that all men are equally entitled to life, liberty, and the pursuit of happiness; and the other, the conviction that such equal opportunity will most advance civilization. Aristocracy, on the other hand, denies both these postulates. It rests upon the principle of the superman. It willingly subordinates the many to the few, and seeks to justify sacrificing the individual by insisting that civilization will be advanced by such sacrifices."

While aristocracy as applied to individuals had been overthrown in parts of the Western world, Brandeis maintained, it still prevailed generally in Europe as applied to peoples: "It was there assumed by the stronger countries that the full development of one people necessarily involved its domination over another, and that only by such domination would civilization advance. Strong nationalities, assuming their own superiority, came to believe that they possessed the divine right to subject other peoples to their sway; and the belief in the existence of such a right ripened into a conviction that there was also a duty to exercise it."

The history of Europe demonstrated that a whole people, like a single person, had irrepressible individuality. ". . . the misnamed internationalism which seeks the obliteration of nationalities or peoples is unattainable," he declared. "The new nationalism adopted by America proclaims that each race or people, like each individual, has the right and duty to develop, and that only through such differentiated development will high civilization be attained."

Without the free development of all peoples he saw no hope for lasting peace. "The world longs for an end of this war," he concluded, "and even more for a peace that will endure. It turns anxiously to the United States, the one great neutral country, and bids us point the way. And may we not answer: Go the way of liberty and justice—led by democracy and the new nationalism. Without these, international congresses and supreme courts will prove vain and disarmament 'The Great Illusion.' "

In an earlier address before the Economic Club in February 1915, and published in *Harper's Weekly*, he took as his subject "An Essential of Lasting Peace" and listed measures usually proposed to attain it: a congress of nations, an international court, an international police force, the democratization of nations enabling the people to choose war or peace, disarmament, and removal of the economic causes of war. All these, he believed, would lessen war, but he pointed to a deeper factor which must underlie any permanent peace—that democratic principles must dominate the relations between nations.

A cause of war deeper than rivalries for markets and raw materials, deeper than treaty violations or armament races, was the desire of different peoples for self-development, self-expression. This longing, he argued, had produced the mistaken belief that development of one people necessarily involved mastery of others. Strong nations arrogated to themselves the right and the duty to subject other nations to their sway. Until equal opportunity to develop was assured all peoples, Brandeis knew that discord and war would wrack the world. Just as democracy denied the superman and insisted on human development as both right and duty, just so the right of each nation or race to seek its own highest development, insofar as it was consistent with the similar right of others, must be recognized in international affairs.

"No peace which is lasting can ever come until the nations, great and small, accept the democratic principle that there is and shall be no supernation to rise through subjection of others, and the truth that each people has in it something of peculiar value which it can contribute to that civilization for which we are all striving. And until that principle is accepted—and that trust recognized—unrest must be unending. Whatever economic arrangement may be made, however perfect and comprehensive may become the machinery for enforcing the treaties of the nations, those people who are not accorded equality of opportunity for full development will prove a source of irritation; injustice will bring its inevitable penalty; and the peace of the world will be broken again and again. . . . Equal opportunity for all people as for all individuals—that is the essential of international as well as of national justice upon which a peace which is to be permanent must rest."

With the war in Europe becoming a grim death struggle and the United States steadily more involved, Brandeis was discouraged and pessimistic about the shape of international things to come. ". . . as the world is topsy-turvy," he wrote Alfred, October 22, 1915, "there is no good reason for expecting peace on earth since there is no good will among men."

CHAPTER TWENTY-NINE

International Justice and the Jews, 1912-1921

Brandeis came to Zionism and Judaism at the height of his career, and as a typical American assimilationist. His ancestral background included no formal religious observance, no nationalist leanings, no racial-cultural interests such as a knowledge of Hebrew and the Talmud. Several members of the Brandeis and Goldmark families had married Gentiles. His law practice and social life had never been identified with any one race, sect, or interest. His friends were indiscriminately Jews and Gentiles. He never attended synagogue services or other religious observances.[1]

Brandeis's grandfather, Sigmund Dembitz, and great-grandfather, Aaron Behr Wehle, were devout members of a Jewish sect called Frankists, but their wives remained orthodox. His mother, Frederika Dembitz, remained a firm believer in deism, yet a rationalist. Her personal identification with Jewry was cultural rather than sectarian. In her own words: "I saw that my parents were good Jews, and yet did not associate with Jews and were different from them, and so there developed in me more affection for our race as a whole than for individuals." The only throwback to tradition was Brandeis's uncle, Lewis Naphtali Dembitz (1832-1907), who reverted to strict orthodoxy at the age of thirteen after making acquaintance with an orthodox classmate at boarding school in Prague. Uncle Lewis later developed into the Jewish scholar of the South and became an early American Zionist. Brandeis was fond of his uncle, and this affection may have planted seeds of sympathy for Zionism.[2]

EARLY JEWISH INTERESTS

Brandeis made small gifts to Boston Jewish Charities, but only as anyone might do.[3] In 1893, while at the Hotel Fusta in Milwaukee, he learned something of the Zionist leader Theodor Herzl from an article in the *North American Review*. On reading of the first Zionist Congress at Basle in 1897, he was supposed to have remarked to Mrs. Brandeis: "Now *there* is something to which I could give myself." [4] One notes also the story that Brandeis addressed a young Zionist group in Boston before 1900.[5] In 1910 he is said to have participated in a meeting at the New York home of Banker Jacob Schiff to discuss the plight of European Jews. He left this meeting a discouraged man, but a little later a Jewish fraternity lad showed him pictures of agricultural work in Palestine which lifted his spirit.[6] Occasionally thereafter he noted references to the history of Zionism, yet it was not until 1911 that he sent a small contribution in reply to a particularly moving appeal on behalf of Jewish émigrés.[7]

Such tenuous sympathy had little to do with an understanding of Zionism's most vital and much disputed aspect—Jewish nationalism. For in 1905 on the 250th anniversary of the first settlement of Jews in the United States, Brandeis praised the contribution made to America by people of "Jewish blood," and went on to condemn what President Theodore Roosevelt called "hyphenated Americanism":

There is room here for men of any race, of any creed, of any condition in life, but not for Protestant-Americans, or Catholic-Americans, or Jewish-Americans, nor for German-Americans, Irish-Americans, or Russian-Americans. This country demands that its sons and daughters whatever their race—however intense or diverse their religious connections—be politically merely American citizens. Habits of living or of thought which tend to keep alive difference of origin or to classify man according to their religious beliefs are inconsistent with the American ideal of brotherhood, and are disloyal.[8]

Brandeis's first contact with Jews as a group came in 1910 when he was called in to help settle the New York garment workers' strike. Brandeis, then fifty-four, met face to face the teeming immigrant masses from Eastern Europe. These men, completely alien to him, aroused no prejudice. He sensed his personal kinship with these working-class people, noted their ability to co-operate, and felt that they had a genius for self-government. He saw clearly reflected in them the hopes and aspirations which he held out for all men. He became poignantly conscious of "his people" and of their plight which had not then reached the depths of Fascist persecution or Palestine White Papers. This experience confronted him with a challenge which no self-respecting person, least of all a successful Jew, could shirk.[9]

The effective stimulus which in 1912 brought Brandeis into the Zionist movement came from an English Jew, Jacob De Haas (1872–1937), who had been associated with Theodor Herzl (1860–1904), the father of modern Zionism, in London. At Herzl's suggestion, De Haas had come to America; he settled in Boston and in 1902 became editor of the *Jewish Advocate*. Brandeis's first meeting with him was in the fall of 1910, when he solicited his support, along with other editors, for savings-bank life insurance.[10] In December that year a reporter for a Jewish paper inquired: "Have you any interest, Mr. Brandeis, with those Jews who are working for the revival of a Jewish state in Palestine?" Brandeis replied: "I have a great deal of sympathy with the Zionists. The movement is an exceedingly deserving one. These so-called dreamers are entitled to the respect and appreciation of the entire Jewish people."[11]

According to Brandeis's recollection in 1940, it was not until De Haas's South Yarmouth visit in August 1912 that his interest in Zionism was fully awakened. They were then consulting at William G. McAdoo's request about funds for the Democratic campaign. Their talk completed, Brandeis accompanied his visitor to the station. De Haas made some mention of Lewis Dembitz as a "noble Jew," and on being further questioned, launched into the subject nearest his heart—Zionism. He told the story of his British birth and of the influence he had been able to exert on Henry Cabot Lodge. That an obscure, London-born Jew could gain the sympathetic ear of that stiff-necked Senator piqued the lawyer's curiosity. When De Haas told further that he had been London secretary to Theodor Herzl, his interest in De Haas's story was so profoundly aroused that he forgot vacation plans and invited his caller to stay for lunch and take a later train.[12] In a letter to his brother, August 14, 1912, Brandeis wrote: "I had by chance, one of the original Zionists at luncheon yesterday who told a better story (Susan and Elizabeth will testify) even than Captain Baker." *

AN AVOWED ZIONIST

Although Brandeis was engrossed in other matters, he considered the movement urgent and joined formally the Federation of American Zionism.[13] This affiliation, his first formal and overt identification with the cause, was reported at the Cleveland Zionist convention of 1912. The goal of Zionism was the small state, political and economic self-government, and as an inveterate foe of bigness, Brandeis found it an impelling cause.

* Baker was a South Yarmouth "sea captain."

In 1912 and 1913 Brandeis appeared frequently on the speakers' platform, practically making cross-country tours on behalf of Zionism. In 1913 he became an associate executive committeeman of the Federation of American Zionists; [14] and, at the Cincinnati convention in 1913, he was elected delegate to the eleventh World Congress to be held in Vienna. Brandeis declined this on the ground of other engagements,[15] but his message, read before the Congress, advocated three major lines of endeavor: the diversion of Jewish immigration to Palestine; negotiations with the Turkish government for large concessions; and the industrialization of Palestine by capital investment.[16]

Brandeis's new interest soon attracted public attention. On August 28, 1913, a Boston reporter telegraphed asking if it were true that he was to be elected head of the movement at the forthcoming Vienna Congress.[17] Soon thereafter the *Atlanta Constitution* carried an editorial entitled "Brandeis Inconsistency." It praised the American Jew as a good citizen, and asserted that he ought not to be asked to return to Palestine. Brandeis could, "if he is sincere," the editorial concluded, "put himself right by catching the first boat for the Mediterranean." [18] Two years later the noted anti-Zionist, Isaac M. Wise, of Cincinnati, made a similar proposal: "But our good Zionist friends prefer luxuries instead of privation. They believe that the Russian Jews should be experimented upon. Mr. Editor, if Mr. Brandeis and one hundred prominent Jews go to Palestine and live, then will their example cause thousands of others to follow suit; will the Zionists accept this challenge?" [19]

During the summer of 1914 Brandeis devoted his vacation to intensive study of the Jewish problem. But before he could complete this research the outbreak of war changed the whole situation. Since the headquarters of the *Actions Comité* was in Berlin, the Zionist centers were separated. American adherents therefore began to think of transferring world headquarters to New York.[20] De Haas asked Brandeis's authority "for proposing your name as the chairman or Directing Head of the Committee which will have to take charge at this time of practically the whole Zionist movement." De Haas pointed out that it was a question not only of the fate of their cause, "but indeed the welfare of $7/10$ of the Jewish race." [21] This bold idea appealed to Brandeis. His consent marked assumption of a new, and to him personally, most pleasing, role: acknowledged leadership of the Zionist movement in the United States.

At a conference in New York on August 30, which one hundred and fifty participants attended, a Provisional Executive Committee for General Zionist Affairs (P.C.) was established and Brandeis unanimously elected chairman. An administrative committee of eleven was named to guide the affairs of the new organization. After a few speeches, the conferees were ready to depart, but the new chairman insisted that the administrative committee stay and consider his plans. They did and deliberated almost all night. They convened again in the morning and conferred throughout the next day. The positions of American Jewry and of the Zionist Organization were thoroughly thrashed out, Brandeis pleading that his distance from the Jewish problem now necessitated his acquiring all basic facts.

"I feel my disqualification for this task," Brandeis said in accepting leadership. "Throughout long years which represent my own life, I have been to a great extent separated from Jews. I am very ignorant in things Jewish. But recent experiences, public and professional, have taught me this: I find Jews possessed of those very qualities which we of the twentieth century seek to develop in our struggle for justice and democracy; a deep moral feeling which makes them capable of noble acts; a deep sense of the brotherhood of man; and a high intelligence, the fruit of three thousand years of civilization." [22]

In the eyes of its founders, formation of the P.C. in 1914 marked a new era. Its members were firmly convinced that this body would take over global direction of the movement. Brandeis took his leadership seriously. While directing P.C. activities through frequent, terse communications to the administrative secretary, Benjamin Perlstein, Brandeis plunged into an extensive propaganda campaign. In the fall and winter of 1914, paired with Dr. Schmarya Levin of the *Actions Comité,* he went on a speaking tour—Philadelphia and Baltimore, Pittsburgh and Rochester. Brandeis's addresses began by admitting that only four years ago he had thought Zionism a wild dream of making every Jew live in Palestine. This remained a stock opening for him. He would define the cause in terms of what it was not:

It is not a movement to remove all the Jews compulsorily to Palestine. In the first place there are 14,000,000 Jews, and Palestine would not accommodate more than one-fifth of that number. In the second place, it is not a movement to compel anyone to go to Palestine. It is essentially a movement to give to the Jews more, not less freedom—it aims to enable the Jews to exercise the same right now exercised by practically every other people in the world: to live at their option either in the land of their fathers or in some other country; a right which members of small nations as well as large—which Irish, Greek, Bulgarian, Serbian or Belgium, may now exercise as fully as Germans or English.[23]

Back in Boston, Brandeis repeated at Symphony Hall his address on *Zionism and Patriotism.* This speech, reprinted in pamphlet form by the Federation of American Zionists in 1915 and again in 1918, soon became a classic. Brandeis, in contrast with his 1905 dictum, told the audience that "practical experience and observation convinced me that to be good Americans, we must be better Jews, and to be better Jews, we must become Zionists." Zionism realized the old Jewish dream; colonizing efforts were working out; the Hebrew language was being revived. This analysis had to be reconciled with the Americanism which Brandeis had long exemplified and advocated:

The Jewish Renaissance in Palestine will enable us to perform our plain duty to America. It will help us to make toward the attainment of the American ideals of democracy and social justice that large contribution for which religion and life have peculiarly fitted the Jews.

America's fundamental law seeks to make real the brotherhood of man. That brotherhood became the Jewish fundamental law more than twenty-five hundred years ago. America's insistent demand in the twentieth century is for social justice. That has also been the Jews' striving for ages. Their affliction as well as their religion has prepared the Jews for democracy.

But as the Ghetto walls are falling, Jewish life cannot be preserved and developed, assimilation cannot be averted, unless there be re-established in the fatherland a center, from which the Jewish spirit may radiate, and give to the Jews scattered throughout the world that inspiration which springs from memories of a great past and the hope of a great future.

From idealism the speaker turned to hard facts. Demoralization was setting in among American Jews, as shown by the Rosenthal murders, by the revelations concerning Jewish lawbreakers and prostitutes. Formerly the Jew was seldom involved in crime, Jewish law and tradition had seen to that; and "in the Jewish colonies of Palestine there are no Jewish criminals." It was clearly a case of "inculcating self-respect," by inspiring in each new generation a pride in Jewish achievement:

Every Irish-American who contributed towards advancing home rule was a better man and a better American for the sacrifice he made. Every American Jew who aids in advancing the Jewish settlement in Palestine, though he feel that neither he nor his descendants will ever be there, will likewise be a better man and a better American for doing so.

In early October, Brandeis went to Cleveland, where he was welcomed by Mayor Newton D. Baker. Four thousand turned out to hear the famous attorney, giving him an ovation that lasted five minutes.[24] Brandeis himself for once was fully satisfied with the crowd and the arrangements. Other addresses were made at the University of Cincinnati and at Harvard. On November 8 he spoke before the Menorah Society of Columbia University on "The Duty of Educated Jews in America."[25] Brandeis stressed their stern sense of duty, as in the Puritans of old, inspired by the Prophets; their high intellectual achievements; their submission to leadership as distinguished from authority; and especially their developed community sense.

Beyond these things the educated Jews must remember their glorious heritage of three thousand years. "Assimiliation is national suicide." There must be a land "where the Jewish life may be naturally led, the Hebrew language spoken, and the Jewish spirit prevail," and that land was "our fathers' land"—Palestine.

At the end of November, Brandeis started with Dr. Levin for the Middle West. In Chicago, before a convention of the Knights of Zion, Brandeis gave the leading address. Again he was subjected to bitter attack. A *Chicago Tribune* editorial, entitled "Patriotism Begins At Home," commented: "We cannot believe the possession of territory is necessary now any more than it ever has been to preserve the noble and inspiring ideals and traditions of the Jew." [26] Brandeis wrote a full report of this and other meetings to his brother, November 27, 1914, saying in part:

The Chicago experience was as successful as the Cincinnati was unsuccessful. In fact Chicago was successful far beyond expectation. . . . There were 2200 present, and my talk, which I limited to thirty-five minutes, was unquestionably effective. [Julius] Rosenwald, who had been quite anti-Zionist in his inclinations . . . insisted that the donors should bind themselves to continue contributions, and he rose and stated that he would give $1,000 a month during the war and for twelve months thereafter. . . . The mass meeting Sunday evening, and the luncheon with the reformed rabbis on Monday, were also successful. In addition there was a banquet on Saturday evening, and a Menorah talk at the University on Monday afternoon. The general feeling was that we had captured the town, and I don't think the editorial in the *Chicago Tribune,* which you doubtless saw, will do any harm. . . .

The Milwaukee meeting also was successful. We had a dinner before the meeting with the Germans, who really had no sympathy with the Zionist movement, and who came to it merely out of personal regard for me—one of them being interested in the Independent Shoe Machinery fight,—another in the Fair Trade. The leader of the German community there stated to me at the dinner that he was opposed to Zionism, and no argument could move him; but when I got through my talk, he said that I had converted him, and I think that was true of some of the others. . . .

I believe that when the war is over there will be a great increase in immigration, and particularly of the Jews. . . . Of course immigration to Palestine would involve far less initial cost than to America.

Brandeis spoke at eastern gatherings during December, among others, a Young Zionist Club in the Bronx and a mass meeting of two thousand at Springfield, Massachusetts. Along with his usual law work ran the current of this impelling interest. He wrote his brother, December 8, 1914, from Washington: "Am here on I.C.C., Oregon Minimum Wage and

California eight-hour law cases. Expect to stay until the 18th and then return to Boston via N.Y. . . . You cannot possibly conceive of the horrible
sufferings of the Jews in Poland and adjacent countries. These changes of
control from German to Russian and Polish anti-semitism are bringing
miseries as great as the Jews ever suffered in all their exiles."

"Things Jewish have been occupying my time largely," he wrote his
brother, March 6, 1915. "Cincinnatians . . . have been very pressing with
invitations, but I have resisted, saying I don't want a public controversy
with [David] Philipson." *

In the spring of 1915 the cause took him to New York every week, and
invitations pressed upon him from all sides. "Zionist affairs," he wrote
Alfred, April 25, 1915, "are really the important things in life now." A year
later Zionism had come to "represent in Jewish life what Progressivism
does in general American life." [27]

In all his speeches Brandeis emphasized relief needs in the Eastern war
zone and advocated Zionism as the only solution of the Jewish problem.
In April 1915 he told a Carnegie Hall audience celebrating the eighth
anniversary of Rabbi Stephen S. Wise's Free Synagogue: "The Jewish
Renaissance has come—the nation is reborn, and the Jewish state in its beginning is already here. We have been faithful over a few things—we are
prepared to rule over many." [28]

Another notable address—*The Jewish Problem, and How to Solve It*—
delivered in April before the Eastern Council of Reform Rabbis in New
York, summed up Brandeis's case. Up to 1919 it went through five edi-
tions, comprising 50,000 copies. Beginning with the assertion that Jewish
disabilities, anti-semitism, Jewish suffering, were in the aggregate worse
than ever before, the speaker proceeded to define Jewishness as a matter of
blood. Both sides admit this, he said, the non-Jews who persecute those
of Jewish faith, and the Jews themselves who take pride "when those of
Jewish blood exhibit moral or intellectual superiority, genius, or special
talent, even if they have abjured the faith like Spinoza, Marx, Disraeli, or
Heine."

Zionism would restore to Jews much of the self-respect they had lost:
"The sole bulwark against demoralization is to develop in each new generation of Jews in America the sense of *noblesse oblige*. That spirit can be
developed in those who regard their people as destined to live and to live
with a bright future. That spirit can best be developed by actively participating in some way in furthering the ideals of the Jewish renaissance; and

* Noted rabbi, scholar, and anti-Zionist. This refusal reflects Brandeis's determination not to
imperil Jewish unity by internal dissension.

this can be done most effectively only through furthering the Zionist movement."

In former days the Jewish students in Vienna had been servile in manner and submissive to persecution. "But Zionism gave them courage. They formed associations, and learned athletic drill and fencing. Insult was requited with insult, and presently the best fencers of the fighting German corps found that Zionist students could gash cheeks quite as effectually as any Teuton, and that the Jews were in a fair way to become the best swordsmen of the university. . . ."

The address insisted more strongly than ever on the compatibility of Americanism with Zionism: "There is no inconsistency between loyalty to America and loyalty to Jewry. . . . Indeed loyalty to America demands that each American Jew become a Zionist. . . . Organize, Organize, Organize—until every Jew in America must stand up and be counted—counted with us—or prove himself, wittingly or unwittingly, of the few who are against their own people."

A California paper commented ironically:

Brandeis, the Boston butter-in, is a high-grade opportunist. He . . . suggests that "the immediate unsettlement and ultimate settlement which must come at the end of the European war gives us Zionists and the Jews throughout the world an opportunity which they have not had since the destruction of Jerusalem"—to acquire Palestine real estate at bargain prices.

It is to be hoped that Brandeis and Gifford Pinchot and Amos Pinchot will open real estate offices in Jerusalem and thrive there—and stay there, above all, stay there.[29]

And a Jewish paper was quite as caustic:

No one will deny, and the *Israelite* least of all, that Mr. Brandeis is entitled to his opinion that Zionism is the panacea for all Israel's ills. But when he says that all those who do not agree with him "are against their own people," he is guilty of uttering that which is not true and of being grossly impertinent at the same time. Who is Mr. Brandeis to judge his brethren? How does he come by the right to say that a Jew, be he ever so faithful, is an enemy of his own people, if he does not believe as Mr. Brandeis does? It is very much to be feared that his success and the psalms of praise that the Jewish press have been singing before him, have turned Mr. Brandeis' head. . . .[30]

THE LEADER OF ZIONISM

These frequent public appearances, assiduously promoted by De Haas, served to fix Brandeis in the public mind as the potential leader of the movement. By January 1915 De Haas thought he could be drafted for world Zionist leadership, "if the Jewish people, particularly those in Europe, are prepared to accept a leader who lives so far away." [31] Eulogies began to fill the air. De Haas assured his public that Brandeis was the logical heir to Herzl's mantle when the death of David Wolfsohn (1856–1914), former president of the World Zionist Organization, left room at the top for a great Zionist personality. De Haas predicted that Brandeis would be the world leader, and that the next international Jewish Congress would be brought to the United States.[32] His enthusiasm knew no bounds: "There has been no such leadership since Theodor Herzl passed away." A poem by Joseph Friedlander, entitled "The New Elijah," sang of Brandeis "on whose shoulders Herzl's mantle falls." [33]

As P.C. Chairman Brandeis personally supervised the inner workings of the office as well as its policy making and political negotiations. His constant demand was for reports and more reports. Three weeks after he had established De Haas as director of the New England Zionist Office in Boston, he was writing him for monthly reports. His mania for reports was insatiable.[34] In the same letter in which he declined an invitation to address some small organization, he would urge its officers to send him monthly financial or other statements.

The struggle for control of their community between the mass of American Jewry and the wealthier element was bitter. Brandeis took the lead on the popular side, inviting the American Jewish Committee, of which Louis Marshall was chairman, to co-operate with P.C. in calling a representative conference of all important Jewish groups in the country. The purpose was to emphasize Palestine before the Great Powers in any negotiations during or at the end of the war.[35] In opposition, Marshall declared that "the very thought of the mass of Jews in America having a voice in the matter of deciding the welfare of the Jews in the world made him shrink in horror." [36]

Nevertheless, Brandeis kept urging the Congress project, and before a crowded Carnegie Hall, January 24, 1916, he reiterated the need for full publicity and open discussion of Jewish affairs:

When one considers the tremendous force of long continued habit and the tendency of oppression to breed methods of indirection, it is easy to understand the misgivings even of able and public-spirited men and women, who long opposed the Congress because they feared to have discussed in public the Jewish Problem, which had theretofore been discussed only in private. The opposition of conservative-minded men, accustomed to the caution which heavy responsibility ordinarily entails, was natural. Patient consideration of the objections was appropriate. But it was also clear that if America can aid materially in the attainment of Jewish rights, it will only be through those forces which an open Congress can mobilize.[37]

Before the Congress of National Jewish Organizations met at the Astor House, July 16, 1916, the Senate Judiciary Committee, after hearings of unprecedented length, had recommended Brandeis's confirmation as Associate Justice of the United States Supreme Court. Amid well-nigh universal acclaim from Progressives, Jews and Gentiles alike, Judah Magnes shook his finger at the Justice, saying that he would be repudiated by the Jewish people.[38] An editor of a Danish Yiddish paper exclaimed: "After all there are higher things than the Supreme Court in the United States."[39] Twenty-six organizations finally agreed to establish a Jewish Congress— a decision hailed as "a notable victory for Justice Brandeis."[40] Four days after the Astor House meeting Brandeis resigned as temporary chairman and honorary president of the Executive Organization Committee for the American Jewish Congress, happy that "the triumph of the Congress movement has been assured." But, he explained, the attack on him was not only "malevolent but premeditated. . . . Respect for the High Court, and therefore, also, for the future of our cause," demanded that he should "guard against a repetition of such incidents."[41] But this withdrawal was far more apparent than real.

THE BALFOUR DECLARATION AND AFTER

Brandeis's role in the Balfour Declaration has long been a moot point. Preliminary conversations had taken place in Great Britain, often without reference to New York or Washington. Brandeis had approached President Wilson as early as the fall of 1914, and later obtained verbal assurances from Wilson and from the British and French ambassadors as to Allied policy on Palestine.

Throughout the winter of 1914 negotiations with the allied ambassadors were carried on by representative American Zionists in behalf of persecuted Russian Jews. Two days before Turkey entered the war (October 30, 1914), Brandeis had a satisfactory talk with Jusserand, the French ambassador in Washington, and promised to draw up a memorandum on the situation.[42] Moderate and judicial in tone, this document described the "abnormal conditions of the Jews in the Russian empire" which had aroused much comment in the United States. It was prepared by Richard Gottheil, professor of Semitic languages at Columbia University, collaborating with Rabbi Wise, and was presented by Brandeis to Jusserand.[43]

Despite pogroms and deportations, Zionist aspirations for autonomy were rapidly becoming more concrete. An editorial in the London *New*

Statesman and Nation, November 21, 1914, advocated a British protectorate over Palestine. This inspired Gottheil, now one of Brandeis's principal advisers, to suggest Zionist reliance on the democratic allies.[44] In May 1915 Brandeis heard that Rufus Isaacs (later Marquis of Reading) and Sir Herbert Samuel were considering the Zionist question, and that Lloyd George and Balfour were distinctly favorable. He placed his hope on England and became increasingly troubled by the anti-allied tone of the Yiddish press.

Toward the end of 1916 Brandeis was more formally concerned with the Department of State. He was vitally interested in having the United States represented in any international Congress which would be given the power to settle the future of Turkey.[45] In December, De Haas cabled Abram Elkus, the American Ambassador in Constantinople, about the possibilities of granting autonomy to the Jews in Palestine. Brandeis expressed his conviction that "Zionism is taking its place in public consideration and is one of the problems the war is likely to settle for us." [46] America's entry into the war, April 6, 1917, seemed to clinch the case for Zionism in the minds of its leaders here. The P.C. spread Sir Harry Johnston's opinion that "the best solution is the re-creation of Palestine as a Jewish state." [47]

The break with Germany made Zionist contacts with the administration easier. A memorandum by Rabbi Wise, who had conversed at length in December 1916 with Colonel House, elicited the latter's reply on February 7, 1917: "I hope the dream which we have may soon become reality." A cable, April 9, from Sokolow in Paris told of his confidence in the realization of "our Zionist aspiration," on the basis of his conversations with the Quai d'Orsay. A joint or British protectorate had been envisioned and hope entertained to persuade the allies to accept mutual "concessions" in carrying it out.[48]

Toward the end of April 1917 contacts with the London negotiators became more frequent. On April 25 James Rothschild cabled from London that the plans called for "the only satisfactory solution—a Jewish Palestine under British protection." Rothschild asked that American Jews "support this scheme for their Government and advised that Brandeis see Balfour."

Brandeis was introduced to Balfour at a White House luncheon, given in his honor almost immediately after his arrival in Washington. "You are one of the Americans I had wanted to meet," the British Foreign Minister said.[49] On May 10 Brandeis had interviews with both Balfour and Wilson, and on May 15 he cabled Louis de Rothschild: "Have had a satisfactory talk with Mr. Balfour, also with our President. This is not for publication."

Brandeis spent the summer in Washington helping with the administration's war labor problems. He conferred from time to time with Secretary of State Lansing about Turkish–Palestine relations and the treatment of Jews in the Holy Land; [50] and he was busy getting American approval for what became the Balfour Declaration and the British mandate for Palestine. He lunched in mid-September with Northcliffe and Reading, to whom he undoubtedly talked Zionism.[51] On September 19 Dr. Chaim Weizmann, eminent chemist and Zionist leader in Britain, cabled the tentative text of the Balfour Declaration:

Following text declaration has been approved by Foreign Office and Prime Minister and submitted to War Cabinet:—

(1) H.M. Government accepts the principle that Palestine should be reconstituted as the national home of the Jewish people.

(2) H.M. Government will use its best endeavors to secure the achievement of the object and will discuss the necessary methods and means with the Zionist organization.

To forestall opposition Weizmann suggested that it would "greatly help if President Wilson and yourself would support the text." Acting on these appeals, Brandeis cabled Weizmann, September 24, apparently at Colonel House's suggestion, advising him to get the French and Italians to make inquiry about the President's attitude. On the same day another cable by Brandeis stated that from previous talks with the President and from the opinion now given by close advisers he could say that the President was in entire sympathy.

On October 9 another cable from Weizmann told of difficulties owing to the "assimilants'" opposition: "They have found an excellent champion . . . in Mr. Edwin Montagu who is a member of the Government and has certainly made use of his position to injure the Zionist cause." As a result, when the British cabinet considered the Declaration formula, some changes were made in the text. Weizmann cabled the new version to Brandeis on October 14:

His Majesty's Government view with favour the establishment in Palestine of a national home for the Jewish race and will use its best endeavours to facilitate achievement of this object; it being clearly understood that nothing shall be done which may prejudice the civil and religious rights of the existing non-Jewish communities in Palestine or the rights and political status enjoyed in any other country by such Jews who are fully contented with their existing nationality and citizenship.

On November 12 Weizmann wrote Brandeis thanking him for his work:

I need hardly say how we all rejoice in this great event and how grateful we all feel to you for the valuable and efficient help which you have lent to the cause in this critical hour. . . .

Once more, dear Mr. Brandeis, I beg to tender to you my heartiest congratulations not only on my own behalf but also on behalf of our friends here and may this epoch-making event be a beginning of great work for the good of our sorely tried people and also of mankind.

In the United States the Balfour Declaration, issued November 2, 1917, was viewed as carte blanche to build the Jewish state. Within three weeks P.C. authorities were discussing a chartered company to maintain law and order there until government, general as well as local, could be assumed by the people in Palestine.[52] In London plans were afoot to dispatch a Zionist commission to Palestine. On January 14, 1918, Weizmann urged that Brandeis join it to "checkmate possible unsympathetic influence against our efforts for British Palestine," meaning, of course, the claims of the French. But Brandeis saw no need for this, and when Weizmann persisted in his entreaties, replied that the "international situation definitely renders American membership impossible now."

The Commission, headed by Weizmann, arrived in Palestine on April 14, 1918, and included a French non-Zionist representative and two Italians. After the Armistice, it was joined by the Americans, D. Lewin-Epstein, Professor H. Friedenwald, and Robert Szold. In all his letters to Weizmann, Brandeis had stressed particularly the economic-social aspects of the Commission's work, writing him on January 13, 1918:

The utmost vigilance should be exercised to prevent the acquisition by private persons of land, water rights or other natural resources or any concessions for public utilities. These must all be secured for the whole Jewish people. In other ways, as well as this, the possibility of capitalistic exploitation must be guarded against. A high development of the Anglo-Palestine Company will doubtless prove one of the most effective means of protection. And the encouragement of all kinds of co-operative enterprise will be indispensable. Our pursuit must be primarily of agriculture in all its branches. The industries and commerce must be incidental merely—and such as may be required to ensure independence and natural development.

These principles he formulated in a five-point social justice code for the Jewish Homeland. This was adopted at the Pittsburgh Convention, June 1918, and became known as the Pittsburgh program.

First: We declare for political and civil equality irrespective of race, sex, or faith of all the inhabitants of the land.

Second: To insure in the Jewish National Home in Palestine equality of opportunity we favor a policy which, with due regard to existing rights,
shall tend to establish the ownership and control by the whole people of the land, of all natural resources and of all public utilities.

Third: All land, owned or controlled by the whole people, should be leased
on such conditions as will insure the fullest opportunity for development and continuity of possession.

Fourth: The co-operative principle should be applied so far as feasible in the
organization of all agricultural, industrial, commercial, and financial
undertakings.

Fifth: The system of free public instruction which is to be established
should embrace all grades and departments of education.[53]

THE PARIS CONFERENCE

On August 31, 1918, President Wilson wrote Rabbi Wise "to express the
satisfaction I have felt in the progress of the Zionist movement . . . since
. . . Great Britain's approval of the establishment in Palestine of a National
Home for the Jewish people." Brandeis shared Zionist rejoicings at the
President's endorsement and wrote: "Since the President's letter, anti-
Zionism is pretty near disloyalty and non-Zionism slackening." [54]

Zionists in Europe were less certain of the future of the mandate, and,
after interviewing Balfour in mid-December, Wise cabled Brandeis from
London that "support must be given to British trusteeship proposition."
In reply, Brandeis suggested that Wise inform the President and House
that "I favor and have long advocated British trusteeship under League of
Nations; the resolution of American Jewish Congress to this effect expressed the will and judgment of vast majority of Jews of America." [55]
Having seen Wilson, January 15, 1919, Weizmann submitted the Jewish
case to the Peace Conference on February 27. The high point was reached
when the Londoner explained that by a Jewish homeland was meant an
immigration of 50,000 a year, until Palestine should be as distinctively Jewish as England was English.

Brandeis's Pittsburgh program was made the basis of every version of
the mandate which the Americans offered to their fellow-Zionists for presentation to the Peace Council. De Haas contended that the repeated rejection of these terms was perhaps the first rift between the European and
trans-Atlantic Zionists who met in Paris.

LONDON, PARIS, AND PALESTINE

Zionists were now so confident of Jewish statehood that in March 1919
Israel Zangwill, former opponent of Zionism, proposed that Brandeis be
elected the first President of Palestine.[56] But if Brandeis had any such

ambition he kept it to himself. Others took the matter seriously. William Jennings Bryan expressed supreme satisfaction with Brandeis's "candidacy" and declared: "I would be pleased to vote for you as President of the United States." [57]

By April 1919 Brandeis had made plans to go to Europe and Palestine. He sailed the second week in June on the *Mauretania* with his daughter Susan and De Haas. It was his first trip abroad since 1887 and Brandeis was well-nigh ecstatic. "I wish I had the six idle days of the voyage," he wrote his wife from London, June 22, 1919, "in which to tell you of the last forty-eight hours. There is an infinitude of the interesting. London is civilization," he went on, "and it would be worth millions of men's lives to preserve it. Our American cities are business machines; London is living. All the horrors of bigness are absent. From Southampton to this hotel [Claridge's]—everything is for man and is man's size—and beautiful in its adaptation to his needs."

In London, Brandeis met Dr. Weizmann for the first time. Impressions on both sides were favorable. "Weizmann is neither as great nor as objectionable as he was painted," Brandeis wrote Mrs. Brandeis, June 22. "But he is very much of a man and much bigger than most of his fellows." Weizmann, in turn, saw "something Messianic" in Brandeis's countenance. [58]

After conferring with British officials, Brandeis was convinced that "My coming was very much more needed than I could have conceived possible and I feel that I may be of real value all along the line with the British, quite as much as with our own people." [59]

In Paris, Brandeis conferred with President Wilson, Colonel House, Lord Balfour, the French cabinet, the Italian ambassador, Louis Marshall, and Baron Edmond de Rothschild. On June 25 Brandeis left for Palestine. Writing his wife, June 27, from the deck of the *Malwa,* he exclaimed, "*Vive* the Mediterranean! Next June we must make this voyage together." On July 1 in Cairo, Brandeis was warmly feted by Egyptian Zionists and welcomed by Colonel T. E. Lawrence and other British notables. The military authorities requested that before entering Palestine the party wait the return of General Allenby, British Commander-in-Chief. Brandeis at once understood that the Army heads were not only carrying out policy, but also dictating it. So far as they were concerned, the Balfour Declaration was merely a forgotten episode of the war.

"The problems . . . are serious, of course," Brandeis wrote his wife, July 1, "but no more so than we anticipated; and, of course, they will be solved, if only the British and we bear constantly in mind, that it is a question not of whether, but of how and when, Palestine shall become in fact the Jewish Homeland; that the irreducible minimum is a Palestine large enough, with the water, land, and ports requisite to a self-supporting and reasonably self-sufficient community.

"The most pervading impression of the East is the dreariness, in comparison, of our American civilization in all save the virtues. In those, America and Great Britain excel; and one feels constantly their superiority in moral merit and physical cleanliness, but why our lack of beauty and joyousness which life here is so full of? And why should Western *women* have made such lamentable failure in utilizing the colors and the flowing gown with which *man* here makes every moment interesting and every scene a picture. . . . If only dressmakers and milliners and their fashions could be completely exterminated there would be hope!"

On July 10 he wrote Mrs. Brandeis from Jerusalem: "We have been in Palestine forty-eight hours. . . . It is a wonderful country, a wonderful city. . . . It is a miniature California; but a California endowed with all the interest which the history of man can contribute and the deepest emotions which can stir a people. The ages-long longing—the love is all explicable now. It has also the great advantage over California of being small. The marvelous contrasts of nature are in close juxtaposition. Not only the mind but the eye may grasp them within a single picture. And the marvelous quality of the air brings considerable distances into it. What I saw of California and the Grand Canyon seemed less beautiful than the view from the Mount of Olives upon the Dead Sea and the country beyond. And yet all say that Northern Palestine is far more beautiful—and that in this extra dry season we are seeing the country at its worst. It was a joy from the moment we reached it at Rafa. . . . The way is long, the path difficult," he concluded, "but the struggle is worth-while. It is indeed a Holy Land."

Brandeis now felt that he really knew the main problems and the difficulties and possibilities. Although his stay in the Holy Land was short, he saw practically all the country, all the cities, and twenty-three of the forty-three Jewish colonies. Brandeis met with people in all walks of life. As usual, he was the listener: "I didn't make speeches in Palestine. The most I said on any one occasion did not exceed a few short sentences . . . mainly sweet nothings. . . ." [60]

In a letter to his wife, August 8, he summed up his views as to the future: "What I have seen and heard strengthened greatly my conviction that Palestine can and must become the Jewish homeland as promised in the Balfour Declaration. The problems and the difficulties are serious and numerous—even more so than I had anticipated; but there is none which will not be solved and overcome by the indomitable spirit of the Jews here and elsewhere."

Back in the United States, Brandeis reported at length to his Zionist followers. He urged, among other things, reforestation and acquisition of more land beyond the Jordan and farther South to include Akaba. Of the land he said: "When you have seen it as we have, you understand how the love and longing of the Jewish people have survived these eighteen hundred years." He spoke earnestly of an agricultural and industrial home for six million European Jews, killed later by the Nazis and their collaborators. "So far as the Arabs in Palestine are concerned, they do not present a serious obstacle. The conditions under which immigration must proceed are such that the Arab question, if properly handled by us, will in my opinion settle itself." [61]

Early in 1920 news came from Palestine of the first Arab demonstrations against Jews and Jewish immigration. In April the disturbances were renewed. Even pro-Arab enthusiasts agreed that the Arab aggressors were hoping to force the British to reconsider their decision to accept a mandate for Palestine.[62] Brandeis was alert to the danger and intervened effectively, preventing the loss of a large part of Northern Palestine to Syria.[63] In a cable to Weizmann on February 16, he said:

Please convey Prime Minister Lloyd George following message from myself and all those associated with me in the Zionist Organization of America: . . . My associates of the Zionist Organization of America cable me from Paris that in Conference on Turkish Treaty, France now insists upon terms of Sykes-Picot agreement. If this contention of French should prevail it would defeat full realization of promise of Jewish home for Sykes-Picot agreement divides country in complete disregard historic boundaries and necessity. National northern and eastern boundaries indispensable to self-sustaining community and economic development of country on North. Palestine must include Litany river watersheds of Hermon on East must include Plain of Jaulan Hauran. If Balfour Declaration subscribed to by France as well as other Allied and Associated Powers is to be made effective these boundaries must be conceded to Palestine. Less than this would produce mutilation promised Home. Balfour Declaration was public promise proclaimed by your Government and subscribed to by Allied Powers. I venture to suggest that in your assuming just settlement boundaries in Palestine statesmen Christian Nations keep this solemn promise to Israel.

ZIONIST—AND AMERICAN

Following the San Remo conference which, on April 26, 1920, awarded the mandate for Palestine to England, preparation began for the London Conference, to be held in July. Brandeis knew that trouble was ahead before he sailed for Europe with Mrs. Brandeis, their daughter Elizabeth, the Frankfurters, and De Haas. Before the Conference convened, there were long meetings with Weizmann, Sokolow, and non-Zionist Reading.

At Weizmann's suggestion Brandeis was elected chairman, and at the opening session came forward with bold ideas, apparently formulated and agreed to at the preliminary meetings. Brandeis began by declaring that now, after the victory of San Remo and the appointment of the Palestine High Commissioner (Sir Herbert Samuel), what was required in Palestine was *action.* Therefore the largely political Zionist Commission was no longer necessary and should be abolished. The crux of the problem was to get men and money into Palestine, which could be done only by putting leaders in charge with special business experience and training, regardless of length of service in Zionist ranks. A small executive committee, at first of three members, should be empowered for a considerable period to do the practical work of making Palestine a place in which men will earn a living. This plan immediately raised the question whether he himself would serve on the commission of three.

Brandeis explained at some length why he could not do so. Since his trip to Palestine the preceding year he had been considering active service more seriously than ever, but had come to the conclusion that he could do the cause more good by staying on the Bench, "the highest Bench of the world," and by remaining in America where he represented the liberal element, the "hope in American life." Stepping down from the Court would constitute an admission of the charge he had long combated; people would say that a man cannot be a Zionist and a good citizen of his country, because there was Brandeis, who was supposed to be one of the most American of Americans, who left his Court and country at the time of its greatest need. It would be much better to stay in his place; to resign from the Court would tend to deprive the movement of that support from the American government which it might sorely need. The most he could accept was the office of honorary president, in which capacity he could tender his advice as he had done in the American organization.[64]

Two days later Brandeis told the American delegation of his refusal to serve even as honorary president. He could no longer assume any responsibility in the international organization "in view of the unreliability of Dr. Weizmann's methods." [65] Apparently Weizmann had originally approved of the Brandeis–Reading reorganization plan for Palestine, but after discovering his followers' distrust of such non-Zionists as Reading, he began to veer away.[66]

Despite Brandeis's cool withdrawal, he expressed toward the end of the conference his "very clear conviction" that "the responsibility for the immediate future in Palestine must be left or placed upon Dr. Weizmann and the British Jews primarily, and that no consideration should permit any taking away of that responsibility from those shoulders." [67] At the same time he warned European Zionists that they must not continue to lean so exclusively on Americans for their financial resources; it was not good for their health or self-respect. Such subtle financial intimidation did not go unnoticed. Henrietta Szold, the soul of patience, complained of the "ugly time" Americans were having in Palestine: "To them [the Palestinians] . . . the whole American action at London seems arbitrary, self-willed, petulant, even pettish, and a bit purse-proud. . . ." [68]

Returning to America late in August 1920 on board the S.S. *Zeeland*, Brandeis drafted a memorandum of the policy he favored. After stating in detail the conditions and facilities which their organization should be prepared to secure, he said: "We cannot attain our objective of a manly self-supporting population unless the settlers are made to realize that they must, and unless they actually do incur, in some form, hardships equivalent to those incurred by hardy pioneers in other lands. . . . The slogan must be 'No easy money in Palestine' and 'No easy living' for any human being. And Zionist officials must set the example in simple living, high thinking, and hard work." [69]

Brandeis continued to insist on his London program and resented Weizmann's refusal to employ people previously unaffiliated with Zionism in the development of Palestine. He repeatedly stressed concentration of effort in the Holy Land, the adoption of sound business methods there, and elimination of "politics." At the end of the London Conference, for example, he had opposed unsuccessfully the establishment of a huge Palestine Foundation Fund, the Keren Hayesod (K.H.), because it commingled investments and contributions and threatened to become an independent rival of the Zionist Organization itself. An English editor, commenting on the London Conference, pointed to a deeper schism: "In one important instance a cleavage did appear, and though Zionist discipline bridged it over, it will possibly appear again. It is the question of work in the diaspora by the Zionist Organization as a whole. The Eastern Zionists have found that the nationalization of the Jews in the lands of the Dispersion is an integral and fruitful part of Zionist activity. . . . In Western lands, particularly in America, the naturalization of the Jews, even of many Zionists, is but skin-deep, and external conditions are unfavorable to such a development." [70]

This charge against Brandeis was carried to the point of identifying him with a policy of assimilation: "Judged by all the standards given above, Justice Brandeis is anything but *nationalgesinnt*. From all that is known of him, he is American first and foremost, and would not dream of applying the term 'Jew' to himself as a national designation." [71]

This was obviously an assertion of partisan opposition. The most that can fairly be said is that Brandeis recognized the importance of cultivating Zionist activities in the countries of the dispersion primarily to secure resources in men and money with which to develop Palestine; that he opposed large expenditures of Jewish energies and money in cultivating Jewish national institutions and culture outside of Palestine, especially after Palestine was assured as a Homeland. "We have reached the parting of the ways," he wrote in his Zeeland memorandum. "We are no longer a propaganda movement except the propaganda that comes from understanding and achieving concrete enterprises. Furthermore, we must never lose sight of the fact that our plans should be such as to elicit the full cooperation of all Jews, those who do not want to build up the Zionist Organization but who do want to share with the Zionist Organization in the upbuilding of Palestine." [72]

On most issues Brandeis was supported by the American delegation in London. But on their return to this country, opposition began to form. Several factors contributed to this ever-widening breach: loyalty to Weizmann and other European leaders who disagreed with Brandeis; resentment against certain of Brandeis's mouthpieces; opposition to the alleged dictatorial methods and aloofness of the Justice himself. Some opponents championed various aspects of diaspora nationalism, which certainly could not be harmonized with Brandeis's conceptions.

THE CLEVELAND CONVENTION OF 1921

The 1921 convention of the Zionist Organization of America in Cleveland was crucial. The first two days were filled with prolonged, almost continuous debate, lasting far into the night. The opposition to Brandeis and his program was confident, self-assured, and obviously reinforced by the receptiveness of a majority of the delegates to hostile views. Weizmann's very presence encouraged opposition. The old argument over the Keren Hayesod was raked up and served to obscure a more fundamental cleavage. Other issues were rehashed pro and con. The pro-Weizmann leaders were Judge Rosenblatt, Emanuel Neumann, Morris Rothenberg, Peter Schweitzer, and Louis Lipsky. They were answered rather more briefly by Judge Mack, Samuel Rosensohn, Nathan Straus, Jr., Rabbi Wise, Rabbi Silver, and Felix Frankfurter.

The vote on whether to approve the administration stood 153 to 71. Thereupon Judge Mack read a prepared statement of resignation for himself, Brandeis, and some thirty-odd others. They could not, Mack explained, continue as active leaders of the movement, but they would continue to work indefatigably in the ranks of Z.O.A. for the cause in Palestine.[73]

Thus the Brandeis regime ended. He had carried American Zionism through World War I, and up from a minor federation almost to the pinnacle of world leadership. His name and prestige had attracted to the organization the loyal work of a large number of outstanding American Jews, non-Zionists as well as Zionists, whose absence in succeeding decades was to be sorely felt. No doubt the power of his fame was such that he could have made peace with the dissidents at any time if he had only said the word. That he did not do so could hardly be attributed to any slackening of interest. Rather he had decided to approach the problem from a new angle.

After the Cleveland convention, Brandeis and his followers met in New York and pledged themselves to "undertake immediate constructive work in Palestine without seceding from Z.O.A. or forming a minority group within the movement." [74] Various bodies were organized to carry out specific economic measures—The Palestine Development Leagues, The Palestine Co-operative Company, The Palestine Development Council, The Palestine Endowment Fund, The Palestine Economic Corporation—these and other such projects felt the touch of his genius. He helped develop basic industries, assisted in low-cost housing and small industrial loans. "In all these economic activities," Robert Szold observes, "Mr. Brandeis was characteristically concerned with 'the little man.' For him Zionism was a segment of the striving for the dignity of man." [75] The basic aim was upbuilding Palestine for a preponderating body of manly, self-supporting Jews. To create such a small state, a Jewish homeland which could support its own culture, required sound economics and good morals. Nor was Brandeis's effort confined to economic enterprises. Even after 1921 he was influential in broader fields of organization and political action and reached out to the four corners of the Zionist world—to Jerusalem, Constantinople, Copenhagen, and London. [76]

AFFINITIES AND AVERSIONS

The feud between Brandeis and Weizmann has remained one of the significant episodes in the Zionist movement. Both men stood well with the political forces in their countries and elsewhere; both enjoyed great popularity among the Zionist rank and file. Friend and foe alike have spoken of Weizmann's great charm.* [77] Brandeis also cast a spell, but

* On one occasion a Jewish Agency representative (non-Zionist) was talking with Dr. Drummond Shield, of the British Colonial Office, about the possibility of Weizmann's resigning. Dr. Shield replied by stating that "he was quite sure that the support of men like Lloyd George, Smuts, Baldwin, and others was not so much an intellectual support as it was support engendered by Dr. Weizmann's charm, and that of course this would be lost." (Memorandum of conversation with Dr. Drummond Shield, January 9, 1931.)

whereas he swayed men by sheer logic, Weizmann was activated by feeling and emotion.[78] Their ultimate goal was the same, the method of achieving it sharply divergent. The cleavage was between propaganda and practical work; between vested organization and newcomers. Brandeis insisted on high efficiency, strict financial accountability, and keeping faith with promises made.[79] Weizmann was, in fact, a man of expediency and compromise, qualities which brought down on his head Brandeis's most violent epithets. Brandeis's followers saw his rival as "utterly incapable of straight-forward and honorable conduct," and the Justice himself characterized his British confrere as "untrustworthy." [80]

A "minor villain" in Zionism for Brandeis was Louis Lipsky, who in the main endorsed the Weizmann large-scale policies, mixed philanthropy and investment (Keren Hayesod). Lipsky openly professed his sympathies with Fabian socialism and distrusted Brandeis's emphasis on private enterprise, individual initiative, and the indispensability of capitalists in Palestine. These differences stirred recrimination, often couched in very strong language. On June 22, 1928, Brandeis wrote De Haas from Chatham:

> The Romans of the great days occasionally lost a campaign. They never lost a war . . . because they never permitted a war to end until they won. Our war is against Lipsky and his ilk. . . .
>
> The terrible demoralization wrought by the Lipsky administration cannot be overcome without teaching Zionists the wages of sin. There must be no suppression in the supposed interest of Palestine—or "to save the movement." The cause cannot be served without saving the souls of American Jewry. . . .

In the light of the fact that De Haas brought Brandeis into the movement, it seems the more regrettable that De Haas's own defects may have prevented Brandeis from exerting the full measure of his influence. In his capacity as go-between De Haas aroused much ill-feeling, not only against himself but also against Brandeis.* As early as 1920 Frankfurter commented: "It's sheer nonsense for a man of his [De Haas's] brains to make the enemies he does." [81] De Haas was the *bête noire* not only of the Weizmann–Lipsky forces but also of many within the Mack–Brandeis group itself. In some quarters he was even more unpopular than Lipsky. In 1928 Judge Mack wrote Brandeis that the only ones in "our group" who did not openly oppose De Haas were Frankfurter and himself. Far from yielding to the well-nigh unanimous sentiment against his mentor, Bran-

---

* De Haas arrogated to himself the prestige of Brandeis's name and stood between leader and people. Judge Mack reported to Brandeis, February 12, 1930: "I spent an hour to-day with Irma Lindheim. Naturally, when she came back from Palestine and wanted to see you, she was deeply hurt when you suggested that she see De Haas instead. In the course of the last ten or twelve years, I have seldom met anyone who does not feel hurt when that suggestion is made. Miss Szold's great grievance always was that the letters came through De Haas."

deis rose to his defense, drafting a letter so extravagant in its praises, that it could not be sent without overruling "the objections of A.G.B. [Mrs. Brandeis]."

"I am sure," Brandeis wrote, "that no one whom I have met has been more devoted, more knowing, and on the whole, more clear-sighted, in all the political aspects and in his judgment of the political characters." De Haas was responsible, Brandeis reiterated, for his own political judgments on Zionism, and it would be the "height of folly" in the strenuous times ahead to try to get along without his knowledge and experience. Finally, the Justice urged Mack to confer with De Haas, saying that he had never known a person with whom it was possible to talk more freely. This was the only part of the original draft that went into the letter as actually sent, which ended with an observation somewhat extraordinary for this man of facts: "You, of course, do not expect me to change my views as to De Haas or as to his usefulness to the cause." [82]

Despite all differences and disaffection, Brandeis remained firm in the Zionist faith, proving his ability to stand alone as in no other cause. Many admirers and friends failed to share the strength of his conviction. "Entre nous," an intimate friend has said of the Justice, "I could never see eye to eye with him on this matter." One day a law clerk, himself a Jew, had the temerity to speak of the Justice's Zionism as "Jewish Hitlerism." Brandeis coldly inquired: "Have *you* read so and so?" reeling off a long list of authoritative books. The young man confessed that he hadn't. "Well," the Justice rejoined, "until you have done so, it will not be profitable to discuss the subject with you." Even Alfred Brandeis, the beloved brother, and his entire family stood aloof from the movement, as did the Goldmarks. In the Justice's own household only Susan became an active Zionist.

This cause, more than any other, fired Brandeis's imagination and captured his heart. It satisfied his love of adventure, brought to the surface his unflagging belief in the power of idealism. Zionism, inspiring as it did achievements of spiritual significance, gave him "understanding and happiness," [83] which even the compromising White Papers and Nazi barbarisms were unable to obliterate. Despite all trials, and throughout the lagging years, Zionism for him was no dream, but a beautiful reality.[84]

CHAPTER THIRTY

The Supreme Court Fight: Alignment

FRIDAY, January 28, 1916, found politics in the nation's Capitol relatively serene. The topic of the day was President Wilson's preparedness speech of the night before until suddenly Washington and the country's financial districts were "stunned as if by a bomb from an unseen Zeppelin." [1] Without taking a single senator into his confidence, Wilson had appointed Louis D. Brandeis to succeed Joseph R. Lamar as an Associate Justice of the United States Supreme Court. "Impossible!" senators exclaimed. Wall Street's groan was "like the echo of a great national disaster"; [2] it must be "a ghastly joke, Sam Untermyer has put one over." [3]

Press comment was sharply divided. The *New York Sun* called the appointment "utterly and even ridiculously unfit." For the *New York Press* it was "an insult to members of the Supreme Court." "Mr. Brandeis," the *New York Times* complained, "is essentially a contender, a striver after changes and reforms. The Supreme Court by its very nature is the conservator of our institutions." The *Boston Transcript* regretted that Wilson should "attempt to force upon the Supreme Court one whom the Senate is reported to have been unwilling to confirm as a member of the cabinet."

The *New York World* saw him as "a radical of unusual ability and character whose elevation to the Bench will be regarded by most people with emphatic approval." "Mr. Brandeis fully measures up to the most rigid standards so necessary in his high position," the *Boston Post* said. "Mr. Brandeis has been a great force for progressive thought and action in the field of political and economic reform" the *Baltimore Sun* observed. Ignoring politics and geography, the *Kansas City Post,* January 18, had seen Brandeis as precisely the logical choice: "The appointee to this great place should not be of the McReynolds type. He should be instead a noted jurist like Louis D. Brandeis."

Early reports spoke of the appointment as a "surprise everywhere in official circles." Since Lamar was a Southerner, certain Democratic senators held that his successor should hail from below the Mason–Dixon line. Massachusetts was already represented on the Court by Justice Holmes. Surely the Bay State's claim to further consideration was slim indeed.

Brandeis was in Washington the day the news broke. "I have nothing whatever to say; I have not said anything and will not," he told newspapermen as he left for Secretary McAdoo's dinner to President Wilson. [4] The guests included, among others, Justices Charles Evans Hughes, Mahlon Pitney, and James C. McReynolds, the latter bitterly hostile to Brandeis. When Wilson noticed this particular Justice very carefully trying to ignore his nominee, the President took him by the arm and said to McReynolds: "Permit me to introduce to you Mr. Brandeis, your next colleague on the Bench." [5]

"I am not exactly sure," Brandeis wrote, January 29, in reply to felicitations from his brother, "that I am to be congratulated, but I am glad that the President wanted to make the appointment, and I am convinced, all things considered, that I ought to take it." Within twenty-four hours a Senate sub-committee had been appointed to sift the mounting charges. "What seems certain," the *Brooklyn Eagle* commented, January 28, "is a protracted struggle in the Judiciary Committee, to which the nomination has been referred. In the course of this fight it is predicted that every detail of Mr. Brandeis's career as a lawyer will be thoroughly gone into. It may be weeks before the nomination is reported back to the Senate."

Writing Alfred, January 31, Mrs. Brandeis described the situation:

The whole thing went most rapidly. It is hardly a week since Louis was asked whether he would consider the appointment. I had some misgivings for Louis has been such a "free man" all these years but as you suggested—his days of "knight erranting" must have, in the nature of things, been over before long. It is of course a great opportunity for service and all our friends here feel that he is the one man to bring to the Court what it greatly needs in the way of strengthening.

It will doubtless be called something of a political appointment, and there is some little of that in it, but the President himself told Louis that he wanted him in the Court because of his high respect for and confidence in him.

The great excitement in the newspapers is amusing, is it not? We never expected that! I tell Louis, if he is going to retire, he is certainly doing it with a burst of fireworks. In Washington they seem to think there was no doubt he would be confirmed—in time.

Whatever Wilson may have had in mind, it was no casual decision. The year before a minor explosion had occurred in the Cosmos Club when the Boston lawyer's name was proposed for membership. "Several members of the Club have started an opposition to Mr. Brandeis," Justice Hitz wrote the President, January 30, 1915, "which bids fair to be successful unless his friends come strongly to his support. The grounds of opposition to Mr. Brandeis are stated to be that he is a reformer for revenue only; that he is a Jew; and that he would be a disturbing element in any club of gentlemen." On February 1 President Wilson wrote the Admissions Committee, as suggested, saying that he held Brandeis in "highest esteem" and "his admission to the Club would not only be an act of justice to him, but would add a member of very fine quality to its list."

Attorney-General T. W. Gregory endorsed the Bostonian as "the greatest lawyer in the United States." * "But I hope you realize," the Attorney-General had warned the President, "what a tempest you will stir up." "Let us see," Wilson said, "I go west next Friday. I will send in the name on Thursday." [6] "I believe," the President wrote Senator Robert L. Owen, February 7, 1916, "that the nomination was the wisest that could possibly have been made, and I feel that few things have arisen more important to the country or to the party than the matter of his confirmation."

Monday, January 31, the Board of Arbitration of the New York dress and shirtwaist industry met in special session. Both employers and union men made speeches warmly congratulatory of Brandeis. It was "the most natural thing in the world," they said, "that the President of the United States should promote their chairman from the position of chief judge of our supreme court to that of judge of the highest court in the land." To all this the nominee simply replied, "Thank you." [7]

"Have you heard that charges have been made to senators concerning your relations with the United Shoe Machinery Company . . . the Lennox case and the Warren will case?" asked a *New York Sun* reporter, as Brandeis left the city for Boston. "No, I have not. I have nothing to say about anything, and that goes for all time and to all newspapers, including both the *Sun* and the moon." [8]

In Boston next morning he wrote a long letter to Norman Hapgood, mapping preliminary strategy for the battle: "La Follette is not only one of my most devoted but politically wisest friends," and the nominee listed prominent people and eminent lawyers who would support him. But political Washington had other ideas. "The Attorney-General is very urgent," his law partner Edward F. McClennen informed Brandeis, February 3, "that no effort should be made by anyone which might arouse any

---

* There has been much speculation as to who was first to suggest Brandeis to Wilson for the Supreme Court. In March 1927 former Attorney-General Gregory told Ray Stannard Baker that soon after Justice Lamar's death he went to the White House and asked Wilson whether he had given thought to Lamar's successor. "No," he said, "I have been waiting to hear from you." "I am going to make a suggestion," said Gregory, "and I am going to ask you not to respond to it for a week. I am going to recommend Louis Brandeis for the Supreme Court. My reason is that he is one of the most progressive men in the United States, and equal to the best in learning and ability." At the end of the week Gregory went back and the question came up again. "You are right," said Wilson, "send his name in." (Baker's conversation with Gregory, March 14, 15, 1927.)

Gregory cannot, however, be given entire credit. "In my opinion," Norman Hapgood wrote Baker, May 10, 1932, "there is no doubt that he [Admiral Cary Grayson] was the first to suggest L.D.B. to W.W. for the Court, and that Gregory's part was limited to agreeing and earnestly fighting for confirmation." The truth of the matter is that by 1916 Wilson knew Brandeis so well as not to need prompting.

suspicion that this appointment sprang from any 'Progressive' source or any other except purely Democratic. The strength is in Democratic party loyalty. This means having Hapgood and Rublee figure as little as possible. . . . Also," McClennen concluded, "he believes activity by the Jews is not likely to help with Bourbon Democrats. They know what this support means in the coming elections, without having it called to their attention." Accordingly Brandeis warned enthusiasts: "I am inclined to think that it would not be advisable for the Jewish members of the Bar to take any concerted action." [9]

From Fargo, North Dakota, United States District Court Judge Charles F. Amidon wrote on February 1: "By your zeal for the common good, you have created powerful enemies. They will do their utmost to defeat your confirmation in the Senate, but they must not be permitted to succeed. . . . You will be accused of everything, from grand larceny to a non-judicial temperament. Fake telegrams will be sent to Washington in the name of persons who never sent them or signed them. Forged signatures will be entered on petitions of protest. I hope you have a friend on the sub-committee who will have charge of your nomination, to keep you fully informed of everything that is presented to the committee. Please do not allow the reluctance which every man of honor feels against defending his own life to prevent your meeting the issue. You owe it to your country as well as to yourself."

On February 2 Brandeis returned to the scene of action. That evening Senator Henry F. Hollis of New Hampshire, a warm supporter, arranged an interview with a member of the recently formed Senate sub-committee. "From a man [perhaps Senator Thomas J. Walsh] who was going to sustain the nomination because the President made it," Hollis reported later, "my friend has changed to an enthusiastic personal supporter of yours." [10] Three other members of the sub-committee were then considered favorable: William E. Chilton of West Virginia, Duncan U. Fletcher of Florida, both Democrats; and Albert B. Cummins, Iowa Progressive Republican. Fletcher had been on the special joint committee investigating the Ballinger-Pinchot feud. Cummins had frequently joined Moses E. Clapp, George W. Norris, R. M. La Follette, and other insurgents in support of progressive legislation. The fifth member, Senator Clarence Clark of Wyoming, was soon replaced by John D. Works of California. Both were old-fashioned Republicans and neither could be counted for Brandeis.

Though newspapers highlighted the fact that only one other Jew had ever been proposed for the Supreme Court,* opposition on the ethnic issue

---

* President Fillmore offered an Associate Justiceship to Judah P. Benjamin, but he declined

was, for the most part, not overtly pressed. The *Boston Morning Globe* of January 31 summed up the anti-case:

That Mr. Brandeis is a radical, a theorist, impractical, with strong socialistic tendencies.

That he is given to extravagance in utterance, inspired by prejudice and intolerance.

That he is a "self-advertiser," reckless in his methods of seeking personal exploitation.

That he does not possess the "judicial temperament" that would fit him for the duties of the Supreme Court judge, in that he would be influenced by personal considerations rather than the merits of the cases submitted for impartial analysis and exact judgment.

It was now certain that the nominee's entire career would be given a thorough going-over, and United States District Attorney George W. Anderson promptly offered his services in defense.[11] Anderson was the only man with whom Brandeis had crossed swords in his battles for the public welfare who strongly supported confirmation.[12] The District Attorney breakfasted with the nominee at the Cosmos Club on February 3. After consulting Attorney-General Gregory, they agreed that Brandeis should leave Washington until victory was assured. McClennen and Anderson remained there for sub-committee hearings. Brandeis stayed several days in New York until McClennen wired he had better return to Boston.[13]

At his law offices George R. Nutter and William H. Dunbar were on the alert, but "carefully saying nothing and doing nothing . . . of a public nature so as not to cross wires." [14] The nominee himself was not inactive. "The Justiceship *ist ein bischen langweilig*," he wrote Alfred, February 12, "but I am leaving the fight to others and we are getting a pretty nice issue built up. As you correctly divined, I should have preferred to be let alone until sixty-five. . . . But the fight that has come up shows clearly that my instinct that I could not afford to decline was correct. It would have been, in effect, deserting the progressive forces. Now my feeling is rather—'Go it husband, Go it bear' with myself as 'interested spectator.'

"Nothing," he added, "could demonstrate more clearly the concentrated power of the interests than some of the incidents, which I will tell you about when we meet."

Had not Morgan, Mellen, and other magnates utilized both state and federal governments in counterattacks against the uprisings led by Brandeis? Of course he was "unfit" in the eyes of these financial and corporate interests with whom he had locked horns. Josiah H. Benton, "a leader of the

owing to his recent election as United States Senator from Louisiana. (Charles Warren, *The Supreme Court in United States History*, Vol. II, p. 519.)

Bar" and formerly an attorney for the New Haven, erupted with shocking disregard for facts:

I consider the nomination unfit to be made not because Mr. Brandeis is a bad man, but because he is not a judicial man. Nobody in Boston would think of selecting him as a referee about anything. That is the test. He has brooded over such subjects as rights of labor until he has reached a point where it is impossible for him to be fair. President Wilson might as well have nominated Samuel Gompers.[15]

To former President Taft, yearning hopefully toward the "sacred shrine," the Brandeis appointment was "a fearful shock. . . . It is one of the deepest wounds that I have had as an American and a lover of the Constitution and a believer in progressive conservatism that such a man as Brandeis could be put in the Court. He is a muckraker, an emotionalist for his own purpose, a socialist," Taft rumbled on, ". . . a man who has certain high ideals . . . of great tenacity of purpose and, in my judgment, of much power for evil. . . . When you consider Brandeis's appointment, and think that men were pressing me for the place, *es ist zum lachen.*"[16]

In effect privilege, openly and for the first time, proclaimed: "Hands off! The Supreme Court is our province. We don't mind if you elect a governor, senator, or congressman now and then. Do anything you please about justice, democracy, and equality of opportunity. With the Supreme Court on duty they can't do much."

Beyond the appointment loomed the presidential election of 1916. The party balance was so delicately poised that both sides hesitated to venture into the perilous realm of radical versus stand-pat social theory. However much Brandeis's reactionary enemies may have feared his "radicalism," they did not force the issue lest the Court be exposed as their protector. Radical friends also were cautious. Confronted with a reuniting Republican party in an election year, they dared not trumpet Brandeis's progressivism in the ears of conservative Democrats.

COLLEAGUE AND PUBLIC BETRAYED

The first protest heard by the Senate sub-committee came from the agrarian Middle West. The last protest was from the simon-pure reformist Edward R. Warren, who went to Washington in March 1916 to tell how, in 1906, the People's Attorney had conspired with Boston Consolidated Gas to defeat the general welfare.

Clifford Thorne, chairman of Iowa's Railroad Commission, had harbored a grievance against Brandeis since the Five Per Cent Rate affair. Senator Cummins, also of Iowa, and Senator William E. Borah of Idaho had heard much of Brandeis's "betrayal." Both were eminently progressive Republicans and members of the Judiciary Committee. "Give me the facts with reference to the conduct of Louis D. Brandeis in the five per cent case," Borah had wired Thorne, January 30. "I will treat the information as confidential unless you consent otherwise." Thorne immediately wired back, saying: "I was an admirer of Mr. Brandeis up until the closing argument in the eastern advanced rate case. His act on that occasion . . . in my judgment had all the essential elements of the act of a traitor." [17]

"The gentleman whom you have under consideration," Thorne told the sub-committee on February 9, "was guilty of infidelity, breach of faith, and unprofessional conduct in connection with one of the greatest cases of this generation." [18] His testimony seemed fatal until Lieutenant-Governor John M. Eshleman of California, who possessed "some slight knowledge of the matter," bluntly advised the sub-committee: "I have never been able to tell why Mr. Thorne felt just the way he did about the conduct of this case; and I have yet to find a single man connected with railroad regulation, up to this time, who agrees with Mr. Thorne's position." [19]

Joseph N. Teal, himself of counsel for the shippers, and James W. Carmalt, I.C.C. attorney, further undermined Thorne. "He [Brandeis] was employed by the Commission to see that all interests were properly represented," Teal told the sub-committee. "He was not retained for the purpose of developing the railroad side . . . nor any particular side," Carmalt testified. "I think he was there to develop the whole case." [20]

Interstate Commerce Commissioner James S. Harlan, who had asked the Boston lawyer "to undertake the task of seeing that all sides and angles of the case are presented of record, without advocating any particular theory for its disposition," testified: "Of course there were two sides to the case. There was the railroad side and there was the shippers' side, and both sides were very ably represented. *But I do not understand that Mr. Brandeis was on either side. He was there in the public interest.*" (Author's italics.) [21]

Thorne's indictment cut two ways. He insisted flatly that the nominee was too favorable to capital, that he wanted to allow the railroads to earn too much money. This contradicted the Wall Street picture of Brandeis "The Railroad Wrecker," as painted by the notorious Clarence W. Barron, whose *Boston News Bureau* had long been in the pay of the New Haven. "The nomination by President Wilson of Louis D. Brandeis to the United States Supreme Court," Barron said, "is an insult to New England. . . . Let any senator at Washington, who thinks the nomination of Brandeis to the Supreme Bench fit to be made, visit Boston for a day and learn how Brandeis has garnered his wealth."

"What is your business?" Senator Chilton asked.

"Farming is my chief business in the town of Cohasset, where I do the largest business of anyone." [22]

This Cohasset farmer had come to Washington with a bag of court records, newspaper clippings, and official reports—all shedding baleful light on Brandeis's past. "I have had the court records of Massachusetts examined," Barron explained expansively, "and have always kept on file in my safe, memoranda in relation to what was of record as to Mr. Brandeis, so that it might be useful and in order, that upon it I might be able to speak when it was required." Barron lacked firsthand information, but could point to an imposing list of persons presumably able to supply it— Charles F. Choate, Jr., Moorfield Storey, Charles S. Mellen, and others— all big names, who were asked to join the fight.[23] "An effort is being made by some members of the Bar here," Nutter reported to McClennen, February 9, "instigated chiefly by Choate [counsel for the New York, New Haven & Hartford Railroad], to have some concerted remonstrance against the confirmation. I learned of it yesterday through Thompson.* The men whom he named as concerned in it outside of Choate were chiefly laughable, and I am inclined to think that the matter will fall by its own weight."

Nutter and McClennen were disinclined to strike back too severely lest such counterattack stir even hotter enmity. "The very fact that there is a division of opinion," Nutter observed, "is in itself unfortunate." But Brandeis realized the futility of trying to soft-pedal. Having been sniped at for ten years and more, he welcomed a show-down. "Every attempt to deal mercifully with the special interests," he had said in an earlier struggle, "simply results in their taking advantage of the merciful. . . . The man with the hatchet is the only one who has a chance of winning in the end."

FIFTY-FIVE BOSTONIANS

By February 11 it was all too evident that the Boston Bar's "concerted remonstrance" would not "fall of its own weight." On that day an imposing petition was published bearing the names of fifty-five Bostonians, with A. Lawrence Lowell, president of Harvard, near the top. The petition said:

We, the undersigned citizens of Massachusetts, are opposed to the appointment of Louis D. Brandeis to the vacancy in the Supreme Court of the United States.

An appointment to this Court should only be conferred upon a member of the legal profession whose general reputation is as good as his legal attainments are great.

We do not believe that Mr. Brandeis has the judicial temperament and capacity which should be required in a judge of the Supreme Court.

* William Goodrich Thompson, Boston lawyer, member of the Union Club.

His reputation as a lawyer is such that he has not the confidence of the people.

For these reasons we express the hope that the Senate will not confirm his appointment.[24]

Besides Harvard's educator, the list included Charles Francis Adams, C. Minot Weld, financier, Hollis R. Bailey, member of the general council of the American Bar Association, William L. Putnam, lawyer and director of American Telephone & Telegraph Company, and Moses Williams, also a lawyer and director of A. T. & T.—all loyal sons of Harvard. "The names read well," Nutter wrote McClennen, "but somewhere there ought to be published a breezy account of who the unknown men are. If the fellows west of the Hudson had any idea of them, they would see that New England humor has not run dry. The tailors of Tooley Street were world renowned by comparison!" [25]

Nevertheless, Nutter found counterattack hard going. "We cannot get a petition signed," he reported wearily to McClennen, February 17. "It takes a long time to get a letter written, at least from the people whom we want to write. Any form of petition will be met in the same way that the requests for letters are met, namely, by a general feeling that it will be best to wait until the conclusion of the evidence." A businessmen's petition made some headway, and at Harvard Law School Professor Felix Frankfurter persuaded several colleagues to write Senator Chilton,* but nothing else had yet been done in the way of preparation for the fight.

Hearings reopened on February 15 to follow up Barron's leads. Appearing as counsel for Boston's Fifty-Five was the pompous and showy New York lawyer, Austen G. Fox, assisted by energetic Kenneth M. Spence. At the sub-committee's request George W. Anderson agreed to "assist the committee." Brandeis's friends and supporters described Anderson's position as *amicus curiae*, "in no sense representing the nominee." [26] "It was suggested that Anderson appear for you," McClennen wrote Brandeis on February 18. "I told him that nobody was to appear for you or your friends. The sub-committee then arranged for Anderson to act for the sub-committee. . . . It is important to keep the spectacle of a trial or contested hearing away." McClennen assisted Anderson and for several days was in the witness chair. Brandeis and Nutter sent him a steady stream of explanatory letters and memoranda.

Barron's side got off to a bad start. They had built their show around Charles S. Mellen, who bluntly refused to perform: "I think it would be a waste of committee's time and mine for me to go to Washington to testify.

* Nine of the eleven members of Harvard's law faculty expressed themselves as favorable to the appointment. Only one, Edward H. Warren, was openly opposed.

I am not at all unfriendly to Brandeis, and I know nothing about his career except hearsay." [27]

But Sidney Winslow of the United Shoe Machinery Company gladly heeded Barron's summons, delaying a Florida vacation until his turn came. Slowly and emphatically he read a lengthy prepared statement on Brandeis's "unprofessional conduct and conduct not becoming an honorable man." Winslow charged that "Mr. Brandeis has, at the instance of new clients, attacked as illegal and criminal the very acts and system of business in which he participated, which he assisted to create, and which he advised were legal, and he has persistently sought to injure our business. . . . I could not understand Brandeis's position, to tell the real truth."

Anderson then pressed the witness to admit that Brandeis had expressly objected to the form of the leases. "Will you state any facts," the District Attorney went on, "which Mr. Brandeis learned as counsel for the United Shoe Machinery Company, or as director of the United Company, that he subsequently, as you say, used in an attack on the United Company?"

Winslow hesitated. "I should like to see just the language I used. If you will call my attention to it, I think I can answer that question for you intelligently." *

"I ask you to state specifically what facts he learned, as counsel or director, that he subsequently used in criticism of, or attack upon, your company?" Anderson repeated.

"I suppose that is a broad question."

"No," Anderson answered. "It is not a broad question. It is a very narrow question."

"It is?" was all that Winslow could find to say.

Cornered at every turn, Winslow resorted to oblique attack. "I do not criticize Mr. Brandeis acting for anyone, if he had at all times scrupulously or, I might say, fairly, confined himself to statements that were correct and true, to the best of his knowledge and belief. . . . I want the committee to understand distinctly," Winslow interposed somewhat apologetically, "that I am not here by any malice toward Mr. Brandeis. I would lean over backward rather than urge anything against him." [28]

Thus beating a retreat, Winslow stepped down and took his trip south.

CLIENTS DESERTED!

"It is not necessary to uncover the grave of Patrick Lennox . . ." Barron remarked, "to show the moral fiber of Louis D. Brandeis and his unfitness

---

* Winslow had said in part: "Mr. Brandeis apparently felt under no obligations to refrain from using such knowledge as he had of the company's business and lease system in an attack upon them."

for the Supreme Bench." [29] Nevertheless considerable exhumation was undertaken. Barron's research man was the ubiquitous William S. Youngman who, as a young lawyer, had volunteered his services to Brandeis in the Boston Elevated fight.

The results, however, were less damaging to Brandeis in 1916 than might have been expected. The key witness, Sherman L. Whipple, whom Brandeis had opposed in the case, turned out to be one of his most effective supporters. Whipple explained that Brandeis "took a broader view, that he was charged with the . . . broader duty to all the interests involved." Lennox had gone to Brandeis's office in search of a lawyer and found rather a "judge" preoccupied with "the whole situation"—the lawyer being "so much absorbed in . . . caring for the situation" that he "overlooked the more human aspect." Brandeis had been wrong but not culpably so, Whipple declared, in that he did not make his position wholly clear, "so that a layman would understand just what he was talking about. I think," Whipple explained, "if Mr. Brandeis had been a different sort of man, not so aloof, not so isolated, with more of the comradery of the Bar, gave his confidence to more men . . . said to them when he was charged with anything that was doubtful, 'Boys, what do you think about it?' and talked it over with them—you would not have heard the things you have heard in regard to him." He rested, Whipple told the sub-committee, "in the security of the purity of his own mind and the purity of his own purpose. . . . He never consults anybody; he gives little thought as to how it is going to affect the mind or minds of other men, and sometimes I have thought he took a delight in smashing a bit the traditions of the Bar, which most of us revere. . . ." [30]

This was indeed an acute analysis of an able, though fallible man suffering somewhat from pride and self-deification, of a lawyer who had to risk being more than a lawyer, regardless of consequences to himself or to anyone else.

Among the blacker pages in his dossier Barron had the Warren will case. On February 15 Hollis R. Bailey, Boston lawyer, signer of the anti-Brandeis petition, told the committee all the horrid details. In the summer of 1940 Justice Brandeis recalled that at Harvard Law School Bailey had been a "commonplace fellow of mediocre ability," who read for "so much an hour" when Brandeis's eyes gave out. Bailey had aided to "the extent of his lights" in inaugurating savings-bank life insurance and in other good causes, but he was now an enemy instrument.

As one of the counsel for Edward P. Warren, Bailey had prepared a bill in equity in which he alleged that Samuel D. Warren in 1889, assisted by Brandeis, carried out a plan for disposing of the family property so that

Edward suffered to the tune of hundreds of thousands of dollars. Actually Brandeis had objected to the disposition of the property as quixotically generous, since it guaranteed to Samuel's relatives 6 per cent of the property and half of the profits of the business, with Sam himself taking all the risk.[31] In 1916 Senator Duncan U. Fletcher also failed to see how the arrangement had operated to Edward's detriment.

"Were those his [Samuel D.'s] earnings or was it the salary that paid him that?" the Florida Senator asked. When Bailey tried to evade making a responsive answer, Senator Walsh intervened: "The Senator [Fletcher] is asking what the lease provided with reference to the salary." The lawyer was forced to admit that the lease provided no fixed salary. "Well," observed Senator Fletcher, resuming his questioning, "the amount of salary would depend altogether on how successfully they operated the business, would it not?" Bailey nodded a reluctant affirmation. "Precisely," Fletcher commented airily. "Then it was not in the shape of salary." [32]

On February 26 Youngman, who had been in this case from the beginning as counsel for Edward P. Warren, displayed before the sub-committee the results of his search. "Mr. Brandeis is on record," he testified, "as producing a sort of chloroform in the form of a legal opinion that put Mr. [Samuel] Warren's brains and conscience to sleep in equity, in this whole thing." [33] Against this McClennen observed: "I think that Mr. Sam Warren drew those contracts, undoubtedly with the advice and assistance of Mr. Brandeis; but I think the actual drafting was Sam Warren's. Of course, you realize that Mr. Sam Warren was likely just as good a lawyer as Mr. Brandeis at that time." [34]

The Warren family was indignant over the resurrection of this whole business. Miss Cornelia Warren wrote Brandeis on February 16, 1916:

I write especially because of the indignation I felt in seeing in last night's papers that your connection with the affairs of my brothers has been made the subject of accusation before a committee of the Senate. I hope the committee was also informed that my brother Edward was alone in conducting the bill in equity referred to, that Fiske and I opposed him, and that the lease complained of has been lived under peaceably since that time until last year when it underwent some unimportant modification.

I hope most sincerely that your nomination will be confirmed, and that the whole country will have the benefit of your ability, and of your unselfish devotion to the public good.

Brandeis replied the next day.

My dear Miss Warren:
    It is a great satisfaction to have your letter of yesterday.

Nine years of persistent abuse had so inured me to personal attack that the renewal of charges in public, under conditions which would compel their being inquired into, brought no regrets, and indeed was most welcome. But I felt with you keen pain that the attacks on me should be made the occasion to attack Sam's memory; and to attempt to make it appear that I was blameworthy because I had been the legal adviser of Sam, who is thus charged practically with breaches of trust. You know, as I know, that Sam was indeed the soul of honor. He was of all people whom I ever knew who had to do with business affairs, the most indifferent to money; and no man have I ever known who sought more eagerly to do justice, and who erred, if he erred at all, in deciding against his own financial interest, when decisions had to be made.

It is in my opinion proper for the protection of his name that you and members of Fiske's family should, in communications to the committee, make clear beyond peradventure the facts; that you should make it clear, among other things, that during all of the period not only you, but your mother and Henry, understood and approved of everything that was done, and of Ed's long approval.

Of course nothing could be more untruthful than the statement of Mr. Bailey that I was on "both sides of the case—the lessor and the lessee." My position was that of being on neither side, but of holding throughout the period of trust, as I had during your father's lifetime, the position of adviser of the family, and during most of the time, of each and every member in their relations to one another, as to outsiders.

If you should care to write, the letter best be addressed to Senator William E. Chilton, Chairman, Sub-Committee, United States Senate, Washington, D.C.

Most cordially yours,

Louis D. Brandeis.

THE RAILROAD WRECKER AND BRIBER

Thorne had pictured the nominee as gratuitously suggesting "extraordinarily high returns, very costly to the American people." Barron, on the opposite tack, condemned him as disastrous to railroads. "Mr. Brandeis," he wrote, "has been the leader of all the political and financial forces smashing the credit of the Boston & Maine and New Haven Railroad systems." [35] As counsel for the New Haven, Moorfield Storey was expected to agree with Barron. "Is it your opinion," Senator Walsh asked Storey, "that the conduct on the part of Mr. Brandeis was calculated unjustly to injure the New Haven road?"

"I do not know that I can or ought to express any opinion on the subject," the New Haven's counsel replied hesitatingly. "The feeling was that there were better ways [i.e., for Brandeis] of conducting that matter than were adopted. . . ." (Author's italics.)

"But his communications through the public press at that time did direct the public mind to what afterwards was disclosed to be a rather question-able system of operation in finance?" Senator Walsh inquired.

"I have no doubt that is correct," Storey somewhat grudgingly replied.[36]

All such testimony tended to endear the nominee to progressives. But another episode was introduced, portraying him as employed by the New Haven itself "to help wreck the New York & New England." "You have to go forward some years," Barron told the sub-committee, "to connect Brandeis with it." [37] But a different light was cast on this matter by Judge William J. Kelly, who had retained Brandeis, and who told the sub-committee: "The reason he was employed was to show that the New England was wrecked at that time and to prevent the further distribution of corporate assets among certain of the directors; . . . it was wrecked already, sir—badly wrecked; there is no dispute about that. These things are all of record in the court." [38]

Barron then tried another tack to show Brandeis on "every side of the case intermittently," and "not anywhere long." Even while he waged war against the New Haven in 1907, Barron charged, Brandeis's own firm, acting as counsel for that transportation bogeyman—Edward H. Harriman, openly solicited proxies in behalf of the Illinois Central Railroad. Surely here was a clear case of playing both sides simultaneously—of con-demning monopoly while aiding and abetting it.

Again investigation destroyed Barron's argument. Brandeis was, in fact, injected into the Illinois case only because Nutter refused to act without his approval. This called for an interview with Waddill Catchings, president of the Central Foundry Company, on whom Brandeis made "the deepest and most lasting impression." The lawyer not only had to be convinced, Catchings told the sub-committee, that no possible inconsistency existed; "he had to be satisfied of the justness of our position. It was," Catchings testified, "an unusual experience. I had occasion to retain other lawyers, and no one ever raised that question." [39]

RESHAPING THE ATTACK

The hearings adjourned on March 8. Throughout Brandeis had been conspicuously silent, but he had not been idle. Besides preparing long letters and memoranda for McClennen in Washington, he held frequent conferences with Anderson and his partners in Boston. This was a new experience; desk work amid battle had never been his forte. Nor was he at all satisfied.

"I . . . feel," he wrote McClennen, March 9, "that our position is not one of apology; but on the contrary in regard to nearly every one of these transactions, we have taken a very much higher standard than ordinarily prevails, and I feel very strongly that that point of view should be emphasized and that harm has been done by allowing an attitude of apparent apology or defense when our real position is one of insisting upon a higher standard than generally prevails."

To illustrate, he cited the Lennox case: "Senator Works talked considerably about obligations which I had assumed toward Lennox. The important thing as to our attitude is the fact that Lennox was untrue to the terms and conditions upon which we agreed to take over the matter. My doing so involved expressly, and even more by implication, honest co-operation on his part and of course an assumption on my part of honesty on his."

Both sides were content to keep the debate within the bounds of that most imponderable of categories—professional ethics. But they did not always succeed in doing so. Divergence of social views rather than ethics constituted the very core of the contest, and at times witnesses ventured somewhat warily into this perilous terrain. Thus Clifford Thorne, having denounced the nominee as favorable to "unreasonably high return" to the railroads, was about to elaborate on "what a tremendous factor a simple little variation of 1 or 2 per cent is," when Senator Chilton cut in: "What do you think now of putting a man on who had a preconceived idea of an unreasonably low surplus?"

"It would be equally objectionable," Thorne admitted.

"And therefore," Senator Chilton inquired, "you are prescribing to us powers that only angels have, are you not? Do you think there is any man on earth who can reconcile these differences of mankind about a matter of opinion in general?" [40]

But Dr. James Cannon, Jr., Bishop of the Methodist Church, blithely took the sub-committee into that very quagmire of rational differences of opinion on controversial subjects. Cannon had nothing against Brandeis personally: "For aught we know, he may be of the highest character and doubtless possesses unusual mentality and legal ability." But the Bishop's resourceful temperance lobby found now that the lawyer had disqualified himself back in 1891 when he appeared before the Bay State Legislature in behalf of the Massachusetts Liquor Dealers' Association.

Senator Fletcher suggested as a possibility "that a judge on the Bench might have some views as to what he believed the law ought to be, but still would enforce the law as it is written."

"Yes, I think that is true," Dr. Cannon admitted, "yet I think it is difficult for men to so divest themselves in interpretation of what they think is a sound public policy and for the moral and material welfare of the state, to be entirely unbiased when it comes to a decision. Judges are men, like everybody else." [41]

The Bishop was right, of course; but Brandeis's critics and supporters alike were necessarily at pains to circumvent this question.

CHARACTER WITNESSES, PRO AND CON

As facts dissipated the critics' direct evidence, they altered their assault. "An appointment to this Court," the Fifty-Five had declared, "should only be conferred upon a member of the legal profession whose general reputation is as good as his legal attainments are great." [42] Republican Senator Clark asked Hollis R. Bailey to testify on this point: "Just state what is the general reputation of Mr. Brandeis?"

"First," Bailey retorted, "that he is a very able lawyer; . . . that he is an able advocate; that he is not entirely trustworthy." [43]

The same question to Mr. Storey elicited much the same reply: "I think his reputation is that of a man who is an able lawyer, very energetic, ruthless in the attainment of his objects, not scrupulous in the methods he adopts, and not to be trusted."

"You say he is not to be trusted," Senator Fletcher inquired. "What do you mean by that?" "I mean to say," Storey replied, "there is a radical lack of confidence in him among a representative class of men in the community in which I live, and which has existed for a good while."

"Is some of that due to these recent activities in connection with the New Haven road?" Senator Walsh interposed.

Storey hesitated. "I judge from what you say," Senator Walsh commented suggestively, "that people associated with that organization [the New Haven] exercise a very powerful influence, socially, politically, and financially in your community?"

"They did, certainly at one time," Storey admitted.

"So," the Senator remarked, "a man would really not be in high favor with some of your best citizens who was engaged in exposing the iniquities of those people?"

Storey stubbornly refused to give in, insisting that "the reputation I speak of was established before that question arose." [44]

But Sherman L. Whipple rejoined: "I think that the Bar is divided. . . . He has antagonized, by an attempt to carry out his ideas, very important and powerful interests, and the feeling of bitterness which they have toward him is something which is very unpleasant to contemplate. But, on the other hand, I believe that they are sincere. I believe that they thought they had been wronged, and that he is mischievous and harmful." [45]

McClennen was much encouraged. "Whipple made a very good impression," he wrote Brandeis on February 18, "better perhaps than if he had not disagreed on many points, as he did. Strangely enough, he is what has done the most to kill the protestants without attacking their good faith."

Meanwhile support was being organized outside the Senate. In Boston, Nutter, assisted by Melvin O. Adams,* encouraged supporters to write letters to the sub-committee, covering the following points:

(1) A statement of who the writer is, particularly of any public offices he has held, and the years of practice.
(2) Statement of his knowledge of Brandeis.
(3) A statement that he approves the confirmation.
(4) Possibly an allusion to the fact that any opposition to him comes from a very narrow circle, and does not represent the real feeling of the community.

Thus, the Reverend A. A. Berle wrote to Senator Chilton on February 18:

It would be fair to say that if any man bearing an old New England name and practicing at the Bar in Boston had everything which is alleged against Mr. Brandeis alleged against him, and were nominated for the Supreme Court, no one would dream of raising these questions.

Long and unchallenged control of everything in the Commonwealth has given many of these gentlemen the perfectly natural feeling that whoever is not approved by them is *ipso facto* a person who is either "dangerous" or lacking in "judicial temperament." . . . They simply cannot realize, and do not, that a long New England ancestry is not *prima facie* a trusteeship for everything in New Engand. That is in my judgment the real spring of most of the opposition.

Special effort was made to counteract President Lowell's opposition and Storey's contention that "lack of confidence" was established even before Barron began mudslinging. "The fact that L.D.B. has been and *is now* on the Committee of the Overseers to visit the Harvard Law School," Nutter wrote McClennen, February 20, "ought to be hammered in. Everyone to whom I mention it is struck by it, and it contradicts Lowell." Storey was also refuted by citing Judge Francis Lowell's invitation to Brandeis of May 21, 1904, to act as special escort for William Howard Taft, recently returned from the Philippines, and the Harvard Medical School's invitation of June 6, 1904, to deliver a course of lectures on the relation of the medical profession to the law and the courts.

Brandeis's Boston aides, though encouraged, were wary of further com-

---

* "Adams," Louis had written Alice Goldmark, December 10, 1890, "is a lawyer of perhaps forty years, whom I like very much—a man of charm and of great kindliness. There is in him much of the native Yankee. Born in a small town of Massachusetts, he worked his way to college and through it [Dartmouth] and has won himself a good position at this Bar."

bat. "Don't get into the position of calling witnesses from Boston on standing in the profession," Nutter nervously warned McClennen. "It will result in breaking the case. The letters ought to be enough."

McClennen also discouraged further demonstration as unnecessary and
unseemly. Nutter said he would resort to it only if the "other side dared
us to produce anybody. . . . We can get plenty of small fry whom nobody
knows. You can judge of our situation by reading the lists of letter-writers
which I have sent. It does not average high." [46] But more pro-Brandeis
sentiment from Boston had to be evidenced. "My present impression is,"
Anderson wrote Nutter on February 26, "that some of the sub-committee
would be disappointed if we do not produce some representative members
of the Bar on our side." Nutter went to work, rounding up Asa French,
former United States District Attorney, Thomas J. Boynton, sometime
Attorney-General of Massachusetts, and others.

Meanwhile Fox daringly produced a character witness likely to carry
great negative weight—former Bay State Attorney-General Albert E. Pillsbury, corporation lawyer, Groton and Harvard, whom Brandeis had routed
in Massachusetts battles.

"His reputation as it has come to me," Pillsbury recited in the now
familiar twang, "is that of a very active, adroit, and successful business
lawyer; a man of unbounded audacity; a man, if you wish to go into questions touching integrity—a man, I should say, of duplicity."

"Of what, sir?" Fox asked, underscoring the point.

"Of duplicity; double dealing; a man who works under cover, so that
nobody ever knows where he really is or what he is really about." [47]

Other character witnesses, in rapid succession, chanted the same refrain.
"A lawyer of great ability, but not straightforward," said Edward W.
Hutchins, vice-president of the Boston Bar Association. "He is untrustworthy, and . . . sails under false colors," General Francis Peabody joined
in. [48]

The Brandeis forces counterattacked March 2 with Newton D. Baker,
reform mayor of Cleveland, and Henry Moskowitz, clerk of the Arbitration Board for the New York garment workers. Moskowitz singled out the
nominee's "capacity to see both sides, his capacity not only for judicial
statement but for judicial thought" as his "one characteristic." Baker presented the social workers' impressive petition laboriously assembled by
Paul U. Kellogg of *The Survey* and social worker Frances Perkins.*
Joseph Walker, lawyer and Bay State legislator, told of Brandeis's public
activities. "If I may analyze it," Melvin O. Adams commented thought-

* Secretary of Labor from 1933 to 1945 in the F. D. Roosevelt administrations.

fully, "there is a group . . . who state and think that Mr. Brandeis is not straightforward in his practice. I think those opinions, when traced, run into some one of these pockets of more or less publicity, namely, the Lennox case, the United Shoe Machinery case, the wrecking of the New England— those allegations." [49]

"He has made enemies, of course," Asa French admitted. "A man cannot be combative as he is, or aggressive as he, fighting as he has been on the firing line all his professional career, without making enemies." Finally, Thomas J. Boynton described Brandeis's general reputation as "good." He had never heard it questioned until (in 1912) he had come across "certain printed matter circulated by the United Shoe Machinery Company." [50] McClennen now considered the counteroffensive helpful. "Things look well," he reported to Nutter on March 4. "The favorable opinion witnesses made a very good showing. Asa French, following soon after Francis Peabody, wrapped the House of Lords in quite a tidy package . . . and left the general reputation as it really is."

The most effective character witness (with the possible exception of Whipple) was another Boston lawyer, Arthur D. Hill, who wrote a long letter to Anderson, which the latter read into the record. Hill, like Whipple, weighed the case with an even hand: "He is a radical * and has spent a large part, not only of his public, but of his professional career, in attacking established institutions, and this alone would, in my judgment, account for a very large part of his unpopularity. . . .

"The fact, too," Hill went on, "that Mr. Brandeis has been the object of constant attack, and in particular of a very skillful and long continued press campaign, engineered on behalf of the New Haven management by C. W. Barron, has probably increased the feeling against him. . . . When you add to this that Mr. Brandeis is an outsider, successful, and a Jew, you have, I think, sufficiently explained most of the feeling against him. . . . Once on the bench," Hill anticipated, ". . . his strong qualities, his great ability, his knowledge not only of law but of economics and social conditions, and his capacity for taking a broad judicial view of any question to which he applies his mind, will be of inestimable value. . . ." [51]

PIERCING THE OPPOSITION'S ARMOR

The Brandeis forces, now led by the nominee himself, tried to outflank opposition by relating every critic to an episode in which he had opposed Brandeis and in which Brandeis had emerged victorious. Thus Brandeis instructed his secretary "to ascertain to what extent I personally have had

* When questioned, June 1944, Mr. Hill agreed that the word "radical" was ill-chosen.

any professional relations with each or any of the fifty-five alleged signers of the protest within the past twenty years." [52] The information resulting was given McClennen for use against unfavorable witnesses.

"I do not recall ever having met Hollis R. Bailey in the Warren case," Brandeis wrote McClennen on February 17. "The last case I had against Bailey . . . was the Henry E. Weston will case. . . . The question in that case was whether Weston was of sound mind. We contended that he was not and undertook to prove that he was affected by general paresis. I think there is little doubt but that the case was won on my closing argument. . . . As I think it over," he concluded, "it must be Bailey's wrong-headedness in this case that started him in opposition to me."

Brandeis believed that a personal grudge antagonized Moorfield Storey, who had had rough-and-tumble treatment in both the New England and New Haven railroad struggles. But Brandeis explained: "My impression is that Storey was less affected by the New England than by my later tussle with him in the New England Mortgage Securities matter which was begun July 28, 1898. . . . In the closing argument I compared Storey's acts with those of the government in the Dreyfus case, quoting the passage from the Merchant of Venice that their contention was 'to do a great right by a little wrong.' [53]

"Somehow Storey's peculiarities should be made clear to the sub-committee," Brandeis persisted. "How this can best be done you and he [Anderson] and the Attorney-General, who knows Storey pretty well, can determine, but there should be no failure to make clear the character of Storey." [54]

To provide ammunition for more counterattacks, J. Butler Studley, a lawyer in the Brandeis office, prepared a chart showing in minute detail the economic and social interrelationships of the fifty-five petitioners. Studley's chart stimulated Walter Lippmann of the New Republic to write an ironic editorial in the March 11 issue, describing Brandeis as "a rebellious and troublesome member of the most homogeneous, self-centered, and self-complacent community in the United States. It was a special community that had found Mr. Brandeis untrustworthy," Lippmann wrote, "the powerful but limited community which dominated the business and social life of Boston. He was untrustworthy because he was troublesome. He was disloyal, if at all, to a group. All the smoke of ill-repute which had been gathered around Mr. Brandeis originated in the group psychology of these gentlemen and because they are men of influence it seemed ominous. But it is smoke without any fire except that of personal or group antagonism. . . . They come of a proud line and are jealous of a noble tradition."

Charles Francis Adams, himself of a "proud line," supported Lippmann's acute analysis. "I have tried Boston socially on all sides," Adams observed; "I have summered and wintered it, tried it drunk and tried it sober, and

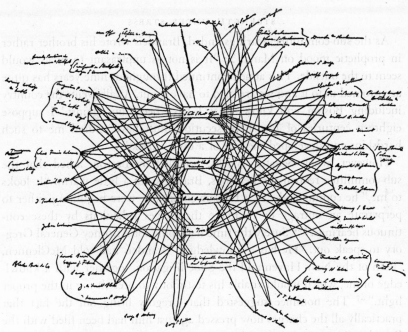

STUDLEY'S CHART OF THE FIFTY-FIVE PROTESTANTS

Center column: State Street officers; trustees and bankers; Somerset Club members; Back Bay residents; Me Too's; large corporate connections and corporate advisers. The marginal inscriptions name the individuals and some of their corporate groupings. The cross lines show interlocking interests.

drunk or sober there is nothing in it save Boston. . . . It is, so to speak, stationary—a world, a Boston world unto itself . . . and, like all things stationary . . . it tends to stagnate." [55]

Still Brandeis was not satisfied. "The matter should be brought out very clearly," he wrote McClennen on February 19, "that libeling did not begin with the Shoe Machinery pamphlet, but that there had been a steady stream since 1907. Of course the purpose of that stream of abuse was to break down the good reputation which I had, and which was recognized as an important factor in carrying through the policies which I advocated."

That this "community campaign" of destructive abuse was both deliberate and cumulative is obvious enough. Barron and other such propagandist scavengers were quite plainly in the employ or under the influence of big interests. What hurt (perhaps due merely to "reasonable misunderstanding") was that men of much better fame were also in opposition. Brandeis's effort to tie these men in as tools or adjuncts of sinister forces was not very successful; nor was it wholly admirable.

STRENGTH UNDER STRESS

As the sub-committee hearings ended, Brandeis wrote his brother rather in prophetic mood on March 2: "It is not as unpleasant to us as would seem to the outside. This attack continued throughout nine years has quite accustomed us to it and we are glad to have it out. At all events the country including Boston will know what I have been 'up against.' I suppose eighteen centuries of Jewish persecution must have enured me to such hardships and developed the like of a duck's back."

However, when Senator Works, prodded by Barron, asked that the sub-committee reopen the hearings, Brandeis got a little warm. "It looks to me," he commented, "as if the sub-committee were beginning either to perpetrate an outrage or to make themselves ridiculous by these continuous hearings." [56] Surely the time had come for Attorney-General Gregory to speak out. "He has a knowledge," Brandeis had told McClennen, "both of the New Haven and the Shoe litigation, together with a knowledge of me, which would enable his testimony to present me in the proper light." [57] The nominee suggested that Gregory bring out the fact that practically all the charges now pressed against him had been filed with the President "in connection with my supposed contemplated entry into the cabinet, and were then investigated for the President, and he concluded that they were unfounded." [58]

"I have carefully refrained from interfering in any way with the conduct of the hearings," Brandeis continued insistently, "or the plans of the Attorney-General in this connection. I have been and am anxious, as you and Anderson know, that the Attorney-General should appear before the committee and make a public statement."

"At the request of the Attorney-General," he reminded McClennen on March 9, "I left Washington on February 2nd [actually February 3] with the understanding that I would not return unless summoned by the sub-committee. I have accepted the opinion that it would be unwise for me to go down to Washington and appear, but if the proceedings continue on the lines which have been taken (making it appear that we are defending ourselves or excusing our conduct), I think I would rather go down and testify."

McClennen disagreed. "What you could say has been said by the papers and witnesses," he wrote Brandeis on March 10. "You would dignify the

adverse claims by coming here. And your presence would surely be miscon-
strued to mean that you were seeking the position. . . . As to the Attorney-General's appearing," he concluded, "it can do no good and might
produce a prejudice. The President and the Attorney-General have said
their word in the nomination itself."

It was agreed that no effort be made, at least openly, to obstruct or delay
further hearings. "Our position ought to be," Nutter wrote McClennen
after the Boston conference on March 10, "that if the sub-committee desires
any information whatever with regard to L.D.B. from his birth up, we
are only too glad to furnish it, or put them in a position where they can
obtain it."

Sub-committee hearings reopened March 14. The opposition now
stressed the Old Dominion Copper case. This controversy had arisen in
1902 when Towle and Fitzgerald, Boston stockbrokers, and their client,
Charles Sumner Smith, became dissatisfied with the company's management and "went out to get control." Brandeis, retained as joint counsel by
Towle and Fitzgerald and Smith, won enough proxies to elect Smith
president and make Towle a member of the executive committee. Fitzgerald was not included as an officer in the new set-up. Brandeis then
brought suit against the former president, A. S. Bigelow, alleging damages caused by mismanagement. In 1903 the company found itself in
financial straits, and Brandeis attempted to raise new money by revising
the company's financial structure. When an injunction suit blocked his
plan, rumors of receivership became rife. Smith and Brandeis suspected
that Fitzgerald was behind both the injunction suit and the talk of bankruptcy, so when the stockbroker sought information concerning the suit
pending against Bigelow, a reply was not immediately forthcoming. Fitzgerald protested. Writing him, January 2, 1904, Brandeis explained: "I am
of course personally always glad to have any suggestions from any stockholder of the Old Dominion Company or from *you,* whether a stockholder
or not, but you will realize that since you are not an officer of the company
and no longer hold the position which you did, of determining the policy
of the company, though not a director, it would be improper for me to
communicate with you on the subject of the company's litigation. . . ."

Brandeis, as counsel, finally entered into an advantageous agreement to
consolidate the Old Dominion with the prosperous and efficiently managed Phelps-Dodge Company. Though not an officer, Fitzgerald had kept
in close touch with developments, and when he sought again to defeat
Brandeis's plans the lawyer advised somewhat colloquially: "Fitz, you
had better come over on the other side. That's where the money is. I have
got on the bandwagon and you had better do the same." [59]

Spence, Fox's assistant counsel, now prepared a detailed "Summary and Proof" on Old Dominion, the nub of his argument being that Brandeis had again defied ethics to maximize his own fees and profits. Apparently the main basis of this charge was an interview in New York between Fox and Fitzgerald. But later when Fitzgerald arrived in Washington to testify he was in an uneasy frame of mind and singularly uncertain of his ground. He was about to conclude his testimony, the sinister effect of that "band-wagon" suggestion not yet having been fully exploited.

"Now, have you not omitted a part of the conversation which you had with Mr. Brandeis?" Fox inquired suggestively, "a part of what he said when you mentioned the 'bandwagon' and so on? I wish to avoid lead-ing you. . . ." [60]

But the witness refused to follow through. Fox kept prodding until Fitzgerald declared flatly: "Perhaps I have given the wrong impression of it. I would say Mr. Brandeis was conserving my interests in telling me to get on the bandwagon, and that my money was there by having a concern that could finance and handle this mine, which was exceptionally rich." [61]

"I want to say that I am not down here of my own volition . . ." the witness had said earlier. "Mr. Brandeis has got himself in the light of being persecuted, and I am not persecuting him, although I dislike him very much." [62]

Brandeis had furnished McClennen with his own version of Fitzgerald's animus on February 11: "I was called back from my vacation in August 1903 for conferences. We undertook to devise some means of raising money. . . . There were rumors of receivership . . . and I had reason to believe that Fitzgerald was behind the rumors. . . . His purpose was made clear by his own statement in which I remember he expressly stated (at all events clearly indicated) a desire to have me put the company into a receivership, and enable him to clear the matter up by acquiring a large interest. . . . Years later [after Brandeis as counsel for others had blocked this effort] I was told that Fitzgerald was short 15,000 shares of Old Dominion at 5, and that he had lost $75,000 by my act."

Fox's one last hope lay in the appearance of Edward R. Warren, Bran-deis's onetime friend and helper in the Public Franchise League. Warren had long been clamoring to be heard, and the committee reluctantly extended the hearing to permit him to testify. Brandeis had sent McClen-nen a six-page special-delivery letter the preceding day. He told how Ed-ward R. Warren in the Public Franchise League and Edwin L. Sprague of the Board of Trade, both "one-idea" men, had protested against his com-promise of the gas problem, and how he successfully presented his plan to the Legislature.

Warren now accused Brandeis of having falsely conveyed the impression that he and Sprague backed his plan. "Now, of course, I do not know personally what happened at that meeting before the legislative committee," Warren told the sub-committee, somewhat inarticulately. "I do not know what was said, nor does Mr. Sprague; but I do know that Mr. Sprague was a bitterly disappointed man. . . ."

Senator Walsh halted such speculation, and when on further questioning it became clear that this protest was stimulated by nothing more than personal pique, Warren implored the committee plaintively: "I tell you what it is, gentlemen; Mr. Brandeis has a wonderful magnetism when he speaks, and he has a wonderful way of carrying his points, and he carried those men right off their feet." [63]

"Gas splendid climax," McClennen wired Brandeis triumphantly on March 15. "Opposition needs pullmotor." That evening McClennen summarized the outcome: "The smile on my face will not come off. I am obliged to hide. My dramatic powers are not up to describing this afternoon properly. . . . Fox looked like after a shampoo before the hair is fully dry. . . . Everybody seemed to think that it was best to hurry for the train and the hearings closed. No general staff could have provided so good a finish as our friends the enemy provided." [64]

THE BAR ASSOCIATION PRESIDENTS DISCHARGE
A PAINFUL DUTY

Before the hearings closed so triumphantly the American Bar Association launched an all-out attack. On March 14 Fox read: "The undersigned feel under the painful duty to say to you that in their opinion, taking into view the reputation, character, and professional career of Mr. Louis D. Brandeis, he is not a fit person to be a member of the Supreme Court of the United States." [65] The statement was signed by William Howard Taft, Elihu Root, Joseph H. Choate, Moorfield Storey, Simeon E. Baldwin, Francis Rawle, and Peter W. Meldrim—all distinguished lawyers, all former presidents of the American Bar Association.* Fox solemnly underscored the statement: "Each of these gentlemen has been, I am told, and I think I know, a president of the American Bar Association." [66]

Brandeis no sooner heard of his excommunication than he planned countermoves. "I think Taft's injecting himself into this controversy," he wrote Hapgood on March 14, ". . . gives opportunity for making clear what we omitted to make clear nearly six years ago—the gravity of Taft's

---

* Taft, Baldwin, Rawle, and Storey all signed on February 7; Choate and Root on March 12; Meldrim's separate letter was dated March 4. Apparently Spence visited Boston on March 11 to secure the signature of Choate.

and Wickersham's act in connection with the antedating [of the Ballinger report]. Taking the hint, Gilson Gardner promptly syndicated an article entitled "Taft's Personal Grievance against Brandeis." And Walter Lippmann wrote another editorial, in the *New Republic* of March 18, beginning: "One would have supposed that ex-President Taft was the last man qualified to express a judgment on Mr. Louis D. Brandeis. . . . It was Mr. Brandeis who demonstrated to the country Mr. Taft's immoral procedure in a disreputable incident."

Other signers were also explained in terms of personal animosity. "You doubtless recall," Brandeis wrote Hapgood on March 18, "that Simeon Baldwin was a New Haven merger man, and an associate of Moorfield Storey in the old New England days. Joseph H. Choate is an uncle of Charles F. Choate against whom I have been persistently opposed in the New Haven and Shoe Machinery matters." Florence Kelley of the National Consumers' League set off Choate's confessed Bourbonism against Brandeis's practical humanitarianism in the columns of *The Survey* on March 16. Mrs. Kelley cited the 1907 Muller brief as one reason for Choate's present opposition. "The outlook of the two men upon industry in relation to the Constitution is," she observed, "irreconcilably divergent."

All this was effective but obscured a basic divergence between Brandeis and his enemies which both were disposed to ignore. Fundamentally, these legalists fought Brandeis because his philosophy of law and of society was alien to theirs. "The government," he had said, "must keep order not only physically but socially. . . . The law must protect a man from the things that rob him of his freedom, whether the oppressing force be physical or of a subtler kind." [67] None of the American Bar Association presidents could say these things, nor could they understand a man who did.

CHAPTER THIRTY-ONE

The Supreme Court Fight: Victory

"There will be some hot work before the vote comes," La Follette warned Brandeis on March 22, "and these hell-hounds must get what is coming to them—I mean the Bar Association presidents, University presidents—these sleek respectable crooks—whose opinions have always been for sale. There are no facts in the case, but these opinions have hurt. It is essential," he continued, "that every foot of the ground be covered and the answers which have been put in to meet the informal objections must be sharpened and given more edge. You know me and can trust me. Take the hearings and make a brief for me just as if I was the man to be confirmed. Don't ask anybody else to do this. You do it—send it to me on plain paper typewritten without any signature. . . ."

At last the nominee himself could move closer to the front and inject his own more militant, less defensive, note. "The dominant reasons for the opposition to the confirmation of Mr. Brandeis," his unfinished brief began, "are that he is considered a radical and is a Jew. The reasons stated are mainly (1) an alleged lack of 'judicial temperament,' (2) an alleged undesirable 'reputation' at the Boston Bar, and (3) certain alleged acts of 'unprofessional' conduct. An examination of these specific acts of alleged unprofessional conduct will show not only that his action was consistent with the highest professional standards, but affords striking evidence of the possession of the judicial temperament, and of the high reputation in which Mr. Brandeis was perhaps universally held until malicious libels undertaken for business purposes, and in spite of them he is now generally held at the Boston Bar as well as elsewhere."

Brandeis then met the several charges head on. Of Thorne's accusation, he said: "Mr. Brandeis's conduct in recognizing the needs of the railroads and, in taking on the subject of income, a point of view far more favorable to the railroads than that entertained by so-called radicals, affords strong evidence of the existence of the judicial temperament which the capitalistic interests have denied him. . . ."

Of the United Shoe matter he wrote: "There is nothing on which to my mind the question not only of judicial temperament, but of high ethical standards and of fitness could be better argued than the shoe machinery case. . . . You have your evidence of reputation; . . . the perfectly deliberate purpose of this whole thing is to destroy reputation. There you have the strongest evidence to overcome all this charge of what reputation was. They were fighting to destroy reputation."

Brandeis described the Warren matter as casting light "upon the quality of Mr. Brandeis as a trustworthy lawyer. He has been counsel for three generations of Warrens, and over a period of more than thirty-five years a man whom a family of large interests and high intelligence, knowing well his abilities and character, were content to trust, knowing that he would decide all questions intelligently and with judicial fairness." [1]

Meanwhile his friends were mapping other strategy. Henry Morgenthau, Sr., concerned as always with the welfare of the Democratic party, was suddenly struck by a brilliant idea. After confirmation Brandeis should decline the Supreme Court appointment and run for the Senate against arch-conservative Senator Henry Cabot Lodge. The two conferred several hours at New London. "You must consider this," the ambassador argued. "The present senators from Massachusetts have both opposed your confirmation and have charged you with dishonorable acts in the practice of your profession in that state. You have a right to present your case in public to your neighbors in Massachusetts . . . and to demand from them a public vindication. This can best be achieved by defeating Senator Lodge for re-election." Brandeis promised "prayerful consideration," but Morgenthau returned to New York disheartened. Brandeis had been "afraid to act." "A great opportunity" had been "missed by lack of courage." [2]

THE SUB-COMMITTEE REPORTS

While Brandeis and Morgenthau talked at New London on April 1, a hopeful telegram came from Mrs. Brandeis: "City editor of *Globe* says Washington advises confirmation 3 to 2."

The three Democrats (Chilton, Fletcher, and Walsh) had found the charges not borne out by the evidence. The two Republicans (Cummins and Works), on the basis of the same evidence, disagreed.

"My conclusion is the result of much reflection," Cummins reported, "and it is with great regret that I announce it." Building his adverse report around the Five Per Cent Rate Case, the Iowan observed: "Mr. Brandeis was employed to take the public side of the question, that is to say, he was to present the side opposed to the claims of the railroads. . . .

"If, under the circumstances of this proceeding," Cummins concluded bitterly, ". . . a lawyer who appears with other counsel in behalf of the public can, after his associates have made their arguments, arise and in open court admit that the carriers were wholly right and the public wholly wrong . . . without incurring the condemnation which follows betrayal, then I confess that I do not understand either common morality among men or the ethics of the profession to which Mr. Brandeis belongs." [3]

The Senator from California was even more harshly emphatic: "He has in many instances been intolerant and offensive in his methods. . . . He has resorted to concealments and deception. . . . He has defied the plain ethics of the profession and in some instances has violated the rights of his clients and abused their confidence. . . ." [4]

In both the majority and minority reports, the United Shoe Machinery and Lennox and Warren cases claimed the greatest space. The same facts invariably led to contradictory interpretations. To Senator Works, Brandeis's role in the United Shoe Case proved lack of appreciation "of the duty of an attorney to his client and a due sense of the proprieties." [5] Senator Cummins concurred. Senators Walsh and Chilton, on the other hand, themselves eminent lawyers, saw the case in an altogether different light. "Mr. Winslow," Walsh observed caustically, "seems to be possessed with the idea that because Brandeis had taken fees from the Shoe Machinery Company he bound himself for ever not to criticize its policies or its practices." [6] Senator Chilton said: *"Three and one half years elapsed after his resignation from the company before he advised any other client on the subject. . . .* How long does an employment mortgage the lawyer's conscience?" [7]

The People's Attorney did not, however, entirely escape censure even at the hands of his supporters. "If in the impetuosity of attack," Walsh observed in mild rebuke, "or the ardor of advocacy he [Brandeis] was led sometimes into giving too vivid a hue to the facts touching the methods of business of Mr. Winslow's company or drew unwarranted conclusions from them, there was no such obliquity of mind disclosed or faults of character revealed as would in any wise unfit him for judicial duties." At the end Senator Walsh cut loose from specific charges and hit out in a bold offensive: "The real crime of which this man is guilty is that he has exposed the iniquities of men in high places in our financial system. He has not stood in awe of the majesty of wealth. He has, indeed, often represented litigants, corporate and individual, whose commercial rating was high, but his clients have not been exclusively of that class. He seems to have been sought after in causes directed against the most shining marks in it. He has been an iconoclast." [8]

HITTING BELOW THE BELT

A month of hearings and testimony, filling well over a thousand pages, had failed to yield conclusive results. For Brandeis's supporters the subcommittee's favorable vote only placed the appointment one step nearer confirmation. But his opponents had added two influential senators to the already impressive weight of seven Bar Association presidents.

Evidence that the opposition would step up its barrage was soon at hand. Even before the sub-committee reported, Fox and Spence had distributed an imposing "Brief," with a title page bearing the imprint "United States Senate,"—all strikingly suggestive of an official document. It opened with a formal question: "Does the evidence show that Louis D. Brandeis has a defective standard of ethics?" The question was answered at great and misleading length. Charges, baseless even in the unsympathetic eyes of Cummins and Works, were again put forth at face value. Thus the Old Dominion case got four pages, though Cummins had expressed his contempt for it, saying: "Mr. Fitzgerald's testimony did not make the slightest impression on me," and Works had brushed it aside in disgust: "There is nothing in this charge worthy of consideration." [9]

A charge, omitted from the Fox brief, but widely circulated by gossips, was the incredible story of Mrs. Peck. A Boston lawyer, Frank N. Fay, passed this yarn on to the Reverend E. S. Meredith to persuade the clergyman to vote against Wilson in 1916. Said Fay:

It seems to me strange that you as a clergyman urge any man to vote for Mr. Wilson. Half the people in the United States know the general facts regarding his expensive acquaintance with Mrs. Peck of Washington. In fact the matter is so generally known that you ask any man who is Peck's Bad Boy, and with a smile, you will be told that it is Mr. Wilson.

Within a very short time from the death of his first wife, he was paying her marked attentions and wrote her a number of amorous letters. . . . Then his engagement was announced to the lady whom he subsequently married. Mrs. Peck promptly claimed breach of promise on his part, and the matter was put into the hands of her lawyers. Suit was threatened if not actually brought. It was settled by Louis D. Brandeis of Boston, and Samuel Untermyer of New York, acting as Mr. Wilson's attorneys, and the amount of money paid Mrs. Peck to secure these letters and prevent any damaging publicity was in the vicinity of $75,000. It is an interesting fact that soon afterward Mr. Brandeis was appointed Justice of the Supreme Court of the United States. [10]

The Reverend Meredith later sent this letter to Brandeis, who replied:

No decent person should have been guilty of circulating this vile slander. For a lawyer to do so is unpardonable. It may interest you to know that I first heard the Peck story some time after my nomination, when my alleged connection with this matter was being whispered about by deliberate liars in the effort to defeat my confirmation. [11]

Other rumors without basis in fact went the rounds in Washington.

THE SUPREME COURT FIGHT: VICTORY

Thus Attorney-General Gregory on April 12 wrote Brandeis: "In conversation with a senator yesterday, he said that he had heard in the cloakroom of the Senate that you had stated that you did not believe in a written constitution." Brandeis wrote back on April 14:

Would it not be possible to follow up such statements to their source and find out who originated them? They must have originated in deliberate lies. I have not only not said any such thing, but not said anything which anybody could have distorted into such a statement. My views in regard to the Constitution are as you know very much those of Mr. Justice Holmes.

It was sufficiently trying throughout two months of the hearings to have lies and misrepresentations spread in regard to me without the opportunity of being heard by the sub-committee and the public, but to have these lies circulated privately after the hearings are closed seems to me not in accord with American conceptions of fair play.

Brandeis sent Gregory's letter to McClennen on April 14, commenting pointedly on how it must "intensify further my strong conviction that the course pursued by my friends, and among other things, the delays, are not only unwise but perilous."

ENLISTING THE LEGAL PROFESSION

While the Senate Judiciary Committee delayed, the propaganda mongers were busily at work. "The 'brief' . . . apparently has been published throughout the country," Nutter wrote McClennen, "and of course will have an important effect. . . . The scheme is to arouse dust, and then argue that because there is dust, the confirmation should be denied."

Daily, Barron's *News Bureau* predicted that confirmation would be denied. Nutter and McClennen were at last convinced that the defensive position was "perilous." But what form should counteractivity take? "There is no use publishing articles," Nutter had commented wearily, "no one reads them." [12] While Nutter and McClennen debated, Barron grew bolder, distributing the Fox brief and minority sub-committee reports under the imprint: "With the Compliments of the *Wall Street Journal*" or the *"Boston News Bureau."* "The constant pushing out of Fox's brief and the adverse reports is only accentuating the situation," Nutter wailed. "Our adherents have nothing to say, because they don't know the facts." [13]

Nutter himself now went to work on a defensive statement. But McClennen was wary: "Nobody believes such things to be spontaneous. You know one of the charges is that 'he works under cover.' " [14] Nutter struck another snag when he asked his friend William V. Rowe, a New York lawyer, to help find a publisher. Rowe raised "questions of *propriety* and *tact* and *advisability*." He thought it better to let "a cold matter rest." Nutter replied: "If this were an ordinary case before a jury, comments upon the evidence before a verdict had been given would be improper; but as in all cases in which politics enter, public opinion plays a very important part in influencing the final result." [15]

Convinced at last that "aggressive publicity" was both necessary and proper, Rowe got busy. He reported that the *New York World* would publish the article, "authorship unknown." Nutter was a "little nervous" over the possibility that authorship might be "traced to me or to my firm," and wished to have it understood that "this statement has not been submitted to Mr. Brandeis at all, and so far as I know he knows nothing about it. It seems to all of us," he concluded, "that it is a perfectly fair statement. At least we have tried to make it so." [16]

On April 25 the *World's* evening edition carried Nutter's article in full. A six-line streamer and the heavily leaded title "War of Interests against Brandeis" made a most effective display. The aggressive captions breaking the article would have done credit to Brandeis himself.

Meanwhile the administration took more aggressive action. On April 25 Hapgood hurried to Washington in response to a telephone call from Attorney-General Gregory. Hapgood wrote Brandeis the next day that Gregory wanted more "publicity by our side, to offset the elaborate work of the stand-patters." But the Brandeis forces could not use Nutter's *World* article because he was still a little nervous about the author being discovered.[17]

Hapgood and Rublee then suggested that the Walsh and Chilton reports be sent to all legal bodies throughout the country. This ambitious project raised two more questions: Who would bear the not inconsiderable expense? Who would sign the covering letter accompanying the reports? "Provision will of course be made for the disbursements," Brandeis assured Hapgood, promptly solving the expense problem.[18] The matter of signers was not so easy. Nutter, who went to New York on this mission, promptly reported to McClennen: "New York names giving difficulty." "This is quite a village and the streets are rather long." [19]

Nutter finally enlisted Charles C. Burlingham, Everett P. Wheeler, and H. deForrest Baldwin.* "Burlingham is interested in the 'fair play' argument," Nutter reported on May 3, "without much 'believer' business. Burlingham objects to having us pay for it. That will have to be managed somehow." Burlingham also insisted on sending minority as well as majority reports, and rewrote the covering letter, eliminating "belief" and reducing the original draft to a cold statement as to "fair play." Burlingham

* Cousin of Simeon E. Baldwin.

had known Brandeis at the Harvard Law School. They had been good friends during the years since. And yet after talking with one of his associates at the Bar, he expressed the feeling that "L.D.B. has really had his innings." *

"This was enough," Nutter wrote McClennen on May 5, "to upset all on the list including Burlingham himself. They will sign if *all* are sent out, but not the majority [reports] only." McClennen, joined by Rublee and La Follette, strongly opposed such procedure. "Those who want fair play," McClennen commented sharply, "ought to be able to see that errors in the minority reports are not in conclusions merely, but in facts stated and omitted. Two whacks on one side and one on the other is not fair play." [20] So on May 6 it was "settled that only the majority reports go out," and four days later ten thousand copies went.† Brandeis's supporters had met the challenge of the Bar Association and of the Fifty-Five in the only way it could be met—by setting lawyers against lawyers.

THE NOMINEE TAKES COMMAND

Four months had now elapsed since Wilson sent Brandeis's name to the Senate. The issue was going stale. Democratic Senator Henry F. Ashurst, in a newspaper interview, accused Republican senators on the Judiciary Committee of deliberately filibustering against a report on the nomination. Senator Sutherland noted this in the Senate and retorted: "No Republican senator is responsible for not having an immediate report. . . . The Republican members . . . are quite ready to vote at any time."

Ashurst lashed back: "This is . . . a contest between that great inarticulate mass of people . . . on one hand, and the great corporations on the other." But Democratic Senators Hoke Smith of Georgia and Lee S. Overman of North Carolina were not so firm in the faith. "I have seen no disposition on the part of any Republican to delay a report on the nomination," Overman observed apologetically. "There has never been a time," Smith confessed, "when Mr. Brandeis could have attained a favorable report from those present at a committee hearing." [21]

Hoke Smith's implied admission that Republican lines stood fast while Democratic ranks wavered seemed to certify Brandeis's defeat. "Debate Reveals Critical Status of Brandeis," a *Boston Herald* streamer said. "Hint

---

* "My memory is still a blank as to my conversations with Nutter," Mr. Burlingham wrote the author, June 12, 1944, "but I am certain my confidence in L.D.B. never weakened in the slightest, and I have no doubt that the reason a few of us did not sign up was because we were unable to obtain the signatures of the Great and thought that if a handful of us came out pro L.D.B., friends of Fox would come out contra."

† A brief covering statement was signed by Everett P. Wheeler of the New York Bar, Stephen S. Gregory of Chicago, former president of the American Bar Association, Joseph N. Teal of Portland, and Joseph B. Eastman of the Public Service Commission of Massachusetts.

Brandeis is Beaten," the *Transcript* commented. "Rejection of Brandeis is Danger Wilson Faces," said the *New York Sun*. Still the Senate Judiciary Committee did not vote. "They say that they have got matters so arranged that the nomination is indefinitely laid on the table in the Judiciary Committee," Nutter had reported to McClennen. "If it can go over until the fall and Wilson is defeated, they feel sure there is a strong chance of getting enough senators to repudiate the nomination." McClennen replied somewhat impatiently: "All of us see the advantage of haste," but "you cannot get it out without a majority vote." [22]

On May 4 Brandeis himself apparently took charge of getting out this vote. "Had conference this morning at City Club with L.D.B., Hapgood, and Wise," Nutter wired McClennen. "Hapgood is going down." The strategy decided upon at the New York conference, and Hapgood's purpose in going to Washington, are indicated in the editor's letter of May 4 to Dr. Cary Grayson, President Wilson's personal physician. "One of the strongest arguments being used by those on the fence," Hapgood wrote, "is that the administration does not care, and this charge has even been made public by the *Boston Herald*. Of course, it is grossly unjust, but it takes the form of supporting the absurd charge that the appointment was made for political purposes and that those political purposes have already been accomplished."

Meanwhile Anderson had suggested to Attorney-General Gregory on May 2 that "someone should write the President a carefully framed letter adverting to the opposition in the Brandeis case and the charge that it was a political appointment, and asking if the President is willing to state some of the reasons which moved him to make the appointment. This would furnish an opportunity for the President to make a reply which we think could be so framed as to put the opponents of Mr. Brandeis hopelessly on the defensive.

"He could emphasize," Anderson went on, "his own personal acquaintance with Brandeis, his impartial, impersonal, orderly, constructive mind, his analytical power, his deep human sympathy, his profound acquaintance with the historical roots of our institutions, the constant evidence he gives of being imbued with the American ideals of justice and equality of opportunity, his knowledge of modern economic conditions and the way they bear on the masses of the people, his constructive work in getting people of diverse views to co-operate and to sense in human, kindly fashion each other's points of view. . . ."

Later the same day Anderson wrote a second letter: "Think how the President with his powers of expression, could deal with the situation. There ought to be a ringing assertion . . . that it is the best possible ap-

CANOEING ON THE POTOMAC, MAY 1919

BRANDEIS WITH HIS BROTHER ALFRED ON HIS LAST VISIT TO LOUISVILLE, MAY 1922

JUSTICE AND MRS. BRANDEIS, WASHINGTON, MARCH 1919

THE BRANDEIS HOME AT CHATHAM, CAPE COD

pointment—that it means the strengthening of that Court in its deliberations and its counsel, as well as in the public confidence in its human and
democratic justice."

Gregory promptly prepared a three-page memorandum for the President. To evade charges of Presidential meddling, Senator Charles A. Culberson, Judiciary Committee Chairman, not Gregory, was to ask Wilson
for the statement—all in strictest confidence.[23]

Wilson's famous letter drew heavily from Gregory's memorandum, inspired by Anderson's two letters. Of his nine paragraphs, only three can be
attributed entirely to the President, the first two and the fourth.[24] The
crowning paragraph was Wilson's:

I perceived from the first that the charges were intrinsically incredible by anyone who had really known Mr. Brandeis. I have known him. I have tested him
by seeking his advice upon some of the most difficult and perplexing public
questions about which it was necessary for me to form a judgment. I have dealt
with him in matters where nice questions of honor and fair play, as well as
large questions of justice and public benefit, were involved. In every matter in
which I have made test of his judgment and point of view I have received from
him counsel singularly enlightening, singularly clear-sighted and judicial, and,
above all, full of moral stimulation. He is a friend of all just men and a lover
of the right; and he knows more than how to talk about the right—he knows
how to set it forward in the face of his enemies. I knew from direct personal
knowledge of the man what I was doing when I named him for the highest
and most responsible tribunal of the nation.[25]

THE OPPOSITION TRIES FLANKING TACTICS

Wilson's letter was published on May 8, and favorable reaction on the
Judiciary Committee was immediate but short-lived. For the first time in
months all Democratic members were present. After listening to the President's letter, the committee adjourned abruptly without even fixing a date
for voting. It looked for a time as if Wilson's letter had been impolitic,
perhaps reckless.

"The opinion was expressed this afternoon," the New York Times reported, May 9, "that the President's letter, ignoring the opposing views of
the members of the sub-committee and brushing aside the voluminous
testimony taken by it, had not helped matters. There was undoubtedly a
feeling of deep resentment at the President's expressions, and this resentment was expressed even by Democratic senators favorable to Mr. Brandeis. . . . The committee is as far from agreement as ever."

Other setbacks were in store. When the committee met on May 10, it
adopted Senator Sutherland's motion to reopen its interminable hearings,

to explore Brandeis's role in the proposed Riker-Hegeman and United Drug Company merger of 1915.[26] United Drug, seeking a controlling interest in the Riker-Hegeman chain, had been frustrated by United States District Attorney George W. Anderson, who threatened prosecution under the Sherman Anti-Trust Act. Brandeis contended that "the proposed purchase is lawful beyond any reasonable doubt." [27] And Senator Works now submitted a mound of material exhibiting Brandeis's views on price maintenance—all designed to show that "L.D.B. is a friend of the trusts when that is in his interest." [28] Anderson told the committee he had conferred with Brandeis on this matter.

"What have been your relations with Mr. Brandeis in the past?" Senator Works asked. Anderson took the opening, apparently unaware that anything he might say was at 100 per cent discount: "I go to him whenever I am at a loss as to what my duty or course may properly be on any matter involving ethics—professional ethics, public ethics—or any other question. . . . He is impersonal, impartial, judicial, powerful." [29]

While the drug merger was under consideration, Brandeis's supporters had noted Senator Borah helping the enemy. "It is all very blind," Hapgood wrote Brandeis on May 11, "but I rather think . . . that right will triumph." But no solid ground could be found for Hapgood's optimism. Apparently the outcome would be decided by politics, not evidence. Some believed that President Wilson's letter could be effective only when and if the people had demonstrated to Democratic senators that they must back the nomination or risk defeat in the 1916 elections. The administration itself felt that "mass meetings held in Boston and New York" might prove effective.

Nutter, who had been willing to take whatever measures the situation seemed to demand, was cold to the mass meeting idea, and when McClennen's special-delivery letter informed him that "reliable sources give possibility of a majority in the committee and good prospects of fifty-five in the Senate," he blew up: "There is no use taking chances if you have the votes. The place will be packed with Jews and Labor men. . . . To subject L.D.B. to these risks is unforgivable. He may well ask to be saved from his friends." [30]

McClennen shared Nutter's misgivings but he felt helpless to block the proposed meeting. "Don't promote it," McClennen counseled, "but if it cannot be stopped, make it appropriate to the Supreme Court. We must exert an influence to see that, if it comes, it is without dancing bears or other features which senators do not associate with the Supreme Court." [31]

Nutter took solace in the thought that Charles W. Eliot, Harvard's glacial president emeritus, might possibly be induced to preside and speak, and two days later he had good news. Eliot refused to speak, but wrote a letter to Chairman Culberson. "A thunderbolt to the other side," Nutter called it in a telegram to McClennen. "Look after publicity." The newspapers featured this liberal triumph by setting it off against President Lowell's protest. Gilson Gardner wrote a syndicated column on it; the Associated Press reported it in full. "I have known Mr. Louis D. Brandeis for forty years," the educator began, "and believe that I understand his capacities and his character." Eliot recalled him as a "distinguished student" and referred to his "practical altruism and public spirit. . . .

"He has sometimes advocated measures or policies which did not commend themselves to me," Eliot conceded, "but I have never questioned his honesty and sincerity, or his desire for justice. . . . Under present circumstances," the letter solemnly concluded, "I believe that the rejection by the Senate of his nomination to the Supreme Court would be a grave misfortune for the whole legal profession, the Court, all American business, and the country." [32]

"Next to a letter from God," McClennen commented cheerfully to La Follette, "we have got the best." Nutter's fears were allayed: "There seems to be a Providence over this mass meeting idea, for it served to call out Eliot, and then died!" [33]

SHORING UP THE PARTY LINE

There had never been any definitely perilous lack of votes in the Senate; the real battle had to be fought in the Judiciary Committee. Unless Brandeis won a majority there, the case would never get to the Senate. Throughout long hearings the opposition party line held fast. Of the G.O.P.'s eight members, only two (Cummins and Borah) had ever offered Brandeis's supporters even a ray of hope. With an eye to the Republican presidential nomination, Cummins held firm. Borah distrusted Brandeis on the price maintenance, trust, and Sherman Act issues.*

Of the Judiciary Committee's eighteen members, ten were of the President's party. But with the Republicans solidly lined up, the administra-

---

* In later years, Senator Borah recanted. See Claudius O. Johnson, *Borah of Idaho* (1936), p. 157.

Senator Borah was invited to meet Brandeis, but spurned the invitation as improper. "A friend of Mr. Brandeis called me up and asked me if I would not have an interview with Mr. Brandeis personally, privately," the Senator explained to Rabbi Wise, June 3, 1916. "I told him I could not do so, that I did not think it quite the proper thing to do either for Mr. Brandeis or for myself. . . . I felt that if Mr. Brandeis and his friends did not want him to come before the Committee, so far as I was concerned I was not in a position to say or do more; I certainly was not in a position to see him privately."

tion had to command unanimous loyalty. The President had only five sure votes—Culberson, Chilton, Fletcher, Walsh, and Ashurst. For confirmation he had to have ten. Democratic leaders and supporters now turned to the delicate task of shoring up the party line.

Democratic Senator Overman was spreading dissent in the cloakrooms when the President invited him and Secretary of the Navy Daniels on a trip to Charlotte, where the Mecklenburg Declaration of May 20, 1775, was being celebrated. Overman had asked the President to make a platform address at Salisbury, his home town, but "could not budge him." Daniels then explained to his chief the strategic importance of placating the "shocked" Southerner, and when the train stopped at Salisbury the President was on the platform, flanked by the Secretary of the Navy and the town's first citizen.

"You have reason to be proud of your Senator," the Chief Executive told the Senator's fellow-townsmen, "and I am very glad to give him the tribute of my praises."

"Do you think Overman's vote is cinched?" the President asked Daniels later.

"There is no doubt of it," Daniels replied elatedly. "He will go back and advocate instead of merely voting." [34]

The next most influential Democrat on the Judiciary Committee was Senator James A. Reed of Missouri. Reed had long been hostile. Some papers, recalling his vindictive fight against George Rublee's nomination for the Federal Trade Commission, dubbed the Missouri Senator "leader of the opposition." One paper had stated that Reed's "chief reason" for opposing Rublee was "intimacy with Brandeis." [35] Reed himself had said he opposed Rublee "because he is in fact the author of what is known as the Stevens fair trade bill." But of course the real author of that measure was Brandeis himself.

Frank P. Walsh, Kansas City lawyer, started war on Reed through the columns of his *Kansas City Post*. But the long-standing Walsh–Reed feud made this campaign ineffective. Earlier Jacob Billikopf, Kansas City social worker, had wired the nominee: "Do you object to my bringing pressure on Reed of Missouri?" Somewhat wary, Brandeis explained to Norman Hapgood: "I thought it best not to answer this; but Billikopf is a first-rate man, the head of Jewish charities there [Kansas City], and could be relied upon to be loyal." [36] Accepting silence as consent, Billikopf went to work, sending hundreds of telegrams to labor leaders in Missouri and other states.

By the time the President's letter came to the committee, May 8, so much "organized heat" had begun to fret the Senator. "Reed and Shields say the President's letter is an attempt to bring pressure on the committee," Mc-

Clennen wrote Nutter on May 9. "Borah is complaining that there is pro-Brandeis propaganda on. . . . Borah and Reed have, it would seem, been getting telegrams."

On May 11 Reed was still reported as "definitely known to disapprove of the nomination," and three days later another approach was tried. Norman Hapgood arranged an informal party at his apartment, Sunday, May 14, to which friends, formerly opposed, were invited to meet the nominee himself. About nine in the evening Reed came in. Apparently intending to make his visit purely formal, he left his wife waiting in the car. The night was damp and cold. Immediately after being introduced, Brandeis took the recalcitrant Senator by the arm and together they sat down before the open fire, discussing every conceivable topic except the one then pressing for solution. At the end of an hour or more, Reed rose suddenly, saying, "I must be going! Mrs. Reed has been sitting in the car ever since I came in here!" [37]

The Brandeis nomination had to be made palatable to still another Southern Democrat—reactionary Hoke Smith. The Georgia Senator had not distinguished himself in Wilson's crusade for the New Freedom and when, in April, rumor circulated that he was leaning toward confirmation, he promptly denied it. "I will say," he explained to a *Boston Herald* reporter, "that I was greatly prejudiced against Mr. Brandeis when the appointment was first announced. . . . If I voted the first day I should have voted against him." [38]

The middle of May found the nomination stalled in the Judiciary Committee and Hoke Smith's vote, along with others, still in doubt. President Wilson was deeply concerned. Far more was involved than Brandeis's confirmation. At stake also were the President's prestige as party chief in election year, his standing as head of a great power in a world at war. Realizing that Brandeis's defeat might in effect "turn the party into the wilderness for forty more years," Henry Morgenthau, Sr., at the President's suggestion, conferred with Hoke Smith and discovered that Smith's recalcitrance was not confined entirely to the Brandeis appointment. "Smith feels keenly," Morgenthau wrote the President on May 18, "that you did not consult any of the Democratic members of the Judiciary Committee about the nomination. . . . He and some of the other Senators have been nursing their discontent. . . . A few soothing words from you will produce a prompt cure." * [39]

Meanwhile Hoke Smith had soothing words from a far more adept tongue. The Senator had met the nominee himself at Hapgood's Sunday

---

* In a letter to the editor of *World's Work*, December 30, 1921, Senator Smith repudiated Morgenthau's account as "interesting but imaginative. . . . He [Morgenthau] certainly in no way influenced my action." (Quoted in the *New York Times*, December 31, 1921.)

evening party. "Hoke Smith is much mollified," Hapgood reported to Brandeis the next day.

Also in the doubtful column, and in a highly strategic position, was another reactionary Democrat, John K. Shields of Tennessee. "Shields appears to be necessary to get the matter out of committee expeditiously," McClennen had written Brandeis, April 15. "It is important to get before him the kind of man you are." McClennen knew "radical" Senator La Follette could not be helpful. "If, as appears to be the case," McClennen added hopefully, "Hoke Smith intends to go right, it may help with Shields. Perhaps regularity will control."

Brandeis had never met Shields and had only a slight acquaintance with Hoke Smith.[40] Meanwhile very high powered pressure was being exerted on the Tennessean. "The President saw him last Thursday or Friday," Hapgood wrote Brandeis, May 18. ". . . I think both Gregory and Burleson are at work now." But no definite assurance was forthcoming. The main reliance still rested on the thought: "Hoke Smith thinks he can carry Shields. Regularity will control."

By May 22 Democrats Overman, Reed, and Smith had been reclaimed, bringing the assured pro-Brandeis ballot in the Judiciary Committee to eight. The solid Republican opposition also stood at eight. Shields and Senator James A. O'Gorman of New York were in the doubtful column. One adverse vote would mean defeat. Earlier reports had O'Gorman favorable, but now, like other fence-sitters, he was said to be weighing the whole case. On April 20 William V. Rowe wrote Nutter: "I am wondering where O'Gorman really stands. Three weeks ago he told me his mind was 'open,' but when I let him talk, I thought he was a little disposed to consider points of criticism."

The final vote of the Judiciary Committee which occurred May 24 was anticlimactic. The meeting lasted only eight minutes. Confirmation had been hanging fire five months. Voluminous evidence had been marshaled and weighed. Editors, columnists, lawyers, politicians, and social reformers had joined in a nation-wide debate. Communiqués from Europe's war fronts competed unsuccessfully for headlines. The mountain labored only to produce a purely political mouse. "Regularity controlled"; the verdict stood 10 to 8. For confirmation: Democrats Culberson, Overman, Chilton, O'Gorman, Fletcher, Reed, Ashurst, Shields, Walsh, and Smith. Against confirmation: Republicans Brandegee, Borah, Clark, Cummins, Dillingham, Nelson, Sutherland, and Works. In the Senate on June 1 only one Democrat, Francis G. Newlands of Nevada, deserted.* Progressive Re-

* "I was very much pained to see that Senator Newlands alone of the Democrats voted against you," William E. Smythe wrote Brandeis, June 2, 1916, from San Francisco. "It reminds me of

publicans La Follette, Norris, and Poindexter lined up with the Democrats to approve the nomination by 47 votes to 22.

"I am relieved and delighted at the confirmation of Brandeis," President Wilson wrote Henry Morgenthau on June 5. "I never signed any commission with such satisfaction as I signed his."

IN RETROSPECT

Throughout Boston and the country Brandeis's friends were jubilant. Congratulatory messages showered upon him. His office received the news with mingled joy and regret. Miss Malloch and Miss Grady planned a surprise party. At his Dedham house there were handclasps, tears, and smiles; everybody was happy and sorry at once.

This triumph found the new Justice quite serene. On Friday, June 2, he went into Boston from Dedham on the 8:15 train as he had done for many years. To congratulations of friends, neighbors, and trainmen, he simply said, "Thank you" and went on to his Devonshire Street office.

Later that month, in reply to Judge Charles F. Amidon's congratulations, Brandeis analyzed the campaign's inner meaning:

As I have thought over the recent struggle I find myself not only without animosity, but almost without indignation at the attacks of those who were active in endeavoring to defeat my confirmation. These opponents fall into two classes: First, the abnormal and lawless—like the men of the United Shoe Machinery Corporation, or the old New Haven management—with whom libeling was deliberate and a business, and whose attacks upon character were comparable to the acts of murderers or robbers. Secondly: men like A. Lawrence Lowell who had been blinded by privilege, who have no evil purpose, and many of whom have distinct public spirit, but whose environment—or innate narrowness—have obscured all vision and sympathy with the masses. In every society there must be some who are abnormal, and some who are blinded by privilege. One cannot properly feel even indignation at either. They are rather subjects for sympathy. But we must seek steadily to nullify their influence, and limit their numbers.

What has seemed to me the really serious features of the attitude of this community during the last nine years were not the attacks of my opponents, however vicious and unfounded, but the silence or acquiescence of those who were not opposed to or were actually in sympathy with me. Most alarming is the unmanliness, the pusillanimity of those who believed that my efforts were

the colloquy you had with him in the committee room some years ago. He rose and asked: 'Mr. Brandeis, what do you think the effect of this measure will be on investments?' You replied: 'Senator, I was thinking of its effect upon the much larger number of our people, who have no investments and no money to invest.' . . . Poor Senator Newlands can never think of anything except the sanctity of the securities in which he invested his wife's money; . . . he lives always in the shadow of those investments."

commendable, but feared to speak out; feared because of either financial or social considerations or for the love of enjoyment or ease. And then the acquiescence of an equally large body of men who felt neither sympathy with nor opposition to my views, but who so lacked an active sympathy with the demands of fair play, that they were willing to remain silent, although they realized fully that my opponents were guilty of foul play.

This silence or acquiescence was due probably quite as much to the overweening power, financial and social, to which our community has been subjected as to a demoralization through prosperity and failure to realize what is really worth while in life. (You may recall the passage in my "Other People's Money," Banker Protectors, pages 132–134, where I cited one of many indications of existing servility.) But whatever the cause—the existence of such servility and lack of manhood is a menace to democratic institutions and ideals.

No one but a fanatic can be *sure* that his opinions—political, economic, or social—are correct. But no man, be he reactionary or progressive, ought to doubt that free thought and free speech are necessary in a democracy; and that their exercise in things public should be encouraged. My opponents throughout long years practically refused to discuss publicly or privately with me the measures under consideration. For opposing arguments they substituted attacks upon reputation. And the community permitted them to do so almost without a protest. This seems to me the fundamental defect. Our task in Massachusetts is to reconstruct manhood.[41]

Responding to a message from Harold Laski, Brandeis wrote: "This case is exceptional, and in some ways unprecedented. Austen Fox and Clarence Barron are the modern substitutes for the bravos of the renaissance period and the assassins of other days. The attitude of the vested interests when attacked is always the same. The weapons change from time to time." [42]

Reactionaries had looked upon the Supreme Court as an invincible fortress protecting vested rights and privileges. Brandeis's confirmation, they argued, "would make every citizen feel insecure." [43] Brandeis was to them a scoundrel, to "their" country a traitor; of his double guilt they were certain. Yet Austen G. Fox, in this very case counsel for the reactionaries, told Amos Pinchot: "It is true that nothing unethical has been proved against Mr. Brandeis. What has been proved against him is that he does not act according to the canons of the Bar. The trouble with Mr. Brandeis is that he never loses his judicial attitude toward his clients. He always acts the part of a judge toward his clients instead of being his clients' lawyer, which is against the practices of the Bar." [44] With incredible irony, his adversaries seized upon his most distinguishing trait as a weapon with which to strike him down. What Fox was trying to show was that by never losing his judicial attitude Brandeis proved he never had any!

In being "judicial," and in his hard drive toward a particular goal, Brandeis sometimes neglected the niceties of human and professional relations. He could be, as Barron truly and yet wrongly said, "on every side intermittently . . . not anywhere long," because he discerned the see-saw of forces in modern society constantly creating new conditions, changed relationships. He realized that when any one group gets legislation passed, or wins other advantages by engrossing public good for private ends, the general will is defeated. Here was a man who saw that the persons who operate railroads as well as those who ship goods, the men who sell liquor as well as those who buy and drink it, that corporate executives as well as union leaders, however divergent, all integrate and combine to make that entity—"the public." [45]

Such austerity at times seems well-nigh inhuman and helps explain how Brandeis could rub even some of his best friends the wrong way.* Fiery and astute, he was "terribly cutting in his devices" of advocacy. The usual spirit of comradery at the Bar did not hinder him from taking instant advantage of any technicality in the law, or from capitalizing on an adversary's every misstep or oversight. In his "sharp practices," so-called, Brandeis went all out to defend the interests of his client. And with this spirit of drastic advocacy he combined an unbecoming assurance of his own capacity for impartiality, an "exasperating spirit of delight in smashing revered traditions."

In Boston, and in a Jew, such idiosyncrasies seemed unforgivable. "A Boston aristocrat," someone has observed, "thinks that the straight and narrow path leads from the front bay window of the Somerset Club to the coupon room of the safe deposit vaults on State Street and back again. You should never plead fraud charges against a fellow State Streeter or Club member. On State Street it was and is bad form to hit too hard." [46]

Brandeis flagrantly and casually violated Boston's unwritten code. Having charted his course, he never swerved no matter what persons or canons

* The following is typical of not a few letters Brandeis received from friends as well as foes in his years as a lawyer.

Boston, October 5, 1896.

My dear Brandeis:

I have been a good deal disturbed over our interview of last Friday, from the fact that I believe we both said much we would not repeat in calmer moments, and so far as I am guilty I apologize. I do not know why your manner of treating a matter in which you were entirely right, should so exasperate me as it did, unless it be that your past kindness and consideration had made me like a spoiled child who always likes to be coaxed; at any rate I ought not to have said many things I did say, and I hope you will forgive and forget all that was harsh and unjust in my language, and believe me as ever,

Sincerely your friend,
William T.

might be involved. Brandeis remained himself—a serious fault in a Bostonian not of Brahmin blood, nor born on Beacon Street. But this is integrity, the test of character—an essential in human greatness. Surely such a man was "guilty of uncommon common morality."[47] Surely "such a man should not be appointed to the Bench. He should be condemned to it."[48]

In the Temple of Law

PART V

In the Temple of Law

CHAPTER THIRTY-TWO

Charting His Course

EVERY available seat in the historic Senate Chamber of the Capitol was occupied at noon on June 5 when Brandeis assumed his seat as Associate Justice of the United States Supreme Court. A few minutes before noon he walked across the corridor to the courtroom and was ready, Bible in hand, when Chief Justice White appeared. The *Boston Globe* [1] noted Brandeis's "extreme nervousness" as he took the oath:

I . . . do solemnly swear that I will administer justice without respect to persons, and do equal right to the poor and to the rich, and that I will faithfully and impartially discharge and perform all the duties incumbent upon me as Associate Justice of the Supreme Court of the United States, according to the best of my abilities and understanding, agreeable to the Constitution and the laws of the United States. So help me God.

Spectators included many members of the Senate and House and the usual government officials. Sitting in the reserved seats were Mrs. Brandeis and daughters Susan and Elizabeth, Miss Pauline Goldmark, Alfred Brandeis, George W. Anderson, Charles P. Hall, and other close friends. Pressure for seats was great, and an unusually large crowd stood in line awaiting admission. One woman remarked: "I am about to see a Jew on the Supreme Court of my country for the first time." The line moved on. She gained a seat. Shortly after she said to one sitting next to her: "What an interesting face the new Justice has." A few minutes later Chief Justice White sent a memorandum by one of the pages to Mr. Justice Brandeis. He read it and leaned forward to bow his acknowledgment to the Chief Justice. The lady then turned to her other neighbor and repeated: "What a beautiful face the new Justice has." [2] Without even a word Brandeis had won a hard case against prejudice. This ceremony closed the current term of Court, which then adjourned until October.

During the day the new Justice received more than two hundred telegrams of congratulations from prominent men in various parts of the

country and some from abroad, including one from Lord Reading, Chief
Justice of England.

BREAKING OLD TIES AND FORMING NEW ONES

Riding down to the Capitol with Chief Justice White before the ceremony, Brandeis broached the matter of proprieties in his new post. He
wanted to make sure that his widely diversified investments, amounting
approximately to two million dollars, would not disqualify him from taking part in any case coming before the Court. Several weeks later he wrote
the Chief Justice in detail about his custom as to investments, how his surplus income went into "absolutely safe investments intended to be permanent and yielding a low rate of return." He followed this policy in order
not to have his "attention diverted by considerations of personal financial
interests from . . . professional or public work. . . . I have thus treated
my property," he explained, "as a highly conservative trust estate, and have
left its management in the past, and should wish to leave it in the future
so far as possible, largely to others." [3] The Chief Justice soon relieved his
anxiety, advising him not to entertain the thought of "disposing of the investments which you have made with so much care." [4]

The days following June 5 were crowded with activity. In preparation
for judicial duties many deep-rooted connections, public and private, had
to be cut. He resigned membership in the National Economic League, the
Utilities Bureau, Mayor Mitchel's Conciliation Council for the Garment
Trades, and all his Harvard Law School connections. His most recent interest—Zionism—continued.

The summer's calm at South Yarmouth was interrupted when President
Wilson asked him to head a Commission to settle Mexican border difficulties with Carranza's government. He accepted the appointment "subject
to the approval of the Chief Justice." Then, after a mid-August conference with Chief Justice White at Lake Placid, he declined the post. "I appreciate the opportunity for high service which membership on the Mexican Commission would present," he wrote President Wilson, August 14,
"but upon consultation with the Chief Justice, I find the state of the business of the Supreme Court at the present time to be such that it is my duty
not to undertake this important additional task."

In personal relations Brandeis had made a good start with Chief Justice
White, and membership on the Court meant renewal of his long friendship with Justice Holmes. While the fight over his friend's nomination had
raged, Justice Holmes had maintained a discreet silence, but he had had no
doubts as to the merits of the case. Privately he had expressed himself in

unqualified terms. "I dined last night with Justice Holmes," Walter Lippmann had written Brandeis, February 18, 1916, "and he spoke of you with such affection and admiration that I came home extremely happy."

"I won't talk about Brandeis," Holmes had written C. K. Poe, Seattle attorney on March 16, "until the Senate acts, except to say that he has called on us for many years, and in my personal relations I always have got the impression of a good man as well as of one with many suggestive ideas. . . . I haven't read the evidence at the hearings, but have a notion that nothing very tangible has turned up and that he does appear to have been more public spirited than most of us." *

When Associate Justice Charles Evans Hughes resigned to accept the Republican presidential nomination, he was succeeded by John H. Clarke, Cincinnati railroad lawyer and federal judge who was known for his liberal views. Brandeis warmly applauded the appointment, and Clarke was equally cordial in his response.† "I am looking forward," Justice Clarke wrote, "with unusual confidence to pleasant association with you because of what I suppose is something of community point of view between us." Clarke had had as his law partner William E. Cushing, Brandeis's friend of early years at the Harvard Law School. "If you think half as much of him," Clarke commented, "as he does of you, there should be a basis for more than formally pleasant relations between you and me." [5]

Early in October, Justice Brandeis and his wife were off to Washington, settling in a modest Stoneleigh Court apartment, leaving behind the entire Boston secretarial staff which had been essential in the large law offices housing his professional and public activities. Everyone assumed that at least Miss Alice Grady, his secretary and co-worker in savings-bank insurance matters, would go to Washington, but the Justice said no. He had decided to write his judicial opinions, as well as carry on a voluminous correspondence, in longhand. During his twenty-three years on the Court his only assistant was a fledgling lawyer, selected for him each year by Professor Felix Frankfurter from among Harvard law graduates.

---

* On the twentieth anniversary of Brandeis's service on the Bench, Poe sent him this letter from Holmes, saying: "Dear Mr. Justice: I hate to part with the enclosed letter from Justice Holmes, but as it contains a materialized prediction about you—feel that you should have it."

† It seems not unlikely that Brandeis may have suggested Clarke's name to President Wilson. Writing the President, July 6, 1916, Norman Hapgood passed along Justice Brandeis's general view as to the vacancy. He had advised against appointing the type of man then being urged, on geographical grounds, from New York City, Brooklyn, or Buffalo. It would, he said, be "a wet blanket and would have a noticeable effect in chilling enthusiasm." The political effect of such an appointment was, Brandeis believed, "so much overestimated as to amount to a superstition." What was important politically and otherwise was the selection of a man "recognized as eminently fit and eminently progressive." On July 14 President Wilson nominated Clarke.

AGGRESSIVE LIBERALISM AND TORY RESISTANCE

Brandeis embarked on his new task with eager enthusiasm. "There is much to be done which promises to be very interesting," he commented in a letter to Alfred, October 1, "and I have the utmost confidence." Of course there were the usual regrets, but a backward glance at the bitter struggle against his confirmation made him believe that "the renunciation was worth-while. My incredulous enemies would probably believe least of all that I was [not] eager for office," he told his brother. In truth, however, Brandeis did not relish the appointment. He had been working for years with complete freedom of action. His objectives were of his own choice. The restraints on his activities and freedom of expression which acceptance of judicial office entailed was a real hardship. "I can see now," Edward F. McClennen recalls, "the expression of terror in his face when I told him that he would have to wear a silk hat. It lasted until inspiration brought him relief, and he said, 'Holmes wears a soft one.'" Wilson's nomination had placed a duty upon him, and "committed him unmistakably to acceptance." [6] Three years later Brandeis was sure of the wisdom of his decision. "Old Boston is unregenerate," he wrote his wife, June 14, 1919, "and I am not sorry to have escaped a struggle there that would have been as nasty as it is unending."

To the clamorous alarm of eminent lawyers and citizens, the first thoroughgoing progressive ever to be appointed to the Supreme Court had taken his seat. No one before Brandeis had brought to the Court such thorough grounding and firsthand experience in modern business technicalities. He had abundantly proved his competence in the economics of labor, public utilities, and railroads, as well as his unusual talent for bringing a great reservoir of fact and shrewd mastery of analysis to bear on the constitutional issues which the Court had assumed power to decide. No lawyer had come to the Court more familiar with legal technicalities and court circumlocutions; nor had any shown greater facility in using these with all the art of both advocate and judge. His ability as a social scientist and business analyst had been so conspicuously demonstrated and so much emphasized that Dean Roscoe Pound was prompted in 1916 to remind the Senate Judiciary Committee that the Bostonian was also "a very great lawyer."

Reformers had long denounced the Court as the keystone of the industrial-financial oligarchy, as the arch-defender of property rights against human rights. Brandeis himself had commented on the Court's predominantly reactionary personnel, but this would not be the first time he would be pitted against die-hard conservatism. Nor did any one doubt his determination to press on beyond legal fiction and judicial precedent to the world of fact and reality. He had never been a conventional lawyer, nor was he likely to be a conventional judge. He came to the Court as an apostle of "the living law"; he would examine old concepts to determine their current value as guiding principles, just as he had done for years as lawyer and public-spirited citizen. His method, his technique, his purpose, would be the same, but from this new forum he would speak with greater prestige, even if in the minority.

Holmes had tried to stem the conservative tide by firmly announcing as his own first judicial commandment, "Thou shalt not decide constitutional questions on the basis of any particular economic theory." In terms of specific results Holmes had failed. Brandeis would follow a different tack, the one he had so successfully charted in his labor briefs. He would meet his conservative colleagues on their own ground. By recourse to facts he would demonstrate that their assumptions were empty of reality. And even if he did not coax them out of their dark closet of abstractions into the light of a living world, he might at least prove to universities, law schools, and perhaps legislative bodies, that his colleagues' world of thought was as dark as it was empty. All this was recognized by opponents of his confirmation, and their fears soon proved well founded.

During his first term Brandeis wrote more than a score of opinions as spokesman for the Court and dissented five times. His first two dissents are notable as setting the pattern which he was to follow through his years on the Bench. His opinion, May 21, 1917, in *New York Central Railroad* v. *Winfield* was the first to focus the professional spotlight on him. It was a case involving the scope of the 1908 Federal Employers Liability Act in relation to state power. His colleagues (except Justice Clarke) held that Congress in passing the act covered the entire field as to compensation for injuries suffered by railroad employees engaged in interstate commerce. Brandeis dissented, and "the importance of the question involved" induced him "to state the reasons." [7] Surely, he argued, Congress did not leave the states powerless to provide the needed protection for railroad workers injured without fault on the part of the carriers. Congress did not intend to preclude state action in this field:

It is the state which is both primarily and ultimately concerned with the care of the injured. . . . Upon the state falls the financial burden of dependency, if provision be not otherwise made. Upon the state falls directly the far heavier burden of demoralization of its citizenry and of the social unrest which attend destitution and denial of opportunity. Upon the state also rests, under our dual system of government, the duty owed to the individual, to avert misery and promote happiness so far as possible.[8]

He bolstered this argument by copious references to judicial precedents, but he did not stop here. Delving into the nature, origin, and purpose of the Federal Employers Liability Act, as well as into "world experience in dealing with industrial accidents," he "uncovered as fiction many an assumption upon which American judges and lawyers had rested comfortably." The conviction has become widespread, he told his incredulous colleagues, that "our individualistic conception of rights and liability no longer furnish an adequate basis for dealing with accidents in industry." [9] This familiar doctrine of "the living law" he had voiced before the Chicago Bar Association in January 1916.

Just before the close of his first term, the Court overturned in a 5 to 4 decision (June 11) a Washington statute prohibiting private employment agencies from taking fees from workers for whom they found jobs.[10] Counsel for the state had contended unsuccessfully that such a business is "economically . . . non-useful, if not vicious, because it compels the needy and unfortunate to pay for that which they are entitled to without fee or price, that is, the right to work." Under the statute, personal placement costs might still be met by the employer, but the Court took the position that for all practical purposes the statute abolished the "business," thus violating the "due process" clause of the Fourteenth Amendment.

In reaching this decision, the Court made no examination whatever into the evils of private employment agencies in Washington or elsewhere. Brandeis, on the other hand, giving comparatively little space to judicial precedents, and much to facts and experience, boldly asserted that no correct decision could be reached in such a case merely by reasoning from past cases. Judges are without authority, he said, to disqualify social legislation unless, by recourse to fact, it "is a clear, unmistakable infringement of rights secured by the fundamental law." [11]

In this he was but adapting to judicial purpose the method he had employed so successfully in his earlier briefs. He was simply saying that under the time-honored principle of judicial presumption of constitutionality, acts of state legislatures are valid until proved otherwise. This rule, he contended, logically demands of those who oppose state legislation a recitation of facts showing that the evil to be corrected either does not exist or that the remedy is inappropriate. "Whether a measure relating to the public welfare," he observed, "is arbitrary or unreasonable, whether it has no substantial relation to the end proposed, is obviously not to be determined by assumptions or by a priori reasoning. The judgment should be based upon a consideration of relevant facts, actual or possible—*ex facto jus oritur*. That ancient rule must prevail in order that we may have a system of living law. . . . What was the evil which the people of Washington sought to correct? Why was the particular remedy embodied in the statute adopted? And, incidentally, what has been the experience, if any, of other states or countries in this connection?" [12]

None of these questions had been raised by Justice McReynolds, who spoke for the majority, and, so far as one can judge from his opinion, no official investigation of these matters might ever have been made. And yet relevant and easily available source material exposed far-reaching abuses— extortionate fees, discrimination, misrepresentation as to conditions of work and as to terms of employment, fee-splitting with foremen, almost a rascal's litany of wrongs against workers. A report of the United States Commission on Industrial Relations showed that many private employment agencies were quite unable to meet the needs for which they were supposed to exist, being operated not to relieve unemployment and secure jobs for men out of work, but actually to congest the labor market and increase irregularity of employment.

Nor had the recognized abuses of employment agencies been accepted as inevitable and unavoidable. Twenty-four states had attempted direct regulation by statute and by municipal ordinances; nineteen had undertaken indirect control by establishing municipal employment offices. This extensive experience had developed the conviction "that the evils of private agencies were inherent and ineradicable, so long as they were permitted to charge fees to the workers seeking employment."

Furthermore, Justice Brandeis saw in the Washington statute a purpose not appreciated at all by Justice McReynolds. The purpose behind the act was positive: to strike at that paramount evil in the workingman's life— irregularity of employment.

The problem which confronted the people of Washington was far more comprehensive and fundamental than that of protecting workers applying to private agencies. It was the chronic problem of unemployment—perhaps the gravest and most difficult problem of modern industry. . . . Students of the larger problem of unemployment appear to agree that establishment of an adequate system of employment offices or labor exchanges is an indispensable first step toward its solution. There is reason to believe that the people of Washington not only considered the collection by the private employment offices of fees from employees a social injustice, but that they considered the elimination of the practice a necessary preliminary to the establishment of a constructive policy for dealing with the subject of unemployment.[13]

This opinion, typical of his research into social and economic problems, was circulated among his colleagues in advance of a vote. Warm praise came from Justices Clarke and Holmes. "Splendidly done!" Justice Clarke scribbled across an advance copy of Brandeis's opinion. "Only the Lord can so harden their heads as well as their hearts as to prevent their confessing their sin of ignorance when voting in so grave a matter. No matter what decision is rendered this will soon be the law of the case," Justice Clarke predicted. "Your selections are admirable and the restraint of comment discreet, having regard to your purposes. The authority attaching to such a statement from a member of this Court will make it a great public service. I am glad you are circulating it in advance. The experiment is worth trying."

"Note me as agreeing with you vehemently," Justice Holmes commented. Interstate Commerce Commissioner Harlan read the opinion through from the beginning to the end, "including the very helpful footnotes. It left me so completely satisfied and delighted," Harlan wrote, "that I cannot refrain from telling you what a splendid document it seems to me to be. . . . It cannot be doubted that the conclusions you have reached must in the end prevail." [14]

Brandeis's early dissents were widely noticed by the legal profession as setting a new and promising departure in judicial technique—use of the dissenting opinion as an educational device to explore and illumine not only the law but also the relations which law governs, bringing to bear relevant law reports, secular literature, information from pertinent sources in a persuasive demonstration of what the law ought to be in terms of social justice. This was judicial pleading "of a very high order, . . . the art of the advocate, subdued to intellectual inquiry, and directed to the ends of social justice." [15] Formerly Brandeis's educational work carried only such prestige as his professional eminence might supply. From the rostrum of the United States Supreme Court, he spoke with high authority and he was determined to make the most of it. His opinions, even in dissent, soon began to carry greater weight and attract more attention than those of the majority. Later these crusading doctrines came to prevail. Brandeis's first term gave some hint of what was to come. Since the Court was reactionary in outlook and temperament, Brandeis was fated to write his most notable opinions in dissent. But this was no new experience. He had never placed the highest value on immediate victory, knowing that the best test of truth is its ultimate power to prevail.

COUNSELING THE WAR EFFORT

Long on the brink of war, America was embarked in the spring of 1917 on gigantic plans in preparation. On the hotly contested preparedness issue Brandeis had stated his views at length in a plank which he submitted for the 1916 Democratic platform:

"Preparedness" implies far more than adequate military equipment and training. It implies conservation and development of all the resources of the nation, human and material. It implies that in industry and in agriculture there will be constant effort to improve the methods and means of production and distribution. It implies that men and women will be trained for the vocations they are to pursue, and that opportunity shall exist to make their labor effective. It implies that conditions of living, as of work, shall be such that every American citizen may, throughout life, be fit to perform the duties of citizenship, and that he may, by participation in its privileges, learn to understand American ideals and become eager to co-operate for their attainment.

For such thoroughgoing preparedness—preparedness social and civic as well as military and economic—preparedness which makes not only for safety but also for the liberties and happiness and the elevation of the whole people—the Democratic Party pledges itself to strive fearlessly and unceasingly.[16]

Mrs. Brandeis was an avowed pacifist, a charter member of the Massachusetts Women's League for Peace and Freedom. The Justice himself undoubtedly sympathized with her views. As late as March 9, 1917, we find him noting Secretary of the Navy Daniels's opinion (passed on to him by Robert Woolley) "that he [Daniels] could see how war could be averted."

"I guess he would be as likely to see peace ahead as any living man—if it were visible," he commented consolingly to his wife.

Even before formal declaration of war, Brandeis had gained much information on the European situation through his friend Herbert White, who had gone to Britain early in the war to take charge of one of the first American medical units. In London, White had met Herbert Hoover, already active as head of Belgian relief. Norman Hapgood had also conferred with Hoover and was greatly impressed. "Herbert Hoover," Hapgood wrote from London on January 10, 1917, "is the most interesting man I know. . . . You will enjoy his experiences in diplomacy, finance, etc., in England, Belgium, France, and Germany." By the end of January, Hoover was in the United States, seeking funds to aid starving Belgium, and in early February he talked with Justice Brandeis. "In one hour," the Justice commented years later, "I learned more from Hoover than from all the persons I had seen in connection with war matters heretofore." [17]

Convinced that the Wilson administration could not afford to let Hoover go without enlisting his services, Brandeis arranged conferences between him and Secretary Baker and Secretary McAdoo. This led to Hoover's later appointment as Food Administrator, thus starting him up the political ladder. It was also the beginning of a warm and mutually helpful friendship. The Hoovers and Brandeises frequently exchanged dinner invitations during the war years and later.

But the Justice had already begun to discern Mr. Hoover's political ineptitude. Shortly after the Court's adjournment in June 1917, Hoover had asked Brandeis to dine with him. In the course of the evening his host told of his troubles with Congress. The Food Administrator was especially insistent in his denunciation of Senator James A. Reed. "You are but giving expression to the common verities," the Justice observed. "I dare say you have not plumbed Reed to the depths." The Justice then related the story of his successful meeting with Reed at Hapgood's apartment during the nomination fight. Hoover might use a similar strategy, he suggested, to win political support for his food control bill then under fire in Congress.[18]

In writing Hapgood a few days later, the Justice observed: "There is clearly progress being made—actually rapid progress—but democratic methods are necessarily slow and often seem unreasonable. And the fact that our instruments are man with his weaknesses and defects, is at times exasperating. Hoover—who seems to me the biggest figure injected into Washington life by the war—has been suffering much from congressional action or inaction, but he has already accomplished much, through organizing public sentiment and introducing definite practical means for food conservation. Indeed he is the strongest argument of recent years for the needlessness of law." [19]

During the trying summer of 1917 Brandeis stayed on in Washington to be of help wherever he could. Each day brought new and complex troubles—policy, shipping, labor, construction, and transportation. "The task is all around of a seriousness to tax all our resources—in brains, money, and manliness," he wrote his wife, September 17, 1917. Control of food was but one job among many—"Even the Germans with their nigh perfect organization have fallen down badly." Coal men were loudly posing the most difficult problem of all—price control. "The price-fixing job is about the hardest economic problem ever tackled. The world has been at it from time to time for a thousand years—never with great success. My own opinion is that in America—inducing lessened consumption through education and exhortation—difficult as the task is—is the factor which will tend most toward a satisfactory solution. But it is comforting to know that Hoover and [Julius] Barnes are on the job. No men can do better than they—with such help as they are bound to get from loyal supporters." [20]

Brandeis found certain authoritarian tendencies most disturbing. In their eagerness "to get things done" powerful financial and industrial leaders urged short cuts. Brandeis found "much criticism, particularly in the Cosmos Club and among financial big businessmen who are prone to forget—if they ever knew—that we are a democracy, that education of the people to new methods and conditions is an essential. . . . The trouble with democracy," he commented emphatically, "is that we Democrats do not wish to pay the price—education, education, education—not in books but in public affairs. Education that is current and persistent." [21]

Besides maintaining close contact with high administration leaders, Brandeis came in contact with foreign emissaries in this country—Jusserand, Northcliffe, Reading, and others. He also associated with less prominent figures—Walter Lippmann, Felix Frankfurter, Herbert Croly, Stanley King, Philip Littell. Passionately optimistic as to the future and confident of their capacity to insure it against war, these young men took counsel with Holmes and Brandeis. Holmes was highly skeptical and dubbed their living quarters on Nineteenth Street "The House of Truth." Brandeis, on the other hand, was more tolerant of their vision and their effort. Herbert White passed along reports of his "great influence," which he emphatically denied. But, as he wrote his wife, "it was as hard to dispel such notions as the legends about my working which you know are unfounded." [22] President Wilson himself added to Brandeis's fame. "I need Brandeis everywhere," Wilson told Rabbi Stephen S. Wise, "but I must leave him somewhere." [23]

In late 1917 freight traffic jammed at important junction points, such as Pittsburgh, Cincinnati, and the terminal yards in eastern New Jersey, threatening to break "Pershing's bridge of ships." A coal famine affected different parts of the country. Hundreds of vessels lay in New York harbor for months, unable to sail for lack of coal as well as cargo. The War Industries Board, whose chief function was to keep supplies moving, proved unable to cope with an unorganized situation. The President then made up his mind to operate the railroads as of January 1, 1918. His great concern was to secure an effective Director General. Obviously no railroad executive would do. He would have too many of his own kind to deal with; favoritism and jealousies would crop up, all to public disadvantage. Many railroad officials, industrialists, and others thought William G. McAdoo the best possible choice. The President's chief objection was that of heaping additional honor and responsibility on a cabinet member who was also his son-in-law. Talk of "the Crown Prince," and "Heir Apparent," reached his ears.

Late Friday afternoon, December 7, 1917, Joseph P. Tumulty, secretary to the President, telephoned Interstate Commerce Commissioner Robert W. Woolley, asking Woolley to go with him for an important interview with Justice Brandeis. Tumulty wanted the Commissioner's assistance in persuading Brandeis to advise the President to appoint McAdoo Director General of the Railroads. The Justice was sympathetic from the start.

McAdoo's appointment was favored provided he relinquish the office of Secretary of Treasury; the two posts carried too much responsibility even for a man of McAdoo's energies and competence. But the Justice flatly refused to go to the White House in McAdoo's behalf.

"What if the President were to ask you to come?" Tumulty inquired. "That would be a command, and I should obey," the Justice replied.

It was then agreed that Tumulty would take up the matter with the President and that Brandeis might expect an invitation from the President to call at the White House the following Sunday afternoon. At 4:45 P.M., Sunday, December 9, no word having come from the President, the Justice telephoned Woolley that he was at a loss as to what to do. Woolley promptly notified Tumulty, who said that he had discussed the matter with Wilson the day before, that his reaction to the suggested invitation had been favorable, and a memorandum had been placed on his desk.

"You see, Bob," Tumulty explained, "Woodrow Wilson is Scotch-Irish. When the Irish in him is on the job, he is wonderful. The Scotch seems to have the upper hand today."

At exactly 5 P.M. the President himself, accompanied by two Secret Service men, appeared unannounced at the Justice's apartment. "I could not request you to come to me," Wilson explained, "and I have therefore come to you to ask your advice."

Some months later (April 20, 1918), Mrs. Brandeis described for her sister, Susan Goldmark, the setting of this unusual meeting: "You know his [L.D.B.'s] study. It is not a very large room and now lined with bookshelves on all sides from floor to ceiling. The room was fairly dark, with only one strong desk light. He had been working at some opinion, consulting authorities, and law books were lying everywhere about—on his desk, on chairs, even on the floor. . . . Here surely was the scholar, the student at his work. And yet it is as a practical man of affairs, a statesman, that Louis's advice is so much sought."

The President, like Brandeis, deemed it improper to ask a Justice of the Supreme Court to the White House on a matter necessarily political. After a conference of about three-quarters of an hour, the President thanked Brandeis, told him he would appoint McAdoo, and left. Both men had exhibited a high conception of the proprieties of judicial office.[24]

Brandeis was also concerned about the new and vexing war labor problem. "Mr. Justice Brandeis has spent two evenings talking with me about the general labor situation throughout the country," Secretary Baker wrote the President, June 18, 1917. "He feels very strongly that, as our munitions contracting business, both on our account and that of our allies, increases in volume, very special arrangements will have to be made to prevent the labor conditions from being lost sight of in the agitation for hurried quantity production." Baker suggested that if the President wanted "a disinterested view of the whole situation," he might get it from "a man who is thinking hard and seeing it all from the outside."

Our war effort suffered, among other things, from gratuitous dislocations due to competitive bidding between military authorities for both labor and materials. The Navy would send field agents from Newport News to West Virginia and lure workers from the War Department's large munitions plant being constructed at Nitro. Whereupon the War Department, confronted with labor shortage, would offer still higher wages and haul the same men back to Nitro. Labor costs, generally, were soaring, and nothing was being done about it.

Early in January 1918 Colonel House turned to Brandeis for advice. The Justice replied at great length:

Stoneleigh Court,
January 9, 1918.

My dear Colonel House:—

You have asked my opinion of the work of the War Department and the War Industry Board and Committees.

I consider the situation very serious—imperiling success abroad and also the ascendancy of the Democratic Party upon which we must rely for the attainment of our ideals at home. Betterment can come only through radical changes in systems:—such as

First: The War Department shall be relieved of all responsibility for the purchase, production, and transportation of munitions; the War Industry Board and Committees shall be abolished; and all their respective functions shall be concentrated in a munitions administration.

Second: The powers of the munitions administration shall be vested in a single head with full power of delegation; and the delegated power shall likewise be vested in single officials with full power of action within the sphere delimited (subject only to veto by the munitions administrator). There shall be no committees within the munitions administration except such advisory committees as the official shall himself appoint for his aid. The sphere of action of the several officials shall be limited to a size consistent with efficient action by him.

Third: The Labor Problem of the munitions administration cannot be effectively dealt with separately by that department. A labor administration should be created to deal with labor problems for all departments of the Government, and the power be vested in a single director with an advisory committee representing the several departments specifically interested.

Fourth: The War Department—dealing then only with purely military matters—should be reorganized so that for purposes of administration

(a) In each branch of the service there be a single directing head;
(b) In each branch of the service by limitation of power the practices and the institutions preventing immediate action be eliminated; and
(c) All branches of the service co-ordinated. Only questions of military policy should be determined by committees or councils.

Fifth: The Intelligence Service of the War Department and of the munitions administration cannot be effectively dealt with by them separately. A Central Intelligence Office should be created to deal with the problem for all departments of the Government and the power should be vested in a single director to co-ordinate and so far as possible consolidate the work of the several departments. He should have an advisory committee representing the several departments.

Sixth: The transportation requirements of the War and Munitions departments cannot be dealt with separately. A single director of shipping with an advisory committee representing the several departments of the Government should have power to allot shipping and make other provision in connection therewith, and the construction of ships should be divorced from the control of shipping.

Seventh: A small war council independent of all departments and composed of men freed from the detail of administration and of executive responsibility should be created to consider the broad questions of policy in internal and external affairs, and submit to the President the results of their deliberations. This instrument essential to the effective conduct of the war is not now provided by any, and cannot be provided, in the aggregate, by all of the several departments of the Government.

The above recommendations rest largely upon the obvious limitation of the power of any one man to deal effectively with many extensive and difficult problems. It is only by freeing Secretary Baker from many of the burdens now improperly resting upon him that the country can get the full benefit of his great ability and fine qualities.

Sincerely yours,
LDB

More ambitious plans for directly enlisting Brandeis's services in the war effort were soon in the making. In the spring of 1918 a small group consisting, among others, of Mark Hopkins, Stanley King, and Matthew Hale—all of subordinate rank in the government service—met at the Cosmos Club to consider the labor situation. Without taking top War and Navy officials into account, they decided to press for the adoption of Brandeis's suggestion for a National Labor Administration. A Herculean job had to be done, and the "insurgents" decided that Brandeis was the man to do it. The President, they thought, could draft him at the end of the current term of Court. Brandeis was willing, but the group had no easy entrée to the President. At this point Hale called in Commissioner Wool-ley, who agreed to take up the group's suggestion with the President.

Wilson was extremely wary of the proposal (adopted more than once during World War II), but left the door ajar by suggesting that Wool-ley tell his story to Secretary of Labor William B. Wilson and get his ad-vice.*

"Woolley," the President commented, "when a seemingly impossible war emergency task looms, I am urged to draft Brandeis to tackle it. At least twice I have put it up to him. Very properly he replied he would take it up with the Chief Justice. In each instance Chief Justice White held that a member of the Supreme Court should confine his endeavors to the work of that Court. I readily agreed. Whereupon Brandeis would offer to resign, which was characteristic of him. My reply was: 'Not on your life. On that Bench you are more important to the country than you could possibly be elsewhere. It was too difficult to get you there to take a chance on losing you through a temporary appointment.' "[25]

As Woolley left the White House, one of the first men he encountered was Felix Frankfurter. They talked of the interview just ended and agreed that further pressure might be brought on the President to set up the office and appoint Brandeis. Woolley then wrote the President a hasty note reiterating his suggestion and sent it to the White House by special messenger. Within two hours Wilson replied, chiding his persistence:

April 27, 1918

My dear Woolley:

Just a note to say go slow, please, in the matter of Justice Brandeis. I admire and trust him as much as you do, but I am not convinced that it would be wise to choose a member of the Supreme Court at this juncture. I am going to give the matter a little further thought.

Cordially and faithfully yours,
Woodrow Wilson †

* Mr. Woolley reported Secretary Wilson's views to the President on April 25, 1918. Though strongly demurring to the suggestion that such an office was necessary, the Secretary of Labor told Woolley that if the President should nevertheless decide to appoint a National Labor Administrator, he considered Justice Brandeis "pre-eminently the man for the post." But there remained the question of judicial proprieties. As to this Woolley reported progress. He dis-covered that "the winning of the war" had "become a passion with the Chief Justice," and he was not likely to hold out against drafting Brandeis. And in case the Chief Justice was still adamant, Felix Frankfurter had a plan for winning him over: Justice Holmes would persuade White of "the propriety of consenting to the drafting of Justice Brandeis." Frankfurter "en-thused" over the idea, saying: "You may depend upon me to deliver Holmes."
† The President had misunderstood Woolley's proposition, which was that Brandeis could be drafted at the end of the current term and serve until the opening of the October term. "In making it," Woolley explained to the President, April 29, "I was mindful of what you said . . . of the 'master and servant' decision [probably the Hitchman case] and the importance of his remaining at his post."

Two weeks later the press announced the creation of the War Labor Policies Board and the name of the chairman—Felix Frankfurter. Brandeis remained at his more crucial post on the Supreme Court.

CHAPTER THIRTY-THREE

Wilson's Adviser—Taft's Colleague

DURING the summer of 1918 Brandeis again remained in Washington, performing services not unlike those rendered during Wilson's first term. Though he saw Wilson only occasionally, he was not unmindful of the war's heavy toll on the President's strength. Nor was he unaware that the days ahead would be trying. Some premonition of what might come inspired him to write President Wilson on Armistice Day:

Throughout the war I have refrained from burdening you with communications. Today, I venture to send you some lines from Euripides: [1]

> "O Strength of God, slow art thou and still,
>   Yet failest never!
> On them that worship the Ruthless Will,
> On them that dream, doth His judgment wait.
> Dreams of the proud man, making great
>   And greater ever,
> Things which are not of God. In wide
>   And devious coverts, hunter-wise,
> He coucheth Time's unhasting stride,
>   Following, following, him whose eyes
> Look not to Heaven. For all is vain,
> The pulse of the heart, the plot of the brain,
> That striveth beyond the laws that live.
> And is thy Faith so much to give,
> Is it so hard a thing to see,
> That the Spirit of God, whate'er it be,
> The Law that abides and changes not, ages long,
> The Eternal and Nature-born—these things be strong!

What else is Wisdom? What of man's endeavour
Or God's high grace so lovely and so great?
To stand from fear set free, to breathe and wait;
To hold a hand uplifted over Hate;
And shall not Loveliness be loved for ever?"

The next day the President thanked the Justice "with such emotion as you may imagine." [2]

DOUBTS AND MISGIVINGS

Throughout Wilson's first administration and during the war years Brandeis held the President in highest esteem and gave full approval to his policies. His personal letters seldom show a trace of criticism. But toward the close of Wilson's second term Brandeis began to distrust the President's course. He deplored Wilson's absorption in international affairs at the expense of closely related and equally urgent domestic problems, such as reconversion and reconstruction. "The President thinks, apparently, there is none of great moment," he wrote his wife, December 2, 1918. Two days later he noted Felix Frankfurter as being "well crushed by the President's expressions on reconstruction. There is nothing for F.F. to do but demobilize his reconstruction group and devote his energies to the United States employment service."

In the international field Brandeis saw Wilson's Russian manifesto of August 1918 as the first indication of physical and mental overstrain. This attempt to compromise a difficult situation was "unnatural to Wilson," and marked the beginning of a series of similar blunders.[3]

Brandeis had occasion to state his views on "the urgency of the Russian question" in November 1918 when Hoover sent his secretary, Lewis Straus, to ask for an appointment with the Justice regarding the forthcoming Peace Conference which Hoover was shortly to join. With typical consideration for another man's time as well as for his own, Brandeis gave Straus his main thoughts for transmission to Hoover:

Justice Brandeis believes that thus far we have misunderstood the Russian people and very much underestimated the situation. None of the commissions which we have sent to Russia has, in his opinion, accomplished the least fragment of tangible result and, in fact, he has some misgivings as to whether they have not been harmful to our prestige among the masses and confusing to individual Russians who may be earnestly trying to discover a way toward stabilization and recovery. Neither military nor diplomatic missions are, in his opinion, capable of bringing the proper help and he believes what is needed is an economic mission which would offer its services in an attempt to promote economic

recovery and heal the wounds which the transportation and production struc-
tures of the Empire have suffered as a result of war and revolution.

He distrusts the ability and the disinterestedness of the Kerensky group as
well as certain cliques of Russian ex-diplomats in Washington, London, and
Paris. These groups, he believes, are probably Czarist and autocratic at heart.
He does not credit a large part of the information which has come to us concerning the present regime, fearing that it may be largely inspired by the group
just mentioned. The present government, he feels, should nevertheless be dealt
with in the utmost caution until its intentions are clear and we are convinced of
its honesty.

The urgency of the Russian question, and the fact that upon its settlement
rests inevitably the proper functioning of economic interdependence in Europe,
indicates to him the necessity that it should be the first matter to be settled by
the Powers at the forthcoming Conference at Paris. Any delay in facing the situation will postpone the restoration of normal world conditions and will allow
the focus of the disorganization to fester and spread.

Brandeis did not hold Wilson alone responsible. Allied leadership generally was storing up trouble for future generations. "I fear that the allies,
since the German surrender, are making as grave errors as the Germans
did in starting the war," he commented in a letter to Alfred, March 25,
1919. "The Russians fear a Napoleon will develop there. To understand
affairs, read the story of the French Revolution and thereafter instead of
the daily press."

Brandeis considered Wilson's mistakes primarily political. The Justice
believed that the President's decision to go to Paris was fatally wrong.
The President should have insisted that the Peace Conference be held in
Washington.[4] His appointments on the Peace Commission, his blunder-
ings in dealing with Senate leaders, were well-nigh unforgivable.

In a letter to his wife, December 2, 1918, Brandeis indicated misgivings
and sized up the situation with uncanny accuracy: "The event of the day
was, of course, the President's message, which Holmes, Pitney, McReynolds, Clark, and I attended. The President was obviously nervous at the
start and much of the audience obviously hostile. But both parties behaved
well. There was enough applause for decency and not enough to belie the
existing dissatisfaction.

"The message was, as you will see, beautifully phrased and in some
ways a clear presentation of needs for congressional activity—as if to make
them feel that they have plenty to work at while he is busy abroad. But I
am inclined to think that the actual silence in regard to his plans will anger
the Senate the more."

Other mistakes followed on Wilson's return from the Peace Conference.

Having negotiated the treaty, the President, Brandeis believed, should have left it on the Senate's doorstep. All these errors, in his opinion, plainly showed that Wilson did not understand the politics of the situation.[5]

Brandeis himself had gained firsthand knowledge of certain international complexities during the summers of 1919 and 1920 when he went abroad on Zionist missions, making short stays in London and Paris. He found the outlook discouraging. "I had three busy and profitable days in Paris," Brandeis wrote his wife, August 8, 1919, "where I lunched effectively with Mr. Balfour and breakfasted with the American Peace Commissioners and have supplemented work there with two busy and effective days in London.

"The world is certainly out of joint," his letter continued. "I suppose American problems will tend to further delay action on the treaty and thus prolong and intensify the agony here. Hoover is in the depth of gloom. Col. House is less gloomy generally, but like all other Americans severe on most that has been done." Brandeis told of walks along the Champs Elysées, the Boulevard, and the Seine, where he noted "faint effort of rejoicing over the peace, but it was microscopic in size. Everyone is dissatisfied and each pretty nearly with everybody. . . . Our own problems are sufficiently serious, but one bears them with becoming lightness in this world of gloom."

In London he emerged from "strictly Zionist circles" long enough to get "a bit of the Radical and Labor flavor; but it is not much relief," he wrote his wife, August 20. "Their problems are quite as serious as ours. All the world cusses Lloyd George and the Peace Performances. . . . We are of course watching American affairs, so far as the English papers permit. The President has his hands pretty full; and even my revered associates on the Bench (of whom I rarely think) must begin to realize that we are not living in the nineteenth century."

British institutions somewhat revived his hopes for mankind and civilization. "I feel again, as I did last year when here," he wrote Norman Hapgood, July 31, 1920, "that England is nearer civilization than any other country. That it is nearer democracy seems clear. As I watch events from day to day I am ever more impressed with the existence of a potent public opinion—expressing itself manfully and with much immediate effect. Our own machinery—referendum, initiative, primary elections, and elective officials galore—is a miserable substitute for the alert, intelligent watchfulness which is reflected generally in the press and which finds, in the interrogations in the House of Commons and in letters to the *Times,* the means of uncovering wrong action before it has become irremediable or has ceased to be of moment."

NORMALCY AND IRRESPONSIBILITY

By 1920 Wilson was broken politically and physically. And when the nation began its long search for new leadership Brandeis quietly supported Herbert Hoover. "I am 100 per cent for him," he wrote Hapgood, February 11, 1920, apparently forgetting earlier misgivings on the score of political ineptitude. "High public spirit, extraordinary intelligence, knowledge, sympathy, youth, and a rare perception of what is really worth-while for the country would, with his organizing ability and power of inspiring loyalty, do wonderful things in the Presidency, and his wife must not be omitted in the category." But Hoover had no political contacts of importance. Even his party affiliation was, to say the least, equivocal. And when the Republicans took the more "practical" course of party normalcy, Brandeis was sorely distressed. The elevation of Harding and Coolidge and the rejection of Hoover embittered him as "a sad story of American political irresponsibility. My hope is in the very extremeness of our present unworthiness," he wrote Alfred, June 21, 1920. "It is essentially un-American and when we awake, we shall cast aside in shame our present mistakes."

After the 1920 reactionary landslide, the G.O.P. promptly retreated from internationalism to isolationism and hastened the country back to "normalcy" by the time-tested G.O.P. panacea—a higher protective tariff. Wilson's administration had been the only period in recent American history when rich men did not have undue influence.[6] But this subordination of economics to politics was short-lived. To the loud acclaim of the business world, Harding sounded the keynote of the next decade of Republicanism: "We want less government in business and more business in government." The change was high-lighted by placing Andrew Mellon, number one businessman, monopolist, and multimillionaire, at the head of the Treasury Department. The Republican party resigned leadership and practically gave over the government to business at a time when a host of problems towered on the national horizon: railroads, prohibition, labor, political corruption—problems in every field, multiplied and accentuated by war. With the eye of a prophet Brandeis commented sententiously: "Europe was devastated by war, we by the aftermath."[7]

Harding's renunciation of the powers of government as our national problems sky-rocketed, filled Brandeis with profound discouragement and evoked pessimism of a sort he seldom expressed. Only the beauties of nature could lift the dark clouds. He wrote his mother-in-law, March 1, 1921, just before Harding took office: "Sun and sky are gladsome today. The trees are jutting forth buds; the grass its tenderest leaves. And the birds are singing their sweetest love songs—all in preparation for your birth-

THE GRANDCHILDREN
AT CHATHAM, 1935

Louis Gilbert, Walter
Raushenbush, Alice Gilbert,
Frank Gilbert

ON VACATION, CHATHAM, 1935

Harris and Ewing portrait

THE JUSTICE, 1937

day. Even the impending gloom of a Republican administration cannot dampen their ardor or suppress their joyousness.

"The Party of Peace and Prosperity," he continued, "will have to lead us through long stretches of Purgatory before they land us in Paradise. And there will not be idle, carefree days for Mr. Harding and his cabinet. Even the doleful, outgoing administration impressed with the ingratitude of Republicans may feel some relief in laying down the burden of government at this time."

As to railroads, finance, politics, Zionism, he saw the deluge. "At all events, I am safe," he wrote Alfred. "I bought a fine pair of Navy officers' shoes (high) for $6.50 yesterday." He approved the administration's determination to lend the railroads $500,000,000. "Ultimately the government will have to take over the railroads," he remarked, "and it is just as well to do it piecemeal in that way"—that is by large government loans. "But it is silly," he added, "to put out this talk that this will start business on the upgrade." The railroads' lament that they had been misunderstood reminded him of Clarence Darrow's answer to the sympathetic lady who said, "You must have suffered terribly from being misunderstood." "Yes," he replied, with a deep sigh, "but I should have suffered far more if I had been understood." [8]

The Harding regime's eagerness to aid business by reduced taxation at the top and increased bounties to special interests, reflected no credit on the wisdom of either political or industrial leadership. "The so-called beneficiaries will rue the day," he predicted in a note to Alfred on June 22. "As compared with them, medieval pawnbrokers—including our ancestors— were saints." He was sure that the new administration's deliberate retreat from international responsibility and its blind disregard for Europe's needs would have repercussions destructive to our best interests. Again he combined clear-sighted comment with cynicism:

I guess we and the entente allies are behaving so stupidly that Germany will run away with the industrial field ultimately. . . . We shall do little for Europe and it looks as if we were determined that no other country should do much for us. The tariff game, as it is to be played, will, I think, run up against reactions hitherto unknown to us. And our whole policy seems directed toward enabling England and Germany to get control of trade elsewhere. I can't imagine that Canada, Australia and the Argentine will sit quietly by and see us place embargoes on their raw materials without kicking back against our manufactured products. On the whole U.S.A. has little to be proud of in its conduct. We have slipped back badly in twenty-five years, in order, security to life and property; in liberty of speech, action and, assembly; in culture; and, in many respects, in morality. Father would have said "Pfui." [9]

"When the governors of mankind," he exclaimed fatalistically, "make such high errors, it is clear that we are not fit for organized society and should dissolve into the primordial atoms. Our ancestor Joseph who realized that there were lean years as well as fat ones knew a thing or two." [10] So did "Old Horace," whose lines he passed along to Norman Hapgood, November 8, 1921:

> The tide of business, like the running stream,
> Is sometimes high and sometimes low,
> A quiet ebb, or a tempestuous flow,
> And always in extreme.

Doubts soon began to plague him as to that "wonder"—Mr. Hoover. The "great engineer" had no sooner landed in the Harding cabinet as Secretary of Commerce, than speculation became rife as to whether he would be able to stay. Brandeis had thought that Hoover could contribute much in many ways if allowed to. "I guess the law of supply and demand still holds," he remarked as the postwar depression deepened, "despite the Republican monopoly of prosperity. . . . Hoover is certainly having opportunity to test any and all his power as an economic leader." [11]

Other observers noted Hoover's "insatiable and absurd graspingness" and "insane longing for publicity." Senator Walsh passed along the general opinion that "he hasn't a friend in the Senate." Hoover was profuse in ideas and plans, domestic and foreign, but Brandeis queried certain of them as unsound or misdirected. "My greatest grievance against him," he commented, "is that eighteen months have elapsed since he said he would grapple with the irregularity of production in the coal industry. . . . That is the bottom trouble. . . . Employment is so irregular that miners can't average more than a living wage now and the rail equipment, etc., is not utilized and the railroads have high coal costs, etc. It is the worst of all evidences of man's inability to organize society." [12]

And official Washington was obtuse generally: "I don't think the folks here have any idea that they can help the unemployment situation. Their real notion is either to build for the future by reducing irregularity of employment in normal times, or to talk for political effect, particularly to get the load off the administration by referring the problem to the local committees for solution. I don't think there is any serious thought of sending any government money to the committees. The government hasn't any and is likely to have less hereafter instead of more. With ships and railroads on its hands, it doesn't crave additional parasites." [13]

While ignoring the bottom trouble at home, Hoover complicated it, as well as our foreign relations, by his aggressive drive for trade and investments abroad. "Because some or most European countries need it," Brandeis remarked, "we foolishly pursue it, like the lady who wanted a mortgage on her house, as all the neighbors had one." "Hoover dined with us the other evening," the Justice wrote Alfred, October 15, 1921. "He was in good form, talkative and interesting. The net result was that 'every prospect pleases, only man is vile.' "

Early in the momentous postwar decade, amid unsound banking, stock and land speculation, unparalleled corruption, and fake prosperity, men cried loudly for "normalcy," for a do-nothing government. "But," the Justice commented to his wife, April 27, 1921, "the U.S.S.C. goes merrily on. The main discussion at luncheon was of shirts—where, when, and how satisfactory ones may be secured, and you fail to appreciate the judicial shirt—why not a chapter like Carlyle's in *Frederick the Great:* 'The King of France changeth his shirt.' " *

GREATNESS IN DISASTER

Woodrow Wilson was now, as Brandeis said, "indeed a lost soul." He had withdrawn to the seclusion of his S Street house, cut off even from many of his former friends and supporters. A small coterie remained friendly and loyal, among them Bernard Baruch, Frank I. Cobb, Thomas D. Chadbourne, Bainbridge Colby, and Brandeis. From the early summer of 1921 to January 20, 1924, Wilson and Brandeis carried on a more or less continuous correspondence. "Paragraphs," "memoranda," "summaries" passed between them, some written on the President's old typewriter and not very legibly, as the President had the use of only one hand. Numerous meetings took place at which this group endeavored to concentrate common council "in the formulation of principles and purposes" on the basis of which the Democratic party might stage a comeback in 1924.

In this "all important enterprise" Brandeis and Colby "generously assumed the laboring oars." [14] But Wilson himself was not idle. "Suggestions form themselves somewhere in the hidden recesses of my system and I am uneasy to get them out," he wrote the Justice somewhat apologetically, December 6, 1921. "I hope that it will not seem to you that I am firing these things at you with inconsiderate frequency and rapidity." Brandeis's response was always warm but was usually stated in general terms.

* In similar vein he wrote, September 25, 1923, of another meeting with his colleagues: "I spent nearly two and one-half hours with the Chief yesterday. First he wanted to read me his opinion (a very long extrajudicial one on 'Costa Rica Arbitration') and then we (with Sutherland who came in after the reading) chatted on many matters—mainly the Chief Justice talked. The most important thing I learned was that autos are worse about his house than Stoneleigh —then that you were quite right about Mrs Harding. She was the real force and made whatever there was in him [Harding]. Sutherland says she didn't die—simply because she refused to do so."

By April 9, 1922, Wilson had assembled the group's several pieces in a single document nearly seven pages long. It was a ringing manifesto for an American conception of social justice. To Wilson's mind it was "satisfactory"—"a very clear and self-consistent document." Republican leadership was bitterly denounced as the "most partisan, prejudiced, and unpatriotic coterie that ever misled the Senate of the United States; . . . the country will never be restored to its merited prestige until their work is undone." A clarion call went out to the Democratic party to return the country to that prestige.

Brief, lucid paragraphs told the meaning of "America First." For Republicans "America First" was only a slogan; it meant "no service to any other nation or people which she can reserve for her own selfish aggrandizement." For Democrats it meant that America, having developed within her own citizenship a sensitive regard for justice in the relations of men, must lead the world in applying the "broadest conceptions of justice and peace." The document deplored the Republican administration's "clamor for payment" of international debts, the "brandishing of our contracts," the "ignorant delusion that we are untouched and unaffected by these all-encompassing conditions." Here was a bold proposal that we use "our accumulated strength, our savings and our matchless resources in the rescue of our sister nations, from which alone our own recovery can arise.

"Our opponents," runs paragraph 11, "have sought to promote the accumulation of wealth as an instrument of power in the hands of individuals and corporations. It is our object to promote it as a means of diffused prosperity and happiness and of physical and spiritual well-being on the part of the great working masses of our people."

The document called for systematic co-ordination, co-operation, and interchange of services by the railroads, and advocated the creation of a Secretary of Transportation as a cabinet officer equal in rank with other great cabinet posts. It advocated the development of transportation by inland water routes and ship canal communications with the Atlantic seaboard. Included also were recommendations of credit institutions for farmers, suggesting that "mutual associations [be] formed among responsible farmers themselves to facilitate production and assist orderly marketing"; an efficient and adequate merchant marine; and, finally, federal regulation of fuel supply and electrical power to "the utmost limit of the constitutional powers of the federal government," to the end that these may be made accessible to "all upon equitable and equal terms."

Paragraphs 14 and 15 sounded an even more Brandeisian note, pointing to the "present menace to political liberty and peaceful economic prosperity" as consisting in the "hasty, passionate, and irrational programs of revolution." Here one notes a significant shift of emphasis. At the turn of the century Brandeis had seen the social menace primarily in terms of the excesses of capitalism. The "Russian business" now threatened danger from another side. Since 1918 his query had been: "How can bolshevism be averted?" [15] "The world has been made safe for democracy," the document reads, "but democracy has not yet made the world safe against irrational revolution. It is the privilege and duty of ours, the greatest of all democracies, to show the way."

The recipe recommended is the one that Brandeis had suggested at the turn of the century for warding off the danger of socialism: "It is our purpose to defeat the irrational programs of revolution beforehand by sober and practical legislative reforms which shall remove the chief provocations to revolution." Among other things, this called for "a practical plan of veritable partnership between capital and labor, in which responsibilities of each to the other, and of both to the nation, shall be stressed quite as much as their respective rights. Our industrial system must command the interest and respect of the wage-earners as an avenue to those liberties and opportunities for self-development, which it is the nature of free men to desire."

In the early twenties this formulation of principles was a veritable oasis in the desert of normalcy. But how could these ideas be made of service to the country? "Do you think there is any immediate use," Wilson inquired of Brandeis, April 9, 1922, "that could wisely be made of the document that would not militate against the realization of our hope that it can be made the official party declaration two years hence?"

Wilson's first thought was to hand it to Cordell Hull, chairman of the Democratic National Committee, with the suggestion that he send copies of it confidentially to Democratic candidates for the House and Senate that autumn, with an intimation that they draw from it declarations of policy for their own local campaigns. In that way the thought of the party might, Wilson wrote Brandeis, "be drawn into common channels before the big tasks of nineteen and twenty-four demand immediate performance." Baruch considered this course unwise and Brandeis agreed. "Ammunition so potent should not be dissipated," the Justice advised Wilson, April 11, 1922. "You have taught us the lesson of watchful waiting."

Strong loyalty to Wilson and his principles pervaded Brandeis's Christmas note the year after the broken President left office.

December 27, 1922

My dear Mr. Wilson:

The year now closing brought you, after much sorrow, the satisfaction which came with the reawakening of the American people. May the years to come bring you and others the happiness which would attend the realization of your ideals.

Most cordially,
Louis D. Brandeis

"Watchful waiting" was still in order for the Democrats in 1924. One brief paragraph at the head of the party's platform embodied something of the spirit of the Wilson–Brandeis confidential document, but the party's Wall Street standard bearer, John W. Davis, afforded little more promise of progressive leadership than G.O.P.'s Calvin Coolidge.

SUPREME COURT NORMALCY

In the meantime the brief tenure of President Harding had enlarged the Court's reactionary majority. At the first opportunity the President appointed William Howard Taft to succeed Chief Justice White, thus satisfying the former President's lifelong ambition. When Justice Clarke resigned in 1922, another Brandeis opponent in the Ballinger investigation and the 1916 nomination fight, former Senator George Sutherland, became his colleague. In striking contrast with the long delay in Brandeis's case, Sutherland, the Colonel House of Harding's 1920 front-porch campaign and a great senatorial leader of Republicanism, was confirmed the day he was nominated without even formal reference to the Senate Judiciary Committee. In rapid succession, without either query or criticism, Minnesota's railroad lawyer Pierce Butler, succeeded Justice William R. Day, and Tennessee's Edward Terry Sanford replaced Justice Pitney. All were safe and sane, true and blue conservatives. Surely Taft had no reason to fear that the Court thus restored and refreshed by Harding would break down "the bulwark of our civil liberties," as he had said it would when Wilson nominated Brandeis.

The relative strength of the Court's liberal wing was weakened by Justice Clarke's resignation to devote all his energies to the League of Nations. "I should die happier," Clarke wrote Brandeis, September 13, 1922, "if I should do all that is possible to promote the entrance of our government into the League of Nations than if I continued to devote my time to determining whether a drunken Indian had been deprived of his land before he died or whether the digging of a ditch in Iowa was constitutional or not." Devoted as Wilson was to the League, he nevertheless regretted Clarke's resignation. Wilson had been counting on Brandeis and Clarke "to restrain the Court in some measure from the extreme reactionary course which it seems inclined to follow"—a course which the former President said would "more and more outrage the common people's sense of justice and cause a revulsion against judicial authority which may seriously disturb the equilibrium of our institutions. . . ." * [16]

For those who recalled the Ballinger episode and the prominent role played in it by Sutherland and Taft and the latter's open vindictiveness toward Brandeis in 1916, this shift in Court leadership seemed most unhappy for Brandeis. His relation with Chief Justice White had been most cordial; Washington had become accustomed to seeing them out walking together. How would he get along with his new chief and with Sutherland? Cordial relations with Sutherland had already been established in 1921. "Your ham, Senator and Mrs. George Sutherland, Vernon Kellogg, the Norman Hapgoods, and the Arthur Ballards, helped to eat last Sunday," Brandeis wrote Alfred, December 16. "Sutherland is English born, whether a Yorkshireman, I can't say, but he and Kellogg ate like experts."

It was rumored that Taft and Brandeis were not on speaking terms. Few knew of the chance meeting which Justice Brandeis described to his wife, December 4, 1918: "Had an experience yesterday which I did not expect to encounter in this life. As I was walking toward the Stoneleigh about 1 P.M., Taft and I met. There was a moment's hesitation and when he had almost passed, he stopped and said in a charming manner, 'Isn't this Justice Brandeis? I don't think we have ever met.' I answered, 'Yes we met at Harvard after you returned from the Philippines.' He, at once, began to talk about my views on regularity of employment. After a moment I asked him to come in with me. He spent a half hour in 809, talking labor and War Labor Board experiences—was most confidential. I told him of the great service he had rendered the country by his action on the Labor Board and we parted with his saying in effect—he hoped we would meet often." [17]

There was little likelihood that either man, least of all Brandeis, would have allowed personal differences to interfere with the effectiveness of the Court's work. Any man who could tolerate serenely, as Brandeis had done for five years, the McReynolds snarling against Jews, would certainly have no difficulty in getting on with the fat and jovial former President.†
Brandeis was always singularly reticent in any discussion of Court personalities. "Try as hard as I may," one of his friends remarked, "to get

* An entirely different version of Wilson's reaction to Clarke's resignation is given in the latter's letter to Brandeis, September 13, 1922: "A letter from W.W. this morning approves my action in the strongest terms and his good wishes come with it in quite the most unreserved way I have ever known him to write."
† Writing, one thinks, with tongue in his cheek, Brandeis told his wife, May 8, 1923, of his technique for keeping on good terms with one who, as Taft said, "takes delight in making others uncomfortable": "My friendly relations with my 'brothers' took a new advance yesterday when I asked McR. to write the dissent in a case in which we two are unable to concur with the majority. He seemed greatly pleased at being asked. Next Saturday has been specially assigned for exclusive consideration of my elaborate memo:—so you see we are very friendly."

an expression of opinion regarding his colleagues, particularly Butler, Mc-Reynolds or Taft—no success." [18] Among his law clerks he was less re-strained. "There was . . . beneath the surface of his kindly gravity a twinkle of gaiety and witty consideration of the strength and weaknesses of his colleagues." [19]

On Taft's appointment as Chief Justice, Brandeis wrote a short note of congratulation and at the same time urged upon his new chief the need of readjusting the machinery of the federal court system so as to accelerate judicial business. "I thank you for your note on this subject," Taft replied, "and look forward with pleasure to joint consideration and co-operation with you in this and all other matters of the Court." "I am looking for-ward with pleasure to meeting you in Washington," he wrote a few weeks later.[20]

Taft continued to distrust Brandeis's "radicalism" but he admired him as "a very hard worker"; also because "he thinks much of the Court and is anxious to have it consistent and strong and he pulls his own weight in the boat." After working with this "dangerous foe" of our institutions two terms, Taft could say: "I have come to like Brandeis very much indeed." [21]

"Have you seen Brandeis lately?" Taft inquired of Edward F. Mc-Clennen in August 1923. "Is he getting a restful vacation? You can imag-ine the thoughts with which I approached a close association with him when I became Chief," Taft told Brandeis's former law partner. "You may not know how close and satisfactory that association has been. I am wor-ried about the way he overworks himself. It is not only the personal friend-ship. It is that I do not see how we could get along without him. Do what you can to make him have a good rest this summer. I have talked to him again and again about his doing so much more on the cases assigned to him than is necessary, but it does not seem to have any effect. He keeps at it." [22]

The cordial relationship between the two men was amusingly dem-onstrated in 1927, when Brandeis received a crank's postal card telling of growing impatience with "rotten imitation celibate Priestcraft." The writer had about decided to become "a reformed Jew." "Are you orthodox or reformed?" the correspondent inquired. "Which is better, Unitarian or Jew?"

It was a challenging question, and the Jew referred the matter to his Unitarian colleague. On the address side of the card Brandeis scribbled: "My dear Chief: I refuse to compete. L.D.B.," and passed the message to the Chief Justice. Two days later Taft wrote: "I beg to acknowledge card from your correspondent. He seems to be a fundamentalist unitarian, and yet he seems to think there is some advantage in stepping into Judaism.

My church is broad enough to house all the cranks there are and I am inclined to think that we can't exclude him. I hope you will conclude to send him an exegesis on the subject of his inquiry. Take the summer to it. As ever yours, W.H.T."

Without compromising his convictions or his self-respect, Brandeis, in his relations with leaders so antithetically apart as Wilson and Taft, proved once more his infinite genius for adapting himself to, and working with, all sorts and conditions of men.

CHAPTER THIRTY-FOUR

Trade Unionism and Public Utilities

IN THIS country, in contrast with England, the rights of labor had been defined, even narrowed and delimited, by the Courts. Legislative effort to correct industrial exploitation and to create for labor a substantial bill of rights had either been set aside or construed away. Labor's helplessness in the face of superior industrial power judicially entrenched was worsened by the fact that the Supreme Court itself had weakened major legislative efforts by Congress to curb combinations in restraint of trade. Having drawn the teeth of the Sherman Act as to industrial combination, the Court then rigidly applied its fangs to the activities of labor unions. The Sugar Refining Company, a confessed 98 per cent monopoly, was held not to be within the language or intent of the Anti-Trust Act,[1] but the United Hatters' Union was covered, and the statute's onerous provisions imposing treble damages were invoked in the Danbury case.[2] The courts also undermined or nullified state and national legislation regulating hours, wages, and working conditions. State legislation was declared void as violating the due process clause of the Fourteenth Amendment,[3] while national legislation was sometimes set aside as encroaching on the sacred domain of state police power.[4]

In addition to halting organized labor's attempts to compensate its unequal struggle against organized capital by self-help and legislation, the Court had introduced in 1895 the notorious labor injunction.[5] The Debs case that year advertised its effectiveness so successfully that the phrase "government by injunction" was soon a national byword. Another employer-instrument carrying judicial sanction was the "yellow-dog" contract—an agreement whereby a worker in accepting employment pre-contracted to quit his union or not to join one. The courts upheld this as a legally enforceable agreement, and when Congress and the states outlawed the device, the legislation was declared unconstitutional.[6] This, in brief, was the legal-constitutional status of labor when Brandeis joined the Court in 1916.

OPPOSING THE YELLOW-DOG CONTRACT

In 1917 Brandeis ran headlong into the Court's support of the judge-made injunctive device and the yellow-dog contract. The Hitchman Coal Company had made individual agreements with its employees not to join the union while in the employ of the company, and when the union began a campaign to compel the employer to rescind these obnoxious contracts, the company secured an injunction against union organizers to maintain and preserve their yellow-dog agreements. Justice Pitney, speaking for the Court, was primarily concerned with the question whether there had been a breach of contract, whether the union had actually threatened to coerce the company to recognize unionism against its will and without its consent. He held that there had been a threat of illegal coercion which the equity courts must protect.

Brandeis, in dissent, ran the full gauntlet of all such technical matters but he did not stop here; he went on to consider the vital need of strengthening the bituminous mine workers' bargaining power, and tied this up with labor's need for security and economic independence. He kept the broader implications, however, within bounds. He did not harangue against either yellow-dog contracts, the labor injunction, or the open shop. He did not deny the company's petition for an injunction of sweeping character, providing its rights were substantially threatened. But whereas Pitney's attention was centered on the legal minutiae of employers' rights, more particularly the contested right to have the mine judicially protected against unionization, Brandeis stressed more important values—the recognized social and legal rights of labor.

Trade unions and collective bargaining, he reasoned, were legal; the methods employed were also legal. Therefore the injunction should be sustained only if the company's contract were considered more important than labor's legally established right to increase its economic power through organization and collective bargaining. The organizers did not induce, nor did they threaten to induce, workers to break their contracts. They were seeking to produce a situation that would force the employer to forego the yellow-dog contract as a condition of employment. Pitney called this illegal coercion. He saw in such labor activity no other than an illegal purpose: to compel the company to change its method of operation. What to Brandeis was plainly necessary to equalize bargaining power between employer and employee, and "to establish the equality of position between the parties in which liberty of contract begins,"[7] was denounced by the majority of the Court as an unconstitutional infringement of that very liberty. In protest Brandeis said:

". . . Coercion, in a legal sense, is not exerted when a union merely endeavors to induce employees to join a union with the intention thereafter to order a strike unless the employer consents to unionize his shop. . . . The employer is free either to accept the agreement or the disadvantage. Indeed, the plaintiff's whole case is rested upon agreements secured under similar pressure of economic necessity or disadvantage. If it is coercion to threaten to strike unless plaintiff consents to a closed union shop, it is coercion also to threaten not to give one employment unless the applicant will consent to a closed non-union shop. . . ."[8]

DEFENDING THE SYMPATHETIC STRIKE

The term "labor dispute," Justice Brandeis observed in the Duplex Case, "includes any controversy . . . regardless of whether or not the disputants stand in the proximate relation of employer and employee."[9] In 1919 the Duplex Company had sought a court order to restrain the union from boycotting its products in an effort to win the union shop, and the Court granted an injunction in spite of the immunity supposedly provided under the labor clauses of the Clayton Act. These provisions had been the outcome of trade union objectives strenuously pursued since 1908 when the United States Supreme Court held the Sherman Act applicable to labor. Designed as corrective legislation, the Clayton Act recognized labor's right to organize and presumably placed certain activities, such as striking, picketing, and boycotting, outside the scope of the Sherman Act. Believing that these aims had been achieved, Gompers triumphantly proclaimed the Clayton Act's labor clauses as labor's Magna Charta and Bill of Rights. The Duplex decision blasted all such high hopes.

Ignoring the function and policy of trade unions, Justice Pitney, again speaking for the Court, construed the act narrowly. He saw labor's refusal to work on the Duplex company's materials, or to repair or install its products, as evidence of malicious intent to injure the employer. He considered it merely a "sentimental or sympathetic . . . dispute." This contest did not arise, he said, out of "terms or conditions of their own employment past, present, or prospective," and therefore the strikers could not properly claim the Clayton Act's exemptions from injunctive relief. "Congress had in mind particular industrial controversies, not a general class war," Pitney observed.[10]

Only when one reads Justice Brandeis's dissent does one come face to face with the economic realities underlying these industrial controversies. From his opinion one learns that the Duplex Company was one of four competing companies manufacturing printing presses in the United States. Three had been unionized. The Duplex Company held out against union recognition, refusing both the eight-hour day and the minimum wage scale. Thereupon two of the three other manufacturers notified the union that they would be obliged to terminate agreements providing for more advanced standards and working conditions unless their competitor, the Duplex Company, also met union requirements. The union was thus faced with the crucial alternative of either accepting lower wages and worse working conditions, or using its organized power to bring the company to fair terms.

On this issue judges as a class had long been sharply divided. The strike had once been illegal at common law. But this was no longer the case. "A better understanding of the facts of industrial life," Brandeis pointed out, has yielded more liberal rulings. Informed judges now recognized economic pressure as justified in terms both of self-interest and social well-being. Pitney was innocent both of the industrial revolution and of subsequent changes in labor law as reflected in Court decisions and legislation. He saw this case merely as a dispute between two litigants and as if in the simpler days of handicraft. Brandeis, on the other hand, realized the dispute in terms of economic conflict in a highly organized industrial society. He saw the issue as involving matters of more far-reaching social consequence than the specific case at Bar. The workers, he contended, had "injured the plaintiff, not maliciously, but in self-defense.

"When centralization in the control of business brought its corresponding centralization in the organization of workingmen, new facts have to be appraised. A single employer might, as in this case, threaten the standing of the whole organization and the standards of all its members. . . . May not all," he asked, "with a common interest join in refusing to expend their labor upon articles whose very production constitutes an attack upon their standard of living and the institution which they are convinced supports it?"[11]

As Brandeis put it: "The Clayton Act substituted the opinion of Congress . . . for that of differing judges," and declared "the right of industrial combatants to push their struggle to the limits of the justification of self-interest." [12] In taking a narrow view of the legislative exemptions provided in the Clayton Act, the Supreme Court, by technical indirection, restored the very evils Congress had sought to correct.

Brandeis held that the defendant's sympathetic strike was justified both at common law and under the Clayton Act, but he pointedly disclaimed any purpose to attach constitutional or moral sanction thereto. No implications were to be drawn from his opinion beyond the issues involved in the case at the Bar. "All rights," he observed, "are derived from the purposes of society in which they exist; above all rights rises duty to the community. The conditions developed in industry may be such that those engaged in it cannot continue their struggle without danger to the community. But it is not for judges to determine whether such conditions exist, nor is it their function to set the limits of permissible contest, and to declare the duties which the new situation demands." [13]

Here he struck a note which in time was to become a compelling refrain: judges have neither the competence nor the power to decide controversial economic and social issues. They have not the staff nor the facilities to amass the facts necessary to form a considered and valid judgment on such matters.

As was to be expected, the already sharp division in the Court on labor cases deepened under the conservative leadership of Taft and Sutherland. Taft was as outspoken in his anti-labor prejudice as Brandeis was in sympathy. The Chief Justice still believed it possible to achieve order amid wretchedness, by force if necessary. "The only class," he wrote Horace Taft, May 7, 1922, "which is distinctly arrayed against the Court is a class that does not like the courts at any rate, and that is organized labor. That faction we have to hit every little while, because they are continually violating the law and depending on threats and violence to accomplish their purpose." [14]

HUMAN RIGHTS VERSUS PROPERTY RIGHTS

Taft had occasion to hit labor in a case involving an Arizona statute that placed much the same limitations on the intervention of state courts of equity in labor disputes as were imposed upon the federal courts by Sections 6 and 20 of the Clayton Act. Chief Justice Taft found the statute wanting under both the equal protection and due process clauses of the Fourteenth Amendment. He held that persons (in this case, employers and property owners) may be as effectively denied equal protection of the laws by conferring a favor (in this case on wage-earners) as by imposing a pen-

alty; that even in the absence of violence an employer may not be deprived
of the only effective protection he has against such tactics of labor, namely
the injunction; that there is a minimum of protection to which a property
owner or businessman is entitled, and of which he may not be deprived
by denial of equitable relief, without invading fundamental rights guaranteed by the Fourteenth Amendment.

Brandeis protested strongly against the Court's decision and underscored
the sort of consideration the case in hand demanded: "What, at any particular time, is the paramount public need, is, necessarily, largely a matter
of judgment. Hence, in passing upon the validity of a law challenged as
being unreasonable, aid may be derived from the experience of other countries and of the several states of our Union in which the common law and
its conceptions of liberty and of property prevail." [15]

Brandeis made detailed investigation of labor in England, showing that
improvement of the workingman's condition there had been deemed the
paramount public need; that resort to the injunction was infrequent; that
it had played no appreciable part in conflicts between capital and labor;
that the history of the rules governing employer–employee relations disclosed a variety of opinion as to what may best serve the public interest.
Turning then to the contrasting American policy, he told how the injunction had been a favorite instrument of employers to safeguard their property at the expense of human freedom.

"The equitable remedy," he said, "although applied in accordance with
established practice, involved incidents which . . . endangered the personal liberty of wage-earners; . . . that the real motive in seeking the
injunction was not ordinarily to prevent property from being injured, nor
to protect the owner in its use, but to endow property with active, militant
power which would make it dominant over men. In other words, that,
under the guise of protecting property rights, the employer was seeking
sovereign power. And many disinterested men, solicitous only for the public welfare, believed that the law of property was not appropriate for dealing with the forces beneath social unrest; that in this vast struggle it was
unwise to throw the power of the state on one side or the other, according
to principles deduced from that law; that the problem of the control and
conduct of industry demanded a solution of its own; and that, pending
the ascertainment of new principles to govern industry, it was wiser for
the state not to interfere in industrial struggles by the issuance of an injunction." [16]

Brandeis went on to stress the essential wisdom of judicial tolerance:
"The divergence of opinion in this difficult field of governmental action
should admonish us not to declare a rule arbitrary and unreasonable merely

because we are convinced that it is fraught with danger to the public weal, and thus to close the door to experiment within the law." [17]

Once again Brandeis warned judges against the temptation to enlarge their own power at the expense of other agencies of government. In the United States judicial intervention in industrial controversies had been frequent; anti-injunction proposals had long occupied the attention of Congress as well as several state legislatures. Nor did the Constitution place any barriers in the way of these efforts. Brandeis held that "states are as free since the adoption of the Fourteenth Amendment as they were before, either to expand or to contract their equity jurisdiction. The denial of the more adequate equitable remedy for private wrongs is, in essence, an exercise of the police power, by which, in the interest of the public, and in order to preserve the liberty and the property of the great majority of the citizens of a state, rights of property and the liberty of the individual must be remolded, from time to time, to meet the changing needs of society." [18]

In his crusade for judicial recognition of the rights of labor Brandeis was frequently at odds with that first-rate lawyer and judicial craftsman, Mr. Justice Sutherland. It was the former Senator from Utah who in 1923 spoke for the Court in outlawing the minimum wage law for the District of Columbia similar to that which Brandeis had successfully defended in 1914 before an evenly divided Court.[19] Disqualified in 1923 on the score of judicial propriety, Brandeis did not vote. Sutherland, speaking for the Court, ruthlessly threw out the mass of reports, opinions of experts and special observers, on which Brandeis's minimum wage brief of 1914 had successfully relied. Brandeis had then convinced four of the Justices, but in 1923 Sutherland found all such data "interesting but only mildly persuasive. These are all proper enough," he said, "for the consideration of the lawmaking bodies, since their tendency is to establish the desirability or undesirability of the legislation; but they reflect no legitimate light upon the question of its validity." [20]

The Court now stood 5 to 4 against the minimum wage. Among the dissenters was Chief Justice Taft, who denied judicial power to void acts of Congress "simply because they are passed to carry out economic views which the Court believes to be unwise or unsound."

UNION LABOR AND THE SHERMAN ACT

Brandeis renewed the battle with Sutherland in 1927 when the journeymen stone cutters tried to unionize the Bedford Cut Stone Company by calling upon all local unions to refuse handling stone cut by non-union labor. For Justice Sutherland the issue was not unlike that involved in the

Duplex case. The Court's opinion there, he said, "might serve as an opinion in this case." Justice Sanford was also unable to distinguish the two cases. Justice Harlan F. Stone, whom President Coolidge had recently elevated to the Court, considered the union's conduct reasonable, but held that the Duplex decision was controlling. Once again, the Sherman Act, supposedly designed to curb industrial combinations, was invoked to restrict union activity even though its propriety, as Brandeis said, "can hardly be doubted by one who believes in organization of labor."

With due bitterness, he observed: "If, on the undisputed facts of this case, refusal to work can be enjoined, Congress created by the Sherman Law and the Clayton Act an instrument for imposing restraints upon labor which reminds of involuntary servitude. . . . The Sherman Law was held in *United States* v. *United States Steel Corporation* . . . to permit capitalists to combine in a single corporation 50 per cent of the steel industry of the United States, dominating the trade through its vast resources. The Sherman Law was held in *United States* v. *United Shoe Machinery Company* . . . to permit capitalists to combine in another corporation practically the whole shoe machinery industry of the country, necessarily giving it a position of dominance over shoe-manufacturing in America. It would, indeed, be strange if Congress had by the same act willed to deny to members of a small craft of workingmen the right to co-operate in simply refraining from work, when that course was the only means of self-protection against a combination of militant and powerful employers. I cannot believe that Congress did so.[21]

But Justice Brandeis was not always in disagreement with Taft and Sutherland even in labor cases. Though a strong advocate of collective bargaining, he denounced trade union irresponsibility and abuses no less strenuously than they. He supported the majority in the Coronado Case, where Taft, speaking for the Court, ruled that a trade union, an unincorporated association, was suable and liable to treble damages under Sections 7 and 8 of the Sherman Act.[22]

The Coronado decision was denounced by labor as a "blow to human freedom," but Brandeis saw it as a real gain for labor. That very immunity from suit and legal responsibility, so much cherished by labor, had in reality paved the way for the greatest injury inflicted by the courts—"government by injunction." In this decision he could see the partial attainment of that for which labor had been working since the Debs case—a possible limitation on the use of injunctions in labor disputes.

As lawyer and judge, Brandeis steadfastly followed the principle that "industrial liberty, like civil liberty, must rest upon the solid foundations of law." [23] Thus, when a trade union official called a strike to compel payment of an ex-employee's disputed wage claim, in violation of the Kansas Industrial Court Act, labor's friend on the Court ruled: "Neither the common law, nor the Fourteenth Amendment, confers the absolute right to strike."

Sounding the conservative note of earlier years, Brandeis, speaking for the Court, said: "The right to carry on business—be it called liberty or property—has value. To interfere with this right without just cause is unlawful. The fact that the injury was inflicted by a strike is sometimes a justification. But a strike may be illegal because of its purpose, however orderly the manner in which it is conducted. To collect a stale claim due to a fellow member of the union who was formerly employed in the business is not a permissible purpose. . . . To enforce payment by a strike is clearly coercion. The legislature may make such action punishable criminally, as extortion or otherwise." [24]

This decision was also denounced by labor spokesmen as a judicial "blow to human freedom." It might be more correctly considered as but another illustration of Brandeis's belief that society does not gain by exchanging tyranny of capital for that of labor. Nor is the opinion as drastic as appears at first glance. Without the Kansas statute, the strike might well have been condemned as a conspiracy at common law. And lest erroneous implications be drawn, Brandeis pointed out that "the question requiring decision is not . . . the broad one whether the legislature has power to prohibit strikes." [25]

THE STABLE BASE AND FAIR RATE OF RETURN

One of the most baffling problems before the Court during the Chief Justiceship of Taft concerned rate-making for railroads and public utilities—a field in which Brandeis had served an exceptionally long and fruitful apprenticeship. As early as 1913 he had been recognized as an expert in this field, receiving inquiries from all sections of the country. Taft frankly confessed his distaste for the whole subject as well as his incompetence to handle it. But, he observed, "we have some experts on our Court. One is Pierce Butler, the other is Brandeis." [26] The situation was complicated, however, by the fact that these judicial experts were in sharp disagreement. Butler believed reproduction cost should be the determining factor in ascertaining the rate base; Brandeis advocated the doctrine of "prudent investment."

The reproduction cost rule so strongly favored by Coolidge–Hoover conservatives has had a varied and curious history. Back in 1893 it was urged on behalf of the community. William Jennings Bryan argued in favor of present value for rate-making purposes as protection against inflated claims and high prices. The long depression after 1893 brought prices to the lowest level of the nineteenth century. Reproduction cost was then invoked in protest against watered stock, recklesss finance, and racketeering contracts. During World War I rising prices caused railroads and other utilities to adopt eagerly the position once fortified by liberals on behalf of the consumer. By the early thirties the way was paved for another shift back to Bryan by those who favored public interests.

The Court has not always been the final forum for the solution of such conflicting issues. It was not until the turn of the century that the Judiciary, fearful lest state legislatures dominated by populists and reformers enact socialism, gratuitously assumed the burden of deciding these social and economic complexities. In 1876 the Court had taken a position of non-interference, claiming that fixing public utility rates was a legislative matter which should remain free from judicial interference.[27] Ten years later at the high point of judicial belief in legislative laissez faire, the Court had shifted its ground to insist that this power of the legislature was not without limit; that utility rates must yield a fair return upon a fair valuation of the property devoted to such a public service. Although the Court two years later retreated somewhat, when it suddenly recognized that it was without any basis upon which to question legislative control over public utility rates, all misgivings on the latter score had vanished by 1890, when the Court held judicial review applicable in public utility cases, maintained that due process of law required the rate to be reasonable, and that of this the Court was final judge.[28] This right of judicial review in the whole field was boldly stated in *Smyth* v. *Ames* (1898), despite the prior protest of a minority which held that judges were not equipped to decide social and economic issues.

Certainly judges could find precious little guidance in the Constitution. What was there in the Constitution that hinted whether 5, 6, or 8 per cent was a fair return on public utility property? What was there to shed light on whether utilities should be valued for rate-making purposes at original cost, or at reproduction cost? Absolutely none. And yet these questions were settled in Court by applying highly controversial accounting measurements and economic theories.

The Court had, it is true, formulated a rule on the basis of which "just compensation" and "reasonable rates" might be determined, but it was so vague as to leave wide latitude for judicial discretion. To be taken into account were "the original cost of construction, the amount expended in permanent improvements, the amount and market value of its [the company's] bonds and stock, the present as compared with the original cost of construction, the probable earning capacity of the property under particular rates prescribed by statute, and the sum required to meet operating expenses, all are matters for consideration, and are to be given such weight as may be just and right in each case." [29]

Unfortunately this judicial formula comprised not one but three different, and not altogether harmonious, bases for determining the value of property for rate-making purposes: historical cost of tangible property plus permanent improvements; capitalization and commercial value of the business as determined by current market prices of the company's stocks and bonds; cost of reproduction.

The adequacy of this rule was fully explored in 1923 in the Southwestern Bell Telephone case. The Telephone Company had appealed to the highest Court when the Supreme Court of Missouri sustained rate reductions ordered by the State Public Service Commission. Justice McReynolds, speaking for the Court, leaned heavily toward the reproduction cost rule. "Estimates for tomorrow," he said, "cannot ignore prices of today." In determining "a fair return" on the properties devoted to the public service, the Court must give "consideration to the cost of labor, supplies, etc., at the time the investigation is made. . . . An honest and intelligent forecast of probable future values is essential." [30]

Brandeis concurred in holding that the particular rate fixed was confiscatory, but "I differ fundamentally from my brethren," he said, "concerning the rule to be applied in determining whether a prescribed rate is confiscatory. . . . The rule [of *Smyth* v. *Ames*] does not measure the present value either by what the utility cost to produce, or by what it should have cost, or by what it would cost to reproduce or to replace it. Under that rule the tribunal is directed, in forming its judgment, to take into consideration all those, and also other, elements, called relevant facts.

"Obviously, 'value' cannot be a composite of all these elements," he continued. "Nor can it be arrived at on all these bases. They are very different, and must, when applied in a particular case, lead to widely different results. The rule . . . as interpreted and applied, means merely that all must be considered. What, if any, weight shall be given to any one, must practically rest in the judicial discretion of the tribunal which makes the determination." [31]

The Court had in fact divided in a long and important line of decisions as to the relative weight to be given the various factors in rate base determination. The time had come to substitute certainty and stability for judicial chaos and muddling. By 1923 twenty-five years' experience had demonstrated that the rule enunciated was "delusive."

"It has failed," Brandeis said, "to afford adequate protection either to capital or to the public. It leaves open the door to grave injustice." [32] The rule was inadequate whether one considered its component factors singly or in combination. He reminded his conservative colleagues that their strong preference for reproduction cost might in the not too distant future prove their undoing. "The present price level," he suggested, with an uncanny forecast of the collapse of 1929, "may fall to that of 1914 within a decade; and that, later, it may fall much lower." [33]

Obviously no rule would be adequate which would not serve as a guide regardless of whether prices were rising or falling. The inadequacy of the rule formulated in *Smyth* v. *Ames* prompted Brandeis to make his usual detailed survey of the whole problem and to propose a substitute.

REALITY AND THE RATE BASE

To give public utility capital its due constitutional protection, Brandeis argued that the rate base be definite, stable, and readily ascertainable; that the percentage to be earned on the rate base be measured by the cost, or charge, of the capital employed in the enterprise.

"Capital honestly and prudently invested must, under normal conditions, be taken," he said, "as the controlling factor in fixing the basis for computing fair and reasonable rates. The adoption of the amount prudently invested as the rate base, and the amount of the capital charge as the measure of the rate of return, would give definiteness to these two factors . . . which are now shifting and treacherous, and which render the proceedings peculiarly burdensome and largely futile. . . . The rate base would be ascertained as a fact, not determined as a matter of opinion. It would not fluctuate with the market price of labor, or materials, or money. It would not change with hard times or shifting populations. It would not be distorted by the fickle and varying judgments of appraisers, commissions, or courts. It would, when once made in respect to any utility, be fixed for all time, subject only to increases to represent additions to plant, after allowance for the depreciation included in the annual operating charges. The wild uncertainties of the present method of fixing the rate base . . . would be avoided; and likewise the fluctuations which introduce into the enterprise unnecessary elements of speculation, create useless expense, and impose upon the public a heavy, unnecessary burden." [34]

It would have been difficult, if not impossible, Brandeis admitted, to apply this actual prudent investment principle when *Smyth* v. *Ames* was decided. Few, if anyone, could then have ascertained what it cost in money to establish the utility; or what income had been earned by it; or how the income had been expended. By 1923 the situation was greatly altered. "These amounts are now readily ascertainable in respect to a large and rapidly increasing proportion of the utilities. . . . It is, therefore, feasible now to adopt, as the measure of a compensatory rate, the annual cost, or charge, of the capital prudently invested in the utility. And, hence, it should be done." [35] Regulated accounting had done its work.

Much dicta in Justice McReynold's majority opinion in the Southwestern Bell case made strongly for the reproduction cost theory. But the rates there involved were so inadequate that they did not bring a fair return even on the actual cost of the properties, much less on the reproduction cost. Therefore Brandeis concurred in reversing the state court. He joined in declaring the rates confiscatory, but did so because they did not bring a fair return on the actual investment.

The same observations may be made with reference to the Bluefield case, where the rates were also held confiscatory. Again the Court, speaking this time through Justice Butler, used dicta which indicated a leaning toward reproduction cost. And again Brandeis concurred, because the rates did not yield a fair return on the actual investment. As in the Southwestern Telephone case, he concurred in the decision, but not in the dicta favoring the reproduction cost principle.[36]

In the similar case of the Georgia Railway & Power Company, also decided in 1923, Brandeis spoke for the Court. The rates fixed were upheld because they yielded a fair return on actual investment of about $7\frac{1}{4}$ per cent though only 4 per cent on reproduction cost.[37]

The Court's decided preference for the reproduction cost theory was shown three years later in Justice Butler's opinion in the Indianapolis Water Company case, and evoked from Brandeis a flat denial that the Court had made any statement to the effect "that value is tantamount to reproduction cost." Again stressing the impracticability of this principle, he observed that it would be impossible even for experts, much less Supreme Court Justices, to make any accurate determination of such cost "without the aid of Aladdin's lamp." [38]

THE INTRICATE PROBLEM OF DEPRECIATION

The rate base problem was considered from a new angle—that of depreciation—in the Baltimore Street Railways case. But the Court's line-up was the same. Here the Maryland Public Service Commission, in fixing the rates of fare, agreed that depreciation should be reckoned on the cost of the thing depreciated and not on its present value, but the Maryland Court of Appeals held this erroneous, contending that depreciation should have been reckoned on present value. This decision the Supreme Court upheld as "plainly right." "It is the settled rule of this Court that the rate base is present value, and it would be wholly illogical to adopt a different rule for depreciation."

Brandeis again made vigorous dissent. He could not concur, as in earlier cases, because the rate was so clearly non-confiscatory. "A net return of 6.26 per cent," he said, "upon the present value of the property of a street railway enjoying a monopoly in one of the oldest, largest, and richest cities on the Atlantic seaboard would seem to be compensatory.

"Acceptance of the doctrine of *Smyth* v. *Ames*," he argued, "does not require that the depreciation charge be based on present value of plant. For an annual depreciation charge is not a measure of the actual consumption of plant during the year. No such measure has yet been invented. There is no regularity in the development of depreciation. It does not proceed in accordance with any mathematical law. There is nothing in business experience, or in the training of experts, which enables man to say to what extent service life will be impaired by the operations of a single year, or of a series of years less than the service life." [39]

Brandeis's study of the economics of insurance had shown him how legal science could solve this intricate problem. "The depreciation charge is frequently likened to the annual premium in legal reserve life insurance," he pointed out. "The life insurance premium is calculated on an agreed value of the human life—comparable to the known cost of plant—not on a fluctuating value, unknown and unknowable. . . . Because every attempt to approximate more nearly the amount of premium required proved futile, justice was sought and found in the system of strictly mutual insurance. Under that system the premium charged is made clearly ample; and the part which proves not to have been needed inures in some form of benefit to him who paid it.

"Similarly," he continued, "if, instead of applying the rules of *Smyth* v. *Ames,* the rate base of a utility were fixed at the amount prudently invested, the inevitable errors incident to estimating service life and net expense in plant consumption could never result in injustice either to the utility or to the community." [40]

His claim that the depreciation charge should be based upon the cost of property rather than upon present value, rested upon experience as well as reason. This method had been adopted by the United States Chamber of Commerce; it was the practice of public accountants and was supported by leading business institutions. It conformed to the policy of public utility commissions. In confirmation of all this Brandeis cited references to hundreds of authorities—studies in economics and in political science, studies as to the practice of administrative bodies and private corporations, works on accountancy, and more. All pointed to the conclusion that any effort to apply reproduction cost or present value was fairly certain, through the fluctuation of values, to operate at one period against the public and in favor of the utilities, and at a later period against the utilities and in favor of the public. Only by adopting actual cost and prudent investment could these difficulties be avoided.

These intra-Court squabbles, however important in law and economics, were of such technical nature as to go unnoticed by the average citizen. It was not until the famous O'Fallon Railway case that the issue came conspicuously to public attention. Under the provisions of the Transportation Act of 1920, railroads earning more than 6 per cent of their valuation were required to pay half the excess into a fund administered by the I.C.C. for the benefit of less prosperous roads. Administration of this provision involved the whole problem of rate base determination, but the act itself furnished no clear guide. The famous Section 15a merely directed the Commission to give due consideration to all the elements of value recognized by the law of the land for rate-making purposes—a formula hardly more definite than that enunciated in *Smyth* v. *Ames*. The Commission was also divided, very much as the Supreme Court had been. A majority found that "the value of the property of railroads for rate-making purposes . . . approaches more nearly the reasonable and necessary investment in property than the cost of reproducing it at a particular time." [41] The O'Fallon railroad experts disagreed; so did a majority of the Supreme Court. Relying on the reproduction cost rule adopted by a minority of the I.C.C., the road insisted that income in excess of 6 per cent had not been earned and therefore refused to contribute to the I.C.C. fund.

Justice McReynolds, speaking for the Court, followed the I.C.C. minority, ruling that sufficient weight had not been given the principle of reproduction cost. Brandeis's dissent is among the most masterful opinions of his career. The rate-making problem in all its intricate aspects is disentangled and clarified by a veritable *tour de force* which is said to have gone through more than a score of revisions. He showed once more, and in greater detail, the practical difficulties of applying the rule of reproduction new. "The Commission was clearly authorized," he contended, "to determine for itself to what extent, if any, weight should be given to the evidence; and its findings should not be disturbed by the Court, unless it appears that there was an abuse of discretion." [42]

His protest was of no avail. The Court had chosen in this instance to follow its other expert, Mr. Justice Butler. Eventually, on major aspects of trade unionism and public utilities control, Brandeis's minority view came to be the law of the land. For the time being, however, he had to find satisfaction in Lord Morley's maxim—"the history of the world is the history of minorities."

CHAPTER THIRTY-FIVE

This Tangled Web of Freedom

IN MIDDLE life Brandeis was strongly impressed by man's growing dependence and interdependence. Industrialism had cut men off from the eighteenth century. The stress formerly laid on the innate rights of man was outmoded. We must go forward, he insisted, to a new order with individual rights and social relations harmonized by trade unions, cooperatives, and government. Individualism and its values were indispensable but the advance of technology and mass production demanded closer governing, greater social control, if liberty was to have any meaning for mankind. The continuing problem to him was how best to adapt institutions and laws to the machine age, while yet retaining the human–economic values of applied science, laissez faire, and individualism.

The web of freedom is tangled. Men are not necessarily made free when immune from rule; nor does freedom spring full grown when the state protects the poor against the rich. The life of freedom is self-wrought, not conferred; it can be aided by many social agencies—all functioning as means and never as ends. "I have just run across the following from Goethe," he wrote Norman Hapgood, November 27, 1927: *"Alles was unsern geist befreit ohne uns die Herrschaft über uns selbst zu geben, ist verderblich."* *

In every institution, every device, in man himself, lurks a diabolical taint. Legislature, trade union, court, corporation, may serve either to liberalize or to enslave. The problem is not merely drawing the line, in general, between political power and economic power. It is the more complicated one of delimitation as between the main forms of economic and political power. At what point does the right of a businessman to conduct his own affairs as he sees fit encroach upon the right of his workers to organize and, through their combined activity, forcibly to extend their own power and control into the employer's business? In conflict should the court take sides through a writ of injunction? Is the injunction itself so essential to the protection of property as to be immune from legislative control and regulation?

There is the further problem of marking barriers between the federal government and the states, between many levels, departments, and agencies of government. No geologic fault-line yawns where state power begins and federal power ends, or fences off Executive from Senate, or hems in

---

* "Everything which frees our spirit without giving us control over ourselves is fatal."

judges who, ignoring their self-restraint, maximize their power to that of a super-legislature.

Conservatives settled these questions by mental prepossessions and reached an easy solution by rule-of-thumb. Eighteenth-century fictions—natural law, natural rights, liberty of contract—gave a ready measure and one easy to apply. This was true, perhaps, even of a liberal Justice such as Holmes. For him the Constitution embodied no particular economic theory; and he himself claimed not to know what was "right." As a naturalist he conceded the strongest power its way, whether that power was economic or political. The problem was more difficult for Brandeis, who saw liberty imperiled on all sides and looked for some more certain test to guide judges in determining constitutional limits of freedom as government extended its power into ever-widening fields.

THE JUDICIAL PRESUMPTION OF FREEDOM

Brandeis's first rule for adjudication was the presumption of constitutionality. The legislature, with better facilities for finding and weighing the facts, must be presumed to have acted within permissible constitutional bounds. Whether it had or had not done so could not be determined by assumptions or by a priori reasoning. Sound judgment must be based on considerations of relevant facts, actual or possible—*ex facto jus oritur.* "That ancient rule," he insisted, "must prevail in order that we may have a system of living law." [1]

When Brandeis spoke for the Court he was content to rely, if he favored the legislation, on the rule of constitutional presumption. If he led the Court in setting aside legislation, judicial precedents were usually available to serve the purpose. In dissent he used masses of lethal facts to smash what he held were but fictions and obsolete judicial assumptions. He deplored the prevalent fashion among lawyers and judges to invoke eighteenth-century conceptual absolutes, such as liberty of contract, to block legislative efforts in correcting the abuses of industrialism, the excesses of capitalism. Whether a law is unreasonable or arbitrary could not, he contended, be determined by examining legal precedents. Nor would the test of "common knowledge," or what a "reasonable man" considers necessary to promote the general welfare, be a safe guide. "Time and change happeneth to them all."

Nothing was clearer to Justice Brandeis than that hotly controverted social and economic policy can be fairly and equitably decided only with the help of accumulated empirical data, "only by a consideration of the contemporary conditions, social, industrial and political, of the community to be affected thereby. . . . Resort to such facts is necessary, among other things, in order to appreciate the evils sought to be remedied and the possible effects of the remedy proposed." And "since government is not an exact science, prevailing public opinion concerning the evil and the remedy is among the important facts deserving consideration." [2] Brandeis, as well as Holmes, paid some deference to what "the crowd wants."

In the expanding scope of regulation so characteristic of modern society, many agencies take part—the voluntary association, the administrative commission, the legislature, and the judiciary. Brandeis assigned the latter a relatively narrow function, particularly in reviewing evidence in anti-trust and rate cases. Thus, when in 1920 the Justices affirmed the judgment of a Circuit Court, annulling an order of the Federal Trade Commission that the offending company desist from imposing upon purchasers the so-called "tying clause," he protested.

"The proceeding is . . . a novelty," he explained. "It is a new device in administrative machinery, introduced by Congress in the year 1914, in the hope thereby of remedying conditions in business which a great majority of the American people regarded as menacing the general welfare and which for more than a generation they had vainly attempted to remedy by the ordinary processes of law. . . .

"Instead of undertaking to define what practices should be deemed unfair, as had been done in earlier legislation, the act left the determination to the Commission. . . . Recognizing that the question whether a method of competitive practice was unfair would ordinarily depend upon special facts, Congress imposed upon the Commission the duty of finding the facts; and it declared that findings of fact so made (if duly supported by evidence) were to be taken as final." [3]

Sixteen years later in a concurring opinion Brandeis protested against judicial review of evidence in a stock yards rate case, arguing that such action would redound to the disadvantage of both administrative bodies and the courts. "Responsibility is the great developer of men," he said, resorting to an old theme. "May it not tend to emasculate or demoralize the rate-making body if ultimate responsibility is transferred to others? To the capacity of men there is a limit. May it not impair the quality of the work of the courts if this heavy task of reviewing questions of fact is assumed?" [4]

He usually insisted that the Court confine its functions and jurisdiction to tasks it could perform intelligently and effectively. Even if the Court entertained doubt as to whether a particular remedy was the best; even if it had reason to believe that the measure might lead to other evils, the Court must not interfere provided the act was of a character that might conceivably "produce results sought to be obtained."

The legislature must, he often said, be given latitude in experimentation: "Put at its highest, our function is to determine, in the light of all facts which may enrich our knowledge and enlarge our understanding, whether the measure, enacted in the exercise of an unquestioned police power and of a character inherently unobjectionable, transcends the bounds of reason. That is, whether the provision, as applied, is so clearly arbitrary or capricious that legislators, acting reasonably, could not have believed it to be necessary or appropriate for the public welfare." [5]

SMALL VERSUS LARGE UNITS

The political liberty and legal equality which eighteenth-century liberals prized are still important; but amid industrial giants, wielding power over small competitors, employees, and consumers, liberty becomes vacuous unless men are free in both industry and finance. Despite various legislative restrictions, business corporations have come through size to dominate the state itself. That is why as a Supreme Court Justice, Brandeis consistently exhibited sympathy for organized labor. He saw the trade union not only as essential to the workers' freedom, but also as a bulwark against overweening industrial power. For the same reasons he favored cooperatives among farmers, consumers, and small businessmen and placed great stress on voluntary co-operation and self-help. These methods could bring men closer to freedom's goal.

Although he spurned various forms of statism advanced under the guise of liberalism, he conceded that government may have to aid individual and group effort if the people are to be saved from enslavement "by the most amazing plutocracy that the world has ever seen." [6] Government must intervene to reduce the size and curb the power of large business combinations and to maintain fair competition among small business units. Some years before 1916 he saw that "the displacement of the small independent businessman by the huge corporation with its myriad of employees, its absentee ownership, and its financier control, presents a grave danger to our democracy. The social loss is great, and there is no economic gain." [7]

His preference for small co-operating business units as against the crushing power of combined capital was shown in the Quaker City Cab case. The Philadelphia Cab Corporation objected to a Pennsylvania statute that placed a relatively heavier tax burden on it than on competitors operating as individuals and partnerships. Speaking for the Court in a 6 to 3 decision, Justice Butler declared the statute unconstitutional under the equal protection clause. The difference between individuals and partnerships on the one hand, and corporations on the other, did not furnish such "a real and substantial difference" as to justify classification for tax purposes.

Brandeis dissented, saying: "In Pennsylvania the practice of imposing heavier burdens upon corporations dates from a time when there, as elsewhere in America, the fear of growing corporate power was common. The present heavier imposition may be a survival of an earlier effort to discourage the resort to that form of organization. The apprehension is now less common. But there are still intelligent, informed, just-minded, and civilized persons who believe that the rapidly growing aggregation of capital through corporations constitutes an insidious menace to the liberty of the citizen . . . that the evils incident to the accelerating absorption of business by corporations outweigh the benefits thereby secured; and that the process of absorption should be retarded. The Court may think such views unsound. But obviously the requirement that a classification must be reasonable does not imply that the policy embodied in the classification made by the legislature of a state shall seem to this Court a wise one." [8]

STATE RIGHTS

Brandeis's tendency to interpret government regulation of trusts, railroads, and public utilities not as infringements on liberty but rather as protection against such infringements, did not always predetermine his stand. He supported Taft in setting aside the federal tax designed to curb child labor. Having failed to destroy this traffic in human lives by means of the Commerce power,[9] Congress sought to achieve the same purpose by imposing a tax so oppressive as to make employment of children highly unprofitable. This was not a tax, the Chief Justice said, but a penalty. It was a disingenuous attempt by Congress to achieve control indirectly over subject matter reserved by the Constitution to the states. "To give such magic to the word 'tax' would . . . break down all constitutional limitation of the powers of Congress and completely wipe out the sovereignty of the states." [10]

These words struck responsive chords for the apostle of localism. "Perhaps it will be recognized someday as the beginning of an epoch, the epoch of State Duties," Brandeis commented in passing Taft's opinion along to Norman Hapgood. "State Rights succumbed to the Rights of Nations. State Duties were ignored and state functions atrophied. The extremes of concentration are proving its failure to the common man. . . . The new Progressivism requires local development—quality not quantity." [11] Here Brandeis foreshadowed sharp differences of later years with the New Dealers whose headlong drive for national power threatened, he believed, to destroy one of the great bulwarks of liberty—federalism.

SEPARATION OF POWERS

Taft and Brandeis disagreed in 1926 when the Court came to consider the problem closest to Taft's heart—executive power. The case grew out of a suit brought by a postmaster to recover salary claimed after he had been removed by the President before the end of the term for which he was appointed. The postmaster based his case on a statute which required that the Senate give its advice and consent to Presidential removal of certain inferior officers. The President had not done this, and government counsel contended that the removal of officers, such as postmasters, was a part of the President's executive power which even Congress could not enable the Senate to share. Chief Justice Taft, speaking for the Court, upheld the government's contention. His own experience as Chief Executive had naturally impressed him with the necessity of broad Presidential power commensurate with great responsibility. Without such power, the President cannot, he argued, discharge the duties of his office with dispatch and efficiency. To achieve this he boldly assumed that the President must have complete power of removal, even though Congress alone, under the Constitution, has power to create offices. In effect the Chief Justice's opinion rendered "all executive or administrative officers of the United States removable by the President at will." [12]

Taft had spent more than a year on this opinion, and when Brandeis riddled the crowning achievement of Taft's judicial career with shafts of criticism, the Chief Justice was outraged: "Brandeis puts himself where he naturally belongs. . . . He is opposed to a strong Executive. He loves the veto of the group upon effective legislation or effective administration. He loves the kicker, and is therefore in sympathy with the power of the Senate to prevent the Executive from removing obnoxious persons, because he always sympathizes with the obnoxious person." [13]

Brandeis's reasons for dissenting bear not the slightest resemblance to those stated by Taft. His purpose was corrective and instructive. He denied Taft's assumption of "an uncontrollable power of removal in the Chief Executive" and amassed historical and documentary material that repudiated Taft's ruling as at war with our most basic political principle. "The doctrine of the separation of powers was adopted by the Convention of 1787," he said, "not to promote efficiency but to preclude the exercise of arbitrary power. The purpose was not to avoid friction, but, by means of the inevitable friction incident to the distribution of the governmental powers among three departments, to save the people from autocracy. . . . In America, as in England, the conviction prevailed then [1787] that the people must look to representative assemblies for the protection of their liberties. And protection of the individual, even if he be an official, from the arbitrary or capricious exercise of power was then believed to be an essential of free government." [14]

Brandeis's purpose in writing his elaborate dissent was not, as Taft asserted, "to stir up dissatisfaction," but rather as he himself said, "to stir interest in political science." [15] And in this he was not disappointed. Authors immediately began publishing articles and books canvassing the entire subject of the President's removal power. It was soon evident that Taft's *tour de force* had not settled anything. Scholars berated the Chief Justice's history, logic, and law. Like Justice Holmes, they likened his argument to "spiders' webs inadequate to control the dominant facts." [16]

The scholarship which Brandeis's dissent helped stimulate bore fruit some years later when President Franklin D. Roosevelt, relying on Taft's broad conception of the President's removal power, summarily ousted Federal Trade Commissioner William E. Humphrey. But a unanimous Supreme Court, relying on the materials amassed by Justice Brandeis and others, held otherwise, confining the President's removal power to purely executive officers.[17] Brandeis's criticism of Taft's broad conception of Executive power had thus resulted in "increasing the appointing power of heads of departments and commissions and raising them from their pitiable positions of chief clerks." [18]

RATIONALIZING COMPETITION TO ENLARGE FREEDOM

While some observers saw in certain of Brandeis's opinions an element of collectivism not far removed from alien doctrines, others were confused when he looked with favor on business arrangements regulating competition. His endorsement of the economic policy embodied in the Sherman Act never committed him to such strict interpretation as would prevent businessmen from rationalizing competition. "The Sherman Law," he asserted, "does not prohibit every lessening of competition; and it certainly does not command that competition shall be pursued blindly, that business rivals shall remain ignorant of trade facts, or be denied aid in weighing their significance." [19] Just as the trade union was a necessity in securing higher wages, shorter hours, and better working conditions, so the trade association was for him commendable in its field.

In the American Lumber case (1921), an association of some four hundred producers was responsible for about 30 per cent of the annual production of hardwood lumber in the country. A large majority of these firms agreed to send to their association's manager of statistics, information on sales, production, and stock at hand. When the manager advised the members to curtail production, prices rose considerably. The Court held that since "the united action of this large and influential membership of dealers contributed greatly to the extraordinary price increase," it contravened the anti-trust laws. Brandeis, however, saw in this open competition plan enormous possibilities for improving conditions in the industry. He also feared that judicial frustration of this association among producers might lead to consolidation and monopoly. It seemed that the Sherman Act (originally intended to secure free competition) had become an instrument by which to destroy the small competitor or force him into the arms of monopoly, and to this he objected:

"The co-operation which is incident to this plan [open competition] does not suppress competition. On the contrary, it tends to promote all in competition which is desirable. By substituting knowledge for ignorance, rumor, guess, and suspicion, it tends also to substitute research and reasoning for gambling and piracy, without closing the door to adventure, or lessening the value of prophetic wisdom. In making such knowledge available to the smallest concern it creates among producers equality of opportunity. In making it available to purchasers and the general public, it does all that can actually be done to protect the community from extortion. . . . The evidence in this case, far from establishing an illegal restraint of trade, presents, in my opinion, an instance of commendable effort by concerns engaged in chaotic industry, to make possible its intelligent conduct under competitive conditions." [20]

FREEDOM OF SPEECH AND THE PRESS

It was one thing for the legislature to expose employers to "coercive" unionist activities by limiting the use of injunctions or to interfere with individual liberty by abolishing the yellow-dog contract or to approve a relatively heavier tax for corporations than for partnership and individual enterprise; it was something else when government restricted man's freedom of thought, speech, and press.

In 1920 the Court invoked the Federal Espionage Act of 1917 to curb those publishing statements alleged to interfere with prosecution of the war. The defendants were convicted for publishing in German, articles contemptuous of our war activities and intended to hint that the war had resulted from machinations of the President. For Justice McKenna the case afforded the curious spectacle of enemies taking shelter under "that great ordinance of government and orderly liberty . . . to justify the activities of anarchy. . . ." [21] But for Justices Holmes and Brandeis the case was not so simple. If, under legislation regulating the labor contract, their argument ran, freedom is the rule and regulation the exception, why do not the same principles apply to limitations on speech and press?

In an earlier case the Court had upheld a jail sentence against a Russian-born American for saying, among other things, that it was a crime for American workers to "fight the Workers' Republic of Russia." [22] "The prevailing notion of free speech" Holmes had explained, "seems to be that you may say what you choose if you don't shock *me*." [23] It was, to say the least, an unsatisfactory judicial test of liberty. Worse still, to Holmes's mind, it lost sight of values for which our forefathers fought and died. Holmes and Brandeis therefore worked out another criterion: "The question in every case is whether the words used are used in such circumstances and are of such a nature as to create a clear and present danger that they will bring about the substantive evils that Congress has a right to prevent." [24]

Brandeis applied this formula in the 1920 case. He could not see how any jury, "acting in calmness, could reasonably say that any of the publications set forth in the indictment were of such a character or were made under such circumstances as to create a clear and present danger, that they would obstruct recruiting, or that they would promote the success of enemies of the United States. . . . Men may differ widely as to what loyalty to our country demands; and an intolerant majority, swayed by passion or by fear, may be prone in the future, as it has often been in the past, to stamp as disloyal opinions with which it disagrees." [25] Surely in this realm of rational differences of opinion, freedom is the rule, regulation the exception.

The Federal Espionage Act was also used against socialists for distributing sample copies of a four-page leaflet entitled "The Price We Pay," written by an Episcopal clergyman, Irwin St. John Tucker. The offending distributors testified that their only purpose was to advance the cause of socialism. Brandeis considered that the tenor of the leaflet indicated this as the sole aim. In any event, its distribution did not, he held, "create a clear and present danger" to the effective operations of our military and naval forces. What to Justice Pitney was a "highly colored and sensational document" intended "to hamper the government in the prosecution of the war," was to Brandeis a more or less harmless discussion of the causes of war. He admitted that the leaflet contained "lurid and perhaps exaggerated pictures of the horrors of war," that its arguments might appear "shallow and grossly unfair," and the remedy proposed "worse than the evil"; but, he said, our scholars and historians seldom agree as to what constitutes the determining factor in a particular war. Historians, like judges, "attach significance to those things which are significant to them." That is why contributing causes "cannot be subjected, like a chemical combination in a test tube, to qualitative and quantitative analysis so as to weigh and value the various elements. . . . Mr. Wilson, himself a historian," Brandeis went on, had used words "before he was President" that smacked strongly of radicalism. "The masters of the government of the United States," Wilson had written in *The New Freedom*, "are the combined capitalists and manufacturers of the United States." [26]

The lesson Brandeis deduced from all this is that truth in the social sciences, no less than in the natural sciences, depends on freedom to think, write, and speak, and, above all, on the right to differ: "The fundamental right of free men to strive for better conditions through new legislation and new institutions will not be preserved, if efforts to secure it by argument to fellow citizens may be construed as criminal incitement to disobey the existing law—merely because the argument presented seems to those exercising judicial power to be unfair in its portrayal of existing evils, mistaken in its assumptions, unsound in reasoning, or intemperate in language. No objections more serious than these can, in my opinion, reasonably be made to the arguments presented in 'The Price We Pay.' " [27]

Brandeis again sprang to the defense of civil rights when Postmaster-General Burleson, under the Espionage Act, revoked the *Milwaukee Leader's* second-class mail privilege. The Court, speaking through Justice Clarke, found no objection to the Postmaster-General's order. There was still available to the *Milwaukee Leader,* the Court reasoned, other classes of mail, and if these were found financially burdensome, the editor could mend his ways to conform to the Postmaster-General's views. To Brandeis such an argument was fatuous; it conceded to an administrative officer discretionary power alien to democratic principles.

The Postmaster-General based his authority to revoke the *Milwaukee Leader's* second-class mail rate on the Mail Classification Act of 1879, which required that a newspaper, to be mailable at the second-class rates, "must be regularly issued at stated intervals as frequently as four times a year. . . ." Inasmuch as the subject matter of the *Milwaukee Leader* contained matter violative of the Espionage Act of 1917, the paper was not, according to the Postmaster-General, "regularly issued."

"The argument," Brandeis observed, "is obviously unsound. The requirement that the newspaper be 'regularly issued' refers, not to the propriety of the reading matter, but to the fact that publication periodically at stated intervals must be intended, and that the intention must be carried out." Brandeis denounced the order revoking entry of the *Milwaukee Leader* to second-class mail as "punitive, not a preventative measure," as a bold reach for power under an act which neither involved nor permitted the exercise of discretionary power. "If, under the Constitution," Brandeis concluded, "administrative officers may, as a mere incident of the peacetime administration of their departments, be vested with the power to issue such orders as this, there is little of substance in our Bill of Rights, and in every extension of governmental functions lurks a new danger to civil liberty." [28]

Anxiety lest radical thought and belief somehow hamper effective prosecution of the war drove the State of Minnesota to even more drastic restrictions. An Act of April 1917 prohibited the teaching of pacifism, not merely as a war emergency but for all time and under all circumstances. Its purpose was to prevent not acts but beliefs. Joseph Gilbert of the Non-Partisan League was sentenced under this act to fine and imprisonment for speaking at a public meeting. "Every word that he [Gilbert] uttered in denunciation of the war was false," Justice McKenna declared. The act was justified, he held, as "a simple exertion of the police power to preserve the peace of the state." In courageous defiance of Voltaire and John Stuart Mill, McKenna again ruled against the curious spectacle of the Constitution being used "to justify the activities of anarchy or of the enemies of the United States." [29]

Brandeis, on the other hand, found the Minnesota statute "inconsistent with the conceptions of liberty hitherto prevailing. . . . The statute invades the privacy and freedom of the home. Father and mother may not follow the promptings of religious belief, of conscience or of conviction, and teach son or daughter the doctrine of pacifism." To him wrong was done to society as well as to the individual. "Full and free exercise of this right by the citizen is ordinarily also his duty," Brandeis observed, "for its exercise is more important to the nation than it is to himself. Like the course of the heavenly bodies, harmony in national life is a resultant of the struggle between contending forces. In frank expression of conflicting opinion lies the greatest promise of wisdom in governmental action; and in suppression lies ordinarily the greatest peril." [30]

Brandeis pointedly called attention to the zeal with which the Court, often against his protest, had invoked the Constitution to strike down legislation regulating property and contract: "I have difficulty," he said with a trace of sarcasm, "in believing that the liberty guaranteed by the Constitution, which has been held to protect against state denial the right of an employer to discriminate against a workman because he is a member of a trade union, the right of a businessman to conduct a private employment agency . . . although the legislature deems it inimical to the public welfare, does not include liberty to teach, either in the privacy of the home or publicly, the doctrine of pacifism. . . . I cannot believe that the liberty guaranteed by the Fourteenth Amendment includes only liberty to acquire and to enjoy property." [31]

THE BURNING FAITH OF FREEDOM

In 1919 Anita Whitney, a member of the Communist Labor party, convicted and sentenced under California's Criminal Syndicalism Act, appealed to the United States Supreme Court. Miss Whitney had not, as she might have done, raised the question whether there was in fact a "clear and present danger" manifest in her acts. She claimed only that the criminal syndicalism statute violated the Constitution. The Justices rejected her plea and confirmed the state court's sentence. Concurring in the result, Brandeis took occasion to summarize in undying words the sanctity of the constitutional protection afforded freedom of press and speech:

"Those who won our independence believed that the final end of the state was to make men free to develop their faculties; and that in its government the deliberative forces should prevail over the arbitrary. They valued liberty both as an end and as a means. They believed liberty to be the secret of happiness and courage to be the secret of liberty. They believed that freedom to think as you will and to speak as you think are means indispensable to the discovery and spread of political truth; that without free speech and assembly discussion would be futile; that with them, discussion affords ordinarily adequate protection against the dissemination of noxious doctrine; that the greatest menace to freedom is an inert people; that public discussion is a political duty; and that this should be a fundamental principle of the American government. They recognized the risks to which all human institutions are subject. But they knew that order cannot be secured merely through fear of punishment for its infraction; that it is hazardous to discourage thought, hope, and imagination; that fear breeds repression; that repression breeds hate; that hate menaces stable government; that the path of safety lies in the opportunity to discuss freely supposed grievances and proposed remedies; and that the fitting remedy for evil counsels is good ones. Believing in the power of reason as applied through public discussion, they eschewed silence coerced by law—the argument of force in its worst form. Recognizing the occasional tyrannies of governing majorities, they amended the Constitution so that free speech and assembly should be guaranteed.

"Fear of serious injury," the Justice continued, "cannot alone justify suppression of free speech and assembly. Men feared witches and burned women. It is the function of speech to free men from the bondage of irrational fears. To justify suppression of free speech there must be reasonable ground to fear that serious evil will result if free speech is practiced. There must be reasonable ground to believe that the danger apprehended is imminent. There must be reasonable ground to believe that the evil to be prevented is a serious one. . . .

"Those who won our independence by revolution," the opinion concludes, "were not cowards. They did not fear political change. They did not exalt order at the cost of liberty. To courageous, self-reliant men, with confidence in the power of free and fearless reasoning applied through the processes of popular government, no danger flowing from speech can be deemed clear and present, unless the incidence of the evil apprehended is so imminent that it may befall before there is opportunity for full discussion. If there be time to expose through discussion the falsehood and fallacies, to avert the evil by the processes of education, the remedy to be applied is more speech, not enforced silence. Only an emergency can justify repression. Such must be the rule if authority is to be reconciled with freedom. Such, in my opinion, is the command of the Constitution." [32]

Justice Brandeis's writing seldom rose to such a pitch of eloquence. Here, surely, one finds in his judicial prose that quality which has been described as "an earthly majesty which springs always from the ground but still reaches outward to the stars." [33]

THE PROPHET STUMBLES

Brandeis stood firm for the ancient liberty comprised in freedom of belief, thought, and discussion. But when he came to consider certain prescriptions "by men of zeal, well-meaning but without understanding," such as the Volstead Act, he was less alert to the invasion of liberty. When confronted with the "experiment noble in motive," the support he had given pacifists, socialists, and other radicals banned by regulatory legislation, was not forthcoming.

In the case permitting the federal government to close breweries and distilleries without any compensation whatever to the owners, he delivered the opinion of the Court. [34] It was Justice Brandeis who held that one conviction for possessing liquor and another conviction for selling the same liquor did not violate the constitutional protection against double jeopardy; [35] he upheld the government's right to confiscate an innocent owner's motorcar simply because a guest-passenger had a small flask of whisky on his person; [36] and he sustained that section of the Volstead Act which prohibited, *inter allia*, physicians from prescribing more than one pint of liquor to the same patient within a period of ten days. [37]

One sees in these cases evidence of paternalism in the moral sphere, and one may wonder if he had forgotten his own warning: ". . . In every extension of governmental functions lurks a new danger to civil liberty." [38]

Nor can these cases be explained away by pointing out that they all involved statutory interpretation only and did not necessarily reflect the Justice's opinion of the wisdom of the Eighteenth Amendment and Volstead Act in terms of public policy.

Brandeis is on record as opposed to repeal. In 1923, at the request of President Wilson, he had prepared a memorandum stating his views in detail: "The Eighteenth Amendment made prohibition the law of the nation. The Volstead Act prescribed for the nation what liquor should be deemed intoxicating. The intention was that each government [federal and state] should perform that part of the task for which it is peculiarly fitted. . . . To relieve the states from the duty of performing [their tasks] violates our traditions; and threatens the best interests of our country. The strength of the nation and its capacity for achievement is, in large measure, due to the federal system with its distribution of powers and duties. . . . But the Eighteenth Amendment should remain unchanged. And the Volstead Act should remain unchanged."

In this statement involving "moral" issues Brandeis took a stand strangely out of key with his customary liberalism. The contrast is even more puzzling in view of his realistic insight into prohibition in 1891. Then he had recognized that "liquor drinking is not wrong, that no regulation can be enforced which is not reasonable." It was not until enforcement of the Volstead Act involved what to him were the more precious rights of privacy and free speech that he protested.

MORAL STANDARDS FOR DOMINANT POWER

The antithetical values Brandeis placed on the right to drink as against the right to privacy were shown when federal agents tapped the telephone wires of men suspected of conspiring to violate the Volstead Act. On the basis of evidence thus obtained the Court sustained the convictions by a 5 to 4 vote. Brandeis's stand had been evidenced earlier in 1928 when the Court sustained convictions in violation of the Harrison Anti-Narcotic Law, against Brandeis's protest that the evidence was inadmissible in that federal agents had themselves induced the violation. Holmes, speaking for the Court, said: "We are not persuaded that the conduct of the officials was different from, or worse than, ordering a drink of a suspected bootlegger." [39]

Brandeis, however, saw the indictment as involving a principle of first importance: "I am aware that courts—mistaking relative social values, and forgetting that a desirable end cannot justify foul means—have, in their zeal to punish, sanctioned the use of evidence obtained through criminal violation of property and personal rights or by other practices of detectives even more revolting. But the objection here is of a different nature. . . . The government may set decoys to entrap criminals. But it may not provoke or create a crime, and then punish the criminal, its creature." [40]

In the famous wire-tapping case Chief Justice Taft, delivering the opinion, overruled the defendants' claim that the evidence obtained when government agents tapped their telephone wires violated either unreasonable searches and seizures or the constitutional protection against self-incrimination. No tapped wires entered their homes and offices, Taft reasoned, so there was neither search nor seizure.

For Justice Brandeis such a narrow construction degraded our great charter of freedom to the level of a municipal ordinance. Quoting Chief Justice Marshall's famous admonition—"We must never forget that it is a Constitution we are expounding"—he pointed out that just as the power of Congress had by judicial interpretation been kept abreast of scientific progress, and extended the Fundamental Law to objects of which the Founding Fathers never dreamed, so also must the judges in construing limitations on the powers of Congress be ever-mindful of changes brought about by discovery and invention. To have a living Constitution, limitations on power no less than grants of power must be construed broadly. "Subtler and more far-reaching means of invading privacy have become available to the government," Brandeis observed. ". . . The progress of science in furnishing the government with means of espionage is not likely to stop with wire-tapping. Ways may some day be developed by which the government, without removing papers from secret drawers, can reproduce them in court, and by which it will be enabled to expose to a jury the most intimate occurrences of the home. . . .

"Our government is the potent, the omnipresent teacher. For good or ill, it teaches the whole people by example. Crime is contagious. If the government becomes a lawbreaker, it breeds contempt for law; it invites every man to become a law unto himself; it invites anarchy. To declare that in the administration of the criminal law the end justifies the means—to declare that the government may commit crimes in order to secure the conviction of a private criminal—would bring terrible retribution. . . .

"The makers of our Constitution undertook to secure conditions favorable to the pursuit of happiness," he emphasized. "They recognized the significance of man's spiritual nature, of his feelings and of his intellect. They knew that only a part of the pain, pleasure, and satisfactions of life are to be found in material things. They sought to protect Americans in their beliefs, their thoughts, their emotions, and their sensations. They conferred, as against the government, the right to be let alone—the most comprehensive of rights and the right most valued by civilized men. . . .

"Experience should teach us to be most on our guard to protect liberty when the government's purposes are beneficent. Men born to freedom are naturally alert to repel invasion of their liberty by evil-minded rulers. The greatest dangers to liberty lurk in insidious encroachment by men of zeal, well-meaning, but without understanding." [41]

Holmes, author of the majority opinion in the narcotics case, now, on Brandeis's insistence, wrote a dissent. "I should not have printed what I wrote," Holmes said, "if he [Brandeis] had not asked me to. . . . Brandeis wrote much more elaborately, but I didn't agree with all that he said." [42]

That the wire-tapping decision shocked Brandeis deeply is indicated by the fact that he broke his generally observed rule not to discuss Court affairs informally. When questioned about the case in 1931 he said: "One can never be sure of ends—political, social, economic. There must always be doubt and difference of opinion; one can be 51 per cent sure." There is not the same margin of doubt as to means. Here "fundamentals do not change; centuries of thought have established standards. Lying and sneaking are always bad, no matter what the ends." [43]

"I don't care about punishing crime," he remarked some years later to his niece, "but I am implacable in maintaining standards"—and that word, as we have seen, he used in the broadest sense. He championed as a moral standard the right of workers to unionize and fight for a larger stake in our industrial society, expanding that concept to include the civil liberties. But he did not consider the power wielded by organized men in exercise of their constitutional liberty unlimited.

To understand Brandeis's judicial contribution to the cause of freedom, each case has to be set in the factual context out of which it arose. For him there was no easy and absolute rule. The facts as he saw them forced him to insist that national power be strong enough to cope with truly national problems. Yet he valued the states as essential laboratories of democracy for sound economic experimentation. A man setting such great store by fact must necessarily assume beforehand that his fellow-men are reasonable and open to persuasion. This is the faith which echoes in his memorable dissents upholding liberty of opinion, of the press, and of speech.

CHAPTER THIRTY-SIX

Holmes and Brandeis Dissenting

"IN A few days," Holmes wrote Sir Frederick Pollock, October 21, 1926, "Brandeis who is next to me in age among the judges will be seventy. . . . I think he has done great work and I believe with high motives." [1]

After his first decade on the Court the phrase "Holmes and Brandeis dissenting" had become classic in the progressive fight to liberalize constitutional interpretation. In their work they usually reached the same goal, but they did not travel the same route. In fact, they differed singularly in technique and approach as well as in conception of the scope of judicial review.

THE TWO FRIENDS

Various factors had brought these "liberals" together as friends. They first met in 1879 through Brandeis's law-partner Samuel D. Warren, who had been for a while in Holmes's office. Brandeis and Warren were accustomed in those Boston days to meet Holmes at the Parker House for beer and talk. Later on when Holmes became an Associate Justice of the United States Supreme Court, occasional notes passed between them, and Brandeis called on the Holmeses in Washington from time to time. In early years on the Court they often walked together, and after Holmes became enfeebled by age they took short motor trips in Virginia. "But for all his philosophy," Brandeis commented in 1940, "Holmes worried." [2] Friendship of the younger man, himself free from worry, was a source of great comfort to Holmes.

Brandeis's letters to his wife often referred to hour or half-hour visits at the red brick house, 1720 I Street. There were opinions to talk over or Holmes wished to read one of his literary creations. "I have practiced solitude," Brandeis wrote his wife, February 4, 1923, "save for a call on Holmes this afternoon. He has finished for the printer his introduction to John Wigmore's book and wanted to read it to me." Brandeis was among the first to ride on Holmes's "beautiful elevator," an experience which reminded him of the "sacred precincts of a safe deposit vault."

A marked spirit of camaraderie pervaded Holmes's note written from the Corey Hill Hospital where he recuperated July 1922 from a serious operation. "Your letter went to my heart, and if the unforeseen does not cut in again, you and I will have another run together. I hope to be in shape by the beginning of the term, as usual, but can't be certain till the term comes. Meanwhile, I can't write, but my reading goes from Frost to Kipling. Nothing doing in things intellectual, but gratitude in those more complex matters with which latterly I have grown more familiar." [3]

As the Court became ever more reactionary in its decisions, Taft suspected Brandeis and Holmes of ganging up out of sheer deviltry, thus blighting the Chief Justice's ambition to "amass the Court" and avoid his pet aversion—the 5 to 4 decision. Taft was sure that Brandeis had gotten "the old gentleman" under his magnetic spell. "I think perhaps his age makes him a little more subordinate or yielding to Brandeis, who is his constant companion, than he would have been in his prime," Taft commented.[4] "He is so completely under the control of Brother Brandeis that it gives to Brandeis two votes instead of one." [5] No doubt Taft's habit of gossip and natural distrust of Brandeis's "radicalism" led him to exaggerate, but we do know from Brandeis's letters that on occasion he urged his elder brother to speak out in dissent. "I have interrupted myself at this point," Holmes commented in a letter to Pollock, November 3, 1923, "to consider a case which Brandeis wants me to be ready with a dissent, because it weighs on my mind, and so I am no longer the careless and happy boy that began this." [6] Thus by Brandeis's persistence the choice phrase, the priceless epigrams of Holmes in dissent, that might otherwise have been lost, were achieved for humanity. A shrewd friend has observed of Brandeis: "I wonder if even in his relations with Holmes he was not chiefly concerned with giving." [7]

Holmes himself may have been conscious of yielding somewhat to Brandeis's persuasive power. One notes a trace of pride, of independence reconquered in his comment to Pollock, February 17, 1928: "I am glad that he dissents from the only opinion [8] I have to deliver. It will indicate that there is no pre-established harmony between us." [9] Just as the Northern Securities case afforded him opportunity to assert his independence of T.R.,[10] so *Casey* v. *United States* provided an occasion to demonstrate his independence of his "upward and onward" brother on the bench.

Holmes was fifteen years older than Brandeis, but both had come to intellectual maturity in an age of cultural crudeness and political turmoil. Business enterprise was beginning to crystallize into a structure of corporate and supercorporate monopoly. Socialist and populist movements had their hour; labor awakened and organized. As popular sovereignty began to assert itself in legislation, lawyers and judges decisively interposed the Constitution, their Constitution, in support of their own social and economic predilections. Both Justices had been sensitively aware of these dynamic pressures and conflicts; but whereas Holmes (save for his timeless words in protest against cases "decided upon an economic theory") remained calm and unmoved, Brandeis became militant, emerging as the People's Attorney.

THE GULF BETWEEN

Holmes regarded neither the rise of business combination nor of trade unionism as unmitigated evil. For him, as for Darwin, struggle was the law of life. If allowed to go on unhindered, the best in politics, in ideas, in economics, as in life itself, would survive. Therefore, when lawyers and judges sought to block change, he branded them "simple-minded men," needing "education in the obvious." We too, he said, need to "transcend our own convictions," to leave room for much that "we hold dear to be done away with short of revolution by the orderly change of law." [11]

Holmes was fully as harsh in criticizing social reformers (a category in which he was rather too much inclined to include Brandeis [12]) who were sure that "wholesale social regeneration" would result from "tinkering with the institution of property. . . . The notion that with socialized property we should have women free and a piano for everybody seems to me an empty humbug." [13]

Holmes's liberalism might perhaps be described as aloof or detached— not in the sense of unawareness of the crucial social and economic struggles of his day but rather as denoting the deeply rooted naturalism that drove him to accept monopolies, trade unions, and legislation as part of the law of social organization, and of life itself. His oft professed humility would not allow him to take sides or to join with those whose passion for change was greater than his, or to agree with lawyers and judges who thought they could thwart change and thus maintain the status quo.

Holmes abjured any and all absolute values. "When I say that a thing is true, I mean," he observed, "that I can't help believing it. . . . I therefore define the truth as the system of my limitations and leave absolute truth for those who are better equipped." [14] Having himself no infallible measure of right and wrong, he upheld programs and policies in legislation even though he personally considered them in error or foolish. As he himself said, "I am so skeptical as to our knowledge about the goodness and badness of laws that I have no practical criterion except what the crowd wants. Personally I bet that the crowd if it knew more wouldn't want what it does—but that is immaterial." [15] One day a friend asked him if he had ever worked out any general philosophy to guide him in the exercise of the judicial function. "Yes," the aged jurist replied. "Long ago I decided that I was not God. When a state came in here and wanted to build a slaughter house, I looked at the Constitution and if I couldn't find anything in there that said a state couldn't build a slaughter house I said to myself, if they want to build a slaughter house, God-dammit, let them build it." [16]

Amid conflicting social forces Brandeis simply could not stand aloof. His uncanny knowledge that man's failure to solve today's problems accentuates and complicates the issues of tomorrow drove him on to take a resolute stand in favor of social control as against the anarchy of private economic power and greed. One with such knowledge and vision simply could not find ease in Holmes's citadel of "enlightened skepticism." [17] Brandeis was passionately convinced that it lay within the power of statesmanship to determine the course of our social development. He held with Holmes that the extension of social control was inevitable, but he knew also that men had the capacity to determine whether such changes were to be along lines of "evolution or of revolution." Failure to heed that responsibility promptly and effectively would, he was certain, seriously limit the alternatives open to statesmanship in the years ahead. Failure to curb the excesses of capitalism would not only insure more extensive and more arbitrary government control, but would in fact jeopardize the very existence of our much vaunted free enterprise.

Thus Brandeis differed fundamentally from both Holmes, the so-called liberal, and Taft, the ultraconservative. Holmes's keen perception of the absurdities and dangers of visionary social reform as well as those of blindly naïve opposition to change drove him to a position of detachment. Taft's lack of education in the obvious, his proved incompetence in dealing with complicated economic issues, his inability to allow that which he held dear to be altered or ended by orderly processes of law, prompted his futile effort to block change. He, unlike Holmes, had in his own mind a measure of truth, of right and wrong; it was absolute as only such abstractions can be; he could and did take sides with complete conviction, blithely unaware of Holmes's wise words: "To rest upon a formula is a slumber that, prolonged, means death." [18]

Brandeis also had a norm or standard to guide his action—knowledge of the conditions out of which modern legislation emerges. That is why his decisions and opinions are alive with deep conviction and carry much heavier wordage than those of Holmes. The latter might uphold state legislation which he detested for no better reason than his belief in the right of legislatures to carry on experiments within their states. Brandeis, on the other hand, while no less ardent in advocacy of legislative experimentation, might well uphold or set aside legislation depending on whether the statute conformed to certain standards of social justice established prima facie by the facts.

No one realized better than the dissenters themselves the chasm separating them. A basic difference as to the role of power in modern industrial society set them apart. Brandeis believed that unrestrained power, as such, and under whatever auspices, was a social menace. As organized and manipulated by monopoly management, it imperiled the rights of employees, entrepreneurs, and consumers; it rivaled and even surpassed the power of the state itself.

Surmising these differences between them, Holmes had written Brandeis as early as April 20, 1919:

Let me not be put in an attitude of opposition when I don't oppose. . . . I agree that wherever a great fortune produces an idler like the chap that shot Stanford White it produces an evil. But that does not seem to me more than an incident, dramatically impressive but not of the first or even great economic importance. The luxuries of the few I believe to be a drop in the bucket. The "sums withdrawn by Capital" that even such able men as Croly talk about seem to me merely the adjustments made by the most competent prophet to the anticipated equilibrium of social desires six months hence. They are not expenditures on luxuries, they are investments—intended to be the most profitable that can be got—and most profitable because they most nearly satisfy the consumer's demands. This adjustment would be as necessary under socialism as under any other system—otherwise the community gets less of what it wants. It never gets or can get as much as it wants. I believe that this man—the poor— now has substantially all there is. . . . Generally speaking I agree with you in liking to see social experiments tried, but I do so without enthusiasm because I believe that it is merely shifting the place of pressure and that so long as we have free propagation Malthus is right in his general view. All of which you know, but I like a moment of leisure to sing my old song over again. I believe it to be responsive in substance, although not so perhaps in form.

Yours ever,

O.W.H.

P.S. You might twit—that it is easy for those who don't appear to philosophize to chide me—I have known some suffering in my day. . . . Philosophy, as an old fellow in a book . . . says of courage, never is proved but always to be proved. I hope, if I am destined to be tried, I shall remember what I quoted yesterday, "They know not what they do."

"It is not far from the mark," Mr. Francis Biddle says of Holmes, "to conclude that his thinking in the field of economics stopped at twenty-five." [19] The important thing, according to Holmes, was to forget money matters, private ownership and control, and consider the more vital question of who consumes the annual product.[20] What difference does it make, he was accustomed to argue, if Rockefeller owns all the wheat in the United States, so long as the wheat is eventually consumed by the people?

Private ownership should be viewed not as a terminus but as a gateway; "large ownership means," as he put it, "investment, and investment means the direction of labor toward the production of the greatest returns." [21]

Anyone inclined to consider Holmes and Brandeis as Siamese twin liberals should put these words alongside those uttered by the People's Attorney in his 1911 testimony before the Senate Committee on Interstate and Foreign Commerce. Holmes entertained the naïve eighteenth-century faith that the economic process worked automatically—that the self-seeking drive of the individual results in gain which would somehow redound to the good of all. "For a man so skeptical about philosophic systems he was curiously uncritical," Mr. Biddle has observed, "about the orthodox economic axioms on which he was brought up." [22]

"I know," Holmes himself said, "no way of finding the fit man so good as the fact of winning it [command] in the competition of the market." [23] Industrial magnates whom Brandeis denounced as guilty of unconscionable social wrongs, Holmes admired as having triumphed in the life and death struggle of competition. "I regard a man like Hill [James J., the railroad giant] as representing one of the greatest forms of human power, an immense mastery of economic details, an equal grasp of general principles, and ability and courage to put his conclusions into practice with brilliant success. . . ." [24]

Holmes was naturally unsympathetic toward any government interference with this struggle, this triumph of the fittest. Those government controls which Brandeis strove to win as essential to social justice, Holmes decried as humbug: "I don't disguise my belief that the Sherman Act is a humbug based on economic ignorance and incompetence, and my disbelief that the Interstate Commerce Commission is a fit body to be entrusted with rate-making, even in the qualified way in which it is entrusted." [25]

Obviously to call two men "liberals" who held views so diametrically opposed is to empty this much abused word of all meaning. Holmes was a liberal primarily in the sense that he enforced (as he himself said) "whatever constitutional laws Congress or anybody else sees fit to pass—and do it in good faith to the best of my ability." [26]

It was this tolerance of social change that constituted an important area of agreement. Both believed in freedom as the way to truth; both understood the essence of politics as involving an unending search for points of equilibrium, for balance between conflicting social forces. Both saw a more stable society resulting from struggle and change—an evolution no force on earth could stop. They agreed that the limits of conflicting social desires must ultimately be defined, and that this is the essence of government. They agreed also in holding that no mechanical rule can determine precisely where Aristotle's Golden Mean is to be found, that "government is not an exact science." *

The dissenters parted company, however, as to the factors to be taken into account when confronted with a specific case. For Holmes the power factor—that is, legislative majorities—was usually decisive, not because the dictates of majorities were necessarily right, but because of the futility of opposing or arguing with a superior force.† For him, "wise or not, the proximate test of a good government is that the dominant power has its way." 27 Though Brandeis did not ignore the power factor, he did stress knowledge as an auxiliary measure. Nor was Holmes unmindful of the effectiveness of Brandeis's approach. There should be, he said, no "slackening in the eternal pursuit of the more exact. The growth of education is an increase in the knowledge of measure . . . ; it is a substitution of quantitative for qualitative judgments." Although the "worth of the competing social ends . . . cannot be reduced to number and accurately fixed," it is of "the essence of improvement that we should be as accurate as we can." 28

Despite such professions, Holmes himself showed no dominant inclination to shape economic forces constructively. His contributions to our liberalism are essentially negative. He not only detected the blindness of conservatives to the inevitability of change, but also exposed the illusions of reformers who believe that by changing property, or otherwise revolutionizing institutions, man can surely reach freedom's final goal. Holmes's liberalism must be measured primarily in terms of his own rare open-mindedness when most judges were singularly obtuse. He failed to contribute constructively, not because he did not value facts, not because he was unaware of the path of progress as hit upon by Brandeis, but because he could not bring himself to undertake "the eternal pursuit of the more exact." For the factual studies in which Brandeis reveled, Holmes expressed "fastidious disrelish." His reaction, amounting almost to inertia, when Brandeis suggested that he spend a summer investigating the textile industry, is typical:

"Brandeis the other day drove a harpoon into my midriff with reference

---

* The following quotation of an opinion handed down by Justice William Johnson in 1821, Brandeis enclosed in a letter to Norman Hapgood, July 22, 1922. It summed up his own view: "The science of government is the most abstruse of all sciences; if indeed, that can be called a science which has but few fixed principles, and practically consists of little more than the exercise of sound discretion. It is the science of experiment." (*Anderson* v. *Dunn*, 6 Wheat. 205.)

† Holmes stated his position in *Tyson* v. *Banton* (273 U.S. 418, p. 446), saying: "If the legislature of the state thinks that the public welfare requires a specified course of conduct, analogy and principle are in favor of the power to enact it. That is to say, as long as the Constitution does not forbid it, the state is at liberty to exercise power as it sees fit."

to my summer occupations," Holmes wrote Pollock, May 26, 1919. "He said 'you talk about improving your mind, you only exercise it on the subjects with which you are familiar. Why don't you try something new, study some domain of fact. Take up the textile industries in Massachusetts and after reading the reports sufficiently you can go to Lawrence and get a human notion of how it really is.' I hate facts. I always say the chief end of man is to form general propositions—adding that no general proposition is worth a damn. Of course a general proposition is simply a string for the facts and I have little doubt that it would be good for my immortal soul to plunge into them, good also for the performance of my duties, but I shrink from the bore—or rather I hate to give up the chance to read this and that, that a gentleman should have read before he dies. . . ." [29]

Brandeis read economics as well as Euripides; Holmes read and reread Plato. The results are clearly reflected in their judicial opinions. Holmes is the enlightened skeptic; Brandeis, the militant crusader.

VARIATIONS ON THE LIBERAL THEME

When the Court set aside social legislation, it was enough for Holmes that the dominant power had embarked on experiments not prohibited by the Constitution. The nub of his quarrel with his conservative brethren was that they used the Constitution as a device for enforcing their own prejudices. Said he: "There is nothing that I more deprecate than the use of the Fourteenth Amendment beyond the absolute compulsion of its words to prevent the making of social experiments that an important part of the community desires, in the insulated chambers afforded by the several states, even though the experiments may seem futile or even noxious to me and to those whose judgment I most respect." [30]

Holmes felt no compulsion or responsibility for making his opinions instructive as to the broader social and economic issues. "It rests with counsel," he said on one occasion, "to take the proper steps [to furnish the Court with relevant facts], and if they deliberately omit them, we do not feel called upon to institute inquiries on our own account." * [31] Brandeis, on the other hand, in disagreeing with the majority, explored and illumined the entire subject. He was not content to deal merely with the constitutional issue. He must go further and make his opinion both persuasive and informative.

* Brandeis states his contrasting view as follows: "Much evidence referred to by me is not in the record. Nor could it have been included. It is the history of the experience gained under similar legislation, and the result of scientific experiments made, since the entry of the judgment below. Of such events in our history, whether occurring before or after the enactment of the statute or of the entry of the judgment, the Court should acquire knowledge, and must, in my opinion, take judicial notice, whenever required to perform the delicate judicial task here involved." (Dissenting in Jay Burns Baking Co.)

Even when Holmes concurred in Brandeis's weighty opinions, he sometimes grew weary reading them. On one occasion Holmes "knit his
brow" over a long opinion, profusely decorated with the usual footnotes
as to economic data, trade journals, and committee reports. Beautifully
clear and no doubt true, Holmes thought, as he leaned back in his chair;
then he wrote on the margin: "This afternoon I was walking on the tow-
path and saw a cardinal. It seemed to me to be the first sign of Spring. By
the way, I concur." [32]

Holmes's and Brandeis's judicial vetoes were not always in agreement.
When, for example, Pennsylvania prohibited mining coal in such a way as
to cause private dwellings to cave in, Holmes held the law an unconstitutional encroachment on property rights.[33] Brandeis, less concerned for the
sacredness of property, was more willing to allow legislative experimentation.

With an entirely different set of values, the positions of the dissenters
were reversed. When legislatures passed statutes affecting freedom of
thought, speech, and press, or when government agents invaded that right
"most valued by civilized men"—the right "to be let alone"—Brandeis did
not hesitate to interpose his judicial veto, though Holmes sometimes ruled
that the legislature be allowed to experiment. Brandeis could not agree,
contending that such statutes denied the fundamental right of free men
"to strive for better conditions." Thus when Nebraska prohibited German-
language instruction in private, parochial, and public schools, Holmes permitted the dominant power to have its way. To Brandeis, "what the crowd
wants" was in this instance no safe guide, and he voted with the majority
to overthrow the statute.[34]

Brandeis's own decisions were not entirely governed by facts alone. Both
as a lawyer and a judge, the decisive factors were "partly legal, partly sentimental, and partly a recognition of economic rights and a sound social
policy." [35] Certain prejudices and certain special preferences formed a
picture of an ideal society and predetermined his stand. His major prejudice was against unconfined and irresponsible power—political or economic—whether it was wielded by Executive or Judiciary, business corporation or trade union. His fundamental maxim was stated in an early
battle for civic betterment: "Power must always feel the check of power."
This he applied in cases involving power conflicts between the federal
government and the states, between President and Congress.

Another prejudice was exhibited in cases posing the conflict between
property rights and human rights. Brandeis never underestimated the
importance and social utility of private property, but he protested strongly
against any tendency to make it dominant over men. This was clearly .

shown in *International News Service* v. *Associated Press* where the Court upheld the Associated Press claim not to have its news items copied so long as they had "commercial value as news." Brandeis objected to this ruling as "an important extension of property rights [by judicial decision] and a corresponding curtailment of the free use of knowledge and ideas." He observed: ". . . with the increasing complexity of society, the public interest tends to become omnipresent; and the problems presented by new demands for justice cease to be simple. Then the creation or recognition by courts of a new private right may work serious injury to the general public, unless the boundaries of the right are definitely established and wisely guarded." [36]

Because the public interest in modern society tends to become omnipresent, Brandeis accorded legislatures wide latitude for their experiments affecting property and contract, while judicial review was correspondingly curtailed. He was especially alert to any tendency to create a property right by judicial decision. Thus when the Court settled on a narrowly technical definition of income that would render stock dividends immune from taxation, he penetrated the corporate veil, digging into the motives of management to prove how financiers, with the aid of their lawyers, had devised the stock dividend as a device for retaining profits while actually distributing them.[37] In ruling that stock dividends are not income, the Court in effect flouted the "terse, comprehensive language" of the Sixteenth Amendment. This disinclination to endorse judicial power when used to protect property against government control was not always shared by Justice Holmes. Nor were recognized liberals, such as Judge Learned Hand, always able to agree.* But Brandeis's position was solidly in accord with his general doctrine that "in order to preserve the liberty and the property of a great majority of the citizens of a state, rights of property and the liberty of the individual must be remolded, from time to time, to meet the changing needs of society." [38] But this remolding process, as he saw it, must be largely legislative rather than judicial.

Brandeis's quarrel with the majority was not that facts were neglected but rather that the Court so often presumed to decide "as a fact" and without full knowledge whether or not measures were necessary, thus

---

* As to the Associated Press case mentioned above, Judge Hand wrote to Justice Brandeis, January 22, 1919: "I thought your opinion the best in the Press case but I believe I should have been on the other side. All you say is quite true about the absence of any principle as yet recognized, yet there seems to me the substance of what ought to be a private wrong which can be rendered without prejudice to the public. . . . It is of course true that any kind of judicial legislation is objectionable on the score of the limited interests which a Court can represent, yet there are wrongs which in fact legislatures cannot be brought to take an interest in, at least not until the Courts have acted. After all it is as easy to remedy a wrong decision which gives relief as one which refuses it."

appropriating the "powers of a super-legislature." It is not, he contended, the business of judges to pass on facts but rather "in the light of all facts which may enrich our knowledge and enlarge our understanding" to decide whether the challenged legislation "is so clearly arbitrary or capricious that legislators, acting reasonably, could not have believed it to be necessary or appropriate for the public welfare. . . . Knowledge is essential to understanding; and understanding should precede judging. Sometimes, if we would guide by the light of reason, we must let our minds be bold." [39]

WHAT TRUTH—AND WHOSE

Brandeis's methods were soon imitated by conservative justices, who now fortified themselves with their own statistical data, picked and polished. Surely the use and abuse of facts to support opposite conclusions makes it seem not unlikely that facts, like syllogisms, will remain for judges as relatively unimportant in the judicial process. As Holmes said: "The felt necessities of the time, the prevalent moral and political theories, intuitions of public policy, avowed or unconscious, even the prejudices which judges share with their fellow-men, have had a good deal more to do than the syllogism in determining the rules by which men should be governed." [40]

These observations are as applicable to Brandeis as to Butler or Sutherland. In letters to Pollock, Holmes sometimes made a point of saying that much of what Brandeis had written was not only irrelevant but "all wrong." [41] Brandeis, like his conservative colleagues, was inclined by the pressures and drives of his own nature to translate his own economic and social views into the Constitution itself. That Constitution, an embalming fluid of status quo to the conservatives, to him was a fiery sword of freedom.

In this respect Holmes's position was unique. He was about equally skeptical of reforming zealots, who would make a new world in their own small image, and of those who would maintain moss-grown social and economic institutions unaltered. His "enlightened skepticism," and inertia, prompted him to take the hands-off, laissez-faire position, whereas Brandeis's moving knowledge of the economic forces of his day developed in him a sense of urgency. "How can you be so sure," a friend once asked, "that a particular line of action is the right one?" "When you are 51 per cent sure that you are right," he replied, "then go ahead." [42] Skepticism was not so generic in Brandeis, but after years of association with Holmes he too could observe: "The economic and social sciences are largely uncharted seas. . . . Man is weak and his judgment is at best fallible." [43]

Brandeis's approach was more constructive, less esoteric. In Max Lerner's words: "Where Holmes had spoken of philosophy, Brandeis spoke of

service to the nation; where Holmes talked abstractly of battle, Brandeis
talked pragmatically of reform; where Holmes fashioned graceful phrases,
Brandeis quarried in the hard rock of social reality." Then Mr. Lerner
adds: "Perhaps by the very fact of his indirections and his lesser urgency
Holmes may ironically prove the more enduring voice." * [44]

Quite apart from the proved effectiveness of Brandeis's method and the
validation of his insight and forecasts, Lerner's hypothesis would seem
persuasive only if the comprehension that knowledge confers is turned to
anti-social ends. Brandeis did not, indeed could not, find all the answers in
his facts, but surely his briefs and opinions were much more than appara-
tus to support a preconceived policy or specific judicial decision. [45] They
led, first of all, to a sharper sense of the questions to be asked. At a time
when conservatives saw the Constitution as synonymous with the laissez
faire of Herbert Spencer, and Holmes spoke of the fundamental law as
embodying no particular economic theory, Brandeis stated the crucial issue
as that of reconciling our political democracy with industrial absolutism.
Can anyone doubt today that his method meant a tighter grasp on the
relevancy of the various possible answers? Can anyone doubt that his command of the facts of industrialism helped produce that sense of "urgency"
unknown to liberal Holmes or conservative Taft? Can anyone doubt that
such comprehension made for clearer insight into the advantages gained
from choosing one answer rather than another? If judges really decide
great constitutional questions according to their social and economic opinions, should they not make those opinions as informed as possible? [46]

Brandeis took his stand and accepted full responsibility for action. He
demonstrated his belief that man does have a measure of control over his
own destiny. He proved that, given leadership, knowledge, persistence,
and wide participation in public affairs, man can lay the foundations of a
society with more security as well as more leisure, broader social responsibility as well as greater social privilege—in short, a nearer approach than
men have ever thought possible to the ideal of an enlarging liberty through
a living law.

* It should be noted that Mr. Lerner's observation is confined to a narrow phase of Holmes's and
Brandeis's activities—"their efforts to change the tone and fiber of the legal profession."

CHAPTER THIRTY-SEVEN

Extrajudicial Activities

In the early nineteen twenties Brandeis bought a small place on Cape Cod not far from the village of Chatham. The house, a small clapboard structure, stood on a lonely hill, amid a wide expanse of sand dune, cotton-wood trees, and scrubby green hillocks. Inside, the rooms were as plain as in his Washington apartment. His bedroom-study downstairs was austere, with an oak table, some hard chairs, a small electric heater, a case of books, and a bed covered with a nondescript blanket. A few simple pictures hung on the walls. During an interview in the summer of 1940, the visitor learned that one was of a Danish folk-school. "There," the Justice said, "were really planted the seeds of democracy." Another, yellowed with age, showed some small children. "Yes, that was my mother's. She gave it to me before she died. The one on the left is of me." There was a picture of Sam Warren at the helm of an old sloop, a newspaper likeness of Norman Hapgood, both hung by thumb-tacks. Turning slowly to a small picture on his desk, a catch came in his voice. "You know that man, Justice Benjamin Cardozo.* He was my very dear friend, a beautiful character. His work raised the standard of the New York Circuit Court of Appeals, and even of our Court. We were very close." [1]

Brandeis's life at Chatham was typical of the man's deep love of simplicity and reflected "the universal element in greatness—the capacity to stand alone, to be independent of the activities and judgments of the rest of mankind." [2]

Amid these bare, familiar surroundings, remote from urban civilization, he pursued his extracurricular activities most assiduously. Men from all walks of life sought his advice and found it generously given. He would sit quietly, listen intently, then with a question or a simple comment he would go to the heart of the matter, and the difficulty would evaporate. As Woodrow Wilson once said: "A talk with Brandeis always sweeps the cobwebs out of one's mind."

Many noted Brandeis's resemblance to Lincoln—the wiry strength, the tall, angular, slightly stooped frame, sharp features, deeply set eyes of blue gray, vastly sympathetic, with a trace of sadness, and remarkably bright. He allowed his gray hair to grow rather long and brushed it carelessly, like a philosopher or prophet of old. Slender, sensitive hands suggested the artist; his skin, of olive hue, gave an appearance of robust health that some-

* Cardozo had died July 9, 1938.

what belied the facts. His body was lithe, its motions perfectly co-ordinated, his walk rhythmic. His inherent grace, both physical and spiritual, was striking. That was his quality to a marked degree and one he appreciated in others.

Between visits and the reading of *certioraris* there was life-giving leisure with his family. "I have, as usual, been working at law a part of the day," he wrote Otto Wehle from Chatham, August 29, 1929. "There were two opinions to write, and endless petitions for *certiorari* to occupy the working time. But there has been time for much else." And so there was. He loved the companionship of his two children from their earliest years, as he did long afterward the companionship with his four grandchildren.

As years went by his life became ever more patterned. On the trip to and from Chatham there was always the overnight stop in Boston at the Bellevue, where Miss Grady, his former secretary, would arrange for meetings with important friends—especially those who might be helpful to savings-bank life insurance. In addition, there were calls from personal friends, such as Felix Frankfurter and Lincoln Filene; and, in case savings-bank insurance was under attack in the Legislature, Judd Dewey was likely to arrange a conference with the Governor and others influential in politics.

Even in these brief sojourns with friends he seemed more concerned to get worth-while things done than to idle away time sociably. Clyde Casady, executive vice-president of the Massachusetts Savings Bank Insurance Council, has told of his first meeting with the Justice in September 1932. Miss Grady had invited Casady, a youngster but recently attached to the S.B.I. staff, to go to the train and see the Justice off to Washington. "I expected merely to sit in a corner of the stateroom," Casady wrote, "and listen to conversation between the Justice and his intimate friends. You can imagine my surprise when he met me at the door, excused himself and took me into the next compartment, and spent practically the entire twenty minutes talking about the need and means of promoting savings-bank insurance." [3]

Through his years on the Bench those working in and for S.B.I. received from time to time concise notes containing serially numbered suggestions, particularly on ways of promoting the system, all set down on the familiar yellow notepaper in his own handwriting. A visitor from Massachusetts could rarely leave his presence without meeting the query: "What are you doing for savings-bank life insurance?" He was not so much interested in who the person was or what he had done in the past. He wanted to know what he was doing or might be expected to do in the near future and about specific things. Judd Dewey, Deputy Commissioner of Savings Bank

Insurance, tells the story of a complaint someone had registered to Justice Brandeis during the fight for savings-bank life insurance in New York. Sidney Wolff, a New York cotton broker, had assumed a most conspicuous role, though some considered him tactless and disqualified generally as leader of the movement. To this criticism Brandeis replied calmly that it was true many among the thirteen million people in New York State were more tactful, could make better speeches, and knew more important people than Sidney Wolff did, "but," said the Justice, "they are not interested in establishing savings-bank insurance in New York. Sidney is—he's the best we have who is willing to do the job." [4]

It was not easy, during the incredible twenties, for a crusader, absorbed and remote in the sacred precincts of the Supreme Court, to hold his peace. Dissenting opinions, however militant, were a far cry from the aggressive war Brandeis had waged as People's Attorney. Those had been active, busy, fighting years. He had seen and heard; and studied and thought. He had gained broad and deep understanding of the country's problems. He had been counselor, advocate, pioneer, inventor, and fighter—all in one.

There is not a little evidence that work on the Court failed fully to satisfy his zeal for constructive endeavor. He had hoped, as we have seen, that he might have carried on his knight-errantry at least until he was sixty-five. After he became a Supreme Court Justice, a lingering nostalgia sometimes affected him. Reminiscing one day in 1940, he told his niece, Fanny Brandeis, that his best years were the fifties. Justice Holmes had not agreed; he favored the seventies. "I sometimes thought," Brandeis commented, "I might have had more education—when I was eighteen and nineteen at the Law School. Now I am not so sure: I am a great believer in starting young. The enthusiasm and fire of youth means more than maturity. So I think the fifties are the best. By that time I had been working thirty years, and the experience of those years was there."

Though still at heart a reformer, his activities now were much circumscribed and not immediately constructive. Furthermore, he gratuitously enlarged even the normal strictures imposed by the judicial function, refusing to make public addresses or write for publication on matters unrelated to his Court work. "He was strongly of the belief," a member of the present Court recalls, "that a Justice of the Court should devote himself, single-mindedly to his duties as a Justice, without undertaking to engage in any outside activities." [5]

HIS CREED IN ESSENCE

A stickler for proprieties, Brandeis refused even Charles Evans Hughes's most cordial and urgent invitation of December 1919 to be the guest of

honor at the annual dinner of The New York County Lawyers' Association. On this occasion, like so many others, he pleaded the judicial proprieties and declined. There were, however, conspicuous exceptions. In February 1922, at the request of Robert W. Bruère and F. Ernest Johnson, Executive Secretary of the Department of Research and Education of the Federal
Council of Churches in America, he spoke informally before a small
gathering. Following his talk, he wrote a letter to Bruère on February 25,
summing up his position. Here in brief compass he pointedly stated his
creed:

Refuse to accept as inevitable any evil in business (e.g., irregularity of employment). Refuse to tolerate any immoral practice (e.g., espionage). But do
not believe that you can find a universal remedy for evil conditions or immoral
practices in effecting a fundamental change in society (as by State Socialism).
And do not pin too much faith in legislation. Remedial institutions are apt to
fall under the control of the enemy and to become instruments of oppression.

Seek for betterment within the broad lines of existing institutions. Do so by
attacking evil *in situ;* and proceed from the individual to the general. Remember that progress is necessarily slow; that remedies are necessarily tentative; that
because of varying conditions there must be much and constant enquiry into
facts . . . and much experimentation; and that always and everywhere the
intellectual, moral and spiritual development of those concerned will remain
an essential—and the main factor—in real betterment.

This development of the individual is, thus, both a necessary means and the
end sought. For our objective is the making of men and women who shall be
free, self-respecting members of a democracy—and who shall be worthy of
respect. Improvement in material conditions of the worker and ease are the incidents of better conditions—valuable mainly as they may ever increase opportunities for development.

The great developer is responsibility. Hence no remedy can be hopeful which
does not devolve upon the workers participation in, responsibility for, the conduct of business; and their aim should be the eventual assumption of full responsibility—as in co-operative enterprises. This participation in, and eventual
control of, industry is likewise an essential of obtaining justice in distributing
the fruits of industry.

But democracy in any sphere is a serious undertaking. It substitutes self-
restraint for external restraint. It is more difficult to maintain than to achieve. It
demands continuous sacrifice by the individual and more exigent obedience to
the moral law than any other form of government. Success in any democratic
undertaking must proceed from the individual. It is possible only where the
process of perfecting the individual is pursued. His development is attained
mainly in the processes of common living. Hence the industrial struggle is essentially an affair of the Church and is its imperative task.

THE RIGHT TO REGULARITY OF EMPLOYMENT

Since the anthracite strike of 1902, Brandeis had seen irregularity of employment as our most perplexing evil. This subject had been an ever-
recurring theme in the various garment trade arbitrations, 1910–16; in
testimony before the House investigation of the United States Steel Corporation, 1911; and in hearings before the Industrial Relations Commission, 1914–15. On March 11, 1918, he wrote Paul Kellogg of *The Survey
Graphic:* "I think the time is here when regularity of employment should
be made an insistent fundamental demand of labor to take its place beside
living wages, shorter hours, proper working conditions."

On April 22 he wrote again: "The prevention of unemployment in hard
times is of course very important; but my thought was more fundamental. It is to do away with day-labor—to obliterate the distinction between the salaried man and the wage-earner—by declaring the right to
continuity of employment. About ten years ago we began to recognize the
right to have the business assume the risk of accidents. They should now
assume the risk of unemployment."

On July 31 another reminder went out: "I trust you are bearing in mind
the policy of regularity of employment as an anti-bolshevist measure." *The
Survey Graphic* editor began to think in terms of a nation-wide survey,
but Brandeis advised that nothing so ambitious be undertaken. "Make the
unit small," he suggested, April 30, 1920. "Call it a preliminary survey. Let
it be done as John Fitch—with aids—would do it. Let it be done by your
publication; and give us the tentative results as soon as possible. We may
have hard times a little later and the report should come before then."

Little had actually been accomplished by 1924, and Coolidge prosperity
then discouraged further effort. Well aware of this fact, Brandeis sent
Kellogg more specific instructions on June 9, 1924. "In the heyday of prosperity," he wrote, "Americans never think. In suffering, they sometimes
do. Business depression is apt to bring much suffering within a twelve-
month. I suggest that the *Survey Graphic* avail of the probable thinking
periods, by three issues—each to be devoted *exclusively* to one of the three
following subjects: 1. Irregularity of Employment. . . . 2. Preserving our
Timber Supply and Planting of Trees. On this, urge strongly state and
municipal action. Massachusetts is setting a fine example. . . . Even Congress . . . is waking up. 3. Soil Preservation. . . .

"The three matters are fundamental," he concluded, "demanding attention from economic statesmen. Our social, industrial, political look-ahead
calls for a different vision than that of the stock-ticker patriots."

No amount of prosperity and stock market booming could stay his sense of urgency. "Now that unemployment has been forced upon public attention," he suggested to Kellogg, March 11, 1928, "would it not be possible for the *Survey* to take up vigorously and persistently the musts of Regularity in Employment? That is the fundamental remedy. All others are merely palliatives. . . . Regularity of employment would go far toward eliminating business cycles—in this country. It is essential to the emancipation of labor."

When the *Survey,* in line with his suggestions, published a series of articles, he was pleased though not entirely so. "Yes, the *Survey* articles are very good. . . . But the most important thing is that this opportunity be taken for the assertion of the Right to regularity in employment—a moral right, in a civilized community, superior to the right to dividends and equal, at least, to the right to regularity in the receipt of income from rents or interest."

In April 1929, some six months before the crash, the *Survey Graphic* came out with a special number devoted to "Unemployment and The Ways Out." * Brandeis was much gratified, but still not content. "You and Beulah Amidon have forged a formidable instrument," he wrote Paul Kellogg, March 31, 1929. "What would you say to giving it full utilization by supporting the attack through a monthly Steady Employment section, which would gather 1. Comment from employers, economists, and social workers on the possibilities, etc. 2. Modern instances of the evils and attempted remedies. Keep your readers *au fait* and stirred up."

The next day he wrote at greater length suggesting specific items for the first monthly installment of the proposed "Steady Employment" section. Paul Kellogg's reply, April 5, 1929, carried the staff's misgivings: "I think our judgment is that it would be a mistake, even if we could, to start an unemployment section of the *Survey.* We have just brought out an issue smashing into people's imaginations from a new side, and helping, we hope, to get a fresh hearing for an old and grim problem in its modern phases. But our feeling is that the subject in itself is a dour one,

---

* This special issue carried on its first page:

The Right to Work
As formulated long since by
Louis D. Brandeis

"For every employe who is 'steady in his work,' there shall be steady work. The right to regularity in employment is co-equal with the right to regularity in the payment of rent, in the payment of interest on bonds, in the delivery to customers of the high quality of product contracted for. No business is successfully conducted which does not perform fully the obligations incident to each of these rights. Each of these obligations is equally a fixed charge. No dividend should be paid unless each of these fixed charges has been met. The reserve to ensure regularity of employment is as imperative as the reserve for depreciation; and it is equally a part of the fixed charges to make the annual contribution to that reserve. No business is socially solvent which cannot do so."

which people have been dodging. Hence the neglect. And the way to get them to skip materials opening up that subject would be to bunch and put them under that title.

"But while our instinct is against a special department," Kellogg's letter continued, "it is decidedly for following through. We have discussed the possibility of hitting the subject in every issue from now on."

In his response of April 7 the Justice said: "No doubt it would be unwise journalistically to establish what is technically called a Section. What I have in mind would be fully met, if you mean by follow-up the thing that is so persistent and distinguished that those who are seeking light will look forward to the next *Graphic*.

"My doubt is not as to the decision. It arises from the argument in support. You treat this as one of the 'good causes.' Things may differ so greatly in degree as to differ in kind. My guess is that for the next decade Unemployment will be our great concern. My thought was that the businessmen whose attention you hoped to secure through the December circular might be led to look to the *Graphic* for light; and that they should not be subject to disappointment. *Persistency is the jewel.*" (Author's italics.)

The *Survey* was his faithful torchbearer. "Over the years," a *Survey Graphic* editor has written, "a great many of our major journalistic projects were undertaken at Mr. Brandeis's suggestion, and again and again the staff rose eagerly to the leads he proposed." [6] Though little or no advance had been made toward finding correctives for this "chronic problem," he remained optimistic and untiringly persistent. "In the United States," he wrote Paul Kellogg, March 13, 1937, "regularization of employment is possible; and without regularization, decent conditions are impossible of attainment."

HELPING A UNIVERSITY TO SELF-HELP

In 1924 Justice Brandeis turned his hand to a subject ever close to his heart—education. He began to lay plans for making the university of his home city, Louisville, a more effective community enterprise. One might think from the hundreds of lengthy letters he wrote on university affairs during the years 1924-29 that this was his sole interest, for he was actively concerned with every phase.

His donations at the outset were not of the conventional sort—money with appropriate memorials. He chose to make the more unusual benefaction—thought, planning, encouragement, inspiration, a compelling vision of the University as a dynamic force in the community. To start with he presented to the University library three collections of books and pamphlets—sociology and economics, fine arts, and the World War. He felt that the need for these non-material gifts was great, since they were so hard to come by. He recognized that University trustees and administrative officers would tend to think exclusively in terms of endowment: "The value of money as a means of achieving things is familiar to them [trustees]. To devote themselves to the obvious and to pursue familiar ways is natural. It does not require vision or thinking. I do not criticize it. I accept it as a fact." [7]

Money alone, however, could not build a university: "Too much money —too quick money—may mar one; particularly if it is foreign money. To be great, a university must express the people whom it serves, and must express the people and the community at their best. The aim must be high and the vision broad; the goal seemingly attainable but beyond immediate reach.[8]

Brandeis knew that the hard, close thinking necessary for laying the foundation for a university would not be done by any Board of Trustees charged with supervising administration. As in any other human endeavor, man was for him the important factor. The University's life and soul was the faculty. Laboratories, books, and endowment—only the "essential tools."

Various members of the family were singled out for special responsibilities. His niece, Adele Brandeis, was assigned the Department of Sociology and Economics; another niece, Fanny Brandeis, Archaeology, Art, and Music; Alfred, Kentuckiana, and so on. It was a task "befitting the Adolph Brandeis family, which for nearly three-quarters of a century has stood in Louisville for culture, and, at least in Uncle Lewis, for learning." [9]

His letters in connection with specific gifts of books leave no doubt as to the kind of university he envisioned. It was to be primarily a Kentucky institution to cherish the best the state has produced in war and in peace. It must represent the people and the community it seeks to serve. In short— "an institution for Kentuckians developed by Kentuckians. . . . Everything in the life of the state is worthy of special enquiry. Every noble memory must be cherished, thus the details of Kentucky history, political, economic, and social, become factors of ultimate importance. . . . The University Library should grow rich in Kentuckiana. It should be a depository of unpublished manuscripts and like possessions associated with the life of the state and the achievements of Kentuckians." [10]

To stimulate interest among Kentuckians, whether resident in or out of the state, was in the forefront of all his thinking and planning. This could best be done by making the institution "essentially Kentuckian." "There is," he wrote, "a large field for effort of those outside the University whose capacity, influence, and position give them a wider view and bolder vision;

whose position enables them to secure for the University's projects the approval and support of the community, and whose means enable them to render financial aid. From them may come also the encouragement without which few achieve, and that informed friendly supervision without which few persevere in the most painstaking labor."

The departmental libraries as finally established included: War Library, Sociology and Economics, Railroads, German Literature, English Literature, Fine Arts and Archaeology, Music, Palestine and Zionism, the Classical Library.* He would have these libraries serve ends which for him seemed good. The purpose of the library of Sociology was "to influence the life of the state socially and economically." The library of Fine Arts and Music would promote that "development which is compounded in the term culture. . . . It [the University] should strive to awaken the slumbering creative instinct, to encourage its exercise and development, to stimulate production." [11]

The purpose of his World War Library was "not only to encourage research and learning, but to influence the political life of the state and the nation by a deep and far-reaching study of history, and inquiring into the causes and consequences of present ills, and a consideration of the proper aspirations of the United States and of the functions of the state. History teaches, I believe, that the present tendency toward centralization must be arrested, if we are to attain the American ideals, and that for it must be substituted intense development of life through activities in the several states and localities. The problem is a very difficult one, but the local university is the most hopeful instrument for any attempt at solution." [12]

Besides the Library, Justice Brandeis's special concern was the Law School, which stood in dire need of a more adequate teaching staff, more complete curriculum, and a new building. Students must, he believed, be able to get their legal education in their home state, since most would return there to practice. In support of his contention he cited for President

---

* A subsidiary purpose in making these gifts was "to provide appropriate memorials for certain persons who had contributed to the intellectual life and the worthy development of the city." He therefore asked that a University book-plate be pasted in each volume indicating the person in whose memory the Library was established.

      Palestine-Judaica—Lewis N. Dembitz
      English Literature—Albert R. Cooper
      German Literature—William N. Hailman
      Railroads—Albert Fink and Milton H. Smith
      Music—Louis H. Hast
      Sociology and Economics
      War Library and Government Publications ⎫ Alfred Brandeis
      Classical Literature and History ⎭

Ford of the University a letter by Pliny the Younger (A.D. 62–113) to Tacitus.* But even given these facilities, Brandeis recognized that they "would fail of attaining what is aimed at, without . . . a strong and active public opinion existing among judges, lawyers, and public men of the state." [13]

Besides contributing small sums to the running expenses of the school, he gave books and other gifts. He arranged for the law school to receive a complete set of the briefs and records of cases decided in the Supreme Court of the United States, beginning with the 1924–25 term. Brandeis thought of this arrangement in terms of "an overt act—making clear our intention to build a law school of distinction."

Brandeis's monetary donations to both the Library and the Law School were relatively small, amounting to not more than a few thousand dollars, usually carefully earmarked to cover cataloguing, binding, and shelving the collections he donated. Nevertheless, the anticipated benefits in terms of higher standards as well as money for equipment and building were soon forthcoming. As a result of Brandeis's influence, Neville Miller, eminent lawyer and public spirited citizen, became Dean, and that same year the Law School was admitted to the approved list of the American Bar Association. On June 6, 1938, the cornerstone of the Law School's handsome new building was laid on the Belknap campus. Mr. Justice Stanley Reed was one of the main speakers.

"It is hard," Dean Miller commented, May 1938, "for one who has not lived through the struggle of the Law School to appreciate Mr. Justice Brandeis's influence and assistance. He always kept in the background, seeking no word of appreciation for himself or for what he had done. It was his vision of the Law School as an active force in the community, rather than just another school turning out lawyers, which really decided me to give up the practice of the law and become Dean. He always anticipated our wishes." [14]

---

* The letter reads in part:

"Being lately at Comum, the place of my nativity, a young lad, son of one of my neighbors, made me a visit. I asked him whether he studied oratory, and where. He told me he did, and at Mediolanum. 'And why not here?' 'Because (said his father, who came with him), we have no masters.' 'No!' said I, 'surely it nearly concerns you who are fathers (and very opportunely several of the company were so) that your sons should receive their education here, rather than anywhere else. For where can they be placed more agreeably than in their own country, or instructed with more safety and less expense than at home and under the eye of their parents? Upon what very easy terms might you, by a general calculation, procure proper masters, if you would only apply toward the raising of a salary for them, the extraordinary expense it costs you for your sons' journeys, lodgings, and whatever else you pay for upon account of their being abroad; as pay indeed you must in such a case for everything. . . . May you be able to procure professors of such distinguished abilities, that the neighboring town shall be glad to draw their learning from hence; and as you now send your children to foreigners for education, may foreigners in their turn flock hither for their instruction.'"
(Quoted in B. Flexner, *Mr. Justice Brandeis and the University of Louisville*.)

Even as the original gifts were made, the University's Board of Trustees engaged in a bitter controversy over policy. "The obstacles, I had foreseen," Brandeis wrote Alfred. "I do not consider indifference insufferable. I guess that by appropriate treatment each one of the trustees can be made not only to see but to feel, the worth-whileness of at least one of the many things we are trying to further. There is in most Americans some spark of idealism, which can be fanned into a flame. It takes sometimes a divining rod to find what it is; but when found, and that means often, when disclosed to the owners, the results are often most extraordinary." [15]

For the successful execution of his plan, Brandeis's main reliance was on his brother. When Alfred's health declined, the Justice became alarmed. "You have handled U. of L. matters with so much wisdom and skill that I have no suggestions to make except one—on that I have had half a century of experience and you none.

"Alice's and my plans for the University extend over the next ten years. We don't want to lose our managing partner. It's just fifty years since my eyes gave out. Since then there has never been a time that I haven't had to bear in mind physical limitations of some sort, the walls curbing activity were always in sight;—and I had to adjust my efforts. Your superb constitution relieved you from that necessity. But age is a fact that may not be ignored. It has added to the limitations to which I have been subject—and there is not a day when I am not reminded of it.

"Your constitution is better than mine. But you are nearly three years older. Remember that—and act accordingly.[16]

By September 1929, when the late Dr. Raymond A. Kent became president of Louisville, the task of rebuilding the University into a worthy institution was well under way. The various collections of books and pamphlets had been classified, bound, catalogued, and shelved. Brandeis now turned his attention to what he called the "second stage of our undertaking." This consisted in a carefully planned effort to turn the spotlight of public attention on what had been accomplished and thus interest various sections of the community and win them as friendly participants in the University's future growth.

Underlying all his effort and his gifts was "the conviction that through the University much may be done toward making the state great; that the University can be made a noble and potent one by Kentuckians—and only by and through them; and that, if interest in various departments of the University can be stimulated in the various classes, sections, layers, occupations, and nationalities of which the population of Louisville is composed, there will develop—somehow and through sources which we cannot guess —an intellectual and spiritual ferment which is the essence of greatness." [17]

Brandeis's hope—to make the University an institution of and for the people—has not yet been attained. Nor perhaps is it likely to be; for he had deliberately fixed on an ideal, believing that "to become great a university must express the purpose and the community at their best . . . the goal seemingly attainable but beyond immediate reach."

ZIONISM—A CONTINUING INTEREST

"He is Zionistically at his best during the summer vacations," Jacob De Haas wrote in 1929. "In an old sweater under his heavy tweed jacket, cap on head, he saunters through the berry paths that lead from his Chatham home to the river inlet and to a chosen companion reveals his longings, hopes, and aspirations." [18] Zionists came to see him, singly and in groups, from all over the world. His daily mail brought him news from Palestine, reports and more reports. After his leadership was repudiated at the Cleveland Convention, June 1921, he appeared infrequently at Zionist functions, refusing even to say "a few words of greeting" lest he give rise to the impression that he still led the movement. He had decided to do no more than "(1) to think on the main problems of the cause; (2) to give moral support; and (3) to give financial support." [19]

But his influence spread far beyond these bounds. He kept a captain's hand on the tiller of American Zionism and warmly supported the so-called Mack–Brandeis group, led by Judge Julian W. Mack and Robert Szold, when they staged a come-back, wresting Z.O.A. leadership from the Lipsky clique. The burden of a large deficit, coupled with a steady decline in membership, proved too much. By February 1932 Brandeis himself agreed that "they would be turned out at the June convention."

Nor did the Justice refrain from participating in the affairs of the World Zionist Organization. When crises arose, as on August 23, 1929, he gave far more than moral and financial support. That date marked the outbreak of Arab attacks on Jews, setting off an orgy of violence that spread through Palestine. One hundred and thirty-two Jews lost their lives and six colonies were destroyed. Great pressure was then brought to have Brandeis address an emergency economic conference of influential businessmen in Washington, November 24, and to this he agreed at the request of Felix Warburg. "The immediate need," the Justice explained to a co-worker, "is large investment funds," and "we must win Warburg completely." [20]

Zionist leaders were sharply divided as to the wisdom of this appearance. In a memorandum to Judge Mack and Jacob De Haas, October 3, 1929, Frankfurter stated his fears: "By this public appearance in Palestinian matters, he will inevitably entangle himself in public and political controversies. . . . Thus far he has insulated himself by the formula, 'Judicial office precludes.' Powerful representations have been made to him from time to time for appearance upon professional occasions and I know that it has been felt that he was overfastidious and austere in not giving personal inspiration on important professional occasions. Professional feeling and opinion will not unnaturally take note of the distinction he makes. . . ."

But Brandeis addressed the first and second sessions of the Conference, on both occasions emphasizing his belief that Jews could and would live amicably with Arabs. "The road to a Jewish Palestine is economic," he began, "and the opportunity is open. I reached that conviction ten years ago when I became acquainted on my visit there with the country and the people, both Arabs and Jews." [21] Of course risks had to be taken, he went on, and in characteristic fashion compared the settlers in Palestine to the Pilgrims in Massachusetts who stacked their guns at the church before they worshiped. But it was not mainly a matter of armed defense against the Arabs; conciliation was possible.

Brandeis had long anticipated these difficulties. In an effort to forestall trouble he had embodied in his Pittsburgh program of 1918 a creed of social justice and mutual service. He had recognized the Zionist commitment to institute in the Jewish National Home of Palestine "equality of opportunity . . . with due regard to existing rights." [22] This was still the policy he urged:

"Last summer, before there was any suggestion of an uprising, I had the opportunity of discussing with some of our people active in the conduct of our affairs in Palestine, and who live there, what our relations with the Arabs should be in enterprises started or planned. While we were reviewing the work of the co-operatives we discussed the advisability of opening the co-operatives to the Arabs, of opening our labor unions to Arabs, of inviting Arabs to participate in our industrial enterprises, and of thus becoming more closely allied to them. We discussed the advisability of learning their language, so that we might familiarly visit them in their homes, as some Jews have been doing. When the recent disorders shall have been overcome the work which has been done by the Jews for Arabs will be appreciated. Through our medical organizations, through the elimination of malaria and other diseases, we have done, for the amelioration of the condition of the Arabs, an extraordinary amount, considering the shortness of time. Arabs, unlike some other peoples, have no inherent dislike of the Jews—certainly they did not have it. Jews lived among them in perfect amity before and during the war. I have confidence they will again do so." [23]

Nor did current disturbances shake his conviction that the growth of

JUSTICE AND MRS. BRANDEIS AT THE WHITE HOUSE, NEW YEAR'S DAY, 1932

BRANDEIS, SCULPTOR EDWARD SIMONE, AND HOLMES, 1930

"SCANDALIZED"
Los Angeles Times, January 30, 1916

"A GREAT LIBERAL AT EIGHTY"
New York World-Telegram,
November 13, 1936

"JUSTICE BRANDEIS
DISSENTS"—
FROM
SOCIAL INJUSTICE.
THE GREED OF PRIVILEGE.
LEGAL ARTERIO-SCLEROSIS.
THE THEORY THAT
PROPERTY RIGHTS
ARE PARAMOUNT.
THAT MAN WAS MADE
FOR THE LAW.

the Jewish community there will "make Palestine perhaps, all things considered, the safest place in the world. . . . Let us take counsel of our hopes, not of our fears." [24]

In March 1930 the Shaw Commission report on the 1929 riots upheld the Arab side and recommended a new statement of policy as well as restriction of Jewish immigration. Brandeis was deeply shocked. He could not understand it; the whole thing was to him "un-English." He advised Felix Warburg to get up a "monster petition" in protest, and he himself conferred with the British ambassador, Sir Ronald Lindsay. The Justice told the ambassador that Great Britain must remain the mandatory "because of the character of her people, the experience of her government, and the possession by the English of the knowledge essential to a practical undertaking; because of her record in respect to Jews; and the absence there of anti-semitism as contrasted with France as exhibited in the Dreyfus incident." He referred to American help in getting the mandate for Great Britain and cited "the monster petition" signed by 532,000 Jews in support of the Balfour Declaration. "As an American," his memorandum recorded, "I again call attention to the danger to the future relations of the U.S. and G.B." [25]

Brandeis felt he had not "omitted anything that it would have been wise to say." Lindsay "made no admission," but listened attentively, and "he knows we are in earnest." [26] Nevertheless, in October 1930, Sir John Hope Simpson's report (claiming lack of available land for colonization) and the Passfield White Paper (asserting that the National Home was "not meant to be the principal feature of the mandate") renewed the very danger Brandeis had sought to forestall—a gradual whittling away of obligations Britain had in fact assumed under the Balfour Declaration. On invitation he saw President Hoover, but "the only important thing that registered," Brandeis learned later, "was your recommendation that he do nothing." [27]

Brandeis's relationship to the Jewish problem now became more and more advisory. He was the elder statesman of Zionism in America. Giving largely himself and helping secure funds from others, much of his interest centered on reopening Transjordania to Jewish immigration. When others, including Weizmann, talked of a bi-national state in whose councils the Jews would have only "parity" with the Arabs,[28] Brandeis strongly protested. "We cannot yield any part of it [Palestine]. We cannot agree to remain a minority. And it ought to be possible to work out a modus vivendi—temporary—with the Arabs. 'My faith is great in time—and that which shapes it to its perfect end.' Reason and virtue will sometime again have their sway. The British, i.e., will return from their erring ways. It is imperative that nothing be done until then in the way of ultimate disposition of the problem." [29]

To the end Brandeis was optimistic. Even after Hitler's rise, he was sure that "the Jewish winning of Palestine and surroundings is Manifest Destiny." [30] But he had no illusions as to what Nazism meant to the Jews. "The Jews must leave Germany," he said, March 11, 1933. He saw that these outrages would prove to Jews everywhere the inadequacy of the assimilationist solution. Nor was watchful waiting (which he had hitherto advised) any longer appropriate. When in March 1933 Rabbi Wise doubted the propriety and expediency of mass demonstration, Brandeis urged: "Make the great protest meeting as good as you can."

Jewish feeling rose so high that when President Roosevelt failed to make formal protest, Brandeis told Secretary Hull: "I feel more ashamed of my country than pained by Jewish suffering." [31] He urged Hull to take the matter up with the President, suggesting a statement, "the kind which W.W. would have made," and "relaxation of immigration curbs in favor of refugees." Still he opposed an official boycott by the United States against Germany, a step soon to be advocated in Congress, and favored voluntary boycott, an idea fought by most non-Zionists.

After further Arab riots in 1936, Brandeis, anticipating trouble with the Axis in the Mediterranean, wanted the British to be made to see "that a large population in Palestine, and Jewish support throughout the world, would be their best ally." [32] And when the British sent to Palestine a royal commission under Lord Peel, Brandeis urged American Jews to present "the American case" before the Commission. [33] His slogan was "British and Arabs will be powerless against us. We are in the right."

A few months later, upon Wise's request, Secretary Hull telephoned Robert W. Bingham, our ambassador to Britain, and a native son of Louisville, that the American government would regard suspension of immigration into Palestine as a breach of the mandate. Soon a message to President Roosevelt came from the British Prime Minister, Neville Chamberlain: "We have given up the idea of suspension because of you (American interests). But we think there ought to be a lessening of immigration for the present." [34]

Chamberlain's statement at least hinted British intention to revoke the obligation which Britain, with the sanction of the world, had undertaken. Yet Brandeis's faith in Great Britain was unshaken. Rabbi Wise visited President Roosevelt to express his gratitude. When Wise added that his own joy was shared by Justice Brandeis, the President interrupted him, saying: "Grand man! You know, Stephen, we of the inner circle call him Isaiah." [35]

Disapproving of terrorism, Brandeis gave full support to Jewish self-defense activities in Palestine. After British disarmament of Jewish colonies previous to Arab attacks, he was convinced that the mandatory would not defend the Jews and therefore encouraged the movement which gave rise to the unofficial Jewish Army—the *Haganah*. Similarly he saw nothing wrong in the practice of evading British restrictions by illegal immigration of Jews into Palestine. Despite bitter experience, the Justice could not for long veer from his basic policy of watchful waiting.

CHAPTER THIRTY-EIGHT

Crusader Amid Prosperity and Depression

JUSTICE BRANDEIS viewed the economic and social trends of the nineteen twenties with increasing concern. The first World War had loosed new forces which, together with accelerated old drives, were heading the nation toward inflation and economic collapse. In these postwar years America, favored by the unhappy exhaustion of her principal business competitors and organized under an autocracy of finance, was able to sell her goods in the most favorable markets, draw the gold of the world into her coffers, and pay it out as profits and wages, thus expanding demand, production, and investment. This incredible boom created a golden age for self-seeking industrialists and financiers. Aiding them for twelve years was an acquiescent Republican administration headed first by Warren G. Harding, then by silent, do-nothing Calvin Coolidge, and finally by the high priest of rugged individualism—Herbert Hoover.

Industrial and scientific war miracles had only made the nation blind to the lessons of history. A terrific domestic struggle of competitive expansion set in, accompanied by the pumping-up of demand through high-powered advertising and forceful installment selling. To promote even greater investment, surtaxes were reduced, and the money saved was devoted to expanding production and foreign loans to win more customers. Production was swelled to a flood without any intelligent regard for the distribution of purchasing power necessary to stabilize such an economy. There was either a cutthroat scramble, wasting natural resources and sweating labor, or consolidation under holding companies and pyramiding of controls so that operating concerns were milked for the profit and further expansion of the big manipulators. Few recognized the transient character of this boom; fewer still understood that genuine security and enduring prosperity must provide for every element in society.

POLITICAL NOTES AND PROPHECIES

Even before the debacle of 1929 Brandeis was extremely skeptical. "I wish to record my utter inability to understand," he commented in 1926, "why a lot of folks don't go broke. These consolidations and security flotations, plus the building boom, beat my comprehension—unless there is a breakdown within a year." He was certain that the New Haven episode would be repeated on a vast scale. Like causes produce like effects. .

In March 1926, when the stock market dropped precipitously, Brandeis surmised that it might be the beginning of the end. "This New York slump may mean," he wrote Alfred, "that Coolidge's honeymoon is over. I guess if the country has *deiges* [common sense] he won't escape. At all events, some gents for whom you and I have little sympathy *haben stark geblutet;* and the blood-letting will doubtless be as good for the body politic as cupping and leeching was supposed to be for humans half a century ago."

By November 1, 1926, he could say that he felt "more interest in politics than for many years." A ray of hope appeared on the political horizon. Shortly before, President Coolidge had gratuitously injected himself into Massachusetts politics in behalf of the senatorial candidacy of his friend, William M. Butler. Brandeis was cheered by the thought that the President's support would prove to be of no assistance to Butler and that "C.C. will come out of the fray badly bruised." "C.C.," he reported to his brother optimistically, "has made his first major political mistake." [1]

Meanwhile, Herbert Hoover assiduously built businessman support by "his extraordinary helpfulness" as head of the Department of Commerce. Through his advocacy of the St. Lawrence Canal route, Hoover had gained an enthusiastic following, particularly in the West. All was not well, however; he had made no headway with the farmers by removing government support of grain prices, and "high government officials were loud in their dispraise of him." The latter agreed, Brandeis was told, "that there is no chance of his ever being President, but that he will be a per-petual candidate." [2]

In the Democratic ranks McAdoo was making still another bid for the Presidency, but the prospects were not promising. "I guess he hasn't much better chance than Hoover. There is considerable talk here of Jim Reed," the Justice speculated. "After timid, safe, and serene Cal, the country may fly to courageous, emphatic, erratic Jim. Certainly Coolidge is making a pitiable mess of our foreign policy. He was on safe ground when say noth-ing, do nothing was his practice." [3]

After the 1927 Jackson Day dinner a spirit of unity seemed to mark Dem-ocratic leadership, and Brandeis suspected that "Al Smith's high political sense is operating and that his influence is being widely felt." [4] "If he leads the Democrats, there will be a good chance of beating any Republican. It looks as if the country were getting sufficiently uneasy to want some change. The farmers may get higher prices for their products, but the industrialists and traders will probably have less joyous times." [5]

His optimism was still rising. "The unemployment situation," he wrote Norman Hapgood, March 4, 1928, "and the continued disclosures of Re-publican corruption in high places, is making Republicans here very uneasy. If the Democrats think hard and act wisely, it will be possible to inaugurate Al Smith a year from today."

Hapgood was an ardent Smith booster, but Brandeis's support seemed at first to have been sympathetic rather than cordial and unqualified. In reading Siegfried's America Comes of Age, he noted the passage: "But what shall we think of a country of British origin where liberalism has to seek its champions among foreigners and Catholics? The reason is clear. In the pursuit of wealth and power, America has abandoned its ideal of liberty to follow that of prosperity." Passing these lines along to Hapgood, June 2, 1927, he submitted the query: "Has it?"

During the middle twenties Brandeis drew inspiration from reading about the contrasting ways of Scandinavian countries, particularly the achievements of the Danes. Largely through co-operation, they had won a large British market and independence for the Danish farmer, established the Folk High Schools, paid the highest wages in Europe to industrial workers, converted peasants into free men of considerable culture, and developed not a little in literature and music—and all this, he wrote Hapgood, June 27, 1928, "on pretty near the poorest land in Europe with-out natural resources enjoyed by its neighbors and with a 10 per cent tariff."

These facts were culled from "Britain's Industrial Future," put out by the Liberal party in 1928. Brandeis described it as "the most comprehen-

sive, reasonable, and generally able modern state paper which I know—
and leaves the lagging Labour party far behind." He urged that Hapgood
take time out from his Shakespeare studies for its perusal. As a postscript
to this letter of June 27, he added: "I suppose your candidate is being
nominated now. Let's elect him." But the Democratic presidential nominee, quite apart from other untoward aspects of his candidacy, proved to
be his own worst enemy. No accusation hurled against him in the carefully
organized whispering campaign was too trivial to be "nailed as a lie." [6]
"The Governor has given new emphasis to Ecclesiastes," he wrote Hapgood, September 13, 1928:

> And the tongue of a man is his fall,
> Be not called a whisperer;
> And lie not in wait with thy tongue.

The Republicans nominated and elected their high priest of private enterprise in a flourish of unbounded confidence. In accepting the nomination, Hoover envisioned poverty banished from the earth. But this optimism was short-lived. The stock market "went over the edge of Niagara
in October and November 1929," and when the business slump became
alarming the country turned to the President for leadership.[7] Hoover had
carefully built up a reputation as a profound student of business, a super-
lative organizer. Whatever may have been his shortcomings in dealing
with politicians, many were sure he knew how to meet a public emergency of this sort. The President appointed numerous committees of experts, called in business leaders for conference, expressed disapproval of
lower wages, recommended a public works program to take up the slack
in unemployment, and other such measures. When these did not turn the
trick, and prospects worsened, the President kept right on assuring the
country that conditions were "fundamentally sound," that "prosperity was
just around the corner." "I am convinced that through these measures we
have re-established confidence," the President said in his annual message
in December 1929.

Brandeis was encouraged, not because the President had actually restored confidence, or was likely to do so, but because his failures gave hope
of political revolution long overdue. Writing Norman Hapgood, May 29,
1930, he observed: "Politically—things American have taken a great turn
since May 1929. The Hoover debacle is more complete than that of Taft
in 1909–10; and the distance between promise and performance is far
greater. The opposition in the Senate—coalition of insurgent Republicans
and Democrats—has been very ably led and has proved very effective. Norris, Borah, La Follette, and others have shown much ability; and the

Democrats (among others, some new men like [Hugo] Black) have done much to redeem the shattered Democratic reputation. The administration forces—*lucus a non lucendo*—have been weaker than anything I can recall."

The breakdown of Coolidge-Hoover prosperity was a bitter dose for the Republican party, which had persuaded itself and the country not only that the prosperity was genuine but also that the G.O.P. had invented it. Early in 1931 there were faint signs of improvement; but by March these uncertain tokens were seen to be false. March 1, 1931, Brandeis noted in a letter to Hapgood: "Hoover has been generally disappointing; and the Democrats have thrown away many opportunities. . . . The depression continues unabated—despite misleading headlines—and vast expenditures of public moneys. The big interests are unthinking as usual. If you were in the old game, I should suggest a new series: 'Is Capitalism bent on committing suicide?' . . . I still think times hopeful for progressives."

Six weeks later he surmised that the seriousness of the breakdown itself might yield the desired results. "The distress incident to the depression is great here," he wrote Hapgood, then on a visit to Europe, "and men are beginning to think. Even the hard-boiled are weakening in their self-satisfaction. Potent punches can pierce their armor. And of the hitherto placid indifferents there are many who are seeking for light. Losses and the prospect of prolonged depression are working beneficently among the people. We and those who can point the way— Come!"

Eagerness to come to grips with the multiplicity of problems confronting the nation well-nigh overcame him as he wrote Hapgood, June 1, 1931: "I regret every minute of your absence from America now. There never was, in our time, such an opportunity for effective blows. Of course, they cannot be dealt without adequate detailed knowledge of past and present; and for this much study is indispensable. But with knowledge and skill—much might be done. For the enemy is demoralized. One of the first tasks is to protect this country from Owen Young."

As the Court adjourned, June 1931, President Hoover sent for Justice Brandeis, saying that he wished to talk on specific matters. Following the interview, the President accompanied the Justice to the elevator. Brandeis bade the President good-by and wished him a good summer. Mr. Hoover's last words were: "Everything is going all right."

"Here even in private conversation," Brandeis observed years later, "Mr. Hoover refused to recognize the most obvious facts." [8]

Hoover, like Owen D. Young and other apostles of bigness and bliss, identified the privileges of the few with the welfare of the many. They had not seen that no group in society can suffer without jeopardizing the security of all. Brandeis looked away from the industrial immensity of America, from the hollow prosperity of the twenties, to the small unit, the true individualism and over-all prosperity of the Scandinavian countries. But how was he, a member of the Supreme Court, to combat the soothsayers of giant finance who had contributed so much to bring on the depression, including that worst of all social scourges—unemployment and want? How was he to block the efforts of those who would substitute "big" government for "big" business?

CLOISTERED WARRIOR IN ACTION

We have already seen how Brandeis ignored the self-imposed restriction on extrajudicial activities to speak before a committee of the Federal Council of Churches. The principles there propounded, he would follow now. Democracy had not failed; rather it had not been tried except for a few specific problems at specific times and places. Private enterprise had not failed; it had been deliberately undermined by the greed and power of mammoth combinations. In the dark days of 1933 when it seemed that the very depths of depression had been reached, a visitor inquired whether he believed the worst was over. "Yes," he replied cheerfully, "the worst happened before 1929." [9]

He would not tinker with the mechanisms of government; rather he would create the conditions necessary for its effective functioning:

I am unwavering in my belief in democracy of the old representative type, when the representative was to exercise his judgment and discretion and not merely voice the will of the electorate. The trouble with our democracy is that we have not been willing to pay the price—that is, educate the electorate. That must be a continuous process—not a quadrennial or annual campaign. And it must involve a much wider participation in government. I think consideration of governmental problems can be made for a large section of the people the most alluring of occupations. And there will be time for this when we have the five-day week and six-hour day. [10]

Above all, he was concerned with the quality of government. The field for special effort should be the state, the city, the village—and each should be led to seek to excel in something peculiar to it. "If ideals are developed locally the national ones will come pretty near taking care of themselves." Brandeis flatly denied that the area dictated by the need for good government necessarily coincided with the capacity for good government.

He was acutely aware of basic error in the easy assumption that since our industrial development is of national dimensions it must follow that the federal government alone can handle the problems set for us by industrialism. Far from following this facile trend, Brandeis had challenged it. In a letter to the editors of the *Survey,* November 7, 1920, he said: "The great America for which we long is unattainable unless the individuality of communities becomes far more highly developed and becomes a common American phenomenon. For a century our growth has come through natural expansion and the increase of the functions of the federal government. The growth of the future—at least of the immediate future—must be in quality and spiritual value. And that can come only through the concentrated, intensified strivings of smaller groups."

Brandeis took an interest in the localities throughout the nation—in Oregon, in Wisconsin, in Missouri, in Idaho. Ordinarily he thought young men should stay where they were brought up rather than rush pell-mell into the big metropolitan centers. This was the best thing not only for their country but also for themselves. He gave this advice in 1933 to Richard L. Neuberger of Oregon, then beginning his work as a newspaperman. Some years later when a tempting offer came from a national magazine, Neuberger wrote Justice Brandeis asking if his opinion remained unchanged. The Justice's reply was brief and to the point:

> Dear Richard Neuberger:
> Stay in Oregon.
>   Cordially,
>   Louis D. Brandeis.[11]

Being disqualified by judicial office from open participation in drives to implement his ideal, he influenced others to follow his lead. By a process of attraction as disciplined, as regulated, as everything else in his life, he brought the world to him. Each Sunday or Monday afternoon through the winter months, a small company gathered for tea in the Brandeis living-room—men and women, from all walks of life, representing all phases of government, each touching some particular interest of the Justice. One did not come unless invited, and the invitation had to be accepted or reasons given for not doing so. "Those teas," Marquis Childs has observed, "became a wonderful and slightly awesome institution. . . . Mrs. Brandeis presided as umpire over a game of musical chairs, designed to give the Justice ten or fifteen minutes of individual conversation with as many of the guests as could be talked to in an hour and a half. The rules were strictly observed. If you stayed too long in the privileged chair, Mrs. Brandeis would gently but firmly supplant you with the next person to be honored." [12] It was all part of a plan to carry on his crusade, to give his ideas force and effect on a wide front.

"I have heard Mrs. Brandeis say," an intimate friend has written, "she had people in because he so much wanted them. Gatherings of that kind probably gave him a sense of human companionship without commitments, so to speak—companionship which some sort of fear of being touched and opened up, of caution, of desire to remain free, prevented his seeking in the usual more intimate ways. As host, while protected himself, he could draw others out, show the interest and little attentions that build up pride in oneself and one's work. The varied assortment of people found at the Brandeis's was due I think in part to his eagerness to get all the facts about everything—and in part to his desire to encourage anyone no matter what he was doing, if he was trying to do a real job. The fact that there were so many young people in any gathering at his house," this writer concluded, "represented his effort to reach out even into the future. He seemed always to be trying to plant a seed in the good ground of a man's best nature or of his moral sense. Also, in contact with the young he was in control of the situation—in giving to others he himself was not exposed. . . . He never thought an individual too unimportant or a group too small to offer his best thought and attention." [13]

There were also small dinners to which six or seven carefully selected guests were invited—usually a newspaperman, social worker, member of a government agency, foreign diplomat, legislator, university professor. A typical list of dinner guests, as of 1927, included Senator Tom Walsh of Montana, who had bucked the Bourbon attack on the Bostonian in 1916; Norman Hapgood, an old friend, dating from 1906; Robert Bruère, contributor of sociological articles to the *Survey;* Monsignor Ryan, whose stout battling for the underdog made Christian doctrine a vital force in American economic life. Mrs. Brandeis sat at the head of the table and served the meat course, the Justice being seated at an inconspicuous corner. Talk moved smoothly, quietly; not infrequently he would single out a guest to carry forward one of his own "worth-while causes," intervening little himself—just enough to induce others to talk of the things for which they cared most. As ten o'clock approached, Mrs. Brandeis became uneasy lest her husband's resources be overtaxed. But the guests knew the custom, and anyone inclined to linger after the appointed hour got a definite hint when the Justice's crackers and milk came in.

Something happened at these informal dinners. "Men of good will once again renewed their faith, their energy, their ideals by the inspiration of his presence. In the company of that eternal fighter for the right, men . . . lost any temptation they may have had to call the battle quits." [14]

Brandeis found still other ways of enlisting his ideas in the dynamics of practical politics. It was not entirely accidental that when the economic collapse bore out his direst prophecies of nearly two decades earlier, men in official positions drew inspiration from his writings. With the 1932 election of Franklin D. Roosevelt, it looked for a while as though it were the triumph of all that Brandeis had long advocated. In fashioning arguments to support corrective legislation, New Dealers, many of them his disciples, cited his book *Other People's Money*. To say that Justice Brandeis was pleased would be understatement.

Until 1932 the book had sold only a few thousand copies. To get wider distribution, arrangements were made with the National Home Library Foundation for a new edition of 100,000 copies, to sell at fifteen cents. Brandeis actively participated, paying the original publisher for permission to reprint. Within a few months after republication of *Other People's Money*, Mrs. Brandeis commented to a visitor: "We are a best seller."

In his lectures of 1933–34 Norman Hapgood vigorously agitated the central Brandeis themes—"Other People's Money" and "The Curse of Bigness." Brandeis himself from time to time offered detailed suggestions for promoting his ideas. "Our publisher ought to seize on the President's talk of *Other People's Money* for an advertisement," he told Hapgood, March 9, 1933, after one of F.D.R.'s fireside chats.

"When you talk on 'Curse of Bigness,' " he innocently wrote Hapgood, "stress 'No man more than one job' as the correlative of 'Every Man a Job.' That is demanded by democracy as well as efficiency. And the job must not be too big a one. The proposition is applicable to government as well as to private business. Hence beware of centralization; and beware also of the mania of consolidating bureaus." [15]

Hapgood was kept primed with data on the progress of savings-bank life insurance and urged to call attention to it as demonstrating the relatively greater efficiency of the small unit. When an insurance man tried to ridicule Brandeis's "greatest achievement" by citing 186 million dollars of commercial insurance issued in Massachusetts in 1933 as against "our puny writings," Brandeis pointed out that "the companies lost in outstanding insurance nearly as much as the year's writings. We held most of our outstanding insurance," he observed. " 'The race is not (always) to the swift.' " [16]

In 1934 Sherman Mittell, editor of the National Home Library Foundation, made tentative plans with the National Broadcasting Company for a series of talks, beginning with a passage from Brandeis's writings. The Justice had no objection to this but found it "impossible to speak personally. A self-denying ordinance adopted when I became a member of the Court, precludes speaking as well as writing except officially." [17] Later on when Norman Hapgood suggested a two-minute radio talk about books, he stood firm: "I must adhere to my resolution not to say anything for publication—either in print or by radio—whether by writing or interview. Of course," he told Hapgood, "I should not object to your referring in your discreet way to my reading habits and my opinion as to the importance in our national development that the habit of reading (and possessing) good books be promoted." [18]

Some considered him too aloof in not giving personal inspiration, at least on professional occasions having no relation to the active promotion of his own social and political ideas. But one may note that the loss entailed by his "self-denying ordinance" was compensated by the inspiration and pressure he brought to bear on hundreds of others. He had emissaries in every conceivable field—politics, universities, law schools, journalism—all of whom he kept supplied with material on his "worth-while causes." Men were catalogued in his mind according to particular tasks which they could be counted upon to further. As the Justice wrote an opinion, or encountered material touching the subject of mutual interest, he was likely to be heard from. "His letters were like communiqués from a battlefield, with the rattle of artillery sounding in their one-two-three memorandum sequence." [19]

"THE RIGHT TO EXPERIMENT"

By 1932, when the Supreme Court began to consider legislation reflective of economic distress, its personnel had undergone considerable change. Taft was dead, and President Hoover had in 1930 nominated the conservative corporation lawyer and former Justice, Charles Evans Hughes, to be his successor, despite a storm of protest from liberals, reminiscent of the assault of the reactionaries against Brandeis in 1916. Admittedly a man of high integrity and great legal ability, Hughes's nomination was nevertheless challenged in protest against "the building up of a judicial system of law that is fast bringing economic slavery in this country." [20]

Earlier President Coolidge had promoted his Amherst classmate and Attorney-General, Harlan Fiske Stone, to the high court. In 1925 Chief Justice Taft had claimed that he "rather forced the President into the appointment"; and for a while Stone, along with the Van Devanter-Sutherland-Sanford-Butler group, was invited to the Chief Justice's Sunday afternoon at home. At these "faintly extracurricular" conferences, "it may safely be assumed, plans were made to block the liberal machinations of Holmes and Brandeis." [21] But it was not long before Stone broke away from the conservative block. In 1929 Taft reappraised him: "He is a learned lawyer in many ways, but his judgments I do not altogether consider safe. . . . He definitely has ranged himself with Brandeis and with Holmes in a good many of our constitutional differences." [22]

But soon thereafter Holmes was lost to the Court. On January 11, 1932, the venerable Justice told the clerk, "I won't be down tomorrow." That night Brandeis's friend of many years, his comrade and close companion, wrote President Hoover: "The time has come and I bow to the inevitable." *

As his successor the President first nominated Judge John G. Parker, but when organized labor's protest defeated Senate confirmation the nation clamored for the appointment of Benjamin N. Cardozo, a famous liberal in the law and at the time Chief Judge of the New York Court of Appeals. The unanimity of public and senatorial opinion in his support reminded Brandeis of the lines from Gilbert and Sullivan's *Iolanthe:*

> Though the views of the House have diverged
> On every conceivable motion, All questions of party are merged
> In a frenzy of love and devotion.

So far as any man might, Cardozo stood for Brandeis in the place of Holmes.

The liberals now numbered three—Brandeis, Cardozo, and Stone—and they could occasionally count on the support of Chief Justice Hughes and Justice Owen J. Roberts, who had succeeded Justice Sanford. As economic distress became ever more severe, certain observers anticipated further breaks in the conservative ranks. All such hopes were blasted early in 1932, when the Court decided the case of *New State Ice Company* v. *Liebmann.* Here the State of Oklahoma, reflecting local emergency conditions, required a certificate of public convenience and necessity of any new ice company desiring to enter the business of manufacturing and selling ice. The New State Ice Company obtained such a certificate, erected a plant, and invested about $500,000. Liebmann, a free-lance dealer, set up a plant and began doing business in competition with the New State Ice Company. The authorized company sued to restrain him, but the state courts sustained Liebmann's plea on the ground that the Oklahoma statute contravened the Fourteenth Amendment, abridged privileges and immunities of citizens of the United States, and deprived persons of their property without due process of law.

For Justice Sutherland, who spoke for the Court, the category of businesses "affected with a public interest" did not include the ice business. And the plain inference from what he said was that economic conditions arising out of depression, however serious, could not possibly have the effect of expanding the judicially constructed category so as to embrace the ice business. "Businesses affected with a public interest" must be strictly confined to the traditional ones—common carriers, gas, water, and other

* Holmes had three more years to live. He passed away March 6, 1935, at the age of ninety-four.

such public utilities—these and no more. Sutherland saw this legislation as warring with those rights on which liberals had placed the highest value. No matter how pressing the conditions out of which such legislation emerged, there were, he argued, "certain essentials of liberty" that must not be interfered with "in the interest of experiments."

Sutherland, who had not heretofore been greatly moved by the specter of economic privilege, saw the statute as creative of monopoly. The act did not "protect the consuming public," he said, "either with respect to conditions of manufacture and distribution or to insure priority of product or to prevent extortion. The control here asserted does not protect against monopoly, but tends to foster it. The aim is not to encourage competition, but to prevent it; not to regulate the business, but to preclude persons from engaging in it." [23]

How could an arch foe of monopoly, a strong advocate of competition such as Justice Brandeis dissent from such views? The answer is to be found in his flexibility of mind, his recognition that our concepts of liberty and property must be remolded from time to time to meet changed conditions, his view that "Time works changes, brings into existence new conditions and purposes. Therefore a principle to be vital must be capable of wider application than the mischief which gave it birth." [24]

In a long and heavily documented dissent Brandeis examined, with an open mind, the conditions out of which the Oklahoma statute emerged. It did not represent an isolated effort. Other states, taking into account unnecessary duplication of plants and delivery service, had enacted controls to "prevent wastes ultimately burdensome to the consumer. The need of some remedy for the evil of destructive competition . . . had been and was widely felt," Brandeis observed. Nor had the category "Businesses affected with a public interest" become closed, once and for all, sometime in the remote past. "The conception of a public utility is not static," Brandeis contended. "The state's power extends to every regulation of any business reasonably required and appropriate for the public protection."

The situation was further complicated by the fact that the emergency was of a novel sort. The community was suffering not from scarcity, as in the past, but from overabundance of productive capacity, unprecedented unemployment, a catastrophic fall in commodity prices, and alarming economic losses. In brief, the question was whether or not the Supreme Court would permit Oklahoma to deal with a novel issue in a novel way; whether or not the Constitution stayed the effort of a community to deal with "an emergency more serious than war." As to this the Justice said:

"Some people believe that the existing conditions threaten even the stability of the capitalistic system. Economists are searching for the causes of this disorder and are re-examining the bases of our industrial structure. Businessmen are seeking possible remedies. Most of them realize that failure to distribute widely the profits of industry has been a prime cause of our present plight. But rightly or wrongly, many persons think that one of the major contributing causes has been unbridled competition. Increasingly, doubt is expressed whether it is economically wise, or morally right, that men should be permitted to add to the producing facilities of an industry which is already suffering from overcapacity. . . . All agree that irregularity in employment—the greatest of our evils—cannot be overcome unless production and consumption are more nearly balanced. Many insist there must be some form of economic control. . . .

"Some people assert that our present plight is due, in part, to the limitations set by the courts upon experimentation in the fields of social and economic science. . . . There must be power in the states and the nation to remold, through experimentation, our economic practices and institutions to meet changing social and economic needs. . . . To stay experimentation in things social and economic is a grave responsibility. This Court has the power to prevent experimentation. . . . But in the exercise of this high power, we must be ever on our guard, lest we erect our prejudices into legal principles." [25]

For more than a decade Brandeis's dissenting opinions had been followed closely by members of the legal profession as indicating the law of the future. His latest effort won much wider notice. "Brandeis, Viewing Crisis 'Worse Than War'—Urges Control of Competition by the State," ran the *New York Times* front-page headlines on March 22, 1932. The *Literary Digest* on April 9 devoted a full page to the case, Brandeis's dissent claiming the lion's share of space. Many newspapers discussed his opinions editorially. "We think this liberal jurist of the nation's highest Bench," the *New York World-Telegram* commented on March 22, "has dealt with a major national need in words that should carry far and wide, exerting profound influence upon judges, legislators, industrialists, businessmen, economists—everyone involved in the carrying out of social and economic readjustments that we can only put off at peril."

The note of urgency running through Brandeis's opinion is obscured somewhat by the phrases—"some people believe," "many insist," "some people assert"—but such reportorial devices did not blind his critics to the fact that he was using this opportunity to crystallize in eloquent words his own mature judgment on these matters—many of which were relevant only because the cast of his mind made them so. They were the things he had been harping on for years in his correspondence with Norman Hapgood and other friends and colleagues. That is why the *Washington Post* sharply condemned the "curious logic" which carried him "dangerously near to socialism." He "put his economic theories ahead of the Constitution," the *Post* declared, and wrote "a dissertation on hard times. . . . The justice took occasion to air his personal views on the American economic structure, with only a casual reference to the legal point at issue." [26]

ECONOMIC ABSOLUTISM OR INDUSTRIAL DEMOCRACY

Among the fulfilled prophecies incident to the economic collapse of 1929, none had been more conspicuous than the "Curse of Bigness" manifested in sprawling public utilities, top-heavy insurance companies, and gigantic bank affiliates. The Justice had hit on this theme in the Quaker City Cab case. In 1933 another opportunity came to hand to give the subject of small versus the large unit full-dress treatment under the most favorable circumstance.

The case involved a Florida statute taxing incorporated chain stores more heavily than individual enterprises or co-operatives. As in the earlier case, the question was whether corporate enterprise could be differentiated in the matter of taxation and still not contravene the equal protection and due process clauses of the Fourteenth Amendment. Is there an advantage gained through incorporation that warrants heavier taxation? A 5 to 4 majority found no such justification and set the act aside. Brandeis might have disposed of his dissent by simply stating, as he did, that those opposing the legislation had not proved the statute unreasonable and arbitrary. "There is nothing in the record," he observed, "to show affirmatively that the provision may not be a reasonable one in view of the conditions prevailing in Florida. Since the presumption of constitutionality must prevail in the absence of some factual foundation of record for overthrowing the statute, its validity should, in my opinion, be sustained." [27]

But he was not content to rest his case on any such narrowly constitutional ground. There followed one of the most masterful opinions of his judicial career. In a detailed and scholarly analysis of the corporation as a form of business activity, he unfolded the entire story of its rise to a dominant position in modern industrial society—how the people at first were reluctant to permit business incorporation at all because of their lurking fear of domination; how corporate capitalization was limited in most states; how these restrictions were relaxed when a few states began a mad rush to lure business within their borders. Formerly there was "Fear of encroachment upon the liberties and opportunities of the individual. Fear of the subjection of labor to capital. Fear of monopoly. Fear that the absorption of capital by corporations, and their perpetual life, might bring evils similar to those which attended mortmain. There was a sense of some insidious menace inherent in large aggregations of capital, particularly when held by corporations." [28]

Such fears were unknown during Coolidge prosperity. The original legal restrictions so carefully thrown around corporations were removed almost without trace. "The states joined in advertising their wares [corporate charters]. The race was one not of diligence but of laxity." Indeed "the prevalence of the corporation in America has led men of this generation to act, at times, as if the privilege of doing business in corporate form were inherent in the citizen; and has led them to accept the evils attendant upon the free and unrestricted use of the corporate mechanism as if these evils were the inescapable price of civilized life and, hence, to be borne with resignation." [29]

Against the Frankenstein monsters resulting from this wholesale relaxation of state charters, Brandeis placed the individual business enterprise, the entrepreneur—necessarily of limited capitalization, "engaging in a struggle to preserve their independence—perhaps a struggle for existence." The Florida statute, he said, was designed to relieve the dreadful plight of private enterprise. The chain-store tax, far from denying unequal protection of the laws as the majority had held, made competition more equitable —enlarged industrial freedom, prevented the "taking" of property by corporations without due process of law.

Brandeis's dissenting opinion reads like a page of his testimony in the Stanley Committee investigation of United States Steel Corporation in 1911, except for the fact that after a lapse of two decades others had also made the discovery: "Able, discerning scholars have pictured for us the economic and social results of thus removing all limitations upon the size and activities of business corporations and of vesting in their managers vast powers once exercised by stockholders—results not designed by the states and long unsuspected. They show that size alone gives to giant corporations a social significance not attached ordinarily to smaller units of private enterprise. Through size, corporations . . . are sometimes able to dominate the state. The typical business corporation of the last century, owned by a small group of individuals, managed by their owners, and limited in size by their personal wealth, is being supplanted by huge concerns in which the lives of tens or hundreds of thousands of employees and the property of tens or hundreds of thousands of investors are subjected, through the corporate mechanism, to the control of a few men. Ownership has been separated from control; and this separation has removed many of the checks which formerly operated to curb the misuse of wealth and power. And as ownership of the shares is becoming continually more dispersed, the power which formerly accompanied ownership is becoming increasingly concentrated in the hands of a few. The changes thereby wrought in the lives of the workers, of the owners, and of the general public, are so fundamental and far-reaching as to lead these scholars to compare the evolving 'corporate system' with the feudal system; and to lead other men of insight and experience to assert that this 'master institution of civilized life' is committing it to the rule of a plutocracy." [30]

Nor was this all. The depression had served to underscore other evils of bigness: "There is a widespread belief that the existing unemployment is the result, in large part, of the gross inequality in the distribution of wealth and income which giant corporations have fostered; that by the control which the few have exerted through giant corporations, individual initiative and effort are being paralyzed, creative power impaired, and human happiness lessened: that the true prosperity of our past came not from big business, but through the courage, the energy, and the resourcefulness of small men; that only by releasing from corporate control the faculties of the unknown many, only by reopening to them the opportunities for leadership, can confidence in our future be restored and the existing misery be overcome; and that only through participation by the many in the responsibilities and determinations of business, can Americans secure the moral and intellectual development which is essential to the maintenance of liberty." [31]

It was the author's good fortune to see something of this opinion while in preparation and to hear Justice Brandeis deliver it from the Bench. On his invitation in 1933, I used the cluttered and dust-laden office above his apartment at 2205 California Street. The adjoining room was occupied by his law clerk, Paul A. Freund, who kindly permitted me an occasional peep at an opinion in process. He told how the Justice wrote his opinions in longhand and sent them to the printer in that form. Then began the arduous work of revision from the printed page. The printed draft was turned over to Freund with the understanding that he might submit memoranda suggesting the citation of pertinent cases or other material to enlarge its informative character. Freund recalled how search for an Italian reference occupied him for hours in the Library of Congress. The Justice had worked out with his secretary an elaborate system of indicating revisions by the use of multi-colored pencils. To the uninitiated, it seemed intricate indeed. This process, which involved many memoranda passing to and from his law clerk, sometimes ran to more than a score of revisions.

On the evening of March 12, 1933, a messenger appeared at the author's lodging in the Brookings Institution, with a note which read: "I think you will want to be in Court tomorrow morning. A card is enclosed admitting you to the reserved seats. You may present it to the clerk shortly before 12."

When it came the Justice's turn to speak, he leaned forward and began in a rather conversational manner, creating a marked spirit of intimacy between himself and his audience. He did not refer to the advance copy of his opinion, nor did he seem to follow notes. In fact, the organization of the opinion as delivered was quite different from that of the written document. As he proceeded one was impressed by a trace of Kentucky in his enunciation, by the fine modulation of his voice, by its sheer persuasiveness and power, but, above all, by the strong conviction which his words carried. It was a rare, never-to-be-forgotten occasion. There were still six more years during which he delivered important opinions, but it is doubtful whether he was ever more successful in fusing clarity and conviction in the presentation of a technical subject. Basic principles and the practical creed he built thereon stood out clear to all men.

CHAPTER THIRTY-NINE

The New Deal: Yes and No

BY NOVEMBER 1931 Brandeis had served fifteen years on the Supreme Court. He had now reached his seventy-fifth birthday—an event widely noticed by newspapers, magazines, and law reviews. From the universal praise now accorded him, one would never imagine that his nomination had been challenged. "The country, and not he, is to be congratulated on the anniversary," the once doubtful *New York Times* commented editorially on November 9. "Year by year his stature as a Judge has increased. He has come to be regarded with general respect and affection such as surrounds his elder brother, Mr. Justice Holmes."

Honors such as university degrees which most public figures accept as a matter of course he consistently declined. A striking instance is recalled by Thurman Arnold: "When I was on the faculty of the Yale law school they asked us to nominate a candidate for an honorary degree. The faculty named Justice Brandeis. President Angell turned it down. Next year they asked the faculty again. We named Justice Brandeis. President Angell gave in, but the trustees turned it down. The third year they asked us again. We named Justice Brandeis. President Angell approved, the trustees approved, but the corporation turned it down. The fourth year they asked us again. Again we named Justice Brandeis. President Angell approved, the trustees approved, the corporation approved, but Justice Brandeis turned it down."

When Harvard was arranging to have his portrait installed in the Law School alongside those of Marshall, Webster, and Holmes, Brandeis refused to sit. The artist had to work from a photograph and hasten each morning to the Supreme Court to catch the expression of life while the Justice sat on the Bench. As was to be expected, the job is not well done. Brandeis himself never took the trouble to look at it.

Leading law reviews in 1931 dedicated their November issue to him and carried articles discussing various phases of his legal and judicial career. Five of these articles were collected by Felix Frankfurter and published in book form. In a brief introduction, Justice Holmes, then retired, spoke of their long friendship interrupted only by "the place and nature of our occupations. But our meetings were renewed when possible, and since he came upon the Bench of the Supreme Court they have been constant. . . . Whenever he left my house I was likely to say to my wife, 'There goes a really good man.' I think that the world now would agree with me in adding what the years have proved—'and a great Judge.' . . . In moments of discouragement that we all pass through," Holmes concluded, "he always has had the happy word that lifts up one's heart. It came from knowledge, experience, courage, and the high way in which he always has taken life." [1]

NEW DEAL ORACLE AT SEVENTY-FIVE

With the presidential election of 1932, the time seemed ripe for wholesale enactment of Brandeis's creed. Recent events had borne out his fears as well as his hopes. There was hardly a phase of the social and economic collapse that he had not foreseen. The New Deal, in its first efforts, seemed guided essentially by his philosophy and spirit. The President spoke of his own program as a response to the country's need for "bold, persistent experimentation."

Roosevelt's utterance was not accidental. Guiding the New Deal policy and legislative program were several of the Justice's disciples, the most notable being Felix Frankfurter. Professor Frankfurter had put his oar into the mainstream of New Deal politics in August 1932, when F.D.R.

invited him to spend a week-end aboard the presidential candidate's train. The candidate listened long and attentively to talk on hard subjects. Nor was the effort unfruitful. The Professor found his pupil attentive and capable of considerable grasp of facts once they were put to him. That October the candidate asked Frankfurter to arrange for a full talk about future policies with Brandeis himself.

During the hectic Hundred Days in the spring of 1933 and later, Frankfurter was tutor to the new administration. The Harvard Law Professor, in turn, sought light and guidance on general policy as well as on specific programs from Justice Brandeis. He consulted the "old counselor" on appointments, great and small. Several of the key administrators during the formative years were pupils of Brandeis—Tom Corcoran, Ben Cohen, A. A. Berle, Jr., Dean G. Acheson, and James M. Landis. Some of them had been his law clerks. Even after appointments had been decided upon Frankfurter saw to it that the nominee was brought under the Justice's influence.

Much early New Deal legislation bears the Brandeis stamp. In 1914 Brandeis had, for example, thrown out the challenge: "We must break the Money Trust or the Money Trust will break us." [2] Under the Banking Act of 1933, national and member banks were forced to divest themselves of their securities affiliates; within a year it became unlawful for any securities company to engage in banking, hitting directly at private banking houses, such as J. P. Morgan & Company, that had been exercising both functions. "Compel bankers when issuing securities to make public the commissions or profits they are receiving," he had advocated back in 1913; [3] and under the Securities Act of 1933 the investor is protected against deceptive and fraudulent securities by the requirement that would-be investors be fully informed as to the facts of the securities offered them for sale.

Brandeis had long favored "regulated competition" as against "regulated monopoly." Having exposed the evils of anarchic competition, he urged co-operation among those engaged in a particular industry. "The functions of government," he had said in 1914, "should not be limited to the enactment of wise rules of action, and the providing of efficient judicial machinery, by which those guilty of breaking the law may be punished. . . . We need the inspector and the policeman even more than we need the prosecuting attorney. . . ." Above all, Brandeis had urged government publicity of current information. "The mere substitution of knowledge for ignorance," he said, "of publicity for secrecy—will go far toward preventing monopoly." [4] Some of these ideas were embodied in the National Industrial Recovery Act of 1933.

President Roosevelt's discussion of this measure, June 17, 1933, stressed these features of Brandeis's philosophy. He spoke of it as a great co-operative movement throughout all industry in order to obtain wide re-employment, shorten the working week, pay decent wages, and prevent unfair competition. The act did not provide, except against recalcitrants, that government impose its own rules, but placed upon industry itself the obligation of putting its house in order. The various trades were not only permitted but urged to frame and adopt their own codes. If these received government approval, particularly as to labor and the consumer, they were mandatory for the trade affected.

But enactment of sound public policy was one thing, its administration something else. This was particularly true of the NRA, and, despite re-markable successes, Brandeis followed New Deal developments a bit anx-iously. Frontal attack had yet to be made on the major curse—industrial and financial "bigness." Also disturbing was the evidence he saw on all sides of that dreaded curse spreading to government itself. "I am glad you are planning lunch talks on the small unit," he wrote Hapgood, October 31, 1934. "There is evidence that the difficulties of bigness are being real-ized in governmental matters." Every sign of the administration's aware-ness of this characteristic American evil he seized upon as making for progress. Hapgood entertained doubt as to whether it was either desirable or possible to reverse such trends. In reply Brandeis quoted these lines:

> Wouldst thou make me weep with dreams
> of hope that never can be won?
> Deeds that were dreamed not of may yet be done.

"Indeed," Brandeis added, "there is evidence that the curb of bigness has set in, in other ways than chain-store legislation. The decentralization of plants by big concerns is a step—; and federal legislation going a little way is imminent." [5]

A few weeks later he was harping on the same theme. "When you are next at the club, look at Hammond's *Rise of Modern Industry* (1925) pp. 87–90, to see how, under the theory of the efficiency of bigness, medie-val villages were destroyed in England; and of the different story in France and Denmark. We must come back to the little unit in business, etc.—as the world is coming everywhere back (except Russia) in agriculture." [6]

NEW DEAL IN COURT—HOPES

How the Justices would stand on the New Deal legislative program no one could foretell. The votes of Chief Justice Hughes and Justice Owen J. Roberts were quite unpredictable. Some indication of the probable alignment was given when in 1934 the Court in a 5 to 4 decision upheld Minnesota's two-year moratorium on mortgage foreclosures; [7] and, again by vote of 5 to 4, upheld a New York state statute fixing the minimum and maximum retail price of milk.[8] Those favorable to the New Deal as well as those opposing it found comfort in the majority opinions. New Dealers looked fondly on those paragraphs of the Minnesota moratorium opinion in which Chief Justice Hughes pointed to the Court's appreciation of the public interest as omnipresent, and to the necessity of finding ground for rational compromise between individual rights and public welfare. They were cheered by his recognition of "an increased use of the organization of society in order to protect the very bases of individual opportunity." All this was in the best Brandeis tradition. At the same time opponents of Roosevelt's legislative program took heart in the Chief Justice's stress on the emergency character of the legislation, but they could find no such comfort in Justice Roberts's opinion upholding the New York milk law. Here legislative price-fixing was upheld without reference to the emergency.

Now Brandeis found himself in the majority on crucial social and economic issues. The die-hard conservatives—Butler, McReynolds, Sutherland, and Van Devanter—dethroned from their customary dominance, were desperate. For them the deeper and more fundamental issue presented by these cases was not whether the New Deal would stand up under the microscope of the Judiciary. The "liberal" triumph threatened the existence of the Constitution itself, and along with it our unique and venerable principle of judicial review. "If the provisions of the Constitution can not be upheld when they pinch as well as when they comfort," Justice Sutherland carped in his Minnesota moratorium dissent, "they may as well be abandoned." In the New York Milk case, Justice Roberts, speaking for the majority, solemnly disclaimed any judicial control over social and economic policy. "With the wisdom of the policy adopted," he said, "the Courts are both incompetent and unauthorized to deal." But Justice McReynolds in dissent vehemently disagreed. He would continue the judicial pre-eminence over policy of former Justices Brewer, Field, Peckham, and Taft—the dogma these sturdy individualists had successfully upheld for forty years. "But plainly," McReynolds declared, "I think this Court must have regard to the wisdom of the enactment."

In this lay the crux of the whole matter. It was not the provisions of the Constitution nor the foundations of the Fathers that were being undermined in these test cases, but only the then dissenting view of what constitutes sound public policy. Certain enthusiastic commentators on constitutional interpretation saw these 1934 decisions as insuring the validity of the entire legislative program; one authority on the Constitution anticipated that judicial review itself might well fall into innocuous desuetude. But those in closer touch with political trends in Washington were quite sure that the Court would not relinquish its self-made role as final arbiter of state and national policy.[9]

NEW DEAL IN COURT—REALITIES

The New Deal was introduced to the Court under most inauspicious circumstances, December 10, 1934, when government attorneys argued on behalf of the validity of certain orders of the President issued under the NIRA * which purported to authorize him to prohibit the transportation in interstate commerce of "hot oil," i.e., of oil produced in violation of state government laws.[10] Counsel in opposition complained that their client was arrested, indicted, and held in jail several days for violating a law that did not exist. The client said he had seen only one copy of the code and that was in the "hip pocket of a government agent sent down to Texas from Washington." Brandeis was immediately aroused. Here, surely, was proof of what happens when bigness afflicts government.

"Who promulgates these orders and codes that have the force of law?" the Justice asked.

"They are promulgated by the President, and I assume they are on record at the State Department," the government's attorney replied.

"Is there any official or general publication of these executive orders?"

"Not that I know of."

"Well, is there any way," Brandeis pursued, "by which one can find out what is in these executive orders when they are issued?"

"I think it would be rather difficult, but it is possible to get certified copies of the executive orders and codes from the NRA," † government counsel replied somewhat lamely.[11]

Administration leaders now might well surmise that the Court was more than incredulous, though Justice Brandeis was still open-minded, writing Hapgood, October 27, 1934: "NRA seems to be tending toward removal of price-fixing and production curtailment;—and toward the lowering of prices, which is essential to lessening unemployment. It is a pity we have wasted so much time in trodding false paths; but good to be on the right one now."

But NRA had still not found the open road on that fatal day, May 27, 1935, when the Court went on a rampage, slaughtering the Blue Eagle,[12]

* National Industrial Recovery Act.
† National Recovery Administration.

setting aside the Frazier–Lemke Act [13] and repudiating President Roosevelt's bold exercise of the removal power [14]—all three by unanimous vote. Although few were more sympathetic with mortgagors in depression, Brandeis wrote the opinion holding unconstitutional the Frazier–Lemke Act for the relief of farm debtors. This act of 1934, depriving creditors of all effective remedy, represented New Deal lawmaking at its worst. It would be difficult to cite a clearer case of class legislation, of legislative transference of property from A to B without ulterior public advantage. Speaking for a unanimous Court, Brandeis showed again his respect for private property and recognized the need for its constitutional protection even in cases where changed conditions clothed it with a public interest.

". . . The Fifth Amendment," he said, "commands that, however great the nation's need, private property shall not be thus taken even for a wholly public use without just compensation. If the public interest requires, and permits, the taking of property of individual mortgagees in order to relieve the necessities of individual mortgagors, resort must be had to proceedings by eminent domain; so that, through taxation, the burden of the relief afforded in the public interest may be borne by the public." [15]

That same day the Court blocked President Roosevelt's removal of Republican Federal Trade Commissioner William E. Humphrey, thereby rejecting the broad implications of Chief Justice Taft's opinion in *Myers* v. *U.S.* Brandeis was greatly pleased to have his earlier dissenting views prevail. In a confidential interview on June 23, 1935, he expressed great satisfaction, saying: "If men on the Federal Trade Commission and similar government agencies are not allowed to exercise their independent judgment we should have in effect a dictatorship or a totalitarian state. What would happen to us," he queried, "if Huey Long were President and such a doctrine prevailed?"

Brandeis's assent to the unanimous decision overturning NIRA aroused curiosity and comment, but on examination his stand becomes entirely consistent. Purporting to set up industrial self-government, the act actually surrendered control of production, prices, and trade practices, to a small group of big corporate employers, thus making for the elimination of competition. Put forward as an incentive to trade unionism and collective bargaining, the act resulted in the growth and extension of company unionism on a scale heretofore unequaled. Brandeis, the inveterate foe of bigness, who had never pinned his faith entirely on government control, who had expressed doubt as to what the mind of the bureaucrat, no less than that of the banker or businessman, can comprehend—joined in declaring the act unconstitutional.

OFF THE RECORD

It was these decisions, particularly that setting aside NIRA, that stimulated President Roosevelt's impulsive and ill-tempered attack on the Supreme Court in his famous "horse and buggy" interview with newspapermen. Justice Brandeis, on vacation in June 1935 at Chatham on Cape Cod, expressed an altogether different view of what had been accomplished. In a confidential interview with two prominent newspapermen, he exhibited little or none of his customary reticence in discussing judicial business. The day on which the Court handed down the three decisions unfavorable to the administration was, he said, "the most important day in the history of the Court and the most beneficent." Following this dramatic opening, the Justice proceeded to enlarge on his favorite theme—that bigness in industry begets inefficiency. Men in high positions, both in public and in private life, spread themselves out too thin. In this country we have "ignored the fundamental importance of cutting our coat to human cloth." No man, however able, can do efficiently what many executives in public and private life undertake. "Many men are all wool," he said, "but none is more than a yard wide."

"The curse of bigness," Brandeis said, "has prevented proper thinking." Therefore the three decisions of May 27, 1935, far from returning us to the "horse and buggy" days, "compelled a return to human limitations." Reverting to the act, he spoke of the great number of codes, some six hundred in all, and emphasized how impossible it was for any administrator to form a sound judgment on each code. The time had come to correct the assumption, the "lie," that the country as a whole could make an advance. This prevalent idea ignored historical fact and a great mass of historical literature showing that great advances had been made in states and localities and in particular industries. NIRA was, as he saw it, a Procrustean bed for sections and industries—a wholesale attempt to regulate wages and hours. It demonstrated again the characteristic American error of trying to get things done the easy way. There is, he said, no easy way to social reform, but only the hard way of education.

The Justice, however, entertained no lack of sympathy for President Roosevelt's purposes. Even the more "radical" views of Henry Wallace did not disturb his usual calm. "I guess you will have to read Secretary Wallace's *New Frontiers*," he commented in a letter to Norman Hapgood, October 5, 1934. "The economic difficulties are great—but his attitude, his approach, and his aims are fine. And what he says of the farm problem is very informing."

Measured statistically, Justice Brandeis was a New Dealer. Of the several New Deal enactments coming before the Court, he turned down only three.* His vote helped win the first judicial New Deal victory, the Gold Clause cases,[16] where the Court split 5 to 4. He joined with seven other Justices in affirming the Tennessee Valley Authority [17] against the lone dissent of Justice McReynolds. He voted for the original Railway Pensions Act [18] which the majority disapproved, and was of the minority of four in defense of the Municipal Bankruptcy Act.[19] He supported the Wagner Labor Disputes Act [20] and Social Security legislation.[21]

Brandeis greatly admired President Roosevelt as a political leader. Comparing him with other Chief Executives, including Jefferson, Cleveland, and Wilson, he commented: "But none of them could match this fellow"— F.D.R. Jefferson he described as "the most civilized and democratic American," and Cleveland as "an honest man, when honest men were rare in American politics." [22] Roosevelt, like Woodrow Wilson, was guided by high purpose but, he declared, "the country will not be saved by even the best motives in Washington. . . . Thank God for the limitations inherent in our federal system." Speaking again with contempt for over-all planners, he asked: "What do they know about the practical problems of business?" No man or group in Washington could possibly know the facts of localities and industries throughout the states, and, besides, to fix wages and hours for the whole country regardless of living standards and wage levels was "uneconomic." The real problem, as he saw it, was to "break up businesses to the point where the states could regulate them." There should be no such thing as a Delaware corporation beyond the power of states. Public utility holding companies had grown too big to be regulated. "You can't control a monster," he said.

But how could the "break-down" be effected? By taxation—a tax on bigness, a tax on resources; a federal tax on corporations doing business outside the state of their incorporation, thus forcing large businesses to incorporate in states in which they do business; a tax on directors doing business with their own corporations. Lack of such a tax had made accumulations of large fortunes possible and permitted directors to betray their trust; and, finally, a tax on intra-organization transactions within a holding company.

Brandeis was critical of the Roosevelt administration for its failure to strike fundamentally at the worst of our industrial evils—irregularity of employment. "We are responsible for unemployment," he said, "because we have tolerated the idea that an employer is free with impunity to de-

---

* The Panama Refining, Schechter Bros., and Louisville Joint Stock Land Bank cases.

crease or increase his force." Here also taxation was a serviceable device of social control, as illustrated in the Wisconsin tax on irregularity which requires employers who want to indulge in it to pay a tax.[23]

FROM RECOVERY TO REFORM

The Supreme Court decisions of May 1935 marked a significant turning point in the evolution of the New Deal. Heretofore the President had maintained a fairly even balance between the objectives of recovery and reform, the stress being laid on the former. A major New Deal recipe for recovery had been artificial limits on production and artificial raising of prices. Brandeis never subscribed to either of these policies. He was strongly opposed to raising prices by government fiat. "Recovery and well-being must come through reducing prices—not by raising them. My own belief is, where there is money available people will buy if prices are not only within their means, but alluring; that quantity of sales is essential to giving employment; and that prices will rise of their own accord through increasing demand." [24]

After May 1935 the President turned sharply from recovery to reform. His answer to judicial set-backs was a bold attack on economic privilege. Within a few months he announced his "soak the rich" tax proposal and forced through Congress the Social Security Act, the National Labor Relations Act, and the Wheeler–Rayburn Holding Company Bill. Throughout the summer and fall of 1935 Brandeis followed Roosevelt's change of temper with growing enthusiasm: "F.D. is making a gallant fight, and seems to appreciate fully the evils of bigness. He should have more support than his party is giving him; and the social worker–progressive crowd seems as blind as in 1912.

"F.D. gives evidence of appreciation of the 'irrepressible conflict with bigness'—and of growing firmness. The lobby * investigation is showing up the lawyers, as are the decisions on applications for rapacious fees in reorganizations. It is a question whether lawyers or life insurance are the more in need of public investigation.

"F.D. is showing fine fighting qualities. As to the political outlook:— This is certainly a period which must give grave concern to F.D. and his following—Liberals as well as Democrats. Happily for F.D.—it is nearly twelve months before election day—and happily also—the enemy has neither leader nor measures." [25]

For some months after the New Deal experiments began, the Tory

---

* Brandeis had reference to the public utilities lobby which defeated the "death sentence" clause of the Holding Company bill, July 1, 1935, by the decisive vote of 216 to 146. On the opening day of the debate several congressmen received as many as five thousand telegrams apiece, many of them bogus.

opposition did not venture into the open. It did not co-operate as the President had hoped, but engaged in "chiseling," muttered doubts, expressed misgiving, and awaited a bit anxiously the final collapse. But after a measure of recovery had been achieved, and Roosevelt came out strongly for reform, New Deal critics spoke out vigorously. "It is about time," President Eugene G. Grace of Bethlehem Steel remarked, "we had a little old-fashioned economy, that we encouraged efficiency and thrift and stopped holding out false illusions."

By mid-1936 the conservative Justices again recovered their composure and again dominated the councils of the Supreme Court. On January 6, 1936, the Court invalidated the Agricultural Adjustment Act of 1933 as exceeding the powers of Congress and invading rights reserved to the states by the Tenth Amendment. Justice Brandeis concurred in the sharp dissent of Justice Stone. "Courts are not the only agency of government that must be assumed to have the capacity to govern," Stone said. "Congress and the courts both unhappily may falter or be mistaken in the performance of their constitutional duty. But interpretation of our great charter of government which proceeds on any assumption that the responsibility for the preservation of our institutions is the exclusive concern of any one of the three branches of government, or that it alone can save them from destruction, is far more likely, in the long run, 'to obliterate the constituent members' of 'an indestructible union of indestructible states,' than the frank recognition that language, even of the Constitution, may mean what it says." [26]

On May 18, 1936, the Court struck down the provisions of the Bituminous Coal Conservation Act of 1933 relating to wages, hours, and working conditions.[27] Justice Brandeis joined in Cardozo's dissenting opinion. Less than a month later a 5 to 4 decision outlawed the New York Minimum Wage Law.[28] Once again Brandeis found himself in the minority. But what the left wing lacked in votes was more than made up by intensity of conviction, giving New Dealers reassurance that their reading of the Constitution was not permanently untenable.

A majority of the Supreme Court thus set aside a substantial legislative effort to deal with conditions which Brandeis described "as more serious than war." During far less trying times Chief Justice White had admitted that the Court "relaxed constitutional guarantees from fear of revolution." Such judicial interposition amid dire economic emergency seemed to mock our vaunted democracy and to elevate the Supreme Court to dictatorship. Would the American people tolerate such bold frustration of representative institutions, or would they dethrone the Court? The answer was soon forthcoming.

THUMBS DOWN ON COURT PACKING

Backed by a huge popular mandate in the 1936 presidential election, and mindful of Charles Evans Hughes's dictum of 1908 that "we are under a Constitution, but the Constitution is what the Judges say it is," President Roosevelt made a bold attack on the Supreme Court—that citadel on which economic privilege had long and confidently relied. Briefly the plan was to give a Supreme Court Justice past seventy, six months in which to retire. If he failed to do so he could continue in office, but the President would appoint an additional Justice—presumably younger and better able to carry the heavy load. Since there were five Justices in this category, the President would have at once five appointments to make.

In presenting his Court packing plan on February 5, 1937, the President justified it in terms of the need for infusing new blood into old judicial veins, so as to clear a crowded Court docket. In his original proposal the President gave no hint of a purpose to change the decisions of the Court or subordinate the Judiciary to Executive and Congress. But in his message to the nation, March 9, 1937, the cloak of sophistry was thrown off and the President frankly explained: "When the Congress has sought to stabilize national agriculture, to improve the conditions of labor, to safeguard business against unfair competition, to protect our national resources, and in many other ways to serve our clearly national needs, the majority of the Court has been assuming the power to pass on the wisdom of these acts of the Congress—and to approve or disapprove the public policy written into these laws. . . .

"We have, therefore, reached the point as a nation where we must take action to save the Constitution from the Court and the Court from itself. We must find a way to take an appeal from the Supreme Court to the Constitution itself. We want a Supreme Court which will do justice under the Constitution—not over it. In our courts we want a government of laws and not of men." [29]

This forthright attack on our sacrosanct institution aroused the nation to a fury of public discussion and debate. Unhallowed hands, even if those of the President, had been placed on the very Ark of the Covenant. Far from saving the Constitution from the Court, far from being designed to achieve a government of laws and not of men, the President's plan was deliberately calculated—it was said—to destroy both Constitution and Court. Months of hearings took place; clergymen, educators, businessmen, and lawyers trekked to Washington to testify for and against the plan.

Hundreds of letters poured in on Brandeis, and from practically every state in the union. Women, children, lawyers, doctors, farmers, grocery clerks—all were represented. "Continue your work and don't be bothered by the verbiage of a would-be dictator," an Albany, N.Y., voter wrote him. "The Court must stand firm to protect us from the reds," a Greenwich, Conn., woman said. "You form the only barrier against destruction, please do not forsake us." A member of the St. Catherine Welfare Association of New York apologized for the "insincerity and brutality of Mr. Roosevelt's attack" and urged the Justice to "retain tenure of office, however irksome." "I am sorry you are not in the fifties," a Van Wert, Ohio, man wrote, "so we could elect you President of the United States about 1940." Ninety per cent of Brandeis's correspondents were opposed to Court reform. Certain of those who urged him to retire did so out of a desire to save the Court. "It seems to me," a prominent Raleigh, N.C., attorney wrote, "that a crowning act of your career would be your voluntary retirement along with the other of the oldest members, in the hope and with a reasonable expectation that thereby irreparable injury to the Court itself may be avoided."

Throughout the hue and cry Brandeis—the eldest of the "age-old judicial destroyers"—maintained his customary reticence. Not even his law clerk, Willard Hurst, heard him express any opinion on the President's Court bill. "He strongly disapproved of it as a method, I know; and of the indirection of its presentation," Hurst has observed. "It was characteristic of him to dislike the 'smart' or 'clever' in public business." [30]

On the Court bill some saw Brandeis as parting company with such ardent friends and New Deal advisers as Felix Frankfurter,* Ben Cohen, and Tom Corcoran, and, in effect, as lining up with American Liberty Leaguers and others, to the aid and comfort of that whole rabble of agitators who had long disliked and scorned him. "Brandeis did not determine his principles by counting heads," Justice Robert H. Jackson has explained. "He simply thought his friends were wrong and his foes for once were right, and that was the end of the matter for him. He believed with all the intensity of his being that the country needed the institution he served, and that a court of courage, character, and independence could exist only in an atmosphere of freedom from political pressure. But he believed the Justices maintain it by self-restraint and open-mindedness, by unbiased patient, and accurate application of the law, and by freedom from political ambition or partisanship." [31]

A vigorous and forthright campaign against the bill was being waged under the leadership of Senator Burton K. Wheeler. Tom Corcoran had

---

* Mr. Frankfurter, now Justice, never stated his own position publicly, but we have it on the best of authority that his sympathies were then favorable to the plan.

tried vainly to dissuade him from making the fight; the President himself told Wheeler of the futility of opposing a measure certain to pass in any event. Still the Senator persisted. "A liberal cause," he said, "was never won by stacking a deck of cards, by stuffing a ballot box, or packing a court." [32] At the height of battle Mrs. Brandeis, an old friend of the Wheeler family, went to call on the Senator's daughter, then living in Alexandria. In making her departure the Justice's wife commented as a sort of afterthought: "You tell your obstinate father we think he is making a courageous fight." The Senator lost no time in making an appointment with Justice Brandeis. As the Montana legislator made his way to 2205 California Street, certain misgivings troubled him. Though Brandeis had been a sort of father confessor since Wheeler's first years in Washington, he wondered whether the Justice's usual insistence on observing the proprieties of judicial office might not cause him to resent the visit. In any event, he must confine his mission solely to search for information. What he wanted to know was the actual state of the Court docket. Was it crowded? Were the Old Men worn out and behind with their work? When Brandeis suggested that the Senator's questions might more appropriately be addressed to the Chief Justice, the Senator opined: "Yes, but I don't know the Chief Justice." "But the Chief Justice knows you, and what you're doing," commented the wiry veteran of many political battles, leading Wheeler to the telephone. [33]

The result was the famous letter of Chief Justice Hughes, hurriedly prepared over the week-end so as to be ready for the Senator's use at the hearing on Monday, March 22. Wheeler led up to his brilliant coup by referring to the President's message accompanying the Court plan as "a serious reflection upon all the members of the Supreme Court, including one of the greatest liberals in the United States . . . Mr. Justice Brandeis. . . . To say that [Brandeis] because of age, has ceased to keep pace with the times, seemed to me to be extremely unkind, to say the least. . . . And I have here now," Wheeler continued, "a letter by the Chief Justice, dated March 21, 1937. . . . Let us see what [he says] about it." [34]

In the coolest language, without a trace of argument on the merits of the proposal, Hughes pointed out in the minutest detail that the Supreme Court was "fully abreast of its work" and that "this gratifying condition has obtained for several years. . . . On account of the shortness of time," the Chief Justice concluded, "I have not been able to consult with the members of the Court generally with respect to the foregoing statement, but I am confident that it is in accord with the views of the Justices. I should say, however, that I have been able to consult with Mr. Justice Van Devanter

To the Senate of the United States:

I nominate Louis D. Brandeis

of Massachusetts, to be Associate Justice of the Supreme

Court of the United States, vice Joseph Rucker Lamar, deceased:

Woodrow Wilson

The White House.

Washington 28 January, 1916

THE WHITE HOUSE
WASHINGTON

February 13, 1939

My dear Mr. Justice Brandeis:

One must perforce accept the inevitable.
Ever since those days long ago, when you first took
your seat on the Supreme Court Bench, I have come to
think of you as a necessary and very permanent part
of the Court — and, since 1933 as one who would continue
his fine service there until long after I had left
Washington.

The country has needed you through all
these years, and I hope you will realize, as all your
old friends do, how unanimous the nation has been in
its gratitude to you.

There is nothing I can do but to accede to
your retirement. But with this goes the knowledge
that our long association will continue, and the hope
that you will be spared for many long years to come to
render additional services to mankind.

Always sincerely,

Franklin D Roosevelt

Honorable Louis D. Brandeis,
Associate Justice of the Supreme Court,
Washington, D. C.

PORTRAIT BUST, 1942, BY ELEANOR PLATT

Original presented to the Supreme Court on behalf of the American Bar,
at the opening of the Fall Term, October 5, 1942, the first anniversary of the
Justice's death

and Mr. Justice Brandeis, and I am at liberty to say that the statement is approved by them." [35]

The reading of the Chief Justice's letter before the Senate Judiciary Committee marked the turning point in the struggle. The Committee flatly rejected the plan.[36] The President's specific reform was defeated, yet practically, and within a year, he had his way. This experience appears to have encouraged caution in wavering Justices Hughes and Roberts, giving rise to a somewhat scurrilous comment—"switch in time saves nine." Even before the fate of the Court plan was settled, 5 to 4 decisions were going in favor of rather than against the administration.[37]

This 1937 New Deal struggle was 1916 in reverse. In the Tory campaign to prevent Brandeis's confirmation, both conservatives and progressives sidestepped social and economic theory, lest it be shown that judges' views thereon really did affect judicial decisions. Participants in the 1937 battle were more experienced as well as more outspoken, making it abundantly clear that "the Supreme Court is the Constitution." [38] The political-economic aspect of judicial interpretation was now publicly declared. The Constitution in actual cases was to mean what the Justices said; and what they said was to be determined by whatever social, political, and constitutional theories were held by a majority of the Court—as jelly takes the shape of the mold in which it is set. After the unsuccessful reactionary drive against Brandeis in 1916 and F.D.R.'s naïve campaign of 1937, only the most credulous could believe that judicial decisions are "babies brought by Constitutional storks." [39]

CHAPTER FORTY

Fulfillment: The Prophet Passes

FEW MEN live to see their ideas become realities, their views accepted, their philosophy enacted into the law of the land. That reward, however, came to Brandeis. In the popular mind he had won fame as a dissenter, but, as in the case of Holmes, this dissenter label is misleading. On the record he was far more often in the majority than the minority. Four hundred and fifty-four of his five hundred and twenty-eight opinions were written for the Court. His "great work was done, not in opposing the Court, but in leading it." [1] His dissenting opinions are of quality, not quantity. These were and are highly significant because in so many instances he stated the law as it was yet to be. When in dissent, he pleaded persuasively for ends and values that at the moment had not gained recognition. In dissent he was relatively the more free in that he did not need to keep his views strictly in step with others. "I alone am responsible," he said. "I expose myself."

In dissent he could, and did, keep on crusading. Never content to state objections solely in terms of constitutional issues, his footnotes referred to trade and professional journals, federal, state, and foreign government reports, magazine articles, ranging from *The Nation* to *Nation's Business,* and all sorts of books, ancient and modern, sometimes references on which certain colleagues cast a dubious eye. "There was the question once" a former law clerk recalls, "of whether in a footnote we might cite a pair of student notes from the *Columbia* and *Harvard Law Reviews,* to the effect that these 'showed' a certain rule to be established; the Justice thought the phraseology had better be simply that 'the cases are collected in Notes in—' . . . 'Mr. Justice McReynolds,' Brandeis remarked with his own private twinkle, 'did not favor *Law Review* citations.' " [2]

Much of his law clerks' work consisted in checking his draft of opinions against the pleadings and evidence in the cases assigned to him to write. Every separate assertion of fact made in an opinion was meticulously checked against the evidence and findings. After an opinion had reached what seemed final revision, he was likely to say to his law clerk, "The opinion is now convincing, but what can we do to make it more instructive?" [3]

THE JUDICIAL PROPRIETIES

It is doubtful whether any Supreme Court Justice in our history ever held that tribunal in higher regard. His reverence was almost mystic. What moved him was not so much "the rich color and high drama of the Court's great past," nor the majesty of judicial office—much less the splendor of the architectural structure in which it is now housed. He preferred the modest quarters in the old basement Senate Chamber of the Capitol to the present magnificent temple. He feared the Court's dignity might consist in marble and columns rather than in wisdom and craftsmanship. He would have avoided all such enrichment of material surroundings lest men fail to see that the Court's enduring strength lies in the final test of reason.

"From the first days with him," Willard Hurst writes, "I was conscious of the depth and austerity of his regard for the proprieties of the functioning of judicial office. The Court's business was to become known only through the proper official channels, and his law clerk was made to feel right from the first and most keenly the obligation of discretion in respect to Court affairs. I learned from the Justice how politely one may withhold even the implication of information from an inquiring news-man by the art of a polite negative." [4]

Brandeis became harsh only if the indiscretion was deliberate or brash. Those innocently committing a *faux pas* were handled deftly and with subtle wit. Samuel B. Pettengill tells of the lady who, at one of Mrs. Brandeis's Sunday afternoon teas, asked the Justice his opinion on a case then pending before the Court. Instead of drawing himself up in frozen dignity, he pointed to Mr. Pettengill and said, "It is fortunate that I can refer you to a very good lawyer for a better reply than I am able to give." [5] In the middle thirties, when a book appeared purporting to reveal the private and public lives of the Justices, a gossiping lady caller asked if he had read the book. "No," he replied, "Mrs. Brandeis tells me there are some things in it I should not know." [6]

LAW AS AN INSTRUMENT OF SOCIAL POLICY

Despite the secrecy of the Justices' conference room, no one can doubt that the clarity, wealth, and exactness of Brandeis's information must have greatly impressed his colleagues. "He brought to us," Chief Justice Taft said of him, "all sorts of information as to economic conditions and other matters of the greatest value which we did not have before and never would have acquired otherwise." [7] "Nothing of importance, however minute," Chief Justice Hughes wrote in 1931, "escapes his microscopical examination of every problem, and through his powerful telescopic lens, his mental vision embraces distant scenes, ranging far beyond the familiar worlds of conventional thinking." [8]

The idea that law can be found but not made formed no part of Brandeis's philosophy. The reordering of law to harmonize it with life was partly the work of the Court, but more truly the function of the legislature. A rule of law once settled may have to yield later on to the impact of circumstances unforeseen. On this principle Brandeis insisted that the judiciary recognize its relatively inferior lawmaking function. "No inconsiderable part of his labors on the Court went into the exacting art of staying the judicial hand lest it decide more than was required by the case at the Bar." [9] Thus when the Court went out of its way to sustain the constitutionality of the TVA, he protested. He did not disagree with the Chief Justice's conclusions on the constitutional question, but he argued that the Court had no business anticipating it. "The fact that it would be convenient for the parties and the public to have promptly decided whether the legislation assailed is valid, cannot justify a departure from these settled rules of corporate law and established principles of equity practice." [10] He also dissented when the Court took jurisdiction of a case under the rule of diversity of citizenship. There was no actual dispute, he argued, but only the prospect of a dispute, the case being brought solely to have the contested act declared unconstitutional. "The well-settled rule that the Court is without power to entertain such a proceeding applies equally, whether the party invoking its aid is a state or a private person." [11]

Brandeis was "a great liberal in the true sense," someone has said, "because he saw law as an instrument of social policy, because he insisted that the various organs of government be kept within the bounds assigned to them by the Constitution. He saw the impact of fundamental and time-honored principles as they met novel conditions. His vision was not obstructed by any barrier formed by the earlier application of those same principles to different conditions. He was not a liberal to impair the barriers set by the Constitution to the attempts of men in Congress to make unauthorized pronouncements as if laws. He was not a liberal in attempts of courts to usurp powers not judicial but belonging to the legislative branch of the government. He was as opposed to using or to promoting the use of other people's powers as he was to the unauthorized use of other people's money." [12]

As a Supreme Court Justice, Brandeis had strong regard for judicial tradition, and no regard for opportunism. And yet his was no blind deference. *"Stare decisis,"* he observed, "is ordinarily a wise rule of action. But it is not a universal, inexorable command." [13] It "does not command that we err again when we have occasion to pass upon a different statute." [14] The peculiar virtue of our legal system, as he saw it, lay in the fact "that the process of inclusion and exclusion, so often employed in developing a rule, is not allowed to end with its enunciation." [15] "The rule as announced must be deemed tentative. The many and varying facts to which it will be applied cannot be foreseen." [16] His research in one case disclosed that the Court on numerous occasions had overruled earlier decisions. "The Court bows," he concluded, "to the lessons of experience and the force of better reasoning, recognizing that the process of trial and error, so fruitful in the physical sciences, is appropriate also in the judicial function." [17]

He did not hesitate to give the law a push in a direction in which he felt sound policy clearly to lie, even if there was nothing to cite in support. A case in point was that sustaining the constitutionality of Wisconsin's Anti-Injunction statute. "It was my good fortune," writes Joseph A. Padway, General Counsel, A.F. of L., "to have . . . briefed and argued it [the case] in the Supreme Court of the United States. I realized from the start that our major hope rested not on any precedents of the Supreme Court but almost entirely on persuading a majority of the Court of the accuracy of the philosophy and the economic and legal arguments that ran throughout Justice Brandeis's [dissenting] labor opinions."

Padway argued that peaceful picketing in furtherance of a labor dispute could not be denied under the free speech guarantee of the constitution. The A.F. of L. attorney's hopes "were more than realized." Not only did Justice Brandeis "lucidly expound the economic justification for the union's conduct in the case, but he accepted the 'free speech' argument and thereby struck a note that has literally revolutionized the law affecting labor." [18]

"Picketing and publicity," Justice Brandeis ruled, "are not prohibited by the Fourteenth Amendment. Members of a union might, without special statutory authorization by a state, make known the facts of a labor dispute, for freedom of speech is guaranteed by the Constitution." [19]

Willard Hurst commented: "After a careful search through the Supreme Court decisions, I reported to the Justice that I could find nothing to cite by way of support to this observation; it stayed in the opinion." [20]

For the first time the majority opinion in an important labor case was written by Brandeis. By a vote of 5 to 4 the basic labor philosophy embodied in his dissenting opinions now became the law of the land and established precedent for major labor decisions of recent years. [21]

THE SUPREME COURT CATCHES UP

By 1931 Brandeis's dissenting opinions had begun to prevail in ever-increasing number and in various fields. For example, during his early years on the Bench the Court not infrequently disregarded its own rule as to the presumption of constitutionality of legislation. But, in 1931, as spokesman for the majority, Brandeis held that under this ancient maxim, legislation clearly within the police power must be sustained "in the absence of some factual foundation of record for overthrowing the statute." [22] Under the rule as revived in 1931, the Court, as Brandeis always insisted, need examine the facts no further than to determine whether, considered as a means, the legislation is necessary to achieve a permissible end. Thus the burden of proving unconstitutionality was again thrown on those contesting the validity of state enactments.

In 1920 Brandeis had observed: ". . . in frank expression of conflicting opinion lies the greatest promise of wisdom in governmental action; and in suppression lies ordinarily the greatest peril." [23] His championing of freedom of speech and press was then defeated. Under Chief Justice Hughes's leadership, the Court in two notable cases broadened the conception of liberty guaranteed by the due process clause of the Fourteenth Amendment so as to embrace freedom of speech and press. In 1931 the Justices set aside a California statute penalizing public display of a flag or banner as a sign, symbol, or emblem of opposition to organized government. Voicing the sentiments of Brandeis's earlier dissents, Chief Justice Hughes held that "all change is, to a certain extent, achieved by the opposition of the new to the old, and in so far as it is within the law such peaceful opposition is guaranteed to our people and is recognized as a symbol of independent thought containing the promise of progress." [24] Justices McReynolds and Butler, formerly in the majority, now protested in dissent. The Court also applied Brandeis's principles to invalidate a Minnesota statute restricting freedom of the press, and again Justices Butler and McReynolds, joined by Van Devanter and Sutherland, dissented.[25]

In the first major valuation case to reflect the depression conditions, Chief Justice Hughes used language strikingly similar to that in which Justice Brandeis in 1923 described the practical and theoretical difficulties of using *present value* as the rate base. "It is apparent," the Chief Justice concluded, "that the estimates of cost of reproduction new of 1929, or 1930, upon which the company relies, afforded no secure foundation for prediction of future values, and the rate base as fixed by the Commission is not to be invalidated as involving confiscation by reason of these estimates which the course of events deprived of credit as trustworthy prophecies." [26]

Even public utilities officials were now on record as agreeing with Justice Brandeis's "prudent investment" principle of valuation set forth in his dissent of 1923 in the Southwestern Bell Telephone case. Said the president of the Philadelphia Electric Company: "If the 'prudent investment' theory of utility property valuation is applied now in the manner indicated by the Brandeis decision, we couldn't help but approve." [27]

Other reverses followed in rapid succession. Brandeis's earlier dissenting view that the substitution of rational competition for ruinous economic warfare furthers rather than restrains commerce, was accepted.[28] The majority opinion in 1937 on the Wisconsin Anti-Injunction case set aside Taft's 1921 decision on the Arizona statute limiting the use of injunctions in labor disputes. In 1937 the Court also upheld an act of Congress forbidding wire-tapping by federal officers,[29] and in 1938 Governor Herbert H. Lehman asked the New York State Constitutional Convention to write into the state's fundamental law a "search and seizure" clause which would bar wire-tapping by prosecuting officials until they had obtained a warrant from a Supreme Court Justice. Lehman quoted at length from Brandeis's dissenting opinion of a decade earlier, recalling the Justice's denunciation of the "pernicious doctrine" that the end justifies the means.[30]

By the Norris–La Guardia Act of 1932, repudiating the yellow-dog contract, and by the National Labor Relations Act of 1935, Congress enacted Brandeis's labor views stated in the Hitchman, Duplex Printing, and other cases. In sustaining the latter act, Chief Justice Hughes recognized the validity of Brandeis's old argument: that a workman's liberty can be interfered with not only by government but also by industry; that it was not enough for the law merely to recognize the right of collective bargaining; that Congress has constitutional power to implement and safeguard that right by legislation. He succinctly expressed the viewpoint which had triumphed: "We refuse to shut our eyes to the plainest facts of our national life and to deal with these issues in an intellectual vacuum." [31]

Even the judicial taboo on minimum wage legislation was finally revoked.[32] After twenty-three years in which two adverse 5 to 4 rulings occurred against the validity of minimum wage legislation,[33] Brandeis's masterly argument of December 1914 became the law of the land. In 1941 the Supreme Court exempted labor from the anti-trust laws, citing Brandeis's dissenting opinion in the Duplex case.[34]

The dissenter had, in his own time, become the prophet of the living law.

THE YEARS BEGIN TO TELL

By 1937 the Justice began increasingly to show signs of ebbing physical strength. During 1937 and 1938, his last full years on the Bench, he wrote thirteen and sixteen opinions respectively, as against twenty-seven in 1917, thirty-seven in 1920, and thirty-three in 1925. Though his latter-day decisions gave no hint of intellectual impairment, the prolonged labor to which he was accustomed was no longer possible. His tea guests found him sitting down rather than greeting each person as he or she came in. Dinner guests noted that the hour of departure was advanced to nine. Mrs. Brandeis watched him more closely lest he overtax his declining strength.

Since 1936 rumors of his leaving the Bench had been rife, but passed unnoticed by him and his friends. Early in his eighty-third year his decision to retire came dramatically—on February 13, 1939, at the end of a day in which he had taken part as usual in the work of the Court. He had returned to the Bench the week before after a month's absence caused by grippe and a heart attack. A brief note to the President read: "Pursuant to the Act of March 1, 1937, I retire this day from regular active service on the Bench."

"One must perforce accept the inevitable," President Roosevelt said in reply. That same day the Justice reassured his sister-in-law, Mrs. Alfred Brandeis:

Washington, Feb. 13/39

Dear Jennie:

My birthday greeting goes to you a bit early. But I want you to know promptly that I am not retiring from the Court because of ill health. Mine seems to be as good as heretofore. But years have limited the quantity and intensity of work possible, and I think the time has come when a younger man should assume the burden.

It was fine to have the photograph of you and the grandchildren.

Louis

On February 17 his colleagues joined in an affectionate letter, praising the years of service rendered with "a vigor and devotion which have never been surpassed. . . . Your long practical experience and intimate knowledge of affairs, the wide range of your researches and your grasp of the most difficult problems, together with your power of analysis and your thoroughness in exposition, have made your judicial career one of extraordinary distinction and far-reaching influence. It has always been gratifying to observe that the intensity of your labors has never been permitted to disturb your serenity of spirit and we shall have an abiding memory of your never-failing friendliness."

His retirement was inevitable, as the President said, and yet it was hard to accept. Not a few, some formerly hostile, had through the years come to associate his presence on the Court with stability, sanity, justice, law and order—anything but the radicalism they had hated and feared. It remained for his daughter Elizabeth to make articulate the feelings of the unnumbered many.

February 14, 1939

Dearest Father:

It is hard for me to write. All the things I want to say sound mawkish—or presumptuous from me to you. I cannot bear to use any words at this time that do not ring true. I hope you know what is in my heart even if I cannot get it said.

I know that there is no cause for grieving. Everything must have an end and the life and work that you can look back upon must give you contentment and satisfaction. As for me, my appreciation of what you are and have done keeps increasing as I grow older and better able to understand.

If the lessons you have taught do not seem to have been learned very well yet, that is not for any lack on your part. Measuring my words, I do not see how any one person could have done more than you have done.

But of course I feel sad—regardless. Ends are always sad. Paul and I, along with hundreds, probably thousands, of others, will be trying to carry on different parts of your work and trying to catch something of the spirit in which you have worked. But we shall all know how inadequate we are and how far we fall short of the standards you set. But I know you will be generous in your judgment of us. And at least, despite our other limitations, our love and admiration for you will continue to be just about unlimited.

Elizabeth

Much speculation followed as to whom President Roosevelt would appoint to succeed him. To the supreme satisfaction of the former Justice, his post went to William O. Douglas, then chairman of the Securities and Exchange Commission. On July 1, 1941, Chief Justice Hughes also retired. "Aren't you delighted with what the President has done in elevating Justice Stone to the Chief Justiceship?" Brandeis inquired of a visitor in the summer of 1941. "No other President has performed such a signal service." When reminded that President Taft, a Republican, had promoted White, a Democrat, to be head of the Court, he replied, "But White cannot be compared to Stone." [35]

MAKING THE BEST OF IT

Brandeis's last years were spent reading, writing letters, motoring, talking with friends, and promoting Zionism. In October 1938 the exterminative phases of Hitlerism moved him to break his accustomed judicial reserve. With steady gait and unflinching mind, the venerable Justice went to the White House for a two-hour interview with President Roosevelt. No announcement was made as to the discussion, but none doubted that he went to see the President in an attempt to avoid the threatened stoppage of immigration into Palestine.

On May 17, 1939, the British government issued the so-called MacDonald White Paper designed to end Palestine immigration within five years. Once more Brandeis spoke out: "A legal obligation assumed by Great Britain is the basis for Jewish construction enterprise in Palestine. That legal right, sustained by humanitarian needs, cannot be obliterated for private advantage." [36] In October 1939 he discussed the refugee situation with President Roosevelt. The President suggested a central organization to deal with the refugee problem, with Bernard Baruch as its head. To this Brandeis rejoined that Baruch would be more likely to consider colonization by Jews on some undiscovered planet than Palestine. The Justice found the President "sympathetic as in the past," and came away feeling that there was "reason to hope that he will say something about Palestine." [37]

During the war crisis the President wrote him:

June 18, 1940

My dear Isaiah:

I do wish I could have seen you before you left but our friends tell me you are well. Do continue to take very good care of yourself.

I fear that you and I have the same feeling of futility in these daily events—but both of us must keep up our spirits and our hopes.

Affectionately,
F.D.R.

As countless multitudes were slaughtered, exiled, made destitute, Brandeis was saddened but never doubted democracy's ultimate triumph. "The Dictators are having their fling now," he wrote a friend, November 14, 1937, "but Democracies will again have their day." [38] Less than six months before his death, when German victories in Greece and Crete threatened invasion of the Near East, perhaps destruction of Russia and Palestine, he still had faith:

This is the time to stand firm and resolute. We must not waver or yield one iota of our position. Assuming that the Germans will do their worst, invade and destroy and obliterate part of what we have created, they cannot destroy Jewish ideals and aspirations with regard to Palestine. There are 500,000 Jews in Palestine now, but there are millions of others prepared to go, when the time comes, and to continue the work.

It has been established that the Jews require a state of their own for their continued existence. The Germans have established that fact. The Jews have established their capacity to build such a state. That is the essential ground work for the future effort. [39]

His health continued good—"as good," he usually remarked, "as my years permit." People from all walks of life continued to seek advice, encouragement, inspiration. Sometimes he grew overwearied and seemed to long for the end. "All I can do now," he told his niece, Fanny Brandeis, May 19, 1940, "is let people talk to me and imagine I help them—I don't, but—" a catch came into his voice, and he changed the subject.

Late in the summer of 1940 Brandeis suffered an attack of pneumonia from which he never fully recovered. He continued to see people and kept up a large correspondence, always brief and to the point and written in rugged straight-up-and-down script that never showed sign of age or infirmity. This was true even of the notes written only a few days before he died. One of the last, dated October 1, 1941, so much impressed a correspondent that he sent it to his daughter at college, suggesting that she "might emulate Mr. Justice Brandeis and exercise a bit more care with her own calligraphy." [40]

These last days were enjoyed to the full, for to Brandeis home life was an essential. It satisfied some of the deepest urgencies of his nature—an inner need for peace, for harmony, for love. These things he instinctively craved, perhaps by way of compensation for his devouring work. "I could not have lived my life without Alice," he had said to a few close friends after the crucifying days that followed his attack on New Haven and United Shoe. "If my wife had been hurt, how could I have had the strength to go on?" [41] Theirs was a union of truly mated minds, of harmonious standards and tastes, alike in their austerity.

FINALE

On Tuesday, September 30, 1941, the last checks were signed, the routine of the month finished. Next morning, following long-established custom, he drove with his wife to Rock Creek Park, there to listen to her reading which he so much enjoyed. He returned home apparently in good health. Soon after midday, without much pain or discomfort, he suffered a heart attack and was taken to the hospital. His condition grew steadily worse, and physicians had lost hope of prolonging his life by Saturday night, when he sank into a coma. The end came Sunday, October 5, at a quarter past seven. On November 13 he would have completed his eighty-fifth year.

Monday morning, October 6, certain close friends were called to express Mrs. Brandeis's desire that they attend the private funeral services at 3:30 next day. There were about fifty present in the apartment at 2205 California Street, including Chief Justice Hughes, retired, the Justices of the Supreme Court and their wives, Mrs. Woodrow Wilson, Mrs. Henry A. Wallace, various representatives of savings-bank life insurance from Massachusetts and New York, Zionist leaders, and several of his former law clerks. A violin quartet played Beethoven selections; then Assistant Secretary of State Dean Acheson spoke briefly on behalf of the men who had "the great joy and the great fortune of serving him so intimately as his secretaries." The talk was exquisitely worded and profoundly moving. "We are the fortunate ones," Acheson began, "but what he has meant to us is not very different from what he has meant to hundreds of young men and women who have grown up under his influence. . . .

"Throughout these years," Acheson continued, "we have brought him all of our problems and all our troubles, and he had time for all of us. A question, a comment, and the difficulties began to disappear; the dross and shoddy began to appear for what it was, and we wondered why the matter had ever seemed difficult. . . . I have heard him speak of some achievement of one of us with all the pride, and of some sorrow or disappointment of another, with all the tenderness of a father speaking of his sons.

"We are the generation," the former law clerk went on, "which has lived during and between two wars. We have lived in the desert years of the human spirit. . . . Years when the cry was 'What is truth?' . . . . These were years during which we . . . saw in action his burning faith that the verities to which men had clung through the ages were verities; that evil never could be good; that falsehood was not truth, not even if all the ingenuity of science reiterated it in waves that encircled the earth. . . .

"But to him," the speaker concluded, "truth was less than truth unless it was expounded so that people could understand and believe. During these years of retreat from reason, his faith in the human mind and in the will and capacity of people to understand and grasp the truth never wavered or tired. In a time of moral and intellectual anarchy and frustration, he handed on the great tradition of faith in the mind and spirit of man which is the faith of the prophets and poets, of Socrates, of Lincoln." [42]

The Justice's body was cremated, and on the first anniversary of his death the urn containing his ashes was buried beneath the porch of the Law School building on the campus of the University of Louisville.

Newspapers far and wide, domestic and foreign, noted his passing.[43] The *New York Times* spoke of him as "one of our elder statesmen and philosophers, truly cast in the American mold, deeply, even mystically, infused with the American spirit." All joined in praise of "his unqualified faith in the civic and moral worth of the individual."

"His vast learning in law, his vaster grasp of the ways of American living, his austere and disciplined personality," the *Toronto Law Journal* recorded, "were instruments which charted his course between laissez faire and *étatisme*—between social chaos and Leviathan. For him there was no puerile Spencerian antithesis between the citizen and the state: the state is the citizens, created by them, endowed by them with power, and armed by them with procedure to safeguard the individual and make his life one of opportunity for the development of personality." [44]

On the very day of his funeral service Brandeis's will was admitted to probate. He had left an estate, before taxes, totaling $3,178,495.75; of this, $2,875,356 was in bonds. The remainder was cash, $294,139; furniture and furnishings at Chatham and Washington, $4,000; summer house at Chatham valued at $9,450; and an 1881 life insurance policy of $5,000. Debts were put at not more than $5,000. The twenty-seven page document, signed January 16, 1939, named as executors Mrs. Alice G. Brandeis,* his wife; Susan Gilbert of New York and Elizabeth Raushenbush of Madison, Wisconsin, the Justice's two daughters; Edward F. McClennen, his former

* Mrs. Brandeis died of heart attack, October 12, 1945, in her Washington, D.C., home.

law partner; and E. Louise Malloch, a former secretary. A trust estate of $400,000 was set up for his widow, and $200,000 for each of his two daughters. "I have made for my wife and daughters," the Justice's will read, "provision larger than will be required for that simple living which we have practiced from conviction and which I assume each will continue. I have done this because I desire that each of them shall have ample means to carry forward or otherwise aid the public work in which she may from time to time be interested. This course will, I believe, best insure the wise application of the surplus to public purposes."

Beneficiaries of the residue of the estate were the Survey Associates, one quarter, "for the maintenance of civil liberty and the promotion of workers' education in the United States"; the University of Louisville, one quarter, for the library and law school; Zionism, the other one-half, to be divided equally between Palestine Endowment and Hadassah for "the upbuilding of Palestine as a national home for the Jewish people."

A conspicuous omission from the beneficiaries was savings-bank life insurance, to which cause he had given well over two hundred thousand dollars. Brandeis's will expressed hope that during "the balance of the calendar year in which my death shall occur and one full calendar year thereafter, my wife and daughters will continue to give, to the persons and causes to which I have customarily contributed, sums as large as I have given in the calendar year preceding my death."

And now Brandeis once again became a storm center of controversy. To the consternation of some ardent admirers, this inveterate foe of money power, this true friend of the common man, had died three times a millionaire. He had always been, as he said in 1940, "a large earner." Through his thirty-five years of leadership in law practice he had received fees commensurate with his professional eminence. Nevertheless, it was his time and his brains—the harder gifts—that he gave to good causes rather than his cash. Add to this the opportunities of his era, his astuteness as an investor, his frugal living, and the mystery is solved.

"His practice was lucrative," Mr. McClennen writes. "This was due to the character and volume of the matters handled and the quality of the work done. . . . From the outset, the practice which came to him was a general one, unusually diversified. . . . He acted for manufacturers, for merchants, for investors, for brokers, for associations of these different ones, for labor unions, for the injured, for the successful, for the unsuccessful, and for benevolent institutions. There was no field not included except it be in the defense or prosecution of alleged criminals, the department of patents and admiralty. Even in these unaccustomed fields he worked occasionally. . . . He made scrupulous effort never to overcharge, and to scrutinize the measure of fairness. The fortune which he left tells the story of the value of the professional work which he did." [45]

The accumulation of a fortune sufficient to make him economically independent had been deliberately embarked upon and successfully pursued so that he might champion without fear or favor whatever causes he might consider right and proper. By 1890, at the age of thirty-four, his income was approximately $50,000 a year and increasing. He was a millionaire by 1907, and a millionaire twice over in 1916. His income, exclusive of salary, was then nearly $100,000 annually, and, prior to 1913, free from income tax. Of this, he spent only about $10,000 per year for living expenses. Interest on his two-million-dollar estate, plus his salary as Supreme Court Justice for twenty-five years, added another million by the time of his death. Despite sizable gifts, his estate grew steadily by conservative accumulation. He thus retained that strength of independence, that freedom of individual action, which were for him life's basic values.

CHAPTER FORTY-ONE

A Free Man's Search

BRANDEIS deserves to be saved from his friends as well as his foes. Both blur his sharp reality. He has been seen as a masterful genius, a crafty Lucifer, an inspired humanitarian. Even Holmes placed him among the "upward and onward fellows." Neither liberal nor conservative found him altogether acceptable: the former distrusted his compromising conservatism, the latter damned his anarchist-radicalism. No single formula can explain him because he had no objective in life in the sense of a set goal to be reached. Nevertheless, he knew where he was headed. He did not drift with wind and tide. His actions, his policies, were too sure and definite for sudden impulse or random opportunism.

The most significant quality in his career was restless curiosity, thirst for knowledge. It was not learning for its own sake but knowledge to put to some use. When he began on a problem, he wanted to absorb it all, to explore all implications. He studied the past, not to adore, but for the light its accumulated wisdom threw on the living present. If he showed unusual moral discernment, as he certainly did, or demonstrated extraordinary understanding of hard problems; if in his own time, and in a variety of fields, he helped to vindicate his prophetic vision, the reason is that curiosity drove him to toil over every inch of the complex segments of modern life. Much of his own scope and power came from infinite capacity for taking pains.

His expert handling of widely dispersed and distorted facts is a matter of common knowledge. What is not so well known is his capacity for moral indignation. This was even stronger in him than his great sense of compassion. He was moved by the wrongs of economic privilege, by human suffering and exploitation, but what moved him more was public apathy and moral obtuseness in face of social abuses. In 1916 the silent acquiescence of those in sympathy with him, not the vicious and unfounded attacks of his opponents, was the alarming aspect of the nomination struggle. He was sorely grieved by the fate of persecuted peoples in Europe, but he felt much more deeply the slowness with which the nations of the world rose in protest. To him "the greatest menace to freedom is an inert people."

As his mind became absorbed, it caught fire. His thinking seemed to gain voltage from his fellows, from the electric play of other minds. Literary composition, a solitary task, was tedious. His laboriously written and rewritten manuscripts lack the literary charm and grace, the apt and cutting phrase, that distinguish those of Justice Holmes. There are, of course, exceptions. In his lines upholding freedom of speech cold facts were set aglow by the warmth of human feeling.

Brandeis's temperament and his mind were adventurous. In old age he liked to tell of the most trivial experiences on canoe trips or with spirited horses, of riding every day, sometimes over icy roads, regardless of weather. Something of the same daring permeated his social thought. Though confident of the soundness of our basic American institutions, he knew that social progress, in the very nature of things, demands bold and courageous experimentation, that there must be change. If a condition was unsound, a policy unwise, he fought it. To him, nothing in human affairs is inevitable, save change itself.

The dominant strain in Brandeis and in his heritage was an urgent zeal for freedom. In a letter to Norman Hapgood, April 6, 1935, he enclosed these lines from General Smuts's address on freedom:

> We fight not for glory, nor for wealth,
> Nor for honour, but for that freedom which
> No good man will surrender but with his life.

Brandeis's public campaigns were guided by a deep sense of continuing responsibility for community welfare, and his life exemplifies what for him were the responsibilities of citizenship. In the *Index Rerum,* prepared during his student days, he had recorded: "Republics are not ungrateful, but the debt of each citizen to his country is so great that no payments, however large, can extinguish it."

For Brandeis, men, not things, are the source and goal of progress, and that society is richest which takes fullest advantage of all its human possibilities, not only those of the able and the astute, but also those of the little people, the small men with one or a few talents. He had faith in little men because he had seen little men grow, and in countless instances had helped them grow. "Democracy, as he saw it," a *New York Times* editorial commented after his death, "was no sullen leveled-down mass—it was a multitude of separate persons working, hoping, striving, willingly co-operating." [1]

Brandeis's lifelong opposition to bigness was no phobia. It was grounded in his conviction that "excessive power is the great corrupter," that "responsibility is the great developer." It was rooted in the belief that men have common limitations as well as common potentialities; that the ablest are too weak to bear unfalteringly the burdens of government or business when units grow too large; that the lowliest are too essential to be denied a sphere of participation befitting their capacities. "I felt," a friend of his writes, "that he was always trying to reach in to the something firm in the other man and to persuade him to stand on that." [2]

Knowledge of men as they are, shortcomings and all, never made him despair. Nor was he carried into ecstasy by any utopia of what ought to be. His concern was for a society as it is and can be. The better life must be won, if at all, by mortal men—the good, bad, and indifferent; the public welfare must be sought and found by men as they are, not as one hopes they may be in a dream world. Once when his daughter Susan complained of some difficulty, a friend heard him say, "My dear, if you will just start with the idea that this is a hard world, it will all be much simpler." [3]

Brandeis had a keen sensitivity to individuals as fellow beings. Visitors found him keenly interested in their ideas and experiences; he drew them out, absorbed everything they had to give. With close friends he was likely to begin by saying, "Tell me the things which you think I ought to know." Interviewers were much impressed when they found this learned man of the law learning from them. All felt at home and thought they really knew the man and had known him for a long time.

Yet those who knew him well discovered an inner sphere of personality vigilantly guarded, which few, if any, could penetrate; thinking they were close to him, they soon found that as they approached the inner man they could go no further.* This aloofness even long association never broke through. Some were hurt and repelled by his spiritual isolation. It was as if his friendships were based not on affection for an individual, but on interest in and appreciation of that individual's function in life.

This is not to suggest that he was coldly impersonal. His quiet charm gained loyal and devoted friends. Not a few valued him as a person even more than as a champion of social justice. "Your friendship has so deeply affected the quality of my life," Robert W. Bruère wrote him, November 3, 1926, "that my gratitude on this personal account outweighs my gratitude for your enriching influence upon the public life of America. I rarely go to my desk or face the perplexities of day-to-day decision without walking with you again over the dunes of Chatham and hearing you meditate aloud on 'the things worth living for.' "

The defects of great men, someone has said, reclaim them to humanity. So it was with Brandeis. Inevitably there were the defects of his qualities. His instinct for freedom and independence sometimes made his stand rather less than clear and unequivocal. In certain complicated situations of which he was the storm center, men of divergent interests could and did mistake his position and his views. He had reserved for himself an area of freedom from specific commitments such as would leave him independent no matter what might later ensue.

---

* William Hurst, his former law clerk, touches on this in his memorandum of November 3, 1941: "I think I would emphasize . . . (1) his faith in the ultimate value of individual men, their goodness (in the good old Roman sense of *virtus*), their potentialities, their capacity to be interesting in and of themselves.

(2) His sense of personal, inner security, which gave one a greater sense of poise and sure balance than one probably had ever gotten from another man.

(3) Closely related somehow to the last, though I'm not quite sure how, *his jealous guardianship of his own privacy*—no niggardly husbanding of resources, but rather, I think, *a sense of personal dignity which would not be consistent with an easy opening of doors to everyone who knocked* (Author's italics), and which was linked also with

(4) a keen sensitivity to time, as a stock held in trust, to be used for the best in one's power— meaning no mere time-saving adage from Poor Richard's Almanac, but almost literally the feeling of holding a trusteeship for one's stock of time and mental and physical energy, that one should put it to account for a good purpose.

(5) The pervading stress on craftsmanship, which one always felt in working for and with the Justice . . . not merely the pride of work of a good technician, but the master craftsman's identification of his own dignity as a person and human being with the doing of master work, insisting always upon the highest standards of performance not so much as a matter of the guild standards as of one's own self-respect and fulfillment."

Brandeis's peculiar talent, on his own testimony, was for figures and finance, but he supplemented accountancy with a rarer endowment—a fertile imagination, the power to single out the item or items of a complicated situation on which everything else hung. "He could do what the lumberman does in a log jam, pick out the key log which, once moved, sets the rest going." [4] In him burned an inner flame which made him more than a superb lawyer, social scientist, great judge. He gave to social data and statistics vitality and significance by meaningful interpretation and apt quotation. When his friends proclaimed the efficiency, the wonder and glory of machinery, of industrial organization and mass production, he was wont to point his moral against them, by quoting his favorite line from Goethe's ballad, "The Magician's Apprentice": "Even if we had the wise man's stone, the stone would be without the wise man." Newly discovered forces, even atomic, have only such social usefulness as men provide. He saw, as did few if any of his contemporaries, the perils of our industrial revolution, the development of corporate and cartel industry as menacing employees, competitors, capitalism, democracy—the state itself.

It was fitting that Brandeis joined the Supreme Court at the height of his fame. Membership on the Court gave him voice and vote in the citadel of corporate–financial power, provided a more effective forum in which to follow his inevitable search. Judicial office forbade the rough and tumble battles of earlier years, but did not impair this crusader's technique nor blight his creed. Individual worth remained his favorite theme, human dignity his unvarying touchstone. The basic test of any institution, economic or political, was whether it valued man as man and not as machine. His vision, his ideal, was of a community within which the individual would develop as a human being; his final value was the common man. Euripides stated his creed:

> And avert thine eyes from the lore of the wise,
> That have honor in proud men's sight.
> The simple nameless herd of Humanity
> Hath deeds and faith that are truth enough for me! [5]

If we hold with Burke that the standard of a statesman is the "disposition to preserve and the ability to improve, taken together," then Brandeis met that test. The actual fulfillment of his forecasts, the impressive validation of his views by subsequent events, may well suggest that a militant liberalism such as his, asserted and persistently pursued from the turn of the century, would have made man far more the master of his own destiny.

Bibliographic Notes

Bibliographic Notes

PROFILE

1. William E. Cushing to Mrs. B. M. Cushing, March 17, 1878. This letter came to me through the courtesy of Justice Brandeis's former law partner, Edward F. McClennen. Mr. McClennen's son-in-law, Bernhard Knollenberg, became librarian of Yale University, July 1, 1938. A friendship with Dr. Harvey Cushing ensued. In the spring of 1939 Mr. Knollenberg was looking at a book in Dr. Cushing's house library and found the letter of comment on Brandeis. It has since been placed among the collected Cushing letters. The photostat was obtained from the Cushings, who kindly gave permission for its use in this biography.
2. This accusation featured the drive against him especially in the New Haven struggle. See Chs. XII and XIII.
3. The most notable incident is that of United Shoe Machinery Company. See Ch. XIV.
4. His position is clearly stated in "The Opportunity in the Law," an address delivered at Phillips Brooks House before the Harvard Ethical Society, May 4, 1905. Reprinted in Louis D. Brandeis, *Business—a Profession,* with preliminary chapters regarding the author by Ernest Poole, Felix Frankfurter, and James C. Bonbright (Boston: Hale, Cushman & Flint, 1933), pp. 329–43.

PART I

CHAPTER I

1. *Reminiscences of Frederika Dembitz Brandeis,* prepared at the request of her son Louis, during the years December 12, 1880–December 27, 1886, p. 44. Translated from the German by Alice G. Brandeis. Privately printed in 1944.
2. Quoted in Josephine C. Goldmark, *Pilgrims of '48* (New Haven: Yale University Press, 1930), pp. 198–99.
3. Goldmark, *op. cit.,* p. 200.
4. *Supra,* note 1, p. 10.
5. *Ibid.,* p. 13.
6. *Ibid.,* p. 4.
7. Goldmark, *op. cit.,* p. 180.
8. *Ibid.,* p. 181.
9. *Supra,* note 1, pp. 36–37.
10. *Ibid.,* p. 45. *See also* Goldmark, *op. cit.,* p. 186.
11. Frederika Brandeis to Louis D. Brandeis (hereafter referred to as "L.D.B."), October 21, 1877. This and other uncollected letters in the early chapters from Frederika and Adolph Brandeis to their children have been translated from the German by the author.
12. Goldmark, *op. cit.,* p. 202.
13. *Ibid.,* pp. 204–205.

14. *Ibid.*, p. 285.
15. *Ibid.*, p. 202.
16. *Ibid.*, p. 206.
17. *Ibid.*, pp. 206–207, *passim.*
18. *Ibid.*, p. 209.
19. *Ibid.*, pp. 209–10.
20. C. E. Heberhart in *The Madison Courier*, February 15, 1939, gives some interesting local color.
21. G. S. Cottman, *Centennial History and Handbook of Indiana*, pp. 131–32; quoted in Goldmark, *op. cit.*, p. 216.
22. Diary of John Lysle King, January 1, 1850.
23. Goldmark, *op. cit.*, p. 222.
24. Quoted in Goldmark, *op. cit.*, p. 221, from Carl Sandburg, *Abraham Lincoln: The Prairie Years.*
25. John Lysle King was born in Madison, Indiana, September 1823, the only son of Victor and Eliza Lysle King, natives of Boone County, Kentucky. Having completed his preparatory education in the private schools of Madison, he entered Hanover College and received the A.B. degree in 1841. He immediately took up the study of law in the office of his grandfather, Judge Wilberforce Lysle, one of the most prominent judges in the Middle West. Later he formed a partnership with one Judge Stevens. A recognized leader at Madison's Bar, he was a member of Indiana's House of Representatives in 1851. He left Madison in 1855, along with the general exodus of business and professional men, and settled in Chicago, acquiring there a lucrative practice. He was unmarried, and died in April 1892.

    The relevant entries in King's Diary were sent, January 1939, to Mr. Justice Brandeis by Joseph M. Cravens of Madison, Indiana. They came to the author's attention through the courtesy of Mr. Bernard Flexner.
26. King's Diary, April 14, 1849.
27. *Ibid.*, April 16, 1849.
28. *Ibid.*, June 1, 1849.
29. *Ibid.*, December 5, 1849.
30. *Ibid.*, June 20, 1849.
31. *Ibid.*, July 13, 1849.
32. *Ibid.*, July 26, 1849.
33. *Ibid.*, January 1, 1850.
34. Goldmark, *op. cit.*, p. 242.

CHAPTER II

1. Ernest Poole, Introduction to *Business—a Profession*, p. xi.
2. Author's interview with Justice Brandeis, January 17, 1940.
3. *Reminiscences of Frederika Brandeis*, p. 20.
4. Author's interview with Justice Brandeis, July 29, 1940.
5. Frederika Brandeis to Fannie and Amy Brandeis, August 13, 1865.
6. Alfred Brandeis to Fannie and Amy Brandeis, August 20, 1865.
7. Report Card of German and English Academy, from September to November 1868.
8. Louisville Male High School, Report of L.D.B., 1871–72.
9. Bert Ford, "Boyhood of Brandeis: An Early View of the Man," *Boston American*, June 4, 1916.
10. Abraham Flexner, *I Remember* (New York: Simon & Schuster, 1940), p. 29.

    Dr. Flexner's memorandum, "The Louisville Library—Louisville, Kentucky," explains how it arose and indicates the extent to which it influenced the town's intellectual life. In the '70's a public library, the Polytechnic, had been planned, but the project was handicapped by poor selection of books. "Thereupon," says Dr. Flexner, "the intellectuals of Louisville, headed by the Brandeis family, Mr. Dembitz, Mr. A. R. Cooper, Major Allen, the Belknap family, the Semples, and others . . . organized a private reading and lending library known as 'The Louisville Library.' It was located at the corner of Fifth and Walnut Streets. . . ."

"The books numbered," Dr. Flexner continued, "about ten thousand and represented very careful and conscientious selection of English and to a slight extent German and French masterpieces. . . . The Library was an immediate success, for all the intelligentsia of the town deserted the Polytechnic and made the Library their meeting place, particularly in late afternoons after business hours. The prominent lawyers, doctors, physicians, and persons interested in literature would assemble in the front room, read *The Saturday Review, The Nation,* and a few similar journals, and engage in conversation. If anybody wanted to read and not be disturbed he would retire to the rear part of the room near the card catalogue. . . .

"I think it would be difficult to exaggerate the stimulating effect of the Louisville Library on the intellectual life of Louisville, for it was not only a storehouse of excellent books, but it was the meeting place of cultivated men and women who for an hour or more in the day discussed things and events."

11. L.D.B. to Fanny Brandeis [daughter of Alfred Brandeis], June 11, 1926.
12. Author's interview with Justice Brandeis, July 24, 1940.
13. *Supra,* note 3, pp. 32–34.
14. The facts as to his years of European travel were related to me by Justice Brandeis in an interview, January 17, 1940.
15. Ford, *op. cit.*
16. Edgar Clifton Bross, "An Analysis of Louis D. Brandeis," *Eastern and Western Review,* August 1916.
17. Poole, *op. cit.*
18. *Ibid.*

CHAPTER III

1. L.D.B., "The Harvard Law School," *The Green Bag,* January 1889, pp. 10–25.
2. *Ibid.,* quoted by L.D.B.
3. *Ibid.*
4. *Ibid.*
5. *Ibid.*
6. James Russell Lowell, "Abraham Lincoln," *My Study Windows* (1884), p. 173.
7. Lowell, "A Certain Condescension in Foreigners," *op. cit.,* p. 62.
8. *Supra,* note 6, p. 166.
9. *The Copeland Reader* (New York: Charles Scribner's Sons, 1926), p. 1413.
10. Author's interview with Justice Brandeis, July 29, 1940.
11. James M. Landis, "Mr. Justice Brandeis and the Harvard Law School," *Harvard Law Review,* December 1941, p. 184.
12. Quoted by Ford, *op. cit.*
13. Quoted by Ernest Poole in "Brandeis, a Remarkable Record of Unselfish Work Done in the Public Interest," *American Magazine,* February 1911, reprinted in *Business—a Profession.*
14. Author's interview with Justice Brandeis, July 27, 1940.
15. Charles W. Eliot to L.D.B., June 14, 1877.
16. Author's interview with Justice Brandeis, January 17, 1940.
17. Landis, *op. cit.*
18. Louis B. Wehle to the author, June 16, 1943.
19. James Taussig to L.D.B., September 22, 1878.
20. Irving Dilliard (ed.), *Mr. Justice Brandeis: Great American; Press Opinion and Public Appraisal* (St. Louis: Modern View Press, 1941), p. 13.
21. James Taussig to L.D.B., January 8, 1880.
22. Author's interview with Justice Brandeis, July 25, 1940.

CHAPTER IV

1. James Taussig to L.D.B., July 7, 1879.
2. L.D.B.'s notebook, November 12, 1880.
3. J. C. Shaw, Jr., to L.D.B., May 3, 1880, January 26, 1882.

4. Mark de Wolfe Howe, "Back Bay Landfall," *Atlantic Monthly*, August 1941.
5. L.D.B. to Amy Wehle, January 2, 1881.
6. S. D. Warren to L.D.B., January 21, 1887.
7. Author's interview with Justice Brandeis, July 28, 1940.
8. J. B. Thayer to L.D.B., November 22, 1879.
9. J. B. Thayer to L.D.B., December 8, 1879.
10. L.D.B. to Frederika Brandeis, January 2, 1881.
11. Author's interview with Justice Brandeis, July 26, 1940.
12. L.D.B.'s notebook.
13. J. B. Thayer to L.D.B., March 1, 1881.
14. Charles W. Eliot to L.D.B., March 28, 1882.
15. E. F. McClennen, "Brandeis—the Lawyer," memorandum prepared at the author's request, February 5, 1942.
16. L.D.B., "The Harvard Law School," *op. cit.,* p. 23.
17. Author's interview with Judge Julian Mack, October 19, 1941.
18. L.D.B. to Dean C. C. Langdell, December 30, 1889.
19. L.D.B. to Charles W. Eliot, April 25, 1893.
20. S. D. Warren to L.D.B., September 22, 1886.
21. Author's interview with Justice Brandeis, April 12, 1941.
22. L.D.B. to Alice Goldmark, December 28, 1890.
23. Roscoe Pound to William Chilton, 1916.

Pavesich v. *New England Mutual Insurance Co.,* 50 Southeastern Reporter, p. 68, was the first case sustaining the right to privacy for which Warren and Brandeis had contended.

In a note, December 1912, the *Columbia Law Review* commented: "An article by Messrs. Samuel D. Warren and Louis D. Brandeis on 'The Right to Privacy,' in the *Harvard Law Review* of December 1890, enjoys the unique distinction of having initiated and theoretically outlined a new field of jurisprudence. The authors first summarize the growth of legal protection with the broadening of the intellectual and spiritual wants of mankind. A stage has now been reached when not only rights of the physical person, of property and reputation must be guarded, but also, immunity should be afforded against the use of one's personality for private gain by others, or to feed a prurient curiosity. The writers ingeniously offered as a germinal analogue the law, not of defamation, but of literary property."

Brandeis and Warren had earlier co-operated in the preparation of "The Watuppa Pond Cases," *Harvard Law Review,* Vol. 2 (1888); and "The Law of Ponds," *Harvard Law Review,* Vol. 3 (1889).
24. L.D.B. to Adolph Brandeis, December 16, 1889.
25. Author's interview with Justice Brandeis, January 12, 1940.
26. The full story is told in Goldmark, *Pilgrims of '48.*
27. L.D.B. to Alice Goldmark, December 5, 1890.
28. Unpublished Reminiscences of Elizabeth Glendower Evans.
29. *Ibid.*

CHAPTER V

1. *New York Herald,* March 3, 1912.
2. Author's interview with Justice Brandeis, July 28, 1940.
3. L.D.B. to Alice G. Brandeis, September 12, 1928.
4. Author's interview with Miss E. Louise Malloch, July 18, 1940.
5. Livy S. Richard, "Up from Aristocracy," *The Independent,* July 27, 1914.
6. *Boston Advertiser,* June 13, 1884.
7. Charles Nagel to L.D.B., June 17, 1884.
8. Author's interview with Justice Brandeis, July 21, 1940.
9. L.D.B.'s argument before the Joint Committee on Liquor Law of the Massachusetts Legislature, February 27, 1891.
10. *Springfield Republican,* December 29, 1894.
11. *Report of the Committee of the Whole Board of Aldermen on the Care and Management of Public Institutions* (1894), Vol. III, pp. 3631-32.

12. *Boston Herald,* December 29, 1894.
13. *Supra,* note 11, p. 3634.
14. *Boston Herald,* January 12, 1897.
15. *Springfield Republican,* January 13, 1897.
16. "An Unusual Man of Law," *New York Times Annalist,* January 27, 1913.

PART II

CHAPTER VI

1. Daniel Webster, *Journal of Debates and Proceedings in the Convention of Delegates chosen to revise The Constitution of Massachusetts, November 15, 1820–January 9, 1821* (Boston, 1821), p. 144.
2. L.D.B., "The Opportunity in the Law," an address delivered before the Harvard Ethical Society, May 4, 1905, reprinted in *Business—a Profession,* pp. 342–43.
3. *Ibid.,* p. 338.
4. Henry B. Brown, "The Distribution of Property," *Report of the American Bar Association,* Vol. 16, p. 225.
5. D. J. Brewer, "The Movement of Coercion," reprinted from *Proceedings of the Sixteenth Annual Meeting of the New York State Bar Association,* Vol. 16, pp. 37–47.
6. R. T. Ely, "Report on Social Legislation in the United States for 1889 and 1890," *Economic Review,* April 1891, p. 236.
7. *Supra,* note 5.
8. Henry F. Pringle, *The Life and Times of William Howard Taft* (New York: Farrar & Rinehart, 1939), Vol. I, p. 128.
9. *Pollock* v. *Farmers' Loan and Trust Co.,* 157 U.S. 429 (1895) and 158 U.S. 601 (1895).
10. F. N. Judson, "Liberty of Contract under the Police Power," *Report of the American Bar Association,* Vol. 14 (1891), p. 259.
11. *Supra,* note 2, p. 339.
12. *Ibid.,* pp. 337–38.
13. Author's interview with Justice Brandeis, July 22, 1940.
14. *Supra,* note 2, p. 342.
15. *Boston Post,* October 27, 1905.
16. *Supra,* note 2, p. 343.
17. *Ibid.*
18. *Ibid.,* pp. 340–41.
19. George W. Alger to the author, June 26, 1944.
20. George W. Alger to C. C. Burlingham, June 12, 1944.

CHAPTER VII

1. L.D.B. to E. F. McClennen, February 17, 1916.
2. L.D.B., "The Experience of Massachusetts in Street Railways," *Municipal Affairs,* Vol. VI (1903), No. 4.
3. L.D.B. to Colonel W. A. Bancroft, May 20, 1897.
4. Robert B. Woods and Joseph B. Eastman, "The Boston Franchise Contest," *The Outlook,* April 14, 1906.
5. *Practical Politics,* April 1, 1905.
6. L.D.B.'s notes of speech before the Committee on Metropolitan Affairs, May 18, 1900.
7. "The Boston Elevated," *Good Government,* May 29, 1901.
8. E. H. Abbot to L.D.B., July 7, 1901.
9. L.D.B. to E. A. Filene, June 1, 1901.
10. L.D.B. to Morton Prince, June 6, 1901.
11. L.D.B. to W. Murray Crane, June 7, 1901.
12. Myron E. Pierce, "The History of the Westminster Chambers Case," February 11, 1902 [pamphlet]; *Boston Herald,* February 24, 1903.

13. L.D.B. to McClennen, February 28, 1916.
14. L.D.B. to M. R. Maltbie, June 27, 1901.
15. "The Veto," *Boston Post,* June 27, 1901 [editorial].
16. House Rept. No. 1449, Commonwealth of Massachusetts, containing Governor Crane's veto, June 18, 1901, pp. 1–6; reported in *Boston Post,* June 19, 1901.
17. *Boston Evening Transcript,* June 18, 1901.
18. *Boston Evening Transcript,* June 19, 1901.
19. "Some Objections to the Matthews-Livermore Terminal Subway Bill," February 17, 1902 [typescript of speech].
20. *Ibid.*
21. *Boston Evening Transcript,* April 16, 1902.
22. *The Beacon,* April 26, 1902 [Boston].
23. "Subway Controversy. Shall the Boston Elevated Railway Co. Be the Servant or Master of the People? L. D. Brandeis Defines the Issue," from the Final Subway Hearing, April 14, 1902. Pamphlet issued by the Associated Board of Trade and the Public Franchise League.
24. "The Washington Street Subway—Comments on the Financial Condition of the Boston Elevated Railway Co., submitted by Louis D. Brandeis on behalf of the Boston Associated Board of Trade to the Committee on Metropolitan Affairs of the Massachusetts Legislature," April 26, 1902.
25. Albert E. Pillsbury to L.D.B., April 30, 1902.
26. Statement by Brandeis, October 22, 1902 [typescript].
27. John T. Boyd to L.D.B., October 21, 1902.
28. "Address of Mr. Brandeis before the Committee on Metropolitan Affairs, on behalf of the Public Franchise League, in Opposition to the Proposed Act to Incorporate the Boston Transportation Company," March 23, 1905 [typescript].
29. L.D.B. to Walter L. Fisher, April 10, 1905.
30. L.D.B. to W. Rodman Peabody, House Chairman, Committee on Metropolitan Affairs, March 24, 1906.
31. *Boston Traveler,* June 13, 1911.
32. *Boston Traveler,* June 21, 1911; *Boston Journal,* June 22, 1911.
33. Norman Hapgood's report to Woodrow Wilson of a conversation with L.D.B., February 13, 1913.

CHAPTER VIII

1. L.D.B. to W. H. McElwain, June 18, 1902.
2. Pamphlet issued October 1903 by order of the Executive Committee.
3. Speech delivered before the Good Government Association, April 8, 1903 [typescript].
4. E. A. Adler to Morton Prince, March 24, 1903.
5. L.D.B. to John F. Fitzgerald, July 21, 1906.
6. *Boston Post,* March 19, 1903.
7. *Boston Journal,* April 9, 1903.
8. *Boston Herald,* April 9, 1903.
9. Speech before the Unitarian Club, April 9, 1903 [typescript].
10. *Boston Journal,* April 9, 1903.
11. *Supra,* note 3.
12. *Boston Traveler,* April 14, 1903.
13. *Ibid.*
14. *Boston Herald,* April 14, 1903.
15. *Boston Record,* April 14, 1903.
16. *Ibid.*
17. L.D.B. to Frank Parsons, July 29, 1905.
18. Speech delivered at Brighton, Massachusetts, December 2, 1904 [typescript].
19. "What Loyalty Demands," speech delivered before the New Century Club, November 28, 1905 [typescript].
20. Author's interview with Justice Brandeis, July 26, 1940.
21. *Boston Post,* September 16, 1904.

22. L.D.B. to Guy W. Cox, March 2, 1906.
23. *Boston Herald,* June 14, 1905.
24. *Ibid.*
25. *Ibid.*
26. *Boston Globe,* November 16, 1904.

CHAPTER IX

1. L.D.B., "How Boston Solved the Gas Problem," *American Review of Reviews,* November 1907, reprinted in *Business—a Profession,* pp. 99–114; L.D.B. to Lawrence Abbot, July 1, 1907.
2. Edward H. Clement, "Nineteenth Century Boston Journalism," *New England Magazine,* September 1907.
3. Text of the bill in the *Boston Evening Transcript,* May 8, 1903.
4. L.D.B. to McClennen, March 14, 1916.
5. *Supra,* note 1.
6. *Supra,* note 4.
7. "Consolidation of Gas Companies and of Electric Light Companies, Argument of L. D. Brandeis on behalf of the Massachusetts State Board of Trade before the Legislative Committee on Public Lighting," March 9, 1905. Pamphlet issued by the Public Franchise League.
8. *Ibid.*
9. *Boston Globe,* March 9, 1905.
10. *Ibid.*
11. Edward R. Warren to L.D.B., March 10, 1905.
12. L.D.B. to Edward R. Warren, March 13, 1905.
13. L.D.B. to McClennen, March 14, 1916.
14. L.D.B.'s *Index.*
15. L.D.B. to McClennen, March 14, 1916.
16. Testimony of Edward R. Warren, *Hearings before the Sub-Committee of the Committee on the Judiciary, United States Senate, on the Nomination of Louis D. Brandeis to be an Associate Justice of the Supreme Court of the United States,* 64th Cong., 1st Sess., Sen. Doc. No. 409, Vol. I, p. 1312. Hereafter referred to as *Nom. Hearings.*
17. *Ibid.*
18. G. W. Anderson to L.D.B., May 6, 1905.
19. *Supra,* note 15.
20. *Supra,* note 16, p. 1312 *et seq.*
21. L.D.B. to Edward R. Warren, May 3, 1905.
22. *Report of the Committee Appointed to Consider the English Sliding Scale, Pursuant to Chapter 101, Resolves of 1905.* Received by L.D.B., January 22, 1906 [typescript, unsigned].
23. L.D.B. to McClennen, March 14, 1916.
24. *Boston Evening Transcript,* April 6, 1906.
25. *Boston Evening Transcript,* April 4, 1906.
26. *Boston Evening Transcript,* April 6, 1906.
27. "An Act to Promote the Reduction of the Price of Gas in the City of Boston and Its Vicinity." Noted on it by Brandeis: "Draft submitted to P.L. Committee, April 23, 1906" [typescript].
28. Remarks of Louis D. Brandeis, *Hearing on Report of Special Committee on the London Sliding Scale of Prices and Dividends as Applied to Gas Companies,* Committee on Public Lighting, State House, April 23, 1906 [typescript].
29. *Boston American,* May 11, 1906.
30. *Boston Evening Transcript,* April 25, 1906. Brandeis expressed his own views in a letter to the *Boston Post,* May 18, 1906.
31. *Boston American,* May 14, 1906.
32. *Boston Herald,* May 26, 1906.
33. *Boston Evening Transcript,* June 7, 1906.
34. G. L. Barnes to L.D.B., June 5, 1906.

35. L.D.B. to Charles P. Hall, July 13, 1906.
36. *Supra*, note 1, pp. 102, 114.
37. *Boston Evening Transcript*, March 9, 1905.
38. Quoted by L.D.B. in a letter to Bernard J. Rothwell, July 23, 1909.

CHAPTER X

1. Hamilton Holt, "Just the Man for Judge," *The Independent*, February 7, 1916.
2. "The Employer and Trades Unions," an address delivered at the annual banquet of the Boston Typothetæ, April 21, 1904, reprinted in *Business—a Profession*, pp. 16–17.
3. "An Economic Exhortation to Organized Labor," an address before the Boston Central Labor Union, February 5, 1905, and published in *Civic Federation Review*, March 1905; reported in the *Boston Globe*, February 6, 1905.
4. The Brandeis–Gompers debate was reported in the *Boston Herald*, December 5, 1902. Brandeis's speech was published as an article, "The Incorporation of Trade Unions," in *The Green Bag*, January 1903, and reprinted in *Business—a Profession*, pp. 88–98.
5. H. D. Lloyd to L.D.B., December 3, 16, 31, 1902; January 29, 1903.
6. *Supra*, note 3.
7. L.D.B. to Charles F. Pidgin, July 26, 1905.
8. Related by E. G. Evans, "Mr. Justice Brandeis, the People's Tribune," *The Survey*, October 29, 1931.
9. *Supra*, note 3.
10. E. A. Filene, "Louis D. Brandeis, As We Know Him," *Boston Post*, March 4, 1916.
11. *New York Times Annalist*, January 27, 1913.
12. William Hard, "Regularization of Shops by a Business Individual," *Philadelphia Public Ledger*, May 16, 1916.
13. *Supra*, note 3.
14. "Business—the New Profession," an address delivered at the Brown University commencement, June 1912, reprinted in *Business—a Profession*, p. 12.
15. *Filene Co-operative Association Echo*, May 1905.
16. L.D.B. to Hayes Robbins, April 28, 1905.
17. Lincoln Steffens to L.D.B., February 12, 1909.
18. L.D.B. to E. A. Filene, April 22, 1908.
19. *Supra*, note 2, p. 18.
20. Reported in *Providence News* and *Providence Evening Bulletin*, April 11, 1905.
21. *Daily Eastern Argus* [Portland, Me.], April 19, 1905.
22. Statement before the United States Commission on Industrial Relations, 64th Cong., 1st. Sess., Sen. Doc. No. 415, Vol. 19, p. 995.
23. *Supra*, note 2.
24. *Civic Federation Review*, May 15, 1905.
25. Statement by Brandeis for the *Boston Globe*, December 18, 1903 [typescript].
26. *New York Times*, April 26, 1903.
27. L.D.B. to F. S. Baldwin, May 5, 1904.
28. *Supra*, note 24.
29. *Supra*, note 2, p. 26.
30. *Boston Post*, February 6, 1905.
31. "Hours of Labor," an address delivered at the first annual meeting of the Civic Federation of New England, January 11, 1906, reprinted in *Business—a Profession*, pp. 29, 32.
32. *Boston Herald*, December 5, 1902.
33. *Boston Post*, February 9, 1905.
34. *Boston Daily Advertiser*, November 17, 1904.

CHAPTER XI

1. *New York Insurance Journal*, July 10, 1905.
2. Author's interview with Justice Brandeis, July 12, 1938.

3. Quoted in Alpheus Thomas Mason, *The Brandeis Way* (Princeton, N.J.: Princeton University Press, 1938), p. 91.
4. "Life Insurance, the Abuses and the Remedies," an address delivered before the Commercial Club of Boston, October 26, 1905, reprinted in *Business—a Profession*, pp. 115–59.
5. *Ibid.,* p. 118.
6. *Ibid.,* p. 141.
7. *Ibid.,* p. 142.
8. *Ibid.,* pp. 144–45.
9. *Ibid.,* pp. 131, 132.
10. *Ibid.,* p. 147.
11. *Ibid.,* p. 138.
12. *Ibid.,* p. 156.
13. *Report of the Joint Committee of the Senate and Assembly of the State of New York Appointed to Investigate and Examine into the Business and Affairs of Life Insurance Companies Doing Business in the State of New York,* Assembly Doc. No. 41, Vol. X, p. 318.
14. Testimony, *Ibid.,* Vol. III, p. 2551.
15. *Ibid.,* Vol. VI, p. 5053.
16. *Ibid.,* Vol. X, p. 445.
17. *Ibid.*
18. This letter is quoted in full in Mason, *op. cit.,* pp. 123–26.
19. Wright to L.D.B., December 13, 1905.
20. L.D.B. to Charles P. Hall, June 12, 1906.
21. Charles Evans Hughes to L.D.B., July 6, 1906.
22. R. F. Herrick to L.D.B., July 5, 1906.
23. Reprinted in Mason, *op. cit.,* pp. 311–25.
24. *Supra,* note 4, p. 158.
25. *Ibid.,* p. 159.
26. Charles P. Hall to L.D.B., July 27, 1906.
27. L.D.B. to Norman H. White, December 8, 1906.
28. Charles H. Jones to L.D.B., March 18, 1907.
29. *Boston Herald,* November 8, 1906.
30. *Practical Politics,* May 4, 1906.
31. Memorandum of argument by Representative Garcelon against House Bill No. 1467.
32. *Charities Magazine,* July 11, 1908.
33. Remarks of L.D.B. at a Workers' Conference, September 23, 1910.
34. Alice H. Grady to L.D.B., April 13, 1915; also author's interview with Judd Dewey, July 20, 1938.
35. For the full report on industrial insurance, *see* "Hearings before the Temporary National Economic Committee of the United States," *Investigation of Concentration of Economic Power,* 76th Cong., 1st Sess., Pt. 10.
36. Gerhard A. Gesell, "A Study of Legal Reserve Life Insurance Companies," Monograph No. 28, prepared under the auspices of the Securities and Exchange Commission for the Temporary National Economic Committee, 76th Cong., 3rd Sess., Sec. XVII, p. 305.
37. *Ibid.,* p. 312.
38. *Ibid.,* pp. 311–12.
39. Author's interview with Justice Brandeis, July 14, 1938.
40. "The Regulation of Competition against the Regulation of Monopoly," an address before the Economic Club, reported in the *New York Times,* November 2, 1912.

CHAPTER XII

1. *New York World,* May 15, 1914.
2. *New York Times Annalist,* May 5, 1913.

3. *Hearings before Massachusetts Committee on Railroads,* June 10, 1907; reported in the *Boston American,* June 12, 1907.
4. *Boston Post,* June 26, 1906.
5. Memorandum from L.D.B. to E. Louise Malloch, November 4, 1907.
6. L.D.B. to Frankfurter, February 26, 1916.
7. Memorandum of L.D.B.'s conversation with Mark Sullivan, January 4, 1908.
8. *Boston American,* June 10, 1907.
9. George W. Batson, "Charles S. Mellen: Railroad Organizer," *Review of Reviews,* August 1907.
10. *Boston Evening Transcript,* June 12, 1907.
11. Quoted by John F. Moors in "Betraying New England," *New England Magazine,* March 1913.
12. *Boston Morning Herald,* June 12, 1907.
13. *Supra,* note 7.
14. *Boston American,* June 18, 1907.
15. *Boston Evening Transcript,* October 31, 1907.
16. *Supra,* note 7.
17. *Ibid.*
18. *Ibid.*
19. *Hartford Daily Courant,* November 14, 1907.
20. *Supra,* note 7.
21. *Boston News Bureau,* January 10, 1908.
22. *Lowell Telegram,* February 23, 1908.
23. *Supra,* note 7.
24. Stenographic report of L.D.B.'s statement before the Commission.
25. L.D.B.'s memoranda show numerous conversations with Douglas and Droppers.
26. *Report of the Commission on Commerce and Industry,* March 1908, pp. 15–21.
27. *Boston Evening Transcript,* May 9, 1908.
28. *Boston Advertiser,* May 13, 1908.
29. *Boston Evening Herald,* May 19, 1908.
30. *Boston Morning Journal,* May 23, 1908.
31. *Boston Evening Transcript,* July 10, 1908.
32. *Ibid.*
33. *Boston Journal,* January 21, 1909.
34. *Boston Advertiser,* February 26, 1909.
35. *Boston Post,* April 28, 1909.
36. L.D.B.'s argument before Committee on Railroads, May 19, 1909 [transcript].
37. Quoted by R. M. La Follette, April 12, 1910, *Cong. Rec.,* 61st Cong., 2nd Sess., Vol. 45, Pt. V, pp. 4549–63.
38. *Ibid.*
39. *Boston Journal,* July 15, 1914.

CHAPTER XIII

1. Quoted in the *Manchester Union,* February 16, 1911.
2. *New York Evening Post,* September 11, 1911.
3. *Boston Advertiser,* September 7, 1911.
4. *Boston American,* May 12, 1912.
5. *Newspaper Enterprise Association,* November 23, 1912.
6. *Boston Evening Transcript,* December 9, 1912.
7. *Boston Journal,* December 13, 1912.
8. *Boston Record,* December 20, 1912.
9. Quoted in *Boston Herald,* December 22, 1912.
10. George R. Conroy, "Schiff and Brandeis," *Truth,* April 18, 1914.
11. *Boston Globe,* March 7, 1913.
12. *Boston Journal,* March 14, 1913.
13. *Boston Evening Transcript,* March 14, 1913.
14. *Boston Traveler,* April 24, 28, 1913.

15. *Boston Post,* April 29, 1913.
16. *Boston Globe,* April 25, 1913.
17. *Boston Journal,* May 8, 1913.
18. *Boston Evening Transcript,* May 7, 1913.
19. *Ibid.*
20. *Boston American,* July 9, 1913.
21. *Ibid.*
22. *New York World,* July 9, 1913.
23. L.D.B., "The Failure of Banker–Management," July 23, 1913, Ch. IX of *Other People's Money and How the Bankers Use It* (Washington, D.C.: National Home Library Foundation, 1933), p. 134. [First published in book form by Frederick A. Stokes Co. in 1914.]
24. *Boston Journal,* September 25, 1913.
25. *Boston Journal,* October 2, 1913.
26. *Washington Post,* December 11, 1913.
27. *New York Times,* February 26, 1914.
28. *Financial Transactions of the New York, New Haven and Hartford Railroad,* 63rd Cong., 2nd Sess., Sen. Doc. No. 543, pp. 712–13.
29. *Ibid.,* p. 874.
30. Author's interview with Justice Brandeis, February 11, 1941.
31. *Supra,* note 28, pp. 37–38.
32. *Washington Post,* June 23, 1914.
33. *Boston Post,* July 22, 1914.
34. L.D.B. to Hapgood, October 1, 1914.
35. *New York Times,* August 28, 1929.
36. *Boston Journal,* March 1, 1911.
37. L.D.B., "Monopoly a Failure," *Business America,* August 1913.
38. *Ibid.*
39. L.D.B., *Other People's Money,* pp. 141–42.

CHAPTER XIV

1. L.D.B. to Alfred Brandeis, July 28, 1904.
2. Miss E. Louise Malloch to the author, July 5, 1944.
3. William Hard, "Brandeis the Adjuster and Private-Life Judge," *Philadelphia Public Ledger,* May 14, 1916. *See also* his article, "Brandeis," *The Outlook,* May 31, 1916.
4. Extract from statement of Louis D. Brandeis at informal meeting with Sidney W. Winslow and most of his fellow-directors, July 12, 1911; reprinted in *Nom. Hearings,* p. 221.
5. *Nom. Hearings,* p. 945.
6. Louis D. Brandeis' Memorandum on House Bill No. 472, enclosed in letter to Sidney Winslow, March 28, 1906; reprinted in *Nom. Hearings,* pp. 255–56.
7. Statement of Louis D. Brandeis before the Joint Judiciary Committee of the Massachusetts Legislature, April 18, 1906; reprinted in *Nom. Hearings,* p. 1047 ff.
8. *Ibid.,* p. 1048.
9. *Ibid.,* p. 1050.
10. *Supra,* note 6, p. 257.
11. *Supra,* note 7, p. 1050.
12. *Supra,* note 6, p. 256.
13. Reprinted in *Nom. Hearings,* p. 259.
14. *Ibid.,* p. 218.
15. W. H. McElwain to L.D.B., May 25, 1906; reprinted in *Nom. Hearings,* p. 722.
16. Reprinted in *Nom. Hearings,* p. 723.
17. *Ibid.*
18. L.D.B. to Erving Winslow, October 5, 1906; reprinted in *Nom. Hearings,* p. 956.
19. *Supra,* note 4.

20. L.D.B. to Sidney Winslow, December 6, 1906; reprinted in *Nom. Hearings,* pp. 958–59.
21. L.D.B. to Moses E. Clapp, February 12, 1912; reprinted in *Nom. Hearings,* pp. 218–19.
22. Testimony of Sidney Winslow, *Nom. Hearings,* p. 219.
23. *Supra,* note 21, p. 219.
24. *Supra,* note 4, p. 222.
25. *Supra,* note 21, p. 219; testimony of E. F. McClennen, *Nom. Hearings,* p. 735.
26. *Supra,* note 21, p. 219.
27. *Supra,* note 4, p. 222.
28. *Ibid.*
29. Charles H. Jones to William Chilton, February 25, 1916.
30. Testimony of E. F. McClennen, *Nom. Hearings,* p. 737.
31. *U.S. Supreme Court Reports,* Vol. 204, p. 673, February 25, 1907.
32. *Supra,* note 21, p. 219.
33. *Ibid.*
34. Memorandum statement of Charles H. Jones, May 5, 1911.
35. Statement of Sidney Winslow, *Nom. Hearings,* p. 166.
36. *Supra,* note 4.
37. *Ibid.,* p. 224.
38. L.D.B. to McClennen, February 19, 1916.
39. *Supra,* note 30, p. 742.
40. *Supra,* note 4, pp. 221–24.
41. On December 14–15, 1911, Brandeis testified in favor of La Follette's bill, *Report of Hearings before the Committee on Interstate Commerce,* United States Senate, pursuant to Sen. Res. 98, Pt. XVI, pp. 1146 *et seq.* Testimony relevant to United Shoe Machinery Company reprinted in *Nom. Hearings,* pp. 1025–31.

   On January 26 and 27, 1912, before House Committee on the Judiciary concerning the Thayer, Lenroot, and Peters bills, *Report of Hearings before the Committee on the Judiciary, House of Representatives, on Trust Legislation,* Serial 2, p. 13 *et seq.* Testimony relevant to the United reprinted in *Nom. Hearings,* pp. 1031–39.

   On May 15, 1912, before the House Committee on Patents, *Report of the Hearings before the Committee on Patents, House of Representatives,* No. 18, p. 3 *et seq.* Testimony relevant to the United reprinted in *Nom. Hearings,* pp. 1039–41.

   On February 16, 1914, before the House Judiciary Committee, *Report of Hearings before the Committee on the Judiciary, House of Representatives, on Trust Legislation,* Serial 7, Pt. 16, p. 637 *et seq.* Testimony relevant to United reprinted in *Nom. Hearings,* pp. 1041–46.
42. Testimony before Committee on Interstate Commerce of the United States Senate, December 14, 1911, reprinted in *Nom. Hearings,* pp. 1028–29.
43. Sidney Winslow to Moses E. Clapp, January 19, 1912; reprinted in *Nom. Hearings,* p. 939.
44. L.D.B. to Moses E. Clapp, February 24, 1912; reprinted in *Nom. Hearings,* p. 217.
45. *Ibid.,* p. 219.
46. *Ibid.,* p. 221.
47. Sidney Winslow to Moses E. Clapp, February 29, 1912; reprinted in *Nom. Hearings,* pp. 957, 958.
48. Reprinted in *Nom. Hearings,* pp. 936–59 *et seq.*
49. *Supra,* note 22, p. 239.
50. See T. G. Joslin's review of James Kerney's *Political Education of Woodrow Wilson, Boston Evening Transcript,* April 29, 1926.
51. L.D.B. to McClennen, February 23, 1916.
52. "The Employer and Trades Unions," Boston Typothetæ address, reprinted in *Business—a Profession,* p. 17.
53. "Life Insurance, the Abuses and the Remedies," Commercial Club address, reprinted in *Business—a Profession,* p. 125.
54. "The Opportunity in the Law," Harvard Ethical Society address, reprinted in *Business—a Profession,* pp. 333, 337.

CHAPTER XV

1. Extracts from Petition dated July 1914, in *U.S.* v. *New Haven & Hartford Railroad Company, et al.* (D.C.S.D. N.Y. Original Petition), reprinted in *Nom. Hearings,* Vol. I, pp. 416–17.
2. Testimony of William Kelly, *Nom. Hearings,* pp. 404–405.
3. *Ibid.,* p. 411.
4. *Ibid.*
5. Extracts from *Report of Hearings before the Joint Standing Committee on Railroads, under the Order for said Committee to Investigate the Conduct of the New York, New Haven & Hartford Railroad,* Massachusetts, 1893, testimony of L.D.B., May 3, 1893, reprinted in *Nom. Hearings,* p. 422.
6. *Supra,* note 2, pp. 403–405.
7. *Supra,* note 5, p. 423.
8. *Ibid.,* p. 424.
9. *Ibid.,* p. 426.
10. *Ibid.,* p. 427.
11. *Ibid.,* p. 428.
12. *Ibid.,* p. 416.
13. Tuttle, William Rockefeller, Morgan, C. P. Clark to Corbin, January 23, 1893; Extracts from testimony in *U.S.* v. *William Rockefeller, et al.* (D.C.S.D. N.Y.), New York, October 25, 1915, quoted in *Nom. Hearings,* p. 449.
14. *Supra,* note 2, p. 412.
15. Testimony of E. F. McClennen, *Nom. Hearings,* p. 699.
16. L.D.B. to McClennen, February 19, 1916.
17. *Supra,* note 5, p. 436.
18. *Ibid.,* p. 436.
19. *Ibid.,* p. 431.
20. *Ibid.,* p. 439.
21. *Supra,* note 2, pp. 406–407.
22. L.D.B. to McClennen, February 18, 1916.
23. *Supra,* note 1, p. 417.
24. Reprinted in *Nom. Hearings,* Vol. I, p. 787.
25. *Ibid.,* pp. 787, 788.
26. *Ibid.,* pp. 789–90.
27. *Ibid.,* p. 287.
28. *Ibid.,* pp. 287–88.
29. *Ibid.,* p. 295.
30. *Ibid.,* p. 288.
31. *Ibid.,* p. 299.
32. L.D.B. to McClennen, February 17, 1916.
33. McClennen's memorandum to the author.
34. *Nom. Hearings,* Vol. I, pp. 140–41.
35. *Ibid.,* p. 278.
36. *Ibid.,* pp. 283–84.
37. *Ibid.,* p. 284.
38. Richard W. Hale, Sr., to Richard W. Hale, Jr., November 11, 1936
39. Hapgood to Wilson, February 21, 1913.
40. Testimony of Asa P. French, *Nom. Hearings,* Vol. I, p. 770.

PART III

CHAPTER XVI

1. *Muller* v. *Oregon,* 208 U.S., p. 412.
2. "The Living Law," an address delivered before the Chicago Bar Association, January 3, 1916, published in *Illinois Law Review,* February 1916; reprinted in *Business—a Profession,* p. 344 *et seq.*

3. *Luke,* 11: 52.
4. *Supra,* note 2, p. 362.
5. "It is but decent respect due to the wisdom, the integrity, and the patriotism of the legislative body, by which any law is passed, to presume in favor of its validity, until its violation is proved beyond all reasonable doubt." Justice Washington in *Ogden* v. *Saunders,* 12 Wheat. 24 (1827), p. 270.
6. *Ritchie* v. *People,* 155 Ill. 98 (1895). Quoted in Josephine C. Goldmark, *Fatigue and Efficiency, a Study in Iudustry* (New York: Russell Sage Foundation, 1912).
7. *Lochner* v. *New York,* 198 U.S. 45 (1905), p. 57.
8. *People* v. *Williams,* 189 N.Y. 131 (1907), p. 135.
9. Brandeis's statement, *Hearings of the New York State Factory Investigating Commission,* January 22, 1915, Fourth Rept., Vol. V, p. 2893.
10. *Ibid.*
11. Alfred Lief, *Brandeis: The Personal History of an American Ideal* (New York: Stackpole Sons, 1936), p. 137.
12. From a memorandum prepared by Josephine C. Goldmark at the author's request, November 6, 1944.
13. *Supra,* note 1, pp. 419–21.
14. *Supra,* note 2.
15. *Supra,* note 8.
16. Judge Hiscock in *People* v. *Schweinler Press,* 214 N.Y. 395 (1915), at p. 411.
17. *Stettler* v. *O'Hara,* 69 Ore. 519 (1914).
18. *Stettler* v. *O'Hara,* 243 U.S. 629 (1916).
 The Supreme Court divided evenly on the constitutionality of the act. Brandeis, having been appointed to the Court after taking part in preparation of the brief, did not vote.
19. L.D.B., "The Constitution and the Minimum Wage," *The Survey,* February 6, 1915.
20. For an elaboration of this theme, *see* Alpheus Thomas Mason, *Brandeis: Lawyer and Judge in the Modern State* (Princeton, N.J.: Princeton University Press, 1933), Ch. 6.
21. F. W. Coburn, "Who is this Man Brandeis?" *Human Life,* February 1911.

CHAPTER XVII

1. *Hearings before Committee of Investigation of Interior Department and Bureau of Forestry,* 61st Cong., 3rd Sess., Sen. Doc. 719, Vol. 7, p. 3805. Hereafter referred to as *Int. Hearings.*
2. *Ibid.,* Vol. 8, p. 4507 *passim.*
3. *Seattle Post-Intelligencer,* September 16, 1909.
4. Pringle, *The Life and Times of William Howard Taft,* Vol. I, p. 491.
5. *Ibid.,* p. 505.
6. *Int. Hearings,* Vol. 4, p. 1226.
7. *See* Alpheus Thomas Mason, *Bureaucracy Convicts Itself* (New York: The Viking Press, 1941), p. 88 *et seq.;* also George Wharton Pepper, *Philadelphia Lawyer, an Autobiography* (Philadelphia: J. B. Lippincott Co., 1944), pp. 83–84.
8. Norman Hapgood, *The Changing Years* (New York: Farrar & Rinehart, Inc., 1930), p. 182.
9. Pepper, *op. cit.,* p. 84.
10. *Cong. Rec.,* January 7, 1910, 61st Cong., 2nd Sess., p. 390.
 Senator Norris tells the whole story in a speech, June 25, 1932, honoring Harry A. Slattery, in Ballinger's time one of Pinchot's righthand men. Printed in full, *Cong. Rec.,* July 15, 1932, 72nd Cong., 1st Sess., pp. 15456–57.
11. George W. Norris to Gifford Pinchot, March 27, 1940.
12. For the milieu of the committee sessions, the author is indebted to E. H. Abbot, "Performance of The Ballinger Case," *The Outlook,* May 28, 1910.
13. *Trenton Times,* May 16, 1910.
14. *Providence Journal,* May 11, 1910.
15. *Int. Hearings,* Vol. 7, p. 3861.

16. *Ibid.*, p. 4130.
17. *Ibid.*, p. 3861.
18. *Washington Evening Star*, February 3, 1910.
19. Pepper, *op. cit.*, p. 85.
20. Alfred Brandeis to L.D.B., April 9, 1910.
21. *Int. Hearings*, Vol. 6, pp. 3171-72.
22. *Ibid.*, p. 3198.
23. *Ibid.*, Vol. 7, p. 3626.
24. *Ibid.*, pp. 3624-25.
25. *Ibid.*, p. 3624.
26. *Ibid.*, p. 3626.
27. *Ibid.*, p. 3627.
28. *Ibid.*, p. 3630.
29. *Ibid.*, p. 4137.
30. *Ibid.*, pp. 4137-38.
31. *New York Sun*, May 2, 1910.
32. *Int. Hearings*, Vol. 7, p. 4139.
33. Author's interview with George Rublee, December 11, 1940.
34. *Int. Hearings*, Vol. 7, pp. 3787-88.
35. *Ibid.*, p. 3594.
36. *Ibid.*, p. 4087.
37. *Ibid.*, p. 4090.
38. *Ibid.*, pp. 4115-16.
39. *Ibid.*, pp. 4074-75.
40. *Ibid.*, pp. 3964-65.
41. *Ibid.*, p. 3862.
42. *Ibid.*, pp. 3865-66.
43. *Ibid.*, p. 3868.
44. *Ibid.*
45. *Collier's Weekly*, October 9, 1909.
46. *Int. Hearings*, Vol. 7, p. 3881.
47. *Ibid.*, p. 3978.
48. *Ibid.*, p. 3807.
49. *Ibid.*, Vol. 3, p. 487.
50. *Ibid.*, Vol. 8, p. 4458.
51. *Ibid.*, Vol. 7, p. 4364.
52. *Ibid.*, Vol. 8, p. 4479; *New York Times*, May 22, 1910.
53. L.D.B. to Frankfurter, March 18, 1916.
54. *Int. Hearings*, Vol. 8, pp. 4507-4508.
55. *Ibid.*, p. 4394.
56. G. W. Pepper to the author, February 10, 1945.
57. *New York Sun*, May 18, 1910.
58. *Int. Hearings*, Vol. 8, p. 4492.
59. *Ibid.*, p. 4493; *Philadelphia Public Ledger*, May 18, 1910.
60. *Int. Hearings*, Vol. 7, p. 3811.
61. *Ibid.*, Vol. 8, pp. 4493-94.
62. *Ibid.*, p. 4495.
63. *Report of Committee of Investigation of Interior Department*, Vol. 1, pp. 90-91.
64. *Ibid.*, p. 94.
65. *Int. Hearings*, Vol. 9, pp. 4922-23.

CHAPTER XVIII

1. *New York Times*, May 8, 1911.
2. *Philadelphia North American*, April 21, 1911.
3. *Philadelphia North American*, April 28, 1911.
4. *Preliminary Examination of Persons Having Knowledge of Controller Bay Matter*, Washington, D.C., July 26, 27, 28, 1911.
5. *Ibid.*

6. Published in *Philadelphia North American*, July 7, 1911.
7. *Boston Herald*, July 11, 1911.
8. *Boston American*, July 9, 1911.
9. J. M. Graham to L.D.B., July 13, 1911.
10. L.D.B. to J. M. Graham, July 14, 1911.
11. *Boston Evening Transcript*, July 12, 1911.
12. *Philadelphia North American*, July 5, 1911.
13. Gilson Gardner to L.D.B., July 17, 1911.
14. Hapgood to Myrtle Abbott, June 5, 1911.
15. L.D.B. to J. E. Lathrop, July 24, 1911.
16. L.D.B. to Gifford Pinchot, August 1, 1911.
17. Message of the President in Response to the Resolution of the Senate, June 27, 1911.
18. Theodore Roosevelt, "Alaska—It Must Be Developed," *The Outlook*, July 22, 1911 [editorial].
19. *Washington Evening Star*, July 27, 1911.
20. *Cong. Rec.*, March 3, 1911, Vol. 46, Pt. 5, p. 4114.
21. *New York Tribune*, July 26, 1911; *Seattle Post-Intelligencer*, August 4, 1911; *Philadelphia Inquirer*, July 24, 1911; *Cong. Rec.*, March 3, 1911, p. 4116.
22. *Philadelphia North American*, July 11, 1911.
23. L.D.B. to Amos Pinchot, September 18, 1911.
24. *Ibid.*
25. "An Alaskan Program," sent by L.D.B. to Gifford Pinchot, July 29, 1911.
26. L.D.B. to Amos Pinchot, August 2, 1911.
27. *Supra*, note 25.
28. *Cong. Rec.*, 62nd Cong., 1st Sess., Vol. 47, Pt. 5, pp. 4262–4306.
29. L.D.B. to Amos Pinchot, September 5, 1911.
30. *Sacramento Star*, September 9, 1911.
31. *New York Sun*, November 7, 1911.
32. *Boston Evening Transcript*, December 4, 1911.

CHAPTER XIX

1. Louis Levine, *The Women's Garment Workers* (New York: The Viking Press, 1924), p. 182.
2. Address of Louis D. Brandeis, published in *The Echo*, March 19, 1913.
3. *New York Call*, July 26, 1910.
4. *Ibid.*
5. *Ibid.*
6. Levine, *op. cit.*, p. 187.
7. *Ibid.*, pp. 187–88.
8. *Minutes of Joint Conference between Ten Delegates of the Joint Board of the Cloak, Suit & Skirt Makers' Unions, and Ten Delegates of the Cloak, Suit & Skirt Manufacturers' Protective Association*, held in New York City beginning Thursday, July 28, 1910.
9. *New York Times*, July 29, 1910.
10. *Supra*, note 8, pp. 273–89.
11. *Ibid.*, pp. 287–92.
12. *Ibid.*, p. 292.
13. *Ibid.*, p. 293.
14. *Ibid.*, pp. 294–98.
15. *Ibid.*, pp. 299–301.
16. *Ibid.*, p. 301. For Mr. Cohen's full story, *see* his *Law and Order in Industry* (New York: The Macmillan Co., 1916).
17. *Ibid.*, p. 308.
18. Argument of Benjamin Schlesinger, *ibid.*, p. 326.
19. *Ibid,*, p. 338.
20. Tentative agreement drawn up by J. H. Cohen, enclosed in letter to Meyer London, August 1, 1910.

21. L.D.B. to Cohen, August 1, 1910.
22. *New York Sun,* August 1, 1910.
23. Levine, *op. cit.,* p. 190.
24. Max Meyer to L.D.B., August 3, 1910.
25. Henry Moskowitz to Meyer Bloomfield, undated.
26. Levine, *op. cit.,* pp. 192–93.
27. Cohen to Max Meyer, December 18, 1941.
28. Levine, *op. cit.,* pp. 193–94.
29. Quoted by Mary Brown Sumner in "A Settlement of the Cloak Makers' Strike," *The Survey,* September 17, 1910.
30. L.D.B. to Jane Addams, November 26, 1910.
31. Board of Arbitration, Session of March 4, 1911, p. 41.
32. *Ibid.,* pp. 75–95.
33. Mary Brown Sumner, "Story of the Cloak Makers' Strike," *The Survey,* December 17, 1910; Edith Wyatt, "The New York Cloak Makers' Strike," *McClure's,* April 1911; Henry Moskowitz, "The Power for Constructive Reform in the Trade Union Movement," *Life and Labor,* January 1912; Henry Moskowitz, "An Experiment in Democratic Industrial Control," *La Follette's Weekly,* April 19, 1913; J. B. McPherson, "The New York Cloak Makers' Strike," *Journal of Political Economy,* March 1911.

   Charles H. Winslow, "Conciliation, Arbitration, and Sanitation in the Cloak, Suit & Skirt Industry in New York City," *Bulletin 98,* January 1912, pp. 203–272; "Industrial Court of the Cloak, Suit & Skirt Industry of New York City," *Bulletin 144,* March 19, 1914, pp. 1–78; "Conciliation, Arbitration, and Sanitation in the Dress & Waist Industry of New York City," *Bulletin 145,* April 10, 1914, pp. 1–196; "Wages and Regularity of Employment in the Cloak, Suit & Skirt Industry, New York City and Boston," *Bulletin 147,* June 13, 1914, pp. 1–197. Issued by the U.S. Department of Labor, Bureau of Labor Statistics.
34. Levine, *op. cit.,* p. 206.
35. Cohen to L.D.B., October 6, 1911.
36. L.D.B. to Cohen, October 7, 1911.
37. Levine, *op. cit.,* pp. 205–206.
38. *Ibid.,* p. 243.
39. Cohen to Max Meyer, December 18, 1941.
40. "Conference between the Representatives . . . ," February 3 and 4, 1913.
41. *Ibid.,* pp. 51, 53.
42. *Ibid.,* p. 80.
43. *Ibid.,* p. 191–92, 195–96, 207–208.
44. *Ibid.,* pp. 213–15.
45. "The Good and the Bad Aspects of the Protocol," translation of an article in the *New Post,* May 23, 1913.
46. *Jewish Daily Forward,* June 21, 1913.
47. Moskowitz to L.D.B., July 17, 1913.
48. Moskowitz to L.D.B., July 24, 1913.
49. *Proceedings of the Meeting of the Board of Arbitration Selected by the Representatives of the Cloak and Skirt Makers' Unions of New York, and the Cloak, Suit and Skirt Manufacturers' Protective Association, with the Representatives of the said unions and the said protective association,* August 3–6, 1913, Vol. II, pp. A22–A23.
50. *Ibid.,* Vol. I, pp. 33–34.
51. *Ibid.,* pp. 218, 221–22.
52. *Ibid.,* Vol. II, p. A29.
53. Levine, *op. cit.,* p. 261.
54. *Proceedings of the Meeting of the Board of Arbitration,* January 24, 1914, p. 13.
55. Morris Hillquit to L.D.B., December 7, 1914.
56. Session of Board of Arbitration, January 29, 1915, p. 558.
57. Moskowitz to L.D.B., February 3, 1915.
58. Session of Board of Arbitration, February 5, 1915, p. 137.
59. *American Cloak & Suit Review,* March 1915.

60. This theme is elaborated in John A. Dyche, *Bolshevism in American Labor Unions: A Plea for Constructive Unionism* (New York: Boni & Liveright, 1926).
61. Session of the Board of Arbitration, April 25, 1915, p. 3.
62. Memorandum of telephone conversation between W. Baxton (answering for Brandeis) and Moskowitz, May 20, 1915.
63. Charles Heineman to L.D.B., June 2, 1915.
64. Report of Council of Conciliation, Proceedings, Vol. III, p. 156.
65. Philip J. Halvosa, interview with L.D.B., *Boston American*, November 12, 1911.
66. Cohen to Max Meyer, December 18, 1941.

CHAPTER XX

1. *Evidence in Matter of Proposed Advances in Freight Rates* (1910–11), 61st Cong., 3rd Sess., Sen. Doc. No. 725, Vol. 4, p. 2567. Hereafter referred to as *Rate Hearings*.
2. *Ibid.*, p. 2415.
3. *Ibid.*, p. 2328.
4. *New York Evening Post*, September 26, 1910.
5. *Boston Evening Transcript*, January 18, 1911.
6. *See* the series of articles by Harry A. Bullock in the *Boston Evening Transcript* of November 12, 19, and 21, 1910.
7. Quoted in "Brandeis, Teacher of Business Economy," *Philadelphia Public Ledger*, December 4, 1910; also published in the *New York Times* and the *Springfield Republican* [Mass.].
8. *Rate Hearings*, pp. 2033–34.
9. *Ibid.*, pp. 2203–34.
10. *Ibid.*, p. 2444.
11. *Ibid.*, p. 2368.
12. *Ibid.*, pp. 2977–79.
13. *Ibid.*, p. 2294.
14. *Ibid.*, pp. 2501–2505.
15. *Ibid.*, pp. 2396–97.
16. "Fluctuations in the Price of Iron and Steel Products for Thirteen Years," *Iron Age*, January 5, 1911.
17. *Rate Hearings*, pp. 5261–62, 5263.
18. *Ibid.*, p. 2507.
19. *Ibid.*, pp. 5254–55.
20. *Ibid.*, p. 2314.
21. *Ibid.*, pp. 2363–64.
22. *Ibid.*, p. 2314.
23. *Ibid.*, pp. 2400–2401.
24. *Ibid.*, pp. 2403, 2617.
25. *Ibid.*, p. 2619.
26. *Ibid.*, p. 2620.
27. *Ibid.*, p. 2734.
28. *Ibid.*, p. 2772.
29. *Ibid.*, p. 2822.
30. *Ibid.*, pp. 2846–47.
31. Quoted by Harry A. Bullock, *Boston Evening Transcript*, November 21, 1910.
32. *New York Tribune*, November 24, 1910.
33. *New York Times*, November 30, 1910.
34. "Brandeis, Legal Hercules, Fights for Principle," *New York World*, December 4, 1910.
35. "Brandeis, Teacher of Business Economy," *Philadelphia Public Ledger*, December 4, 1910.
36. "A Soldier of the Common Good," *Louisville Courier-Journal*, December 2, 1910 [editorial].
37. "Mr. Brandeis and the Railroad Men," *New York Sun*, December 2, 1910 [editorial].
38. "Sincerity Answers Sarcasm," *New York Times*, November 30, 1910 [editorial].

39. " 'Go It, Husband; Go It, Bear,' " *Chicago Tribune*, January 18, 1911 [editorial].
40. *Louisville Evening Post*, December 2, 1910 [editorial].
41. "Efficiency and Economy," *New York Tribune*, November 22, 1910 [editorial].
42. *Chicago Record-Herald*, December 1, 1910.
43. "Brandeis," *Railroad Herald*, December 1910 [editorial].
44. "Railway Rates and Railway Efficiency," *Railway Age Gazette*, December 2, 1910.
45. "President Brown Scoffs at Brandeis Plan," *New York American*, December 2, 1910.
46. *New York Times*, December 11, 1910.
47. Samuel Gompers, "Miracles of Efficiency," *American Federationist*, April 1911.
48. "Emerson on Efficiency," *Boston Evening Transcript*, November 26, 1910.
49. "Railroad and Other Economies," *American Metal Market*, December 7, 1910 [editorial].
50. "Householders Will Welcome This," *Chicago Tribune*, December 7, 1910 [editorial].
51. "Brandeis' Idea Is Worth Trying in Municipal Rule," *Louisville Herald*, December 17, 1910.
52. "A Brandeis for the Kitchen," *Boston Evening Transcript*, December 23, 1911 [editorial].
53. *New York Evening Post*, November 22, 1910.
54. "Financiers Go West to Probe Railroad Economy," *Philadelphia Evening Times*, December 3, 1910.
55. "Accepting the Brandeis Plan of Saving," *The Financial World*, January 28, 1911 [editorial].
56. *Rate Hearings*, Vol. 8, p. 4845.
57. Report of the I.C.C., 1911, p. 305.
58. *Boston Traveler*, February 24, 1911.
59. L.D.B., "A Victory for Conservatism," *Moody's Magazine*, March 1911.
60. "Wall St. Surprised by Commission's Decision," *Boston Journal*, February 24, 1911.
61. "The Financial Situation," *Commercial and Financial Chronicle*, March 4, 1911 [editorial].
62. "Railway Men Will Meet," *New York Evening Post*, February 24, 1911.
63. *Boston News Bureau*, February 24, 1911.

CHAPTER XXI

1. Reported in the *Boston Post*, October 10, 1913.
2. Ernst Freund to L.D.B., October 27, 1913.
3. *New York Times*, November 27, 1913.
4. H. S. Gauss to L.D.B., November 26, 1913.
5. S. W. Stratton to L.D.B., November 28, 1913.
6. L.D.B. to J. W. Carmalt, November 13, 1913.
7. J. S. Harlan to Daniel Willard, November 20, 1913.
8. L.D.B. to J. B. Eastman, November 18, 1913.
9. *New York Commercial*, October 16, 1913.
10. E. E. Clark to J. Russell Marble, November 6, 1913.
11. G. S. Patterson to J. S. Harlan, December 15, 1913.
12. *The Manufacturers' News*, February 19, 1914.
13. *Five Per Cent Case* (1913–14), Sen. Doc. No. 466, 63rd Cong., 2nd Sess., Vol. 2, pp. 1390–91.
14. For Brandeis's full statement of Free Services, *ibid.*, Vol. 2, pp. 1735–36.
15. Gilson Gardner, *Newspaper Enterprise Association*, February 7, 19, 1914.
16. Statement of H. C. Barlow, *supra*, note 13, Vol. 3, p. 2170.
17. Edward F. Henson, cross-examined by L.D.B., *ibid.*, Vol. 4, pp. 3441–42.
18. *Ibid.*, p. 3437.
19. *Supra*, note 13, Vol. 6, pp. 5233–34.
20. *Ibid.*, pp. 5235, 5246–48, 5254–55, 5264, 5265.
21. *Ibid.*, pp. 5260–62.

22. Quoted in the *New York Sun*, May 7, 1914.
23. *Supra,* note 13, Vol. 6, p. 5421.
24. *Ibid.,* pp. 5437, 5443.
25. *Ibid.,* pp. 5443–44.
26. *Ibid.,* p. 5445.
27. *I.C.C. Report on Five Per Cent Case* (June–October 1914), Vol. XXXI, p. 384.
28. *Nom. Hearings,* p. 36.
29. Notation by L.D.B. on letter from J. S. Harlan, dated August 22, 1914.
30. J. S. Harlan to L.D.B., August 8, 1914.
31. *New York Evening Post,* September 10, 1914.
32. *Boston Herald,* September 18, 1914.
33. "Fools or Knaves," *Boston Traveler,* September 23, 1914 [editorial].
34. "Too Much Brandeis," *Philadelphia Press,* October 25, 1914 [editorial].
35. *Supra,* note 28, pp. 37, 39.
36. *Supra,* note 13, Vol. 7, pp. 6328, 6334.
37. A detailed eleven-page memorandum from L.D.B. to J. S. Harlan, November 26, 1914.

CHAPTER XXII

1. *Hearings before the Committee on Interstate Commerce* (1911), United States Senate, 62nd Cong., Sen. Res. 98, p. 1278.
2. *Ibid.,* pp. 1163, 1166.
3. Ida M. Tarbell, *The Life of Elbert H. Gary* (New York: D. Appleton & Co., 1925), p. 134.
4. J. B. Bishop, *Theodore Roosevelt and His Time* (New York: Charles Scribner's Sons, 1920), Vol. I, p. 184.
5. "Social Justice and the Trusts," an address before the undergraduates of Harvard University, December 18, 1912.
6. *Supra,* note 1, p. 1161.
7. L.D.B. to Wilson, September 30, 1912.
8. *Supra,* note 1, pp. 1147, 1278.
9. *Ibid.,* pp. 1147–48.
10. *Ibid.*
11. *Ibid.*
12. *Ibid.,* p. 1149 *et seq.*
13. *Ibid.,* pp. 1170–71.
14. *Ibid.,* p. 1208.
15. *Ibid.,* p. 1157.
16. *Ibid.,* p. 1156.
17. *Ibid.,* pp. 1188, 1291.
18. *Ibid.,* pp. 1156–57.
19. *Ibid.,* p. 1166.
20. Author's interview with Robert W. Woolley, April 20, 1941.
21. *Hearings before the Committee on Investigation of United States Steel Corporation,* House of Representatives, January 29, 1912. Quoted by Brandeis, p. 2836.
22. *Ibid.,* pp. 2836, 2842.
23. Address at Ethical Culture Meeting House, February 10, 1912. Reported in the *New York Times,* February 11, 1912.
24. *Supra,* note 21, pp. 2841–43.
25. *Ibid.,* p. 2857.
26. *Ibid.,* p. 2865.
27. *Supra,* note 1, p. 1151.
28. *Supra,* note 21, p. 2863.
29. *Ibid.,* p. 2856.
30. *Supra,* note 1, p. 1258.
31. *Ibid.,* pp. 1152, 1185.
32. *Ibid.,* p. 1155.
33. *Ibid.,* p. 1180.

34. *Ibid.*, p. 1174.
35. *Boston American*, March 17, 1912.
36. *Supra*, note 1, pp. 1225–26.
37. *Boston Globe*, December 16, 1911.
38. *Boston Herald*, December 18, 1911.
39. *Boston Evening Transcript*, December 20, 1911.
40. M. E. Pew passed Poindexter's letter on to Brandeis, February 25, 1912.
41. L.D.B. to J. P. Yoder [Poindexter's secretary], February 26, 1912.
42. Poindexter to L.D.B., February 29, 1912.

PART IV

CHAPTER XXIII

1. Henry F. Pringle, *The Life and Times of William Howard Taft*, Vol. II, p. 761.
2. L.D.B. to Gifford Pinchot, July 5, 1911.
3. *Kansas City Times*, February 5, 1911.
4. *Boston Journal*, September 22, 1911.
5. *Chicago Evening Post*, January 3, 1912.
6. Matthew Josephson, *President Makers; the Culture of Politics and Leadership in an Age of Enlightenment, 1896–1919* (New York: Harcourt, Brace & Co., 1940), p. 240.
7. R. M. La Follette, *Autobiography* (Privately printed, 1913), p. 479.
8. L.D.B. to Alfred Brandeis, February 7, 1912.
9. La Follette to L.D.B., December 30, 1910; *La Follette's Weekly*, February 4, 1911.
10. Josephson, *op. cit.*, p. 400.
11. *Ibid.*, p. 407.
12. *Boston Journal*, September 22, 1911.
13. *Boston American*, October 19, 1911.
14. *Boston Journal*, September 23, 1911.
15. *New York American*, October 31, 1911.
16. *Boston American*, October 15, 1911.
17. Pringle, *op. cit.*, Vol. 1, pp. 552–53.
18. L.D.B. to W. L. Houser, December 27, 1911.
19. *Chicago Tribune*, January 4, 1912.
20. *St. Paul Daily News*, January 4, 1912.
21. *Cleveland Plain Dealer*, January 2, 1912.
22. *Chicago Tribune*, January 4, 1912.
23. *Chicago Record-Herald*, January 3, 1912.
24. *Minneapolis Evening Tribune*, January 4, 1912.
25. Rublee to L.D.B., March 15, 1912; Frankfurter to L.D.B., March 18, 1912.
26. Interview given the United Press, April 3, 1912.
27. L.D.B. to C. O. Whedon, April 15, 1912.
28. *San Diego Union*, May 18, 1912.

CHAPTER XXIV

1. L.D.B. to Alfred Brandeis, April 3, 1912.
2. Josephson, *op. cit.*, p. 443.
3. L.D.B. to Hapgood, July 3, 1912.
4. L.D.B. to Alfred Brandeis, May 13, 1910.
5. Rublee to L.D.B., July 18, 1912.
6. *Boston American*, July 10, 1912.
7. L.D.B. to Alfred Brandeis, July 28, 1912.
8. L.D.B. to Hapgood, July 3, 1912.
9. L.D.B. to Alfred Brandeis, August 29, 1912.
10. *New York Times*, August 29, 1912.
11. L.D.B. to Dickinson S. Miller, September 4, 1912.
12. For the story of Perkins's grip on T.R.'s Bull Moose party, *see* Harold L. Ickes,

"Who Killed the Progressive Party," *American Historical Review*, January 1941, pp. 306–337.
13. L.D.B., "Competition," *American Legal News*, January 1913.
14. Hapgood to L.D.B., August 8, October 31, 1912.
15. "Vested Wrongs," manuscript of an article sent to Hapgood, October 2, 1912.
16. "Trusts and the Interstate Commerce Commission," manuscript of an article.
17. L.D.B. to Arthur K. Stone, September 4, 1912.
18. Hapgood to L.D.B., August 29, 1912.
19. L.D.B. to Charles Henry Davis, October 4, 1912.
20. *New York World*, August 28, 1912.
21. *Supra*, note 19.
22. Memorandum among L.D.B.'s notes, dated September 16, 1912.
23. "Wilson the Progressive," undated manuscript of an article.
24. *Boston American*, September 8, 1912.
25. "The Great Trust Problem and How the Democrats Would Solve It," L.D.B.'s suggestions to Wilson, September 30, 1912.
26. *Ibid.*
27. Homer S. Cummings to L.D.B., August 31, 1912.
28. *Cleveland Press*, October 11, 1912.
29. *Boston Post*, September 19, 1912. This speech was published in pamphlet form and widely distributed under the title, "Third Term-Trust-Scheme to Deceive Labor. Exposed by Louis D. Brandeis, Republican lawyer and supporter of La Follette."
30. "Efficiency and Trusts," address delivered before the Town Criers, Providence, October 7, 1912.
31. *Supra*, note 13.
32. L.D.B. to Samuel Untermyer, September 23, 1912.
33. Arthur N. Holcombe to L.D.B., September 30, 1912.
34. L.D.B. to Arthur N. Holcombe, October 3, 1912.
35. L.D.B. to Alfred Brandeis, October 15, 1912.
36. L.D.B. to Alfred Brandeis, October 25, 1912.
37. L.D.B. to Alfred Brandeis, November 2, 1912.
38. *Supra*, note 35.
39. *Supra*, note 37.

CHAPTER XXV

1. Lincoln Steffens to Laura Steffens, November 11, 1912, *Letters of Lincoln Steffens* (New York: Harcourt, Brace & Co., 1938), p. 312.
2. Lincoln Steffens to E. A. Filene, July 6, 1908, *ibid.*, p. 200.
3. *Collier's Weekly*, June 10, 1911.
4. *Boston Traveler*, July 22, 1911.
5. L.D.B. to Alfred Brandeis, July 10, 1912.
6. L.D.B. to Mrs. Charles Edward Russell, February 14, 1912.
7. Henry H. Hunter to L.D.B., November 14, 1912; L.D.B. to Henry H. Hunter, November 15, 1912.
8. L.D.B. to Julius Helburn, February 7, 1913; *Chicago Journal*, January 14, 1913.
9. J. F. Rhodes to Wilson, December 19, 1912.
10. W. S. Youngman to Irving Fisher, January 18, 1913.
11. E. R. Warren to Wilson, November 18, 1912.
12. *Boston Post*, February 13, 1913.
13. *Boston News Bureau*, February 10, 1913.
14. *Boston News Bureau*, February 13, 1913.
15. *Boston News Bureau*, March 3, 1913.
16. *The Philistine*, July 1913.
17. *Life*, December 26, 1912.
18. *The Philistine*, July 1913.
19. Henry Moškowitz to Hapgood, February 11, 1913.
20. E. B. M. Brown to Joseph Tumulty, February 26, 1913.
21. Hapgood to Wilson, January 30, 1913.

22. Hapgood to Wilson, February 21, 1913.
23. E. A. Filene to Hapgood, February 3, 1913.
24. E. A. Filene to Wilson, December 21, 1913.
25. Frankfurter to Hapgood, February 12, 1913.
26. C. R. Crane to Wilson, February 10, 1913.
27. Dickinson S. Miller to Wilson, February 21, 1913.
28. G. W. Anderson to Wilson, December 24, 1912.
29. G. W. Anderson to Wilson, February 20, 1913.
30. L.D.B. to Mary P. Morgan, February 7, 1913.
31. C. H. Jones to Wilson, February 11, 1913.
32. J. M. Minton to E. E. Moore, February 24, 1913.
33. *Boston American,* February 12, 1913; also article by Gilson Gardner, "Privilege Seeks to Bar Brandeis," *Boston Post,* February 13, 1913.
34. *Boston Evening Transcript,* February 8, 1913.
35. *Boston Record,* February 8, 1913.
36. *Boston Evening Transcript,* February 11, 1913.
37. *New York Sun,* February 20, 1913.
38. E. A. Brandies to L.D.B., February 20, 1913.
39. *New York World,* February 27, 1913; *Boston Post,* February 28, 1913.
40. *Boston Post,* March 3, 1913.
41. James Kerney, *Political Education of Woodrow Wilson* (New York: Century Co., 1926), pp. 284–86.
42. Hapgood to R. S. Baker, July 23, 1928.
43. *Supra,* note 18.
44. *Boston News Bureau,* March 4, 1913.
45. *Boston Advertiser,* March 3, 1913.
46. L.D.B. to Hapgood, July 9, 1913.
47. L.D.B. to Carl Snyder, March 11, 1913.
48. *Boston Advertiser,* March 12, 1913; *Boston Journal,* March 13, 1913.
49. Ray Stannard Baker, *Woodrow Wilson: Life and Letters* (New York: Doubleday, Doran & Co., 1931), Vol. IV, p. 36.
50. L.D.B. to Wilson, May 19, 1913.

CHAPTER XXVI

1. *Boston Post* and *Boston Journal,* March 11, 1913; L.D.B. to Hapgood, March 13, 1913.
2. *Boston Globe,* April 5, 1913.
3. Baker, *op. cit.,* Vol. IV, p. 165; Carter Glass, *An Adventure in Constructive Finance* (New York: Doubleday, Doran & Co., 1927), pp. 113–14.
4. Baker, *op. cit.,* p. 162.
5. L.D.B. to Wilson, June 14, 1913.
6. *Ibid.*
7. *Ibid.*
8. Baker, *op. cit.,* p. 166.
9. *Ibid.,* pp. 357–58.
10. L.D.B. to Franklin K. Lane, December 12, 1913.
11. *New York Times,* January 3, 1914; Baker, *op. cit.,* p. 367.
12. Baker, *op. cit.,* p. 370.
13. *Ibid.*
14. L.D.B. to Alfred Brandeis, January 23, 1914.
15. *Hearings before House Committee on Interstate and Foreign Commerce* (January 30, 1914), 63rd Cong., 2nd Sess., pp. 4, 9.
16. *Ibid.,* pp. 5, 6.
17. *Ibid.*
18. *Ibid.,* p. 15.
19. L.D.B. to Hapgood, March 12, 1913.
20. L.D.B. to Wilson, May 19, 1913.
21. L.D.B. to Wilson, May 26, 1913.

22. W. G. McAdoo to L.D.B., July 15, 1913.
23. L.D.B. to Wilson, October 10, 1913.
24. L.D.B. to F. K. Lane, October 15, 1913.
25. G. W. Anderson to L.D.B., December 11, 1913.
26. G. W. Anderson to L.D.B., December 17, 1913.
27. Clarence E. Hanscom to L.D.B., December 17, 1913.
28. L.D.B. to J. C. McReynolds, August 13, 1913.
29. L.D.B. to Hapgood, December 31, 1914.
30. L. R. Glavis to L.D.B., October 20, 1914; and L.D.B. to B. W. Marshall, October 22, 1914.
31. L.D.B. to Treadwell Cleveland, November 27, 1914.
32. Henry F. Hollis to L.D.B., November 5, 1914.
33. C. H. Jones to L.D.B., April 17, 1915.

CHAPTER XXVII

1. *Boston American*, December 14, 1911.
2. "Breaking the Money Trust," *Harper's Weekly*, November 22, 1913.
3. L.D.B. to Alfred Brandeis, July 29, 1912.
4. Hapgood to L.D.B., August 29, 1912.
5. Hapgood to L.D.B., October 18, 30, 31, 1912.
6. L.D.B. to R. J. Collier, November 11, 14, 1912.
7. L.D.B. to R. J. Collier, November 7, 1912.
8. L.D.B. to Hapgood, November 14, 1912.
9. L.D.B. to C. R. Crane, February 15, 1913.
10. C. R. Crane to Wilson, May 23, 1913.
11. L.D.B. to Hapgood, July 15, 1913.
12. L.D.B. to Alfred Brandeis, January 1, 1914.
13. L.D.B. to J. R. Smith, February 2, 1914.
14. *Chicago Journal*, January 4, 1913.
15. L.D.B. to Samuel Untermyer, March 8, 1913.
16. Samuel Untermyer to L.D.B., September 10, 1913.
17. L.D.B. to Hapgood, September 30, 1913.
18. L.D.B. to Clinton Rogers Woodruff, July 28, 1913.
19. L.D.B. to R. S. Lovett, October 29, 1913; R. S. Lovett to L.D.B., November 5, 1913.
20. Jacob Schiff to L.D.B., November 5, 1913.
21. Garet Garrett to L.D.B., November 8, 1913.
22. L.D.B., *Other People's Money*, p. 118.
23. L.D.B. to Samuel McCrea, September 29, 1913.
24. W. G. McAdoo to L.D.B., October 3, 1913; L.D.B. to W. G. McAdoo, October 6, 1913.
25. *Supra*, note 22, p. 4.
26. Lawrence Chamberlain, "Mr. Brandeis and Investment Banking," *Harper's Weekly*, January 17, 1914.
27. Lawrence Chamberlain, "A Reply to Mr. Brandeis," *Harper's Weekly*, April 4, 1914.
28. Quoted in *Harper's Weekly*, May 23, 1914.
29. "The Employer and Trades Unions," Boston Typothetæ Address, reprinted in *Business—a Profession*, p. 17.
30. H. B. Joy to L.D.B., January 28, 1914.
31. "Interlocking Directorates," *Annals of American Academy of Political and Social Science*, January 1915.
32. James McCarthy to the editor of *Harper's Weekly*, January 3, 1913.
33. *Harper's Weekly*, December 13, 1913.
34. B. H. Meyer to L.D.B., December 22, 1913.
35. K. M. Landis to L.D.B., December 3, 1913.
36. *Philadelphia North American*, November 8, 1913.
37. *Philadelphia Public Ledger*, November 8, 1913.

38. Charles W. Hobbs to L.D.B., November 8, 1913.
39. Marlen E. Pew to L.D.B., November 8, 1913. .
40. Carl Kelsey to L.D.B., November 9, 1914; Samuel S. Fels to L.D.B., November 9, 1914.
41. *Final Report and Testimony of the Commission on Industrial Relations* (1915), 64th Cong., 1st Sess., Sen. Doc. No. 415, Vol. 26, p. 7761; *supra*, note 31, p. 45. *See also Hearings before the Committee on the Judiciary*, Trust Legislation (February 25, 1914), 63rd Cong., 2nd Sess., Pt. 22; and *Hearings before Sub-Committee of the Committee on Banking and Currency* (February 21, 1928, March 1, 2, 1933), 72nd Cong., 2nd Sess., Sen. Res. 84 and Sen. Res. 239.
42. Ferdinand Pecora, *Wall Street under Oath, the Story of Our Modern Money Changers* (New York: Simon & Schuster, 1939), pp. 71, 76.
43. "How the Combiners Combine, Interlocking Directorates," *Harper's Weekly*, December 6, 1913.

CHAPTER XXVIII

1. *Boston Herald*, June 12, 1911.
2. *Boston Herald*, June 14, 1911.
3. *Boston Evening Transcript*, June 27, 1911.
4. *New York Herald*, March 3, 1912.
5. *Ibid.*
6. L.D.B. to Alfred Brandeis, October 10, 1914.
7. *Dr. Miles Medical Co.* v. *Park and Sons Co.*, 220 U.S. 409; *Bobbs-Merrill Co.* v. *Strauss*, 210 U.S. 339; *Bauer* v. *O'Donnell*, 229 U.S. 1.
8. L.D.B., "Cutthroat Prices, the Competition that Kills," *Harper's Weekly*, November 15, 1913.
9. L.D.B. to A. W. Shaw, July 11, 1913.
10. L.D.B. to E. J. Frost, July 12, 1913.
11. L.D.B. to J. F. McElwain, July 14, 1913.
12. L.D.B. to Bureau of Labor Statistics, July 14, 1913.
13. L.D.B. to E. A. Van Valkenburg, June 13, 1913.
14. Typed Manuscript on Price Maintenance.
15. Hearings on H.R. 13305 before House Committee on Interstate and Foreign Commerce (January 9, 1915), quoted in *Nom. Hearings*, Vol. 2, p. 120.
16. *Ibid.*, pp. 135–36.
17. L.D.B. to W. H. Ingersoll, March 1, 1915.
18. L.D.B. to E. A. Whittier, March 1, 1915.
19. L.D.B. to W. E. Smythe, September 22, 1915.
20. V. G. Iden to L.D.B., September 16, 1931.
21. *Final Report and Testimony of Commission on Industrial Relations* (1914), 64th Cong., 1st Sess., Sen. Doc. No. 415, Vol. 19, pp. 995, 997.
22. *Ibid.*, p. 991.
23. *Ibid.*, Vol. 26, p. 7666.
24. *Ibid.*, Vol. 19, p. 995.
25. *Ibid.*, Vol. 26, pp. 7667, 7668.
26. *Boston American*, March 17, 1912.
27. *Supra*, note 21, Vol. 26, p. 7663.
28. *Ibid.*, pp. 7659–60.
29. *Ibid.*, Vol. 19, p. 1005.
30. *Ibid.*, pp. 7660, 7664.
31. L.D.B. to Robert W. Bruère, February 25, 1922.
32. *Supra*, note 21, Vol. 26, p. 7660.
33. *Ibid.*, p. 7662.
34. *Ibid.*, p. 7677.
35. *Boston Post*, February 14, 1915.
36. 1912 memorandum on "Efficiency in Your Home and in Your Business."
37. McClennen's memorandum to the author.
38. F. W. Coburn, "Who is this Man Brandeis?" *Human Life*, February 1911.

672

BRANDEIS: A FREE MAN'S LIFE

39. Notes from Fanny Brandeis's interview with L.D.B., May 19, 1940.
40. *Minneapolis Journal,* January 4, 1912.
41. Manuscript on Legal Reform, May 2, 1912.
42. Quoted by Ernest Poole, "Brandeis, a Remarkable Record of Unselfish Work Done in the Public Interest," *American Magazine,* February 1911, reprinted in *Business— a Profession.*
43. L.D.B. to John H. Wigmore, May 8, 1912; L.D.B. to Herbert Harley, November 13, 1912.
44. L.D.B. to Charles F. Johnson, June 1, 1912.
45. L.D.B. to Frankfurter, January 28, 1913.
46. L.D.B. to Herbert Harley, November 13, 1914.
47. L.D.B. to Maurice Hutchinson, October 28, 1914.
48. Reprinted in *Business—a Profession,* p. 364 ff.
49. Horace M. Kallen, "Philosopher of Americanism," *Jewish Frontier,* November 1936.

CHAPTER XXIX

1. Author's interview with Justice Brandeis, July 29, 1940.
2. For L.D.B.'s attitude toward his uncle, see Bernard Flexner, *Mr. Justice Brandeis and the University of Louisville* (privately printed, 1938), pp. 36-37.
3. Jacob De Haas, *Louis D. Brandeis, a Biographical Sketch, with Special Reference to His Contributions to Jewish and Zionist History.* (New York: Bloch Publishing Co., 1929), p. 50.
4. Memorandum from Stephen S. Wise to Julian W. Mack, November 29, 1937.
5. De Haas, *op. cit.,* p. 51.
6. This story was told by Brandeis himself at a Zionist meeting in St. Louis on January 1, 1915. *St. Louis Globe-Democrat,* January 4, 1915.
7. Author's interview with Justice Brandeis, July 28, 1940.
8. "What Loyalty Demands," New Century Club address, November 28, 1905 [manuscript copy].
   Brandeis gave much of the same material, including the paragraphs quoted herein, in his interview for the *Jewish Advocate,* December 9, 1910; *see* De Haas, *op. cit.,* p. 152.
9. At a banquet given in honor of Meyer London in December 1914, Brandeis made a touching reference to the debt he owed the New York garment workers. *Daily Independent-Times,* January 2, 1915.
10. De Haas, *op. cit.,* pp. 51-52.
11. "An Interview with Louis Dembitz Brandeis," *The American Hebrew,* December 10, 1910.
12. Author's interview with Justice Brandeis, July 28, 1940.
13. *Jewish Advocate,* March 7, 1913, p. 12.
14. L.D.B. to Louis Lipsky, July 18, 1913.
15. L.D.B. to Louis Lipsky, July 23, 1913.
16. N. Sokolow to L.D.B., September 15, 1913; *New York Times,* September 8, 1913.
17. W. A. Troys to L.D.B., August 28, 1913.
18. *Atlanta Constitution,* September 16, 1913.
19. *The American Israelite,* December 23, 1915.
20. Minutes of the Executive Committee, Federation of American Zionists, August 13, 1914.
21. De Haas to L.D.B., August 26, 1914.
22. De Haas, *op. cit.,* pp. 161-62.
23. "Zionism and Patriotism," a 1915 address, published by Federation of American Zionists, p. 1.
24. *Cleveland Plain Dealer, Cleveland Leader,* October 8, 1914; L.D.B. to De Haas, October 9, 1914.
25. Henry Hurwitz to L.D.B., November 16, 1914. This address was first published under the title "A Call to the Educated Jew," in *The Menorah Journal,* January 1915, pp. 13-19.

26. *Chicago Tribune*, November 25, 1914.
27. L.D.B. to Jacob Billikopf, June 16, 1916.
28. *Jewish Advocate*, April 16, 1915.
29. *Los Angeles Times*, June 4, 1915.
30. *The American Israelite*, July 1, 1915.
31. Jacob De Haas, "The Possible Jewish Leader—Louis D. Brandeis of Boston," *The American Jew*, January 8, 1915.
32. *Boston Herald*, June 30, 1915.
33. *Jewish Advocate*, July 2, 1915.
34. L.D.B. to De Haas, January 25, 1915.
35. *Jewish Advocate*, August 13, 1915.
36. *Boston Post*, October 4, 1915.
37. Manuscript of Brandeis's speech at Carnegie Hall, New York, January 24, 1916.
38. *New York Tribune*, July 17, 1916.
39. Report of *Actions Comité* from Copenhagen, Mimeograph, August 20, 1916.
40. *Boston Herald*, July 17, 1916.
41. L.D.B. to Judge Hugo Pam, July 21, 1916.
42. L.D.B. to R. Gottheil, October 29, 1914.
43. L.D.B. to J. J. Jusserand, November 16, 1914.
44. *New York Sun*, November 29, 1914.
45. Memorandum in letter of J. I. Peyser to L.D.B., December 4, 1916.
46. Provisional Executive Committee Minutes, April 2, 1917.
47. *New York Times*, April 7, 1917.
48. Wise to L.D.B., April 9, 1917.
49. Blanche E. C. Dugdale, *Arthur James Balfour* (London: Hutchinson & Co., 1936), Vol. II, p. 231.
   Mrs. Dugdale recalls her uncle's remark that Brandeis "was in some ways the most remarkable man he had met in the United States," and she adds, "It seems from such notes of these conversations as survive, that Balfour pledged his own personal support of Zionism."
50. Robert S. Lansing to L.D.B., June 4, 1917.
51. "Your letter re Lord N. and Lord R. piques my curiosity as to what happened at the luncheon." De Haas to L.D.B., September 19, 1917.
52. Proposed Provisional Executive Committee draft to Rothschild, Weizmann, and Sokolow, enclosed in a letter to L.D.B., November 21, 1917.
53. De Haas, *Louis D. Brandeis,* pp. 96–97.
54. L.D.B. to Mack, September 3, 9, 1918.
55. L.D.B. to Wise, December 29, 1918.
56. *New York American*, March 25, 1919.
57. W. J. Bryan to L.D.B., March 27, 1919.
58. De Haas, *op. cit.,* p. 113.
59. L.D.B. to Alice G. Brandeis, June 22, 1919.
60. L.D.B. to Alice G. Brandeis, August 1, 8, 1919.
61. L.D.B.'s report to National Executive Committee, Zionist Organization of America, September 9, 1919.
62. J. M. N. Jeffries, *Palestine: The Reality* (London: Longmans, Green & Co., 1939), p. 329.
63. David Lloyd George, *The Truth about the Peace Treaties* (London: Victor Gollancz, Ltd., 1938), Vol. II, pp. 1179–80.
64. L.D.B.'s address before American Delegation, London, July 14, 1920. Reprinted, and somewhat edited, in De Haas, *op. cit.,* pp. 241–59.
65. L.D.B.'s remarks, Meeting of the American Delegation, London, July 16, 1920.
66. For Weizmann's point of view, see his letter of August 20, 1920, *The New Maccabean*, June 1, 1921.
67. *Supra*, note 64, July 19, 1920.
68. Henrietta Szold to De Haas, September 2, 1920.
69. For this document, known as the Zeeland Memorandum, see De Haas, *op. cit.,* pp. 260–72.
70. "A New Chapter," *The Zionist Review*, August 1920, p. 58.

71. "Zionism and Assimilation," *The Zionist Review*, November 1920, p. 120.
72. De Haas, *op. cit.*, p. 272.
73. Minutes of the Cleveland Convention, 1921.
74. Minutes of Conference, Palestine Development Associates (New York), June 10, 1921.
75. Robert Szold, "Louis Dembitz Brandeis," *Hadassah Newsletter*, December 1941–January 1942.
76. *The New Palestine*, November 13, 1936 [editorial].
77. Jeffries, *op. cit.*, p. 90; R. J. Feiwel, *No Ease in Zion* (New York: A. A. Knopf, 1939), p. 110.
78. Ben V. Cohen to Mack, November 12, 1920.
79. Memorandum prepared by Robert Szold at the author's request, January 22, 1946.
80. For opinion on Weizmann, see *Chaim Weizmann* (New York: Dial Press, 1944).
81. Frankfurter to L.D.B., December 11, 1920.
82. L.D.B. to Mack, April 25, 1928.
83. From a statement made in acknowledgment of a testimonial signed by 10,000 Zionists on the occasion of his sixtieth birthday, November 13, 1916.
84. From an address before New England members of the Palestine Land Development League, Boston, June 24, 1923. Published in *Brandeis on Zionism*, a Collection of Addresses and Statements by Louis D. Brandeis (New York: Zionist Organization of America, 1942), p. 137.

CHAPTER XXX

1. Gilson Gardner, *Shreveport Times*, February 3, 1916.
2. Wall Street reporter for the *New York Times*, quoted in the *Kansas City Post*, February 12, 1916.
3. *New York Tribune*, January 29, 1916.
4. *Washington Post*, January 29, 1916.
5. *Daily News Bulletin*, Vol. V, No. 25, February 4, 1924.
6. Hapgood, *The Changing Years*, p. 192.
7. *Boston Journal, Boston Trade Record*, February 1, 1916.
8. *New York Sun*, January 31, 1916.
9. L.D.B. to S. R. Stern, February 10, 1916.
10. H. F. Hollis to L.D.B., February 4, 1916.
11. G. W. Anderson to L.D.B., January 29, 1916.
12. Author's interview with Justice Brandeis, July 27, 1940.
13. G. W. Anderson to L.D.B., February 2, 1916; Hollis to L.D.B., February 4, 1916; McClennen to L.D.B., February 5, 1916.
14. Nutter to McClennen, February 4, 1916.
15. *New York Times*, January 29, 1916.
16. Quoted in Pringle, *Life and Times of Willam H. Taft*, Vol. II, p. 952.
17. Interchange of views quoted in the *Des Moines Register & Leader*, January 31, 1916.
18. Testimony of Clifford Thorne, *Nom. Hearings*, Vol. I, p. 8.
19. Testimony of John M. Eshleman, *ibid.*, p. 62.
20. *Ibid.*, pp. 68, 78.
21. Testimony of J. S. Harlan, *ibid.*, Vol. II, pp. 161–63.
22. Testimony of Clarence W. Barron, *ibid.*, Vol. I, p. 116.
23. *Ibid.*, pp. 117, 123.
24. *Boston Herald*, February 12, 1916.
25. Nutter to McClennen, February 13, 1916.
26. William V. Rowe to Senator James A. O'Gorman, April 6, 1916.
27. Quoted in *Nom. Hearings*, Vol. I, p. 136.
28. Testimony of Sidney W. Winslow, *ibid.*, Vol. I, pp. 160, 185, 200.
29. Clarence W. Barron, "An Unfit Appointment," *Boston News Bureau*, January 29, 1916 [editorial]. *Nom. Hearings*, Vol. I, p. 124.
30. Testimony of Sherman L. Whipple, *Nom. Hearings*, pp. 299–301.
31. Hapgood to Wilson, February 21, 1913.

32. Testimony of Hollis R. Bailey, *Nom. Hearings*, Vol. I, p. 144.
33. *Ibid.*, p. 476.
34. *Ibid.*, p. 873.
35. Quoted, *ibid.*, p. 123.
36. Testimony of Moorfield Storey, *ibid.*, pp. 270–71.
37. *Nom. Hearings*, p. 129.
38. *Ibid.*, p. 406.
39. *Ibid.*, p. 343. For Brandeis's own full statement of his relation to the Illinois Central case, see his letter of May 1908, to Joseph Walker, printed in *Nom. Hearings*, pp. 352–53.
40. *Ibid.*, Vol. I, p. 34.
41. *Ibid.*, pp. 1054–55, 1072.
42. As quoted in the *Boston Globe*, February 12, 1916.
43. *Nom. Hearings*, Vol. I, p. 153.
44. *Ibid.*, pp. 271–72.
45. *Ibid.*, p. 308.
46. Nutter to McClennen, February 26, 1916.
47. *Nom. Hearings*, Vol. I, p. 653.
48. *Ibid.*, pp. 611, 750.
49. *Ibid.*, p. 766.
50. *Ibid.*, pp. 770, 771.
51. *Ibid.*, pp. 619–20.
52. L.D.B. to Miss E. Louise Malloch, February 13, 1916.
53. L.D.B. to McClennen, February 24, 1916.
54. L.D.B. to McClennen, February 19, 1916.
55. Charles Francis Adams, *An Autobiography* (Boston: Houghton Mifflin Co., 1916), pp. 39, 205.
56. L.D.B. to McClennen, March 9, 1916.
57. L.D.B. to McClennen, February 10, 1916.
58. L.D.B. to McClennen, February 24, 1916.
59. *Nom. Hearings*, Vol. I, p. 1226.
60. *Ibid.*, pp. 1233–34.
61. *Ibid.*, p. 1239.
62. *Ibid.*, p. 1232.
63. *Ibid.*, pp. 1310, 1312–13.
64. McClennen to Brandeis, Dunbar & Nutter, March 15, 1916.
65. *Nom. Hearings*, Vol. I, p. 1226.
66. *Ibid.*, p. 1227.
67. Quoted in the *Boston Journal*, February 3, 1916.

CHAPTER XXXI

1. Stenographic transcript of Brandeis–McClennen conference, March 22, 1916, pp. 1–6.
2. Henry Morgenthau, Sr., "All in a Life-Time: The Campaign of 1916," *World's Work*, December 1921, p. 141.
3. Report of Senator Cummins, *Nom. Hearings*, Vol. II, pp. 309, 313–14.
4. Report of Senator Works, *ibid.*, p. 371.
5. *Nom. Hearings*, Vol. II, p. 335.
6. *Ibid.*, pp. 231–32.
7. Report of Senator Chilton, *ibid.*, pp. 182–83, 190.
8. Report of Senator Walsh, *ibid.*, pp. 232, 234.
9. *Nom. Hearings*, Vol. I, p. 1251, Vol. II, p. 365.
10. Frank N. Fay to E. S. Meredith, November 2, 1916.
11. L.D.B. to E. S. Meredith, November 11, 1916.
12. Nutter to McClennen, March 30, 1916.
13. Nutter to McClennen, April 6, 1916.
14. McClennen to Nutter, April 11, 1916.
15. Rowe to Nutter, April 10, 1916; Nutter to Rowe, April 12, 1916.
16. Rowe to Nutter, April 13, 1916; Nutter to Rowe, April 14, 1916.

17. Eugene E. Prussing to Brandeis, Dunbar & Nutter, April 25, 1916.
18. L.D.B. to Hapgood, April 28, 1916.
19. Nutter to McClennen, May 1, 1916; Nutter to L.D.B., May 2, 1916.
20. McClennen to Nutter, May 5, 1916.
21. *Cong. Rec.,* 64th Cong., 1st Sess., April 28, 1916, pp. 6970–73.
22. Nutter to McClennen, April 22, 1916; McClennen to Nutter, April 24, 1916.
23. McClennen to L.D.B., May 6, 1916.
24. I am indebted to John P. Furman's detailed analysis in his unpublished Senior thesis, "The Brandeis Nomination Fight" (1942), pp. 420–27.
25. Wilson to C. A. Culberson, May 5, 1916, reprinted in *Nom. Hearings,* Vol. II, pp. 5–7.
26. *Boston Record,* May 11, 1916.
27. *Nom. Hearings,* Vol. II, p. 13.
28. McClennen to Nutter, May 10, 1916.
29. *Nom. Hearings,* Vol. II, pp. 100–101.
30. Nutter to McClennen, May 13, 1916.
31. McClennen to Nutter, May 15, 1916.
32. Charles W. Eliot to C. A. Culberson, May 17, 1916.
33. McClennen to Nutter, May 24, 1916; Nutter to McClennen, May 18, 1916.
34. Josephus Daniels, *The Wilson Era* (Chapel Hill, N.C.: Univ. of North Carolina Press, 1944), pp. 545–47.
35. *New York Evening Mail, Washington Post, New York World, Boston Traveler,* January 29, 1916; *New York American,* January 30, 1916.
36. L.D.B. to Hapgood, February 1, 1916.
37. Author's interview with Justice Brandeis, July 23, 1940.
38. *Boston Herald,* April 11, 1916.
39. *Supra,* note 2.
40. L.D.B. to McClennen, April 17, 1916.
41. L.D.B. to Charles F. Amidon, June 27, 1916.
42. L.D.B. to Harold Laski, May 9, 1916.
4 . Alexander Sidney Lanier in the *Kansas City Post,* February 12, 1916.
44. Wise to L.D.B., March 23, 1916.
45. William Hard, "Brandeis," *The Outlook,* May 31, 1916. In sending this article to Brandeis, May 23, 1916, Hard commented: "I want to tell you frankly that the success of your enemies in poisoning the minds of editors against you is one of the most appalling things I have found in my journalistic experience. Three magazines which never before have refused an article from me on any subject have refused to take anything from me about you." But Brandeis thought "that it was not so much the result of enemies 'poisoning the minds of editors' as the lack of freedom in the editors to do what they would have preferred to do. I am quite sure that in certain other quarters this has been the explanation not only of silence but of attack." (L.D.B. to William Hard, May 26, 1916.)

Hard was the only newspaperman whom Brandeis took into his confidence. After several interviews Hard wrote a series of three meaningful articles, published in the *Philadelphia Public Ledger,* May 12, 14, 16. "I like you in the capacity of portrait painter," Brandeis wrote Hard, May 26, 1916.
46. R. W. Hale to C. C. Burlingham, October 20, 1941.
47. Mark Sullivan, *Collier's Weekly,* April 22, 1916 [editorial].
48. Hard, *op. cit.*

PART V

CHAPTER XXXII

1. *Boston Globe,* June 6, 1916.
2. Edward F. McClennen, "Better than a Man's Own Works," *The New Palestine,* November 14, 1941.
3. L.D.B. to Edward D. White, June 29, 1916.
4. Edward D. White to L.D.B., July 17, 1916.

5. J. H. Clarke to L.D.B., August 18, 1916.
6. *Supra*, note 2.
7. *New York Central v. Winfield*, 244 U.S. 147 (1917), p. 154.
8. *Ibid.*, p. 166.
9. *Ibid.*, p. 165.
10. *Adams* v. *Tanner*, 244 U.S. 590 (1917).
11. Quoted, *ibid.*, p. 599, from *Otis* v. *Parker*, 187 U.S. 606, 609.
12. *Supra*, note 10, p. 600.
13. *Ibid.*, p. 613.
14. J. S. Harlan to L.D.B., October 25, 1917.
15. Walton Hamilton, "The Jurist's Art," in *Mr. Justice Brandeis*, edited by Felix Frankfurter, with Essays by Charles Evans Hughes [and others], Introduction by Oliver Wendell Holmes (New Haven: Yale University Press, 1932), p. 188.
16. This memorandum is among the papers in the Woodrow Wilson collection, Library of Congress.
17. Author's interview with Justice Brandeis, July 22, 1940.
18. *Ibid*.
19. L.D.B. to Hapgood, July 21, 1917.
20. L.D.B. to Alfred Brandeis, September 16, 1917.
21. L.D.B. to Hapgood, November 16, 1917.
22. L.D.B. to Alice G. Brandeis, September 18, 1917.
23. Lief, *Brandeis, the Personal History of An American Ideal*, p. 409.
24. Author's interview with Robert E. Woolley, April 25, 1941. Also Woolley's letter to the editor of the *Saturday Evening Post*, January 14, 1939.
25. Author's interview with Robert E. Woolley, April 25, 1941, and his letter of May 28, 1945, to the author.

CHAPTER XXXIII

1. From *The Bacchae* by Euripides, translated by Gilbert Murray.
2. Baker, *Woodrow Wilson, Life and Letters*, Vol. VIII, p. 594.
3. Notes of R. S. Baker's interview with Justice Brandeis, March 23, 1927.
4. *Ibid*.
5. *Ibid*.
6. *Ibid*.
7. L.D.B. to Alfred Brandeis, April 10, 1921.
8. L.D.B. to Alfred Brandeis, May 14, July 12, May 29, 1921.
9. L.D.B. to Alfred Brandeis, March 26, 1921.
10. L.D.B. to Alfred Brandeis, June 17, 1921.
11. L.D.B. to Alfred Brandeis, July 12, 1921.
12. L.D.B. to Alfred Brandeis, May 6, 1921.
13. L.D.B. to Alfred Brandeis, October 8, 1921.
14. Wilson to L.D.B., November 6, 1921.
15. L.D.B. to Hapgood, September 18, 1918.
16. Baker, *op. cit.*, Vol. VI, pp. 116–17.
17. *Cf.* Drew Pearson and Robert S. Allen, *The Nine Old Men* (New York: Doubleday, Doran & Co., 1936), p. 176.
18. Jacob Billikopf to Lloyd Garrison, October 9, 1941.
19. Willard Hurst to the author, November 3, 1941. *See also* Pearson and Allen, *op. cit.*, pp. 182–83.
20. William H. Taft to L.D.B., July 24, August 19, 1921.
21. William H. Taft to Helen Manning, June 11, 1923; quoted in Pringle, *The Life and Times of William Howard Taft*, Vol. II, p. 970.
22. McClennen's memorandum to the author, February 5, 1942.

CHAPTER XXXIV

1. *U.S.* v. *E. C. Knight*, 156 U.S. 1 (1895).
2. *Loewe* v. *Lawlor*, 208 U.S. 274 (1908).

3. *Lochner* v. *N.Y.*, 198 U.S. 45 (1905).
4. *Adair* v. *U.S.*, 208 U.S. 161 (1908).
5. *In re Debs*, 158 U.S. 564 (1895).
6. *Supra*, note 4; *Coppage* v. *Kan.* 236 U.S. 1 (1915).
7. Justice Holmes dissenting in *Coppage* v. *Kan.*, p. 27.
8. *Hitchman Coal & Coke Co.* v. *Mitchell*, 245 U.S. 229 (1917), p. 271.
9. *Duplex Printing Co.* v. *Deering*, 254 U.S. 443 (1921). *Cf.* 47 Stat. 73., c. 90. Sec. 13 (1932), 29 U.S. Code, Sec. 113.
10. Duplex case, *ibid.*, p. 472.
11. *Ibid.*, pp. 481, 482.
12. *Ibid.*, p. 486.
13. *Ibid.*, p. 488.
14. W. H. Taft to Horace Taft, May 7, 1921; quoted in Pringle, *op. cit.*, Vol. II, p. 967.
15. *Truax* v. *Corrigan*, 257 U.S. 312 (1921), p. 357.
16. *Ibid.*, pp. 366, 368.
17. *Ibid.*, p. 357.
18. *Ibid.*, p. 376.
19. *Stettler* v. *O'Hara*, 243 U.S. 629 (1916).
20. *Adkins* v. *Children's Hospital*, 261 U.S. 525 (1923), pp. 559–60.
21. *Bedford Cut Stone* v. *Journeymen Cutters' Ass'n.*, 274 U.S. 37 (1927), p. 65.
22. *United Mine Workers* v. *Coronado Coal Co.*, 259 U.S. 344 (1922).
23. *Business—a Profession*, p. 26.
24. *Dorchy* v. *Kan.*, 272 U.S. 306 (1926), p. 311.
25. *Ibid.*, p. 309.
26. W. H. Taft to R. A. Taft, October 21, 1928; quoted in Pringle, *op. cit.*, p. 1066.
27. *Munn* v. *Ill.*, 94 U.S. 113 (1876).
28. *Chicago, Milwaukee, St. Paul R.R. Co.* v. *Minn.*, 134 U.S. 418 (1890).
29. *Smyth* v. *Ames*, 169 U.S. 466 (1898), pp. 546–47.
30. *Southwestern Bell Tel. Co.* v. *Public Service Comm.*, 262 U.S. 276 (1923), p. 288.
31. *Ibid.*, pp. 290, 294–95.
32. *Ibid.*, p. 292.
33. *Ibid.*, footnote 16, pp. 303–305. The entire footnote contains a most illuminating discussion of the shift in price levels before and after World War I.
34. *Ibid.*, pp. 306–307.
35. *Ibid.*, pp. 309–10.
36. *Bluefield Water Works and Improvement Co.* v. *Public Service Comm.*, 262 U.S. 679 (1923).
37. *Georgia Ry. & Power Co.* v. *R.R. Comm.*, 262 U.S. 625 (1923).
38. *McCardle* v. *Indianapolis Water Co.*, 272 U.S. 400 (1926).
39. *United Railways and Electric Co.* v. *West*, 280 U.S. 234 (1930), pp. 254, 255, 262.
40. *Ibid.*, pp. 278–79.
41. Quoted by Justice Brandeis, *St. Louis & O'Fallon Ry.* v. *U.S.*, 279 U.S. 461 (1929), p. 541.
42. *Ibid.*, p. 494.

CHAPTER XXXV

1. *Adams* v. *Tanner*, 244 U.S. 590 (1917), p. 599.
2. *Truax* v. *Corrigan*, 257 U.S. 312 (1921), pp. 356–57.
3. *Federal Trade Commission* v. *Gratz*, 253 U.S. 421 (1920), pp. 432, 436–37. *See* in this connection L. L. Jaffe, "The Contributions of Justice Brandeis to Administrative Law," *Iowa Law Review*, Vol. 18, p. 213.
4. *St. Joseph Stock Yards Co.* v. *U.S.*, 298 U.S. 38 (1936), p. 92.
   In *Crowell* v. *Benson*, 285 U.S. 22 (1932), Brandeis also argued at great length for judicial recognition of facts as established, or capable of being established, by administrative officers or agencies. In this case he pleaded for judicial acceptance of the deputy commissioner's findings under the Longshoremen's and Harbor Workers' Act. The Court, speaking through Chief Justice Hughes, ruled that the employer was entitled to a judicial trial *de novo*, enabling him to admit new evidence. Brandeis in dissent contended that such a holding ignored the difference

between the functions of an expert examiner and a court of law. "To permit a contest *de novo*," he observed, "in the district court of an issue tried, or triable, before the deputy commissioner will, I fear, gravely hamper the effective administration of the Act. The prestige of the deputy commissioner will necessarily be lessened by the opportunity of relitigating facts in the courts. The number of controverted cases may be largely increased. Persistence in controversy will be encouraged. And since the advantage of prolonged litigation lies with the party able to bear heavy expenses the purpose of the Act will be in part defeated."

5. *Jay Burns Baking Co.* v. *Bryan*, 264 U.S. 504 (1924), p. 534.
6. Language of Sir William Archer, quoted by G. R. Farnum, *Some Men of the Law*, p. 20 [pamphlet].
7. L.D.B., "Cutthroat Prices, the Competition that Kills," *Harper's Weekly*, November 15, 1913.
8. *Quaker City Cab Co.* v. *Pa.*, 277 U.S. 389 (1928), pp. 410–11.
9. *Hammer* v. *Dagenhart*, 247 U.S. 251 (1918).
10. *Bailey* v. *Drexel Furniture Co.*, 259 U.S. 20 (1922), p. 38.
11. L.D.B. to Hapgood, June 1, 1922.
12. Edward S. Corwin, *The President's Removal Power under the Constitution*, published in the National Municipal Monograph Series, 1927, p. 7.
13. Pringle, *op. cit.*, Vol. II, p. 1024.
14. *Myers* v. *U.S.*, 272 U.S. 52 (1926), pp. 292–95.
15. L.D.B. to Hapgood, October 28, 1926.
16. Corwin, *op. cit.*, p. 66.
17. *Rathbun* v. *U.S.*, 295 U.S. 602 (1935).
18. *Supra*, note 15.
19. *American Column and Lumber Co.* v. *U.S.*, 257 U.S. 377 (1921), p. 415.
20. *Ibid.*, pp. 418–19.
21. *Schaefer* v. *U.S.*, 251 U.S. 466 (1920), p. 477.
22. *Abrams* v. *U.S.*, 250 U.S. 616 (1919).
23. M. D. Howe (ed.), *Holmes–Pollock Letters* (Cambridge, Mass.: Harvard University Press, 1941), Vol. II, p. 163.
24. *Schenck* v. *U.S.*, 249 U.S. 47 (1919), p. 52; Holmes in dissent.
25. *Supra*, note 21, pp. 483, 495.
26. Quoted in *Pierce* v. *U.S.*, 252 U.S. 239 (1920), pp. 267, 270, 272.
27. *Ibid.*, p. 273.
28. *U.S. ex rel. Milwaukee Social Democratic Co.* v. *Burleson*, 255 U.S. 407 (1920), pp. 425–26, 436.
29. *Gilbert* v. *Minn.*, 254 U.S. 325 (1920), pp. 331–33.
30. *Ibid.*, pp. 335–36, 338.
31. *Ibid.*, p. 343.
32. *Whitney* v. *Calif.*, 274 U.S. 357 (1927), pp. 375–77.
33. J. M. Landis, "Mr. Justice Brandeis," *The Legal Intelligencer*, January 29, 1942.
34. *Ruppert* v. *Caffey*, 251 U.S. 264 (1920); Justices Day, McReynolds, and Van Devanter dissenting.
35. *Albrecht* v. *U.S.*, 273 U.S. 1 (1927).
36. *U.S.* v. *One Ford Coupe*, 272 U.S. 321 (1926); Justices Butler, McReynolds, and Sutherland dissenting.
37. *Lambert* v. *Yellowley*, 272 U.S. 581 (1926).
38. *Supra*, note 28, p. 436.
39. *Casey* v. *U.S.*, 276 U.S. 413 (1928), p. 419.
40. *Ibid.*, p. 423.
41. *Olmstead* v. *U.S.*, 277 U.S. 438 (1928), pp. 473–74, 478, 479, 485.
42. Howe, *op. cit.*, Vol. II, p. 222.
43. Fanny Brandeis's notes of an interview with Justice Brandeis.

CHAPTER XXXVI

1. Howe, *op. cit.*, Vol. II, p. 191.
2. Fanny Brandeis's notes on an interview with Justice Brandeis, spring of 1940.

3. O. W. Holmes to L.D.B., July 27, 1922.

4. Taft to Helen Manning, June 11, 1923, quoted in Pringle, *op. cit.,* Vol. II, p. 969.

5. Taft to H. L. Stimson, May 18, 1928, *ibid.,* p. 970.

6. The case, Mr. Howe thinks, was *Craig* v. *Hecht,* 263 U.S. 255. *See* Howe, *op. cit.,* Vol. II, p. 124.

7. Mrs. R. M. Boeckel to the author, March 9, 1944.

8. *Casey* v. *U.S.,* 276 U.S. 413 (1928).

9. Howe, *op. cit.,* Vol. II, p. 215.

10. For a brilliant discussion of the psychology of the Northern Securities case, *see* Max Lerner (ed.), *The Mind and Faith of Justice Holmes* (Boston: Little, Brown & Co., 1943), pp. 217–22.

11. O. W. Holmes, *Collected Legal Papers* (New York: Harcourt, Brace & Co., 1920), p. 295.

12. Comment of Justice Holmes after discussing informally with Justice Brandeis the issues involved in the California syndicalism statute of 1919. *See* Silas Bent, *Justice Oliver Wendell Holmes* (New York: Vanguard Press, Inc., 1932), pp. 280–81.

13. Holmes, *op. cit.,* p. 306.

14. *Ibid.,* pp. 304–305.

15. Howe, *op. cit.,* Vol. I, p. 163.

16. Raymond Clapper in the *New York World-Telegram,* May 22, 1936.
    For an analysis of the authoritarian implications of Holmes's relativism, *see* Ben W. Palmer, "Hobbes, Holmes and Hitler," *American Bar Association Journal,* November 1945.

17. Holmes, *op. cit.,* p. 186. *See also* Francis Biddle, *Mr. Justice Holmes* (New York: Charles Scribner's Sons, 1942), pp. 9–10.

18. Holmes, *op. cit.,* p. 306.

19. Biddle, *op. cit.,* pp. 86–87.

20. Holmes, *op. cit.,* p. 279; Howe, *op. cit.,* Vol. I, p. 141.

21. Holmes, *op. cit.,* p. 293.

22. Biddle, *op. cit.,* p. 88.

23. Holmes, *op. cit.,* p. 281.

24. Howe, *op. cit.,* Vol. I, p. 167.

25. *Ibid.,* p. 163.

26. *Ibid.*

27. Holmes, *op. cit.,* p. 258.

28. *Ibid.,* p. 231.

29. Howe, *op. cit.,* Vol. II, pp. 13–14.

30. *Truax* v. *Corrigan,* 257 U.S. 312 (1921), at p. 344.

31. *Quong Wing* v. *Kirkendall,* 223 U.S. 59 (1912), p. 64.

32. Biddle, *op. cit.,* p. 152.

33. *Penna. Coal Co.* v. *Mahon,* 260 U.S. 393 (1922), pp. 415, 416.

34. *Meyer* v. *Nebr.,* 262 U.S. 390 (1923).

35. *Testimony before the Commission on Industrial Relations* (1915), 64th Cong., 1st Sess., Sen. Doc. No. 415, Vol. 26, p. 7681.

36. *International News Service* v. *Associated Press,* 248 U.S. 215 (1918), pp. 262, 263.

37. *Eisner* v. *Macomber,* 252 U.S. 189 (1920).

38. *Supra,* note 30, p. 376.

39. *Jay Burns Baking Co.* v. *Bryan,* 264 U.S. 504 (1924).

40. O. W. Holmes, *The Common Law,* p. 1.

41. Howe, *op. cit.,* Vol. II, p. 61.

42. *Supra,* note 7.

43. *New State Ice Co.* v. *Liebmann,* 285 U.S. 262 (1931), p. 310.

44. Lerner, *op. cit.,* pp. 28–29.

45. *See* Thomas Reed Powell's suggestive review of Alpheus Thomas Mason, *Brandeis: Lawyer and Judge in the Modern State, New York Herald Tribune,* January 14, 1934.

46. See *The Nation,* October 11, 1941 [editorial].

CHAPTER XXXVII

1. Related by Harold Putnam, *Boston Globe,* October 6, 1941.
2. Philip Bernstein, "My Pilgrimage to Brandeis," *The Reconstructionist,* December 1941.
3. Clyde S. Casady to the author, December 11, 1941.
4. *Ibid.*
5. Harlan F. Stone to the author, January 10, 1946.
6. Beulah Amidon to the author, November 20, 1945.
7. L.D.B. to Alfred Brandeis, January 16, 1927.
8. L.D.B. to Alfred Brandeis, February 18, 1925.
9. *Ibid.*
10. *Ibid.*
11. *Ibid.*
12. *Ibid.*
13. From a statement by Robert N. Miller to the Board of Trustees, incorporating Justice Brandeis's ideas as expressed in notes and conversations. Quoted in Bernard Flexner, *Mr. Justice Brandeis and the University of Louisville* (privately printed, 1938).
14. Neville Miller to Bernard Flexner, quoted in Flexner, *op. cit.,* p. 63.
15. L.D.B. to Alfred Brandeis, January 16, 1927.
16. L.D.B. to Alfred Brandeis, May 26, 1927.
17. L.D.B. to Alfred Brandeis, August 11, 1926.
18. De Haas, *Louis D. Brandeis,* p. 149.
19. L.D.B. to De Haas, March 28, 1928.
20. L.D.B. to Mack, October 20, 1929.
21. *Brandeis on Zionism,* p. 144.
22. De Haas, *op. cit.,* p. 96.
23. *Supra,* note 21, pp. 151–52.
24. *Ibid.,* p. 152.
25. L.D.B.'s memorandum of a talk with Sir Roland Lindsay, June 19, 1930.
26. L.D.B. to Mack, June 19, 1930.
27. Frankfurter to L.D.B., November 23, 1930.
28. "Actions Committee Meets; Declines Weizmann's Resignation," *The New Palestine,* September 5, 1930.
29. L.D.B. to Wise, September 23, 1937.
30. L.D.B. to Robert Szold, November 19, 1933.
31. L.D.B. to Wise, May 11, 1933.
32. L.D.B. to Frankfurter (in London), July 9, 1936.
33. L.D.B. to Robert Szold, July 31, 1936.
34. As reported by President Roosevelt to Wise. From a report of a visit to President Roosevelt by Wise, October 5, 1936.
35. *Ibid.*

CHAPTER XXXVIII

1. L.D.B.'s comment was stimulated by a *Boston Evening Transcript* clipping sent him by Miss Grady.
2. L.D.B. to Alfred Brandeis, October 26, 1926.
3. L.D.B. to Alfred Brandeis, January 30, 1927.
4. L.D.B. to Alfred Brandeis, January 14, 1927.
5. L.D.B. to Alfred Brandeis, August 18, 1927.
6. See *New York Times,* September 13, 1928.
7. Frederick Lewis Allen recovers the spirit of the times in *Only Yesterday, an Informal History of the Nineteen-Twenties* (New York: Harper & Bros., 1931).
8. Author's interview with Justice Brandeis, June 26, 1940.
9. Remarks of Paul A. Freund, in an address at Temple Israel, St. Louis, November 10, 1941.
10. L.D.B. to Hapgood, November 23, 1932.

11. R. L. Neuberger, "A Citizen of the Entire Country," *The Progressive,* October 25, 1941 [Madison, Wis.].

12. Marquis W. Childs, *I Write from Washington* (New York: Harper & Bros., 1942), p. 43.

13. Mrs. R. M. Boeckel to the author, March 9, 1944.

14. J. M. Landis, "Mr. Justice Brandeis," *The Legal Intelligencer,* January 29, 1942.

15. L.D.B. to Hapgood, June 22, 1934.

16. L.D.B. to Hapgood, May 6, 1934.

17. L.D.B. to Sherman Mittell, August 10, 1934.

18. L.D.B. to Hapgood, December 11, 1934.

19. Lerner, *op. cit.,* p. xli.

20. Senator Dill, *Cong. Rec.,* p. 3642 (1930).

21. Pringle, *op. cit.,* Vol. II, pp. 1043–44.

22. Taft to C. P. Taft, II, May 12, 1929, quoted in Pringle, *op. cit.,* p. 1044.

23. *New State Ice Co.* v. *Liebmann,* 285 U.S. 262, pp. 279–80.

24. *Olmstead* v. *U.S.,* 277 U.S. 438, pp. 472–73.

25. *Supra,* note 23, pp. 280, 308–11.

26. Quoted in Lief, *op. cit.,* p. 449.

27. *Liggett* v. *Lee,* 288 U.S. 517 (1933), pp. 542–43.

28. *Ibid.,* pp. 548–49.

29. *Ibid.,* pp. 548, 559.

30. *Ibid.,* pp. 564–65.

31. *Ibid.,* p. 580.

CHAPTER XXXIX

1. Frankfurter (ed.), *Mr. Justice Brandeis,* Introduction.

2. L.D.B., "The Inefficiency of the Oligarchs," *Harper's Weekly,* January 17, 1914.

3. L.D.B., "What Publicity Can Do," *Harper's Weekly,* December 20, 1913.

4. "Constructive Co-operation v. Cutthroat Competition," address of L.D.B. before the National Rivers and Harbors Congress, Washington, D.C., December 9, 1914.

5. L.D.B. to Hapgood, November 23, 1934.

6. L.D.B. to Hapgood, January 20, 1935.

7. *Home Building Loan Asso.* v. *Blaisdell,* 290 U.S. 398 (1934).

8. *Nebbia* v. *N.Y.,* 291 U.S. 502 (1934).

9. See Alpheus Thomas Mason, "Has the Supreme Court Abdicated?" *North American Review,* October 1934.

10. Before the Court were the so-called "hot-oil" cases—*Panama Refining Co.* v. *Ryan* and *Amazon Petroleum Corp.* v. *Ryan,* 293 U.S. 388 (1935). The Court stood 8 to 1 against the government, Justice Cardozo dissenting.

11. *Washington Post,* December 11, 1934; quoted by E. S. Corwin, *Constitutional Revolution, Ltd.* (Claremont, Calif.: Claremont Colleges Administration Office, 1941), pp. 39–41.

12. *Schechter Bros.* v. *U.S.,* 295 U.S. 495 (1935).

13. *Louisville Joint Stock Land Bank* v. *Radford,* 295 U.S. 555 (1935).

14. *Rathbun* v. *U.S.,* 295 U.S. 602 (1935).

15. *Supra,* note 13, p. 602.

16. *Norman* v. *Baltimore & Ohio R.R.,* 294 U.S. 240 (1935); *Nortz* v. *U.S.,* 294 U.S. 317 (1935); *Perry* v. *U.S.,* 294 U.S. 330 (1935).

17. *Ashwander* v. *T.V.A.,* 297 U.S. 288 (1935).

18. *Railroad Retirement Bd.* v. *Alton R.R. Co.,* 295 U.S. 330 (1935).

19. *Ashton* v. *Cameron County Water Improvement District,* 298 U.S. 513 (1936).

20. *National Labor Relations Bd.* v. *Jones & Laughlin Steel Corp.,* 301 U.S. 1 (1937).

21. *Stewart Machine Co.* v. *Davis,* 301 U.S. 548 (1937); *Helvering* v. *Davis, ibid.,* p. 619; *Carmichael* v. *Southern Coal & Coke Co., ibid.,* p. 495.

22. Interview of Harold Putnam, *Boston Globe* reporter, with Justice Brandeis in the summer of 1940.

23. For this material the author is indebted to the confidential memoranda of two newspapermen who interviewed Justice Brandeis, June 23, 1935, at Chatham.

24. L.D.B. to Hapgood, May 24, June 12, 1936.
25. L.D.B. to Hapgood, August 1, 9, and November 23, 1935.
26. *U.S.* v. *Butler,* 297 U.S. 1 (1936), pp. 87–88.
27. *Carter* v. *Carter Coal Co.,* 298 U.S. 238 (1936).
28. *Morehead* v. *People,* 298 U.S. 587 (1936).
29. *Report on the Reorganization of the Federal Judiciary,* 75th Cong., 1st Sess., Rept. No. 711, Appendix D, pp. 42–43.
30. Memorandum prepared at the author's request by Willard Hurst, November 3, 1941.
31. Address of Justice Robert H. Jackson, Brandeis Memorial Colony Dinner, June 24, 1943.
32. Raymond P. Brandt, *Washington Evening Star,* April 21, 1940.
33. Author's interview with Senator Wheeler, February 25, 1944.
34. *Hearings before the Committee on the Judiciary, United States Senate, on the Reorganization of the Federal Judiciary,* 75th Cong., 1st Sess., Pt. 1, p. 487.
35. *Ibid.,* pp. 488, 491–92.
36. *Supra,* note 29, pp. 1–23.
37. For the full story, *see* Corwin, *Constitutional Revolution,* Ch. 2.
38. Felix Frankfurter, *Current History,* May 1930.
39. Max Lerner, "The Fate of the Supreme Court," *The Nation,* March 26, 1936.

CHAPTER XL

1. Justice Robert A. Jackson's address, June 24, 1943.
2. Hurst's memorandum to the author.
3. Remarks of Paul A. Freund at a meeting of the United States Supreme Court in memory of Justice Brandeis, December 21, 1942.
4. *Supra,* note 2.
5. *Pittsburgh Post Gazette,* October 14, 1941.
6. Related by Paul A. Freund in an address delivered at Temple Israel, St. Louis, November 10, 1941.
7. Remarks of Charles C. Burlingham on the presentation of portrait of Justice Brandeis to the Harvard Law School, November 14, 1938.
8. Frankfurter, *op. cit.,* pp. 3–4.
9. *Supra,* note 3.
10. *Ashwander* v. *T.V.A.,* 297 U.S. 288 (1935), p. 345.
11. *Pa.* v. *W. Vir.,* 262 U.S. 553 (1923), p. 610.
12. McClennen's memorandum to the author.
13. *Washington* v. *Dawson & Co.,* 264 U.S. 219, 238 (1924).
    For citation of cases in which the Court has disregarded the principle of *stare decisis,* see *ibid.,* Brandeis's footnote 21 at p. 238. For a more recent collection of such cases, *see* his dissenting opinion in *Burnet* v. *Coronado Oil & Gas Co.,* 285 U.S. 393, p. 406 *n.* 1 (1932).
14. *DiSanto* v. *Pennsylvania,* 273 U.S. 34 (1927).
    Speaking for the Court in the significant case of *Erie Railroad Co.* v. *Tomkins,* 304 U.S. 64 (1938), he said, at p. 79, "The doctrine of *Swift* v. *Tyson* is 'an unconstitutional assumption of power by courts of the United States which no lapse of time or respectable array of opinion should make us hesitate to correct.'"
15. *Jaybird Mining Co.* v. *Weir,* 271 U.S. 609 (1926), p. 619.
16. *Supra,* note 13, p. 236.
17. *Burnet* v. *Coronado Oil & Gas Co.,* 285 U.S. 393 (1932), p. 408.
18. J. A. Padway, "Brandeis and Labor," *American Federationist,* December 1941, p. 32.
19. *Senn* v. *Tile Layers' Protective Union,* 301 U.S. 468 (1937), p. 478.
20. *Supra,* note 2.
21. See *Thornhill* v. *Ala.,* 310 U.S. 88 (1940); *Carlson* v. *California,* 310 U.S. 106 (1940); *A.F. of L.* v. *Swing,* 312 U.S. 321 (1941).
22. *O'Gorman & Young* v. *Hartford Insurance Co.,* 282 U.S. 251 (1931), p. 258.
23. *Gilbert* v. *Minn.,* 254 U.S. 325 (1921), p. 388.

24. *Stromberg* v. *Calif.*, 283 U.S. 359 (1931), p. 366.
25. *Near* v. *Minn.*, 283 U.S. 697 (1931). More recent cases reinforce Brandeis's more liberal stand. See *Herndon* v. *Lowry*, 301 U.S. 242 (1937); *Cantwell* v. *Connecticut*, 310 U.S. 296 (1940).
26. *Los Angeles G. & E. Corp.* v. *Railroad Co.*, 289 U.S. 237 (1933), p. 312.
27. *New York Times*, December 22, 1937.
28. *Appalachian Coal, Inc.* v. *U.S.*, 288 U.S. 344 (1933).
29. *Nordone* v. *U.S.*, 302 U.S. 379 (1937).
30. *New York Times*, June 14, 1938.
31. *National Labor Relations Bd.* v. *Jones & Laughlin Steel Corp.*, 301 U.S. 1 (1937), p. 41.
32. *West Coast Hotel* v. *Parrish*, 300 U.S. 397 (1937).
33. *Adkins* v. *Children's Hospital*, 261 U.S. 525 (1923); *Morehead* v. *N.Y.*, 298 U.S. 587 (1936).
34. *U.S.* v. *Hutcheson*, 312 U.S. 219 (1941).
35. Jacob Billikopf to Lloyd Garrison, October 9, 1941.
36. From a statement presented to Dr. Solomon Goldman, President of the Zionist Organization of America, in May 1939.
37. L.D.B. to Wise, October 24, 1939.
38. L.D.B. to Elisha Friedman, November 14, 1937.
39. Report of L.D.B.'s conversation with Emanuel Neuman, April 18, 1941.
40. *Supra*, note 35.
41. Elizabeth Glendower Evans, "Alice Goldmark Brandeis," *The Progressive*, July 26, 1930.
42. Mr. Acheson's remarks are printed in full in Dilliard (ed.), *Brandeis, Great American*, pp. 125–36.
43. For press opinion, *see* Dilliard, *op. cit.*
44. *The University of Toronto Law Journal*, Lent Term, 1942, p. 402.
45. McClennen's memorandum to the author.

CHAPTER XLI

1. *New York Times*, October 6, 1941.
2. Mrs. R. M. Boeckel to the author, March 9, 1944.
3. *Ibid.*
4. John Buchan's characterization of Lord Milner in *Pilgrim's Way* (Boston: Houghton Mifflin Co., 1940), p. 98.
5. Enclosed in a letter to Lincoln Steffens, May 26, 1909.

Appendix

Chronology

1856   Born, Louisville, Ky., November 13.

1874–1875 Student, Annen-Realschule, Dresden.

1875–1878 Harvard Law School.

1878   Admitted to the St. Louis Bar, November.

1879–1897 Lawyer, Warren & Brandeis, Boston.

1889   Admitted to the Bar of the United States Supreme Court.

1891   Married Alice G. Goldmark of New York, March 23.

1897–1916 Senior, Brandeis, Dunbar & Nutter, Boston.

1897–1911 "People's Attorney" for Public Franchise League and Massachusetts
          State Board of Trade.

1905   Unpaid Counsel for the New England Policy-Holders' Protective
          Committee.

1907–1913 Unpaid Counsel for William B. Lawrence in New Haven merger
          controversies.

1907–1914 Unpaid Counsel for the State in defending hours of labor and
          minimum wage statutes of Oregon, Illinois, Ohio, and California.

1910   Counsel for *Collier's Weekly* in Ballinger–Pinchot dispute.

1910–1911 Unpaid Counsel for Commercial Organizations in I.C.C. Advance
          Railroad Rate Case.

1910–1916 Unpaid Chairman, Arbitration Board, New York Garment Work-
          ers' strike, and under subsequent protocols.

1911–1915 Worker and adviser in Progressive Politics.

1912   Joined Zionist Movement.

1913–1914 Special I.C.C. Counsel in Five Per Cent Rate Case.

1916   Nominated for Associate Justice, United States Supreme Court,
          January 28.

1916   Confirmed by Senate, 47 to 22, June 1.

1916   Took Oath of Office from Chief Justice Edward D. White, June 5.

1939   Retired, February 13.

1941   Died, Washington, D.C., October 5.

Selected Writings

BY LOUIS D. BRANDEIS

Law Review Articles

"Liability of Trust-Estates on Contracts Made for Their Benefit," *American Law Review*, Vol. 15 (1881), pp. 449–62.

"The Watuppa Pond Cases," with S. D. Warren, Jr., *Harvard Law Review*, Vol. 2 (1888), pp. 195–211.

"The Harvard Law School," *The Green Bag*, Vol. 1 (1889), pp. 10–25.

"The Law of Ponds," with S. D. Warren, Jr., *Harvard Law Review*, Vol. 3 (1889), pp. 1–22.

"The Right to Privacy," with S. D. Warren, Jr., *Harvard Law Review*, Vol. 4 (1890), pp. 193–220.

Books and Pamphlets

Notes on Business Law. Lectures, Massachusetts Institute of Technology, 1894–96, 2 vols., privately printed.

Financial Condition of the New York, New Haven & Hartford Railroad Company, and of the Boston & Maine Railroad. Privately printed, 1907.

Other People's Money and How the Bankers Use It. New York: F. A. Stokes & Co., 1914. Preface by Norman Hapgood. Republished in 1932 by the National Home Library Foundation.

Business—a Profession. Boston: Small, Maynard & Co., 1914. Introductory article by Ernest Poole. A new edition was published in 1933 by Hale, Cushman & Flint, with supplementary notes by Felix Frankfurter and foreword by James C. Bonbright.

The Social and Economic Views of Mr. Justice Brandeis, edited by Alfred Lief. New York: The Vanguard Press, 1930. Foreword by Charles A. Beard. A collection of abstracts from judicial opinions, extracts from articles, addresses, and statements on various subjects.

The Curse of Bigness, edited by Osmond K. Fraenkel. New York: The Viking Press, 1934. Miscellaneous papers of Louis D. Brandeis. Contains a good bibliography and a topical list of opinions from October 1931 through June 4, 1934.

Mr. Justice Brandeis and the University of Louisville, letters collected and arranged by Bernard Flexner. Privately printed by the University of Louisville, 1938.

The Brandeis Guide to the Modern World, edited by Alfred Lief. Boston: Little, Brown & Co., 1941. Classified extracts from letters, opinions, speeches, memoranda, oral and other statements.

Brandeis on Zionism, edited by Solomon Goldman. Washington, D.C.: Zionist Organization of America, 1942. Foreword by Justice Felix Frankfurter. A collection of addresses and statements.

ON LOUIS D. BRANDEIS

De Haas, Jacob. *Louis D. Brandeis, a Biographical Sketch, with Special Reference to His Contributions to Jewish and Zionist History.* New York: Bloch Publishing Co., 1929. Contains full text of many of Brandeis's Zionist addresses and statements from 1912 to 1924.

Dilliard, Irving (ed.). *Mr. Justice Brandeis: Great American; Press Opinion and Public Appraisal*. St. Louis: Modern View Press, 1941.

Frankfurter, Felix (ed.). *Mr. Justice Brandeis*. New Haven: Yale University Press, 1932. Introduction by Justice Holmes. Contains articles by Charles Evans Hughes, Max Lerner, Felix Frankfurter, Donald R. Richberg, Henry Wolf Biklè, and Walton H. Hamilton—all of which appeared in various law reviews, November 1931, in honor of Justice Brandeis's seventy-fifth birthday. Included is a list of cases in which opinions were written by Justice Brandeis, December 4, 1916 to June 1, 1931.

Lief, Alfred. *Brandeis: The Personal History of an American Ideal*. New York: Stackpole Sons, 1936. Contains an excellent bibliography.

Mason, Alpheus Thomas. *Brandeis: Lawyer and Judge in the Modern State*. Princeton, N.J.: Princeton University Press, 1933. A new and revised edition was published in 1936 by the National Home Library Foundation with an introduction by Norman Hapgood.

———. *The Brandeis Way*. Princeton, N.J.: Princeton University Press, 1938. A case study in the workings of Democracy.

———. *Bureaucracy Convicts Itself*. New York: The Viking Press, 1941. The Ballinger–Pinchot controversy of 1910.

MEMORIAL ISSUES (SELECTED)

The New Palestine, November 14, 1941. Articles by Benjamin V. Cohen, Louis E. Levinthal, E. F. McClennen, H. M. Kallen, Jacob J. Kaplan, Harry Friedenwald, Max Radin, and others.

Opinion, A Journal of Jewish Life and Letters, November 1941. Tributes by William O. Douglas, Stephen S. Wise, Irving Lehmann, Robert Szold, Chaim Weizmann, and others.

Harvard Law Review, December 1941. Articles by Felix Frankfurter, James M. Landis, Dean Acheson, Calvert Magruder, and Paul A. Freund.

Proceedings of the Bar of the Supreme Court of the United States and Meeting of the Court in Memory of Associate Justice Louis D. Brandeis, December 21, 1942. Contains remarks of Solicitor-General Fahy, Circuit Judge Calvert Magruder, Circuit Judge Learned Hand, Paul A. Freund, Senator George W. Norris, Attorney-General Francis Biddle, and Chief Justice Harlan F. Stone.

Law Clerks to Justice Brandeis

(Selected by Professor Felix Frankfurter and accepted sight unseen)

Calvert Magruder	1916–1917	U.S. Circuit Judge, C.C.A., First Circuit
William A. Sutherland	1917–1919	Lawyer, Atlanta, Ga.
Dean Acheson	1919–1921	Undersecretary of State
William G. Rice, Jr.	1921–1922	Professor of Law, University of Wisconsin
William F. McCurdy	1922–1923	Professor, Harvard Law School
Samuel H. Maslon	1923–1924	Lawyer, Minneapolis, Minn.
Warren S. Ege	1924–1925	Lawyer, St. Paul, Minn.
James M. Landis	1925–1926	Dean, Harvard Law School
Robert Page	1926–1927	Lawyer, New York City
Henry J. Friendly	1927–1928	Lawyer, New York City
Irving B. Goldsmith	1928–1929	Deceased
Harry Shulman	1929–1930	Professor, Yale Law School
Thomas H. Austern	1930–1931	Lawyer, Washington, D.C.
Henry M. Hart, Jr.	1931–1932	Professor, Harvard Law School
Paul A. Freund	1932–1933	Professor, Harvard Law School
Louis L. Jaffe	1933–1934	Professor, University of Buffalo Law School
Nathaniel L. Nathanson	1934–1935	Professor of Law, Northwestern University
David Riesman, Jr.	1935–1936	Professor of Law, University of Chicago
Willard H. Hurst	1936–1937	Professor of Law, University of Wisconsin
William G. Claytor, Jr.	1937–1938	Lawyer, Washington, D.C.
Adrian S. Fisher	1938–1939	U.S. Army, Nuremberg

Income and Finances

During the years for which figures are available (1901–1915), Brandeis's income from law practice totaled approximately $1,096,489 and averaged about $73,000 a year, the extremes being $45,116 in 1902 and $105,758 in 1912. In 1906–1907, after his father's death, he inherited $70,488. His total estate as of 1915 and subsequent years and annual income follow:

YEAR	INVESTMENTS	INCOME FROM BRANDEIS, DUNBAR & NUTTER	GROSS INCOME (INCLUDING SUPREME COURT)	NET INCOME
1915	$1,953,211	$47,694	$ 88,041	$ 81,483
1916	2,056,996	37,919	99,164	90,551
1917	1,929,752	27,527	108,835	101,670
1918	1,996,177	2,714	111,085	90,046
1919	1,923,481	2,598	113,695	83,537
1920	1,849,693	2,180	113,294	94,964
1921	2,092,683	1,591	115,152	96,723
1922	2,246,515	1,290	121,344	97,777
1923	2,264,299	587	122,835	99,371
1924	2,379,072	642	122,732	105,014
1925	2,464,229		124,477	107,214
1926	2,590,380		129,559	114,665
1927	2,750,393		138,310	123,887
1928	2,699,075		144,325	130,074
1929	2,575,910		137,372	124,305
1930	2,586,141		138,783	127,056
1931	2,284,756		135,717	125,965
1932	2,301,327		135,875	127,783
1933	2,292,834		134,676	126,044
1934	2,732,332		139,120	130,650
1935	2,903,064		137,422	128,930
1936	3,130,700		139,399	131,197
1937	2,891,154		137,266	129,131
1938	2,948,131		136,395	128,146
1939	2,991,744		136,965	131,035
1940	3,138,441		133,821	124,551
Total		$124,742	$3,159,942	$2,951,769

Gifts (1890-1939)

YEAR	JEWISH CHARITIES AND ZIONISM	SAVINGS-BANK LIFE INSURANCE	EDUCATIONAL	RELATIVES AND FRIENDS	MISCEL-LANEOUS	TOTALS
1890–1904 (totals)				$ 3,285.00	$ 3,275.00	$ 6,560.00
1905	$ 125.00			1,314.00	201.00	1,640.00
1906	145.00	$ 227.00	$ 10.00	1,541.00	451.00	2,374.00
1907	295.00	4,539.84		1,711.75	5,720.00	12,266.59
1908	175.00	976.05		1,756.25	15,925.01	18,832.31
1909	175.00	7,221.72		1,790.00	11,375.99	20,562.71
1910	175.00	9,373.63		1,570.00	795.34	11,913.97
1911	175.00	9,030.00		2,055.00	1,213.54	12,473.54
1912	200.00	9,275.00		4,285.00	4,152.95	17,912.95
1913	860.94	7,475.00		2,165.10	5,084.70	15,585.74
1914	3,160.87	7,100.00		1,515.50	1,895.96	13,672.33
1915	12,227.52	8,075.00		1,535.00	822.27	22,659.79
1916	12,995.41	10,347.70	500.00	2,395.00	264.01	26,502.12
1917	8,491.94	6,033.26		1,485.00	567.22	16,577.42
1918	28,379.87	2,777.40		3,405.00		34,562.27
1919	53,614.95	1,999.98	1,000.00	3,396.10		60,011.03
1920	34,120.87	2,000.00		1,797.10	200.00	38,117.97
1921	18,546.90	1,872.59	100.00	2,545.00	505.04	23,569.53
1922	13,800.40	1,500.00	1,000.00	1,420.00	105.00	17,825.40
1923	16,985.84	1,500.00	1,000.00	2,190.00	1,100.00	22,775.84
1924	43,646.50	4,887.34	3,500.00	3,408.34		55,442.18
1925	5,509.50	5,271.98	10,000.00	27,767.54	25.00	48,574.02
1926	2,526.80	2,350.00	12,641.00	4,250.00		21,767.80
1927	1,735.40	2,500.00	10,021.71	2,420.00		16,677.11
1928	13,505.00	5,350.00	6,702.00	47,398.50	100.00	73,055.50
1929	9,920.50	12,110.55	7,627.00	177,410.39	2,000.00	209,068.44
1930	38,434.29	10,784.69	5,934.50	71,279.82		126,433.30
1931	20,236.82	17,571.90	6,300.63	44,055.00		88,164.35
1932	13,074.96	6,679.96	4,813.20	23,787.50		48,355.62
1933	6,334.48	12,774.96	4,147.95	9,800.02		33,057.41
1934	10,711.67	6,733.49	7,009.92	4,602.02	2.00	29,059.10
1935	29,716.29	6,331.08	4,727.40	12,725.00	125.00	53,624.77
1936	62,297.00	6,331.08	10,570.60	7,701.10	14.44	86,914.22
1937	77,325.50	7,692.08	3,882.40	12,545.04	500.00	101,945.02
1938	35,589.00	6,991.08	5,862.26	5,739.96		54,182.30
1939 (10 months)	39,635.00	4,813.40	2,549.45	6,380.02		53,377.87
Total	$614,849.22	$210,497.76	$109,900.02	$504,427.05	$56,420.47	$1,496,094.52

Index

Abbot, Edwin H., 70, 110, 112, 152, 158
Abbott, Lawrence, 301
Abbott, Myrtle, 283, 285–86, 288
Abe Stein & Company, 233–34
A. Brandeis & Son, 50
Academy of Political and Social Sciences, 419
Acheson, Dean G., 615, 637–38
Actions Comité, 444–45
Adair v. *U.S.*, 382
Adams, Charles Francis, 188–89, 473, 485
Adams, Henry, 42
Adams, Melvin O., 76, 481–82
Adamson, William C., 402
Addams, Jane, 76, 301, 378, 422
Addicks, J. Edward, 127
Adler, Felix, 75, 313
Adriatic, 28–29
Advance Rate case, 315–34, 404
Agricultural Adjustment Act, 623
Alexander, James W., 153, 156
Alexander & Green, 84
Allen v. *Woonsocket*, 61
Allenby, General E. H. H., 456
"All Together for Boston," 125
Amalgamated Association of Iron and Steel Workers, 87
American Bar Association, 101, 103, 105, 473, 489–91, 494, 497, 591
American Cloak and Suit Review, 303
American Fair Trade League, 426–27
American Federation of Labor, 168, 293, 381, 631
Americanism, 16, 438–39, 442, 446, 459–461, 565–68, 603
American Jewish Committee, 450
American Jewish Conference, 455
American Jewish Congress, 450–51

American Law Review, 36, 53
American Liberty League, 625
American Lumber case, 560–61
American Metal Market, 332
American Mining Congress, 288
American Railroad Employees and Investors' Association, 317
American Telephone & Telegraph Company, 473
American Tobacco Company, 226, 353
American Tobacco Trust, 355, 378, 403, 426
Ames, James B., 36–38, 65, 240
Amidon, Beulah, 587
Amidon, Charles F., 206, 418, 468, 505
Anderson, Chandler P., 68
Anderson, George W., 129, 134–35, 138–139, 210, 227, 395, 404–405, 407; on L.D.B.'s suggested cabinet appointment, 391; supports L.D.B. for Supreme Court, 469, 474, 478, 482, 484, 486, 498, 500, 511
Anderson v. *Dunn*, 576
Angell, Henry, 76
Angell, J. R., 614
Ann Arbor Railroad, 333
Annen-Realschule of Dresden, 30–31, 35
Anti-Merger League, 197
Anti-Stock-Watering Act, 129–30, 211
Anti-Trust Division of the Department of Justice, 194
Arbitration, of labor disputes, 430–31
Aristotle, 576
Armstrong, William W., 156–57
Arnold, Matthew, 39–40, 94
Arnold, Thurman, 613–14
Arnold, W. E., 217
Ashurst, Henry F., 497, 502, 504

693